The Mediaeval World

LITERATURE AND WESTERN CIVILIZATION

The Mediaeval World

GENERAL EDITORS

David Daiches

Anthony Thorlby

ALDUS BOOKS · LONDON

Aldus Editor   Kit Coppard

Copy Editor   Maureen Cartwright

SBN 490 00241 2

Printed in England by Unwin Brothers Limited, Old Woking, Surrey

Contents

Preface

The intellectual history of the Middle Ages, as Gordon Leff points out in Chapter 7, involves a continuing attempt to fit increasing natural knowledge into the unquestioned doctrinal and institutional framework of Christianity. The claims of Christianity represented something that had been unknown in the ancient world, whose tolerant polytheism encouraged the proliferation of local cults. There is no chapter in Volume I of this work that can compare in scope or length with Professor Leff's, for the simple reason that, in spite of the great intellectual and scientific achievements of individual Greek thinkers, there was in the ancient world no all-embracing ideology of the kind represented by mediaeval Christianity. The mediaeval mind continually sought a *summa*, a comprehension of all knowledge as it became available within the framework of basic Christian dogma. The struggle to achieve this *summa*, the contradictions to be resolved and the adjustments and re-definitions to be made, are reflected in the literature and art as well as in the philosophy of the Middle Ages.

A great deal of mediaeval literature is about the gap between the facts of human desires and aspirations and the power structure that is built on them, on the one hand, and Christian faith and ideals, on the other hand. Feudal service, knighthood, and military prowess are continually being pressed into a Christian context and continually resisting the pressure. Courtly love is pagan and adulterous, yet it can be related to the worship of the Virgin Mary; the ritual of courts, the practices of knighthood, the codes of the *trouvère* and the troubadour, and the world of the Arthurian romances—all are part of the brute facts of power and passion, yet time and again they are manoeuvred into the world of Christian values. The knight seeks the Holy Grail, the courtesy of the lover becomes associated with Christian charity, and military adventure becomes a crusade. The process of union is continually breaking down and continually renewed. The interplay of secular entertainment and religious motivation is perhaps seen most clearly in the development of mediaeval drama, which began as a dramatization of part of the service of the Church. That service itself had its innate dramatic elements, and the literary imagination was quick to seize on the possibilities for drama not only of antiphonal elements in religious ritual but also of the facts of biblical story.

With more and more to accommodate, the mediaeval ideal of a Christian *summa* could never be final, which might mean that it was fated always to remain an ideal, never permanently realized. But the story of how the ideal worked in mediaeval thought and art is central to mediaeval cultural history. After the fragmentation of mediaeval Christendom, it was left to the rare individual to try to produce a philosophy that claimed to embrace everything that could be known. In the 19th century Hegel was to attempt just that, and Marx, who learned his method from Hegel, claimed to have produced his own secular *summa*. With the enormous increase in knowledge in our own time, when no single mind can hope to embrace or accommodate into a system more than a fraction of it, the whole idea of a *summa* has faded. This makes the mediaeval situation all the more interesting as we look back to it now.

THE EDITORS

CHAPTER I

The Survival of Culture

Pierre Riché[*]

When the scholar Cassiodorus was born, about A.D. 480, the Germanic barbarians had established their own kingdoms amidst the ruins of the Western Empire. Roman civilization still survived in the Mediterranean area, however, and as a young man Cassiodorus did not suffer under the new overlords. The rich citizens in the towns could still divide their time between the forum and the baths. On the great country estates farms and slaves continued to work as before. To govern their kingdoms the barbarians made use of Roman civil servants, and Cassiodorus's father was employed in this way. Thus the practice—which had been such an important feature of Roman civilization in the West—of recording public and private transactions in writing, and of making funerary inscriptions, continued. The barbarian kings may not have been literate, but they were sufficiently romanized to appreciate Roman civilization and intelligent enough to use its cultural equipment. Theodoric the Ostrogoth (c. 454–526), for instance, wanted to appear as a successor of the Roman emperors and to guarantee peace throughout the Mediterranean.

Classical literary culture benefited from the restoration of peace at the beginning of the 6th century, and it was more or less kept alive in aristocratic circles until the beginning of the 7th. Thanks to the work of Ennodius, bishop of Pavia (c. 473–521), we know something about Italian literary life, in Rome and in the north, during Theodoric's reign. He describes the literary debut of young Milan aristocrats, such as Arator, the future deacon, who was to write an epic on the Acts of the Apostles; and he gives us an idea of the schools of grammar and rhetoric in Milan, Ravenna, and Rome. It is clear that, as in former centuries, culture there continued to be essentially literary and oratorical: the students read and re-read the classical authors, writing commentaries upon them and doing imitative exercises in an oratorical style known as *dictiones*, in order to

* Professeur d'Histoire Médiévale, University of Paris.

perfect their Latin. Ennodius laid down a whole series of models for his young disciples, in which he demonstrates both his virtuosity and his preciosity.

At Ravenna and at Rome, high Roman officials took an active interest in classical literary works and revised the texts of 4th-century authors. The senator Faustus devoted himself to poetry and spent long hours in his great library. In the family of his colleague Symmachus the cult of *belles-lettres* had long been traditional. (The most distinguished member of this family was Quintus Aurelius, a statesman and orator of the late 4th century, whose *Relationes*, or official correspondence, is of great historical interest). Unlike his contemporaries, Symmachus did not confine himself to the study of Latin writing; he knew Greek, and established contact with the Roman grammarian Priscian, who became professor of Latin at Constantinople and whose 18 books of *Institutiones grammaticae* constitute a comparative grammar and syntax of the two classical languages that was to become widely known in the Middle Ages. The family was related by marriage to the great Boethius (*c.* 480–524), and it was at the request of his father-in-law that this Roman philosopher, so well versed in Greek, undertook the task of making the riches of Greek literature and thought available to his Latin contemporaries. Boethius's never-completed translation of Aristotle became the basis of much mediaeval philosophy, and he also wrote commentaries on the scientific works of Euclid and Ptolemy. His ambitious plans were interrupted in 523, when he was arrested on a false charge of treason, thrown into prison (where he composed his most famous work, *De consolatione philosophiae*), and then executed. He had tried to employ philosophy in the service of politics, and accepted the high offices that Theodoric offered him; but he aroused jealousy and incomprehension, and was accused of plotting against the king in favour of the Eastern Emperor.

After Boethius, another aristocratic scholar rose to the post of *magister officiorum* (chief of the civil service): Flavius Magnus Aurelius Cassiodorus. His illustrious family had allied itself with Odoacer, commander of the barbarian auxiliaries who overthrew the Empire of the West, and later with Theodoric. It was by writing a panegyric of Theodoric that Cassiodorus first found official favour and obtained the post of *quaestor*. From then on, he became the intellectual and political adviser of the king. Theodoric, who wanted to be seen as an educated monarch, commanded Cassiodorus to write a *History of the Goths*—a work that has been lost but is the foundation of Jordanes' *De rebus Geticis* (*c.* 550). Cassiodorus's official position obliged him to stay at Ravenna, particularly after 523,

when he took over from Boethius, but he did not forget Rome, still the
literary capital of the Latin world. He gave orders for the restoration of
ancient monuments, and later, during the reign of Athalaric, the grandson and successor of Theodoric, he sent a memorandum to the Roman
senators urging them to maintain recruitment into the schools. This
memorandum begins with a passage in praise of grammar, "the foundation stone of literature, ornament of the human race, mistress of the
spoken word, and teacher of all the lessons of antiquity through the
practice of good reading." Cassiodorus continues:

> If we pay actors for the entertainment of the people, there is even
> better reason to support those who maintain eloquence and civility
> in the manners of our great houses.

It is clear that for Cassiodorus the purpose of literary education is both
moral and political, and this attitude was to persist in later centuries.
Admittedly, the senators cannot have spent very much on this project,
to judge from the small number of names that are known of persons
engaged as public teachers at Rome. That is why Ennodius of Pavia
recommended his young friends to the educated senators themselves, who
in this way took the place of the inadequate professional teachers.

The same development occurred in regions that were politically more
or less dependent on the kingdom of Italy, such as Spain, Provence, and
Burgundy, where public schools were no longer functioning. Cordova,
Seville, and Merida remained as provincial capitals sufficiently alive in
terms of literary culture to experience later a kind of intellectual renaissance. Refugees from Africa, such as the grammarian Pomerius, enriched
the life of Arles; Vienne, the capital of the kingdom of Burgundy, continued to enjoy the reputation won for it at the end of the 5th century by
the Christian bishop Claudianus Mamertus and by Sapaudus. The later
archbishop of Vienne, Avitus, is a typical cultured aristocrat of the period,
exchanging highly literary letters with his friends in Provence and
Aquitaine, just as the Christian writer and bishop Apollinaris Sidonius
had done a generation earlier. Although the schools of southern Gaul
were closed about 474, the great senatorial families preserved enough
contact with classical culture to ensure that it was not lost. Private tutors
or parents undertook the task that was no longer being performed by
professional teachers.

This survey of the cultural condition of the barbarian kingdoms at the
beginning of the 6th century would be incomplete without some reference
to the revival in Vandal-occupied Africa. Teaching had begun again in

the schools of Carthage. Here Martianus Capella (*fl. c.* 420) produced his famous work, *De nuptiis Philologiae et Mercurii* (The Wedding of Philology and Mercury), an elaborate and encyclopaedic allegory that treats of the seven liberal arts that then constituted all human knowledge. This compendium of the liberal culture of the age quickly enjoyed wide circulation and continued to be highly esteemed by the scholars of the Middle Ages. In or around Carthage were to be found such poets as Dracontius—who was once imprisoned for neglecting to praise the triumphs of the Vandal king and had to write a special poem pleading for release—and others whose charming occasional poems are to be found in the *Anthologia latina*, which was compiled in Africa during the 6th century. (Anthologies of this kind played an important role during the Middle Ages, providing mediaeval authors with the greater part of their learning.) St Fulgentius of Ruspe, who grew up in Byzacium (a province of Roman Africa), was soundly educated in Latin literature and even in Greek. North Africa was re-integrated into the empire after the successful campaigns of Justinian in the mid-6th century, and it remained a repository of classical culture (or what remained of classical culture) until the end of the 7th century, when the region was invaded and occupied by the Arabs.

The cultural level of the kingdoms in the Western Empire of the 6th century was, of course, inferior to that of the Eastern Empire. On the one hand, educated men no longer set themselves the task of mastering the seven liberal arts. Despite Martianus Capella, they studied only grammar and rhetoric. And despite Boethius, Greek was no longer understood, with the result that the study of philosophy was neglected. The contemporaries of Boethius understood so little about philosophy, in fact, that they confused it with the occult sciences that were condemned by both Church and State. It is not difficult to understand how Boethius himself could have been accused of being an astrologer and magician. And on the other hand, such culture as there was remained a privileged possession of the senatorial aristocracy in Rome and in the provinces. The purpose of study was to prove that one was worthy to belong to good society. The fate of this secular culture, therefore, depended on the existence of an aristocratic class, on the preservation of urban civilization, and on the residence of these aristocrats in a city. Gradually members of this class began to settle more and more on their rural estates and to forget their cultural obligations to other citizens—a tendency that Cassiodorus laments. An educated man could be kept in a town only by the promise of an administrative career. The immediate goal of a classical education, in the Western as in the Eastern Empire, was a post in the civil administration. The barbarian kings maintained the administrative machine as best they could, but what Theodoric could still achieve—being an educated man and an admirer of antiquity—other princes were to have greater difficulty in doing. Literary culture depended therefore on the durability of the political apparatus bequeathed by Rome.

The success of Justinian's policy of regaining provinces lost to the Empire in Italy and North Africa naturally gave rise to hopes for a cultural revival. One of his first acts as Emperor triumphant was to restore to the professors of Carthage and Rome their privileges and salary. Among the series of measures designed to re-establish the social and economic well-being of Italy (known as the Pragmatic Sanction of 554), he required that teachers of grammar, rhetoric, medicine, and law should be paid by the state, "so that there shall be an abundance of young people instructed in the liberal arts." This injunction certainly seems to have been applied, for the knowledge and practice of law were maintained throughout Italy and Byzantine Africa, even in small towns. The art of medicine was taught within the general framework of Byzantine science in Rome and in Ravenna. Aristocrats were being educated about the middle of the 6th century according to the same syllabus as Ennodius or Cassiodorus had followed 50 years earlier. For instance, the poet Fortunatus (*c.* 530–609), who was born at Treviso and eventually became bishop of Poitiers, reports that at Ravenna he had already learnt grammar, rhetoric, and even law before his departure for Gaul around 565.

The other famous example is that of Pope Gregory the Great (*c.* 540–604). Born of a Roman patrician family, he spent his earliest years in their palace on the Caelian Hill; to fit him for an administrative career, his education was entrusted first to a grammarian and then to a rhetorician. His contemporaries noticed what the study of his work still confirms: Gregory is one of the rare writers of his time to command a correct and elegant Latin. In his sermons he remains faithful to many principles of classical style, using rhyme, the rhetorical sentence ending known as *clausula*, and the *cursus*, or prose rhythm, that was to become characteristic of the pontifical chancery in the high Middle Ages. Gregory liked to polish his style and "to make a well-composed piece of work," to quote his own expression in the prefatory letter to *Moralia in Job* (a monumental commentary on the Book of Job, couched in a Latin that is full of classical echoes). Like many other scholars of his time, Gregory had a taste for scientific learning, interesting himself in the arts of medicine, zoology, and history. He resembled them too in his lack of experience of the study of philosophy, for he knew no Greek although he had spent several years at Constantinople. Gregory cannot be considered a scholar of the calibre of Augustine or even of Cassiodorus, but an attentive reading of his work shows nevertheless how strongly he was attached to the intellectual traditions of the Roman aristocracy. He never speaks directly about his masters or his studies, but this is because he was converted to the monastic life in his early 30s and he wished to expunge everything profane from his thought. Yet he was obviously well aware of the fascination of classical literature for a Christian scholar. In the famous letter in which he reprimanded Didier, bishop of Vienne, Gregory reproached him for expounding classical authors instead of the Gospel, and thus of forsaking his calling as a pastor for the profession of teacher.

The fact that Bishop Didier could assume such a role is clear enough evidence that a taste for classical literature still persisted in southern Gaul at the beginning of the 7th century. Many features of Roman civilization were preserved throughout the Merovingian kingdom of the Franks, which embraced Provence, Burgundy, and Aquitaine, and stretched from the Mediterranean to the Loire. Civilized urban life continued, and with it the cultivation of the written word, as can be seen from inscriptions and from the work of municipal notaries who drew up documents of all kinds. The great senatorial families were anxious to give their children a classical education. In Provence, one educated circle included the patrician Dynamius of Marseilles, the Duke Loup, and the senator Felix, who, according to Bishop Gregory of Tours, studied Virgil, Roman law, and computation with the aid of his slave. At Avignon, at Vienne, and at Lyons, educated readers and literary works were not uncommon. In Aquitaine, the family of Sulpice from Bourges, that of Felix from Nantes, and above all that of Didier from Cahours all kept up the tradition of classical culture. Didier, who was born about 590 at Albi, enjoyed a literary education within his family before being sent to the court of Clotaire II, where he had a brilliant administrative career.

The pattern of literary culture in Gaul at this time was very similar to that in Italy. Priority was given to grammar and rhetoric, both in prose and in verse, and also to law, for learning of this kind could open the way to administrative office. The principal advisers of the Merovingian rulers in the 6th century and at the beginning of the 7th were educated aristocrats. After serving a period of office at the court, some of them were nominated as bishops by the king, on the strength less of their doctrinal knowledge than of their secular culture—a practice that was to lead eventually to a religious crisis in Gaul.

From the beginning, then, "Roman" Gaul—the area south of the Loire—formed part of the Mediterranean cultural community. But with time these links with the past grew weaker. The level of learning fell with each generation, and by the second half of the 7th century scarcely a trace of classical lore remained. Barbarian influences seem everywhere to have prevailed over Roman traditions. The situation is complicated, however, by the fact that, prior to this period, the culture of southern Gaul had been vigorous enough to infiltrate the northern Germanic areas. The Gallo-Roman scholars in service under the Merovingians had every reason to rejoice at the arrival of Venantius Fortunatus at the court of Sigebert, king of Austrasia. Fortunatus was an inspiration to these men, being the most admired Latin poet of his time and familiar with earlier Latin poetry, both pagan and Christian. In the *epithalamium* he wrote for the marriage of Sigebert and Brunhilda, Fortunatus invokes Venus and Cupid and other pagan deities propitious to love according to the classical tradition. The barbarian aristocracy were evidently impressed by and ready to accept this alien culture. Brunhilda's personal adviser after the death of her husband, and the tutor of their son, the future Childebert II, was a poet and rhetorician by the name of Gogo. Chilperic, the brother of Sigebert and king of Neustria, composed liturgical hymns in the manner of Sedulius, a Christian poet of the 5th century whose bombastic style imitates Virgil's. Chilperic even tried to reform the Latin alphabet and to impose on the Church his treatise concerning the Trinity, assuming thereby the same kind of authority as the Roman and Byzantine emperors.

The reason why the Frankish sovereigns and nobles of the second half of the 6th century were so receptive to Roman literary influences was that classical culture had been brought down to their level. In fact, these barbarians preserved only its more superficial and showy aspects, and they were mainly amused by poets who could entertain them with verbal tricks. They also liked to cherish the illusion that they were the successors of the great Roman tradition. When Fortunatus wrote his *Vita Radegundis*, he did not hesitate to compare the conquest of Thuringia by Clotaire I—Queen Radegund's former husband—to the capture of Troy. The legend that the Franks were of Trojan origin, which is reported in the *Historia francorum* (a contemporary chronicle of Frankish history attributed to a certain Fredegar), probably grew up about this time. In this way the Franks established a noble ancestry for themselves, and other barbarian races did the same, to prove their right to be accepted in the civilized world.

Meanwhile, south of the Pyrenees, a truly classical renaissance was taking place in both learning and letters. The explanation for this phenomenon is to be sought in terms of Byzantine influences, of the political stability of the region, and of the survival of the old aristocracy. Justinian had not succeeded in re-conquering the whole of Spain, but he had established his empire solidly in the south, from Cartagena to Seville. The presence of civil servants and dignitaries from the Eastern Empire ensured the continuance of ancient institutions. Moreover, the Visigoth kings installed at Toledo wanted to imitate the example of Byzantium. Spanish towns remained great social and economic centres, where Greek merchants were to be found who kept in contact with their native land. As in the Byzantine parts of Italy, a civilization based on written documents lasted throughout the 6th and 7th centuries. The *Lex wisigothorum* of 654 is modelled on Byzantine codes, and lays down the form for drawing up wills, donations, and deeds of sale. From it can be inferred the level of medical and legal practice in the lay sections of Spanish society. The great senatorial families who held out against the Arian persecutions of the 6th century, and who provided the monarchy with a reliable social structure after the conversion of King Reccared in 589, kept a high respect for literary tradition. Leander, bishop of Seville, and his more celebrated younger brother Isidore (*c.* 570–636), who succeeded him and was one of the most prolific writers of his age, came of an aristocratic family from Cartagena, and both of them clearly enjoyed a familiarity with the classics.

The converted Visigoth nobility, for their part, were eager to acquire literary culture. Whereas in Gaul the intermingling of barbarians and Gallo-Romans tended to result in the disappearance of classical culture, the opposite happened in Spain. All the scholars about whom anything is known gravitated toward the court, regardless of whether they were of barbarian or Hispano-Roman origin. Visigoth princes played the part of patrons of the arts and were themselves sometimes learned men, such as Sisebut, the author of a poem on an astronomical subject, as well as letters and the life of a saint. Again, grammar and rhetoric were the two arts most widely studied. The superior quality of Visigoth Latin is to be explained by looking at the grammarians of the time. The celebrated *Ars grammatica* of Donatus, the 4th-century Roman grammarian and teacher of rhetoric, was known to lay readers in Spain before Isidore included a resume of it in his *Etymologiae*, a summary of all knowledge accessible to him (and known by this title because of his etymological explanations of various subjects). The art of rhetoric was particularly esteemed for purposes of letter-writing and for legal procedures. Isidore also recognized the educative role of history, declaring that "a knowledge of the facts of the past helps to form the men of today"—an idea that was to be repeated by Julian of Toledo at the end of the century. One of the most remarkable features of the "Isidorian renaissance" is that it lasted so long: laymen and ecclesiastics knowledgeable in classical culture were to be found at Toledo and Saragossa right up to the end of the Visigoth monarchy early in the 8th century.

Such classical learning as survived was employed in the service of the Church. To construct a Christian scheme of knowledge based equally on the pagan liberal arts and on the Bible had been the wish expressed by St Augustine in *De doctrina christiana*. The Christian scholars of the 6th and 7th centuries had to pursue this goal on the basis of what was left of classical culture after the barbarian invasions. Like Augustine, Cassiodorus considered that a knowledge of the liberal arts was suitable preparation for a study of the Bible; that it was necessary, in fact, to learn how to read and understand the sacred text. In 533 he planned to establish at Rome a "Christian university" that would rival the schools of the rhetoricians, for, as he says in the preface to his *Institutiones*, he had been "saddened to see that holy scripture was not taught, whereas brilliant teaching was making profane authors famous." Unfortunately this plan was never realized, despite the support Cassiodorus received from Pope Agapetus I, because of the war that had broken out between Justinian and the Ostrogoths. Twenty years later Cassiodorus took up his idea again; he founded a monastery at Vivarium, which he turned into a centre of high religious culture. He transported to this remote place (in what is now Calabria), where his family estate lay, a large part of his rich library, which included both profane and religious works; he expanded it with new acquisitions and Greek translations, and produced a sort of catalogue that is at the same time an analytical bibliography for the use of educated monks. It is this that constitutes the most important part of the *Institutiones divinarum et secularium litterarum*, which lays down an educational programme for his monks, with instructions on the use of manuscripts. Cassiodorus also wrote a commentary on the Psalms in which he shows how the liberal arts are to be used. He tried to prove that the liberal arts existed in the Bible before the pagan masters discovered them for themselves, and that Scripture as a whole contains all the figures of classical style, as well as the fundamentals of music, geometry, and arithmetic; thus, a man who has been schooled in the classics will find it easy to become a biblical exegete. Admittedly, the exegesis practised by

Cassiodorus was rather more literary and formal than religious, for he himself remained all his life a professor of grammar and rhetoric. The last work he wrote (in his 93rd year), the *De orthographia*, is a compilation from the works of various grammarians, intended to instruct his monks in good writing.

While Cassiodorus was ending his days at Vivarium, the Roman aristocrat Gregory the Great was transforming his house into a monastery, and he too used his classical education in the service of religious study. Contrary to what has often been asserted, Gregory never abjured all interest in the classics he studied in his youth, but employed them rather as servants of Scripture. In his commentary on the first Book of Kings he declares that the study of secular literature can be useful if it leads to a greater comprehension of the Bible. Human learning provides the language for knowledge of the divine, in the same way that God became incarnate by assuming the voice of a man. Gregory is following here the line adopted by St Augustine, exploiting all the resources of his native culture in order to explain the great books of the Old Testament. The prime example of his exegetical method is to be found in *Moralia in Job*, where he goes through the Book of Job verse by verse, and gives literal, moral, and allegorical explanations of each one. Whereas Cassiodorus had been mainly interested in questions of literary interpretation, Gregory shows himself to be above all a moralist and a mystic. He was addressing himself to a small elite of monks, among whom was the future founder of the Christian Church in England, St Augustine of Canterbury (d. 604). After becoming pope in 590, Gregory could not expect his secular and ordinary clergy to share his taste for such learned religious study. But by his reorganization of the Lateran library and perhaps also by his influence (the extent of which is still not exactly known) on the so-called Gregorian sacramentary and music, he gave to his ill-educated clergy the means of spiritual self-improvement.

Gregory dedicated *Moralia* to his friend Bishop Leander of Seville, knowing that in Spain monks who had become bishops would be able to understand him. The monasteries in the Visigoth kingdom had, in fact, attained a level of religious culture comparable with that at Vivarium or the monasteries of Africa. Africa was in every sense close to Spain—Cartagena, for instance, had been founded by a Carthaginian and was called New Carthage to distinguish it from the African city—so it was quite natural that African monks fleeing from the ravages of the Arabs or the religious persecutions of Byzantium should establish themselves, about 570, in the one case near Merida (in Extremadura) and in the other case near Valencia. The latter group, according to a contemporary chronicle, brought with them a large quantity of books. By the 7th century, large monasteries with a flourishing literary culture were to be found near the cities of Seville, Toledo, Merida, and Saragossa. Isidore's encyclopaedic knowledge owed much to the wealth of manuscripts in the library of the monastery at Seville. He acknowledged that "grammarians are not mere heretics, for their knowledge can be useful to our way of life provided that it is put to good use." Like St Augustine, he thought it necessary to use these academic disciplines in the service of Christian learning. Isidore's study of the diacritical signs that have to be understood to establish a proper text of the Bible, and his observations about the literary figures of speech present in Scripture, are in the scholarly tradition of Augustine and Cassiodorus. His search for a sacred meaning in words and their etymology renewed an older Judaeo-Christian tradition and presented exegetes with vast possibilities of research. Following up an idea already expressed by Augustine and by Eucher of Lyons, he wrote a *Liber numerorum*, a treatise on the art of numerology. Isidore also followed Augustine in his injunctions to Christian orators to eschew preciosity and the elaborate styles of profane rhetoric that were still in fashion. He wanted to revive the classical tradition of Cicero and Quintilian, and urged bishops to speak in a style of sober elegance.

Although the writings of Isidore are important, they do not, of course, bear comparison with those of St Augustine. In fact, no great work of exegesis or theology was composed by Isidore or any of the learned bishops of Saragossa and Toledo who came after him. Isidore's chief contribution to Christian culture was the composition of practical manuals, compendiums of very varied information on subjects such as biblical toponomy, numerology, and ecclesiastical institutions. In the same way that his *Etymologiae* was successful as a reference work, making fragments of classical culture available in simple form at a time when such knowledge was badly needed (almost 1000 mediaeval manuscripts of the work are still in existence), so his manuals were useful to Christian readers because they gave the basic knowledge necessary for a fruitful reading of the Bible. Isidore was well aware of the intellectual level of his contemporaries and realized that literature as a whole, whether sacred or profane, could find a home amid only a very restricted circle of people. Not even all the bishops of Spain shared the intellectual curiosity of Isidore and his disciples, being more often men of action than scholars. The "Isidorian renaissance" affected only a small number of literate clergy. In his own day, Isidore's manuals were addressed to an elite; only later, as these manuals became more widely known, did his work bear its full fruit. Like Cassiodorus in Italy, Isidore of Seville worked for the future.

At the end of the 7th century, then, Christian culture in the humanist style seemed to have little impact on the world. It was the preserve of a tiny minority, most of them of aristocratic birth, and it did not reach the great majority of monks and clergy, to say nothing of the lay populace, Christian though their beleifs might be. There was, moreover, a sharp distinction and sometimes conflict between two types of religious culture, one of them humanist in tendency, the other exclusively spiritual in character. This distinction had existed for centuries, for it corresponded to two categories of Christians. One group wished to reconcile the liberal arts of antiquity with the Christian revelation, whereas the others adhered to the Bible alone. This more rigorous persuasion had originated in the monasteries of the Middle East and then spread to the West. Its adherents declared that there was no need to study the liberal arts, because the Bible contained within itself all branches of culture: history was to be found in the Books of Kings, poetry in the Psalms, natural history in Genesis, dialectic in the Epistles of St Paul, and so on. To study these topics in profane literature was harmful, because the songs of the pagan poets cultivated sensuality, the ancient philosophers were the masters of the heretics, and rhetoric was an art that attached more significance to words than to the reality of things. At the beginning of the 6th century, Bishop Césaire of Arles—formerly a monk at Lerinum, near Cannes, a monastery that had produced a number of eminent churchmen— denounced the evils of the *sermo scholasticus*, or artistic style of prose, and affirmed that the first duty of a Christian writer was to make himself comprehensible to all. The Gospel had been preached by fishermen, not by rhetoricians. Césaire's own sermons are in a simple and colloquial style, and illustrate his belief that "there is no need to have been to school with a rhetorician in order to bring home to people the truths they should believe and the duties they should practise." It was for pastoral reasons, in fact, that Césaire and other bishops wanted to see the scholarly tradition of a Christian culture abandoned. Because the rural and urban masses were illiterate, or had at best an exceedingly rudimentary education, there was no point in presenting religion to them in any very intellectual form. What they needed was to read the Bible, or rather to have the Bible read to them, and to sing the psalms and hymns of the monks in order to imbibe the word of God and to drive out of their minds any memory of worldly and generally immoral songs.

The culture of emergent Christendom was thus predominantly a biblical one. The simple goal pursued by Césaire of Arles closely resembles that of his great contemporary, St Benedict (*c.* 480–543). Benedict is reported to have fled from the Roman schools, where he was sent as a boy, because of their licentiousness; but he became *scienter nescius et sapienter indoctus* (knowledgeably ignorant and wisely unlearned), to quote his biographer Gregory the Great. This knowledgeable ignorance of St Benedict's did not, of course, mean a refusal of all learning as such; on the contrary, it was for the work he began, and his monks continued, toward not only the evangelization but also the civilization of Europe that he has since been proclaimed Europe's patron saint. And his monks needed a basic education in order to give them access to the Bible. In Benedict's monastery at Monte Cassino the monks had to learn to read the Psalter so that they could follow the holy office and meditate day and night on the sacred word. They also had to spend several hours each day reading quietly to themselves, in the low voice prescribed by St Benedict's Rule, passages from the Bible or the lives of the Church Fathers. This was a difficult task, both for those of aristocratic birth (who were accustomed to being read to by a slave) and for those of plebeian origin (who at the start were illiterate). This way of life became normal in most monasteries, each of which possessed a small library and a scriptorium. The intellectual level of these copyists should not be exaggerated, however, for their work was often an ascetic rather than an intellectual exercise. A monk had first to acquire this ascetic "culture" in order to refine his spirit, and the object of meditating on the Scriptures was to contemplate God.

This programme of monastic training was also adopted for the secular clergy. In Provence and in Spain the bishops endeavoured to establish residential schools where the clergy could receive a practical and theoretical education in their religion. This was the beginning of diocesan and presbytery schools; the former were directed by an archdeacon, who would teach the clergy to read the office, to intone, and to administer the sacraments, and the latter were entrusted to parish priests and might be open to young laymen. They thus became the first rural primary schools. But in neither case was there any question of teaching secular subjects.

While the cultural pattern of the barbarian kingdoms around the Mediterranean remained broadly ascetic and religious, with only a few aristocrats still faithful to classical traditions, the British Isles enjoyed an intellectual revival in the 7th century that was in no way presaged by what had gone before. Britain had been only superficially romanized, and later abandoned to the Celts; it was then repeatedly invaded by the Anglo-Saxons from the beginning of the 5th century onward. The Anglo-

Saxons had little knowledge of Greek or Roman civilization and they
remained pagan until the 7th century. The only areas in which Christianity survived were in Wales and Ireland. There the monasteries were
rather like rural cities, and Christian literature was preserved in them in a
quite distinctive form. The monks who wished to study the Bible had
first to learn Latin, which was for them an entirely alien language, and
to do this they needed books of grammar. As they did not have to protect
themselves against the dangers of classical paganism, they did not feel
the same reluctance as the monks on the Continent toward using the
works of profane authors. And as they did not have to adapt their written
style to the intellectual level of the people, because the natives of the
British Isles spoke a totally different language, there was no need to react
against the excesses of classical rhetoric. Anyone who has read the
Hisperica famina (a 6th-century British or Irish collection of mediaeval
learning) will have been struck by the unusual and mannered style. The
vocabulary is a medley of words borrowed from ecclesiastical Latin,
Greek, and Hebrew, and of neologisms formed from classical words.
Preciosity of this kind was undoubtedly attractive to the Celtic mind,
which delighted in complex and elaborate forms. This refinement of
artistic taste can be seen in works of Celtic jewellery and miniatures, with
their complicated lines of interlacing spirals and a fluidity that reflects no
earthly shapes. Besides this there was a native bardic tradition in both
Wales and Ireland, where poets competed to show their skill in narrating
the exploits of warriors, the adventures and loves of heroes, and the
voyages of sailors in search of the marvellous islands of another world.

During the 6th century Celtic culture developed in complete seclusion
from other influences, but in the 7th the situation radically changed.
England became the scene of a direct confrontation between Celtic and
Christian ideas as a result of the arrival of Roman missionaries in the
country. There emerged from this encounter a new kind of Christian
culture: a blending of elements that was to form the basis of the quite
distinctive culture of the Middle Ages.

Various stages can be distinguished in this new cultural development,
which took place in different parts of the country over a period of a
century and a half. During the first three decades of the 7th century
Latin culture rarely passed beyond the level of asceticism. The monasteries
founded by Augustine of Canterbury and his companions were intellectually modest; their primary interest was to preach and convert rather
than to pursue religious studies. But gradually, thanks to materials sent
from Rome, small monastic libraries were established at Canterbury,

London, Rochester, and Dunwich (an important commercial centre in Anglo-Saxon days on the coast of Suffolk; it has since been engulfed by the sea). In the north of England, where the first Roman missionaries were unsuccessful, Irish monks finally succeeded in establishing themselves on Holy Island (Lindisfarne, just off the coast of Northumberland) in 635, and from there they spread the faith. At this monastery, founded by St Aidan at the invitation of King Oswald, monks, clergy, and laymen learned to read the Psalter and to meditate upon the Scriptures; even ransomed Anglo-Saxon slaves were educated and prepared to enter the priesthood. Further south, at Whitby, King Oswy of Northumbria established in 658 a double monastery for monks and nuns that acquired renown under the abbess Hilda. She it was who encouraged the poet Cædmon to translate the Gospel into Anglo-Saxon verse for the benefit of people who had no knowledge of Latin. Lindisfarne, Whitby, and their offshoots introduced into northern England a culture that was markedly Celtic, even though none of these centres was ever really comparable with those in Ireland. Many Anglo-Saxons, in fact, went over to "the island where science blossoms," to find there not only their daily bread free of charge but also the books that they needed. At the same time, Roman monks were renewing their attempt to penetrate the northern parts of the country. Their progress was impeded by their liturgical differences with the Celtic rites, but the contact between monks of two such different backgrounds was valuable in itself. Under Oswy, the Anglo-Saxons began to be reconverted to the Roman discipline, and the Celtic party was finally overthrown at the Synod of Whitby in 664. The decisive voice was that of Wilfrid, the future bishop of York, who had been sent to visit Rome as a young man after finding favour at Oswy's court. With the acceptance of the Roman liturgy a new period began in the religious and cultural history of England.

Celtic influences also made themselves felt on the continent of Europe, after St Columban left Ireland with 12 other monks about the year 585 and settled first at Luxeuil in the Vosges; Columban was later banished, preached without success in Switzerland, and finally retired to Italy, where he founded another monastery at Bobbio (in the Apennines above Genoa). Although he was a learned man and a writer, he did not make either of these foundations institutions of learning. He did not place much importance on intellectual training in his Rule, which was intended rather to produce ascetic and missionary monks. A Columbite monk was expected to devote his life to manual work, personal or collective prayer, and acts of mortification. Nevertheless, by their monastic example the

27

followers of St Columban reawakened in both the clergy and the laity with whom they came into contact a taste for meditating upon the Scriptures. Columbite monasteries attracted young aristocrats of both sexes from Neustria and Austrasia, with the result that Gaul also began to witness a spiritual revival. Even the court of Clotaire II and of his son Dagobert (king of the Austrasians *c.* 623–9) was touched by this religious influence. It was for these kings that the gifted goldsmith Eloi created his jewelled masterpieces; later he acquired a distaste for worldly life, became a missionary priest, and founded many churches and monasteries, at Paris, Solignac, and elsewhere. Another prominent figure at Dagobert's court was Dadon, who was responsible for monastic foundations at Rebais (near Jouarre), at Faremoutiers, and at Lagny—all of them based on the parent house at Luxeuil. Their ascetic culture seems to have been respected everywhere.

In Italy, St Columban was able to establish his monastery at Bobbio thanks to the support of the Lombard king Agilulf. He wanted it to shine as a beacon of Catholicism in an Arian kingdom. After Columban's death, the religious zeal of his monks was largely concentrated on defending themselves against the persecutions of the Lombard Arians. The only writer associated with Bobbio at this period was an Italian from Susa, Jonas, the biographer of Columban and his successors. Jonas revealed in his preface and in the manner of his work as a whole that he had had some contact with the Latin rhetoricians of the 6th century before entering the monastery at Bobbio; the Celtic influences he experienced there merely reinforced a prior tendency toward preciosity. Certainly the library at Bobbio itself was quite modest and contained only religious works, records of ecclesiastical councils, books by Gregory the Great and some Christian poets, and the like.

No monasteries in Italy, however, could long remain immune to the cultural and religious forces at work within the peninsula. Despite the wars between Byzantium and the Lombards, northern Italy was in contact with Rome and with the monasteries of central Italy. And it was from there that the Rule of St Benedict was gradually radiating outward. Monte Cassino had been destroyed by the Lombards, but the Benedictine monks had sought refuge in Rome. Gregory the Great took it upon himself to write the biography of St Benedict, and by so doing he helped to make the father of monasticism known throughout the West. The monastic rule itself did not gain recognition everywhere so quickly. It was still unknown in Spain, and was only gradually becoming accepted in England, while in Gaul the diocese of Albi was the first to adopt it in about the year

630. At Bobbio the Benedictine Rule was probably not introduced before about 645. As a result of the strong ties between Bobbio and the Columbite monasteries of Gaul, as well as of the influence of Jonas himself, who travelled widely, there were significant opportunities for encounter between the Celtic and Benedictine types of monasticism. From the middle of the century onward many monasteries in Gaul allowed some form of compromise to emerge between the Benedictine Rule and the practices of Luxeuil, tempering the rigour of Celtic asceticism with Roman *discretio* and urbanity. This had a noticeable effect upon their cultural life; instead of devoting themselves to manual or missionary work, monks turned increasingly toward more scholarly pursuits. The cultural contacts that developed between Ireland, Gaul, and Italy allowed ideas and books to circulate widely; Rome became a great source of manuscript material, which found its way to Gaul and to England.

During the last third of the 7th century, uninterrupted relations existed between England and Rome. Five years after the Synod of Whitby, Rome sent Theodore (a Greek from Tarsus) and Hadrian (an African abbot of a monastery near Naples) to reorganize the Church in Britain. Both were well-educated men, and the School of St Peter and Paul that they set up at Canterbury attracted a great number of clergy and monks, and soon became famous for its teaching. According to Bede, they taught prosody, astronomy, computation, medicine, exegesis, and even Greek. New monasteries were founded in the north of England about 674 at Wearmouth and at Jarrow by Benedict Biscop, a friend of Wilfrid's. In order to equip these foundations, Benedict, who had already travelled to Rome in his youth, repeatedly returned to the Continent and Rome in search of manuscripts. It has been shown that some of these manuscripts came originally from Vivarium, passing from there to the Lateran library before being given or sold to Benedict Biscop. The famous 8th-century illuminated manuscript of the Bible known as the *Codex Amiatinus* was inspired by one of these acquisitions from abroad.

The monastery at Jarrow became famous, of course, chiefly as the lifelong residence of Bede (673–735). He went there at the age of 12 and remained for 50 years: "Observing the discipline of the Rule and reciting daily the Offices of the Church, my pleasure was in learning or teaching or writing." He is the prime example in his age of a great scholar who adhered strictly to the monastic way of life until his dying day. He had at his disposal the rich library that Benedict had succeeded in collecting, and it was by becoming acquainted with many classics of profane and sacred literature that he developed the clear and regular style that distinguishes him to such advantage from most Celtic writers and their disciples. He knew how to use Latin as a fine instrument for historical, scientific, and exegetical work. His style has a dignity and weight— *gravitas romana*—that is superior to the mannerism of Celtic writing. Centres of Celtic learning still survived in Bede's lifetime, particularly in Wessex. At the end of the 7th century the monastery at Malmesbury, which had been founded by a Scot, was headed by a prolific and gifted writer, Aldhelm, whose poetry and prose are both marked by typical traits of Celtic preciosity. A generation later at the monastery of Nursling, in Hampshire, Wynfrid (the future St Boniface) established a reputation for learning and (like Aldhelm) composed two grammatical treatises for his numerous disciples. He wrote these before 716, when he left England for the Continent, and it is remarkable how he loads his style with rare words, mixes his Latin with expressions drawn from Greek, and decorates his poems with laboured phrases.

The influence of Rome can be seen at other centres of learning in the north of England besides Jarrow: for instance at Ripon and at York, where Wilfrid had been abbot and bishop. In 732, one of Bede's disciples, Egbert, brother of the king of Northumbria, became bishop of York and entrusted the school there to his relative Ælbert. Among the pupils at the school was a boy called Ealhwine, later to become known as Alcuin (735–804), one of the most celebrated and influential ecclesiastics of the century. One of Alcuin's poems, dedicated to the bishops of York, recalls the syllabus and authors he studied at the episcopal school, and it is evident that York then occupied in England the place that the Canterbury school had held under Theodore. By the time Alcuin left for the Continent about 780, he had developed his learning and literary gifts to a level that was to enrich the court of Charlemagne, where he became educational adviser to the emperor.

Was the cultural level of continental Europe—from the German territory that Pope Gregory II commissioned Boniface to evangelize (Frisia, Thuringia, Bavaria) to western Gaul, where Alcuin was to end his days (at the monastery of Tours)—as low as is generally supposed? Certainly, the racial fusion, and linguistic confusion, of the Gallo-Romans and the Germans caused the last vestiges of culture among the laity to disappear; the invasions and wars in Provence and Aquitaine destroyed the last centres of intellectual and artistic life; and the material and moral crisis experienced by the Frankish Church resulted in the clergy becoming even more ignorant. The monasteries north of the Loire, however, were better able to preserve themselves, and in the first half of the 8th century they were the only centres where learning was kept alive. At the abbey of Corbie (Picardy), which had links with Luxeuil, scribes invented a new type of handwriting that combined features of an originally Irish script with others of Roman origin. There was an active scriptorium at Laon (near Rheims), which produced manuscripts of Origen, Augustine, Orosius, and Isidore of Seville. The monastery Dagobert founded at St Denis (near Paris) enjoyed royal protection (most of the kings of France have been buried there), and built up a rich library. Fleury-sur-Loire had close relations with Italy, especially after the relics of St Benedict had been transported there. Saint-Martin de Tours, which was an important starting-place on a pilgrim route, took in refugees fleeing from the Moorish invasion in Spain; the magnificently illustrated manuscript of the Pentateuch had found its way there by the end of the 8th century. These monasteries may not have boasted scholars of the calibre of Bede or Boniface, but they were at least preparing the ground for a revival of learning. They were encouraged by the arrival on the Continent of Irish and Anglo-Saxon monks intent on evangelizing the Germanic territories.

These missionaries were supported by Rome and were for the most part educated men. Willibrord, "the apostle of the Frisians," was educated at Ripon under Wilfrid; the monastery of Echternach, near Trier, which he founded and where he died, produced a famous Gospel Book. For three years Willibrord was assisted in his missionary work by St Boniface, who brought out to Germany former pupils from Wessex, men "formed by their knowledge of reading and writing, as well as of the other arts." It was not long before the abbots and abbesses of the new monasteries in Germany began to create their own libraries and to order books from England and from Italy. Boniface's own correspondence is typical of its time in his repeated requests to friends for books both religious and secular. In his moments of leisure he wrote poems, and he completed a grammatical treatise. When he set out on his last mission to Frisia, which ended in his murder by the pagans, he took with him a small library, and according to tradition he was holding a book in his hand when he was killed.

The growth of monastic culture in northern Europe, which was to provide the basis of the Carolingian renaissance, had its counterpart in Italy. Thanks to collaboration between the Lombard rulers, Pope Gregory II, and the Anglo-Saxon bishop of Eichstätt (who spent some time in Italy during a pilgrimage to the Holy Land), the monastery at Monte Cassino was restored in 720. A school was established there of a cenobitical kind (that is, as a true community rather than as a group of hermits) to teach the Benedictine Rule. The community included Italians, Anglo-Saxons, and Spaniards; the Lombard historian Paulus Diaconus (Paul the Deacon) used the reconstituted library there to begin his major literary work, the *Historia gentis langobardorum** (History of the Lombard People). At about the same time, the monastery at Bobbio began to take an interest in profane culture, and its scriptorium, which had hitherto produced only ecclesiastical works, started to transcribe the works of grammarians (Charisius, Servius, Probus), historians, and philologists (Macrobius), as well as glossaries. Manuscripts of biblical texts were actually effaced to make room for extracts from grammarians. Henceforward the monks at Bobbio could claim to be regarded as "humanists," and the monastery benefited culturally from the links that tied it to Ireland and to the nearby court of Pavia. Artists and poets had found patronage at this court ever since the reign of Cunincpert (d. 700). The poet Etienne, who celebrated the Synod of Pavia in verse at the command of the king, probably came from Bobbio. The grammarian Felix, who was a deacon, was also honoured by the king; and his nephew Flavian was the teacher of Paulus Diaconus. The cultured court at Pavia was regarded as a model by other princes in Bavaria and Friuli (between modern Italy and Yugoslavia); it was even imitated to some extent by the first Carolingians, Charles Martel and Pépin III, the grandfather and father of Charlemagne.

In the year 781, when Alcuin met Charlemagne in Italy and accepted the post of director of the palace school at Aachen, the literary culture of Europe may be summarized as follows. It was a culture accessible more and more to only an ecclesiastical elite. It was maintained and developed within a more or less closed circle of teachers and pupils, and its programme of studies was rather distantly linked with the classics of antiquity. Its exclusively ecclesiastical character is to be explained by the fact that the lay, senatorial aristocracy no longer existed. The aristocracy that had taken its place in the service of the barbarian rulers was more interested in fighting than in learning: it was as ignorant of Latin as were the common people. The clergy who were responsible for instructing the laity had to adapt their teaching, and particularly their preaching, to this public. Among the canons drawn up for the reform of ecclesiastical discipline at the synod of Cloveshoe in 747 was the injunction that priests must explain the Creed and the text of the mass in the vernacular. The rare instance of a lay person being able to understand Latin is invariably due

---

* The work is included in the *Monumenta germaniae historica*, ed. by G. H. Pertz *et al.* (1887).

to his having been taught the language originally by monks. In England it was not uncommon for princes and princesses to be educated by monks, even if they did not intend to embark on a religious life. The future Pépin III was sent to the monastic school at St Denis by his father.

It was within this restricted ecclesiastical milieu that Latin culture was preserved. Here students would read the Psalter, which was linguistically much more elementary than the moral maxims, such as the *Distica Catonis* (*c*. 300), that had once been given to the Roman schoolboy. The rules of Latin were taken from the grammar or commentaries of Donatus, and there were glossaries containing rare and obscure words with which scholars could embellish their prose. Bede's *De orthographia* is at once a glossary, a grammar, and a treatise on spelling. He gives the meaning of certain words in alphabetical order, the classification of nouns and the basic tenses of verbs, some etymology, and variant spellings; but the book scarcely bears comparison with the scholarly work of Cassiodorus on the same subject. From glossaries of this kind the monks and learned clergy of the early Middle Ages would have learnt the few words of Greek that they liked to introduce into their writings. The grammarians of antiquity had been expected to explain the classics but in the 8th century this was no longer what was wanted. The only classical verse that a monastic scholar might have been able to appreciate was what he found in the pages of some grammarian. Doubtless this would sometimes have inspired in him the desire to read the complete work, or at least further extracts in the anthologies then in circulation, but the primary object of his grammatical studies was a better understanding of Holy Scripture from a spiritual rather than a literary point of view.

Such were the historical conditions in which the Anglo-Saxon scholars were working as they re-made a body of Christian learning, and they preserved only a few of the ancient scholarly disciplines. Rhetoric and dialectic seemed to them useless, indeed dangerous; arithmetic, on the other hand, because it could be used for symbolic computation, they accepted as important, along with music. These 8th-century scholars perhaps enjoyed a certain advantage in being able to organize their studies along purely religious lines, for they no longer found themselves in the embarrassing position of standing between two cultures, as Cassiodorus or even Isidore had done. They were separated from ancient Rome by so great a passage of time that they could begin to invent a purely Christian culture; they could share the conviction of Boniface that no knowledge could exist outside the boundaries of God's law.

Contrary to what is sometimes asserted, the Anglo-Saxon revival of

C

learning did not restore the classical programme of the liberal arts. Although the monastery at Jarrow obtained books from Vivarium *via* the Lateran library, Bede did not simply follow Cassiodorus to the letter. He did not think it necessary to employ the liberal arts in the service of Christian thought, for the simple reason that he had only a fragmentary and secondhand knowledge of what the liberal arts were; and in this respect he stood well outside the patristic tradition represented by Augustine, Cassiodorus, and even Gregory the Great. Bede thought of Gregory as fourth in the line of the Church Fathers, coming after Jerome, Augustine, and Ambrose; indeed, all the Anglo-Saxons thought of Gregory as their "pedagogue." But Gregory had lived at a time and place still sustained by classical tradition, from which Bede was cut off by historical and geographical circumstances. It is revealing to compare Gregory's commentary on the Book of Kings with that of Bede. Whereas Gregory had accepted the liberal arts as a legitimate study for the purpose of learning to read Scripture, Bede condemns Christians who are tempted by Satan down from the heights of God's word toward worldly learning; he does not speak of any possible upward movement from liberal studies toward God. Elsewhere he frequently warns his readers against the dangers of secular literature, which he likens to "the thorns about a rose, the poisonous sting of the bee—one cannot touch such things without harm." The doctors of the Church, he says, have been reproached for being Ciceronians rather than Christians.

Alcuin may have been more attracted by classical culture, even though he was educated by Anglo-Saxons, but the new Athens he set out to build in Gaul was a city of God. As he wrote to Charlemagne:

> The only channels of learning for the old Athens were the sciences of Plato. Our city would have besides the sevenfold fullness of the Holy Spirit and would surpass all the dignity of worldly wisdom.

When Cassiodorus was planning his "Christian university" he intended to give equal importance to profane and religious studies. Isidore still respected the autonomy of the liberal arts. The scholarship of the 8th century is markedly different in being entirely orientated toward Christ and the interests of Christ's disciples in his pilgrim Church on earth. And thus it was to remain for all the centuries of the Middle Ages.

Bibliography

H. MARROU, *Saint Augustin et la fin de la culture antique* (Paris 1937).

P. COURCELLE, *Les lettres grecques de Macrobe à Cassiodore* (Paris 1943).

P. RICHÉ, *Education et culture dans l'occident barbare*, 3rd edn (Paris 1973).

J. FONTAINE, *Isidore de Seville et la culture classique dans l'Espagne wisigothique* (Paris 1959).

W. LAISTNER, *Thought and Letters in Western Europe (500–900)*, 2nd edn (London 1957).

CHAPTER 2

The Romance Languages

J. Cremona*

Classical, Low, and Vulgar Latin

The adjective "Romance" is used to qualify those modern European and American languages that have derived from Latin. Originally an adverb, to speak *romanice* was to speak the Roman way, to use the language of the Romans, as against that of the other peoples of the ancient world, especially the barbarians. The Romance languages are therefore those languages that can trace their ancestry back to Latin in a direct line. If we probe a little deeper, however, we shall find statements to the effect that the Romance languages did not develop from the Latin we know, the Classical Latin of school textbooks, but from a variant form of it generally called Vulgar Latin. Our first task, then, should be to consider what is meant by this statement.

By definition, Vulgar Latin was essentially the Latin of the *vulgus*, or common people. Contemporary terms were *sermo vulgaris* and *sermo plebeius*, to which we may add the near-synonyms *sermo rusticus*, *sermo cotidianus*, and *sermo familiaris*. In effect, Vulgar Latin is the term applied to the spoken form of the language in its many varieties, particularly the ones used by the uneducated, for it was customary to oppose to it the polished *sermo urbanus* of the educated. What we know as Vulgar Latin, then, may be defined along at least two semantic dimensions. The first, essentially social, opposes the educated and socially superior to the less-educated lower classes of society (*urbanus* as against *vulgaris* and *plebeius*). The other, essentially stylistic, sets what was written against what was spoken. In this case, however, we have no contemporary Latin adjective with which to label the literary "pole" and to set against the *cotidianus* or *familiaris* descriptive of the everyday language: *urbanus* was a term common to both dimensions.

* Lecturer in Romance Philology, University of Cambridge, and Fellow, Librarian, and Director of Studies in Modern Languages, Trinity Hall, Cambridge.

There is also a third dimension: the geographical or spatial. The spoken language varied with place, and featured identifiable regional characteristics; the written language, on the other hand, was essentially uniform. But in this case the opposition was not quite as simple as in the earlier dimensions, for we must take into account the notions of town and country and their accompanying social connotations: the large provincial towns appear not to have displayed regional features to anything like the same extent as the rural areas, and major cities would often mirror faithfully the model set at Rome. Hence, the two opposing terms along this dimension are *urbanus* again and *rusticus* or *provincialis*. Differences of language along this dimension were to play an important part in the subsequent linguistic and cultural history of the Empire, for they were the seeds of the dialectalization of the huge territory, and helped to break it up into the smaller areas that correspond to the individual modern Romance languages.

Yet another dimension should be mentioned here: the chronological. Linguistic differences that set in and grow with the passage of time are again more noticeable in the spoken than in the written language. These differences, too, were to play an important part in the development of the several Romance languages, although they need not detain us for the moment, because it seems that the ancients were only dimly aware of the process of linguistic evolution: no ancient grammarian appears to have systematically distinguished between "archaic" and "modern" with reference to Latin.

It seems as if the dimension that most attracted the attention of ancient writers as regards the language they spoke and wrote was the stylistic one: that in which the literary language was opposed to the spoken language of everyday exchanges. There is little difficulty in finding suitable comments—for instance, from a rhetorician of the end of the 1st century A.D.:

> There are still some critics who deny that any form of eloquence is purely natural, except that which closely resembles the ordinary speech of everyday life, which we use to our friends, our wives, our children, and our slaves.[1]

Thus, we have on the one hand Classical Latin, a rigidly codified, literary language taught in the schools and modelled very considerably on Classical Greek; and on the other hand a fluid vernacular, spoken over a large expanse of the empire by men and women in almost every walk of life.

Differences between spoken and written forms arise as soon as a society reaches a certain size or degree of complexity. They become very noticeable the moment a literary tradition in the vernacular becomes well established. The forms exhibited by spoken English in the world today are more varied and more numerous than those reflected in written English, in spite of the fact that modern literary English tends to keep remarkably close to the spoken forms. Modern spoken French, although it is the mother tongue of a more homogeneous society, differs very considerably from literary ("school") French. The difference is more marked in French than in English owing to the strength of the academic tradition in France. In short, literacy tends to encourage uniformity in the means of expression: to a greater or lesser extent it involves the imitation of models, and the critical evaluation of the "best" models. It may be worth pointing out here that, throughout antiquity and the Middle Ages, permanence and uniformity were ideals much admired and striven for in the idioms of the arts. It was partly owing to its uniformity that Latin remained the main vehicle of literacy throughout and beyond the Middle Ages, only gradually retreating before the emerging vernaculars: being no longer spoken, Latin could only remain fixed. In the *Convivio* (*c.* 1305), written in Italian, Dante sets Latin above the vernaculars on three counts, the first being its "nobility": Latin is perpetual and incorruptible, the vernaculars unstable and corruptible.[2] When the time came for the vernaculars to be fixed in their turn, in order to promote the new literacies, their grammars were largely modelled on Latin grammar, and rules were drawn up to ensure that they should no longer "wander" with time and space, from author to author, or (later) across social classes.

In dealing with such a complex matter as the diversification and co-existence of linguistic forms, it becomes important not to oversimplify the description: for instance, the constant interaction of spoken and literary models upon each other must be taken into account. In the case of literary Latin, an important change in the direction of the spoken language took place with the spread of Christianity toward the end of the Empire, and it produced a new literary model that we now call "Low" or "Late" Latin. Low Latin tends to adopt the vocabulary and syntax of the spoken vernaculars of the time (particularly their word-order), while maintaining the spelling and the grammatical forms of the classical language largely intact. It is the Latin used by St Jerome in his Vulgate translation of the Bible, and represents a conscious attempt on the part of Christian authors to "democratize" their language in order to reach as wide a public as possible: "Better for you to understand, though my speech be uncouth,

than be unable to follow because of my fine words," exclaimed St Augustine in one of his sermons.[3]

The Features of Vulgar Latin

How far and in what ways does Vulgar Latin differ from Classical Latin?
The question is of some importance, because the structure of Vulgar
Latin underlies the earlier stages of all Romance languages as a common
denominator and can still, for the most part, be discerned in the modern
languages: their common latinity is, in fact, a common vulgar latinity.
But before embarking upon a description of the differences we find, it
is as well to state that most can be located in time, i.e. as differences
between earlier and later stages of the language. A feature such as the
loss of the consonant *h* can be shown to have occurred over a period of
time. However, they can also be located in one or more of the other
dimensions that we have noted: a neologism frequently tends to appear
in the lower, less-literate strata of society and to spread upward in the
course of time. This seems to have been the case with the loss of *h*, so that,
at any given moment during its decline, the presence or absence of the
consonant in a given context may have distinguished one social group
from another, one "style" of speech from another. Moreover, differences
can also be traced geographically: successful innovations generally
spread from centres of high prestige (e.g. large cities) to peripheral rural
areas, which thus tend to appear linguistically backward and archaic
with respect to them. It is as well to keep these complexities in mind when
considering a basically chronological account of the changes that took
place.

The features that distinguish Vulgar Latin—particularly that spoken
soon after the breakdown of the empire—from Classical Latin are
numerous enough to rule out the possibility of our describing even the
most important of them here. Many can be successfully described only
in specialist terms that are out of place in a review of this nature. We
can, however, attempt to give a representative sample from which to
draw some conclusions.

To begin with grammar, we see the noun and adjective presenting a
noticeably simpler picture in Vulgar Latin than in Classical Latin. There
is a reduction from three to two in the number of genders, as a result of
the elimination of the neuter; a reduction from five to three in the
number of declensions, resulting from the absorption of the fourth and
fifth declensions by the first three; and a reduction in the number of
cases, difficult to specify for any given time and place but seldom featuring

more than three or four cases. The morphology of the verb shows similar simplifications: the passive voice is eliminated as a distinct set of forms and there are reductions, varying with time and place, in the number of tenses, perhaps the most interesting being the disappearance of the future as a formally distinct tense throughout Romance-speaking territory.

When we consider these and similar examples of simplification and reduction in the number of forms, we should beware of concluding that the means of expression became thereby more limited. This need not necessarily be so. Apart from the difficulty of establishing semantic functions for many of the grammatical categories that were reduced (e.g. declensions and gender for the noun, conjugations for the verb), the elimination of distinct forms for those categories whose semantic function is much clearer (e.g. case for the noun or tense for the verb) did not make it impossible to express their original semantic content. A virtually equivalent function could be performed by other means: *amor* (I am loved) came to be replaced by a more "analytical" *amatus sum* (Fr. *je suis aimé*)*; *ibo* (I shall go) by *ire habeo*, *ire debeo*, or *ire volo* (I have to go, I must go, I will go; Fr. *j'irai* from *ire habeo*); the "synthetic" *Petri* in *filius Petri* by a more "analytical" *de Petro* in *filius de Petro* (Fr. *le fils de Pierre*). In many instances it is clear that acceptable alternative expressions were already current in the classical language and that the spoken vernacular did no more than prefer the "analytical" to the "synthetic"; Sallust's *conscientia de culpa* was as acceptable as Livy's *conscientia culpae*. In other cases one function was expressed by two distinct forms within the same utterance, so that one of the forms was clearly redundant: for example *eo in urbem*, where "movement toward" is expressed by both *in* and the accusative *urbem*; or *venio de urbe*, where "provenance" is expressed by both *de* and the ablative *urbe*. The use of either preposition or case was sufficient to convey the required meaning (already implied, in any case, in the verbs *eo* and *venio*): the spoken language rejected one of the redundant forms and relied solely on the more analytical prepositional use.

Vulgar Latin appears thus to have lost much of the "synthetic" conciseness of Classical Latin, and to have become a far more analytical language, more articulated, and, as a result, more flexible. The same tendency may be seen working on most other aspects of grammar: e.g. *binas* (two by two, two at a time) is glossed by *duas et duas* (cf. Fr. *deux à*

* The original "past" function of *amatus sum* was lost as the result of the analogical action of expressions such as *romanus sum*.

deux), and *optimum* by *valde bonum* (cf. Fr. *très bon*) in the 9th-century North French Reichenau Glossary.

The trend toward simplification of the means of expression was accompanied by a parallel movement working toward the regularization of inflexions—that is, the gradual elimination of a large number of forms that did not conform to the statistically most frequent patterns in the grammar. Thus *caro-carnis* became *carnis-carnis* on the analogy of *canis-canis*; *acer-acris-acre* became *acer-acra-acrum* on the analogy of *niger-nigra-nigrum*; and *esse, posse, velle* became *essĕre, *potēre, *volēre† by analogy with the many infinitives in *-ere* present in the language.

Gradually, in this way, the paradigms of Latin became simpler and more regular. These changes were to a large extent inherent in the evolution of the language, and may be seen to have been working from the earliest times for which we have texts. But although they were inherent, reflection will show that a movement toward all-round paradigmatic simplicity and the constant preference for analytical rather than synthetic constructions cannot be explained simply in terms of an essentially spoken language left to its own devices. Paradigmatic simplicity means an economy in the number of choices to be made in the forms of a word at any given point in the chain of speech: when *filius de Petro* was preferred often enough to *filius Petri*, the form *Petri* disappeared from the paradigm *Petrus-Petrum-Petri-Petro*, which thus became reduced to *Petrus-Petrum-Petro*. But such a simplification could occur only at the cost of lengthening the speech chain by the addition of an element, here the preposition *de*. In technical terms, paradigmatic simplicity entails a compensatory lengthening of the syntagmatic chain. Now, a language left to its own devices and spoken in a restricted society tends to shorten rather than lengthen the speech chain, for the sake of economy of effort. This can be achieved only by increasing the number of paradigmatic choices facing the speaker. The movement toward analysis and paradigmatic simplicity that we have seen working in Vulgar Latin therefore betrays the working of an outside factor: as we have seen, it is not wholly explicable in terms of inherent tendencies.

Vulgar Latin does in fact show all the internal signs of having been spoken by a non-homogeneous society, a society in which it seems to have been the second language for the majority over a comparatively long period of time. It is the adult learner of a second language who

---

† An asterisk marks forms that are not attested in contemporary texts; they are generally "reconstructed" from later forms by the comparative method: cf. *èssere, potére, volére*; Old Fr. *estre, pooir, voloir*.

simplifies the choices he has to make at the cost of longer phrases and sentences, who prefers a more "analytical" construction for building up his phrases, and who tends to eliminate exceptions. The rapid spread of Latin over huge territories during the centuries of conquest confirms this internal evidence. Both inside and outside Italy, the language was acquired by peoples whose mother tongue differed from Latin to a greater or lesser degree, and among whom only a tiny minority were schooled in the "correct" use of the classical language. With one important exception, the prestige of the indigenous, non-Latin languages was not sufficient to effect a successful and widespread penetration of their structural elements—words and constructions—into Latin. Even a language enjoying as relatively high a prestige as Etruscan appears to have left very little trace of itself in the vernacular of the territory where it was originally spoken. All who could do so learned to speak Latin as well as ability and opportunity allowed, but they did so by taking, wherever possible, lines of least resistance. This movement was pronounced at the time of the Empire, but it became noticeably more rapid and effective after the breakdown of the central authority, when most linguistically conservative and centralizing forces, such as the administration and the schools, weakened to the point of disappearance over large areas.

The one important example of a language enjoying high enough prestige to affect the structure of Latin is provided, not surprisingly, by Greek. The enormous cultural influence of the Greek world over the Italic and Roman worlds had affected the history of Latin from its very beginnings: it was the Greeks who introduced the alphabet into Italy, and Greek had been a constant literary and linguistic model for Latin writers. Most educated Romans of imperial times had some knowledge of the language. Greek was in fact the chief language of culture and of international communication over most of the eastern half of the Empire. We should not be surprised, therefore, to find that it considerably influenced the development of the vernacular of the western half, although there is a tendency to undervalue the role it played in the history of Vulgar Latin. Large numbers of Greek words and expressions may be found (as in the vernacular sections of Petronius's *Satyricon*), even if we discount the large "technical" component represented by the specialized language of Christianity, which had reached the Western world largely through the medium of Greek. A number of grammatical features of the spoken vernacular can also be ascribed to Greek, although here we are on more uncertain ground: the Rumanian and southern Italian

43

dialects are imbued with Greek grammar, for instance, and it is possible that the development of a definite article—a feature unknown to Latin—out of the Latin demonstrative adjective system owed much to the presence of a definite article in Greek. Greek also affected the phonetic development of some vernaculars: for instance, it gave the Italian dialects a new consonant sound, the voiced *z* found in *zelo, zona*, and so on.

The elements of Vulgar Latin, then, reveal it to be a "mixed" language only to the limited extent that it incorporated a sizable Greek component. For the rest, it was formed almost entirely out of Latin ingredients—but ingredients that were modified and sifted by speakers of different native languages. As a result, even though the ingredients were basically Latin, the general aspect of Vulgar Latin betrays the characteristic structure of a mixed language.

Much the same phenomena may be seen working in the syntax of Vulgar Latin. Lessening reliance on a case system for the noun throws greater weight on such features as word-order to mark the function of the constituents of a sentence. Three elements of a basic Classical Latin sentence such as *Petrus Paulum amat* (Peter loves Paul) could in theory be placed in any order, because the case endings marked clearly enough the function of each noun. The choice of one particular order was determined by factors of a predominantly stylistic nature, such as the wish to stress one of the constituents more than the others. The fact that certain sequences were by far the most common introduced into the system an element of redundancy that we have already seen operating elsewhere. Vulgar Latin exploited the redundant element and fixed on the order subject + predicate for the sentence, and verb + object for the predicate, resulting in the order subject + verb + object for the sentence as a whole. As soon as this particular choice was made frequently enough, it was the turn of the case endings to become the redundant element, and thus relatively dispensable. Ultimately, word-order was preferred to mark the functions of subject and object, for a fixed word-order had the great advantage of being universally applicable and regular, whereas case endings changed their form according to declension, number, and gender. The fixing of word-order is another illustration of the move toward analysis, paradigmatic simplicity, and syntagmatic complexity.

Similarly, we find a predominance of co-ordinate over subordinate phrases in sentence constructions in texts that best illustrate the traits of Vulgar Latin. At this point, however, we should remember the nature of the sources we have at our disposal, and that, by definition, there cannot be such a thing as a Vulgar Latin text, because the language we

44

have been characterizing is essentially a spoken one. Few authors[4] set out to *write* what we have been calling Vulgar Latin: the sources at our disposal consist mainly of attempts at writing good Classical or Low Latin on the part of imperfectly schooled men and women. It is through these attempts that colloquialisms make their appearance: the model remains basically the same. A good example is the *Peregrinatio Silviae vel Aetheriae ad loca sancta* (The Pilgrimage of Silvia or of Aetheria to the Holy Places), an account of a pilgrimage to the Holy Land related by an unknown nun, probably of Spanish origin, whose schooling had taken her far enough to avoid spelling mistakes and the more obvious pitfalls of grammar, but not so far as to eschew glaring colloquialisms in syntax, style, and choice of vocabulary.

When comparing Vulgar Latin with Classical Latin we should also remember that the two had very different functions to perform. This becomes especially apparent when we compare their vocabularies. Many of the pairs of synonyms or near-synonyms present in the classical language are absent from Vulgar Latin: for instance, of the classical pair *tellus* and *terra*, only *terra* survived in Vulgar Latin (Fr. *terre*). But we must take into account that *tellus* was a highly poetical term that belonged to the traditional *carmina* and had not been in current use since the archaic period. When comparing the two vocabularies, then, we are comparing the vocabulary of an essentially spoken, everyday vernacular with that of a literary, often poetic, language polished and refined through centuries of cultivation. Even so, even if we grant the many losses from the vocabulary of Classical Latin, it would be a mistake to conclude that the vocabulary of Vulgar Latin as a whole was substantially impoverished. No statistical studies have been made on this point, but the evidence seems to indicate that the losses were more than compensated by neologisms of all kinds: loan-words from languages with which Latin had come into contact, metaphorical creations, and, especially, new derivatives built up from inherited lexical material.

The Dialectalization of Romania

We have described Vulgar Latin as featuring some of the typical characteristics of a mixed language, and we have seen that, apart from a sizable Greek element, these characteristics had not involved the incorporation of foreign components as much as the selection, from among alternatives available to Latin, of those means of expression that best suited the needs of a large, mixed population for whom Vulgar Latin played the role of a second language. Despite the vastness of the Empire and the heterogeneous nature of the original languages spoken within it, Vulgar Latin does present the student with a picture that is uniform enough to substantiate this view. We should remember that the presence of a single literary model, Latin, constituted a powerful unifying force that exerted its influence all the way down the social scale. The political, administrative, and cultural reality of the Empire during the first centuries A.D., followed by the weaker but still effective reality of a Church centred on Rome, gave the Latin literary model a sufficient hold over the vernacular to act as a brake on its evolution and even to influence it in the direction of uniformity.

The collapse of literacy that followed the breakdown of the Empire at the end of the 5th century naturally brought with it a considerable weakening of the conservative and unifying influence of the literary model over the vernacular. The rate of development increased, but—perhaps more to the point—Vulgar Latin evolved differently at different points of the Latin-speaking portion of the Roman world (or *Romania*, as it has come to be called). The earlier movement toward linguistic unity, which had been slow and precarious because of the vastness of the Empire, gave way before the forces that led to increased differentiation. Each locality began to develop its own form of the vernacular, and henceforward we must refer to a multiplicity of vernaculars. Differences between the speech of one locality and that of another had always been present, of course; but whereas they had tended hitherto to even out with time, from the close of the 5th century they tended to become more pronounced. Thus, from this time onward meaningful statements can no longer be made about Vulgar Latin in general, but only about the Vulgar Latin of such and such a province or town. Although it is still too early to speak of Romance dialects proper, some scholars prefer to avoid the use of the term "Vulgar Latin" altogether for the Dark Ages of the 6th to the 8th century, and to replace it by the awkward word "proto-Romance."

As we have seen, forces leading to linguistic differentiation are ever present in a community that is socially heterogeneous, especially when distributed over a vast territory with poor and infrequent communications. These forces were now given a comparatively free rein in Romania, assisted by the fragmentation of the Roman world into a number of politically independent states, the new kingdoms of the invading barbarians: Germanic (Frankish, Visigothic, Burgundian, and Langobard) in northern and central Romania; Arab in southern Romania; and Slav in eastern Romania. Linguistically conservative forces—chiefly the

Roman Church, buttressed for a few decades by Charlemagne's Holy Roman Empire—exercised their influence, but they were too weak to stem a movement that reflected so faithfully the contemporary development of European society.

It is important to realize that the linguistic developments we have been describing took place largely unnoticed: no one, as far as we are aware, was conscious of the fact that the vernaculars had developed far enough away from Latin, or had differentiated sufficiently among themselves, to warrant, for instance, the use of a new name by which to call them. Few, in any case, attached much importance to the spoken language: it was generally considered to be no more than an imperfect reflection of the literary form. Moreover, the very arrangement of the new dialects on the terrain offered few clues to the extent of radical change: with few exceptions, the dialectalization of Romania did not involve the creation of sets of clear-cut linguistic frontiers that parcelled out the domain into a number of well-defined speech areas roughly corresponding to the old provinces or the new kingdoms. The differences that set in or became more clearly marked were gradual and continuous. There was, for the most part, mutual comprehensibility between the dialect of one locality and that of its immediate neighbours, so that it was possible to communicate, village by village, from one end of Romania to the other (a situation that endured, incidentally, in many areas until the late 19th century). It was not till later that groupings of the new dialects came to be formed around emerging political and cultural centres.

This state of affairs is reflected by the contemporary nomenclature for the vernaculars. As we have said, no specific term was used to distinguish the new vernaculars from Latin or from each other. All we have are new terms opposing the languages of the "Romans" with those of the "barbarians," and these new terms themselves became current only where they were most needed—on the frontiers of the Romance speech area as a whole. We thus have *romanus* (whence *Rumanian*, to distinguish Romance from Slavonic in the Balkans; and *Romagnolan*, to distinguish Romance from Greek or Germanic in northern Italy); *romanicus* (whence *romanice*, giving *Rumantsch* in the valley of the Grisons, to distinguish Romance from Germanic); *romaichos* (to distinguish Romance from Greek in the Balkans); and *latinus* (whence *Ladin*, to distinguish Romance from Germanic in northern Italy, and *Ladino*, to distinguish Romance from Arabic in Spain).[5]

Despite the fact that little patterning can be discerned in the early history of the emerging Romance dialects, there is nevertheless a relatively clear early division of Romania into a western half—Gaul, Spain and northern Italy—and an eastern half—central and southern Italy, Dalmatia, and Dacia (now Rumania). The basis of this division is a number of divergences in the development of Vulgar Latin: the west has shown itself more conservative in some aspects of its phonetic development, for example by retaining Latin final *s* (cf. Fr. *temps, trois*, as opposed to It. *tempo, tre*, from Lat. *tempus, tres*), or the Latin diphthong *au* (cf. Fr. *taureau*, as opposed to It. *toro*, from Lat. *taurus*). A similar division is repeated in some aspects of the vocabulary. An example is the gender of Lat. *dies* as reflected in the neologism *dies dominicus/dies dominica*, coined from the Greek: it is masculine in the west (Fr. *dimanche*, Sp. Port. *domingo*), but feminine in the east (It. *domenica*, Rum. *duminică*). The relative conservatism of the western compared with the eastern provinces of Romania has been ascribed to differences in the manner of their latinization: the west appears to have been latinized mainly through "learned" agencies (the administration and the schools); it thus reflects a type of Latin that was closer to the literary standard than was the Vulgar Latin of Italy proper or that of the Balkan provinces, which were latinized largely through the settlement of colonies of veteran legionaries from Italy.

In much the same way, it is possible to discern other early divisions of the Romance speech area: there is, for instance, a clear opposition between an innovating central region and archaic peripheral regions in the vocabulary of Romance. The central distribution of a Vulgar Latin innovation such as *bellus* (beautiful: Fr. *beau*, Prov. *bel*, It. *bello*) contrasts with the peripheral distribution of an older Latin *formosus* (Port. *formosa*, Sp. *hermoso*, Rum. *frumos*).* It is also possible to oppose an "innovating" north to a "conservative" south in a whole series of examples drawn from the phonetic and grammatical development of Vulgar Latin. Northern dialects, for instance, tend to reduce the number of syllables in a word more drastically than do the southern ones; in other words, northern dialects have developed closer to monosyllabism. For example, Lat. *cannabis* has given Fr. *chanvre* and Prov. *cànep*, as against Port. *cânamo*, Sp. *cáñamo*, It. *cànapa*, and Rum. *cînepă*. Or again, the Latin demonstrative adjective system indicating three degrees of distance (near, middle, and far, represented by *hic, iste*, and *ille*) has been reduced to one indicating only two degrees in the north—e.g. Fr. *ce (livre)-ci, ce (livre)-là*, as against the retention of the Latin system in its essentials in the south, e.g. Sp. *ese, este, aquel*, It. (Tuscan) *questo, codesto, quello*. It is harder to ascribe causes for north-south differentiations than in the case of other types;

* Latin *pulcher* leaves no trace in Romance.

it is clear, however, that in several instances we are witnessing the influence of Germanic on Romance, the result of the new bilingualism that arose in areas thickly settled by Germanic invaders.

It is thus possible to ascribe the dialectalization of Romania to a number of causes: the way in which the various provinces were latinized; the very size of the speech area, making contacts difficult, if not impossible, to maintain by any but a powerful central administration, resulting in the uneven penetration of neologisms when the administration was still effective, and the eventual fragmentation of Romania when it collapsed; and the influence of Germanic and other invaders, positive when they directly affected the evolution of the language or negative when they encouraged the development of smaller, largely independent speech areas.

We have so far left out of account what many linguists have considered to be the chief cause for the break-up of an original Vulgar Latin unity: the influence of the languages over which Vulgar Latin had spread. Here it is not so much a question of the manner as of the degree of latinization. In those provinces that had been deeply latinized over the centuries, the period of bilingualism during which Vulgar Latin played the role of second language ceased comparatively early, and the pre-Latin languages, as we have seen, did not directly affect the structure of Vulgar Latin to any noticeable extent: at most, local lexical elements penetrated the vocabulary. But in those areas where, for a number of reasons, latinization had not been so thorough and where the native first language enjoyed a comparatively high prestige, there does seem to have been some influence on Vulgar Latin structure, and consequently on its development. In these cases we are justified in describing the Vulgar Latin of a particular area as a fully mixed language.

Such is the purport of the *substratum* theory, which has been hotly debated for many decades by Romance scholars because we know very little about most of the pre-Latin languages spoken in Romance territory. The arguments are often intricate and technical, and we have no room to summarize them here. The existence of a small but clear nucleus of vocabulary of pre-Latin origin in most Romance dialects is not disputed. These "fossil" words are found especially in rural terminology, and are often detectable in place-names: words denoting the configuration of the land, names of local plants or animals, and household words (e.g. Fr. *lande, combe, jachère, chêne, alouette, suie, landier*—all of Celtic origin). It is chiefly in the peculiarities of the phonetic history of each area, however, that substratum influence has been seen and debated: for example, the idiosyncratic development of Latin *f* and *v* to *h* and *b* in Castile and

Gascony, which is attributed to the influence of a Cantabro-Aquitanian linguistic substratum related to the ancestor of present-day Basque, a pre-Latin, non-Indo-European language. The influence of the substratum on grammar is far less obvious. This may be a reflection of our ignorance of the grammatical structure of pre-Latin languages, but we should remember that most grammatical changes (as indeed most phonetic changes) are intelligible without recourse to "external" influences. Nevertheless, in those areas where we have some knowledge of the grammatical structure of the substratum language (e.g. southern Italy, where Greek was widespread), the influence on grammar is clearly detectable; but again we should remember that Byzantine rule and the high prestige enjoyed by Greek prolonged the period of bilingualism in this portion of Romania and probably increased the possibility of direct influence. Celtic influence on the Vulgar Latin of Gaul may help to explain the survival of a rudimentary case system in Old French, although the "learned" character of the latinization of Gaul may be sufficient, as we have seen, to explain this archaic feature.

Similar (and equally debated) influences on Vulgar Latin development have been ascribed to the languages of the invading settlers, the *superstratum*: Germanic, Arabic, and Slavonic. Variable factors, such as the nature of the superstratum language, the degree of prestige of the newcomers, and the density of their settlement, all played a part in increasing the depth of differentiation. The northern French dialects appear to have been particularly affected by Germanic in vocabulary (e.g. Fr. *blanc, bleu, gris, fauve, blond, brun,* to quote only adjectives of colour, are all of Frankish origin) and in phonetic structure (for instance, the consonant *h—h aspiré*—was reintroduced with words such as *hanche, hérisson, hache, haie,* and remained pronounced until the 16th century); evidence of grammatical influence, on the other hand, is scant.

Vulgar Latin, then, may not have been very uniform as it spread over Romania, but it is clear that during the first 500 years of our era the forces working toward unification were stronger than those working toward diversification. At the fall of the Roman Empire, the trend was reversed, and disruptive forces, whether latent or overt, took the upper hand. The results of the invasions appear to have encouraged this process, not so much by affecting the internal development of the several dialects as by creating political obstacles to a continued common evolution: they isolated one area from another and placed each on an equal footing with its neighbours. The vernacular of each followed its own peculiar development, the product of a unique combination of external and internal factors. The overall picture of dialectal differentiation that resulted was quite remarkable in its variety, and it remained substantially unchanged until the beginning of the 20th century.

The Emergence of Texts in the Vernacular

We have seen that, in the centuries following the breakdown of the Empire, the comparatively rapid and differentiated evolution of the vernaculars passed largely unnoticed: they had been and continued to be regarded as spoken, colloquial variants of one language, Latin, whose canons had been fixed by the writers and grammarians of the past. The farther the vernaculars evolved from the literary standard, however, the greater was the rift between the spoken and the written language among the few people able in some measure to handle the written form. As a result, a new bilingual situation gradually developed, somewhat reminiscent of the unconscious bilingualism found among educated speakers in present-day France.

An awareness that a new bilingual situation had developed was long delayed. One reason for this is the fact that the knowledge and study of Latin reached its lowest ebb in almost every province of the old Empire during the Dark Ages of the 7th and early 8th centuries. Written Latin was increasingly reflecting the characteristics of the spoken vernaculars, and was developing traditions far removed from the Low Latin of the 5th and 6th centuries. Contemporary documents from the chanceries of France, Spain, and Italy illustrate well the lowering of standards. Early-8th-century texts from Merovingian France include such forms as *ligedema* for *legitima*, *baseleca* for *basilica*, *estromenta* for *instrumenta*, and generally betray features of the spoken language in haphazard fashion. When the 7th-century Lombard king Rotharis wished to set down a code of laws for his subjects, the *Edictus Rothari* (on the model of the Frankish *Lex Salica* and *Lex Ripuaria*), the only scholars he was able to muster in his chancery in Pavia wrote a Latin so full of errors as to be frequently incomprehensible. In Spain, a similarly mongrel form of notarial Latin flourished in the kingdom of León until the end of the 11th century. Known as *latinum circa romancium*, it was opposed to the no-longer-understood *latinum obscurum* of more learned documents. From the mid-7th to the mid-8th century, in fact, grammar and rhetoric were effectively taught in only a few centres; apart from Rome, they were mostly outside Romania, in northern England and Ireland.

The Carolingian reforms of the second half of the 8th century radically altered the situation. Begun under Pépin the Short, they were vigorously pursued by Charlemagne through the agency of a body of scholars under the direction of Alcuin of York (*c.* 735–804). The reform movement was highly effective and soon spread throughout most of Europe. The renewed study of Latin in this Carolingian renaissance mainly entailed the elimination of all traces of vernacular influence from the orthography and grammar of Latin texts. This resulted in a dramatic widening of the gap between the spoken and the written language, and the critical point was reached where the fact of bilingualism was formally acknowledged. A contemporary document unmistakably marks this passage: the ordinance by the Council of Tours in 813 requiring the clergy to abandon Latin for their sermons and to preach in the vernacular:

> Each should strive to translate his sermons clearly into the rustic Roman tongue or the Germanic, thus enabling the congregation to understand more easily what is being said.

It is worth noting in passing that the ordinance implies a reasonably high standard for the Latin of contemporary sermons.

Two inevitable consequences followed the passage from unconscious to conscious bilingualism: the appearance of yet another set of names for the vernaculars, this time in opposition to Latin itself, and the appearance of texts in the vernacular.

The first example of a name for the vernacular that clearly opposes it to Latin occurs in the ordinance we have been quoting: the expression is *rustica romana lingua* (the rustic Roman tongue). Earlier references to a *romana lingua* do occur, but the term was clearly used in a general way to oppose Latin or Vulgar Latin to languages belonging to other stocks. Its use in the 813 ordinance, on the other hand, is unequivocal, reinforced as it is by the qualifying *rustica*. The full expression, *rustica romana lingua*, occurs a little later, again in northern France, in a poem commemorating the death of Adelard, Abbot of Corbie, in 826. From the 9th century onward, the expression appears increasingly, often bereft of the now redundant *rustica*.

It is not by chance that the first appearance of a term to denote the new vernaculars has come to us from northern France: it was in northern France that the vernaculars had evolved furthest from the common Latin norm, especially in their all-important phonetic development. The southern Romance vernaculars were not to be recognized in this manner for some time. In Italy, the earliest mention occurs in a poem composed not later than 923, the *Gesta Berengarii*, celebrating the coronation of Berengarius I, king of Italy, at Rome in 915. The author describes the populace acclaiming the new king in their *nativa voce*, and contrasts it with the *patrio ore* used by the Roman senators. Such are the birth certificates of the new Romance vernaculars: it was not until much later that terms differentiating one vernacular from another appeared.

The earliest known Romance documents also come from northern France. These are the Strassburg Oaths, consisting of two oaths in Gallo-Romance and two in the Franconian Germanic dialect, quoted in a Latin chronicle recording the agreement made at Strassburg in 842 between Charles the Bald of France and Louis the German. Each leader had to swear one of the oaths in his brother's language and before his brother's army; each camp swore the other oath in its own language. It has not proved possible to identify the Gallo-Romance oaths with any one specific northern French dialect: its language is too undifferentiated, and, in the opinion of some, may be a witness—albeit the only one—to the emergence of a form of chancery French.

The most striking aspects of these first texts in the vernacular are perhaps the practical nature of their purpose and the close relation they bore to the spoken language. Oaths meant to be pronounced and understood by men who knew no Latin had necessarily to be in the vernacular, and their preservation for possible later juridical use entailed setting them down in their original form. The first documents from Italy that are unmistakably in the vernacular also consist of oaths: a series of four, written between 960 and 963, attesting the ownership of lands belonging to the monasteries of Monte Cassino, San Salvatore di Sessa, and Santa Maria di Cengla, between Rome and Naples. What is believed to be the first document in Rumanian, written in 1485, consists of an oath of allegiance; but in spite of its late date, we have only indirect information about it, and it is possible that it was written in Venetian. On the other hand, it is best to discount a much earlier text from North Italy, the *Indovinello veronese*, written in the late 8th or early 9th century, consisting of a short riddle of the type "The land was white/The seed was black/It will take a good scholar/To riddle me that."[6] Its early date would give it priority over the Strassburg Oaths: but, although it is undoubtedly written in a language akin to what we deduce the Veronese vernacular to have been at the time, the absence of context (it appears, together with a short Latin prayer, to have been jotted down by a man trying out a pen) makes it impossible to be certain that the writer was consciously writing in a language that was no longer Latin—a crucial point in attempting to decide the matter. Moreover, the very nature and function of the text argue strongly against regarding it as truly "Italian."

Other Romance texts from the 9th and 10th centuries come mainly from northern Romania and fall neatly into three categories:

(i) *Charters, notarial documents, and inventories*: León, *Nodicia de kesos* (10th century). Other Romance languages with first (though later) texts that fall within this category include Sardinian (1080) and Portuguese (1192).

(ii) *Sermons*: northern France, *Fragment de Valenciennes* (10th century). Sermons constitute the first (though later) texts in several Romance languages: Catalan (*c.* 1200), Ladin (12th century), and North Italian (late 12th century). These early sermons generally consist of a Latin original with the sentences interspersed with paraphrases in the vernacular.

(iii) *Religious epics*, a form derived from the vernacular sermon: northern France, *Séquence de sainte Eulalie* (880), the earliest French text after the Strassburg Oaths; the *Passion du Christ* and the *Vie de saint Léger* (both late 10th century); southern France, *Boecis* (*c.* 1000), based on Boethius's *De consolatione philosophiae*.

Glosses make their appearance from the 9th century onward, but have been left out of this account, even though several are extensive and translate whole phrases or passages. They do not testify to the presence of a fully conscious bilingualism, although they probably played an important part in its development.

As we can see, most of these early texts have a clear practical function and many are closely connected with the spoken word (oaths and sermons). Some, however, already show independence both from speech (charters) and from the basic, practical needs of society (religious epics). From the very start of its conscious life, Romance was beginning to take over some of the functions of Latin.

The Development of the New Literary Languages

(a) Latin and Romance

As far as we are able to tell, the problem of getting away from Latin did not present major difficulties in the composition of early texts in the vernacular, once awareness of the new bilingual situation had been reached. Although a number of texts written before the 13th century are in fact translations or adaptations of Latin originals, the influence of the parent language was generally surprisingly small. Only occasionally do we come across obvious latinisms, and then usually in formulas or set phrases (for example, the purely Latin genitive construction *parte sancti Benedicti* in the 960 Monte Cassino Oath). One possible explanation is that the vernaculars first found their identity in the very contrast that they made with Latin. Keeping away from Latin may have come more easily than might at first sight seem possible. Another factor must have been the oral basis of many of the new texts. As we have seen (and as we shall see again), writing in the vernacular was restricted largely to the recording of the spoken word. Hence the essentially phonetic, non-etymological basis of the spelling of words, even when their Latin etymology was very obvious, as in Old Fr. *on/om/ome* from Lat. *homo* (Fr. *homme*); *cors* from Lat. *corpus* (Fr. *corps*); *bele* from Lat. *bella* (Fr. *belle*); *ke* from Lat. *quid/quod* (Fr. *que*).[7]

In this respect, the linguistic situation of the 12th century is far from typical of the history of the Romance languages as a whole. For long periods, there was tension between Latin and the local vernacular. It existed, first, in the allocation of genres to one or the other medium. Latin continued to be used and written, and was a powerful rival to Romance, so that Romance took over only very gradually what had previously been written in the earlier medium. The process was to last for many centuries: it cannot be said to have been completed until the 17th with Descartes's *Discours de la méthode* (1637). Looked at from another angle, the separation of the media meant that a tendency gradually developed for the different literary activities to be conducted by different classes of writers. Again, tension built up with the elaboration of a literary linguistic standard that would also be true to the vernacular and independent of Latin grammar at its various levels: orthographic, morphological, and syntactical. This process again took long to achieve, although, as we have seen, the initial moments were relatively free of Latin influence. In contrast with the history of genres, the history of the influence of Latin on the literary vernaculars is not one of gradual emancipation; periods of deep Latin penetration alternate with others relatively free from interference, and the language of each genre was affected differently at different periods. Again, we have to come down to comparatively recent times before we can observe the permanent independence of the Romance literary languages in all their uses. The process of getting away from Latin was particularly arduous in Italy: Tuscan, the basis of the national literary language, is in many ways the most archaic of the major Romance dialects, and the absence of a political and administrative centre for the whole of the peninsula tended to restrict the use of the written language to purely literary uses and to detach it from its spoken, vernacular roots; the language of Italian poetic tradition, for instance, was, with few exceptions, saturated with latinisms until the end of the 19th century.[8] For a proper appreciation of the development of Romance languages and

55

literatures, it is essential to keep in mind that most writers went on being bilingual and that each nation went on possessing a double literature, one in Romance and one in Latin, throughout most of its history. In varying degrees, Latin was, ambiguously, both a foreign and a mother tongue.

At the end of the 11th century, however, when literary texts of substantial length were beginning to be written in appreciable numbers, the long contest between Latin and vernacular was yet to come. In the 11th and 12th centuries, vernacular writing concentrated mainly upon those genres with closest ties with the spoken word: the epic and the lyric. The great early monuments of Romance literature belong to these genres: in France, the *Chanson de Roland* (late 11th century) and the Provençal lyric (late 11th and 12th century); in the Iberian peninsula, the *Poema de mio Cid* (early 13th century) and the Galician lyric (13th and 14th century). Epic and lyric were genres that did not, for the most part, take over territory traditionally dominated by Latin: writers in the vernacular were essentially recording oral literature, in texts meant to be read aloud or sung. The existence of an oral lyric in 11th-century Mozarabic Spain is known through the presence of *ẖarǧas*[9] in the local Romance vernacular.

The linguistic influence of Latin on the vernaculars became significant after the renaissance of the 12th century. By the beginning of the 13th century, vernacular literature was established firmly enough to begin to take over new functions (such as narrative prose) or to look toward contemporary Latin literature for new fields to take over (such as chronicles). Prose had had an early start in southern France, where charters and notarial documents were translated or composed in the vernacular from the early 12th century; it was much developed in 13th-century Spain by the composition of *fueros* (municipal franchises) in the vernacular. Moreover, new developments were to blur the hitherto relatively distinct borders between what belonged to Latin and what to the vernacular. The general development of literacy among the lay upper classes meant that the tradition of reading aloud before an audience declined: the enjoyment of literature became essentially a private activity. A need was thus born for vernacular texts suitable for reading in private. It was met by the development of vernacular prose, both fictional (romances, stories) and non-fictional (chronicles, hagiographies, scientific treatises, and works of reference: bestiaries, lapidaries, works on astronomy, and so on). The fictional genres derived mainly from earlier vernacular verse-forms, whereas the non-fictional consisted at first mainly of translations or adaptations of earlier works in Latin or Arabic. Thus the Romance vernaculars began to take over some of the more typical functions of

Latin, and Latin began to exert an increasingly important influence on the development of the new literary languages.

Latin influence can be seen most clearly in the development of Romance vocabulary and syntax, both particularly susceptible to the influence of the translated language: vocabulary because of the new kinds of subject-matter adopted, and syntax because of the effect of translation itself and also because of the greater complexity required by the exposition of a line of argument. The latter effect was especially noticeable, as it tended to model the Romance sentence on its Latin original: the co-ordinated sentences typical of the narrative mode were enriched with subordinate clauses typical of intellectual exposition and commentaries. The process required the forging of a series of new subordinating conjunctions, more explicit than the multi-purpose *quid/quod* that had survived in Vulgar Latin and Romance (Fr. *que*; Sp. *que*; It. *che*).

The modelling of vernacular patterns on Latin originals helped to foster a taste for latinisms that was ultimately to work to the detriment of the vernaculars. The prestige of Latin and its literature gave rise to a general conviction that the vernaculars did not constitute as suitable a medium as the classical language for "serious" literary genres. A tension was thus built up in the minds of creative writers in the vernacular, best illustrated by Dante's ambiguous attitude to the two media. It led to a protracted crisis in the history of each vernacular, which each had to overcome in turn. The first to resolve it appears to have been Castilian: the wealth and compass of late-13th- and early-14th-century vernacular prose written in Castile under the direction of Alfonso the Wise (1221–84) and his successors is unparalleled in contemporary Romance. Castile's tremendous output appears to indicate that it was the first of the new nations to realize that its vernacular was potentially able to stand on a par with Latin for most purposes. An explanation of the Castilian phenomenon may well reside in the fact that Latin was not the exclusive language of culture in 13th-century Spain: the sharing of this function with other languages possessing a classical literature—Arabic and Hebrew—may have reduced the dominant position of Latin and furthered the development of Castilian to the position of yet another language of culture, and one, moreover, that properly belonged to the Castilians.

(b) The Formation of National Languages
Much of the vitality of the new literary media derived from the close contacts they maintained with their roots, the spoken vernaculars. In vying with Latin, however, this natural advantage was considerably

offset by a serious disadvantage: their very multiplicity. Linguistically, the basis of the new literatures was essentially dialectal, and few of the languages of early Romance texts had full currency beyond the confines of a relatively circumscribed region, even though the actual manuscripts in our possession (mostly late copies of varied origin) tend to blur some of the dialectal differences. The literary output of 12th-century northern France, for instance, was entirely couched in one or another of a number of regional vernaculars: Picard, Norman, Champenois, or Francien (the name given to the dialect of the Paris region, the Île-de-France). Until well into the second half of the 12th century, Picard, Norman, and Champenois texts were considerably more numerous and varied than texts in Francien.

This local, regional basis of vernacular media was of no great consequence as regards the diffusion of literary works so long as reading was largely confined to a professional class of readers or reciters, skilled in adapting originals to the particular vernaculars of their different audiences. With the development of more widespread literacy, however, the dialectal nature of vernacular texts tended to limit seriously the spread of new writing. The need arose for a literary medium resting on a more than purely local basis, and this came to be satisfied in one of two ways: either by the forging of a *koinē* (common language) with currency over an area wider than the region, or by the dominance of one dialect over its immediate neighbours.

Early attempts at the formation of a *koinē* are typical of the Provençal and Italian domains; both lacked the presence of a single, dominating political centre to act as a linguistic focus. The great mass of mediaeval Provençal lyric poetry is written in a vernacular of no clear local origin: its relatively standard language (for the times) incorporates forms characteristic of a number of dialects spread over a wide area. Individual Provençal troubadours did not write in their native idiom but in the Provençal *koinē*: none of the early Gascon poets, for instance, wrote in their native Gascon, which was clearly differentiated linguistically from the other southern French dialects. In northern Italy, a similar (though less significant) movement to fashion a locally based *koinē* was started in the 13th century; it may be detected in the addition of final vowels to consonant-ending words occurring before a pause—that is, in the avoidance of consonant-ending phrases (typical of, say, Veronese) in favour of the more acceptable vowel-ending phrases that typify Venetian and the more central Italian dialects.[10]

The linguistic situation developed in a different way in areas where a strong centre of political power emerged; there, one dialect came to dominate over its neighbours. Such was the case of northern France, where, from the second half of the 12th century, we witness the gradual dominance of Francien. The growth and prestige of Paris, seat of a central monarchy and a centre of learning since the foundation of its university, elevated Francien to the position of a standard that a growing number of writers from other regions of northern France wished to follow. "My language is good, for I was born in France [i.e. in the Île-de-France]," exclaimed Guernes de Pont-Sainte-Maxence, author of a life of St Thomas à Becket (*c.* 1172). Writers whose native dialect was other than Francien apologize for their language: "I apologize for my rough, uncouth, and barbarous language, for I wasn't born in Paris," writes the author of a 13th-century poem (*Boèce*). Another writer, Conon de Béthune, who was related to the houses of Hainault and Flanders, and was an eminent diplomat, soldier, and orator, protests:

> Encor ne soit ma parole françoise,
> Si la puet on bien entendre en François,
> Ne cil ne sont bien apris ne cortois
> Qui m'ont repris se j'ai dit moz d'Artois,
> Car je ne fui pas noriz à Pontoise.

> (Though my speech be not French [i.e. Francien], yet it can be easily understood in French [i.e. by speakers of Francien], and those who have corrected me for using words from Artois are ill-bred and discourteous, for I wasn't brought up in Pontoise [a town near Paris].)

Similarly in Spain, the prestige and power acquired by the Castilian monarchs during the reconquest of the peninsula from Moslem rule, and the siting of their capital at Toledo, elevated Castilian over its neighbours, although the old literary language was tempered at first when traits common to Mozarabic, Leónese, and Aragonese were not shared by Castilian.[11] A widespread tradition, first documented in the 16th century, claims that Alfonso the Wise decreed in the Cortes of 1253 that the disputed meanings of all ambiguous words were to be settled by reference to their use in Toledo.

The establishment of Tuscan as the national literary language of Italy took place as the result of both processes acting at the same time: Tuscan not only constituted the basis for an Italian *koinē* but also dominated, albeit only in the literary field, its dialectal neighbours. As a central Italian dialect, Tuscan had enough points of common development with both northern and southern dialects to serve as a bridge between them.

Moreover, the archaic nature of its phonetic development meant that Tuscan was closer to Vulgar Latin than any of the other dialects, so that on the time axis too, as well as on the spatial one, it could be said to be more "common." Tuscan was, in fact, so constituted that it was ready to function as an adequate basis for an all-Italian *koinē*. The incorporation into the literary language of many features from northern and southern dialects completed the process: Sicilian features were particularly prominent as the result of the development of a Sicilian school of lyric poetry, derived from the Provençal, during the first half of the 13th century. Dante's description of the *vulgaris illustris*—a term he applied to the new *koinē* in the first book of his *De vulgari eloquentia* (*c.* 1305)—is a classic example of an artist supremely conscious of the medium in which he worked.*

At the same time, Tuscan owed much of the success of its diffusion and its adoption as the national language to the prestige of the three great 14th-century Florentine writers who followed one another in quick succession: Dante, Petrarch, and Boccaccio. To this extent, Tuscan came to dominate the other vernaculars, though dominance was not achieved through political agencies (as in the case of Francien and Castilian) but as the result of literary success.

Even though fairly large territories could be reached as a result of the movements we have been describing, there still remained the fact that the literary vernaculars were local, whereas Latin was universal, and that the vernaculars were many, whereas Latin stood alone.[12] For reasons of prestige and practical utility, Latin still remained dominant as the language of culture of each of the several emergent Romance nations. In Spain, where, as we have seen, Latin did not stand alone as the medium of a learned and classical culture, the local vernaculars appear as a result to have grown more rapidly in status. In Italy, on the other hand, where—in spite of the great 14th-century writers—the formation of a national *koinē* was slow and limited to purely literary uses as a result of political fragmentation, the status of Latin grew until it almost eclipsed the vernacular for most of the first half of the 15th century.

The growth in status of the new "national" languages was further handicapped by a stylistic notion, current in mediaeval and later times, that certain languages were better suited than others to certain genres. Dante reports that Provençal was considered to be particularly well suited to the writing of lyric poetry, and French to the narrative genres.

* The fact that he was unable to identify it with Tuscan (chiefly because of the presence of non-Tuscan elements) detracts very little from the insight of his description.

Such opinions were encouraged by the practice of many authors of writing particular genres in languages that were not native to them. This was encouraged by the absence of clear dialect boundaries between the various Romance linguistic areas, a phenomenon to which we have already referred. The linguistic boundaries of southern France were especially indistinct, and lyric poetry in the Provençal *koinē* was composed by 12th- and 13th-century court poets such as Sordello in northern Italy and Raimon Vidal in Catalonia. Castilian writers of the 13th century wrote lyric poetry in Galician-Portuguese; Alfonso the Wise's *Cantigas de santa Maria* are an example. Occasionally, hybrid forms of language were produced, as in the Franco-Italian epic poetry written in northern Italy (for instance, an anonymous 14th-century version of the *Chanson de Roland*). Such widespread bilingualism helped to foster the prestige of a language possessing a considerable body of literature, and when this prestige was buttressed by political success, it could lead to international use in the modern sense. This was the position of French in Italy during the second half of the 13th century, exemplified by one of Dante's teachers, the Florentine Brunetto Latini, who, on a visit to France, wrote an encyclopaedic compendium in French (*Li livres dou tresor, c.* 1265), and by Marco Polo's record of his journeys, dictated in the same language (1296). The relevant passage from Latini's preface is often quoted in histories of the French language:

> And should any ask why, because we are Italian, this book is written in Romance according to the idiom of the French, I would answer that it is for two reasons: one, that we are in France, the other because its speech is more pleasing and more common to all peoples [than Italian].

The growth of national consciousness in western Romania is closely associated with the passage from dialect to national language that we have been describing. The new languages constituted a source of national pride; and their very number, from being a source of weakness, became a source of strength. Each nation had its own language, different from the others and different from Latin, which, because it belonged to all, ended by belonging to none. It is difficult to sort out the components that went to make up the concept "nation" in Western Europe. We should beware of ascribing the growth of the feeling of belonging to a political community to the feeling of belonging to the same linguistic community: homogeneous linguistic communities arise only out of a shared political and cultural life. There is no doubt, however, that in western Romania this feeling crystallized on a linguistic foundation and that it expressed itself in linguistic terms.

(c) The Codification of Romance Standards

Multiplicity was at first, however, not the only source of weakness of the Romance vernaculars with respect to Latin in the new roles they were being called upon to play. Another derived from their multiformity: whereas Latin was orderly, uniform, and unchangeable, the vernaculars were variable and impermanent. Latin possessed a "grammar," but the vernaculars had none. The very concept of grammar was inextricably confused with the Latin language in the minds of mediaeval writers and thinkers: *grammatica* was virtually synonymous with Latin grammar.[13] The Latin language was long considered to be an artefact, based on a vernacular but fashioned out and away from it by the writers and grammarians of antiquity. The notion of "grammar" (i.e. Latin grammar) thus stood in contrast to that of "vernacular," because the latter was thought to be of natural or spontaneous origin. It was not simply a question of there being no grammatical codification of the vernaculars: in the forms in which they were known, the vernaculars were believed not to be amenable to grammatical analysis. They were too irregular, too protean and variable, for analysis to be possible. These notions were encouraged by the diverging structures of Latin and vernacular[14] as well as by the number of graphic and morphological variations allowed by vernacular written traditions.

Many examples of these polymorphisms can be quoted for any of the mediaeval Romance languages. Forms varied from text to text, and frequently within the same text: for instance, the alternatives *ot/eut* (Fr. *eut*); *iestes/estes* (Fr. *êtes*); *fai/fac* (Fr. *fais*); *gieu/jeus/jus* (Fr. *jeu*), all culled from one manuscript, a carefully written, early-14th-century copy of Jean Bodel's *Jeu de saint Nicholas* (*c.* 1200). Some variations in form were due to the very process of formation of a *koinē*, others to the close relationship then existing between spoken and written language, for polymorphism is a phenomenon characteristic of the spoken language when developing without the restraints imposed by literary models.

Nevertheless, the first systematic descriptions of the grammatical structure of a Romance vernacular were written with the intention not of regularizing the language, but of teaching it to non-native users, particularly writers, who could not be expected to have developed a native's feeling for what was acceptable. It is only incidentally that they tended to regularize, chiefly because they drew much of their linguistic material from the language of the "best" authors and because they modelled their descriptions on the framework provided by Latin grammar. Thus, the first accounts are prescriptive and deal with those languages that were most used on foreign soil: Provençal and French.

Pride of place goes to the *Razos de trobar*, written before 1210 by the Catalan poet Raimon Vidal: its function was to guide Vidal's compatriots in the composition of lyric poetry in Provençal. Two other Provençal "grammars" followed in the 13th century: Uc Faidit's *Donatz proensals* (*c.* 1240) and Jofré Foixa's *Regles de trobar* (*c.* 1290), the first destined for Italians and the second for Catalans. It was only in the middle of the 14th century that a work was composed specifically for use in southern France, the anonymous *Leys d'amors*. But this later work, too, written at a time when the writing of Provençal verse had fallen into decadence, has been interpreted as an attempt to restore the language and its literature to its pristine glory—that is, as a guide needed by writers for whom the medium had to some extent become an alien tongue.

It is worth noticing that the primary concern of all four accounts was with rules governing the composition of verse in the vernacular rather than with rules of grammar. Because of this concern, Dante's unfinished *De vulgari eloquentia* takes its place among the Provençal treatises, even though it does not include a grammatical description of Italy's *vulgaris illustris*. The aim of the first "grammar" of French, on the other hand, was different. Although also intended for the use of non-native speakers, John Barton's *Donait françois* was written in England in the early 15th century to serve as a guide to correct speaking and writing. It reflects the special position of French in England at a time when the language had ceased to be widely known.*

As we have already mentioned, these early accounts of the grammatical structure of Romance languages modelled the presentation of their material on the framework provided by the current textbooks on Latin grammar: the *Ars minor* and *Ars grammaticae* of Donatus, and Priscian's *Institutiones grammaticae*. They tended to have little regard for the differences that existed between Romance and Latin grammatical structures: as an instance, we may cite Uc Faidit's silence on the presence of a definite article in Provençal. Such apparent lapses of insight are numerous, and it is difficult to decide how to interpret them. Did they arise from the desire to bring the vernaculars closer to *grammatica* and thus to ennoble

---

* We are ignoring a number of less important texts composed in England in the 14th and 15th centuries; their purpose was more that of correcting the most common mistakes of usage among English speakers of French than of teaching the rudiments of the language.

them, or were they the result of the aim of presenting the language to non-native speakers, as has been suggested? The latter view would interpret these omissions as the consequence of a contrastive approach: there would have been no need to mention features common to the two vernaculars.

The earliest known true description (in the modern sense) of a Romance language appears not to have had a prescriptive function of any kind. This is a brief, anonymous manuscript account of Tuscan, the *Grammatichetta vaticana*, now known to have been composed in Florence or Rome by the Italian humanist Leon Battista Alberti about the year 1450. Extraordinarily original in its conception, the *Grammatichetta* provides a full statement of Tuscan forms in 32 short pages. We cannot be sure what Alberti's aim was in writing it, but he probably wished to demonstrate the regularity of the vernacular, and to show that Tuscan was as amenable as Latin to grammatical rules. This would mean that Latin was no more an artefact than Tuscan was, and that what had been done for Latin could also be done for Tuscan. The work thus takes its place in the dispute about the origin of Latin that was being conducted in Italy in the first half of the 15th century, and was itself part of a larger debate on the question of which language, Latin or vernacular, was more appropriate for serious literary work. Seen in this light, the *Grammatichetta* appears as a pioneer work in Romance grammar, quite distinct in conception from its predecessors. At the same time, it seems to have been very little known at the time, and to have played only a minor part in the history of Italian grammatical work.* Moreover, Alberti was not so much concerned to prescribe rules for the vernacular, as to demonstrate that the language was already regular.

The first grammar of a Romance language to be printed, and the first work of its kind to apply the word "grammar" to a modern vernacular, was the *Gramática de la lengua castellana* (published at Salamanca in 1492) by the Seville humanist Elio Antonio de Nebrija, who had studied for 10 years (1461–71) at Bologna. The prologue clearly states its threefold aim. First, it was to help to fix the language, because regularity leads to nobility and permanence, as shown by Latin and Greek. Nebrija writes:

> Until now, our language has been loose and unregulated, and for this reason, it has undergone many changes in the course of a few centuries: if we compare what it is now with what it was 500 years ago, we find as much difference and diversity as there can be between

* It was known to Cardinal Bembo, author of the most influential 16th-century work on Italian, the *Prose della volgar lingua* (1525).

two languages. . . . I have therefore made up my mind, before anything else, to set to rule [*reduzir en artificio*] this our Castilian tongue,
so that what may be written in it from now on may remain uniform
[*quedar en un tenor*] and extend for the whole duration of times to come,
as we see was done with the Greek and Latin tongues, which, because they were placed under a new set of rules [*debaxo de arte*],
although many centuries have passed over them still remain uni-
formly one.

Nebrija thought that Castilian literature had reached its apogee in the
15th century and could not be expected to rise further: it was a good
moment, therefore, to codify its rules. His second aim was to teach
Spanish to non-Spaniards and to help Spaniards to acquire Latin. And
lastly, he saw a normalized language as a political instrument: "Language has always been the companion of empire." The prologue quotes the
words of Nebrija's patron, the Bishop of Avila, on the occasion of the
presentation of the grammar to Queen Isabella of Castile:

When Your Highness has placed under her yoke many barbarian
peoples and nations of unsettled tongues [*peregrinas lenguas*], these will
find it necessary after their conquest to receive the laws that the
conqueror imposes on the conquered and, with them, our language;
then, by means of this my grammar [*Arte*], they shall be able to
acquire knowledge of it. . . .*

Nebrija's grammar gives a full account of the forms of Castilian and
includes sections on rhetoric and versification. It is the first Romance
grammar of any consequence, in intention and insight, if not in all the
details of its execution. Differences in structure between Latin and
Romance, for instance, are clearly set out: for instance, "Castilian does
not decline the noun, except from the number of one to the number of
many [from singular to plural], but distinguishes between the meanings
of the cases by the use of prepositions." It is very likely that Nebrija's
apprehension of the differences in grammatical structure (also observable
in the *Grammatichetta vaticana*) was a consequence of the study of Greek,
then at its beginnings in Western Europe, and the inevitable comparison
between Greek and Latin grammar. Nebrija also compiled a Spanish-
Latin and Latin-Spanish dictionary as part of his conscious, sustained
effort at raising Castilian to the status of a *grammatica*, of an instrument in
all respects equal to Latin.

Nebrija's grammar was the first of a long series of grammars in the

---

* The reference was not, of course, to Columbus's venture to America, but to Queen Isabella's
well-known ambitions in Africa; nevertheless, the words constitute a fine piece of prognostication.

several Romance languages. Spain's expansion in Europe (Italy, the Netherlands) and its conquests overseas ensured its rapid and widespread influence. It is no exaggeration to say that the modern linguistic history of Romance begins with Nebrija's *Gramática* and *Diccionário*. They raised the whole question of which criteria to adopt for linguistic selection, and inaugurated debates on questions of language, in which new principles (such as good taste) came to play a preponderant role, as illustrated by the writings of Bembo and Castiglione for Italian and of Juan de Valdés for Spanish. These new developments, however, form part of the complex linguistic history of Europe in the 16th century and lie outside the scope of this essay.

Conclusion

Since 1500, the linguistic history of Romania has seen the fulfilment of the movements initiated during its formative period: the final victory over Latin, the further consolidation of the national languages over the whole of national territory, and the fixation of literary standards in the form of grammars and dictionaries describing the usage of "classical" authors. It was the second of these movements that took longest to achieve, for although the establishment of a written standard for the whole territory was accomplished by the end of the 16th century (with the consequent reduction of the dialects to the status of a patois), the corresponding development of a spoken standard, entailing the disappearance of the dialects, took much longer to accomplish and belongs for the most part to the 20th century. This last process is, in fact, still uncompleted, although 20th-century means of communication are rapidly bringing it to its conclusion. It has been particularly weak in Italy, where the influence of political unification has been felt for barely a century. It has been estimated that, at the beginning of the 20th century, about half the Italian nationals were incapable of speaking or understanding Italian.

On the other hand, the fixation of the literary languages has meant that, once again, spoken and written variants have tended to fall out of step: where the first evolved, however slowly, the second fell behind. Once again we witness a clear dichotomy between popular, spoken vernacular and classical, literary language, and the growth of tension between them: it is the perennial background to the linguistic history of a complex and literate society.

References

1. Quintilian, *Institutio oratoria* XII, x, 40.
2. *Convivio* I, v, 7. Dante was later to change his mind: in *De vulgari eloquentia* I, i, 4 the vernaculars are said to be nobler, partly because they were the first to be used by mankind, partly because they are found the world over and are natural, whereas Latin is artificial. Dante's later view, however, was atypical of learned opinion in his day.
3. St Augustine's consciousness of the two "styles" emerges from a comparison of the language in *De civitate Dei* (addressed to a pagan, humanistic circle) with that in his sermons: see L. R. PALMER, *The Latin Language* (London 1954), p. 190. Augustine's works are collected in *Patrologia latina*, ed. by J. P. Migne (Paris 1844–55), 32–47. Useful editions of his writings include *De civitate Dei*, ed. by J. E. C. Welldon (London 1924), and *Sermones de vetere testamento*, ed. by C. Lambot (Tournai 1961). See also Vol. I, "The Two Cities: Christian and Pagan Literary Styles in Rome."
4. The exceptions are chiefly: snatches of popular language placed in the mouths of their characters by writers such as Plautus, Terence, Petronius, and Apuleius (which remain, nonetheless, "art" forms); private letters, such as Cicero's *Ad familiares* and *Ad Atticum*; and the remarks of normative grammarians on incorrect usage, as in the *Appendix Probi* (see W. A. BAEHRENS, *Sprachlicher Kommentar zur vulgär-lateinischen Appendix Probi* [Halle 1922]).
5. In other areas it was the "barbarian" term for the Romans that gave the Romance vernacular its name, as in *Walloon* of northern France (from Germanic *walhos*; cf. *Welsh* in Britain and *Valachian* in the Balkans).
6. The actual text reads:

   > se pareba boues
   > alba pratalia araba
   > & albo uersorio teneba
   > & negro semen seminaba.

   > (He drove the oxen,
   > Ploughed a white field,
   > And held a white plough,
   > And sowed a black seed.)

   The answer to the riddle is: a hand pushing a pen in writing.
7. The use of individual letters, however, tended to be etymological. The contemporary values of Latin letters already approximated to the sounds of the vernaculars because the clerical pronunciation of Latin had kept in step with local phonetic development. The Romance reflex of the first sound of Lat. *cilium*, for instance, was rendered with a *c* in both French and Italian, although it was pronounced *ts* (as

in *bats*) in O. Fr. *cil*, and *ch* (as in *church*) in It. *ciglio*. In other words, clerical pronunciation of the Latin word rendered *c* as *ts* in France and as *ch* in Italy.

8. Countless examples could be cited: for instance,

> Tu lo mio stabilire e in tempo corto
> puoi ridrizzar il tuo caduto seggio . . .

> (You can consolidate my throne and in a short time restore your fallen one. . .)

from *La Gerusalemme liberata* (X, liii, 5–6) by Tasso (1544–95). From a more modern poet, it is interesting to examine the last line of Giosuè Carducci's sonnet "Il bove" (*Rime nuove*, 1861–87):

> Il divino del pian silenzio verde.

The line is open to two interpretations: a "latinizing" one ("the divine silence of the green plain") and a more modern, synaesthetic one ("the divine, green silence of the plain"). In both, the word order is quite foreign to Italian. E. De Michelis upholds the second interpretation in "'Il silenzio verde' o della sinestesia in Carducci," *Nuova Antologia* 493 (Rome 1965), pp. 463–82; E. Paratore argues for the first in "Il problema del 'silenzio verde' nel sonetto carducciano 'Il bove'," *Atti della Accademia Nazionale dei Lincei*, Serie VIII, Vol. XX (Rome 1965), pp. 242–5.

9. The term *ḫarǧa* is given to the final strophe, or envoi, in two types of Arabic or Hebrew poems, the *muwaššaḥ* and the *zajal*. To be valid, the *ḫarǧa* had to be written in a colloquial vernacular, Semitic or Romance.

10. For example, the lines

> Quel non è bon amigo,
> anci fai soz engano,

> Qi l'amig met en luogo
> onde li vegna dano. . .

in which *o* has been added to *amig* when it appears at the end of the first hemistich, but has been omitted when *amig* appears in the middle of the third. The lines are from the *Splanamento de li proverbi di Salamone* by a 13th-century poet, Gerardo Pateg, of Cremona.

11. An example is the retention of the letter *f* in words where, in Castilian, it had been replaced by *h*. For instance, *fazer* (Old León., Old Arag., Old literary [Toledan] Cast.) corresponds to *hacer* in Mod. Cast.

12. Contemporary opinion on the number of Romance languages may be gauged from a 12th-century, multilingual *descort* by the Provençal troubadour Raimbautz de Vaqueiras, composed in five languages,

one for each stanza—Provençal, Italian, French, Gascon, and Galician-Portuguese. Dante recognized only three major literary vernaculars—the *lingua oïl* (French, proper of the Franci), the *lingua oc* (Provençal, proper of the Yspani), and the *lingua si* (Italian, proper of the Latini)—in *De vulgari eloquentia* I, ix, 2. The rule of the mediaeval Order of the Knights of St John of Jerusalem (Knights of Malta) divided its members into a number of *langues* under the Grand Master; the Romance *langues* were France (French), Provence, Auvergne (Gascon), Italy, Portugal, Castile, and Aragon (Catalan).

13. The word has a curious semantic history in English and French. From meaning "Latin" (whence *grammar-school*), the word *grammar* acquired successively the meanings "learning," "recondite learning," and "magical learning"; whence Eng. *glamour* (mysterious, alluring beauty; cf. *gramarye*) and Fr. *grimoire* (unintelligible scribble).

14. One example is the relative lack of inflexions in the vernaculars. Even today the statement "English has no grammar," based on the same criterion, is often heard. The earlier Romance grammars tended to describe contemporary languages in terms of Latin, and to ascribe, for instance, a case-system to the noun; the French noun would thus be given a paradigm of the type: nom. *le livre*, voc. *ô livre*, acc. *le livre*, gen. *du livre*, and so on.

Bibliography

The standard works in English are:

W. D. ELCOCK, *The Romance Languages* (London 1960).

W. J. ENTWISTLE, *The Spanish Language* (London 1936); this should be supplemented by R. LAPESA, *Historia de la lengua española*, 3rd edn (Madrid 1955).

A. EWERT, *The French Language*, 2nd edn (London 1943).

B. MIGLIORINI and T. GWYNFOR GRIFFITH, *The Italian Language* (London 1966).

M. K. POPE, *From Latin to Modern French* (Manchester 1934).

No standard work on Vulgar Latin or Provençal has been published recently in English. The best introductions to these languages are the books by Väänänen and Bec listed below; but see also J. H. MARSHALL (ed.), *The Donatz Proensals of Uc Faidit* (London 1969).

I have also made use of the following works:

E. AUERBACH, *Literary Language and its Public in Late Latin Antiquity and in the Middle Ages*, trans. by R. Manheim (London 1965).

P. BEC, *La langue occitane* (Paris 1963).

F. BRUNOT, *Histoire de la langue française des origines à 1900*, Vol. I (Paris 1905).

J. CREMONA, "Dante's Views on Language," in U. LIMENTANI (ed.), *The Mind of Dante* (Cambridge 1965).

G. DEVOTO, *Profilo di storia linguistica italiana*, 4th edn (Florence 1964).

P. GALINDO ROMEO and L. ORTIZ MUÑOZ (ed.), *Antonio de Nebrija—Gramática castellana* (Madrid 1946).

C. GRAYSON (ed.), *Leon Battista Alberti—la prima grammatica della lingua volgare* (Bologna 1964).

A. MONTEVERDI, *Manuale di avviamento agli studi romanzi: Le lingue romanze* (Milan 1952).

L. R. PALMER, *The Latin Language* (London 1954).

A. RONCAGLIA, *La lingua dei trovatori* (Rome 1965).

C. TAGLIAVINI, *Le origini delle lingue neolatine*, 2nd edn (Bologna 1952).

V. VÄÄNÄNEN, *Introduction au latin vulgaire* (Paris 1963).

B. E. VIDOS, *Manuale di linguistica romanza* (Florence 1959).

W. VON WARTBURG, *Évolution et structure de la langue française*, 3rd edn (Berne 1946).

CHAPTER 3

The Origins of German Language and Literature

Gerhard Eis[*]

I

The origins of a distinctive Germanic language coincide with that point in time when the Germanic peoples began to detach themselves from the complex of Indo-European parent races to which they belonged and to develop into a separate group characterized by certain distinguishable features. On the question of the primeval home of the earliest Indo-Europeans, scholars are divided. Many take the view that they advanced from Asia into Europe, whereas others believe that they were originally domiciled in Europe and from there dispatched sections of their population to the east and south; scholars holding the latter opinion postulate regions by the Baltic Sea or in south-east Central Europe as points of departure for such migrations.[1] At all events the Indo-Europeans were evidently a restless people, filled with a spirit of enterprise that prompted them to migrate to distant lands and there set up their own kingdoms. The Tocharians penetrated into Central Asia; in the 7th century A.D. we find them living in the Tarim Basin in what is now Sinkiang, where traces of their language are preserved in numerous manuscripts. They were followed later by the Slavs, who subjugated the whole of northern Asia as far as the Pacific Ocean. The Hittites, the Indians, and other Indo-European tribes migrated to western Asia and the Indian sub-continent; other tribes, including those that were eventually to be known as the Greeks, Thracians, and Albanians, settled in the Balkan peninsula; and the Italic peoples and some Illyrian and Celtic tribes occupied the Italian peninsula. It was only at a relatively late stage that the Germanic

* Ordentlicher Professor für Deutsche Philologie und Volkskunde, University of Heidelberg.

peoples broke away from the Indo-European complex. They, too, then made their way southward—to southern Russia, the Balkans, Italy, Spain, and North Africa. Many of the states established by Indo-European tribes perished, as did several founded by Germanic peoples.

The date at which the Germanic peoples began to diverge from the Indo-European parent race cannot be fixed precisely. Estimates vary between the second millennium B.C. and the time of the birth of Christ.[2] The most important sign of their incipient independence was the appearance of the first distinctive linguistic features. This process of individualization took place gradually. Many linguistic changes made by Germanic tribes were common to the languages of neighbouring peoples; some remained exclusive to Germanic. The sum total of such criteria enables us to draw conclusions as to where tribes were settled in relation to one another during the prehistoric era.

One linguistic feature split the Indo-Europeans into two groups of approximately equal size: the development of the *k*-sounds. In the half to which the Germanic tribes belonged, velar *k* and palatal *k̂* (which were differentiated in primitive Indo-European) coalesced into one and the same sound, *k*. This new sound could further be changed in individual languages of the group according to the specific sound laws of each; for example, in Latin, where $k > c$ (*kentum > centum*) and in Germanic where $k > h$ (*∗oktōu >* Goth. *ahtau* [eight]). The languages that retained *k̂* as *k* are known as the *centum* languages (after Indo-Eur. *∗k̂m̥tóm*, Lat. *centum* [hundred]); included in this group are Greek, Italic, Illyrian, Hittite, Tocharian, and Germanic. In the second of the two groups into which Indo-European is divided, *k̂* developed into a sibilant (*∗k̂m̥tóm >* Sanskrit *satam*, Avestic *satem*). These languages are called *satem* languages and they include Sanskrit, Iranian, Armenian, Phrygian, Thracian, Albanian, Baltic, and Slav. The labio-velar sound *ku̯* is retained in the *centum* languages, but loses the labial element in the *satem* languages. For example the equivalent of the Indo-European interrogative *∗ku̯i*, *∗ku̯o* is *quis* in Latin, *kuiš* in Hittite, and *hvas* in Gothic, but *káh* in Sanskrit, *kó* in Avestic, and *kàs* in Lithuanian. A similar distinction is apparent in the development of velar *ĝ* and palatal *g*. From these facts it emerges that the peoples who subsequently comprised the Germanic tribes formed part of the *centum* family in the earliest stages of their existence.

By the same method the position of Germanic within the *centum* group can be defined with greater accuracy. The Germanic race must have been direct neighbours of that part of the Indo-European population that later emigrated to Italy, for Germanic has in common with Italic both

individual words ("isoglosses") that do not occur elsewhere and peculiarities of word formation. The following are found only in these
languages: Lat. *haedus* (he-goat), Goth. *gaits*, Old High German *geiz*
(she-goat); Lat. *clamare*, OHG *hlamōn* (roar, rage); Lat. *tacere*, Goth.
þahan (be silent); Lat. *silere*, Goth. *ana-silan* (grow silent); and there are
many more. Only Germanic and Italic can form adverbs of place
answering the question "whence?" with the suffix *-ne* (Lat. *super-ne*
[from above], Goth. *uta-na*, OHG *ūza-na* [from outside]). On the other
hand, the homeland of the Illyrians before they advanced into Italy
also bordered on Germanic territory. This is evident from the extant
remains of the languages of the Veneti and Messapians, both Illyrian
peoples. Venetic is the only language to have an accusative personal
pronoun, *meχo*, with the same ending as the nominative, *eχo* (I), just
as Old Norse *ek* and OHG *ih* have the accusatives *mek* and *mih* respectively.
In the vocabulary of Messapic we find *burion* (dwelling place), which is
formed from the same root as Anglo-Saxon *būr*, OHG *bûr* (dwelling);
Illyric *teutana* (queen) has the same derivative suffix as Goth. *þiudans*
(king). There is also a considerable number of Celtic-Germanic isoglosses,
for instance O. Irish *luaide* (lead), Anglo-Saxon *lēad* (lead), Middle
High German *lôt* (plumb-line, lead); O. Irish *oeth* (oath), Goth. *aiþs*,
OHG *eit* (oath); Gaulish *nemeton* (sacred grove), Old Saxon *nimid* (sacred
grove). Since these and other words[3] are found only in Celtic and
Germanic, we must conclude that the two peoples were at one time
neighbours, and in fact this theory is convincingly supported by the
historical evidence. Observation of the sound laws enables us to determine which words were originally the common property of both Celts
and Germans and which were later borrowed by one race from the
other. Thus Goth. *reiks* (ruler, powerful) and OHG *rīhhi* (powerful)
were borrowed from Gaulish *rīx* (in names such as *Vercingetorix*) and
O. Irish *rī* (genitive *rīg*: king); and Gaulish *brāca* (breeches) was borrowed
from AS *brōk*, ON *brōk*, and the earlier form of OHG *bruoh* (breeches).

In many other cases common linguistic features extend to three or,
less frequently, even to four neighbouring peoples. The transition of
dt > *tt* > *ss* is shared by Germanic, Italic, and Celtic. If an Indo-
European root ending in *-d* and a suffix with the initial consonant *t* are
juxtaposed, the result is the sound combination *dt*, which appears in
actual individual languages as *tt* (*uid-to*, Skrt *vittaḥ* [found]; *sed-tos*,
Skrt *sattaḥ* [seated]). Correspondingly we find ON *viss* (sure, certain),
O. Irish *fiss*; Lat. *obsessus*, ON *sess* (seat). Examples of isoglosses for
Germanic, Italic, and Celtic are Lat. *lacus*, O. Irish *loch*, AS *lagu* (lake);

Lat. *cribrum*, O. Irish *criather*, AS *hrīdder* (sieve), which still survives in
some New High German dialects as *Reiter*; Lat. *verus*, O. Irish *fīr*, OHG
wār (true). From certain characteristics it shares with the Baltic and
Slav tongues, it is evident that Germanic had bordered directly on the
satem languages spoken in the East since its earliest days. Whereas
in all the other Indo-European languages the dative and instrumental
plurals are formed by adding a *-bh-* suffix (or forms developed according
to the sound laws of individual languages), the eastern variety of the
Indo-European parent tongue, out of which Germanic, Baltic, and Slav
later developed, had an *-m-* suffix. Thus we find on the one hand Skrt
dēvēbhyah (gods), Lat. *hostibus* (enemies), Gaulish *matrebo* (mothers),
Venetic *louzerophos* (children), but on the other hand Goth. *wulfam*,
OHG *wolfum* (wolves), Goth, *gibōm*, OHG *gebōm* (gifts), and on the same
principle Lithuanian *vȳrams* (men) and Slav *ženami* (women). With one
peculiarity Thracian can also be included in this group. In the Germanic-
Baltic-Slav language group, and in Thracian too, the sound combination
sr is expanded to *str*. For example, in Indo-European the root of the
word meaning "to flow" is *∗sreų̯*; it exists in Skrt *srávati* (it flows) and
in O. Irish *sruth* (river). However, the corresponding form in OHG is
stroum (river), in Lithuanian *strove* (current)—although *srove* is also found
in Lithuanian—in Slav *ostrow* (island), and in Thracian *Strumon* (the
name of a river in the Balkans). In this way we can to a certain extent
localize the original homeland of the Germanic peoples. Because the
Baltic languages are particularly archaic in character and the Baltic
peoples probably did not venture upon any migration to distant lands,
we may presume that the Germanic tribes occupied areas flanking their
own present-day territories. Baltic is the only language that forms the
numerals 11 and 12 in the same manner as Germanic—that is, with the
numbers 1 and 2 plus a compound element that can be traced back to
∗likų. The Germanic form of this element is *-lif* (Goth. *ainlif*, *twalif*,
OHG *einlif*, *zwelif*) and the Baltic variant *-lika* (Lithuanian *věnuolika*,
dvýlika). Isoglosses such as OHG *glat* (smooth) and Lith. *glodus* (tight)
also testify to the early proximity of the two races, as well as numerous
later borrowings such as Goth. *reiks*, which appears in O. Lithuanian
as *rikỹs* (kingdom), and Pr. Ger. *∗kuningaz* (king), which was taken over
in Baltic as *kuningas* (prince, priest). At the extreme north-eastern
frontier some of the oldest Germanic words broke through the confines
of Indo-European and were taken over by the Finns. Among the
Germanic expressions that survive in the Finnish tongue are: *liina* (flax:
Goth. *lein* [linen]); *vantus* (glove: Goth. *∗wantus*, Fr. *gant*, ON *vǫttr*);

haikaro (heron: OHG *heigaro*); *rengas* (ring: Pr. Ger. *hringaz, OHG ring); and many others.

The factor that lifted Germanic out of its more limited status within a larger whole and enabled it to develop into an independent language was the appearance of a number of innovations in which no other Indo-European language group participated. One of these was the transition from the musical to the dynamic accent, by which the stress became fixed on the first syllable of a word. Connected with this was the process of smoothing off word endings according to specific rules governing the treatment of final syllables. The most striking innovation was the disintegration of the Indo-European system of plosives, which were altered by the first Germanic sound-shift, giving rise, *inter alia*, to a new set of spirants. A further consequence was the simplification of the inflexional system. A whole series of cases belonging to the nominal and pronominal declensions disappeared as a result of "syncretism"; several grammatical forms were also lost, notably verbal moods and tenses. At the same time new features came into existence. Vowel gradation (*Ablaut*), which was already present in Indo-European, underwent systematic extension, and the *n*-declension of Indo-European substantives developed into the so-called "weak" class of nominal declension and a second (weak) adjectival declension. The creation of the "weak" preterite and past participle enabled tenses to be formed in an alternative manner. With regard to the phonology of Germanic we must stress the development of the syllabic nasals and liquids *m̥, n̥, l̥, r̥,* to *um, un, ul, ur,* and the coalescence of *a* and *o* into *a,* and *ā* and *ō* into *ō.* The vocabulary of Germanic shows many special features that were partly incorporated as a substratum from the pre-Indo-European languages of tribes subjugated by the Germanic peoples, and were partly new creations. Such words are drawn in particular from places of dwelling and settlement, agriculture, cattle-raising, crafts, warfare, navigation, and law. We may assume that it was in these fields that the Germanic peoples made the greatest progress on becoming permanently settled. Only in Germanic do we find the roots of the following NHG words: *Haus* (house), *Burg* (castle), *Rind* (cattle), *Kalb* (calf), *Lamm* (lamb), *Wisent* (bison), *Storch* (stork), *Aal* (eel), *Helm* (helmet), *Schild* (shield), *Bogen* (bow), *Segel* (sail), *Steuer* (rudder, *Thing* (court of law, parliament), *König* (king), *Volk* (people), (*Rechts-*) *Sache* (thing, affair, [legal] case), and many others. The king of the animals is not the lion, which was unknown in Germania, but the indigenous bear (ON *bjǫrn,* OHG *bero*; but Skrt *r̥ksha,* Gk ἄρκτος, Lat. *ursus*).

It is possible that these innovations in the language were connected with the migrations of the prehistoric age or even sparked off by them. Research into the prehistoric era has established that in about 2000 B.C. the Megalithic culture of Scandinavia merged with another culture, whose chief characteristics were corded pottery and individual graves, to form a new Bronze Age civilization, a development that could correlate with the origins of the Germanic race. In the Late Bronze Age (*c.* 1200– 800 B.C.) this new culture spread to Further Pomerania as far as the estuary of the Vistula, and it is feasible that it was borne by those tribes who later appear as the East Germanic peoples. The territory to their south-east was occupied by the Illyrians, that to their south-west by the Celts. In the early Iron Age (6th century B.C.) this culture advanced up the Elbe: the tribes involved may well have been the Irminones (Elbe Germans), as Tacitus was to call them. To the south there were now only Celts. Later the Germanic tribes pushed further westward across the Weser and the Rhine. Many names clearly demonstrate the successive chronological states of this expansion. The Germans reached the *Mosa* before they had changed *o* to *a*, hence the name participated in this sound change and the river became known as the *Maas*. Considerably later, however, when the Germans reached the *Mosella*, this sound law no longer operated: the river retained its old name *Mosel*, and did not become known as the *Maasel*.

From their homes in Scandinavia and North Germany, fresh bands of Germans continued to embark on large-scale migrations. The Alemanni reached the Alpine valleys of Switzerland, and the Goths from Gautland made for the Balkans and South Russia (where traces of them were preserved in the Crimea up to modern times), and later for Italy and Spain. The Burgundians severed their connections with Bornholm (*Borgundarholm*) and founded a new kingdom on the middle Rhine, which was destroyed in A.D. 436 by the Huns; the survivors migrated to the south of France, and in A.D. 534 were incorporated into the Frankish Empire. The Vandals, originally from Denmark (*Vendsyssel*), journeyed via Silesia to Spain, which they reached in 409. They then crossed over to North Africa where, in 429, Geiserich established himself in Carthage; their kingdom was destroyed in 533 by the Emperor Justinian. The Langobards emigrated from northern Germany (*Bardowick*) through Hungary to northern Italy in 568, where their language remained in use until about A.D. 1000. Most of these migrations to southern regions, where other Indo-European peoples had already gained a firm footing, had a tragic outcome, for the Germanic tribes were not strong enough to assert themselves successfully. By contrast, the occupation of central

Europe, the British Isles, Iceland, and the North American continent (which was "discovered" twice) was of permanent duration. Of the languages of the Germanic tribes in southern Europe only Ulfilas' Gothic translation of the Bible, some proper names, and a few legal terms contained in the so-called *Volksrechte* (codes of common law), compiled in Latin between A.D. 400 and 800, are preserved. But we should not omit to mention the opening of a Vandal prayer, *Frōja armēs* (= *Miserere domine*), and a Crimean Gothic glossary that the Fleming G. A. Busbecq took down in Constantinople in the 16th century.

II

The Germanic tongue as it was spoken in the first centuries after the birth of Christ is called Primitive Germanic. There are no extant literary documents of this language, which at that stage of its development showed little dialect variation. We must reckon, however, that gnomic statements in poetic form from the Indo-European era were handed down, and that the Germanic peoples produced poetical works of their own that were circulated orally, for historians repeatedly mention the songs of the ancient Germans. The themes of such poems will have been the deeds of heroes, gnomic religious wisdom,[4] and similar subjects. Of all the old German languages there are only five of which we possess written literary works composed before A.D. 1000.

Only at the third attempt did the Germanic peoples succeed in making a permanent transition from the oral to the written form of language. The runic alphabet, which was probably adopted before the birth of Christ, was not used for recording whole poems or didactic prose, but only for brief communications and magic formulas. The Gothic script, invented in the 4th century for the purpose of copying down the West Gothic Bible, disappeared with the fall of the Goths, and was not taken over by any other Germanic tribe. Not until the adoption of the Latin script, which took place after the Age of Migrations (the *Völkerwanderung*) as a consequence of the conversion to Christianity, was any lasting success achieved. It was introduced by the Anglo-Saxons, who in the 7th century were already producing works of literature in their own tongue. In Germany, written vernacular literature first began to appear in the 8th century, partly influenced by Anglo-Saxon writings, and traces of Anglo-Saxon are clearly evident in the script. It was due to Anglo-Saxon influence that in German scriptoria, too, a few runic symbols came to be written down on parchment, for example the rune ᚹ for *w* in the *Hildebrandslied* and the rune ᚷ for the prefix *ga* in the *Wessobrunner Gebet*. In some OS documents we also find the AS symbol ᚧ for the voiced dental spirant. In Germany itself we must distinguish between two forms of literary language, Old High German in the south, and Old Saxon (which came into use somewhat later) in the north. Together with Anglo-Saxon they are classified as the so-called West Germanic group of languages, although we must not interpret this in genealogical terms, as if Old High German, Old Saxon, and Anglo-Saxon were each descended from a parent language, West Germanic. The fifth old Germanic literary language is Old Norse, which was developed to a particularly high level in Iceland; however, it was not written down until the 12th century.

In the two German languages (OHG and OS) there is a considerable body of extant literature. Some documents are a continuation in both form and content of the type of literature common during pagan times, but the examples we still possess are by no means outstanding for their originality. The most important are the two *Merseburger Zaubersprüche* (Merseburg Charms), and the *Hildebrandslied* (*c*. 800), all composed in alliterative verse. The purpose of the first charm is to obtain the release of a prisoner of war from his fetters, and to this end the assistance of certain merciful women (*idisi*, presumably Celtic-Germanic matrons) is invoked. The second is a cure for a lame horse. A similar horse charm is to be found in the old Indian *Vedas*, whence the formula presumably travelled across southern Europe to the Germanic peoples. In the Merseburg version the gods invoked have been given names from Germanic mythology; however, in a parallel version from Trier the same roles are taken by Christian characters.[5] The *Hildebrandslied* relates the universal story of the home-coming hero who is forced into single combat with his warrior son. The names used here are derived from Gothic historical legend. These and other small remains of pre-Christian poetry show that artistically it attained a high level of development; individual lines are full of verve and have the natural vitality of the spoken word. It is much to be regretted that a collection of old Germanic heroic lays compiled at the instigation of the Emperor Charlemagne has been lost, for it may well have been of the same high literary standard as the *Poetic Edda*, which was also a collection (*c*. 1250) of old heroic lays but in Old Norse. The contents of some of these missing poems can be constructed from adaptations in Latin chronicles and saints' legends. The period immediately after the conversion to Christianity was not a propitious time for the writing down of pre-Christian lays; nevertheless they survived in oral tradition, and in the High Middle Ages many poets still drew on this store for their thematic material. Also preserved (from the end of the 9th century) is a German encomium on the victory of the young King Louis III of the West Franks, who defeated the invading Norsemen at Saucourt in French Flanders. This, the *Ludwigslied*, still retains certain elements of the Germanic lays (*Preislieder*), but its contents are Christian and it is written in rhyming, not alliterative, verse. In the *Waltharius manu fortis* an episode of Germanic heroic legend is narrated by a monk in Latin hexameters, probably in the 10th century. The same theme is dealt with in the extant fragment of an Anglo-Saxon alliterative poem; in the High Middle Ages it was also taken up by a Middle High German epic poet and by the author of the Old Norse *Þiðrekssaga*.

The need to distinguish between Old Saxon and Old High German is occasioned by far-reaching differences of language. Old Saxon retained the consonantal system that emerged from the first sound-shift, and in this respect it resembles Anglo-Saxon and Old Norse. On the other hand it introduced certain innovations in common with Anglo-Saxon but absent from Old High German. One of these "North Sea Germanic" innovations, as they are called, is the loss of nasals before voiceless spirants, with simultaneous lengthening of the preceding vowel; AS/OS *fîf* corresponds to Goth./OHG *fimf*, and AS *ûs* to OHG *uns*. Another peculiarity is the introduction of a uniform plural for OS and AS verbs. The plural of *beran* (bear, carry) in Gothic is *báiram, báiriþ, báirand,* and in OHG *berumês, beret, berant*; but in OS and AS the form in all three persons is *beraÞ* (OS also *berad*). These and other differences between Old Saxon and Old High German indicate that the former was more closely related to Anglo-Saxon than to Central and Upper German. However, the most pronounced feature that distinguishes Old High German from the language of the North Germans is a second shift involving the consonants. This change was so fundamental that it was considered to be the chief characteristic of High German; hence it is called the "High German Sound-Shift." It has been convincingly established in recent years that this sound-shift did not originate among Upper German tribes, but that the latter were merely among those affected by its progress. It was in fact also introduced by the Goths in Italy, Spain, and Portugal, the Vandals in Africa, the Burgundians in France, and the Langobards in Italy, and it was adopted by these peoples before being taken over by the South Germans.[6] It is therefore a Germanic sound-shift like the previous one, but one that affected only the southern half of the Germanic world. The boundary runs right across the middle of Germany. The Bavarians, the Alemanni, and some of the Franks participated in the shift; the Low Germans, including the Low Franks, did not.

In Old Saxon the alliterative verse-form retained its hold longer than in Old High German; it was still used after the conversion to Christianity, and was employed in the service of ecclesiastical propaganda. There are in Old High German only two short Christian texts in alliterative verse, the *Wessobrunner Gebet* (early 9th century), dealing with the Creation, and the *Muspilli*, which gives an account of the Last Judgment. In northern Germany, by contrast, a poet skilled in traditional literary techniques celebrated the life of Christ in a great alliterative epic, the *Heliand* (*c*. A.D. 830). This somewhat long-winded but powerful Old Saxon work is supplemented by a poem about Genesis in the same form, of which only fragments are preserved; these were probably composed by the same author. These manuscripts show us that ancient Germanic alliterative poetry also reached a high standard in Germany. However, contrary to what happened in England and Scandinavia, it did not remain the dominant poetic medium, but was soon superseded by the new art of rhymed verse.

The main body of Old High German and part of early Middle High German literature is dependent for its themes on the religious texts used in monastery schools, and for its style and verse techniques on mediaeval Latin models. The earliest literary documents are concerned with the *artes liberales* (the seven liberal arts) and the *artes mechanicae* (the useful arts). They begin with a glossary that is called *Abrogans*, after its first *lemma*, or preliminary proposition. It originated in Freising about the year 765 and was modelled on a Latin-Latin dictionary that itself carried on the traditions of late antiquity and had probably been brought to Bavaria from a Langobardic school. It contains rare expressions that could be used to embellish solemn addresses and sermons. This first vocabulary list was quickly followed by others, of which the most important was the *Vocabularius St Galli* produced in the monastery of Fulda, in modern Hesse, toward the end of the 8th century. Similarly derived from the traditions of late antiquity were the *Basler Rezepte*, which an Anglo-Saxon compiler copied down in a German monastery; they were intended to ward off cancer and fever, and are free of any magical elements. The technique of composing rhymed verse also developed in the monastery schools. During his period of study every cleric became acquainted with Latin hymns written in this style; they were learnt by heart and recited or sung in Divine Service. To imitate them in German was an obvious next step. Thus in the Alsatian monastery of Weissenburg the monk Otfrid (*c.* 800–*c.* 870) took the same subject that the *Heliand* poet had treated in alliterative verse, and refashioned it into tetrameters of rhyming verse. His *Evangelienbuch*, clumsy in expression, full of expletive words and phrases, with many violations of natural word-order and meagre rhyme invention, was nevertheless greeted enthusiastically by Otfried's ecclesiastical superiors, who had the work copied and dispatched, with dedications, to King Louis the German, the bishop, and neighbouring monasteries. Otfrid's *Evangelienbuch* was the pioneer of German rhymed poetry, which enjoyed absolute domination throughout the Middle Ages and beyond. His pioneering feat was soon followed by smaller religious poems in the same form, such as *Christus und die Samariterin* and the *Georgslied* (written in Reichenau monastery, *c.* 900). However, all these early works in rhymed verse do violence to the German language to an extent that is remarkable when we compare them with extant alliterative poetry.*

Religious prose also provides examples of a natural-sounding rhetorical style, for instance the translation of a polemical tract by St Isidore of Seville (*c.* 570–636) and a German version of Tatian's *Gospel Harmony*. An outstanding characteristic of the Isidore translator was his ability to reproduce in lucid terms the abstract concepts of the original.

Religious literature gives but a one-sided picture of contemporary vocabulary in its entirety. The number of words occurring in Otfried is 3355, in Tatian 2030, and in Isidore 788; altogether 6173 words. The vocabulary of Notker Labeo of St Gall (*d.* 1022), whose attention was also turned to the technical prose of the secular sciences (in so far as these were studied in the monastery schools), was much larger: a total of 7800 words has been listed in his works.[7] The increase is due to his writings on mathematics, music, rhetoric, dialectics, and so on; but even these constitute only a part of the then existing vocabulary, because only what was of educational value came to be written down.

III

The language of Old High German and Old Saxon literature is in neither case uniform. In the Low German area there are fewer noticeable dialect distinctions because less was written there; hence it is not possible

* See Appendix: A.

to draw any precise dialect frontiers. We can note only the division between Old Low Franconian in the west and Old Saxon in the east. Little that is certain can be said about the individual literary centres; we cannot even locate the main work, the *Heliand*, with any accuracy. Various places in the large region stretching from Fulda via Utrecht to the south of England have been postulated as its source of origin.

With regard to Old High German we can distinguish three main dialects in the written language: Bavarian, Alemannic, and Franconian; the last of these is clearly subdivided into South Rhine Franconian (the dialect of Otfried) and East Franconian. Orthography is still closely related to the spoken language, for the development of a script that did not correspond to phonetic transcription was only beginning to take place in the 10th and 11th centuries. In each of the three main dialect regions there were several literary centres: in Bavaria, Freising, Regensburg, Wessobrunn, Tegernsee, Monsee, and Salzburg; in Alemannia, St Gall, Reichenau, and Murbach; in Franconia, Fulda, Bamberg, Würzburg, Lorsch, Mainz, Weissenburg, and others. With the help of modern dialect geography we can to a certain extent define more precisely the line taken by dialect frontiers. However, this is of no great consequence for Old High German literature, because the literary centres of that period sprang up like islands from the surrounding areas where the art of writing was not practised, and there are enough obvious differences between them to make the task of locating extant manuscripts a relatively easy one.

We can observe how vocabulary was affected in various ways by new developments. Archaic words such as *frō* (the Lord), *itis* (woman), *mornēn* (to mourn), gradually disappeared during the Old High German period. Many old expressions, dropped by German, were retained in other Germanic languages, for example OHG *ēwa*, which survives in Dutch as *eeuw* (century), and OS *trio*, which corresponds to the English word *tree* (NHG *Baum*). Conversely, new words came into existence during the Old High German period, particularly in the ecclesiastical sphere. Lat. *scola* was taken over into German as *scuola* (school), Lat. *scribēre* as *scrîban* (to write), Lat. *tractare* as *trahtōn* (to strive), Vulgar Lat. *segnum* (= *signum*) as *segan* (blessing, prayer). Other expressions were created by means of loan translations, such as *armaherz* (*misericors*: mercy), *gifateri* (*compater*: godfather), *hēriro* (comparative of *her*: older). Various influences from Old French, Anglo-Saxon, and Greek can be attributed to the agency of the Church. The Church Latin term *eleemosyne* appears in O. Fr. as *almosne* and this gives OHG *alamuosan* (alms); OHG *priestar* (priest) does not trace back directly to the Greek-Latin word *presbyter*, but to its O. Fr. derivative *prestre*.

The presence of the Anglo-Saxon mission in Germany explains why *Samstag* (Saturday) is also known as *Sonnabend*: OHG *sunnūnābant* is an imitation of AS *sunnanæfen* (eve of Sunday). That Lat. *evangelium* is reproduced in OHG not by the term *guotspel* (glad tidings: *guot* = good) but by *gotspel*, is due to AS *gōdspel*, of which the determinative word *gōd* was erroneously interpreted as "God" instead of "good." It is not possible to arrive at any definite conclusions with regard to a few words that were ultimately of Greek origin. OHG *chiricha* (church) is derived from Gk χυρικόν (not Lat. *ecclesia*), OHG *pfaffo* from Gk πάπας, which designates the cleric of low rank, whereas Lat. *papa* signifies the head of the whole church. Attempts have been made to find an explanation for such phenomena in the existence of a Gothic mission, which is supposed to have been active from south-eastern Europe right up to the Rhine. However, no historical proof of any such mission exists, and the explanation lies more probably in the influence of the Burgundians from south-eastern France, who were likewise of Arian faith. The pagan Germanic terms used to designate the days of the week *Dienstag* and *Donnerstag* (*Dienstag* [Tuesday] was the day of the assembly watched over by Ziu; *Donnerstag* [Thursday] was Donar's day) were ousted in Bavarian by Greek-Gothic expressions. Bav. *ertag* (Tuesday) went back to Gk ῎Αρεως ἡμέρα (the Gothic form of which will have been *areinsdags*), and Bav. *pfinztag* (Thursday) to Gk πέμπτη (in Gothic probably *paintē*). Some new words were invented by Notker Labeo of St Gall, who coined loan translations of Latin concepts for use in his writings. He devised such apt terms as *nōtfolgunga* (*consequentia*: logical conclusion), *unspaltīg* (*individuus*: indivisible), *geskīdotlīh* (*disiunctivus*: disjunctive), and others, although most of them did not survive. A Latin dictionary glossed in German, which was compiled during Notker Labeo's lifetime (*c.* 1010) in or near Worms, appears to have had a more permanent effect. It contains vocabulary drawn from the liberal and useful arts and also specialized legal expressions. It is called the *Summarium Heinrici* and exists in two versions, of which 33 copies have come down to the present day.

Whereas Old Saxon literature ceased to make its voice heard in the 10th century, Old High German underwent an increasingly varied development. In the 11th and 12th centuries the Old High German language was transformed into Middle High German by a series of incisive changes. The most striking is the weakening of the vowels *a, o, u,* and *i* to *e* in unstressed final syllables. This weakening is probably linked with a strengthening of the expiratory accent: the difference between stressed and unstressed syllables increased, so that the vowels in unstressed syllables weakened. In Notker this change can already be observed in the closed final position: in his writings OHG *uuesan* appears as *uuesen*; OHG *zîtin* as *zîten*; OHG *enti* as *ende*; in MHG the OHG endings *-ag*, *-îg*, and *-ing* all become *-ec* (*heilag* > *heilec*, *sâlîg* > *sælec*, *kuning* > *künec*). In the 12th century the unstressed short vowels become *e* even in the open final position: OHG *demu, demo* > MHG *deme*; OHG *fogala* > MHG *vogele*; OHG *edili* > MHG *edele*; OHG *sunu* > MHG *sune*; OHG *fihu* > MHG *vihe*. Regular syncope and apocope, as in *hêrisôn* > *hêrsen*, *eichila* > *eichel*, *grôziro* > *groezer*, simplify words even further. The unstressed prefixes *ga-* and *gi-* become *ge-*; *ant-* becomes *ent-*; *ur-* becomes *er-*; and there are others. The old diphthong *iu*, the umlaut of *û*, and the umlaut of *iu* all coalesce into a single long vowel *ǖ*, of which the written symbol is *iu* (*biutu* > *biute*, *brūti* > *briute*, *tiuri* > *tiure*), and several other diphthongs coalesce into *ie* (*tiuf* > *tief*, *eo* > *ie* [always], *diota* > *diet* [people], *Kriach* > *Kriech* [Greek], and so on). By comparison—and in contrast to New High German—some full vowels are still preserved in the secondary stress position: *-ære* (OHG *scrîbâri*, MHG *schrîbaere*, NHG *Schreiber*), *-în* (MHG *guldîn*, NHG *gülden*), and so on. Gradual progress is made toward the phonological system of normal "classical" Middle High German; however, scribes copying from older manuscripts frequently retained the older form of transcription, even in later times.

From the second half of the 11th century, monastic literature came more and more to be written in the vernacular. Sermons were now composed more frequently in German, and were preserved in large manuscripts comprising several works. They were intended not only for an audience of monks but also for laymen, both in the villages and in the towns. The author of the rhymed sermon *Vom Rechte* wished to instruct peasant listeners on the rights and duties of marriage, and the *Ezzolied* of the Bamberg canon Ezzo was directed at an audience of educated townspeople.

But in this period few authors indeed achieved a satisfying level of artistry in their writings. Early Middle High German poetry does not in general afford us any special aesthetic delights.* Rhymes are inaccurate, rhythms tend to be irregular, and there is a particular preference for over-long lines. Even religious vernacular poetry cannot stand com-

* See Appendix: B.

parison with the achievements of contemporary Latin lyricists. The themes treated are chosen mainly from the Scriptures, such as the Song of Songs, the story of Judith, and the Creation. The horrors of Death and Hell are depicted in vivid colours in such works as *Antichrist* and *Jüngstes Gericht*, and other poems relate the lives of famous saints, such as the *Annolied* and the poems and sequences celebrating the Virgin Mary. Among the latter class there is a group of poems composed by a certain Ava, a pious Austrian lady. A more colourful element is introduced into German literature by the fantastic biographies of Celtic saints (*Brandan, Patricius, Tnugdalus*), which retell old seafaring legends. Such poems were a manifestation of the current interest in foreign lands, which was stimulated by the Crusades, and led at an early date to the composition of works of secular literature. Although Lamprecht (*fl.* 1120), the author of the *Alexanderlied*, was a cleric—a *Tobias* is also attributed to him—in the Alexander story he adapted a non-religious narrative of the pre-Christian era that contained accounts of miraculous events in the Orient. His source was the 12th-century Old French *Roman d'Alexandre* of Alberich de Pisançon.* Examples such as this are evidence that these poets did not have only a clerical audience in mind when they were writing.

That many secular epics have failed to survive can be gathered from interpolations and allusions in mediaeval Latin works, such as the *Ruodlieb*, which was composed in the Bavarian monastery of Tegernsee in about 1030. Some survive in Scandinavian adaptations, such as *Þiðrekssaga*, many chapters of which—including one telling the story of Jarl Iron—are based on German *Spielmann* (wandering minstrel) material.[8] Almost all the secular lyric poetry of the period is also lost. From the 10th century there remains only a single short satirical poem, which tells of a father whose newly married daughter is brought back to him by her husband.[9] There were numerous ballads celebrating isolated deeds and heroes such as Adalbert of Babenburg and Churzibolt. Throughout this epoch the heroic legends of the Age of Migrations lived on in the form of orally transmitted poems; after the turn of the 13th century these were transformed into book-length epics.

The finest works of literature composed during the transitional period are three epics that treat themes from Germanic and German history in fictitious form. In about 1170 a cleric of Regensburg named Konrad composed an epic poem on the military expedition undertaken by Charlemagne and his paladin Roland against the Moors in Spain. At a very early stage the theme had already been incorporated into French

* See Appendix: C.

85

heroic legend (the *Chanson de Roland*) and it was this that provided the source for the German *Rolandslied*. However, Konrad had no knowledge of French, and so Henry the Lion (Duke of Bavaria), who commissioned the German version, first had the French text translated into Latin. The war against the Saracens was considered just, and Roland and his heroes were made out to be saints who died like martyrs: the epic was not intended as a legend, but set out to glorify the knights of the crusading era. Artistically the *Rolandslied* is not of a very high order, the metrical form being imperfectly handled; but the language is rich in archaic formulas and full of pathos.

Another epic, this one drawn from motifs of Germanic history, is *König Rother*, composed by a *Spielmann* of the Rhineland. The name of the hero recalls the Langobardic king Rothari, and the courtship that forms the theme of the work seems to trace back ultimately to the historical wooing of the Bavarian princess Theodelinde by the Langobardic king Authari. In the poem, however, the action has been removed southward to the Norman kingdom of Roger of Sicily, who takes the place of Rothari. The poet employs a simple narrative form and uses a language abounding in formulaic expressions to achieve the crude burlesque effects that suited the primitive tastes of his audience. The essential mood is light-hearted, and the end is a happy one. This appealing short poetic work was—as we can infer from the extant manuscript evidence—popular reading until the end of the 12th century.

The third outstanding work of the transitional period is *Herzog Ernst*, which originated in Franconia about 1170–80 and portrays events of more recent German history. It is named after Ernst II, Duke of Swabia, who rebelled against the Emperor Konrad II (1024–39). Also from the same elevated level of society is the figure of the loyal friend Wetzel, in whom is embodied the historical Wernher von Kyburg. The first theme is fused with elements of an older legend surrounding the feud of an earlier duke, Liudolf, with his father, the Emperor Otto; it is from this latter source that the poet took the name of the parents, Otto and Ottegebe, and a few other details. The adventures that Ernst experiences in the East are crusading tales drawn from the literary tradition of Sinbad the Sailor. *Herzog Ernst*, which is presented with all the pathos of an outlaw legend, was later revised several times, and as late as the 16th century was circulated in popular printed versions with wood-cut illustrations. Composed in a similar style to these secular epics (and likewise in rhyming verse) were the popular religious legends of *St Oswald*, *Orendel*, and *Salman and Morolf*.

The monks were also the first to compose individual specialized works in the vernacular on the arts (*artes mechanicae*) to supplement the text-books on the liberal arts used in their schools. *Merigarto*, written in rhyming verse shortly after 1100, relates the experiences of a voyage to Iceland, and also describes certain noteworthy hydrographic phenomena in Italy. A prose version of the *Physiologus* (*Reda umbe diu tier*), composed toward the end of the 11th century, was the first work in the field of zoology, and it was soon followed by a further adaptation in rhyming verse, and yet another prose version. These books concentrated not upon the physiology of animals but upon their symbolic significance in Christian teaching.

About this time medical treatises began to appear in abundance. The *Arzneibuch Ipocratis*, which is preserved in the *Züricher Arzneibuch* (dispensatory) and in a manuscript fragment from Bamberg, was probably composed in about 1100 by a monk with medical knowledge; it includes more than 60 directions deriving from early mediaeval prescription formulas, and is arranged in a system of *a capite ad calcem* (from head to foot). Not long afterwards the Innsbruck-Prül book of medicinal herbs was compiled by a Bavarian. The work is preserved in two manuscripts and, drawing on sources collected during late antiquity in Salerno, names and describes 18 different medicinal plants. This book is the first of the mediaeval German herbals, of which there were a great number in the later Middle Ages. The Prül manuscript also contains a German *Lapidarius*, which lists the medical and magical powers of precious stones. The *Innsbruck Arzneibuch*, written by an anonymous expert, is interspersed with Latin extracts that suggest sources dating from late antiquity and the early Middle Ages; it is preserved in two manuscripts of the 12th and 13th century.[10] In addition to these fairly large-scale writings we must also mention a considerable body of short works dealing with many aspects of contemporary scientific knowledge.

The legal formulas governing the marriage ceremony, the swearing-in of Jews, and trial by ordeal were also put into writing during the early Middle High German period. In the *Kaiserchronik*, composed during the first half of the 12th century, we possess the first large-scale history of the world (more than 17,000 lines). Although the mediaeval theory of knowledge classed historiography as one of the liberal arts, the *Kaiserchronik* aimed far beyond the requirements of the schools.

The close of the 12th century saw the composition of the *Nibelungenlied*. Although not without artistic failings, it is the most important work in the history of Germanic poetry in the Middle Ages, for it puts into poetic form—and moreover a form worthy of the story, and one that was to remain effective for many centuries—the theme that more than any other had engrossed the attention of the Germanic peoples ever since the Age of Migrations. The same cycle of legendary tradition is also alluded to in Anglo-Saxon literature; in Iceland it was included in the *Poetic Edda* in the form of short lays; and in Norway it was adapted into the prose *Þiðrekssaga*. The German *Nibelungenlied* did not succeed in uniting harmoniously all the contradictory strands that form the multi-layered Nibelungen tradition; nevertheless the poet has created an integral work that makes a powerful and moving impression on its audience.* It became the model for the reshaping of several other heroic legends of early Germanic history into book-length epics, in particular the *Kudrun*, which unites the various Germanic traditions from the North Sea regions, and the Dietrich cycle, in which Gothic heroic legend survives. Unfortunately we have no precise information about the poet of the *Nibelungenlied*. We cannot exclude the possibility that he was a cleric, yet his work is in no way a religious poem but a profoundly heroic one.

About the same time as the *Nibelungenlied* was composed, aristocratic laymen began to participate increasingly in literary life. Whereas hitherto they had occasionally manifested their interest by acting as patrons, they themselves now began to set pen to parchment. Their main sources of inspiration were the latest literary vogues from France, which were then making a great impression at German courts. Even an emperor, Henry VI (d. 1198), took pleasure in writing love poems, and several other princes followed his example. For a few decades popular lyric poetry, which had always existed, was forced into the background by the new art of courtly poetry.

French literary fashions penetrated into Germany across the western frontiers, especially the Lower Rhine and Switzerland. One of the first poets to be influenced in this way was Heinrich von Veldeke, in the Maastricht area; another was Count Rudolf von Fenis, who owned property on Lake Biel (in Switzerland), and who was related to the royal house of Burgundy.† Courtly lyric poetry was limited to a few themes. The essential requirements were that in courtship it was the man who should take the initiative, that the woman whose praises were being sung should be married and of high social position, and that the *Minnedienst* (the service offered by the lover-poet to his unattainable

* See Appendix: D.
† See Appendix: E.

mistress and all that it entailed) should remain secret. The thoughts expressed and the situations presented were fairly limited in range, as were the accessories and background. Emotions were not expressed spontaneously, but reflected upon. Even the vocabulary was sparing. Great care was taken over versification, stanzas were constructed according to strictly prescribed forms, and rhymes were accurate. The development of the *Leich*—an ode-like, carefully structured lay that was recited in public and reserved for elevated (frequently religious) themes—brought with it a richly decorative and highly rhetorical style. However, this meticulous and studied art-form was cultivated by only a small circle, and its weaknesses were immediately recognized by the knightly class.

The first to poke fun at the pining love, the discreet and formal atmosphere, typical of the courtly lyric was the Bavarian Neidhart von Reuenthal (*c.* 1180–*c.* 1250). He went so far as to permit women to express their amorous desires, and introduced the figure of the peasant girl into his poetry. The sprightliness and realism characteristic of Neidhart's verse met with a favourable response and led to the emergence of a second courtly genre.* It was, however, the target of much abuse. Even Walther von der Vogelweide (*c.* 1170–*c.* 1230), the most outstanding of the *Minnesänger* (poets of courtly love), called the new poetry *unhovelîch* (uncourtly), although he too subscribed in some of his poems to the concept of *niedere Minne*—which replaces the high-born lady by a maiden of low degree—in accordance with which he described love as a simple, unsophisticated emotional experience. Walther was a well-balanced, self-sufficient person of a fundamentally happy and optimistic disposition. He had complete mastery of the art of the courtly lyric, and was the most versatile of the lyric poets writing at the turn of the 13th century. He also established the genre of the political *Spruch* (originally a single-stanza poem of a didactic or satirical character). Although an ardent Christian, he was not blind to ecclesiastical abuses, which he castigated sharply and courageously. He is the only lyricist who continued his poetic activities throughout his whole life and not just during the brief period when it was the fashionable pastime; even so, his collected works fill only a slim volume.

In addition to lyric poetry the Middle High German period also saw the emergence of the courtly epic. Once again French influence is clearly visible, particularly in the preference for French sources, which were in their turn partly based on Celtic legends. The first poet to write in this genre was Eilhart von Oberg, who around 1175 adapted the French

* See Appendix: F.

estoire of Tristan the lover. He was followed by Ulrich von Zazikhoven, who composed a version of the Lancelot story (*c.* 1195), Hartmann von Aue (*fl. c.* 1190–1210), whose lengthy epics *Erec* and *Iwein* are based on those by Chrétien de Troyes, and Wirnt von Grafenberg (*fl.* 1204–10), who wrote his Arthurian *Wigalois* in about 1205. The courtly epic reached its zenith in Wolfram von Eschenbach, who, between 1200 and 1220, composed *Parzival,* the unfinished *Willehalm,* and *Titurel* (of which only a fragment exists). Among the epic poets we also find men of the new bourgeois class, such as Gottfried von Strassburg (*fl.* 1210), whose incomplete *Tristan* is artistically the most accomplished of all versions of this story, and Der Stricker, who composed his Arthurian romance *Garel vom blühenden Tal* about 1220. The strong impression that French epic poetry made even on Wolfram is apparent in the fact that he claimed to have used a French source when he apparently did not have one: he refers to a certain poet, Kyot, whose literary achievements cannot be substantiated. Moreover, he refused to follow the new trend initiated by Neidhart, which was a reaction against French influence. Wolfram's style found many imitators, and *Parzival* (based on Chrétien's *Perceval*) in particular remained in circulation until the close of the Middle Ages.*

Although the influence of courtly literature made itself especially felt in the literary style and versification of the following centuries, it also left its traces in the vocabulary. Its chief contribution consisted of substantives taken over from the French, dealing with the various aspects of knighthood: *aventiure* (adventure), *panzier* (armour), *massenîe* (Fr. *maisnie*: retinue), *granmarzi* (Fr. *grand merci*: thanks), and so on. A new method of word formation was acquired by taking the verbal ending *-ieren* from the French (MGH *regnieren* < O. Fr. *reignier*: to rule; MHG *loschieren* < O. Fr. *logier*: to lodge). About 160 verbs in all were taken over during the 50 years or so when French influence was predominant. Most of them fell into disuse later, but down to the present day, verbs have been formed by means of this convenient ending. The substantive ending *-îe* in words such as *prophezîe* (prophecy), and *zouberîe* (magic), can also be traced back to French origin, as can the adjective ending *-lei* (O. Fr. *ley*: kind) in words such as *maneger leie* (of several kinds) and *allerlei* (all kinds of). Many new words were loan translations of French expressions, for example *hövescheit* (O. Fr. *cortoisie*: courtliness), and *dörperîe* (O. Fr. *vilanie*: uncouth behaviour). Some poets delighted in inserting whole

* See Appendix: G.

groups of words from the French, especially Gottfried von Strassburg—e.g. *Tristan*, line 3138 f.:

> juvente bele et riant, diu schoene jugent, diu lachende.
>
> (the beautiful and laughing young.)

Nevertheless, however impressive the evidence may be, there is a strong tendency to over-estimate the total effect of French influence. Moreover, the one-sided emphasis placed on courtly literature and the habit of extolling it as representing a classical epoch in German literature do not do justice to historical reality. Neither in the esteem of contemporaries, nor in respect of the length of time that it remained popular and the extent of its effect, did courtly literature take pride of place among the various literary genres practised during the Middle Ages, even in its heyday around 1200. By taking as our basic criterion the number of extant manuscripts of individual works, we can assess their former popularity and compare the impact made by each. Whether for every manuscript preserved 10 or 1000 have been lost or about 150, as seems most likely for various reasons[11]—the proportion always remains constant, for if twice as many copies of one work are preserved as of another, we can only conclude that the former enjoyed double the esteem and popularity of the latter. The editor of *Parzival* is guilty of a traditional misjudgment when he states[12]: "Of all the literary works composed during the Hohenstaufen period, none has such a rich manuscript tradition as *Parzival*, the text of which is preserved in 84 different copies (17 complete MSS and 68 fragments)." In reality, technical literature had a much greater effect during the Hohenstaufen period than any poetic works. The *Praktik* of Meister Bartholomäus, composed as early as the 12th century, is preserved in over 100 versions, the *Rossarzneibuch* (veterinary handbook) of Meister Albrant in over 200, and the *Sachsenspiegel* (code of Saxon law) of Eike von Repgow in about 270. However, it is symptomatic of present-day scholarly research that the *Praktik* is hardly known at all. It has been edited several times by medical historians, but a complete critical edition is still lacking. The work is not even mentioned in the *Verfasserlexikon*.[13] It is a systematic medical textbook probably based on material originating in Salerno. Albrant, the author of the *Rossarzneibuch*, was Master of the Horse to the Emperor Frederick II (1212–50), and his work was circulated from Prague to the *Deutschordensland* (the Prussian territories administered by the Order of Teutonic Knights), as far as the Bulgarian frontier in the south-east, and to western Germany. It was disseminated among all social classes, from the Imperial Court to the lowest shepherd's hut; it was revised on innumerable occasions, expanded, and even translated into foreign languages. Yet more important was the *Sachsenspiegel*, the first comprehensive codification of German law, embracing both common and feudal law. Its author, Eike von Repgow, was a knight of Anhalt and an expert in Eastphalian law. He drew on daily life and the legal practices with which he had become familiar as an attendant of the influential Ascanian family, who were well disposed toward the Hohenstaufen cause. The *Sachsenspiegel* became a model for many subsequent codes of law until the indigenous legal system was supplanted by Roman law in 1495, when the Supreme Court was established.

IV

During the course of the 13th century two events took place that at first sight had nothing to do with language and literature, but that were to bring about changes of a fundamental nature in these two spheres. The first was the introduction of spectacles for people whom approaching old age had rendered long-sighted. The second was the expansion of German territories in the east.

When introduced into Europe the reading lens invented by the Arabs was rapidly developed into what we now know as spectacles. As a result older people were now able to read, which meant that they could participate in and influence literary life. Previously literature had been a province reserved for people up to the age of about 45, and as such it naturally reflected the tastes and interests of that age group. Those more advanced in years, who could not claim recognition as an active force in literary life and substantiate that claim by producing their own works, had had more experience of life, and were more knowledgeable, less impetuous, and far less susceptible to illusions. Romantic, pining love poetry no longer had much meaning for them; they placed more and more importance on literature of a realistic character, serving practical ends in everyday life. As a result both technical and scientific writing and edifying religious literature received an impetus.

A new literary genre now emerged, more suitable for men of greater age, namely the *Meistergesang*, which is clearly distinguishable from the younger man's art of the *Minnesang*. It is not so fresh and vivacious, but contains a greater variety of themes and more complicated forms. The *Meistergesang* treats in verse new branches of ecclesiastical doctrine and the secular liberal arts; its poets display their erudition and their experience of life. Long stanzas, contrived rhythms, and abundant rhymes are the characteristic features of their more mature style.* A fresh trend in lyric poetry was initiated by the new florid style of writing, which attempted to surpass all previous poetic achievements by the use of affected adjectives, far-fetched similes, puns, pleonasms, and so on. We encounter it among the early *Meistersinger* Frauenlob (Heinrich von Meissen), Heinrich von Mügeln, and Muskatblüt, and it can also be found in epic poetry, for example in Albrecht's *Jüngerer Titurel*, in *Lohengrin*, and in the love allegories. In the place of youthful directness, older poets preferred to clothe their thoughts in metaphorical language, and they preferred the abstract to the concrete—features that can also be regarded as typical of modern literature.

It was now that the allegory began its triumphant advance. The love allegory was already fashionable at the turn of the 14th century, beginning with the *Sekte der Minner* (Sects of Lovers), continuing with the *Urkunde der Minner* (Charter of Lovers) and *Des Kranichhalses neun Grade* (The Nine Degrees of the Crane's Neck), and ending with *Warnung an hartherzige Frauen* (*c.* 1470; Warning to Hardhearted Women). Side by side with the love allegory we also find the hunting allegory (*Der entflogene Falke, Die drei Hunde als Beschützer*, and so on). Townspeople and the noble classes alike participated in these literary movements. When, with old age approaching, the Emperor Maximilian I (1459–1519) set about composing his autobiography, he chose the allegory as his medium (*Teuerdank, Ehrenpforte, Freydal, Weisskunig*).

Reading glasses enabled the writer to put the finishing touches to his rough drafts on paper and to piece them together into the final version. Hence, even an old man suffering from cerebral sclerosis could insert quotations and selected passages into his works as he so desired. The collected works of late mediaeval authors are much greater in quantity than those of their predecessors in the early and high Middle Ages because writers could continue their literary activities for twice as long. Connected with this is the increase in the copying and collecting of manuscripts. The 14th century shows a steady rise in the import of paper from Italy, and toward the end of the century a paper-mill was even set up in Germany itself. This cheap new writing material also made it possible for the less wealthy sections of urban society to buy books of their own. In many towns manuscripts were copied in large numbers, and illuminators illustrated them with hastily dashed-off drawings. The

* See Appendix: H.

most famous book-makers before the introduction of printing were Diebold Lauber in Strassburg and Klara Hätzler in Augsburg. However, these new developments in manuscript production were soon to be overtaken by Gutenberg's invention (about 1439) of a printing press with movable type, which enabled even the earliest printed books to be produced in far greater quantities than before. Warnings against excessive reading soon made themselves heard.

We can also attribute to the influence of older writers that greater use was now made of prose as a literary medium, and it became common practice to produce specialist works of both secular and religious literature in prose. During this period the first prose romances were composed. "*Kluge Sach will Reimens nicht*" (Wise words need no rhyming), declared Heinrich von Wittenweiler in his *Ring* (line 3520), which dates from about 1390. Works originally written in verse were adapted into prose versions, with the aim of achieving greater precision of statement. Thus the first great collection of religious legends, the *Heiligenleben, Sommer- und Winterteil* (The Saintly Life, Summer and Winter Part), includes many works from the verse *Passional* and the *Märterbuch* (Book of Martyrs), which were recast into prose.

It had also become fashionable to compile anthologies from many varied sources. Parables, warning examples, short stories, prayers, and meditations were all combined to form large-scale devotional books that were intended to provide reading-matter for a whole year. Even the inmates of almshouses have been considered as a possible audience, as we can observe from the titles of certain books: *Seelentrost* (The Soul's Consolation), *Kunst des heilsamen Sterbens* (The Art of Dying Wholesomely), *Schatzbehalter* (Keeper of Riches), and others. Geiler von Kaisersberg stated explicitly that he wished his religious tracts to be read out by "persons who are accustomed to frequent churches or hospitals and to nurse the sick."[14] In order to keep pace with the increase of pastoral duties in the populous towns, the new mendicant orders launched themselves vigorously into a new field of activity; in the 13th century the Franciscan order produced such outstanding men of letters as David von Augsburg and Berthold von Regensburg, and these were followed in the 14th century by the Dominican mystics, all of whom wrote in prose. The most important of them, Meister Eckhart (*c.* 1260–1327), turned his thoughts to the problem of the presence of God in the human heart, which he depicts as the birth of God in the soul of the righteous man. Although many of his ideas were over-subtle and obscure, his purely literary achievements were considerable. He coined new expressions for abstract concepts, and mastered the art of making clear-cut paradoxes appear plausible.[15] He exercised a great influence on mystics who wrote in the following centuries, such as Johannes Tauler, Jan van Ruysbroeck, Heinrich Seuse, and others. The most popular work of all was Seuse's *Buch der ewigen Weisheit*, of which about 250 copies are preserved. Mysticism thrived in monastic and urban circles, for instance in the *Kreis der Gottesfreunde* (Society of the Friends of God) in the Upper Rhine region, whose leader was the rich merchant Rulman Merswin. However, mysticism cannot always be sharply differentiated from the scholasticism from which it originated and to whose prosaic level it was to sink back again.

Nevertheless, scholasticism not only determined the education given at monastery schools but also took note of the secular arts and sciences and classified them according to its system of assessment. The division of the various fields of knowledge into liberal arts (*artes liberales*) and useful arts (*artes mechanicae*) provides the guiding principle for classifying the large quantity of literature produced in these fields. The origin of this division is to be found in the theory of knowledge evolved by an early exponent of scholasticism, Hugh of St Victor (1096–1141). The liberal arts formed an introductory course that was the prerequisite for all higher studies. They comprised the *trivium*, which embraced the three linguistic disciplines of grammar, rhetoric, and dialectics, and the *quadrivium*, which consisted of the four mathematical sciences of arithmetic, music, geometry, and astronomy, the last-named being closely connected with astrology. Although Latin had long been used as the language of textbooks and oral instruction, the essential texts were now translated into German, because the knowledge they contained had an effect far beyond the confines of the school and was of great practical value in many professions. Latin-German dictionaries had been compiled during the earliest period of literary life in Germany, and Notker Labeo had already translated mathematical and scientific textbooks. Toward the close of the Middle Ages there was a superabundance of literary works dealing with the liberal arts in the vernacular, and the subject that stimulated the greatest number of printed books was astronomical prognostication. The term *artes mechanicae* embraces seven fields of practical activity that were based on the liberal arts, but these were only partly taught in the schools. They were practised by members of all professions, such as noble men-at-arms, falconers, middle-class craftsmen and merchants, peasant fruit-growers, and itinerant entertainers. The first of the useful arts takes in all the crafts, including alchemy and building; the second covers the

95

art of war in all its branches; the third, navigation, trade, and geography; the fourth, housekeeping, horticulture, and agriculture; the fifth, hunting, fishing, and forestry; the sixth, the medical sciences and pharmacy; and the seventh, games, sporting activities, and the theatrical arts. We must also mention the third category of *artes*, forbidden by both religious and secular authorities, namely the arts of magic, soothsaying, and sharp practices. There existed a highly developed specialist literature on these arts, for the use of their practitioners. Although relevant writings from antiquity were translated into German, the principal concern was to extend the frontiers of knowledge and civilization. This was done on the one hand by translating technical works that appeared in other countries, such as Italy, France, England, and Spain, and on the other hand by recording practical experiments made in Germany itself. Books on the useful arts are therefore of tremendous value for the history of science, lexicography, and etymology; such writings lay particular emphasis on the technical vocabulary of the newly flourishing arts of cathedral-building, ballistics, and tree-grafting, to name only three. The later Middle Ages brought many new discoveries, notably gunpowder and printing, progress in chemistry and astronomy, the treatment of congestive heart failure with an extract from the lily-of-the-valley plant, the use of artificially induced fever to cure certain diseases, and methods of combatting the new pestilences that were becoming widespread at that time (after 1348 the plague, after 1494 syphilis).

The impression we obtain is that technical literature constitutes the most important part of mediaeval German literature. A further, more objective standard of comparison by which to judge its significance can be developed by considering the number of German texts translated into foreign languages. Neighbouring peoples did not show any interest in German lyric poetry; not even the poems of Walther von der Vogelweide were translated into another language. The Old Norse poet who adapted the *Iwein* story disregarded Hartmann's version in favour of the Old French original. In the case of technical literature, however, the situation is very different. A whole series of sizable specialist works in German were translated, many of them several times and with lasting success; examples are Albrant's *Rossarzneibuch*, Gottfried von Franken's handbook on tree-grafting, travel books, legal collections, and medical texts. One work achieved success on a truly international scale: Eucharius Rösslin's guide to midwifery, *Der swangern frawen rosengarten*, was translated into Latin, French, Italian, Spanish, English, Dutch, Danish, and Czech. Such translations are also important for a knowledge of the vocabulary of the foreign languages concerned. The original works, however, provide the richest sources we possess of German lexicography. The variety of expression and vocabulary of the German language are—as Leibniz remarked[16]—exceedingly wide, particularly with regard to the crafts, mining, navigation, and hunting. The lexicon of the mediaeval hunt alone lists about 1300 specialized terms in German.[17]

The richness and diversity of German language and literature in the late Middle Ages were also evident in all their vigour in the newly colonized territories in the east. Indeed, the towns in those regions, which were undergoing rapid development, soon began to set the pace intellectually for the rest of Germany. The clearest illustration of this is the fact that the first four central European universities were established in the east: Prague in 1348, Cracow in 1364, Vienna in 1365, and Fünfkirchen (Pécs, in Hungary) in 1367. Old High German and even late Middle High German were confined to the small geographical area comprising Bavaria, Swabia, and Franconia, whereas ever since the emigration of the Germanic population during the Age of Migrations the adjoining lands in the east had been inhabited by Magyars, Slavs, and Balts. The process of resettlement by Germans from the west commenced in the 10th century and was in full swing by the 13th. The lands in the northeast were appropriated in the course of the missionary campaigns undertaken by the military Order of Teutonic Knights, and the central and southern regions were acquired by peaceful immigration following invitations from the sovereigns concerned. In this way the German-speaking world more than doubled in area. New dialects and written forms of the language emerged, and of these East Central German was the most widely used. In 1269 a memorable event took place in Jaroslav (in modern Poland), when for the first time a trade agreement with Russia was concluded by a document in German.[18]

The intellectual centres founded by the Teutonic Order in its strictly administered territories produced considerable literary achievements. However, the *Minnesang* and the romantic adventure story were not the genres patronized; on the contrary, systematic encouragement was given here to historiography and to devotional and technical literature. In the fortified houses typical of that period, daily readings from such works were the rule. The military campaigns of the Order, and its expansion, were described in lengthy verse chronicles, of which the most important are the *Livländische Reimchronik*, the *Chronik von Preussenland* by Nikolaus von Jeroschin, and a similar work by the King-of-Arms Wigand von Marburg. As in western Germany, the lands in the east under the control

G

97

of the Teutonic Order soon went over to the prose narrative as a literary medium; its outstanding exponent was the historian Johannes von Posilge, who took as his theme the history of the Order from 1360 to 1405.

The second of the prevailing literary genres mentioned above embraces religious legends in poetic form and adaptations of the Bible, mostly of great length and preserved in very ornate manuscripts. In the *Passional* and the *Väterbuch* (Book of the Fathers), which together comprise 150,000 lines, a knight of the Teutonic Order created the most valuable compilation of Church legends of the High Middle Ages; it was also circulated widely in the estates belonging to the Teutonic Knights in the old western part of Germany. No less significant were the paraphrased versions of individual books of the Bible (Judith, Job, the Prophets, and so on), which are among the most important forerunners of Luther's Bible translation. The Teutonic Order also required specialized handbooks on the art of war and on peace-time construction work. Large numbers of military laws and customs were collected together and issued in the *Statuten* (Regulations) and the *Neue Soldbuch* (a book of new statutes), and the *Wundarznei* (Surgery) of Heinrich von Pfolspeundt gave guidance for the care of the wounded. All the basic works on veterinary surgery (Albrant, Albertus Magnus, Jordanus Ruffus), falconry, horticulture (Gottfried von Franken), and so on were revised for use on the estates owned by the Order, and in the *Geometria Culmensis* we possess the oldest German manual of surveying. Although the territories governed by the Teutonic Order lay in the north, Central German was the language in which it conducted its affairs, for several Grand Masters came from Thuringia.

The eastern territories bordering on the southern part of Germany were also colonized by Central Germans. The literary language they developed was a fairly uniform East Central German, and the region where it prevailed extended beyond the Carpathians as far as central Hungary. The language of the Transylvanian Saxons in Rumania was also Central German. In all these territories a lively interest was taken in intellectual life: many towns had *Meistersinger* schools and their own printing works. East Central German was also spoken in Cracow, which, like Leipzig, was an important centre for the dissemination of astronomical and astrological pamphlets. A series of exemplary legal codes came out of Saxony, the most outstanding being the *Magdeburger Weichbildrecht* (laws of the Magdeburg district) and the *Meissner Rechtsbuch* (the Meissen law book), whose authority penetrated far into Slav territory. Mining law was evolved in the Saxon mountain range known as the Erzgebirge. On the Bohemian side of the range, it was codified as the *Joachimstaler*

Bergrecht (Joachimstal mountain law), and in 1548 these statutes formed the basis of the imperial mining regulations, the *Kaiserliche Bergordnung* (imperial regulations for the mountains), which remained in force until 1854, when a general mining law was passed in Austria. The earliest handbook on mining was written by Ulrich Rülein von Calwe, the mayor of Freiberg; his *Bergbüchlein* (Little Book of Mining) became the progenitor of a whole series of mining books down to the 18th century.[19] In 1508 a Leipzig tin-merchant, Christoph Kuppner, brought out a book on trade and commerce entitled *Ein schönes büchlein,* which was the first work to discuss the nature of commerce in the vernacular; it was dedicated to the Archbishop of Magdeburg and the Grand Master of Prussia.

V

In the lands under the jurisdiction of the Bohemian crown, literary evidence of the German tongue goes back as far as the 10th century, when a bishop was greeted with an Old High German *Leis* (a short religious poem) on the occasion of his enthronement. The poets of the 13th century, with King Wenceslas II at their head, took a lively interest in the courtly *Minnesang.* In the rapidly developing German towns of Bohemia, all literary genres were cultivated, and there were particularly close links with Nürnberg and Meissen. The event that was to be of the greatest importance for the history of German language and literature, the emergence of the modern standard language (*neuhochdeutsche Schriftsprache*), is attributable to the conditions prevailing in Prague during the 14th century. Because the mediaeval German Empire had no fixed capital city, the emergence of the modern standard tongue—unlike that of its counterparts in England and France—was dependent on the combination of several factors.

The New High German standard language exhibits an approximately equal number of Central and Upper German features. One Middle German characteristic is the monophthongization of the MHG diphthongs *ie* to *ī* (*liet* > *Lied* [spoken as *līt*], *uo* to *ū* (*guot* > *gut*), and *üe* to *ü* (*güete* to *Güte*); a different, Upper German, element is the diphthongization of the MHG monophthongs *î* to *ei*, *û* to *au*, and *iu* (spoken as *ü*) to *eu* (*mîn* > *mein*, *hûs* > *Haus*, *vriunt* > *Freund*), and others. It follows, therefore, that the modern standard language could have developed only in an area where these two main dialects adjoined one another. In fact this criterion was valid for a very long frontier belt that stretched from the linguistic frontier in the west, along the Mosel and Main valleys to the Eger, continuing through Bohemia, to disappear finally among the scattered settlement in the east. The real problem is not the demarcation of dialect boundaries as accurately as possible, for dialects in this frontier zone are all so alike that, from a purely linguistic standpoint, any one of them could have become the standard tongue. The crux of the matter lies much more in the question: at which point in this zone did literary life become most representative and exercise the greatest effect and influence? It should be noted, however, that these factors were determined in part by the geographical location of the imperial chancery. The Emperor Charles IV (1316–78) had raised Prague to the position of imperial capital. This in itself would not have been sufficient to induce neighbouring territories to adopt Prague German, but there was an additional factor: Prague possessed the oldest and most important of the four ancient universities.[20] Although the language of instruction at Prague and all other universities was Latin, the town was nevertheless a centre of highly concentrated and productive literary activity in the vernacular, because many of the scholars who gathered there used their native language when writing works for publication. Theologians preached in German; lawyers, doctors, and astronomers wrote their treatises in German—and these scholars, who for the first time were working in large numbers at the same place, were reckoned among the most important of their time.

The decisive factor in the spread of the standard language was not poetry but prose. In the decades immediately after the foundation of the university of Prague in 1348, Johannes von Neumarkt and Heinrich von St Gall composed religious works in a flowery prose style (the latter's *Leben Jesu* [Life of Jesus] is preserved in 136 manuscripts), and Albich von Prag, a doctor, and Johannes von Tepl, the town clerk of Saaz—and author of *Der Ackermann aus Böhmen* (The Ploughman from Bohemia)—wrote prose works on secular themes. The most important technical works written elsewhere were also known in Prague; some of them were imported by the authorities and their language altered to suit the local conditions. Among such works was the most widely circulated of all mediaeval German books, the code of common and feudal law (*Das kaiserliche Land- und Lehenrecht*), which in the 17th century was given the misleading title *Schwabenspiegel*. More than 400 manuscripts of this work are preserved.

It was a happy coincidence that the first written language fitted to become the unifying standard tongue had sufficient time to consolidate its position and acquire prestige in adjoining regions. When the standing of the German language in Bohemia was undermined during the Hussite wars, and the imperial chancery was transferred to Vienna, the centre of influence in matters of language passed to Meissen. The Viennese chancery switched to the official language currently prevailing in Austria, which was pure Upper German, and thus had no chance of asserting itself in the rest of Germany; but the language of the Saxon chancery retained the same hybrid character that it had developed in Prague. The traditions of Prague university were assimilated by the new university of Leipzig, founded in 1409, and it was Leipzig German that Martin Luther was writing 100 years later. Through his Bible translation it acquired such a high reputation that it was acknowledged as the best form of the German language. However, the ultimate consolidation of the standard language, and its spread to the towns of Bavaria and Austria on the one hand and to Low Germany on the other, did not take place until modern times.

Appendix

A The difficulties presented by religious prose and verse during this early period can be illustrated by examples. In its OHG version the following magic charm, which is derived from pagan times and is directed against a worm disease of horses, is perfect in form:

> Gang ūz, nesso, mit niun nessinchlīnon,
> ūz fonna marge in deo ādra,
> fonna dēn ādrun in daz fleisk,
> fonna demu fleiske in daz fel,
> fonna demo felle in diz tulli.

> (Go out, worm, with nine little worms,
> out of the marrow into the veins,
> from the veins into the flesh,
> from the flesh into the hide,
> from the hide into the horn [of the horse's hoof].)

There is not a word too many or too few, the word order corresponds exactly with that of natural speech, and there is a strong, effective rhythm. Compare this charm with the following OHG translation from I Samuel II: 1–2, copied by a Rhine-Franconian cleric at about the same time (9th–10th century):

> Ervrouwit herza mīnaz in drohtīno unde ūferhaben ist horn mīn in gode mīnemo; zesprēt ist mund mīn uber vīende mīne: wanda gevrouwet bin in heilī dīnemo. Nist heilegēr alsō ist drohtīn noh gewisse nist ander vone dir unde nist stirker also got unsēr.

(My heart rejoiceth in the Lord, mine horn is exalted in the Lord:
my mouth is enlarged over mine enemies; because I rejoice in thy
salvation. There is none holy as the Lord; for there is none beside
thee: neither is there any rock like our God. [Authorized Version])

The word order in the OHG canticle is completely un-German: it
corresponds exactly to the Latin original. It would be difficult to grasp
even the meaning of these sentences if we did not have the text of the
Vulgate for comparison:

Exultavit cor meum in domino, et exaltatum est cornu meum in
deo meo: dilatatum est os meum super inimicos meos: quia laetata
sum in salutari tuo. Non est sanctus, ut est dominus: neque enim
est alius extra te, et non est fortis sicut deus noster.

About A.D. 1000 the same passage was translated into German by
Notker Labeo of St Gall, whose language is much more spontaneous and
natural:

Mîn hérza fréuta sih an trúhtene und mîn gewált ist hôh irbúret an
imo: mîn múnt ist wīto indān úber mīne fīenda, wanda ih an dīnemo
háltāre gefróuwet pin. Samohéiliger unde sámostárcher neíst sō
trúhten gót únser nóh ánderer neist āne dih héiliger unde stárcher.

The same difficulties are apparent in OHG rhymed verse. The following is a sample from Otfried von Weissenburg's *Evangelienbuch*; it bears
the title "Jesus fatigatus ex itinere":

Sid tho thésen thingon · fuar Krist zen héimingon,
  in selbaz géwi sinaz; · thio buah nénnent uns tház.
Thera férti er ward irmúait, · so ofto fárantemo duit;
  ni lazent thie árabeit es fríst · themo wárlicho mán ist.
Fúar er thuruh Samáriam, · zi einera burg er thar tho quám,
  in themo ágileize · zi eínemo gisaze.
Tho gisaz er múader, · so wir gizáltun hiar nu ér,
  bi einemo brúnnen · (thaz wir ouh púzzi nennen).
Ther evangélio thar quit, · theiz móhti wesan séxta zit;
  theist dages héizesta · joh árabeito méista.

Thie júngoron iro zílotun, · in kóufe in múas hóletun,
  tház sie thes giflízzin, · mit selben Kríste inbizzin.
Unz drúhtin thar saz eíno, · so quam ein wíb thara thó,
  thaz si thes gizíloti, · thes wázares gihóloti.
"Wíb" quad er innan thés, · "gib mir thes drínkannes;
  wírd mir zi gifúare, · thaz íh mih nu gikúale!"
"Wio mág thaz" quad si "wérdan · (thu bist júdiisger mán
  inti ih bin thésses thietes!), · thaz thús mir so gibíetes?"
Thaz óffonot Johannes thár, · bi thiu si só quad in wár,
  bi wíu si thaz so zélita, · thaz drínkan so firságeta.

(Soon afterwards Jesus returned to his homeland, to his own district,
so the Gospels tell us. He was tired from the journey, as often happens
to travellers; he who is truly a man is not spared bodily pain. He

journeyed through Samaria, and there he came to a town where
he eagerly sought a resting place. Tired, as we have already
told, he sat down by a well (which we also call a spring). The
Gospels say that it was about the sixth hour; that is, the hottest
time of day and the most unbearable. The disciples hurried away
in order to buy food so that they could eat with Jesus. While the
Lord was sitting there alone a woman came to the well to draw water.
"Woman," he said then, "give me something to drink; do me this
service that I might refresh myself." "How can it be," she said,
"that you make this request, for you are a Jew and I am a
Samaritan?" It is related by John that she did truly speak thus, and
that she refused to give the Lord something to drink.)

In the space of 20 lines the poet refers three times to his source of information. He labours the point that Jesus was tired, and four lines later he
tells us so again, his reference back being solely to achieve a rhyme.
Possessive and attributative adjectives (*géwi sinaz*, dages *héizesta*) are
placed after their respective nouns, again for reasons of rhyme. On the
other hand, where rhymes are available the natural word order appears:
gibietes rhymes with *thesses dietes* (not with *dietes thesses*).

B As an example of German verse of this period, we may quote the
closing lines of the *Summa theologiae* (*c.* 1100):

> Hêrro, di dir dînint, ist daz rîchi.
> Wî mûgen wir dir gilôni?
> du dir nidir ginîgi ûf zi heuini den man,
> der uon sundin was giuallin.
> du dir wesin woltis (unsir ginôz)
> dragint unsir burdin sô grôz.
> nu hâstu, hêrro, dînen milten rât
> allin dînin holdin zi urowidi brâcht,
> daz dih, unsir irlôseri, alliz daz lobi.
> suaz dir ist undir deme himili ioch dâr obi.

(Lord, those who serve you, theirs will be the kingdom. How can we
repay you, you who have come down to raise up Man who had
fallen through sin, you who wanted to be our companion and bear
our great burden? And now, Lord, you have given great joy to all
your servants with your generous advice, that everything that is
both in and below heaven praises you as our Saviour.)

Difficult as it is to believe, many scholars are certain that all these lines
were intended to be four-footed.

C Lamprecht's art is very simple. He is concerned not so much with a
polished and vigorous style as with being easily understood; his aim is to
give a faithful rendering of the *Roman d'Alexandre,* and he goes out of his

way to saddle Alberich with responsibility for everything that appears in the *Alexanderlied*:

> Alberich von Bisinzo
> der brahte uns diz lit zu
> er hetez in walhisken getihtet.
> nu sol ih iuh es in dutisken berihten.
> niman enschulde sin mich;
> louc er, so liuge ih.

> (It was Alberich of Pisançon
> Who gave us this song.
> He composed it in the French tongue.
> Now I shall tell it in German.
> Let no one impute anything to me;
> If he lied, I lie too.)

D The poet combines two cycles of legends that had long existed side by side. In the first part, which deals with Siegfried's wooing of Kriemhild, Günther's wooing of Brunhild, and the weddings and festivities, bright colours and joyful sounds prevail. Courtly life is on display, knightly sports are held, the heroes are happy and confident, the women young and charming. Even the hunting episodes that precede Siegfried's murder are full of vigour and gaiety. This bright, free-and-easy world, which incorporates fairy-tale motifs, is clouded by the death of its most dazzling hero. The murder, which concludes, and is the most significant event of, the first part of the *Nibelungenlied*, is presaged with increasing clarity in the cantos that lead up to it. Dreams are given ominous interpretations, which are not taken seriously; Hagen tells vague accounts of strange deeds accomplished by Siegfried in his youth; Brunhild's temper is revealed not only in her insolent challenge to Kriemhild but also in the supernatural, demonic side of her nature. The most dangerous factor, however, which remains unsuspected right up to Siegfried's death, emerges violently in the character of Kriemhild: her grief turns into hatred, and the immensity and duration of this hatred determine the second part of the epic, where the planning of revenge, the bleak inevitability of fate, and the bloody out-come in the glare of the burning halls is unfolded with immense power.

The murder of Siegfried has parallels in many other ancient epics, but the downfall of the Burgundian heroes and of Kriemhild, which is elaborated with cold ruthlessness, is unique in character. Whereas the introductory scenes of the epic draw on fairy-tales, the middle of the work is based upon a combination of various legends whose theme is the fate of nations; the last part of the poem involves profound problems of the human soul. The *Nibelungenlied* is a most poignant account of human suffering, exemplified by a struggle that has its roots in the mutual hatred of kinsmen. It derives from a pagan ethos: the Christian trimmings remain external.

The whole epic is composed in strophes comprising four long lines with a paired rhyme scheme (aabb), with each line divided in two by a caesura. This strophic form, which in earlier times was to be found only in the poetry of the *Minnesinger* Kürenberger, was perhaps expressly re-created for the *Nibelungenlied*. Owing to the length of the epic the strophes, repeated as they are several thousand times, achieve a monotonous but powerfully suggestive effect.

E Not only the form but also the content of courtly lyric poetry were occasionally indebted to French poetry of the same period. The following stanza is by Heinrich von Veldeke:

> Tristrant mûste âne sinen danc
> stâde sin der koninginnen,
> want poisûn heme dâ tû dwanc
> mêre dan di cracht der minnen.
> des sal mich di gûde danc
> weten dat ich nine gedranc
> sulic piment ende ich si mine
> bat dan hê, ende mach dat sin.
> wale gedâne, valsches âne,
> lât mich wesen din
> unde wis dû min.

(Tristan, against his will, remained faithful to the queen, for he was compelled more by the philtre than by the power of love. Therefore my love should thank me that I never drank such a concoction and that I love her better than he could do, and let it remain so. Fair and true, let me be yours, and you be mine.)

Compare this with these lines by Chrétien de Troyes:

> Ains del beveraije ne bui
> dont Tristans fu enpuisunés.
> car plus me fait amer que lui
> fins cuers et boine voluntés.
> bien en doit estre mieus li grés,
> c'ains de riens esforciés n'en fui
> fors tant que les miens iex en crui,
> par cui sui en la voie entrés
> dont ja n'istrai n'ains n'en issi.

(I never drank any of that drink with which Tristan was poisoned. I was made to love more by a fine heart and good will [than by the philtre]. He should be grateful to me that I was not compelled by force, but only by what my eyes could see, which brought me into this path from which I never did nor shall depart.)

The Latin verse of the wandering scholars also influenced German lyric poetry of the High Middle Ages. The *Carmina Burana*, the most famous collection of poems by these scholars, contains a mixture of vernacular and Latin poems. This Latin wooing song (*Car. Bur.* 142) was probably composed by a German *Minnesinger*:

> Tempus adest floridum,
> Surgunt namque flores
> Vernalis, mox in omnibus
> Immutantur mores.
> Hos, quod frigus leserat,
> Reparant calores,
> Cernimus hoc fieri
> Per multos colores.
>
> Stant prata plena floribus,
> In quibus nos ludamus!
> Virgines cum clericis
> Simul procedamus,
> Per amorem Veneris
> Ludum faciamus,
> Ceteris virginibus
> Ut hoc referamus!
>
> "O dilecta domina,
> Cur sic alienaris?
> An necis, carissima,
> Quod sic adamaris?
> Si tu esses Helena,
> Vellem esse Paris—
> Tamen potest fieri
> Noster amor talis."

(The time for flowers is here, for the spring flowers are blossoming, soon all our ways will change. What the cold has damaged the warmth of summer will restore. We shall see this happening through the many colours.

The meadows are full of flowers, and there let us play. Let us go forth, girls and students together. Let us play a game for the love of Venus, so that we can tell the other girls all about it!

"O beloved mistress, why do you stay away? Or don't you know, dearest, that you are loved passionately? If you were Helen, I would like to be Paris. In spite of everything, our love can become as theirs.")

F One of the finest of Neidhart's songs tells of a young girl's confident love:

> "Der meie der ist riche:
> er fueret sicherliche
> den walt an siner hende,
> der ist nû niuwes loubes vol: der winter hât ein ende.

Ich fröu mich gegen der heide,
ir liehten ougenweide,
diu uns beginnet nâhen,"
so sprach ein wolgetâniu maget, "die wil schône enpfâhen.

Muoter, lâtz âne melde!
jâ wil ich komen ze velde
und wil den reien springen;
jâ ist es lanc, daz ich diu kint niht niuwes hôrte singen."

"Neinâ, tohter, neine!
ich hân dich alterseine
gezogen an mînen brüsten.
nu tuo ez durch den willen mîn: lâz dich der man niht lüsten."

"Den ich iu wil nennen,
den muget ir wol erkennen;
ze dem so wil ich gâhen.
er ist genant von Riuwental: den wil ich umbevâhen.

Ez gruonet an den esten,
daz alles möhten bresten
die boume zuo der erden.
nu wizzet, liebiu muoter mîn, ich volge dem knaben werden.

Liebiu muoter hêre,
nâch mir sô klaget er sêre.
sol ich im des niht danken?
er giht, daz ich diu schoenest sî von Beiern unz in Vranken."

("May is so strong: he leads the woods, which are now covered with new leaves, firmly by the hand. Winter has ended now.

I rejoice in the splendid sight of the open fields as they approach us"—thus spoke a beautiful girl—"I shall give them a fine welcome.

Mother, don't tell anyone! I want to go and join in the dancing; it is a long time since I heard the young people singing something new."

"No, daughter, no! All alone I nursed you at my breast. No, for my sake, don't amuse yourself with that man."

"I shall tell you his name and you will probably recognize him by it; then I'll hurry to join him. He is called Reuental: I shall greet him with a kiss.

The leaves on the branches are growing so green that the trees almost bend to the ground. Know this, mother dear, that I shall follow that noble lad.

My dear lady mother, he yearns for me so much. Shouldn't I be grateful to him for that? He says I am the most beautiful girl from Bavaria to Franconia.")

In contrast, Walther von der Vogelweide poses as a guardian of courtly *Minnesang* in the strict sense: in the following poem he takes a stand against the poetry of Neidhart:

Owê, hovelîchez singen,
daz dich ungefüege doene
Solten ie ze hove verdringen!
daz die schiere got gehœne!
Owê, daz dîn wirde alsô geliget,
des sint alle dîne friunde unfrô.
daz muoz eht alsô sîn: nu sî alsô!
frouw Unfuoge, ir habt gesiget.

Der uns fröude wider bræhte,
diu reht und gefuege wære,
Hei wie wol man den gedæhte,
swâ man von im seite mære!
Ez wær ein vil hovelîcher muot,
des ich iemer gerne wünschen sol.
frouwen und hêrren zæme ez wol:
owê, daz ez nieman tuot!

Die daz rehte singen stœrent,
der ist ungelîche mêre,
Danne die ez gerne hœrent.
doch volg ich der alten lêre:
Ich enwil niht werden zuo der mül,
dâ der stein sô riuschent umbe gât
und daz rat so mange unwise hât.
merkent, wer dâ harpfen sül.

Die sô frevellîchen schallent,
der muoz ich vor zorne lachen,
Daz in selben wol gevallent
mit als ungefüegen sachen.
Die tuont sam die frösche in eime sê,
den ir schrîen alsô wol behaget,
daz diu nahtegal dâ von verzaget,
sô si gerne sunge mê.

Swer unfuoge swîgen hieze,
waz man noch von fröuden sunge!
Und si abe den bürgen stieze,
daz si dâ die frôn niht twunge.
Wurden ir die grôzen höve benomen,
daz wær allez nâch dem willen mîn.
bî gebûren liez ich si wol sîn:
dannen ist si her bekomen.

(Alas, courtly singing, that crude melodies should ever supplant you at court. May God put them promptly to scorn! Alas that your honour is laid low—that is why all your friends are miserable. Since that must be so—well, let it be so. Dame Coarseness, you have conquered.

He who would bring us back our pleasure again, which would be of the right and proper kind, what a high opinion people would have of him, wherever his name were mentioned. What I should always wish for would be a truly courtly disposition. That would be fitting for both ladies and gentlemen. Alas that no one does it!

Those who spoil the true way of singing are incomparably more [numerous] than those who like to listen to it. I, for my part, still follow the old teaching. I do not want to go wooing at the mill, where the stone goes round and round so noisily and the wheel produces so many discords. Just look at who plays the harp there.

I can only laugh at and despise those who brazenly make a noise and who are satisfied with such crudity. They are like the frogs on a lake who are so pleased with their croakings that the nightingale loses heart, although she would gladly sing on.

If only someone would bid Coarseness be silent and expel her from the castles, so that she could oppress happy people no longer—how we should sing of joy again! If the great courts were barred to her, that would be just what I want. As far as I'm concerned, the peasants can have her: that's where she came from, anyway.)

It is evident from Walther's lines that so-called village poetry was popular even at the highest courts in the land; indeed, most people preferred it to the formal *Minnesang*. But Walther is wrong when he says that the village-poetry movement sprang from peasant circles; on the contrary, it was knightly poetry and it is doubtful if it ever reached the level of the peasantry. Both movements were popular for a long time, as is evident from the number of poets who imitated Neidhart and Walther.

G Wolfram's *Parzival* is intellectually the most considerable of the classical epics of the Arthurian cycle. Its hero is the son of an adventurous French knight in the service of the Caliph of Baghdad and of a sensitive mother who dies of grief when her son leaves her to go in search of adventure. Parzival associates with many important knights of the Round Table, and the action is set in the Celtic fairy-tale landscape common to the French and German Arthurian epics.

Parzival's humanity is more problematic and more subtly delineated than the heroes of the other epics. In his search for proper recognition of the existence of God and for the ideal form of knighthood he is plagued by inner conflict. He is gripped by doubts of God that (one might think) were almost inconceivable during the Middle Ages—doubts that lead him to the edge of madness. In his struggle to attain true knighthood he loses the prerequisite for all resolute action—his self-respect. His trust in God and his faith in himself alike shattered, Parzival endures a life of failure and humiliation. What saves him from total catastrophe is his honesty and personal goodness. His recovery, helped by the love of noblewomen, is due to God's *triuwe* (fidelity): at the castle of the Grail Parzival's name as the future Grail King is revealed by supernatural means. Parzival is reunited with his wife Condwiramurs; she goes with him to his fabulous kingdom accompanied by his pagan half-brother Feirefiz, who is received into the Christian Church.

Wolfram writes with an extraordinary, unflagging power. Even the more insipid episodes are rich in luminous images. Wolfram had no formal education, but he understood French and may well have travelled to the Middle East; he was widely read in contemporary literature and was familiar with the *Nibelungenlied*. *Parzival*, like Wolfram's second epic *Willehalm*, is composed in four-foot rhyming couplets; the extant fragment of his third work, on the *Titurel* theme, is written in a four-line strophe similar to that of the *Nibelungenlied*, from which it probably derived.

H A good example of this more mature style is the following *Meisterlied* by Heinrich Frauenlob (*d.* 1318); it is directed against the *Minnesang*:

> Adâm den êrsten menschen den betrouc ein wîp,
> Samsônes lîp
> wart durch ein wîp geblendet;
> Dâvît wart geschendet,
> her Salomôn an gotes rîch durch ein wîp gepfendet;
> Absôlôns schône in nicht vervinc, in het ein wîp betôret.
> Swie gewaltic Alexander was, dem geschach alsus:
> Virgilius
> trouc wîp mit valschen sitten;
> Olofern versnitten
> wart und ouch Aristotiles von eim wîbe geritten.
> Troyâ die stat und al ir lant wart durch ein wîp zerstôret.
> Achillî dem geschach alsam:
> der wilde Asahel wart zam,
> Artûses scham
> von wîbe kam;
> Parzivâl grôze sorge nam.
> sît daz ie vûgt der minnen stam,
> was schadet ob ein reinez wîp mich brennet unde vrôret?

(Adam, the first man, was deceived by a woman, Samson was blinded by a woman; David was brought into dishonour by a woman, Solomon was deprived of Paradise by a woman; Absolom's beauty did not help him, he was duped by a woman. The same happened to Alexander, in spite of his power; Virgil was deceived by a false woman; Holofernes' head was severed, and even Aristotle was ridden by a woman. The city of Troy was destroyed and all its lands devastated because of a woman. The same fate befell Achilles: the wild Asahel grew tame, Arthur's shame was caused by a woman; Parzival was burdened with troubles. Since love is the cause of all this, what harm can it do if a pure woman burns and freezes me?)

References

1. ALFONS NEHRING, "Idg. mari, mori," *Festschrift für Rolf Schröder* (Heidelberg 1959), pp. 122–38.
2. VITTORE PISANI, "Nachträgliches zur Chronologie der germanischen Lautverschiebung," *Mélanges de linguistique et de philologie, Fernand Mossé in memoriam* (Paris 1959), pp. 378–86.
3. C. S. ELSTON, *The Earliest Relations Between Celts and Germans* (London 1934).
4. FELIX GENZMER, *Germanische Schöpfungssagen* (Jena 1944).
5. GERHARD EIS, *Altdeutsche Zaubersprüche* (Berlin 1962).
6. OTTO HÖFLER, "Die zweite Lautverschiebung bei Ost- und West-germanen," *Beiträge zur Geschichte der deutschen Sprache und Literatur 77* (Tübingen 1955), pp. 33 ff.
7. EDWARD H. SEHRT and WOLFRAM K. LEGNER (ed.), *Notker-Wortschatz: Das gesamte Material zusammengetragen von Edward H. Sehrt und Taylor Starck* (Halle 1955), p. ix.
8. GERHARD EIS, "Die deutschen Vorstufen der Ironsaga," *Arkiv för Nordisk Filologi 67* (Lund and Copenhagen 1952), pp. 182 ff.
9. HANS NAUMANN and WERNER BETZ, *Althochdeutsches Elementarbuch, Grammatik und Texte*, 3rd edn (Berlin 1962), pp. 167 f.
10. GUNDOLF KEIL, "Nachträge zum Verfasserlexikon," *Studia Neophilologica 39* (Uppsala 1967).
11. GERHARD EIS, "Vom Werden altdeutscher Dichtung," *Literarhistorische Proportionen* (Berlin 1962), pp. 13 ff.
12. EDUARD HARTL, "Die deutsche Literatur des Mittelalters," *Verfasser-lexikon*, ed. by W. Stammler and K. Langosch (Berlin 1933–55), Vol. IV, Col. 1067.
13. *ibid.*
14. *Der dreieckicht spiegel* (Strassburg 1510).
15. JOSEPH QUINT, "Die Sprache Meister Eckharts als Ausdruck seiner mystischen Geisteswelt," *Deutsche Vierteljahrsschrift für Literaturwissen-schaft und Geistesgeschichte 6* (Stuttgart 1928), pp. 671–701.
16. GOTTFRIED WILHELM LEIBNIZ, "Unvorgreifliche Gedanken, betreffend die Ausübung und Verbesserung der deutschen Sprache" (1687), in K. E. PH. WACKERNAGEL, *Handbuch deutscher Prosa* (Berlin 1837), p. 544.
17. DAVID DALBY, *Lexicon of the Mediaeval German Hunt* (Berlin 1965).
18. GUSTAV KORLÉN, "Die mittelniederdeutschen Texte des 13. Jahrhun-derts," *Lunder germanistische Forschungen 19* (Lund and Copenhagen 1945), pp. 180 ff.
19. JUDY MENDELS, "Das Bergbüchlein" (thesis: Baltimore 1953); WILHELM PIEPER, *Ulrich Rülein von Calw und sein Bergbüchlein* (Berlin 1955).
20. The oldest university in the western part of the German-speaking territories was Heidelberg, founded in 1386.

CHAPTER 4

The British Languages and their Evolution

Kenneth Jackson[*]

By "British" we mean the Celtic language spoken in this island south of the Forth and Clyde by what used to be called the "ancient Britons" and by their successors down to the early part of the 6th century A.D. Toward the end of this period we can glimpse the formation of two main dialects of Late British: a western and northern dialect (in Wales, the West Midlands, northern England, and southern Scotland), from which later Welsh, and the "Cumbric" spoken in the north-west in the Dark Ages, were descended; and a south-western dialect (in Devon and Cornwall, and parts of Somerset and Dorset), which on the one hand evolved into the now extinct Cornish, and on the other—carried across the Channel by emigrants between the 5th and 7th centuries—became established in Brittany as the Breton that still flourishes there today. There must doubtless have been an eastern dialect or dialects also, but if so, the Anglo-Saxon occupation of England stifled any descendants, and nothing is known of them but what can be deduced from place-names. The language of the far north was Pictish, a Celtic tongue apparently very closely allied to British, though perhaps not wholly identical.

"British" seems to have been introduced, early in the 3rd century B.C., by a series of immigrations of tribes from France, Belgium, and elsewhere, who were an offshoot from the Gauls of those regions and whose language was therefore a dialect of contemporary Gaulish. These people brought with them the culture called "La Tène" by archaeologists. There had been Celtic immigrations before this, and it is not improbable that the Picts represent in part the northernmost settlers from those older move-

---

[*] Professor of Celtic, University of Edinburgh.

ments. Enough is known of the structure of this early British society to show that it was organized into large tribal units governed by kings, with lesser sub-divisions; each main tribe having a primitive "capital" and often smaller towns too, either one of the vast hill fortresses of Iron Age Britain such as Maiden Castle, or a lowland "city" like that at Verulamium near St Albans, capital of the Catuvellauni. Everything known about early Celtic society suggests (and we can glimpse this directly too) that there was a class of nobles besides the kings, and that the structure in Britain was not only monarchical but also aristocratic.

There is ample evidence to show that such Celtic societies were not merely supported on military and economic power, but were also upheld by an idea—the idea that honour, glory, reputation for the aristocratic virtues of courage and liberality, and noble descent in the king or chief were essential to their stability as societies. It was therefore necessary to foster a class of propagandists attached to the individual nobles and their families, whose function it was to uphold and spread the fame of their patrons by composing their praises in verse. These were the celebrated "bards"—the *bardi* of classical observers of Gaulish civilization, and the *beirdd* of Wales and *baird* of Ireland in the Middle Ages. (Some secondary modifications in the status of the mediaeval bards need not concern us here.) These public relations officers underwent a lengthy training in the art and metres of poetry before they qualified as pract'- tioners, and once they had done so they were free to seek patrons and were entitled, either by custom or by law, to a tariff of rewards for their praises. In short, the primary business of the Celtic poet was eulogy, and in discharging this function he was maintaining the structure of the aristocratic society. It is probable that the traditional, conservative nature of the bardic training and the formalized character of the panegyrics tended to foster a static literary language, and thus to act as a brake on linguistic evolution, at any rate among the upper classes. In other words, we begin in Britain with a Celtic language that probably had certain accepted "grammatical" standards.

There are no British texts extant (it was never, properly speaking, a written language), and its character is largely a matter of inference. All we have is names of persons, tribes, and places preserved in the works of Greek and Roman historians and officials and in the Latin inscriptions set up in the Roman province. From these we can get an idea of the phonetic system of British, but they can tell us virtually nothing of its grammar, for which we must rely on inference from the familiar methods of comparative philology; we see that it was an Indo-European language in much the same stage of evolution as its cousin Latin. Starting shortly before the beginning of our era and of the Roman conquest, we find that British seems to have had the five short vowels and four long ones (lacking only *ō*); three short *u*-diphthongs (*au, eu,* and *ou*), perhaps already in process of simplification, and a long *āu*; and two *i*-diphthongs *ai* and *oi*. Its consonants were *p, t, k, b, d, g; j* (=*y* in "yes"), *w; s; f, χ* (=*ch* in both the varieties seen in German *doch* and *ich*); and *m, n, l,* and *r*. All but *j, w, f,* and *χ* could exist double as well as single, and all but these last two seem to have had two fundamental varieties of intensity: a strong, tense one (*fortis*) and a weak, slack one (*lenis*). As to grammar, British inherited the Indo-European system of noun declensions, with results very like Latin. Thus taking the word **epos* (horse) as an example, its declension was evidently singular accusative **epon*, genitive **epī*, dative **epū*; plural nominative **epī*, accusative **epūs*, genitive **epon*, perhaps dative **epobis*. We recognize the virtually identical declension of its Latin cognate *equus* or *equos*, genitive *equī*, dative *equō*; plural *equī*, *equōs, equum* (the *-ibus* ending, related to Celtic *-obis*, is found in other Latin declensions). A noun with consonant stem is *rīx* (king), accusative **rīgan*, genitive **rīgos*, dative **rīgī*; plural **rīges, *rīgās, *rīgon, *rīgobis*; with a close parallel in the cognate Latin *rēx, rēgem, rēgis, rēgī*; plural *rēgēs, rēgēs, rēgum, rēgibus*. In the verb, too, there are many similarities, e.g. third singular present **carāt* (loves), plural **carant*; or **torrīt* (breaks), compared with Latin *amat, amant, audit*.

The occupation of most of the island by the Romans in the course of the 1st century A.D., and the establishment of the Imperial province of Britain, naturally brought about, within its confines, the downfall of the native monarchical and aristocratic organization. Kings and nobles disappeared, to be replaced by the normal Roman administrative structure. The tribal territories and their capitals, however, were adopted as the basis of regional government, so that for instance the tribal lands of the Belgae in Wiltshire and Hampshire became the Roman *civitas* of the Belgae, and their capital Venta was made its administrative centre—whence *Win*-chester. During the succeeding period, society developed in such a way that beneath the top layer of an overall Roman governing class a new stratum of country gentry grew up, the owners of the numerous villas, that is, manor houses with rural estates, scattered widely in many parts of eastern and central England, and as far south-west as the Devon border and the Wye and as far north-east as Yorkshire. These people seem to have been mainly a native squirearchy, who now came to the fore and played their due part in local government and local affairs.

Their whole inclination would have been towards the civilization of Rome and away from the native tradition. In such circumstances the professional poets maintained by the old nobility could not possibly have survived because they had lost their entire function and British had now ceased to be a language of prestige and had become something of a patois. This would mean a certain acceleration in its evolution, once the conservative influence of the literary elite was removed.

These remarks apply, however, to some parts of Britain less than to others. Outside the bounds of the Roman province, north of Hadrian's Wall, where the Roman occupation was quite brief and superficial, the native social organization is likely to have continued almost undisturbed. Even within the province the economically unattractive regions of the north and west, which archaeologists call the Highland Zone, were comparatively little romanized. The intensive agriculture of the villa system did not penetrate there, and romanization consisted largely of organizing the country into military districts watched over by numerically small army garrisons, with the natives left much to their own devices, provided they discharged their financial and other obligations and gave no trouble. In such a case the chances were good that the old Celtic customs would survive not only in Scotland, but also for instance in Wales; and in fact it is clear that some did survive, as we shall see. There would therefore be less likelihood of linguistic breakdown in these regions, though we must set against that the probability of influence by the British of the Roman province, which must have carried prestige and weight. Within the province the language of official government, of law, of the army, of education and writing, of the higher reaches of trade, and to a great extent of the population of the towns must have been Latin. Outside these spheres, the common people, even in the highly romanized south and east, seem to have spoken British. The position of the squirearchy would make it essential that they should know Latin, but there is reason to think that they also spoke British, either with their tenants only or perhaps as their own ordinary colloquial home language too. For them, Latin may well have been an acquired language, something to be taught in school or by tutors, rather like French among the Russian aristocracy before the Revolution. The whole situation may have been not unlike that in mediaeval Ireland, where French was the language of government in the normanized Pale and French and English were that of the towns and large-scale international trade, but Irish was that of the rest of the country; and while even the rural Norman nobility quickly learned Irish though retaining their French, the native Irish aristocracy acquired some French though continuing to speak Irish. During the four centuries of Roman rule in Britain a large number of Latin words were borrowed into British, chiefly nouns and a few verbs, largely words that stood for things or ideas which were foreign to British civilization, such as *civitas* (the Roman-organized tribal-geographical unit), *molina* ([water-]mill), *fenestra* (window), *vitrum* (glass), *pluma* (pen), *papyrus* (paper), and the like. Some 800 such Latin loanwords are known; they were easily assimilated into British because the native sound-system was so like the Latin one, and very little change was therefore needed.

As we should expect, this mass of Latin words shows features characteristic of the ordinary colloquial Latin of the Empire, such as the pronunciation of *coquus* (cook) as *cocus*, of *mensa* (table) as *mēsa*, of *populus* (people) as *poplus*, and so on. But what is surprising, and requires explanation, is the fact that the speakers of Latin by whom the loanwords were introduced into British nevertheless used certain other pronunciations that were far from colloquial, and were indeed archaic and pedantically "correct." Thus whereas final disyllabic *-eus*, *-ea*, *-eum* in words such as *oleum* (oil) had become *-jus*, etc., in ordinary speech (thus *oljum*, which would have given Welsh *ail* or *yl*), these speakers of Latin were careful to keep two distinct syllables and even emphasized their separateness by introducing a glide consonant, *olewum*, so that in fact the Welsh descendant is *olew*. The consonant written *u* or *v*, pronounced *w* in the Republican period, had become *v* in regular Latin speech in the 1st century A.D.; nevertheless our British Latinists kept the archaic *w*, so that for instance *civitas* yielded *kiwet* in mediaeval Welsh, not *kivet*. Latin *c* before *e* and *i*, a *k*-sound in earlier Latin, became a kind of *tsj* colloquially in the late Empire, hence *tsjivitas* and the French *cité*, but in British Latin the *k* was preserved by these "classy" speakers, with the result just seen.

This is peculiar. Who, in Roman Britain, would affect an archaic, "educated" Latin and be at the same time in a position to pass Latin words on to the common speakers of British in that pronunciation, by being in frequent contact with the latter and able to speak British with them? I have suggested elsewhere a probable answer: the native British squirearchy, people whose Latin was acquired artificially in school from pedantic "grammarian" teachers, or by imitation from the genuine high-ranking Romans and not from the vulgar tongue of the army or the townee; people who would readily teach their servants for instance that a pair of scissors was *cisellus*, not *tsjisellus*, or a cradle of improved Roman type was *cawella*, not *cavella*.

During the Roman occupation the British language was slowly evolving, both within and without the province. There appears to have been nothing in the nature of any drastic breakdown, in spite of the disappearance of the old aristocracy and the literary classes referred to; perhaps the British-speaking squirearchy may have been a restraining factor. The main developments are as follows. Original *ū* became something like the *u* in French *une* (printed here *ǖ*); meanwhile the short *u*-diphthongs became a close long *ō* and this, together with the close *ō* newly acquired in Latin words, itself gave a new *ū* by the end of the 3rd century. So, the name of Queen *Boadicea*, really **Boudīca*† in her own lifetime, was now already **Būdīca*; and **dūnon* (fortress) was **dūnon*. The *ai*-diphthong had become an open *ē*; and the old lenis *s* was further weakened to some kind of only faintly sibilant, lisped sound (printed here *Σ*). The old *x*, which had really been *χs*, was now *χΣ*. Hence the British place-name **Lētocaiton* ("Grey Wood": Lichfield) appears as Romano-British *Lētocētum* about the year 300, the second *ē* being open. However the Romans, who evidently heard *Σ* as *s*, still rendered the above two as *s* and *x* respectively, so that we have the Romano-British place-names *Gabrosentum* ("Goat Path": an unidentified place on Hadrian's Wall), and *Uxellodunum* ("High Fort": Castlesteads, in Cumberland) for what were now already **gabroΣenton* and **ūχΣellodūnon*. Nevertheless these and the few other phonetic evolutions do not amount to any drastic disturbance of the system.

When the Roman army and administration were obliged to withdraw, in the early part of the 5th century, there is no reason to suppose that this brought about an instant collapse of Roman life or of the use of Latin. Indeed there is evidence that it did not, and that the real break-down did not begin until about the middle of the century, when the Anglo-Saxon raids on Britain took a serious turn, leading to a fairly rapid conquest and occupation of south-eastern England by the early part of the 6th century, and a more gradual colonizing spread westwards and northwards for some two centuries thereafter. Whatever may have been the extent of survival of the native population—a point discussed below—it is evident that the British upper classes in town and country cannot have outlasted the initial occupation, and we know that organized town life broke down and the landed gentry and their villas vanished away. With all this there must have disappeared also, in the regions conquered by the Anglo-Saxons, the knowledge of writing, the institution of schools, and to a large extent—perhaps almost entirely—the general knowledge

† *Boudicca,* the form commonly given today, is erroneous.

of the Latin language. There is indeed little evidence that Latin survived at all as a living speech in these parts of Britain after the elimination of the upper classes, except among the clergy, and it is incorrect to think, as some have done, that we should now have been speaking a Romance language in England if the Anglo-Saxon invasions had never taken place. All this suggests that it is no coincidence that during the earlier part of the occupation period, about A.D. 450 to 600, the British language underwent the violent upheaval discussed below, so that it is indeed no longer possible to speak of "British" at all after about the middle of the 6th century. The influences which lent themselves to linguistic conservatism were suddenly removed, and the rapidly innovating tendencies of the uneducated classes, to whom the speaking of British was now abandoned within the English boundaries, went forward unchecked.

This social disaster did not apply to the same degree in those parts of Britain which were outside the reach of the Anglo-Saxons—those same parts which, as we have seen, were relatively little romanized, and still basically Celtic, in the previous period. *A priori*, one would therefore expect to find not only that the disruptive effects of the upheavals in neighbouring England had little impact on the Highland Zone, but also that the anti-Celtic consequences of romanization had themselves done little to change its essentially Celtic way of life. These questions need examining.

In the first place, there is reason to think that one result of the Anglo-Saxon onslaught in the Lowland Zone was that the Highland Zone underwent a temporary access of Latin influence. Refugees must have flooded into the safer hill country, bringing with them a more Roman civilization and a greater knowledge of Latin; Latin loanwords into British that had not yet found their way into the dialects of the Highland Zone may have come there now, the Latin in question being the "educated" speech of the old provincial upper classes. This is the period of the rise of the "tyrants" in post-Roman Britain; typical Celtic chiefs, not Roman magistrates and elected representatives, but hereditary over-lords or small kings ruling by right of military power, and probably representing an upsurge of the previous petty chiefs who may have controlled the people in the Highland Zone on behalf of the Roman government. In spite of their "Celtic" character, these chiefs admired and imitated the civilization of Rome while it existed and carried on some aspects of its nature after it collapsed. Thus they often called their children by Roman names, such as Aeternus, Donatus, Tacitus, Paternus, Potentinus, Agricola, Pascentius, Romanus, and so on. When they died, their successors set up rough stone funerary monuments with Latin inscriptions giving their names and sometimes other information, in imitation of Roman custom and obviously with the intention of making them appear as the heirs of Roman civilization. One who was buried in North Wales about the end of the 5th century is described as the cousin of a *magistratus*, a Roman administrator, and another who died in South Wales in the middle of the next century is called *protector*, a high Roman title to which he can have had no right, but which his family tried to pretend he held. One Welsh tombstone is dated to the year 540 by a reference to the consulate of Justinus, in the true Roman manner; and there is even an epitaph of the early or middle 6th century in rough hexameters:

> Servatvr fidaei patrieqve semper amator,
> ic Pavlinvs iacit, cvltor pientisimvs aeqvi.

> (Preserver of the Faith, and ever lover of his country, Paulinus lies here, a most scrupulous fosterer of justice.)

A king who died in Anglesey about 625 is described in his epitaph as *Catamanus rex, sapientisimus opinatisimus omnium regum* (King Catamanus, wisest and most celebrated of all kings), though he seems to have been the last for whom such pretensions were made. How far all this really means that the upper classes themselves understood Latin so late seems doubtful. Gildas, addressing a Welsh king about 540, says, "You had as tutor the refined teacher of almost the whole of Britain," and whatever this means it certainly seems to imply some education in Latin learning. The linguistic consequences of this early Dark Age movement are difficult to assess, beyond the obvious fact that it would bring more Latin loanwords to the Highland Zone, but at least it is not likely to have encouraged the rapid evolution of British.

On the contrary, we have seen that romanization must always have been rather superficial in the Highland Zone. It is remarkable that when the earliest native literature known to us begins, near the end of the 6th century, it is not in the least an imitation of Latin; it is quite simply a direct continuation of the bardic panegyric in praise of the nobility which was the classic concept of poetry among the Celts from the beginning and had survived four centuries of romanization. It may be significant that almost all the oldest known specimens come from southern Scotland, which had been outside the boundary of the Roman province (though doubtless subject to Roman influence) since the Antonine Wall was abandoned near the end of the 2nd century, and where the Celtic tradition might therefore have been strongest; the subsequent flowering of literature in Wales may well have been encouraged by an impetus from the north. The Welsh eulogistic poems attributed to Taliesin in praise of the heroic Urien, king of Rheged in Cumbria in the late 6th century, and the long elegy called *Gododdin* on the warriors of Edinburgh killed fighting the Northumbrians at Catterick about 600, belong essentially to the ancient Celtic tradition of bardic verse—as indeed do many other Welsh poems of much later times, for this tradition lasted in some form down to the modern period. In other words, in spite of four centuries of Roman rule, the Celtic idea of the highest kind of poetry continued unbroken in this island for over 2000 years. Nor was poetry the only intellectual activity bearing witness to the survival of the Celtic element in Britain, for it is clear from the later code of Welsh laws ascribed to the 9th-century Hywel Dda that Britain and Ireland inherited memories of a common legal tradition going back to the primitive days of original Celtic unity. This evidence for the persistence of Celtic learned tradition would suggest that the old British intellectual classes and the native nobility that supported them had outlasted the Romans in the Highland Zone, and once again this does not lead one to expect a rapid breakdown of the ancient language in the Highland Zone in the post-Roman period.

However that may be, such a breakdown certainly took place, between about 450 and 600, and if it really was the consequence of violent social disturbances and the disappearance of a linguistically conservative class, as one might well suppose, it is to the Lowland Zone that we should look, as already explained. If so, the influence of the new, "popular" Late British of the Lowland Zone must in some way be responsible. An influx of Lowland refugees may perhaps be part of the explanation. Linguistic fashions may spread very rapidly in suitable circumstances, as we see in the wholesale americanization of English since World War II; and possibly the "Cockney" brought by refugees from the Lowland Zone may have become as much the vogue among young people in the Highland Zone as modern Midland Cockney appears to be doing in England today; the two are really aspects of one social movement. "Late British" lasts from about 450 to 550, and the succeeding Primitive Welsh (and Cumbric), Cornish, and Breton from about 550 to 750. The chief direct evidence for these things, apart from names in Latin inscriptions and in one or two Latin texts, is the body of Celtic place-names borrowed by the Anglo-Saxons as their occupation of England went forward. These make it possible, within limits, to trace a chronological progression. They were adopted, naturally, in the form they took in the speech of the time, and adapted to the Anglo-Saxon phonetic system, with sound-substitution when the phonemes were difficult for English tongues; but after that, they developed as if they had been English names. We can peel off the layers of English development and arrive at roughly what the native pronunciation must have been when the name was taken over. And since we can give an approximate date to this, that is, the probable date when the English reached the region in question, we can get some idea of the chronology of phonological evolution of the dialects descended from British. The poems and other texts referred to above cannot be regarded as direct evidence, since unfortunately they are preserved in very late manuscripts and in a later linguistic dress, though something can be learnt from them.

The most drastic development, about the middle of the 6th century, was that the unstressed final syllables of all words, and certain unstressed interior ones in words of more than three syllables, were wholly dropped. These changes mark the end of Late British and the beginning of Primitive Welsh and the rest; at no period in the history of the language did a set of more thorough-going linguistic evolutions take place, and one can say that the Welsh, Cornish, and Breton which are their consequence have changed relatively little from then till now. They considerably altered the whole feel of the language by shortening the elements of speech rhythm and by causing modifications in the consonants now brought together in "difficult" groups through loss of the intervening vowels. But they did much more: we have seen that British had been a language of case-endings, and because these now disappeared, the syntax had to be rearranged to compensate, just as happened in Romance with the loss of the Latin case-endings. The distinction between nominative and accusative merely vanished, but for the dative it became necessary to make the noun governed by a preposition; all this is just as in Romance. Unlike Romance, however, the genitive relation was not now expressed with prepositions meaning "of" (cf. *canis mei patris* but *le chien* de *mon père*), but by the word order; the genitive qualifying another noun comes immediately after that noun, as it must have in British, but now without a genitive termination (as if in French one said *le chien mon père*). The Taliesin and *Gododdin* poems show that all this was already fully established before the time when they were composed, because otherwise their metres would have been disrupted by the extra syllables.

Another important early change is that most of the British lenis consonants underwent a further weakening during the Late British period. Lenis *p, t, k, b, d, g,* and *m* became respectively *b, d, g, v, ð* (=*th* in "bathe"), *ʒ* (the voiced spirant corresponding to *χ*), and *μ* (a very nasal *v*). So, the name that had become *Būdīcā* was now *Būðīga*, and the British river-names *Itunā* and *Σabrinā* are now respectively *Eden* and *Severn* in English. The history of *μ* is particularly interesting. The nasality of this sound grew weaker until by the 12th century it had wholly disappeared and the result was a *v* indistinguishable from that arising from *b*. But nasal *v* is an odd sound to English ears, and the Anglo-Saxons were driven to sound-substitution. When they noticed chiefly its nasality they rendered it by their *m*, and when chiefly its character as a labial spirant they substituted their *v*; hence a series of names with British *m*, Late British *μ*, appear in English with *m* in some cases and *v* in others. So British *Tamēsis* has given *Thames*, but *Tamiatis* in Roxburghshire and *Tamios* in Devon are *Teviot* and *Tavy*. There are several rivers Frome, from British *Frāmā*, later *Frōμ*, and one of the Fromes flows past Frampton and Framilode, but also past Frocester (Domesday Book: *Frowecester*), where the *μ* had been heard as *v* or *w* by the English.

A further striking modification is a type of *umlaut*, whereby the vowel *a*, *o*, *u*, or *e* in a preceding syllable were modified when the following contained an *i* or *j*. Thus British *Sorvio(dunum)* (Salisbury) was already *Σerw* when the name was learnt by the English, who made it their *Searo-burh*; and *Tamiatis* giving *Teviot* is another instance. The English *feet* versus *foot* is closely analogous.

Like classical Latin, British was a language in which vowels were long or short because they had been long or short in the parent Indo-European. As in late colloquial Latin, this system was replaced, about the end of the 6th century, by one in which all unstressed vowels became short, short stressed vowels were lengthened if they stood before a short consonant, and long stressed vowels were shortened if they stood before a long consonant or group of consonants. Hence we find that the British river-name *Tĕsā* gives English *Tees*, not *Tess*, because under the new quantity system it had first become *Tēs* in Cumbric.

A few other developments may be mentioned. In the sound *Σ* the tongue had lost all contact by the middle or later part of the 6th century, resulting in an *h*. Hence British *Σabrinā* is now Welsh *Hafren*. But in the Roman period the sound was still sibilant enough to be heard by the Romans as *s*, hence their *Sabrina* and the same is true of the early Anglo-Saxons, therefore *Severn*, not *Hevern*. Contrast *Hamps* in Staffordshire, from British *ΣamoΣispā*, borrowed rather later and therefore with *h*. The development of *ai* to open *ē* has been mentioned; this gave *oi*, probably in the first half of the 8th century, while the old close *ē* became *ui*, rather earlier. In English names, however, these things are naturally not found in the east, and the first is very rare east of Devon, owing to its late appearance. So, Romano-British *Lētocētum* (*ē*'s respectively close and open) was later **Luidgēd* and is now Welsh *Llwytgoed*, but the Anglo-Saxon *Lyccid-feld* (now *Lichfield*) does not show the *oi*, although it does show the *ui*. Similarly British **Mailobrunnios* ("Bald Hill") and **Mailorostā* ("Bald Moor"), later **Mēlvrinn* and **Mēlros*, Welsh *Moelfryn* and *Moelros*, are still English *Malvern* and *Melrose*.

It used to be believed that the Anglo-Saxon conquest left very few surviving Britons, and that almost all were either killed or expelled to the west or to Brittany—the theory called the "clean sweep." Some colour was lent to this by the striking fact that the English borrowed scarcely any British *words* (unlike names); probably not more than a dozen all told, of which the most notable are *ass* and *brock* (badger). How, it was argued, could hundreds of words not have been adopted into English if a British population survived in any numbers and intermarried with the conquerors? The modern study of place-names has put a different complexion on this, and it is realized that though there are admittedly quite few British place-names in the south-east—the region of primary conquest—they become progressively commoner northwards and westwards, in the regions of the Anglo-Saxon secondary colonization which began roughly in the early part of the 6th century. The only explanation must be that once the first rush of conquest was over, considerable British-speaking populations stood their ground and mingled in varying proportions with the incomers. Moreover, place-names offer some evidence for bilingualism; thus *Dover* was a plural name both in British and in Anglo-Saxon ("The Waters"), and must have been handed on by people who knew what a British plural was and could speak Anglo-Saxon. Such things suggest a period of some length when both languages were spoken by the same people. The reason why there are not more ordinary British words in English may be quite different from the rather simple one supposed by the advocates of the "clean sweep." For instance it has been pointed out that the English spoken in those parts of Wales where general Welsh-speaking has died out only in recent times, and without a change of population, does not itself show any larger quantity of Welsh words in it than general English does.

Lastly, we must consider the question of style. We know nothing about prose style in the period under discussion, since the oldest Welsh prose passage of any length dates from the beginning of the 10th century. It has already been remarked that the very early poetry does not survive in contemporary copies, and that the phonetic developments it shows can therefore not be assumed *ipso facto* for the late 6th century. But this scarcely affects the metre and style, and it is legitimate to assume that these are essentially what they were when the poems were composed. All early Welsh metres are syllabic, the number of syllables in the line and the disposition of the rhymes defining the metre. The high-class traditional panegyric is composed in *tirades* of varying length; the lines may or may not all rhyme together (if not, the rhymes are arranged in some other pattern); the pattern varies according to the metre. There is a good deal of internal rhyme, alliteration, rhetorical contrast, and other such features, and a strong tendency to archaic language and heavily heaped-up grandeur of expression: it is stately poetry, slow-moving, highly decorated, and often obscure. These characteristics may be seen, and something of the flavour of bardic heroic elegy perceived, in the following verse from the *Gododdin* poem:

> Gwyr a aeth Gatraeth, oed fraeth eu llu,
> glasved eu hancwyn a gwenwyn vu;
> trychant trwy beiryant en cattau,
> a gwedy elwch tawelwch vu.
> Ket elwynt e lanneu e benydu
> dadyl dieu agheu y eu treidu.

> (The men went to Catterick, swift was their army, the pale mead was their feast and it was their poison; three hundred fighting according to plan, and after the glad shout of battle there was silence. Though they went to churches to do penance, the sure meeting with death overtook them.)

Or again:

> Kywyrein ketwyr, kyuaruuant
> y gyt, en vn vryt yt gyrchassant;
> byrr eu hoedyl, hir eu hoet ar eu carant;
> seith gymeint o Loegrwys a ladassant;
> o gyvryssed gwraged gwydw a wnaethant,
> llawer mam a'e deigyr ar y hamrant.

> (The warriors arose, they met together, together with single purpose they attacked; short were their lives, long the mourning for them among their kinsmen; seven times as many English they slew; in fight they made women widows, and many a mother with her tears on her eyelids.)

These are fragments from one of the oldest poetic traditions in Europe, at a stage of evolution comparable more to Homer than to *Beowulf*. Its conventions had survived the linguistic catastrophe of the earlier part of the same century, and must have been transformed to suit the new form of British—in this case, Primitive Cumbric—in which Aneirin composed the *Gododdin* about A.D. 600. Not the least remarkable of the many amazing aspects of mediaeval Celtic literature is the fact that the ancient tradition of bardic panegyric, with various modifications, lasted not merely to the 6th century but to the 16th and beyond.

Bibliography

For evidence and greater detail on the matters summarized in this chapter, see K. JACKSON, *Language and History in Early Britain* (Edinburgh 1953); and "The British Language during the Period of the English Settlements," in N. K. CHADWICK (ed.), *Studies in Early British History* (Cambridge 1954), pp. 61–82.

CHAPTER 5

The Development of English

Richard N. Bailey*

I

In 597 St Augustine, much against his inclination, arrived in Kent. The Lowland Zone of Britain had changed radically in the preceding two centuries. Two hundred years earlier it had been part of the Roman Empire, Celtic and Latin had been its spoken languages, many of its inhabitants had been Christians, and towns had still played an important role in the economy. Something of that world still survived in Augustine's time but it was confined mainly to the non-urban Celtic societies around the Irish Sea. Further east, Christianity, town life, and the use of Latin and even Celtic had been almost completely obliterated by the 5th-century settlement of the Anglo-Saxons. The language of these settlers is the earliest form of English: for the linguist their coming marks the beginning of the Old English period.

Christianity reached the Anglo-Saxons from two sources: the Roman mission of St Augustine, and the various missionaries of the Irish Church. Whatever the immediate origin, however, its advent was accompanied by the books and learning of the early mediaeval Mediterranean world. Throughout the literature of the Anglo-Saxon period can be seen the influence of the writings of the Christian Fathers, of the great compilations of men such as Isidore of Seville (c. 570–636), and of the detritus of classical literature. This influence is most obviously present in the Latin writings of monks such as Aldhelm, Bede, and Alcuin, but recent work has also demonstrated its thorough permeation of vernacular literature in studies of, for instance, the consolationary *topoi* of *The Wanderer*, the *ubi sunt* motif in both this poem and *The Seafarer*, and the allegorical elements in *Exodus*.[1]

More important in this immediate context is that with Christianity came scriptoria and the Latin alphabet, and thus the possibility of

* Lecturer in English Language and Medieval Literature, University of Newcastle-upon-Tyne.

recording and preserving Old English. This is not to deny the existence of inscriptions dating from the pagan period, because, like other Germanic peoples, the Anglo-Saxons knew and used the runic alphabet.* But runes were never used primarily as a means of lengthy written record, and the linguistic information to be derived from the few pagan inscriptions that survive is often highly debateable. It remains true that the main source of our knowledge of Old English comes from the manuscripts of the Christian period.

These manuscripts are inadequate as the basis for a complete description of the language, even if we take account of other sources, such as place-names and the inscriptions on coins and sculpture. One important limitation on any description is that we have direct knowledge only of *written* Old English. We cannot assume that this is in any way a transcription of the spoken language when recent work on Modern English[2] has shown that there are fundamental differences between the structure of the two types of language.

More obviously there are limitations that stem from the fact that the manuscripts have come down to us through the Church. There were educated laity—such as King Aldfrith in the 7th century, King Alfred in the 9th, or Ealdorman Æthelweard in the 10th—but they had been educated by the Church and relied upon ecclesiastics for their secretariat. None of the surviving documents has come down to us through lay hands. The selection of what to commit to writing and, even more important, its subsequent preservation, was thus almost entirely vested in the Church. Alcuin's views about the place of secular literature in a monastic community—"What has Ingeld to do with Christ?"—were not universal, but, even so, work that was not obviously religious or didactic stood only a slender chance of achieving a written form in the Anglo-Saxon period. It stood even less chance of survival in the reformed monasteries of post-Norman England, where Anglo-Saxon sermons were catalogued as *vetust. inutil* (ancient useless) or marked *non apreciatum propter ydioma incognita* (valueless because of the unknown idioms).[3]

The resulting limitation on the subject-matter of surviving texts has an immediate linguistic impact in the lexical field, because many words that, on other grounds, we can infer were in existence in the pre-Norman period are never recorded in the manuscripts.

Closely related to this is another type of limitation. What has survived

---

* The bibliography lists studies of topics, such as this, that are only allusively treated in the text. Editions of literary works that are briefly mentioned will be found in the works listed in the bibliography under Bennett, Greenfield, Stanley (1966), and Wrenn.

reflects the taste of the monastery and, to a certain extent, of the aristocracy. We have very little information about differences in language
usage at various levels of society or of the type of language used in informal
situations. These are serious losses, because there is good evidence that such
distinctions did exist. Bede, in a letter to Bishop Egbert of York in the
early 8th century, advised him to use a speech "more elevated than
common diction," and the context makes it clear that he recognized a
distinction between formal and informal language.[4] Only hints of this
remain: it seems, for example, that the use of the verb *swætan* in the sense
of *sweat* was less elevated than its use in the sense of *bleed*, but there are too
few texts like the obscene *Riddles* to yield information of this kind.

Differences in class usage are perhaps even more important because the
hierarchical nature of Anglo-Saxon society is one of its characteristic
features. A man's position in society, whether he was a nobleman or a
peasant, was established and codified by an elaborate system of valuation
that could be invoked in cases of crime, injury, death, or oath-giving.
These social divisions remained throughout the period, despite the dis-
ruptions of Viking settlements and the growth of a merchant and trading
class, and they were certainly reflected linguistically. The best evidence for
this comes again from Bede, who tells of a captured nobleman's attempt
to pass himself off as a peasant, and of his betrayal by his countenance,
dress, and speech (*sermonibus*).[5] Unfortunately, we have very little idea
of which features of his speech would have indicated that he was not
from the lower classes.

The limited subject-matter and the lack of information about informal
and lower-class usage result in curious gaps in the historical record of
words and constructions. It is highly unlikely that the ancestral forms
of modern *kill* and *cut* were never used in English before *c.* 1200, yet that
is the date of their first written occurrence. Similarly, if it were not for
their presence in place-names formed during the Anglo-Saxon period,
the demonstrable written history of words such as *clod* and *ball* would be
a very short one.

This depressing list of inadequacies can be closed with one final entry.
It is sobering to reflect that Ker's *Catalogue of Manuscripts Containing
Anglo-Saxon* lists less than 150 manuscripts, including fragments, that
were written entirely or mainly in Old English before *c.* 1200. These few
are our main sources for the language of the Anglo-Saxon period. The
value of even this number is diminished by the fact that they are not
distributed evenly across every century or every part of the country.
There are naturally none from the pagan period, but there are also few

from Wessex before the late 9th century and virtually none of any period from East Anglia.

II

Despite their limitations, our sources do allow some positive statements about Old English. Within the Indo-European system, its highly inflected language shares certain marked characteristics with the Gothic of the Bible of Ulfilas (*c.* 311–83), the languages of mediaeval Scandinavia and Iceland, and those once spoken in Switzerland, Holland, and Germany. Modern English—like Danish, German, and Dutch—still preserves many of these Germanic features.

In all these languages the stress within words falls on the root syllable and does not vary its position with grammatical function: the dominant Old and Modern English pattern is that seen in the series *love*, *lover*, *lovingly*, rather than that of *family*, *familiar*, *familiarity*, because this latter group still preserves the stress system of the non-Germanic language from which the words were borrowed. Similarly Germanic in origin is the fact that the verb inflexion distinguishes only between the past and every other time of an action: there is no inflected future tense in English, only periphrastic expressions (employing *will*, *shall*, *going to*) that have been developed to supplement this binary Germanic system. At the phonetic level, Old English and its Modern English derivative show the results of common Germanic sound changes that account for the regular alternation of certain plosive and fricative sounds between cognate words such as *pater* and *father*, *fish* and *piscis*, in Germanic and non-Germanic languages. These three examples are far from exhausting the list of Germanic features, but suffice to place Old English in its historical context.

Other features show that Old English is most closely linked within this Germanic group to the so-called West Germanic, or Ingaevonic, languages of Old Saxon, Old Frisian, and (to a lesser degree) Old High German. The Frisian link is the most important, because the closeness of the two languages is strikingly illustrated by their common development of identical runic letters to express two sounds produced by shared phonetic changes. The linguistic evidence thus confirms the Frisian element in the settlement, which is asserted by Procopius and attested archaeologically.

In this discussion of the Germanic setting we have taken no account of the fact that the term "Old English" covers a range of language types. The selection from this range is dependent upon such controls as the medium employed, the class of the user, and the formality of the linguistic situation. One type of variety, however, does demand more extensive treatment. The earliest texts show that there were already dialectal variations in Old English by the 8th century. Over the whole period it is possible to distinguish four main dialects: West Saxon, Kentish, and the "Anglian" dialects of Mercian and Northumbrian. The differences between them are not of syntax nor, to any great extent, of morphology, but affect lexis and phonology. It is thus possible to distinguish West Saxon *eall* from its Anglian equivalent *all*, and, on the evidence of place-names, to identify *þrop** (hamlet, farm) as a word with a limited popularity in the West Saxon area. Our knowledge of the development and boundaries of these dialects is very limited because, even when texts are available from an area, their information is often relevant only to the scribal conventions of a particular scriptorium at a certain date. The study is further complicated by the mobility of the churchmen who staffed and administered the monastic scriptoria and by the lack of natural barriers within the country. The problems are well exemplified by the fact that one of the main sources of our knowledge of the Mercian dialect is a gloss written in the Canterbury *Vespasian Psalter*.

Some of the earliest distinctions may result, at least indirectly, from the differing origins of the 5th-century settlers. This assertion should not, however, be tied to Bede's identification of these settlers as Jutes, Angles, and Saxons, and his rigid apportioning of the Anglo-Saxon kingdoms to these races.[6] The archaeological evidence makes it clear that the settlements involved peoples living along the whole of the North Sea littoral from the mouth of the Rhine to Norway and Sweden. Although tribal names can be assigned to them, these groups were not sharply divided from each other on the Continent: the material culture shows many signs of movement and mixture, which must have had its linguistic corollary. Further mixture of these peoples is evident in the earliest phase of settlement archaeology in Britain. Such intermingling was the inevitable outcome of land-taking by small groups emigrating as separate units, and of a settlement that involved war-lords whose success drew followers from a wide area. Most areas of 5th-century England must have contained a population speaking a variety of West (and even some North) Germanic dialects. The linguistic variety that eventually emerged from this welter depended upon the emergence of

* The symbols þ and ð both have the value of the sounds now represented by *th* in *thin* and *then*.

dominant individuals or groups whose language was modified, to a greater or lesser extent, by the range of types spoken in a particular area.

Not all dialectal distinctions belong to the settlement phase, and the later ones are certainly not attributable to racial origins. It has been argued that some reflect the influence of continental Germanic languages on areas in trading contact with the European mainland, but the majority —such as the most obvious of the Kentish features, which emerge only in the 9th century—must reflect the political and cultural polarization of societies around certain dominant centres of influence.

In the 10th century one of these dialects achieved something of the status of a standard written language. Other dialects, notably Mercian in the course of the 9th century, may temporarily have gained this status, but only West Saxon was adopted so permanently and so widely by scribes who did not use the dialect as a spoken form. There are three basic reasons for the emergence of West Saxon in this function. The first is purely political: the dominant power in late-9th-century England was in the south of the country. Mercia and Northumbria were already in decline when Viking invasions and settlement caused further disruption. Wessex under Alfred (871–99) was the only Anglo-Saxon kingdom to survive the Scandinavian invasions, and it was his successors who, in the course of the 10th century, established their control over the Danelaw. Not all of them could claim, as did Athelstan (924–39) on his coins, that he was REX TO[TIUS] BRIT[ANNIAE], but throughout the 10th century the kings of Wessex were the rulers of England.

Political factors therefore favoured the dominance of West Saxon in the 10th century. Probably another element was the fact that Alfred deliberately chose to use the vernacular as a medium of instruction when he set out to translate into English what he called "some books that are most needful for all men to know."[7] The success of his effort is difficult to measure, but it did ensure that, by the 10th century, West Saxon was associated with attempts to use the vernacular for communicating learned material.

The last factor that guaranteed the ascendancy of West Saxon as a literary language was the Benedictine reform movement. Regular monasticism was reintroduced into England in the middle of the 10th century from continental houses such as Cluny and Fleury, and had enthusiastic royal support during the long and peaceful reign of Edgar (959–75). It had an impressive effect upon the art and architecture of late Saxon England, but its importance here is that the Benedictine attention to scholarship and teaching not only stimulated the production of works in Latin but also brought a revival of literary activity in the vernacular. To this period we owe the copying of much of the surviving Anglo-Saxon literature, including nearly all the poetry, but it was also a period of original composition by writers such as Abbot Ælfric of Eynsham and Archbishop Wulfstan of York.

The relevance of this religious movement to the status of West Saxon can be seen from a map showing the distribution of the reformed houses.[8] Nearly all are in the south of the country, and there is a marked concentration in the Wessex area. Even the Fenland monasteries outside this area were founded largely by monks from Wessex. There are none in the north of England, where the Viking invasions had had a disastrous economic effect on the Church. The work produced in such quantities from these reformed monasteries naturally leaned toward the West Saxon dialect, which was already politically prestigious and was historically associated with scholarship in the vernacular.

It would be wrong to claim that West Saxon was inevitably employed as a written standard in all parts of the country; there are many texts that remain completely dialectal. But it did have sufficient status to be used in 10th-century Worcester charters, in 11th-century manuscripts from Canterbury, and (most interesting of all) in 11th-century material in the *York Gospels*.[9]

III

On the opening leaves of the Bodleian manuscript Hatton 20 is a letter from King Alfred addressed to Bishop Wærferth of Worcester.[10] Written just after the near-annihilation of Wessex by the Vikings, it lays out proposals for the education of the sons of freemen "as long as they cannot be of use in any other employment, until the time that they can read English well." He argues that educational policy must be directed, in the first place, at an understanding of vernacular writings, and that it will also involve the translation into English of the major works of mediaeval scholarship. In this task of translation he solicits Wærferth's help.

This decision to base education on the vernacular was forced upon Alfred by the current state of Latin learning. His letter traces the decline in classical learning to the period before the Viking raids, and his argument is well supported by the injunctions of the synod at Cloveshoe (747) and by the curious Latin of the 9th-century charters.

This letter, prefaced to a translation of Pope Gregory's *Cura pastoralis*, does not mark the beginning of Old English prose, although some of the implications of its more polemical passages would seem to indicate this. In the official usage represented by the Anglo-Saxon laws, Bede records[11] that English was being employed in the 7th century; charters in the 8th century and wills in the 9th show other functions of vernacular prose. Alongside these can be placed vernacular glosses to sacred texts (particularly the much-used psalter) and translations of biblical passages that, on the evidence of Bede and his disciple Cuthbert, were available in England from an early date. Bede had even translated passages from Isidore of Seville.[12] What is new in Alfred's period is the conscious attempt to use the vernacular to communicate a wide range of historical, geographical, and philosophical material. Its success can be judged by the fact that by *c.* 900 many of the basic documents of mediaeval learning were available in English.

In its European context the existence of this vernacular prose is remarkable. It cannot be denied that there are vernacular prose texts from Ireland and in some of the continental Germanic languages, but the surviving material gives no indication of anything comparable with either the range or the competence of works in English.

Some of the late-9th-century translations are certainly not by Alfred. The king's biographer, Bishop Asser, states that the translation of Pope Gregory's *Dialogues* was the work of Wærferth, and the Old English version of Bede's *Historia ecclesiastica* was also a Mercian product. More closely associated with Alfred are the translations of Gregory's *Cura pastoralis*, Boethius's *De consolatione philosophiae*, Orosius's history, the *Soliloquies* of St Augustine, and possibly the prose version of the *Paris Psalter*. The interesting sections of these works are the prefaces and the sections for which there was no Latin exemplar. These show Old English to be fully capable of accommodating a variety of prose styles. Alfred's preface to the *Cura pastoralis* is at one extreme, full of literary echoes, recondite vocabulary, and repeated structures. By contrast Ohthere's account, included in the Orosius, seems to catch the short, non-subordinated sentences of colloquial speech with its typical modifications of an idea expressed in an abutted structure:

> Se hwæl bið micle læssa þonne oðre hwalas: ne bið he lengra ðonne syfan elna lang; ac on his agnum lande is se betsta hwælhuntað; þa beoð eahta and feowertiges elna lange, and þa mæstan fiftiges elna lange; þara he sæde þæt he syxa sum ofsloge syxtig on twam dagum.[13]

> (The whale is much smaller than other whales; it is no longer than 7 elns; but in his own land is the best whale hunting; there they are 48 elns long and the biggest are 50 elns; he said that he and five companions had killed 60 in two days.)

The range of the prose produced during the Alfredian period is impressive. There was certainly homiletic work in the vernacular, of which the *Life of St Chad* is probably a survivor, and it was at about this date that the romantic tale of *Appolonius of Tyre* was first translated into English. The extant versions of the *Anglo-Saxon Chronicle* derive from a single exemplar of Alfred's period, although the tradition of historical writing in the vernacular can probably be carried back to the middle of the 9th century. Its value lies in its being a further example of original prose composition associated with the West Saxon court.

The full realization of the potential of the English language as a prose instrument comes during the Benedictine reform period. It can be seen in the *Chronicle* entries of Æthelred II's reign in the late 10th and early 11th century. The language is organized not only to convey the historical facts, but also to convince the reader of the validity of the author's interpretation and attitude.

This organization of language is seen at its most sophisticated in this period in the religious prose of Ælfric and Wulfstan. Their use of the vernacular can be attributed not to any linguistic nationalism in the reform movement in England (indeed, as the movement gathered strength it dispensed more and more with English) but to the limitations of the audience they were addressing. The audience was either the priesthood, whose Latin was of the type Ælfric (*c*. 955–*c*. 1020) lamented in the preface to his first set of *Catholic Homilies*, or the common people, who could not be expected to know Latin. The use of the vernacular in exposition and preaching to this latter group was constantly urged on the Church throughout the period, because in general, as one 10th-century writer put it, "it is certainly of no importance by what language a man is acquired and drawn to the true religion so long as he comes to God."[14]

Some of the pre-Benedictine homiletic material has survived. The *Life of St Chad* and the Blickling and Vercelli collections may all belong to a date before *c*. 950. They all show the rhetorical organization of language, with archaic and emotive vocabulary, alliterative phrases, and the repetition of words, phrases, and sentence structures. It is on this tradition that Ælfric and Wulfstan drew for their highly distinctive prose styles.

Ælfric is the earlier of the two. He developed the characteristic rhythmic features of his English prose style at an early stage in his career. Its nature can be judged by an extract from the opening passage of the *Life of St Edmund*:

Eadmund se eadiga · Eastengla cynincg
wæs snotor and wurðful · and wurðode symble
mid æþelum þeawum · þone ælmihtigan God.[15]

(Edmund the blessed, King of the East Angles, was wise and honourable and ever glorified almighty God with his noble virtues.)

Printed in this way it is easy to see that the sentence is made up of short phrases, each with two stressed elements in them, and that the pairs are joined by alliteration. The fact that the sentences were built up in this way is recognized in the manuscript punctuation. This is obviously a very formal type of prose, which in some of its features is close to Anglo-Saxon poetry (though only a misunderstanding of the nature of Anglo-Saxon verse could lead to the belief that Ælfric was trying to write poetry). What Ælfric has done is to take as the basis of his prose the phrasal unit with two stresses, which constantly occurs in Modern (and presumably occurred in Old) English speech. Within these self-imposed limits he can achieve his oratorical effects by varying the relationship between the stressed and unstressed elements of the phrase, and between these elements and the alliteration. He may have been influenced in his choice of this formal prose by the existence of a contemporary rhythmic Latin prose, but his own style rests firmly on the very English two-stress phrase and alliteration.

A similar type of formal language, whose persuasive effect depends upon its sound, is found in Wulfstan's work. In what has been called the "Age of Bishops," the mark of his strong personality was impressed across the reigns of Æthelred (978–1016) and Canute (1017–35). This personality is mirrored in his language, in the vocabulary peculiar to his work—such as *manswican* (deceivers) and *woruldstruderas* (spoliators)—in his persistent choice of one synonym instead of another (*lagu* and not *æ* for law), in his individual use of *þeod-* as an intensifier, and in the phrases—such as *mid rihte* (rightly) and *swyðe georne* (very eagerly)—that are so much the hallmark of his work that they occur even in his translation of the Lord's Prayer.

The movement of his sermons is elaborately planned, and so is the smaller organization of sentences and paragraphs:

Ne dohte hit nu lange inne ne ute, ac wæs here ⁊ hunger, bryne ⁊ blodgyte on gewelhwylcan ende oft ⁊ gelome; ⁊ us stalu ⁊ cwalu, stric ⁊ steorfa, orfcwealm ⁊ uncoðu, hol ⁊ hete ⁊ rypera reaflac derede swyðe þearle, ⁊ ungylda swyðe gedrehtan, ⁊ us unwedera foroft weoldan unwæstma. . . .[16]

(Things have not gone well at home or abroad for a long time, but there has been the raiding army and famine, burning and bloodshed, time and again in every district; and we have been sorely injured by theft and murder, plague and pestilence, murrain and disease, envy and hatred, and by the robbery of plunderers, excessive tax has severely oppressed us and storms have very often brought about failure of crops. . . .)

The links with Ælfric are clear, because this is another type of rhythmic prose based on the two-stressed phrase. Wulfstan's phrases are crisper than Ælfric's, however, and the alliteration serves to bind together (and rhetorically to emphasize) the members of the phrase, and not the phrases to each other. The effect of the sentence relies upon the common Wulfstan practice of an accumulation of nouns, but it is important to notice the complexity within this accumulation: the paired nouns vary in their semantic relation to one another, rhymed pairs and alliterated pairs interweave their way through the passage, and there is a constant play between the expectation of a repeated structure and its non-realization. Other passages show words and parts of words being repeated from line to line, such as *geweorþað on eorðan* (become on earth).

This sophisticated use of the vernacular in prose is unparalleled elsewhere at this date. Yet our admiration for its growth should be tempered by the memory that it was a growth forced by a decline in scholarship and by the demands of an uneducated audience.

IV

The language of the surviving poetry differs in important respects from that of prose. The lexical differences are the most noticeable, and among these the *kenning* holds pride of place. This Icelandic term describes the periphrastic expression of an object or idea by means of an implicit simile. Kennings are formed by the compounding of elements that are familiar as separate words in prose but whose combination is a poetic device. Their effect is dependent upon the resolution of the apparent incongruity between the object and one of the members of the compound. Thus *nædre* (adder) has little in common with a javelin or arrow, but combined with *hilde* (battle) in the kenning *hilde-nædre* it becomes an effective description of a swift, sharp, and deadly weapon.

Closely related to the kenning are other nominal and adjectival compounds that do not carry any simile function. Compounds such as *gold-wine* (gold-friend, lord) occur as frequently as once every three lines in *Beowulf*. The difficulty for the modern student lies in assessing the originality of both these types of compound and in deciding how far a poet is using them with a degree of awareness of the meaning of their constituent parts. It is never possible to be certain of originality, in view of the small surviving poetic corpus, but poems such as *Beowulf* and *The Dream of the Rood* do show how effectively and relevantly both types of poetic device can be used.

Some kennings and compounds, although possibly not found elsewhere in Old English, do recur in other Germanic languages. This points not only to the danger of arguing originality from negative evidence, but also to the antiquity of the device and many of the compounds. It should not be forgotten that these long-lived expressions must have carried with them, for an Anglo-Saxon audience, the associations of the previous contexts in which they had been heard. These are associations that a poet could exploit, but they are inevitably hidden from the modern critic.

Both kennings and compounds are used in another characteristic device of poetic language. This is the double or multiple statement of frequently recurring concepts such as warfare, weapons, and warriors, as in *Beowulf*, lines 325–8:

> Setton sæmeþe · side scyldas,
> rondas regnhearde · wið þæs recedes weal;
> bugon þa to bence, · —byrnan hringdon,
> guðsearo gumena. . . .

> (Weary from the sea they set down their broad shields [side scyldas], the wonderfully hard shields [rondas regnhearde], against the wall of the hall. They sat down then on the bench, the corselets [byrnan] rang, the war gear [guðsearo] of men. . . .)

The words used here for shield and armour are clearly not synonyms: *rondas* stresses the round nature of the shield, and the compound *guðsearo* emphasizes the warlike purpose of the corselet. Unfortunately our present vocabulary is ill-equipped to express the slight distinctions and shifts of emphasis involved in this technique of variation.

Less noticeable than this type of poetic language is the occurrence in poetry of the words that either—like *mece* (sword)—are totally confined to poetry or carry meanings in poetry that they do not have in prose. *Dream* belongs to this second group: although poetry shares with prose the meanings of *noise* and *sound*, its dominant poetic sense of *joy* is not found in most prose.

Morphologically there are differences between poetry and prose.

Sisam's careful examination of the non-syncopated verbal inflexions (*bindest*, not *binst*) in the poetic manuscripts seems to show that, although this may originally have been a Mercian dialectal trait, it came to be regarded in the south of England as a form suitable to poetry.[17] As a result Alfred used such forms in his verse, but rarely in his prose.

The other differences can best be discussed in relation to the formal requirements of Anglo-Saxon poetry. This type of poetic metre is found in the other Germanic languages, and almost certainly stems back to the continental period. This is not the place to make a detailed examination of its nature, but its main features can be seen in the passage from *Beowulf* printed above. Each line of verse is made up of two metrical phrases, which are usually self-contained grammatical units. These phrases, or half lines, are of equal musical length, although they vary in the number of syllables contained. The factor that ensures the consistency of musical length is that each has two stressed long syllables. The half lines are linked by alliteration, which falls on the first stressed syllable in the second half line and on either or both stressed syllables in the first half line. Sievers' classic analysis[18]—still the best starting-point for the student —defined five different permitted combinations of stressed and unstressed syllables in the half line.

This system may seem highly artificial but, in fact, is not so. The half-line types are merely a selection of rhythmical groups from the range available in spoken Old and Modern English. The two-stress phrase, as was seen in the Ælfric discussion, is a basic element in English speech, and the various patterns that the poetry uses can be illustrated from that speech. Thus Sievers' Type A has the pattern of /x(x. . .)/x and this can be seen in *sídě scýldǎs* of the passage above and in the Modern *régǎl spléndǒur eárlӯ mórniňg*, *wáshiňg pówděr*, and *Engliš Stúdiěs*. The half lines are language patterns.

Although demonstrably based upon speech rhythms, these half-line units and their alliterative requirements inevitably condition the syntax and much of the lexis of poetry. The choice of kennings and compounds, for instance, often reflects alliterative demands.

It is the metrical requirements that, directly or indirectly, lie behind the much-discussed formulaic half lines of the poetry. These have been the centre of much controversy since Magoun argued that they betray the extempore oral composition of the poems in which they are found.[19] Using the evidence of 20th-century oral singers, he demonstrated that poetic composition by illiterate poets was possible only when formulas were available to the extemporizing singer that he knew would fit the metrical requirements of his verse-form. The problem is to decide how far the formulaic element in the surviving corpus of Anglo-Saxon poetry reflects similar oral composition—even if by authors as learned as Cynewulf (*fl. c.* 800) or the *Phœnix*-poet—and how far they are literate, pen-in-hand creations continuing to use and exploit traditional collocations evolved by earlier or contemporary illiterate poets. The evidence seems to favour the latter explanation, but in this context it is sufficient to note the presence of whole phrases that are repeated exactly or with trifling variation across the poetic corpus. Thus *wordhord onleac* (open a store of words) occurs twice in *Andreas* as well as in *Widsith*, *Beowulf*, and Alfred's Boethius. Some of these formulas are creations of the Christian era, but the existence of parallels between Old English and Old Saxon formulas— *Beowulf*'s *fuse to farenne* (eager to go) and the *Heliand*'s *fûsa to faranne*— argues that others were creations of the continental period. It follows that these formulas, like the kenning and compounds, could carry with them the associations of the other contexts in which they had been used, and that a skilful poet could build tensions between these accumulated over-tones and the new context. Equally, a pedestrian poet such as the writer of *The Death of Edgar* cannot prevent them from unbalancing a poem in which they appear among a fairly humdrum list of regal activities.

One last difference between prose and poetic language has recently been revealed by another approach to the problem of the formulas. W. O'Neill and G. L. Gattiker, seeking to define the formula so as to include the repetition of sequences of morphological and syntactic entities, have shown that the half lines of the surviving poetry are reducible to only 25 syntactic patterns.[20] This limitation on the syntactic frames does, in fact, embrace a wide variety of types, but it represents a further distinguishing feature and is much more important than the minor syntactical differences, such as the unexpected adjectival declension or adjectival postponement, noted hitherto.

One of the most startling features of Christian Old English poetry is its attention to warfare and its expression of the figures and concepts of the Christian religion in terms of the relationships and ethos of secular Germanic society: Christ in *The Dream of the Rood* is a warrior hero and the Cross is his faithful follower; Satan is a disloyal member of God's *comitatus* in *Genesis B*; the disciples in *Andreas* are eager leaders in the field of battle. Clearly this treatment would make Christianity more immediately relevant to the audience's experience and, less obviously, much of this approach has its basis in the Scriptures, patristic doctrine, or exegetical teaching. It also reflects, however, the limitations of the inherited poetic language. This language was well developed to fulfil the functions Tacitus and other Latin writers describe it as performing—the praise of leaders and of the ideals of society, the recollection of martial glories, and eulogy of the dead—but it was ill-equipped to deal with subjects such as redemption and salvation. The choice of theme was conditioned by the language available and the adaptability of the one to the other.

The earliest recorded instance of this adaptation is in Bede's story of the illiterate Whitby herdsman Cædmon.[21] This particular narrative is full of interest, not least because of its acceptance of the fact that poetic performance was expected from all ranks of society, whether they were literate or not. The *Hymn* that Cædmon composed at the angel's prompting is reminiscent of the preface to the Canon of the Mass, and describes God in terms that had previously, one assumes, been reserved for a secular lord.

Cædmon's *Hymn* is not a particularly subtle piece of work, but other poets were aware of the potentialities of using language traditionally associated with secular society in a religious context. The poet of *The Seafarer*, for example, deliberately plays upon the ambiguous worldly and heavenly application of words such as *dream, blæd, lof,* and *dryhten* (joy, prosperity, praise, and lord), and much of the complexity of the poem depends upon this linguistic exploitation. Not all poets were so successful, but there is much in the 30,000 or so lines of surviving poetry that repays close study and attention to the use of poetic language.

V

Only two languages, Latin and Scandinavian, had any great influence on English during the Anglo-Saxon period. Old Irish—the language of many of the early missionaries, and of the country where many Anglo-Saxons studied—left little trace beyond the odd ogham inscription and the loan words *dry* (magician) and *ancora* (anchorite), although the Irish modification of the Latin alphabet forms used by the Anglo-Saxons has already been noted. The indigenous British language has left much onomastic evidence but, as the language of the defeated, seems to have remained so unintelligible to the Anglo-Saxons as to be identifiable with the language of the devils who assailed St Guthlac.[22] Nor is it possible to trace any influence from the continental languages spoken by the numerous foreign traders and ecclesiastics who visited and lived in England, although the existence of a common coinage in the 8th century in south-eastern England and Frisia argues that there was probably some linguistic interaction between the two closely related languages. The poem we know as *Genesis B* survives, however, as a reminder of these continental contacts, with its traces of Old Saxon metre, vocabulary, and syntax—the translation of a continental Saxon whose poem is much more impressive than his Old English.

The influence of Latin is a much less peripheral matter. This is not unexpected, because Latin, as the language of the Church, was the medium through which mediaeval culture and learned discourse were transmitted. Our emphasis on the vernacular should not obscure the fact that there are fewer Old English texts than Latin ones surviving from the period. Indeed the use of any language other than Latin by an educated man for his text was a choice forced upon him by considerations of his audience or by the educational situation of his period.

In view of the prestige of Latin and of the fact that so many Old English texts were translations from Latin, it is surprising that the classical language had little impact on vernacular written syntax. Traces can be seen in Wærferth's *Dialogues* and the *Life of St Chad*, but they are usually of the order of Ælfric's *gewunnenum sige* (victory being won) imitation of an ablative absolute construction, or his Latin-inspired idiom *to þas Hælendes spræce* (to speak with the Saviour). The only sign of any importance of Latin in this field is that the Old English development of the progressive forms of the verb (Mod. Eng. *am/was going*) may have been based on Latin constructions such as *consecutus est*. Nickel's recent investigation of this development, however, indicates that it cannot be attributed entirely to foreign patterns.[23] This lack of syntactic influence must be attributed to a widespread awareness that *þæt Leden and þæt Englisc nabbað na ane wisan on ðære spræce fandunge* (Latin and English do not have the same manner of expression).[24]

One starting-point for assessing the influence Latin did have is in the scientific manual produced by Byrhtferth of Ramsey in the early 11th century. In the course of a section on the leap year he complained that "these things are difficult to express in English."[25] It was a cry that was echoed again in the 16th century: the problem of expressing in English the thought and the culture of the Mediterranean, for which Latin had a developed terminology.

One solution was to borrow words from Latin. The advent of Christianity in the late 6th century led inevitably to the introduction of words such as *preost, abbod, candel, ymen,* and *mæsse* to express the physical details and organization of the new religion. Other loans have an even more venerable history, because words such as *stræt, win, disc, deofol,* and *cyrice* (street, wine, dish, devil, and church) were taken into the Germanic languages in the pre-5th-century period to express the material civilization, and some aspects of the religion, of the Roman Empire to the south. Vulgar Latin and Old English sound changes can be used to impose some chronological order on these borrowings, but the process is a complex one that cannot always yield certain results. What is clear from the occurrence of doublets such as *sealm* and *salm* (psalm) is that borrowing continued right through the period, because although both are based on the same Latin word, only the first reflects the early Old English diphthongization before a velar consonant group. Although the chronology is often doubtful, it is possible to make some distinction between those loans that are completely integrated into the English stress, phonetic, and inflexional system and those that are only partly assimilated. *Biscop* (bishop) certainly falls into the first group, because it is sufficiently anglicized to generate derived words such as *biscopian* (confirm), *biscopscir* (diocese), and *biscophad* (episcopacy). Partial assimilation—and there is a series of fine grades involved—can be illustrated by Ælfric's vacillation between *apostoli* and *apostolas* as a nominative plural form, or by his preservation of the Latin ending of *discipuli* in the nominative plural of a noun for which he uses a regular Old English dative plural form of *discipulum*. Many of these learned loans may never have been used outside their written occurrence in a monastic scriptorium.

Ælfric's *Grammar*[26] is a useful text for illustrating other aspects of the impact of a Latin-speaking culture on English. He was well aware that the production of a Latin grammar in the vernacular was a fresh departure and that terminology posed him particularly difficult problems. His ultimate aim was to popularize the technical Latin vocabulary, and to this end he uses a large number of Latin terms, although he is always careful to programme their introduction and to ensure their comprehensibility by a vernacular explanation such as *pronomen, se spelað þone naman* (pronoun, which replaces the name). Other terms, however, are rendered into English by being broken down into their constituent parts, translated into English, and then reassembled into an English compound. This process can be illustrated by the rendering of *interjectio* by *betwuxalecgednys*, built up from *betwux* (between), *alecged* (positioned), and the feminine noun ending *-nyss*. Not all are as clumsy as this—*forgyfendlic* for *dativus* is eminently usable—but this example of loan translation does show how English resources could be used to solve Byrhtferth's problem, besides fulfilling Ælfric's immediate aim of aiding the understanding of the Latin term itself.

The *Grammar* also illustrates the redefinition of words already in the language. This extension or restriction of the meanings of words is perhaps the most interesting response to the changes in Anglo-Saxon culture after the conversion. Ælfric uses *tid* and *cynn* as equivalents of *tempus* and *genus* in a way that suggests that these words, in current pedagogy, had added a specialized grammatical meaning to their usual sense of *time* and *race*. This process can be seen occurring, in the language of the psalter glosses between the 8th and 11th centuries, to the word *giefu*, which takes on the function of expressing *divine grace*—a meaning that was only temporarily attached to other *gift* words, such as *est* and *wuldor*.

The examples in the last paragraph are all of words that acquired meanings they had not previously carried. Some of the most basic ideas of Anglo-Saxon Christianity are similarly expressed by words that certainly existed in the pagan period, but whose earlier field of reference has been entirely changed: *God, husl* (sacrament), *halig* (holy), *weofod* (altar), and *bletsian* (bless) are words of this type.

The influence of a Latin-using Mediterranean culture on English was clearly very great, but the influence of the Latin language itself, outside the monastic scriptorium, can be exaggerated.

The effect of the Scandinavian languages of the Viking settlers was of a totally different kind. Settlement is first recorded around York in 876, and further land-taking occurred a few years later in East Anglia and Mercia. Less well documented is a Norwegian-Irish settlement in north-west England at the start of the 10th century. There is good evidence for the rapid coalescence of the Scandinavian and Anglo-Saxon populations of these areas, and for the rapid conversion of the Vikings to Christianity. The evidence for the numbers involved in the settlement is debatable, though the orthodox view of a dense occupation seems the more acceptable.

Distinctions between the Danish and Norwegian languages of the Vikings at this period are much less important than the fact that both were dialectal variants of a Germanic language that shared its roots and much of its structure with Old English. The differences between the nature of Scandinavian and Latin influence can be ascribed partly to this close identity and partly to the fact that the former was a language spoken by a wide range of society, and not, like Latin, the written language of a small group.

The surviving pre-Norman documents show few signs of Scandinavian influence. This is not an indication of the late acceptance of elements from the settlers' language, but is due to the fact that most texts from the Late Saxon period come from the reformed monasteries of the south of the country (where there was no Viking settlement) or are written in the *Schriftsprache* based on the language of the south. There are some traces in the poem *The Battle of Maldon* (991), which uses the loan words *grið* (peace) and *dreng* (warrior), and an anglicized version of *askr* (ship). Further north the vernacular gloss to the *Lindisfarne Gospels*, written by the conventionally *indignus et misserrim(u)s* (unworthy and most wretched) Aldred at Chester-le-Street in the late 10th century, contains other lexical loans and traces of phonetic influence. Wulfstan's work is full of Scandinavian terms for the classes of society, and employs derivatives such as *griðian* (make peace) and *griðleas* (without peace) based upon Scandinavian loans. But the total is very small, and few of the terms used in Old English texts have survived into the modern period, because they refer, in the main, to a Viking ship-building prowess that was later superseded, or to the legal and social system of Danelaw that was changed in the Norman period.

Middle English texts, dating from after the Norman Conquest, give much more information about the adoption of Scandinavian vocabulary in the original Danelaw area and its acceptance beyond the settlement area. The differing nature and uneven survival of Middle English texts make it difficult to trace the chronology of this acceptance, but the texts do show that there were marked differences in the Scandinavian element between the dialects of northern and southern areas. Thus the *Ormulum*, a work produced *c.* 1200 near Stamford, uses the Scandinavian-derived *take* (take) almost exclusively, whereas the contemporary southern poem *The Owl and the Nightingale* always uses a verb derived from Old English *niman*. Similarly, the 14th-century *Ayenbyte of Inwyt* from Kent excludes parts of the Scandinavian personal pronoun system that had been adopted into English two centuries earlier in the north.

The closeness of the two languages undoubtedly encouraged the adoption of many words. The Scandinavian *deyja* (yielding Mod. Eng. *to die*) was the more acceptable as the basis of a verb in a language that already had *dead* (death) and *diedan* (put to death), but whose native verbs for this were *steorfan* and *sweltan*. The closeness also results in interesting interactions between the forms and meanings of cognate words in the two languages: Wulfstan uses the Old English poetic term *eorl* with the meaning (an administrative official) that was carried by the Scandinavian *jarl*—a term he must have heard frequently as Archbishop of York. Similarly the present meanings, but not the forms, of *dream*, *bread*, and *dwell* come from Scandinavian.

Die, take, dream, bread, and *dwell* have no common factor beyond their

K

very ordinariness. It is the language of everyday intercourse that is affected by Scandinavian speech, in words such as *sister, window, odd, crawl, ill, wrong, awkward,* or of words that never rose above dialectal status, such as *claggy, flit,* and *muggy.* The very fact that these words replaced their Old English equivalents provides a contrast with the area of vocabulary affected by Latin.

A deeper penetration is indicated by the adoption of grammatical words such as *þoh* (though) and *til,* because these are not the class of items that one language normally borrows from another. An even more unusual borrowing is that of the Scandinavian pronoun system for the third person plural. The pressure for the adoption of forms that developed into *they, them,* and *their* is not difficult to recognize, because phonetic changes operating in Old English had obscured a vital distinction between singular and plural forms in the third person of the Old English system. This lack of distinction was much more important than any homonymic clashes that resulted from borrowing from the Scandinavian system.

A similar lack of distinctiveness in the third person feminine nominative form *heo* forced the adoption of a variant, eventually yielding *she,* which used a rising diphthongal pronunciation of Scandinavian type.

Apart from this important area of vocabulary it is difficult to be certain of Scandinavian influence on Old English. The case for syntactic influence, for example, is inconclusive. It has been suggested that the rapid loss of inflexions in northern England during the late Old and early Middle English periods is the result of an attempt to remove barriers to intelligibility between the two languages. This cannot be proved, although it is true that the linguistically radical area throughout the early Middle English period lies in the north of the country.

VI

Consideration of Scandinavian loan words has carried us past the Norman Conquest and into the Middle English period.

It has become fashionable to emphasize the essential continuity of social organization between the late Anglo-Saxon and the Norman periods, and to see Norman feudalism as based upon the Anglo-Saxon lordships with the added imposition of knight service. Much of this is true, but in the present context what must be emphasized is the change in nationality of the leading figures in the Church and aristocracy. Of the 12 earls in England in 1072, only one was English, and he was to be executed four years later. Only one English bishop, Wulfstan of Worcester, survived after 1075. Foreign monks, abbots, retainers, and craftsmen flocked into the country for many years after the Conquest, and French influence endured long after 1066. Lands were jointly held on both sides of the Channel until John's tactless marriage resulted in the loss of Normandy in 1204; and for nearly a century and a half after the Conquest, England was regarded as a place for French fortunes to be made. Even in the 13th century the influx of Frenchmen was sufficient to enrage chroniclers such as Roger of Wendover and Matthew Paris. Nor should it be forgotten that the French-speaking court in 12th-century England patronized a flourishing Anglo-Norman literature, and that the prestige of French culture in the following two centuries guaranteed the continual spoken and written use of the Romance language among the aristocracy and those with any social pretensions.

The effect of all this on spoken and written English needs careful examination, because there are important distinctions to be made between the spoken and the written language, and between the impact of the Anglo-Norman language of the 12th-century English aristocracy and of Central French in the following period.

As a spoken language English never dropped out of use. It merely lost prestige and for a time became the language of the lower classes and of informal intercourse. Evidence for the changing status of the spoken language is often difficult to evaluate, but the material that Wilson has assembled shows that, in the period before *c.* 1300, a knowledge of English alone was a sign of rusticity.[27] More important, it shows that English was understood and used in informal situations well up the social scale. During the course of the 13th century, after the loss of Normandy and in a period of growing nationalism and awareness of the provincial nature of Anglo-Norman, English as a spoken language regained its former position. The production during the late 13th century of manuals giving instruction in French as a foreign language indicates the artificial nature of the preservation of spoken French by that date.

English also lost status as a written literary language. It is clear that the court was much more interested in the lively Anglo-Norman literature of the 12th century than it was in English products. But work still continued to be produced in the vernacular, and—as Wilson cogently observed—it is only the great mass of Anglo-French work in the 13th century that obscures the increasing output of English material. Much of this English work was aimed at an audience who knew neither French nor Latin, yet the existence of the sophisticated *Owl and the Nightingale* shows that there were audiences in the late 12th century in the south of England for an

English poem that drew on French verse-forms and touched assuredly but lightly on the religious and moral problems of the age.

The Owl and the Nightingale is written in a form of English that differs from that of Ælfric. Much of the difference lies in the loss of a sense of a standard literary language. In places, the West Saxon *Schriftsprache* survived the Conquest for nearly a century: the Kentish exemplar of the early sections of the *Peterborough Chronicle* certainly used it up to 1121, and the Fenland scribe who copied it out at that date saw no need to modernize it.[28] Texts from Worcester and Durham also show its continued use into the 12th century. Alongside these comparatively pure texts can be placed others (such as the *Peterborough Chronicle* sections from 1122–31) that show survivals of this literary language, including archaic words, mixed with local forms not proper to that written standard.

Such texts, nevertheless, are part of a dying tradition, because Wessex was no longer of political, cultural, or economic importance in Norman England. The standard language based upon that superiority also died, because Norman scribes and their English pupils, working in the context of an intellectually revived monasticism, had no reason to follow the traditional spelling and language observances of an earlier age. The fact that no fresh standard emerged until the late 14th century is strikingly indicative of the reduced status of the vernacular as a written language.

This increasing ignorance and non-acceptance of any sense of standard written forms lies behind the differences that are commonly believed to distinguish Old from Middle English. The bewildering complexity of forms in Middle English manuscripts was the result of individual, not to say idiosyncratic, attempts by scribes to represent their own pronunciations and to impose their own dialectal forms on the exemplar they followed. But this difference concerns the written representation of the language and does not involve any sudden change in the spoken language. The separation of late Old English and early Middle English is a distinction, based upon the written texts, that obscures the continuum of the spoken language. The conservative written tradition of late Anglo-Saxon England had failed to represent changes occurring in the language in that period, and it is the loss of this tradition that results in the sudden appearance of changes in written form.

Our dependence upon the scribe for impressions of language change is seen at its most dramatic in the final 10 folios of the *Peterborough Chronicle*.[29] At the top of folio 81r is the entry for 1121, written in perfect Late West Saxon. The entry for 1122 is written by the same scribe, but he is no longer copying from his exemplar, and the language immediately changes to a mixture of East Midland forms and traditionalist West Saxon. On folio 88v is the last of the entries from this first scribe, and no entries were made between 1131 and 1154. At some date after 1154 a second scribe completed the history of the intervening years, using language forms and spelling that are even further removed from the pre-Norman standard. Thus, in a period of less than 40 years two scribes produced three widely differing types of written language, yet the spoken language cannot have changed a great deal in that time.

It follows that many so-called Middle English features were already present in the spoken language of the late Old English period, although they are traceable from that date only in scribal slips and the more dialectal texts. This applies not only to minor matters such as the loss of the Old English diphthongs *eo* and *ea*, but also—more importantly—to a set of closely interlinked language changes whose progression and completion varies from area to area of the country in the centuries before and after the Norman Conquest. These are the loss of sound distinctions between the unstressed vowels of the inflexional endings, the levelling of distinctions in the noun and adjective classes, the syncretion of cases, the loss of grammatical gender, and the increased use of word-order and prepositions to signal relationships between the units of the sentence. The orthodox view is that these changes are initially purely phonetic, and that the loss of sound distinctions resulted in the loss of morphological functional differences and a compensatory introduction or strengthening of other methods of indicating relationships. Recently, however, powerful voices have argued that the reduction of final unstressed vowels in inflexions was the result of the redundancy of those inflexions as distinctive markers, their role having been taken over by word-order and prepositions.

Whichever is the truth (and the latter seems more plausible), the essential point remains that all these movements began in the Old English period. The levelling of vowels in unstressed positions can be seen affecting the back vowels in Kentish charters of the 9th century, and the movement was complete in Northumbria and Kent by the 10th century. In the early part of the 11th century, scribal slips indicate that all unstressed vowels in inflexions had been levelled on a common [ə] sound. The 10th-century glosses to the *Lindisfarne Gospels*[30] and the *Durham Ritual*, both strongly dialectal, show the spread of an originally masculine type (with its -*as* plural) into other classes where it would not be expected historically, and the same texts betray the syncretion of dative and accusative cases and vacillation on grammatical gender. These northern documents are useful reminders that the boundary between Old and Middle English is largely a conventional one. Recent demonstrations of the relative stability of word-order in Old English, and large areas of conformity with modern usage, also tend to diminish any contrast between the two periods.

The change of pre-Norman scribal practices in monastic scriptoria also affected the spelling of manuscripts, because writers in all dialects adopted certain features of the French and Latin systems. The effect of this is to make Middle English texts appear much more modern than those of the late Anglo-Saxon period, but again this is a distinction between written representations, and does not indicate sudden changes in the spoken language. Some of these spelling adoptions represent a useful advance in that they distinguish sounds that were not separately symbolized by the Anglo-Saxon system in its latest stages: thus the Old English *c* represented both the initial sounds heard in modern *kill* and *chill*—an ambiguity that was clarified by the introduction of *ch* and the extended use of *k*. The replacement of *sc* by, ultimately, *sh* was a further useful change, but other innovations—such as the substitution of *qu* for *cw* (O. Eng. *cwen*, Mod. Eng. *queen*) and the replacement of *þ* and *ð* by *th*—were of doubtful advantage. These spellings were not universally or consistently adopted in the 12th and 13th centuries, and the lack of a written standard is once more to blame for the individuality of the systems found in any group of manuscripts.

One final feature of Middle English texts that flows from this loss of a written standard is the presence of highly colloquial forms. Among these are the words that Smithers has called *ideophones*—of the types seen in *liklakyng* and *knusshe* (words for the sound made by clashing swords and for battering)—in whose make-up there is a strong element of sound symbolism.[31] Similarly colloquial are the phrases that have never risen above slang status, such as *ouwer bolt is sone ischote* in *The South English Legendary* (*c.*1225). Forms such as these reflect the loss of any sense of what types are appropriate to a written language.

Dialect differences within the language seem to have become more marked in the Middle English period. This increasing divergence, which affects inflexions as well as vocabulary and sounds, was presumably due to the lack of the unifying and conservative influences of a written standard and of the use of English in formal, educated contexts. Writers in the period often refer to these differences, which they must have noted in manuscripts from different parts of the country. A Cambridge manuscript describes its text as having been

translate oute of northarn tonge into sutherne that it schulde the
bettir be vnderstondyn of men that be of the selve countrie. . . [32]

and, for the spoken language, we have William of Malmesbury's evidence
that Northumbrian speech could not be understood by southerners.[33]
In contrast, the Anglo-Saxon period does not seem to have been greatly
worried by what differences there were.

Some of the Middle English dialect distinctions are rooted in the Old
English period and thus emphasize the continuity across the conventional
division. The Middle English Northern and North-Midland use of *-es* as
the third person singular present tense ending of verbs is already visible,
under certain phonetic conditions, in the 10th-century gloss to the
Lindisfarne Gospels. Similarly, many of the phonetic distinctions, such as
that between *hill/hell/hull*, can be traced back to Old English developments. Other differences, such as the rounding of Old English long *a* to *o*
south of the Humber and the development of *-ing* as a present participle
ending, belong entirely to the Middle English period.

VII

The evidence used in the preceding section implies a continued use of
written English in the post-Conquest period. What is now important is to
define its area of usage, and to trace how far there is a continuity in
such specialized language as that of Old English poetry.

Written English continued to be used and studied in the monasteries of
Norman and Angevin England. Old English texts were transcribed and
modernized throughout the 12th century, and many important texts—
such as the Kentish Laws or the most complete version of Alfred's Boethius
—survive only in copies made at this period. At Worcester the extensive
glossing of the famous "tremulous hand" carries the history of interest
in earlier English writings into the 13th century, although by this date
such study was rare and of an antiquarian nature.[34]

The use of English for original prose compositions also continued until
the late 12th century: the *Peterborough Chronicle* was kept up until 1154,
and there are traces of the same tradition of vernacular historical writing
at Winchester as late as 1183. There was even an extension of the known
usages of English in the post-Conquest period, in the production of a
now-lost biography of Bishop Wulfstan of Worcester, written in the late
11th century.

By the end of the 12th century, nevertheless, English was no longer used
for official, legal, or historical prose. Its disuse cannot be ascribed to

the linguistic nationalism of a newly arrived Norman aristocracy or Norman abbots: it was replaced, at least initially, in all of these functions by Latin, not by French. Rather, it was the educational standards of 12th-century English monasticism that were largely responsible for the change.

English still retained one role, that of religious instruction. A Worcester poet, probably writing at the end of the 11th century, looks back with longing to the period when bishops such as Dunstan (*c.* 909–88) "taught our people in English" and contrasts that happy time with his own.[35] His analysis of the post-Conquest situation is over-pessimistic, however, for the need to use the vernacular for religious instruction was widely realized both by individuals and in the edicts of the Church Councils. It was the resulting continuity of vernacular religious prose that was the main theme of R. W. Chambers' seminal essay published more than 30 years ago.[36] The development of this type of prose now appears to be more complex than he allowed, but much of his argument is still valid.

The main texts concerned in any argument for continuity are products of the early-13th-century West Midlands area. They include the *Ancrene Riwle*, the so-called *Wooing* and *Katherine* groups, *Sawles Warde*, and *Hali Meiðhad*. These texts share many features, not least the fact that their audience appears to be female, "gentle and lettered," but not expected to know Latin. There are, however, important differences between them.

The opening line of *Seinte Iuliene*, one of the *Katherine* group, shows the links with Anglo-Saxon homilists:

> I ure lauerdes luue þe feader is of frumscheft, ant i þe deore wurðmunt of his deorewurðe sune. . . .[37]

> (In our Lord's love who is father of creation, and in the glorious worship of his precious son. . . .)

There is the same use of alliterative phrases, each with two stresses, and the same verbal play that is found in the work of Ælfric and Wulfstan. The *Katherine* group also shows a strong traditionalism in the use of language that was either archaic or obsolescent by this period, such as the preservation of compounds in *driht-* (noble) or of alliterative collocations that recall those of Old English, such as *heanen and heatien* (humiliate and persecute; cf. *Beowulf*'s *hatode and hynde*).

The *Katherine* group supports Chambers's case better than does the *Ancrene Riwle* on which he focussed his attention. The latter certainly shares lexical and thematic links with the *Katherine* group, but its rhythm and alliteration are much less obvious, its sentence structures are simpler, and the French element in vocabulary and phraseology is much higher.[38] It does have complex verbal patterning but, like that of the *Wooing* group, this may owe as much to current teaching of rhetoric as to inherited traditions. The stress upon the past in the study of these texts must not obscure the fact that they are not all equally indebted to the pre-Norman tradition. The use of the terms of courtly love (*gentilesse, largesce*) as religious concepts in the *Wooing* texts is but one example of much that is new in the group.

Emphasis on the West Midlands texts must not make us forget that a continuity of religious prose can be traced in other parts of the country, in texts such as *Vices and Virtues* or the *Trinity Homilies*. These are less ornate than the *Katherine* group, but their style seems to stem back to that used occasionally by Ælfric and, in his quieter moments, even by Wulfstan.

Alliterative poetry and the language associated with it also survived the Conquest. The continuity of this alliterative tradition in poetry derives from a popular type of verse that evolved in the 10th century, rather than from the classical type of *Beowulf*, for this latter type hardly survived the end of the 11th century.

The popular poetry of the late Anglo-Saxon period is exemplified by some of the poems in the *Chronicle*: their distribution in the various versions of the *Chronicle* led McIntosh to suggest that this new kind may have had only a regional popularity in its earlier stages. The differences between the two types are that the later verse admitted rhyme and assonance more freely than the classical, that its alliterative rules were freer, and that the metrical lifts were no longer required to fall on syllables that were long as well as stressed. This latter provision was especially important at a time when the vowel quantity system of English was undergoing great changes.

The links between the *Chronicle* poems and those of the 14th-century alliterative revival can now be traced only with difficulty, because much of the intervening material was probably never written down, but it is clear that this type of poetry flourished more in the north and west than in the south and east. At all stages of its development, much of its language was quite distinct from that used in the non-alliterative poetry of the other parts of the country.

Laȝamon's *Brut* is the first poem of any length produced in this metre after the Conquest, and thus affords an opportunity for assessing the persistence of features of the Old English poetic language.[39] It can be dated to the late 12th century, and comes from Worcestershire, an area where there was a strong tradition of post-Conquest use of, and interest in, the vernacular. As we have seen, this was the area that produced a vernacular biography in the 11th century and the "tremulous hand" in the 13th century, and was not far from the home of the *Ancrene Riwle* and the associated texts. Something in this continuity may be owed to the long tenure of the Worcester see by Bishop Wulfstan, but the powerful conservative families of the Western Marches must also have played some part.

The *Brut* is certainly written in the tradition of earlier verse. Half lines contain phrases such as *mid orde and mid egge* (with point and with edge [of weapon]) that are restricted to poetic usage at this period, and that echo the half-line formulas of Old English poetry. Words such as *uul* (cup) and *ærde* (earth) are totally archaic in any but alliterative poetic usage by Laȝamon's date. Variation has disappeared from this type of poetry, but the tradition of using nominal compounds is still sufficiently alive to ensure both the use of compounds coined earlier and apparently original compounding within the poem. It should be stressed, however, that the compounds are much less frequent than in *Beowulf*.

The poems of the alliterative revival in the later part of the 14th century exhibit a great variety of subject-matter and style. Linguistically the most interesting is the work of the *Gawain*-poet (*fl.* 1370), from somewhere near the north-west border of Staffordshire.[40] His audience is clearly a cultivated one with a sophisticated taste and an awareness of French culture, but also with an interest in some of the traditional elements in the language of alliterative poetry. The identification of the audience with the rebellious aristocracy of the west is plausible, but unfortunately not capable of proof.

Some of the peculiarities of the *Gawain*-poet's language are the results of his ambitious verse-forms. This is particularly marked in *Pearl*, where his efforts to echo a word from stanza to stanza but to vary its meaning result in highly individual extensions of meaning in the refrain words.[41] Other features are part of the inheritance of the alliterative tradition, and are preserved only in this poetry. The tradition of nominal compounding has disappeared since Laȝamon, but the many poetic synonyms for *man* (*burn, freke, gome, schalk, segge*) are typical of alliterative poetry, as is the generalized sense of *move* given to a range of verbs with usefully differing initial sounds *boȝe, dresse, helde, sech*). There are other sides to the language of the *Gawain*-poet, however, apart from the traditional: there is a large element of local dialect material that must have rendered the poems incomprehensible outside a small area, and alongside this there is the French-derived language of courtly love and venery. As with the *Ancrene Riwle* and its associated texts, we miss something if we concentrate attention on the traditional elements. Indeed, over-emphasis of the highly ornate nature of the poetry of the north-west as a whole would cloud the fact that these poems, unlike the linguistically less esoteric *Piers Plowman*, had no audience outside their own area. By the late 14th century the traditional language of alliterative poetry had become a barrier to widespread appreciation.

VIII

Our emphasis, so far, has been upon the continuity of language from the Old English period. This has been at the expense of the very great contribution that French language and literature made to English in this period. The extent of the literary influence is everywhere apparent in the syllabic rhymed metres and the subject-matter of Middle English works; the linguistic influence was inevitable against a background of trilingual competence, and many of the patterns of the culturally influential French language were transferred to English. The degree of this transference is apparent in the French -*s* endings given to the singular forms of native nouns in, for instance, *Kyng Alisaunder* (*c.* 1300), and in the Harley Lyrics' assignment of *moon* to a feminine gender on the analogy of Latin *luna* and French *lune*.

There are some traces of French vocabulary in the late pre-Norman period, and 12th-century texts contain many French-derived words— such as the *Peterborough Chronicle's prisun*, *iustise*, and *castel*—that express the new organization of society. Some of this vocabulary was widely enough accepted by *c.* 1200 to be used in the alliterative formulas of *Seinte Iuliene*. But, despite this evidence of early borrowing, the surviving documents show that the peak period of French influence was in the later part of the 13th and the early part of the 14th century, when English was once more being used in formal, educated contexts by speakers who freely borrowed terms from the prestigious French language.

The French element in Middle and Modern English is certainly very large. Most of our present vocabulary concerned with the court, the Church, the law, administration, architecture, and many of the arts is derived from French. The borrowing of these terms involved the loss of many Anglo-Saxon and Anglo-Scandinavian words: *cyning* remains in *king*, but the associated Old English terms yielded place to *royal*, *throne*, and *crown*; the Scandinavian-derived *lagu* remains in *law*, but the highly developed terminology linked with it has given way to French terms such as *judge* and *crime*. There is, of course, no simple pattern of acceptance and loss: in many cases both English and French terms have been preserved with differing overtones of formality and association of the kind seen in *begin* and *commence, depth* and *profundity*.

A mere word count of Modern English survivals does not do justice to the French element in Middle English, because many texts show individual adoptions that never gained general acceptance in the language. *Kyng Alisaunder*, a romance of the late 13th century, is a salutary reminder of the extent of this type of borrowing; its bilingual author freely uses words such as *antecessoures* (forebears) and *hontage* (humiliation) that are rare or never occur again in English.[42]

This romance is also full of phrases lifted directly from the French, such as *Dieu mercy* and the more familiar *parde*. More importantly, it also employs calques such as *nymeth gode cure* (pay attention), whose structure is that of French idioms. Phrasal influence is, in fact, an important aspect of French influence on English in this period. The great growth of phrases made up of verb with noun object is the result of the impact of French patterns such as *faire homage* on a similar pattern in English that had not proved very productive in the pre-Norman period. The importance of this group to Modern English can be judged by a few examples: *give offence, take a rest, have the heart*.

French elements in Middle English are not limited to the borrowing of complete words or the adoption of phrases and phrasal patterns. Morphologically they can be traced in the spread of *-ess* and *-age* as noun formers. Phonetically the *oi* diphthong of Middle English is a new French-based sound, and the most convincing explanation of the spread of the present participle ending *-ing* attributes some influence to the fact that French also had an identical inflexion for present participle and gerund. The loss of a second person singular pronoun form in English is directly due to the adoption of French practices.

Other contacts, notably with the Low Countries, undoubtedly involved some additions to English in the period, but none can compare with the influence exerted by French.

IX

Toward the end of the Middle English period, in the late 14th century, a standard written form of English began to emerge once more. There had been a few Middle English writers, such as Orm (*fl. c.* 1200), who attempted some form of consistency in their own texts. There are even traces of a local literary dialect in the 13th-century texts of the *Ancrene Riwle*, but neither this nor the individual attempts had any permanent influence.

Signs of a move toward a written standard are first seen in the language of the Wyclifite manuscripts. This standard was based upon the language spoken in the Central Midlands area (where the Lollard strength lay), and its spread from that area must be attributed to Lollard activity. The hold of this language type, which was used for secular as well as religious texts, can be judged by the fact that it persisted in use until the late 15th century, long after any spoken equivalent had disappeared. Reference to the Wyclifite manuscripts reminds us that the evolution of a standard English written language is far from being a simple matter of the rise of a London dialect to national importance at a time when that dialect was under strong East Midland influence. The more complex history of its emergence is one of the results of the Middle English Dialect Survey work of McIntosh and Samuels.[43]

Samuels' summary shows that the written standard was certainly based upon the dialect used in London, and there is no need to question the traditional view that this basis reflects the economic, social, and political importance of the capital. But the language of London changed a great deal in the course of the 14th century, and the type that served as a basis for the standard written form was quite different from that found in texts dating from *c.* 1300. At that time the language of London was closely linked to that of Essex and Kent. The changes that occurred in the language of the capital in the course of the 14th century have been illuminated by Ekwall's study of the personal names of the population during this period. His work shows that toward 1300 and during the course of the 14th century there was a large influx from the populous and wealthy areas of Norfolk, together with immigration from Essex, Hertfordshire, and the Home Counties.[44] The language of these immigrants, whose wealth came from the wool trade, gave a much more Anglian character to London's dialect, and this partly accounts for the differences between the language of *Kyng Alisaunder* in the early part of the century and that of Chaucer in the later part.

It does not account for all the differences, however. In the course of the 14th century the pattern of immigration changed in an important way. Movement from the Home Counties ceased, but there was a dramatic rise in the number of people coming from Northamptonshire and Bedfordshire. This Central Midlands contribution has not hitherto been given sufficient stress.

Chaucer's language is thus that of London under strong East and Central Midlands influence. His language is not quite identical with the one that eventually emerged as the written standard, though it clearly has something of this status. The lasting standard is that used in documents emerging from Chancery in the course of the 15th century. Their wide dissemination and official standing ensured the success of the type. Its difference from Chaucer's language can be expressed as an increased debt to the language of the Central Midlands—to a centrally situated area that had provided much of London's population and whose language had already (through the Lollards) achieved a status beyond the purely dialectal.

References

1. See, for example, J. E. CROSS, "*Ubi Sunt* Passages in Old English," *Vetenskaps-Societetens i Lund Årsbok* (Lund 1956), pp. 25–44, and "On the Genre of *The Wanderer*," *Neophilologus* XLV (Groningen 1961), pp. 63–75; J. E. CROSS and S. I. TUCKER, "Allegorical Tradition and the Old English *Exodus*," *Neophilologus* XLIV (Groningen 1960), pp. 122–7; G. V. SMITHERS, "The Meaning of *The Seafarer* and *The Wanderer*," *Medium Ævum* XXVI (Oxford 1957), pp. 137–53, and XXVIII (1959), pp. 1–22.
2. R. QUIRK, "Colloquial English and Communication," *Studies in Communication* (London 1955), pp. 169–82.
3. These notes are cited in N. R. KER, *Catalogue of Manuscripts Containing Anglo-Saxon* (Oxford 1957), pp. xlii-l.
4. C. PLUMMER (ed.), *Venerabilis Baedae Opera Historica*, Vol. I (Oxford 1896), p. 406.
5. B. COLGRAVE and R. A. B. MYNORS (ed.), *Historia ecclesiastica* (Oxford 1969), Bk IV, Ch. 22.
6. *ibid.*, Bk I, Ch. 15.
7. H. SWEET (ed.), *King Alfred's West Saxon Version of Gregory's "Pastoral Care*," Early English Text Society, o.s. 45 (London 1871), p. 7. The text of this letter is printed in most Old English readers.
8. H. R. LOYN, *Anglo-Saxon England and the Norman Conquest* (London 1962), p. 244.
9. W. H. STEVENSON, "Yorkshire Surveys in the York Gospels," *English Historical Review* XXVII (London 1912), pp. 1–25.
10. Printed text as Note 7, above. Facsimile in N. R. KER (ed.), *Early English Manuscripts in Facsimile* ,Vol. VI (Copenhagen 1956).

11. COLGRAVE and MYNORS, *op. cit.*, Bk II, Ch. 5.
12. See Cuthbert's letter in COLGRAVE and MYNORS, *op. cit.*, p. 582.
13. H. SWEET (ed.), *King Alfred's Orosius*, Early English Text Society, o.s. 79 (London 1883).
14. O. COCKAYNE (ed.), *Leechdoms, Wortcunning and Starcraft*, iii (Rolls Series XXXV: 1866), p. 442.
15. G. I. NEEDHAM (ed.), *Lives of Three English Saints* (London 1966), p. 43.
16. D. BETHURUM (ed.), *The Homilies of Wulfstan* (Oxford 1957), p. 262.
17. K. SISAM, "Dialect Origins of the Earlier Old English Verse," *Studies in the History of Old English Literature* (Oxford 1953), pp. 123–6.
18. E. SIEVERS, *Altgermanische Metrik* (Halle 1893). For a more recent study, see J. C. POPE, *The Rhythm of Beowulf*, rev. edn (New Haven 1966).
19. F. P. MAGOUN, "The Oral-formulaic Character of Anglo-Saxon Narrative Poetry," *Speculum* XXVIII (Cambridge, Mass. 1953), pp. 446–67.
20. This work is summarized in F. G. CASSIDY, "How Free was the Anglo-Saxon Scop?" in J. B. BESSINGER and R. P. CREED (ed.), *Medieval and Linguistic Studies in Honor of F. P. Magoun* (London 1965), pp. 75–85.
21. COLGRAVE and MYNORS, *op. cit.*, Bk IV, Ch. 24.
22. B. COLGRAVE (ed.), *Felix's Life of St Guthlac* (Cambridge 1956), Ch. XXXIV.
23. G. NICKEL, *Die "Expanded Form" im Altenglischen* (Neumünster 1966).
24. S. J. CRAWFORD (ed.), *The Old English Version of the Heptateuch*, Early English Text Society, o.s. 160 (London 1922), p. 79.
25. S. J. CRAWFORD (ed.), *Byrhtferth's Manual*, Early English Text Society, o.s. 177 (London 1929), p. 76.
26. J. ZUPITZA (ed.), *Ælfrics Grammatik und Glossar* (Berlin 1880). For the material in this paragraph, see E. R. WILLIAMS, "Ælfric's Grammatical Terminology," *Publications of the Modern Language Association of America* LXXIII (New York 1958), pp. 453–62.
27. R. M. WILSON, "English and French in England, 1100–1300," *History* XXVIII (London 1943), pp. 37–60.
28. C. CLARK (ed.), *The Peterborough Chronicle* (Oxford 1958).
29. Facsimile edition in D. WHITELOCK (ed.), *Early English Manuscripts in Facsimile*, Vol. IV (Copenhagen 1954).
30. See the edition of A. S. C. Ross and E. G. Stanley in T. D. KENDRICK (ed.), *Codex Lindisfarnensis*, Vol. II (Olten/Lausanne/Fribourg 1960), Pt 3.
31. G. V. SMITHERS, "Some English Ideophones," *Archivum Linguisticum* VI (Glasgow 1954), pp. 73–111.
32. A. MCINTOSH, "A New Approach to Middle English Dialectology," *English Studies* XLIV (Amsterdam 1963), p. 8.
33. N. E. S. A. HAMILTON (ed.), *Gesta pontificum* (Rolls Series LII: 1870), p. 209.
34. N. R. KER, "The Date of the 'Tremulous' Worcester Hand," *Leeds Studies in English* VI (Leeds 1937), pp. 28–9.

35. B. DICKINS and R. M. WILSON (ed.), *Early Middle English Texts* (Cambridge 1951), p. 2.
36. As introduction to E. V. HITCHCOCK (ed.), *Harpsfield's Life of More*, Early English Text Society, o.s. 186 (London 1932), pp. xlv–clxxiv. Chambers' essay was also published separately.
37. S. R. T. O. D'ARDENNE (ed.), *Þe Liflade ant te Passiun of Seinte Iuliene*, Early English Text Society, o.s. 248 (London 1961), p. 3.
38. The Early English Text Society has published several texts of this work since 1952.
39. G. L. BROOK and R. F. LESLIE (ed.), *Laȝamon's "Brut,"* Early English Text Society, o.s. 250 (London 1963).
40. J. R. R. TOLKIEN and E. V. GORDON (ed.), *Sir Gawain and the Green Knight*, 2nd edn (Oxford 1967).
41. E. V. GORDON (ed.), *The Pearl* (Oxford 1953).
42. G. V. SMITHERS (ed.), *Kyng Alisaunder*, 2 vols, Early English Text Society o.s. 227 (London 1952), and o.s. 237 (1957).
43. MCINTOSH, *op. cit.*; M. L. SAMUELS, "Some Applications of Middle English Dialectology," *English Studies* XLIV (Amsterdam 1963), pp. 81–94; M. L. SAMUELS, "The Role of Functional Selection in the History of English," *Transactions of the Philological Society* (Oxford 1965), pp. 15–40.
44. E. EKWALL, *Studies on the Population of Medieval London* (Stockholm 1956).

Bibliography

Mediaeval Texts

References to the major editions of the texts of the period will be found in the following.

J. A. W. BENNETT and G. V. SMITHERS (ed.), *Early Middle English Verse and Prose*, 2nd edn (Oxford 1968).
S. GREENFIELD, *A Critical History of Old English Literature* (New York/London 1965).
E. G. STANLEY (ed.), *Continuations and Beginnings: Studies in Old English Literature* (London 1966).
C. L. WRENN, *A Study of Old English Literature* (London 1967).

General

The following works are recommended in addition to those cited in the references.

E. BJÖRKMAN, *Scandinavian Loan-Words in Middle English*, 2 vols. (Halle 1900–2).

A. J. BLISS, "The Appreciation of Old English Metre," in N. DAVIS and C. L WRENN (ed.), *English and Medieval Studies Presented to J. R. R. Tolkien* (London 1962), pp. 27–40.

A. G. BRODEUR, *The Art of Beowulf* (Berkeley 1960).

A. CAMPBELL, *Old English Grammar* (Oxford 1959).

E. EKWALL, *Selected Papers* (Lund 1963).

R. L. KELLOGG, "The South Germanic Oral Tradition," in J. B. BESSINGER and R. P. CREED (ed.), *Medieval and Linguistic Studies in Honor of F. P. Magoun* (London 1965), pp. 66–74.

H. KURATH and S. M. KUHN (ed.), *Middle English Dictionary* (Ann Arbor 1953 ff.).

B. V. LINDHEIM, "Traces of Colloquial Speech in Old English," *Anglia* LXX (Tübingen 1951), pp. 22–42; "Problems of Old English Semantics," in G. I. DUTHIE (ed.), *English Studies Today*, 3rd series (Edinburgh 1964), pp. 67–77.

F. P. MAGOUN, "Colloquial Old and Middle English," *Harvard Studies in Philology and Literature* XIX (Cambridge, Mass. 1937), pp. 167–73.

K. MALONE, "When Did Middle English Begin?" in J. T. HATFIELD (ed.), *Curme Volume of Linguistic Studies* (Baltimore 1930), pp. 110–7.

A. MCINTOSH, "Wulfstan's Prose," *Proceedings of the British Academy* XXXV (London 1949), pp. 109–42.

F. MOSSÉ, *Handbook of Middle English* (Baltimore 1952).

J. A. H. MURRAY, H. BRADLEY, W. A. CRAIGIE, and C. T. ONIONS (ed.), *The Oxford English Dictionary*, 13 vols (Oxford 1933).

L. MUSSET and F. MOSSÉ, *Introduction à la runologie* (Paris 1965).

T. F. MUSTANOJA, *A Middle English Syntax*, Pt I (Helsinki 1960).

J. P. OAKDEN, *Alliterative Poetry in Middle English*, 2 vols (Manchester 1930–5).

J. C. POPE (ed.), *Homilies of Ælfric*, Early English Text Society, o.s. 259 (London 1967).

A. A. PRINS, *French Influence in English Phrasing* (Leyden 1952).

R. QUIRK, "Poetic Language and Old English Metre," in A. BROWN and P. FOOTE (ed.), *Early English and Norse Studies* (London 1963), pp. 150–71.

A. RYNELL, *The Rivalry of Scandinavian and Native Synonyms in Middle English* (Lund 1948).

M. S. SERJEANTSON, *A History of Foreign Words in English* (London 1935).

K. SISAM, *Fourteenth Century Verse and Prose* (London 1921); *Studies in the History of Old English Literature* (Oxford 1953); "Canterbury, Lichfield, and the Vespasian Psalter," *Review of English Studies*, n.s. VII (Oxford 1956), pp. 1–10 and 113–31.

A. H. SMITH (ed.), *English Place Name Elements*, 2 vols. (London 1956).

E. G. STANLEY, "Old English Poetic Diction . . . ," *Anglia* LXXIII (Tübingen 1956), pp. 413–66.

J. R. R. TOLKIEN, "*Ancrene Wisse* and *Hali Meiðhad*," *Essays and Studies of the English Association* XIV (Oxford 1929), pp. 104–26.

R. VLEESKRUYER (ed.), *The Life of St Chad* (Amsterdam 1953).

R. M. WILSON, "On the Continuity of English Prose," *Mélanges de linguistique et de philologie: F. Mossé in Memoriam* (Paris 1959), pp. 486–94; *Early Middle English Literature*, 3rd edn (London 1968).

C. L. WRENN, "Standard Old English," *Word and Symbol* (London 1967), pp. 57–77.

D. H. WRIGHT and A. CAMPBELL (ed.), *The Vespasian Psalter*, in *Early English Manuscripts in Facsimile*, Vol. XIV (Copenhagen 1967).

Author's note: I am grateful to former colleagues in the University of Wales, Dr D. Kirby and Mr J. Eadie, who commented on an early draft of this chapter.

CHAPTER 6

Byzantium and the Emergence of an Independent Russian Literature

D. S. Likhachev[*]

I

The terms "Russian" and "Old Russian" are applied, as far as the 9th–13th centuries are concerned, to all the East Slavs—the common ancestors of the present-day Great Russians, Ukrainians, and Belorussians. This is how the East Slavs are named in all historical sources of that period too. The appellations "Ukrainian" and "Belorussian" did not then exist; to this day, indeed, some inhabitants of Western Ukraine and Belorussia call themselves simply "Russians." The population of ancient Russia was a single people (though divided into tribes); it had one language and entered history as one unit. It settled the territory from the mouths of the Neva in the north to the Danube estuary in the south. It moved toward the south and south-east, forming compact settlements in Tmutarakan' (the district of present-day Taman') and Korsun' in the Crimea. It also gradually moved to the north-east, and in the 10th century it had already formed important cultural centres there with the cities of Vladimir, Rostov[†], and Suzdal'. In the 11th and 12th centuries the Russians were constricted by powerful steppe peoples from the south; Tmutarakan' and the Crimea were cut off from the remainder of Russia, but peaceful movement northward and eastward continued: Russians reached the Volga and began to move on toward the Urals. In the vast semi-inhabited territories of the north-east, Russians peacefully settled down with the Finno-Ugrian populace, at the same time conceding the southern steppes in numberless bitter wars to the militant peoples of the steppe, against

[*] Academician, Institute of Russian Literature, Leningrad.
[†] Rostov "the Great," north-east of present-day Moscow, not to be confused with Rostov-on-Don [translator's note].

163

whose ferocious and deeply penetrating raids they had to defend themselves along the whole sector from the Volga to the Carpathians.

Despite wars, princely feuds, dispersal over a huge territory, and the heavy labour of farming in hostile natural conditions, the Russian tribes conserved linguistic unity, unity of culture, and a highly developed consciousness of nationhood—recognizing themselves to be representatives of European Christian culture, common to all the Slavs and to Byzantium.

The Old Russian language had very weak distinctions of dialect, and was even closer to the other Slavonic languages than is modern Russian. This closeness was a matter not only of vocabulary but of the whole grammatical system: in the Old Russian and South Slav languages not only the roots of individual words, but also word-formative suffixes and terminations, were identical. The resemblance extended to declensions and conjugations. Certain of the differences obeyed regular laws and could thus be easily grasped and remembered in reading. For example, one characteristic of Old Russian is "full vocalization," whereby a Common Slavonic sound-group on the pattern of *tort,** *tolt,** gives in the East Slavonic languages the "fully vocalized" formations *torot,** *tolot,** while in the other languages these Common Slavonic groups are altered according to different rules (compare Common Slavonic *borda* [beard], Russian *boroda*, Serbian *brada*, Polish *broda*). Other important East Slav peculiarities were the early loss of nasal vowels, the change of *ie* into *o* and *iu* into *u* (compare Old Slavonic *iezero* [lake] with Russian *ozero*), the change of the consonant-groups *kv*, *gv* into *tsv*, *zv* (compare Czech *kvet* [flower] and Pol. *kwiat* with O. Russ. *tsvet*, or the Czech *hvezda* [star] and Pol. *gwiazda* with O. Russ. *zvezda*), and so on.

Because the Old Russian language differed only slightly from the other Slav languages, and such distinctions as there were had a regular, easily and instinctively determined character, the culture of Old Russia was not sharply fenced off by linguistic barriers from the cultures of the other Slav countries. Books and other works written in Bulgaria, Moravia, Bohemia, or Serbia could easily be read and understood in 10th- to 13th-century Russia.

Popular Oral Literature

We do not know the precise nature of Old Russian lyrical song, fairy-tale, or ritual folklore in the 9th–13th centuries. We possess only faint hints of their existence in chronicles, church homilies, and the lives (*vitae*) of saints. We are better acquainted with proverbs and sayings: these are

* These are imaginary words [translator's note].

encountered (though not very often) in the chronicles. In the chronicles and lives we may also observe a reflection of the laments for dead princes and saints. But what we can assess best of all is the historical epos (oral epic poetry) of the 9th–13th centuries. Evidence of ancient historical epos can be gathered both from modern transcriptions of *byliny* (as Russian oral epic poems are called) and from 11th- to 16th-century chronicles. On the one hand, 19th- and 20th-century transcripts include *byliny* that (because of references to the names of personages, to events described, and to historical circumstances) can be assumed to relate to an early epoch. On the other hand, we can find a reflection of historical tales, toponymic legends, and *byliny* in the ancient chronicles. Both kinds of testimony tell us of the exceptional significance of the era of Prince Vladimir I (St Vladimir, called "Bright Sun" in the *byliny*).

The reign of Vladimir (*c.* 978–1015) became the "epic period" of the so-called Kievan Cycle of Russian heroic epos. It coincided with the greatest flowering of the Old Russian early feudal state. Vladimir I united an enormous area under his rule; his numerous expeditions to south, east, and west strengthened Russia's position *vis-à-vis* her neighbours. He introduced Christianity to Russia; he increased cultural and political links with Byzantium, the south Slav countries, and western Europe. In Vladimir's reign, too, the importance of the *druzhina* (princely retinue) increased. Vladimir (according to the chroniclers) loved his *druzhina* and took its advice. This is the reason why *bogatyri* (heroes) of the *byliny* constitute Vladimir's *druzhina*, feast together with him, and perform exploits in his service in the defence of Kiev and all the Russian lands.

The heroic *byliny* that have come down to us reflect stories both from pre-Kievan epos and from later centuries. In each case, however, the *bylina* remained a *bylina*, with its action simply transferred to Vladimir's court. Enriched as it was by various 13th- to 17th-century motifs, the *bylina* epos nevertheless reproduces the world of social relationships and the historical circumstances characteristic of the reign of Vladimir the "Bright Sun." Naturally these social relationships and historical circumstances are reproduced far from precisely. It was a period idealized by the people. For example, although entry into the *druzhina* was already difficult for the common people in the 10th and 11th centuries, the *byliny* continued to depict relationships between the prince and the *druzhina* whereby anyone might gain admission to the latter by virtue of his personal merits, bravery, strength, and great deeds. In the *byliny* people remembered a *druzhina* from which they were not yet completely debarred. One reflection of a *bylina* story in the chronicles can be seen in the account of a young leatherworker, included under the year 992. The tale relates how the Pechenegs came to Russia, and their prince summoned Vladimir and proposed that the war between them should be resolved by a duel between the best warrior of each side. The Pechenegs produce their own gigantic and alarming champion, but in Vladimir's *druzhina* there is nobody who will volunteer to fight him. Vladimir begins to "repine," when finally an "aged man" appears and says that he has five sons. He had gone to war with the four oldest, but the youngest, a leather-worker, had remained at home. From childhood nobody had been able to vanquish him. "Once" (relates the old man) "I was angry with him, and in a rage he tore up the skin he was working." It is this youngest son, a simple craftsman "of no great stature," who defeats the Pecheneg cham-pion. Vladimir then makes the young leatherworker "a great man," includes him in the company of his *druzhina*, and returns to Kiev with great glory. The popular bias of this tale is unmistakable: the young leatherworker, a humble artisan and a youngest son, performs a feat beyond the power of the prince's warriors. He succeeds thanks to the powerful hands of his trade: with these hands he crushes the Pecheneg to death.

Many recently transcribed *byliny* not only depict the time of Vladimir but also evidently originate in his period. Among such are the *byliny* "Dobrynia and the Dragon" and "Dobrynia the Matchmaker." The hero of these *byliny* is Dobrynia Nikitich, who, according to the chronicle, was Vladimir's uncle on his mother's side; Vladimir's mother had been a simple "stewardess" in the court of Princess Ol'ga. Dobrynia became a hero for two reasons: because he was a "plebeian" member of the *druzhina*, and at the same time a relative of Vladimir. He represented, as it were, the people's participation in the building of the Russian state. Other *byliny* are connected with the names of such heroes as "the peasant's son" Ilia Muromets, Sviatogor, Vol'ga, Mikula Selianinovich, Mikhail Kazarenin, and others. The popular *bylina* hero Alesha Popovich was originally active in a later historical setting (13th century), and was only later transferred to the "epic period" of Prince Vladimir.

Compared with the popular epics of most eastern and western nations, the fantastic element in the Russian *byliny* is not particularly great; the exploits of their heroes are unusual but not excessively exaggerated. What is represented is not a purely imaginary period, but the history of Russia as the people envisaged it. The *byliny* tell stories about a past that had actually happened.

Besides the *byliny* that depict the exploits of *bogatyri*, there is another epic cycle from which these heroes of the *druzhina* are absent. The action takes place in Novgorod. The principal heroes are the minstrel Sadko and Vasily Buslaev, leader of the poor people of the city. Their exploits are not military; these men struggle to live, one by his skill in playing the *gusli* (a zither-like instrument), the other by his daring and recklessness. Sadko is a professional minstrel; Buslaev, the son of a civic dignitary and a person of privileged birth, nevertheless stands out against the rich and noble, and gathers supporters about himself without distinction.

We do not know what form epic and lyric poetry took from the 10th to the 13th century. The majority of epic works are described or referred to in the chronicles; but the chroniclers were interested in them as historical sources, and have given us almost no idea of their form. However, occasional echoes of folklore in literary works suggest that the folk poems themselves were close to what has been preserved in transcriptions of the 17th–19th centuries. Thus, for example, in his letter to Prince Oleg Sviatoslavich, Vladimir Monomakh, the Prince of Kiev, compares the comfortless widow of his son with a turtle dove cooing on a dry tree—an image used to this day in popular lyric song. The *Tale of Igor's Campaign* also links man's fate with birds, animals, and plants—just as in the modern folk poetry of the Russians, Ukrainians, and Belorussians—and we find images from folk poetry again in *The Petition of Daniel the Captive* and in *The Tale of the Ruin of the Russian Land*.

Besides *byliny* that reflect the popular view of the world, Kievan Russia also produced specimens of *druzhina* epos: poetry associated with the upper levels of a feudal society already in process of formation. Echoes of this *druzhina* epos are to be heard in chronicle accounts of the expeditions to Constantinople of feudal chieftains such as Askol'd and Dir, Oleg, Igor', and Sviatoslav. The *druzhina*'s knowledge of its own strength and importance is clearly expressed in the chronicle description of a feast, which was composed on the basis of *druzhina* tradition or song. The *druzhina* is complaining to the prince because its members have to eat out of wooden spoons rather than silver ones. Because he loves his *druzhina* above anything else in the world, Vladimir orders silver spoons to be sought for them; thereupon he pronounces a maxim that occurs in other tales preserved in the chronicles: "With silver or gold I cannot obtain a *druzhina*, but by my *druzhina* I shall obtain silver and gold."

The favourite hero of the *druzhina* epos is Prince Sviatoslav, who devoted his life entirely to military expeditions, scorning riches, treasuring only his weapons, courageously and straightforwardly warning his enemies before setting forth: "I intend to march upon you." But this is not the place to review the whole range of *druzhina* traditions mentioned in the chronicles—the traditions, for instance, of other noble families, or the plots of historical songs, which were clearly intended for performance in the upper classes of feudal society. What we have to consider now is the phenomenon of an emergent folk literature in which differentiation between classes is already marked and which is imbued with both historical and patriotic consciousness. It is a folk literature at a comparatively advanced stage of social development.

II

The Formation of a Literary Language

Anyone who considers the earliest period of Russian literature will be struck by the sudden appearance in Russia in the late 10th and early 11th centuries of a well-developed and comparatively mature literature; the appearance, that is, of complex works and of a written language capable of expressing not only stylistic and emotional nuances, but also the profound ideas of mediaeval theology. An almost miraculous leap forward had taken place. We do not know the men who brought it about; we cannot identify the geniuses who participated in it. However, this leap forward—so astonishing if we regard it in isolation, within the boundaries of one country and of a single short period—becomes comprehensible if we examine the whole cultural-historical situation in the Byzantine-Slav world in eastern and south-eastern Europe during the 9th and 10th centuries.

The official acceptance of Christianity by Russia in 988 naturally played a very large part in the development of writing and the appearance of literature. However, the need for writing was very great in various spheres of social life even before the acceptance of Christianity. The transition to a highly organized system of writing was prepared by the whole trend of development of Old Russian society.

Traces of various writing-systems have been discovered by archaeologists in several parts of what was once heathen Russia, chiefly on pottery vessels. Writing was used as early as the first half of the 10th century in concluding treaties with the Byzantine Greeks: the written agreement of Prince Oleg with the Greeks in 911 was composed in the Greek and Russian languages. In this treaty there is evidence of the existence among the Russians of written testaments. In the subsequent treaty with the Greeks of 944 there is an article that bears witness to the existence of written documents in the ordinary commercial relations of Russia with other countries. The article mentions documents the Russian prince is sending to other lands; by the terms of the treaty the Russians were bound to equip their ships sailing to Byzantium with written documents. According to the early-10th-century Arab writer Ibn-Fadlan there was set up on the grave of a Russian (whose burial he described) a pillar bearing the name of the deceased and that of the Russian prince in whose reign he lived. There is evidence that Russian idols carried inscriptions with their names. There were also inscriptions on vessels in which goods were kept. Finally, there existed written indications of ownership.

From all the material we have adduced it is plain that the need for writing and writing itself existed in several not very highly developed forms even before the acceptance of Christianity. Writing by means of various alphabetical systems arose, with every appearance of spontaneity, in various parts of Russia. The demand for writing was determined by the appearance of private property, the growing complexity of trade, the emergence of regularized relations with other states, the effort to preserve the memory of the deceased, the growth of historical consciousness, and similar factors. Consequently the transfer to Russia of a highly organized Slavonic system of writing and its diffusion there were not so unexpected and sudden as might at first appear.

A need for the appearance of literature proper was also growing, but it was encouraged by more complex factors, which are harder to elucidate. First we should note the appearance in Russia of a stage of historical consciousness that could no longer satisfy itself with epic poems (*byliny*), for these were dominated by a view of the past that was not divided into chronological periods. In the *byliny* only one epoch exists: "epic time," within which Vladimir the "Bright Sun" eternally reigns. Historical consciousness demanded the rise of more complex local traditions, each telling of events linked with this or that active historical moment, with the reign of this or that known prince. The past begins to emerge in these local traditions as a process; in them we observe attempts to explain the origin of a city, the provenance of geographical names, the formation of some particular custom, or even the derivation of a saying.

The historical epos reached such a state of maturity in the 10th and 11th centuries that it could serve as the soil on which historical literature proper might grow: such forms as chronicles, historical tales, and biographies of saints and of major figures in Russian history. Simultaneously (as class differentiation in society became more and more distinct), works created verbally needed to have a "stable" form; this could be provided only by writing.

In a pre-class society, folklore served everybody and reflected common ideas, outlooks, and concepts. With the development of classes and the appearance of differences in upbringing, views, and interests, and of the personal impulse in culture, a verbal work could no longer express views and attitudes common to everyone. In addition, a dissociation between performers and audience took place: the former might belong to the common people, the latter to the top reaches of feudal society. In such circumstances the ideological homogeneity of folklore could no longer satisfy everybody. The need was felt to express complicated views and world outlooks; and differing views had to be expressed through different kinds of writing. Folklore expressed only what was common to and generally accepted by all; written literature could express the individual ideas of one author or the separate ideas of one particular section of the population or another. Consequently, the indeterminate character of the "text" in folklore no longer fulfilled society's demands. Thanks to the "fixing" of the written word, various forms of literary expression could show more "tolerance" than folklore, i.e. they could reflect diverse interests and ideologies and could answer to the needs of a society having different classes and groups with differing experience, differing ideas, differing upbringing, and a differing circle of contact with neighbouring cultures. Only written literature, moreover, could accept translated works—a fact of particular importance for the further development of Russian culture.

Folklore, too, began striving toward the fixing of its texts in a more-or-less rigid verbal framework: a wealth of traditional forms and formulae and a lack of flexibility in many folklore genres (particularly the epic) testify to just this. Folklore itself was beginning to tend toward literature proper.

Finally let us turn our attention to the preconditions for the formation of a specific literary language. Its formation was also prepared by a lengthy process of development in society. The creation of a written literary language was foreshadowed by an oral "literary language"—that of oral literature. The language of folklore is to this day somewhat distinct from that of everyday life. It is elevated and to some degree purged of many prosaic aspects. But it is not only a matter of the existence of this special language in the high genres of folklore. The social order of ancient Russia in the 9th–12th centuries demanded the development of a highly organized verbal speech in a variety of forms: speeches at the *veche* (the Old Russian popular assembly), at meetings of elders, and at feasts, addresses by princes to their warriors before battles or expeditions, and so on. Speeches of this kind, or parts of them, have survived in the notes made by chroniclers of the 11th–13th centuries; they are brief and expressive, and clear, easily memorized images are used in them. Certain precepts of Russian law subsequently included in the so-called *Russkaia pravda* (the Old Russian written legal codex) were originally also oral and had to have a concise, rigid, and strictly determined form. Characteristic too are the so-called "ambassadorial speeches." In negotiations, princes about to despatch emissaries instructed them to deliver such speeches in a strictly determined form that would not admit of varying interpretations.[1] There were also speeches made by princes at a variety of oath-taking ceremonies, and verbal resolutions accepted by princes at their assemblies. These latter had to define briefly, expressively, and precisely the policy of the princes.

Thus, the appearance of a highly organized system of writing, of a complex literature, and of an exact literary language was prepared long before the introduction into Russia of Christianity with its high intellectual culture. The very acceptance of Christianity by Russia was itself the result of definite social needs and of a government that was becoming more highly organized and developed. An indication of what these needs were can be seen in the attempts made by Prince Vladimir I of Kiev, the future baptizer of Russia and saint, to reform the traditional Russian pagan religion before he accepted Christianity and baptized his people. He first tried to create a unified religion for the whole country and all its tribes by bringing all the heathen gods into a single pantheon and singling out within this pantheon one main god, Perun.[2] But this attempt was incomplete and did not satisfy Vladimir himself, who quickly took a new decision to have Russia baptized. It was impossible to reform the traditional heathen religion sufficiently to satisfy the needs of a developing and complex society—one, moreover, that had to enter into the company of other nations having highly developed cultures.

The Russian plain was never cut off from influences coming from the south, the north, and the west. In the 9th and 10th centuries the most significant of these influences were two. One, brief but intensive, came from the Scandinavian north. The other came from Byzantium;[3] it was already centuries old, being a continuation of the influence exercised already by ancient Greece on the northern shores of the Black Sea. Christianity arrived on the crest of a wave of Byzantine influence. This influence was extraordinary in its character and significance, and in turn elicited further new cultural demands. In order to understand the nature of this Byzantine influence, we must first briefly consider the cultural situation that prevailed at that time throughout the Byzantine-Slav world.

III

The Byzantine-Slav Cultural Milieu

The term "Byzantine influence" is far from exact. Byzantine Christianity did not "influence" Russia; it was *transferred* to Russia from Byzantium and Bulgaria. The same applies to Byzantine culture in its totality: architecture, painting, music, Byzantine concepts about the world, Byzantine political ideas, and so on. In Russia these phenomena of Byzantine culture continued their development, adapting themselves to local needs and the local "cultural climate." There occurred not simply a movement of culture and cultural phenomena so much as their transplantation—as though they were living organisms ("transplantation" is the most accurate word to define the transfer of Byzantine and general European cultural values that took place in the 9th, but particularly in the 10th, 11th, and succeeding centuries). This living culture was transplanted into new conditions while it was still in the process of growing. In Russia it continued to develop, adapting itself to local cultural traditions and needs. Old Slavonic translators and scribes introduced addenda and elucidations into their translations; they simplified or complicated the language and inserted whole passages from other works, adapting their versions to the needs and tastes of their readers. Sometimes Old Russian scholars re-ordered the composition of a work or, on the basis of several translations of different works, created large compendia (composite works dedicated to important subjects such as Old Testament history, the history of Byzantium, and so on).

The character of this remarkable life of a literary work in new Russian circumstances can be shown by several examples. In the translated *Word of Paul the Apostle on Temerity*, where the apostle exhorts his flock not to be idle in listening to sermons, the following insertion was made in order to illustrate this thought by means of material close to the everyday life of the Russian reader:

> ... as if the Polovtsian hordes had come upon us and taken all into captivity, and then their ruler had ordered them to destroy our city... and subsequently he were taken into captivity by our ruler and brought into the city—should we not all run with our wives and children to look at him?

From the middle of the 11th century until the Tatar (Mongol) invasion in the 13th, the Russians suffered particularly from raids by a steppe people—the Polovtsians (Cumans). Thus an example using Polovtsians who had sacked a city and taken its prince into captivity must have had a particularly powerful effect on Russian readers.

Translated lives of saints were also re-worked on Russian soil. For example, the *Life of St Nicholas the Wonder-worker* was supplemented with four new stories, two of which are set in Kiev. The Russian translator of Josephus's *Jewish War* (known as *The Story of the Destruction of Jerusalem*) made a number of insertions in which there were appeals for heroism, praise of those who died on the field of battle, and condemnation of those who preferred to die at home from natural illnesses. Characteristically, the first scholars to study the Old Russian translation of Josephus, unaware of this peculiarity in the work of Old Russian translators, assumed that these insertions had existed in some Greek or Aramaic text that had not come down to modern times and lay at the basis of the translation.

Of course, not every translated work was subjected by translators and scribes to such liberal additions and re-workings. Works that were liturgical or in general had the authority of the Church behind them (translations of Holy Writ, of the Fathers of the Church, and so on), underwent very little change. In such cases translators and scribes would have been afraid of being accused of heresy, and held scrupulously to the canonical texts. Basically, however, translated works continued to live, to change, and to be augmented on Russian soil. The text was not ossified, but alive and growing.

The same can be said about all products of Byzantine culture transplanted into new conditions of existence among the Slavs. What needs to be stressed again here is that individual phenomena were transplanted not in isolation but as part of a certain cultural totality. If Byzantine masters arrived in Russia or any other country in order to paint a church, that would mean that the church itself was constructed in a pattern at least similar to the Byzantine, that the Christian Orthodox liturgy existed in that country, that there were also representatives of the Church hierarchy, and that Byzantine religious concepts were to some degree accessible to the worshippers. It should be added, however, that Byzantine culture was transplanted not in its full Constantinopolitan form, but somewhat adapted to the needs of the Slavs.

Byzantine culture among the Slavs, then, was an offshoot of Byzantine culture proper and grew up on its foundations, but was not identical with that of the metropolis. It was a sort of common culture for the southern and eastern Orthodox Slav lands that evolved simultaneously as a single totality in various Slavonic countries as the result of the transplantation of Byzantine culture into them. It was a supranational cultural milieu, and within it there developed intensive communication of the southern and eastern Slavs among themselves and with Byzantium.

In fact, Byzantine culture first came to Russia less as the result of direct contact between Russia and Byzantium than by way of Bulgaria. In this process Bulgaria was far from being a mere passive medium of transmission. Of course anything that did not need translation from one language to another (visual art, building, handicrafts, and so on) could enter Slavonic lands direct from Byzantium; but the huge verbal segment of culture came to Russia originally from Bulgaria, in Bulgarian translations and in translations made in Moravia-Pannonia into Old Bulgarian (so-called Church Slavonic), which had become the literary language of the southern and eastern Slavs. In the first instance canonical, liturgical, and other ecclesiastical works were translated; without them the life of the Church could not exist. To these were added works about the world in general, universal history, and natural science: the chronicles of George Hamartolos (*fl. c.* 850) and John Malalas (*c.* 491–578), the *Christian Topography* of Cosmas Indicopleustes (*fl. c.* 525), the Hexaemeron, many apocryphal works, patericons, collections of aphorisms, and so on. New compilatory works, essential in the conditions of a new Christian Slav culture, were made on a Byzantine literary basis.

Soon afterwards, however, in the reign of St Vladimir's son Iaroslav the Wise at the beginning of the 11th century, Russia began to have its own school of interpreters as well—a fact that is directly recorded in the chronicles. Apparently about a couple of dozen varied works of literature were translated in Russia; in addition, individual translations were made from the Ancient Hebrew,[4] from Latin,[5] and even from Syriac.[6] Despite the fact that there was no Greek intermediary in the case of the translations from these three languages, the translations have to be regarded in the general context of the Byzantine-Slav cultural milieu outlined above. They not only corresponded with the spirit of this culture, but entered quickly and securely into its totality, and were distributed in all the South and East Slav lands. During the formation of the cultural milieu a continual process of selection went on of works that had been produced or translated in Bulgaria, Moravia, Russia, Serbia, and elsewhere. Independent Slavonic compilations (for example, the wide-ranging *Prolog*, a collection of short lives of saints, stories, and sermons) were composed on the basis of Byzantine works. The general store of Slavonic literature was further enriched by several lives of Slavonic saints (among them Russians: Boris and Gleb, Vladimir, Ol'ga), the best sermons (for example, those of Kirill of Turov), and so on. It should not be supposed, however, that the growing corpus of Slavonic literature included only ecclesiastical works. Slavonic translators made versions of narrative and historical works: *The Tale of Alexander the Great, The Story of the Destruction of Jerusalem* by Josephus, the Byzantine epic poem about Digenes Akritas (The Frontiersman)—in Slavonic, *Devgenievo Deianie*—various chronicles, and others.

A leading role in enriching the common store of translated literature and in the creation of a Byzantine-Slav cultural milieu was played by the centres where Slavs and Byzantines came into cultural contact: the monasteries of Mount Athos, Jerusalem, Sinai, Constantinople, Salonika, and elsewhere. Another most important factor in the creation of this milieu was that representatives of the high clergy often travelled about from one Slavonic country to another. Teams of artists, translators, and scribes similarly travelled from country to country and city to city. Icons, manuscripts, and jewellery were carried from one place to another. It could happen that a luxuriously made edition of the Gospels was copied in Novgorod and bound in Kiev, with individual parts of its binding ordered from Constantinople.[7]

This peripatetic—one might almost say "nomadic"—character of the feudal intelligentsia and of literary and artistic works lasted for a long time. It was intensive at the time of the Byzantine-Slav pre-renaissance in the 14th and first half of the 15th centuries; to some degree it persisted right up to the 18th century, when representatives of the black (i.e. monastic) clergy were still often found moving from one country to another, taking with them manuscripts and printed books in Church Slavonic.

IV

The Church Slavonic Language in Russia

What, then, was the situation of this cultural milieu with relation to the local, popular cultures of the individual southern and eastern Slav nations? It is characteristic of every feudal society that there is a sharp division between the culture of the higher members of that society and popular culture: the former possesses national traits while the latter develops local, geographically limited features. The position of a supranational feudal culture with features of universalism is to some extent analogous to the position in a feudal society of the learned, literary, religious languages with which this supranational culture is closely bound up. Mediaeval Latin united many countries in Western Europe; the classical Arabic language united the countries of the Caliphate from Gibraltar to the boundaries of China; a little later the Persian literary language united some of the eastern countries; Sanskrit stood above the modern Indian languages in India, as did classical Chinese above the Chinese dialects, and so on. There is evidently a regular pattern here: feudalism developed written languages that united a number of countries and a number of ethnic cultures. These written, supranational languages exist on the basis of supranational cultures, a characteristic feature of which is their connection with a religion.

The role of the Church Slavonic language was analogous to the role of Latin and Arabic.[8] The difference, however, was that the Church Slavonic language was not that of the maternal (in this case Byzantine) culture, but was a special language close to the popular Slavonic languages. For this reason the Byzantine-Slav cultural milieu was closer to the popular cultures of the Slavonic countries than were the Latin- and Arabic-speaking cultures to those of the countries united by them.

The Church Slavonic language was developed on the basis of the Old Bulgarian language, in which during the 9th century the first translations from Greek were made by the creators of the Slavonic alphabet—Constantine (*c.* 827–66, better known by his monastic name, Cyril), his brother Methodius, and their pupils. It assumed the functions of a language of high literature, and of a literature that was also basically ecclesiastical (translations of biblical, liturgical, and patristic works), that was common to all the Orthodox Slavs and even to some non-Slavs, such as the Rumanians. It was in this language that all the literature that travelled from one Orthodox country to another and linked the cultures of separate nations of eastern and south-eastern Europe was written.

Church Slavonic was used in different spheres from the popular languages (which, as we shall see, developed independently their own written languages upon the basis of the popular ones), and as a result it soon acquired special stylistic functions as well. What was originally one and the same word began to appear in a Church Slavonic form that indicated a high, religious, or learned style, and in a popular form having an everyday, commercial, or "low" significance. Thus as early as the 11th century stylistic distinctions can be found between words such as *vrata* (gate) and *vorota*, *glava* (head) and *golova*, *glas* (voice) and *golos*, *grad* (town) and *gorod*, *drevo* (free) and *derevo*, *mlad* (young) and *molod*, *mraz* (frost) and *moroz*, *sram* (shame) and *sorom*, *khlad* (cold) and *kholod*, *khrabry* (brave) and *khorobry*, and many others.

In the wake of stylistic distinctions, and almost simultaneously with them, there appear distinctions of meaning as well. Generally Church Slavonic words begin to be distinguished from Russian words of the same origin by the fact that they develop abstract significance. A language does not tolerate two distinct words that are totally identical in meaning. Distinctions in shades of meaning appear, and these distinctions follow on from distinctions in style and usage. Thus the words *glava* and *golova* are essentially distinct in usage: as early as the 11th century *glava* could be used in an abstract or metaphorical sense more easily than *golova*. The latter word was more often used in a concrete, "material," and narrow sense. The same distinctions appear in the words *nrav* (habit) and *norov*, *mrak* (gloom) and *morok*, and the like.

The stylistic function inherent in Church Slavonic aided its preservation as a special language designed for high ecclesiastical, ceremonial, and scholarly works. This preservation of the special role of Church Slavonic was helped also by the continual exchange of books between the Orthodox Slav (and to some degree the non-Slav) countries of southern and southeastern Europe. The tendency toward confusion with languages close to it in usage, which is natural in the life of any language, was counteracted in the case of Church Slavonic by the powerful factors that kept it as the language of religion, and of high style and learnedly literary reference.

Quite different factors were at work in the case of the popular languages, and in particular of Russian. Here there was far less of a tendency toward self-preservation. While the demand for stylistic elevation produced a certain hermetic quality in Church Slavonic, the everyday language of business and conversation required no linguistic etiquette, and it changed easily and quickly. Individual words and expressions from Church Slavonic penetrated the written and spoken popular language. As a result, Church Slavonic continues to be preserved among the majority of Orthodox Slav peoples as the single traditional language of their liturgy, while the popular languages, having undergone far-reaching evolution, contain a considerable element of Church Slavonic vocabulary and certain of its grammatical forms. Present-day Russian has a significant proportion of Church Slavonic forms and words, whereas the Church Slavonic language itself has become very little russianized, and such russianization as there is chiefly affects phonetics and "hidden," scarcely noticeable morphological forms.

Between the Church Slavonic language on the one hand, and the popular Slavonic languages among which it lived on the other, there existed for many centuries a unique symbiotic relationship. This symbiosis continually enriched the popular Slavonic languages, while the

Church Slavonic language—gradually narrowing its sphere of usage, and sealing itself off within the confines of exclusively ecclesiastical genres— preserved its traditional quality and aided the literary contact and linguistic interaction of Slav peoples within the limits of the cultural milieu described above. For example, it was through the Church Slavonic language in the 14th and 15th centuries that certain South Slav forms and orthography penetrated Russia.

In Russia, then, two literary languages existed, each with its own sphere of use. Where it was a question of higher or ecclesiastical themes, Church Slavonic was used; but in writing connected with everyday affairs, the Russian literary language, which had arisen on the basis of the popular language, was used. The latter language is used in the treaties with the Greeks, the *Russkaia pravda*, to some extent in the chronicles, and so on. It must be admitted that it is not always possible to distinguish clearly between the two literary languages. Thus the chronicle basically makes use of a language similar to that of the *Russkaia pravda*, but where it speaks of events of ecclesiastical significance the solemn Church Slavonic language takes over.

For example, when the chronicle tells of the death of the heathen prince Oleg, it uses the Russian literary language that arose on the basis of the popular language:

> And autumn came, and Oleg remembered his horse that he had put out to graze, resolving not to ride it. For he had asked wizards and soothsayers: "From what shall I die?" and one wizard had answered him: "Prince! That favourite horse of yours which you ride—from that will you die." Oleg took these words to heart, and said: "Never shall I mount it again, nor shall I set my eyes on it." And he ordered that it should be fed but not brought to him; and he lived several years without seeing it, until he marched against the Greeks. And when he had returned to Kiev and four years had gone by, during the fifth he remembered his horse from which the soothsayers had predicted his death. And he summoned the senior among the grooms and said: "Where is my horse which I ordered to be fed and looked after?" The groom answered: "It has died." Oleg laughed and re-proached the wizard, saying: "The soothsayers speak not the truth, but only lies: the horse has died, but I am alive." And he ordered a horse to be saddled for himself. "Let me see its bones!" And he reached the place where the bare bones and bare skull lay, dis-mounted, and said, "Is death to come for me from this skull?" And he kicked the skull with his foot, and out of it crawled a snake and bit him on the foot. And from that he fell ill and died. And the people all raised a great lamentation for him, and took him and buried him on the hill called Shchekovitsa; his tomb is there to this day, and is called Oleg's Tomb. And he reigned in all for 33 years.

A different language was used in the chronicle for obituaries dedicated to a saint. Here is how the chronicler Nestor praises Theodosius, abbot of the Kiev Monastery of the Caves, in "The Tale of Bygone Years" (translated as *The Russian Primary Chronicle*):

> But I, your sinful slave and pupil, lack wit to praise your admirable life and your restraint. But this little shall I say: "Rejoice, our father and preceptor! Rejecting the clamour of the world, loving silence, you have served God in quietude, in the monastic life, gaining God's gifts; you have elevated yourself through fasting, acquired a hatred of fleshly passions and temptations, rejected worldly beauty and desires, following in the steps of the learned Fathers, vying with them, exalting yourself through silence and adorning yourself with humility, taking joy in written books. Rejoice, having strengthened yourself with hope for eternal joys, which having accepted, and having laid low fleshly desire, the source of lawlessness and rebelliousness, you, most holy one, have avoided devilish wiles and snares, have gained repose with the righteous, o father, who have won reward for your labours, being their inheritor, having followed their precepts and observed their laws."

In his *Testament*, Prince Vladimir Monomakh (1053–1125) writes in Church Slavonic in those passages where he admonishes and moralizes, but when he recounts his campaigns and hunting exploits he reverts to the everyday Russian language.

We must not suppose that both the literary languages of Old Russia were developed and delineated to the same degree. Church Slavonic was indeed a defined and homogeneous language (although some russicisms penetrated it), but the written Russian language was far from homogeneous and certainly not stable. It is particularly striking that Church Slavonicisms penetrated Russian far more intensively than russicisms into Church Slavonic. Church Slavonic had greater powers of resistance and a greater traditionalism; it was accepted as the language of a defined stylistic system. Indeed, it is inseparable from the system of images, metaphors, and symbols that were taken from Byzantine literature, the Bible, liturgical works, and the writings of the Church Fathers: it is closely bound up with an ecclesiastical viewpoint and habits of thought. More or less any literary work might be translated into most other modern literary languages—but not into Church Slavonic. It is regrettable that this link between Church Slavonic and a defined stylistic system has not been studied at all.

The Russian literary language, which had grown up on the basis of popular speech, was another matter altogether. It was not linked with a particular stylistic system, and it included works as diverse as *The Tale of*

Igor's Campaign (1187), *The Petition of Daniel the Captive* (*c.* 1250), and *The Tale of the Ruin of the Russian Land*. In these works we find some images, symbols, and similes that are typical of a Byzantine-biblical stylistic system and others that are borrowed from folklore. The latter were used in a number of Old Russian works in an attempt to create a "high" style that would be distinct from the customary Church Slavonic style based on the Byzantine-biblical system.

Very early in the South and East Slav lands there began to appear local forms of literature of the upper feudal classes; these local writings had only limited national importance, and did not travel from country to country. In spite of their local and "static" character, however, it was precisely works like these that played a crucial role in the development of each Slavonic nation. They reflected local actuality to a greater extent than supranational works; new features came to the forefront, and they were less subject to the traditions and strict rules of the mediaeval genres.

V

The Birth of an Independent Old Russian Literature

It was during the 10th and 11th centuries that Russia adopted the rich system of literary genres that by then had been successfully developed within the Byzantine-Slav cultural medium we have described. It included various types of saints' lives, sermons both ceremonial and instructive, ecclesiastical hymnography and prayers, chronicles, and compendia of different kinds—liturgical, patristic, collections of sayings, and so on.

Some of these genres were accepted merely as a kind of literary import and did not develop any further on Russian soil. Others inspired imitation, however, and formed a basis for Russian writing on Russian themes. Thus the first work of Russian literature, *The Philosopher's Speech*,[9] which evidently dates from the end of the 10th century and was included in the 11th century in the Russian chronicles, is written in a form that had long existed in Byzantine literature: the so-called socratic dialogue. In this work the Russian Prince Vladimir questions a Christian teacher, called the Philosopher, about the faith, and the latter answers his questions at length, elucidating the fundamentals of Christian doctrine and sacred history. Works of this type were intended for the propagation of Christian teaching in the newly converted country.

Subsequently, in the 11th century, there appear lives of the first Russian saints: Boris and Gleb, the Princess Ol'ga, Prince Vladimir I (the later-canonized baptizer of Russia), and others. There is a tale of the martyrdom of two Varangians—father and son—who had been killed before the conversion of Russia because they had accepted Christianity. Other tales tell of the building and consecration of churches (Santa Sophia and St George in Kiev). Ilarion (the first Russian-born Metropolitan of Kiev) and, somewhat later, the Kievan prince Vladimir Monomakh both composed prayers for the Russian land. Luka Zhidiata, Archbishop of Novgorod, and Theodosius, the leading spirit of the Kiev Monastery of the Caves, compiled the first Russian doctrinal works during the 11th century.

However, as early as the first half of the 11th century new genres unconnected with the genre system of the Byzantine-Slav literary milieu that had been accepted into Russia began to be created in response to the needs of Russian life. Thus, we find chronicles being compiled during the early 11th century in Kiev and in Novgorod, the two chief centres of Russian government. These are in no way imitations of Byzantine chronicles; events are set out in a strictly chronological form, year by year, quite unlike that of the chronicles from abroad that were known in Russia. The latter were histories; the Russian chronicles were collections of documentary notes, lives, historical tales, and so on. It is true that the *Primary Chronicle* compiled in Kiev also opens with a unified historical narrative, but this narrative is thoroughly idiosyncratic: it was founded on data from folklore (traditions, local legends, historical songs) and from Byzantine sources, and it heroizes the Russian past.

Chronicles are among the most unusual and important phenomena of Old Russian culture.[10] Thousands of copies of various chronicles have come down to us. They were compiled in all Old Russian cultural centres of any importance up to the 18th century—at the courts of princes, metropolitans, and bishops, in monasteries, and sometimes in ordinary churches. The writers of chronicles made notes of local occurrences, but certainly did not limit themselves to these notes: they combined in their works earlier chronicles, historical writings, and documents. When they had collected all the material accessible to them, the chroniclers united it in their year-by-year exposition. In order to avoid repetition, the chronicler would relate the document to the year with which it was concerned, would place the life of a saint under the year of his death, and would divide up a historical tale that embraced a span of time, placing each portion under its appropriate year. The construction of a chronicle by years provided its writer with a convenient form for the accommodation of more and more new items of information, literary works, and documents. As a result the chronicles turned into uniquely broad historical encyclopaedias, in which Russian history appeared as a kind of continuation of world history (in the sense that this was understood in the Middle Ages).

The writing of chronicles, then, was a form of expression very characteristic of Old Russian culture, which was permeated with historical feeling.* Old Russian literature was devoted to historical persons and events; it did not allow overt invention—authors and readers alike believed in the truth of all that was described. In pictorial art the chief subjects were events of sacred or universal (and later of Russian) history. Churches were built not only in honour of saints and of sacred events, but also to commemorate particular occurrences in Russian history. Old Russian diplomacy was argued above all in terms of historical precedents. It was thanks to this all-pervasive spirit of history in early Russian culture that the chronicles acquired such literary and cultural importance.

One of the first chronicles, "The Tale of Bygone Years,"[11] was composed at the beginning of the 12th century on the basis of earlier chronicles and folklore (both written and oral). It begins with an account of the division of the lands among the sons of Noah, and continues with an account of the separation of languages at the time of the Tower of Babel. It then tells of the division and migration of the Slavs and of the invention of Slavonic writing, and goes on to describe the formation of the Russian state, the deeds of the first Russian princes, the baptism of Russia, and the whole of subsequent Russian history up to the beginning of the 11th century. This work, which extols the wisdom and courage of the first Russian princes, actually goes so far as sharply to criticize princes contemporary with its compiler (evidently the monk Nestor of the Kiev Monastery of the Caves). Characteristic in this respect is the *Tale of the Blinding of Prince Vasilko of Terebovl'*, which is placed in "The Tale of Bygone Years" under 1097. The introduction to the Novgorod chronicle of the 11th century also opens with sharp criticism of contemporary princes. Old Russian writers, and in particular the chroniclers, felt a deep sense of duty toward their country and were aware of their civic responsibility as writers.

The Problem of Genre

Every literary system of genres that has any sort of dynamism reponds to the demands of changing circumstances. The most unstable part of the Old Russian genre system was that which was closely bound up with

* See the discussion of this subject for Western Europe in Ch. 8, "Mediaeval Ideas of History."

local and national demands. During the 11th and 12th centuries there emerged in Russian literature a whole series of works that are clearly influenced by actual social and historical situations, and whose genre is difficult to determine. These are immature works as regards their form and it is not clear what genre they belong to, but out of them there subsequently evolved independent genres of Old Russian literature that had no analogy in the Byzantine world.

One of the earliest works of Old Russian literature, the *Discourse on Law and Grace* (*c.* 1045) by the Kievan Metropolitan Ilarion,[12] diverges in its genre features from those traditional to ecclesiastical, ceremonial sermons. The work is a ceremonial sermon infused with politico-philosophical content. Ilarion attempts to show the significance of Christianity in world history and the significance of Russia's baptism in the development of world Christendom. In this work there already appears a characteristic feature of Old Russian culture: its universalism—its desire to examine all the events of Russian history in the light of world history, not limiting itself narrowly to national matters, but seeing in the Russian people a peculiar historical mission in the history of the universe. From the point of view of genre this work has no analogy in Old Russian literature. It is unique and stands by itself.

The *Instruction* of Vladimir Monomakh, Prince of Kiev, is also unique.[13] It is a kind of political testament, addressed not only to Monomakh's sons, but to all the Russian princes. The first editor of this work—Count A. I. Musin-Pushkin (whom we shall meet again as first publisher of the *Tale of Igor's Campaign*)—called it a "spiritual primer," but we have no knowledge of any similar "testaments" or "primers" for children. Vladimir Monomakh was married to Gita, the daughter of the last Anglo-Saxon king, Harold Godwinsson, and he was undoubtedly acquainted with the Anglo-Saxon *Fæder Larcwidas*[14] (the *Precepts* in the Exeter Book). But Monomakh's *Instruction* differs sharply from such paternal works of precept. Nor is there any analogy to the autobiography of Monomakh, in which he in effect illustrates the political ideals expressed in his *Instruction*. Another illustration to the *Instruction* was its attached letter to Monomakh's defeated enemy and murderer of his son, Oleg Sviatoslavich, in which Monomakh forgives Oleg and begs him to return to Russia and reoccupy his rightful throne in Chernigov. The political ideal of Vladimir Monomakh (expressed in his *Instruction*, his autobiography, his letter to Oleg Sviatoslavich, in the chronicle writing he patronized, in the cult of the innocently murdered Boris and Gleb that he furthered, in his personal speeches at meetings of the princes, and so on) was fundamentally that everyone should content themselves with their inherited territory, steadfastly observing the interests of sub-ordinates and respecting senior princes. Monomakh saw the cosmic and natural order as the exemplar of the feudal hierarchy of sovereign and vassal. He stands before us as a characteristic Old Russian ruler, striving to propagate his political ideals both with the help of the chroniclers and through his own literary works (just as Ivan the Terrible was to make himself the typical ruler of the 16th century).

Also unique from the point of view of genre is the *Patericon* of the Kiev Monastery of the Caves.[15] The *Patericon* is in the form of a corre-spondence (between Bishop Simon of Vladimir-Suzdal' and the monk Polikarp of the monastery) interwoven with tales. The world of phantasy and legend revealed in the tales about the most important monks in the monastery is set against a background of real historical events of the 11th and 12th centuries. We meet historical personages familiar to us also from the Russian chronicles, and learn something of the day-to-day details of monastic life. The *Patericon* was one of the most popular texts in Russia until the 18th century and even later.

The 12th-century *Petition of Daniel the Captive*[16] likewise has no counter-parts in Byzantine or Old Russian literature. The beginning of the *Petition* recalls the way a *skomorokh* (popular minstrel) would solicit his audience's attention. Thereafter Daniel, like a *skomorokh*, entreats the prince's bounty and reward, praising his wealth and generosity, and describing his own need and the hopelessness of his situation. At the same time Daniel strives to entertain the prince with jests and witticisms, displaying his intelligence and his worldly experience, depicting various scenes from everyday life, and also making satirical sallies against boyars and rich folk in general. But this is no mere transcription of a minstrel's introduction. Daniel is a man of wide education, and the *Petition* was undoubtedly written as a book; but it rests on a groundwork of popular tradition. There is in this work both superficial lightheartedness of manner and a fundamentally serious intention. Daniel is propagating the idea of strong princely power, and terminates his work with a prayer that God may preserve Russia from the rule of strangers who are ignorant of the true God.

Very different, again, from Byzantine "travel books" (guides to the Holy Land) is the *Journey* of Abbot Daniel to Palestine (1106–8).[17] He describes everything he sees in a concrete, circumstantial, and business-like manner. Highly detailed also, and not comparable with anything else from the point of view of genre, is the *Tale of the Capture of Constan-*

tinople by the Crusaders in 1204,[18] compiled by a Russian witness of this event.

It is no accident, therefore, that there should have been much scholarly debate about what genre the 12th-century *Tale of Igor's Campaign* should be assigned to.[19] Its first editors considered the *Tale* to be a "heroic song"[20]; later investigators saw in it a "military tale,"[21] a "*bylina* of the 12th century,"[22] or a "solemn lay" in honour of Igor' Sviatoslavich.[23] Others regarded the *Tale* simply as an "epic poem." Finally there are those who, pointing to its isolated position among Old Russian literary monuments, refuse to see in it a work of Old Russian literature at all, the more so since its manuscript was burnt together with the whole large manuscript collection of A. I. Musin-Pushkin in the Moscow fire of 1812.[24] But although the *Tale* may be *sui generis* as regards genre, it is by no means unique in all other respects among Old Russian literary works. Like *The Petition of Daniel the Captive* it unites in itself both folk and learned elements. Like many works of its time it aims to teach the princes to unite in their struggle with the external foe, and bases its lesson on the tale of the fearful defeat of the Russians on the River Kaiala in 1185, when not only was the whole Russian army destroyed, but the wounded leader of the expedition—Igor' Sviatoslavich, Prince of Novgorod-Seversk—was taken prisoner. Scholars have found many parallels in Old Russian literature to the images and formulae of the *Igor' Tale*, as well as to its author's views of the world and of political events, to his methods of describing nature, and to the character depiction of his main personages.

Among comparable works of world literature the *Igor' Tale* stands closest to the *Chanson de Roland* (*c.* 1100), which was produced in similar historical circumstances. The poems resemble each other in theme, in their political ideas, and in individual motifs, imagery, and poetic formulae. To some extent they belong to the same genre, since the *chansons de geste* have much in common with the "tales of laborious deeds" (the achieving of a difficult feat), of which the *Igor' Tale* is one; these tales tell of some military exploit and combine popular lament and popular encomium. The *Igor' Tale*, like the *Chanson de Roland*, commemorates the defeat of a Christian army, fighting far from home against the heathen for reasons of national honour, so that long-lost territories might be regained. As a consequence of defeat Igor' is captured, while Roland perishes. In both works the author sorrows for the loss of a hero and his army. In both, the nation's grief at this loss is expressed by the senior feudal overlord: by grey-bearded Charlemagne in the *Chanson de*

Roland, by wise, grey-haired Sviatoslav the Great of Kiev in the *Igor'
Tale.* Both poems describe the heathen enemy in similar manner: in
one it is as if they wall off the steppe country with their shouts; in the
other, there is frequent reference to their wild howls. The authors hold
similar concepts of military honour and glory; evil omens accompany
both expeditions; and in both works Nature herself grieves in similar
fashion over the loss of the armies. Popular symbolism is woven into the
fabric of each poem, as are popular folk-epithets, metaphors, lyrical
refrains, and so on. One could adduce further similarities in the form
and content of the two epics. They are to be explained not only by
equivalence of historical situation, but also by a similar stage having
been reached in each case in the development of popular epic poetry,
which had been assimilated by an emergent written literature and led
to the formation of similar genres of lyricizing epos among different
peoples.[25] (All these works, incidentally, exceptional as they are from the
point of view of genre, are written not in Church Slavonic but in Old
Russian, close to the popular language of commerce and folklore.)

It should not be concluded, however, that all the finest works of Old
Russian literature stand outside the traditional system of genres. The
works of Bishop Kirill (Cyril) of Turov,[26] dating (like the *Igor' Tale*)
from the last quarter of the 12th century, bear better witness than anything else from the pre-Tatar period to the high quality of Russian
literary culture. Most of them are solemn compositions on the occasion
of this or that Christian festival, and theological commentaries on these
festivals and exaltation of their significance. Kirill of Turov's compositions
are written according to all the rules of Byzantine rhetorical prose in
splendid Church Slavonic; they are profound in content and excellently
constructed. For five centuries they were copied and re-copied in all the
South and East Slav countries, and ranked with the writings of the
Church Fathers.

We have been able to mention only a tiny proportion of the literature
produced in Russia before the Mongol invasions; in fact, the number of
known Russian writers and works for the period from the 10th to the
early 13th century runs into hundreds. A list of Russian writers from the
late 10th and 11th centuries alone, compiled early in our own century
by Academician N. K. Nikol'sky, contains some 30 names and more
than 100 titles.[27] In the 12th and early 13th centuries, literary works
were produced in most of the Russian feudal capitals—Kiev, Novgorod,
Chernigov, Vladimir-Zalessky and Vladimir-Volynsky, Pereiaslavl'-
Zalessky, Rostov, Suzdal', Smolensk, Pereiaslavl', Galich, and even in

little Turov and in individual monasteries, some of them in the depths of the countryside.

Then again, a large number of literary works have been lost without trace in the course of numberless wars and fires, and from sheer carelessness in subsequent ages. The existence of many works is known to us only from their being mentioned in other writings (neither the oldest life of St Anthony of the Monastery of the Caves nor the works of Kliment Smoliatich [Clement of Smolensk] have come down to us), and have been preserved in single chance copies that are often late and defective. For example, the works of Prince Vladimir Monomakh survive in a single copy; *The Petition of Daniel the Captive* has reached us in a few late copies; a single copy of *The Tale of the Ruin of the Russian Land* was discovered at the end of the 19th century, and only quite recently was a second copy found; *The Tale of Igor's Campaign* was discovered in a single manuscript.

During the Tatar period (1240–1480), Russian literature at first responded to the Mongol invasion with a series of superb lyrical-elegiac works: the *Tale of the Ruin of the Russian Land* (which has much in common with the *Igor' Tale*), several stories of the Russian defeat on the Kalka, the *Story of the Destruction of Riazan' by Batu Khan*, the Kitezh legend (which has reached us only in late reconstructions), and many others. But after this brief flowering, Russian literature underwent a decline lasting more than a century, and began to recover only at the end of the 14th century— a revival that once again owed much to the connections of Russian literature with Byzantium and the whole of the Slav world.

VI

The Style of the Epoch

The more ancient a civilization, the more homogeneous are its cultural components and manifestations: the arts, sciences, theology, even everyday life are all so interconnected as to be quite indivisible. That is why elements of an aesthetic world-view penetrate not only the various arts, but science, political thought, theology, and social institutions. Because of this quality of community and lack of differentiation, and the operation within social life of an aesthetic impulse, a broad tendency develops towards a single "style of the epoch," which lends a recognizable unity to its diverse parts. During the period from the 10th to the early 13th century, Old Russian culture is characterized by a single style of this kind, which linked Russia not only with the Byzantine-Slav intermediary culture but with the whole of Europe.

This common style of the epoch is known in Western Europe by the somewhat imprecise term "Romanesque" (in England by the name "Norman"). It is a style that embraced all Europe, not excluding Byzantium and Russia, and one of its fundamental characteristics is a striving toward generalized and monumental forms, and an emphasis on the significant, the majestic, the timeless, and the eternal. It makes a striking effort to link man with the universe, and to see symbols and signs of the eternal in everything. In Russian literature this style of the epoch can be related to so-called "monumental historicism."[28] The latter was an idiosyncratic style; it persisted in Russian literature until the mid-14th century and continued to exercise some influence even after that, particularly in chronicle-writing. Russia was thus bound to the rest of Europe by a single aesthetic world-view, and was not divorced from it in cultural, political, or economic respects.[29]

References

1. D. S. LIKHACHEV, "Russkii posol'skii obychai XI-XIII vv.," in *Istoricheskie Zapiski*, Vol. 18 (Moscow 1946).
2. E. V. ANICHKOV, *Iazychestvo i drevniaia Rus'* (St Petersburg 1914), pp. 308–28.
3. On Byzantine influences, see G. LITAVRIN, A. KAZHDAN, and Z. UDAL'TSOVA, "Otnosheniia drevnei Rusi i Vizantii v. XI-pervoi polovine XIII v.," in *Thirteenth International Congress of Byzantine Studies: Main Papers* (Oxford 1966); D. S. LIKHACHEV, "The Types and Character of the Byzantine Influence on Old Russian Literature," in *Oxford Slavonic Papers*, Vol. XIII (Oxford 1967).
4. Translations from the ancient Hebrew made in Kievan Russia include the Book of Esther and the *Jewish Antiquities* of Josephus: see N. A. MESHCHERSKY, "Problemy izucheniia slaviano-russkoi perevodnoi literatury XI-XV vv.," in *Trudy otdela drevnerusskoi literatury*, Vol. XX (Moscow-Leningrad 1964), pp. 198 ff.; this article also discusses Old Russian echoes of the Qumran texts.
5. A. I. Sobolevsky considered that the following texts preserved in Russian copies had been translated from Latin: the *Gumpol'd Legend* (about Viacheslav the Czech), the Lives of St Vitus, of Apollinarius of Ravenna, of Anastasia the Roman, and of Christogonos, and a number of prayers. See A. I. SOBOLEVSKY, *Materialy i issledovaniia v oblasti slavianskoi filologii i arkheologii* (St Petersburg 1910), pp. 43, 95 ff.

6. *The Story of Akir the Wise* was apparently translated from a Syriac original.

7. See I. DUJČEV, "Tsentry vizantiisko-slavianskogo obshcheniia i sotrudnichestva," in *Trudy otdela drevnerusskoy literatury*, Vol. XIX (Moscow-Leningrad 1963.)

8. V. D. LEVIN, *Kratkii ocherk istorii russkogo literaturnogo iazyka* (Moscow 1968); V. O. UNBEGAUN, "Le russe littéraire est-il d'origine russe?" in *Revue des Études Slaves* 44 (Paris 1965).

9. See *Povest' vremennykh let*, ed. by V. P. Adrianova-Peretts (Moscow-Leningrad 1950), Pt I, pp. 60–74 and 259–72.

10. D. S. LIKHACHEV, *Russkie letopisi i ikh kul'turno-istoricheskoe znachenie* (Moscow-Leningrad 1947); *Russian Reprint Service* XXXI, ed. by A. Soloviev (The Hague 1966.)

11. *Povest' vremennykh let*, Pts I and II; S. CROSS, "The Russian Primary Chronicle," in *Harvard Studies and Notes in Philology and Literature* (Cambridge, Mass. 1930); N. CHADWICK, *The Beginnings of Russian History: an Enquiry into Sources* (Cambridge 1946.)

12. L. MÜLLER, *Des Metropoliten Ilarions Lobrede auf Vladimir den Heiligen und Glaubesbekenntnis* (Wiesbaden 1962), Slavistische Studienbücher series.

13. See *Povest' vremennykh let*, Pt I, pp. 158–67 and 354–68.

14. M. P. ALEKSEEV, "Anglo-saksonskaia parallel' k Poucheniiu Vladimira Monomakha," in *Trudy otdela drevnerusskoi literatury* II (Moscow-Leningrad 1935).

15. D. I. ABRAMOVICH, *Kievo-Pecherskii paterik* (Kiev 1931); *"Das Paterikon des Kiever Höhlenklosters"* nach der Ausgabe von D. Abramovič, ed. by Dmitrij Tschiževskij (Munich 1964).

16. *"Slovo Daniila Zatochnika"* [The Petition of Daniel the Captive] *po redaktsiiam XII i XIII vv. i ikh peredelkam*, ed. by N. N. Zarubin (Leningrad 1932).

17. V. V. DANILOV, *K kharakteristike "Khozhdeniia" igumena Daniila*, in *Trudy otdela drevnerusskoi literatury* X (Moscow-Leningrad 1954).

18. *Novgorodskaia pervaia letopis' starshego i mladshego izvodov*, ed. and introd. by A. N. Nasonov (Moscow-Leningrad 1950), pp. 46–9.

19. *Slovo o polku Igoreve*. Introductory article by D. S. Likhachev; text established and edited by L. A. Dmitriev and D. S. Likhachev (Leningrad 1967), in *Biblioteka poeta* (Bol'shaya seriia); see *The Song of Igor's Campaign*, trans. by Vladimir Nabokov (London 1960); H. GRÉGOIRE, R. JAKOBSON, and M. SZEFTEL, *La geste du Prince Igor* (New York 1948), which includes notes and translations into English, modern Russian, French, and Polish; *The Penguin Book of Russian Verse*, ed. and introd. by D. Obolensky (Harmondsworth 1962).

20. *Iroicheskaia pesn' o pokhode na polovtsev udel'nogo kniazia Novagaroda-Severskogo Igoria Sviatoslavicha* (Moscow 1800).

21. A. S. ORLOV, *Slovo o polku Igoreve* (Moscow-Leningrad 1938), p. 22.

22. A. I. NIKIFOROV, *Slovo o polku Igoreve-bylina XII v.* (Leningrad 1941).

23. I. P. EREMIN, *Literatura drevnei Rusi* (Moscow-Leningrad 1966), pp. 144–69.

24. A. MAZON, *Le Slovo d'Igor* (Paris 1940); A. A. ZIMIN, "Spornye voprosy tekstologii 'Zadonshchiny'," in *Russkaia Literatura* I (Moscow 1967); the collection *Slovo o polku Igoreve-pamiatnik XII veka* (Moscow-Leningrad 1962); D. S. LIKHACHEV, "The Authenticity of the 'Slovo o polku Igoreve': a Brief Survey of the Arguments," in *Oxford Slavonic Papers*, Vol. XIII (Oxford 1967).

25. For more detailed comparisons of the *Tale of Igor's Campaign* with the *Chanson de Roland*, see V. DYNNIK, "'Slovo o polku Igoreve' i 'Pesn' o Rolande'," in *Starinnaia russkaia povest'. Stat'i i issledovaniia*, ed. by N. K. Gudzy (Moscow-Leningrad 1941), pp. 48–64; A. N. ROBINSON, "Literatura Kievskoi Rusi sredi evropeiskikh srednevekovykh literatur (tipologiia, original'nost' metod)," in *Slavianskie literatury, Doklady sovetskoi delegatsii na VI Mezhdunarodnom s'ezde slavistov* (Moscow 1968), pp. 75–81.

26. I. P. EREMIN, "Literaturnoe nasledie Kirilla Turovskogo," in *Trudy otdela drevnerusskoi literatury* XI (Moscow-Leningrad 1955), XII (1956), XIII (1957), XV (1958).

27. N. K. NIKOLSKY, *Materialy dlia povremennogo spiska russkikh pisatelei i ikh sochineniy* (X–XI vv.), rev. edn (St Petersburg 1906).

28. D. S. LIKHACHEV, *Chelovek v literature drevnei Rusi* (Moscow-Leningrad 1958), pp. 27–69.

29. See the following works on Old Russian literature: N. GUDZY, *History of Early Russian Literature* (New York 1949); A. STENDER-PETERSEN, *Anthology of Old Russian Literature* (New York 1954); R. PICCHIO, *Storia della litteratura russa antica* (Milan 1959); *Medieval Russia's Epics, Chronicles, and Tales*, ed., trans., and introd. by S. Zenkovsky (New York 1963).

CHAPTER 7

Christian Thought

Gordon Leff[*]

Mediaeval thought was governed by its Christian framework. This was at once doctrinal and institutional. Its tenets derived from God's word given in the Bible and the writings of the Fathers, which were taken as canonical; but they were defined and enforced by the Church. The unique authority of the Church as spiritual and doctrinal—and so intellectual and moral—arbiter of society distinguished the Middle Ages from both the classical and the modern epochs. It meant the existence of a binding orthodoxy, conformity to which was the criterion of acceptance; it determined the validity of all judgment and experience, whether intellectual or imaginative. For that reason they could not be autonomous. All independent knowledge and vision, to be tenable, had to be assimilated to the prevailing Christian ethos; this did not prevent deviations or divergences, but they were evaluated dogmatically.

Consequently there is an identifiable continuity in the evolution of the mediaeval outlook from the 4th to the 15th century. It was founded upon the hegemony of Christian truth as interpreted by the Church. This provided at once its unity and its tension. On the one hand, the universalism of the Church's authority was the source of the unity of a Christian outlook; on the other hand, it could be maintained only by Christianizing human experience. The progressive extension of the Christian over the non-Christian was the *leit-motiv* of mediaeval intellectual development. Beginning with conversion and the definition of dogma in the early centuries, it reached its culmination in the 12th and 13th centuries in assimilating the growing naturalism in every sphere: in love, poetry, the study of nature, and the body of pagan knowledge that came with Greek and Arabian philosophy and science. In that sense the dynamic of mediaeval Christian thought consisted essentially in a con-

* Professor of History, University of York.

frontation at every level between natural experience and revealed truth: not only within the Church, over abstract concepts or refinements of doctrine, but in the universal conflict between the demands of precept and practice that sprang from the inherent dualism between spirit and the senses so prominent in Christian teaching. As man's experience changed, so did the need to set it within the unchanging fundamentals of faith—in God the creator, Christ the redeemer, the immortality of the soul, the indispensability of the sacraments, the authority of the Church, the Last Judgment, and so on—demand new adjustments. It was here that the mediaeval society differed from anything that had gone before, and its outlook so susceptible to strains and crises. There was a constant obligation to reconcile the temporal with the eternal, to transcend the developments of the moment in the timelessness of God's decrees.

The pervasiveness of Christian belief is one of the hallmarks of mediaeval society. Although much of it was mere formalism, all the main intellectual, and many of the artistic, themes of the Middle Ages were Christian or given a Christian interpretation; at the same time the main institutions of higher learning were under the aegis of the Church, and the majority of thinkers and teachers were ecclesiastics or members of religious orders. Hence the close convergence of the main phases of life and thought.

As far as Christian thought is concerned, we can distinguish four temporal divisions. First, the end of the Roman Empire in the West, in which the two most formative figures of subsequent thought were St Augustine and Boethius. Second, the period from the 6th century to the 11th, which, although it contributed little new intellectually, transmitted some of the most important elements from the classical heritage and established a lasting pattern of learning in the service of Christian faith and largely in the hands of the Church. Third, the 11th, 12th, and 13th centuries, which saw the renewal of letters and speculation, and a new awareness of the world in every aspect, until it could no longer be contained within a comprehensive Christian framework. The great condemnations at Paris University in 1277 began the final phase of the progressive disengagement of natural knowledge from support of the tenets of a natural theology or a naturalistic ethic; Ockhamism and mysticism, the two most widespread outlooks of the later Middle Ages, each expressed the polarization between belief and natural experience.

There is no need to attempt an empty exercise in seeking a causal relation between these developments and those in society at large; it is enough to recognize that in every case they were the accompaniments of changed social circumstances. The comparative intellectual stagnation from A.D. 600 to 1000 belonged to a period of chronic unsettlement, in which invasion followed invasion, and the only comparative security was in the seclusion of a monastery or an out-of-the-way estate. Intellectually it was the age of the monks, whose highest ambition was to keep learning from extinction and to harness it to the needs of maintaining a literate priesthood. Its most characteristic intellectual products were propaedeutic: the compilations of Isidore of Seville (560–636) and Bede (673–735), the educational reforms of Alcuin (735–804), the handbook of learning of Raban Maur (d. 836). Theologically, apart from John Scotus Erigena, it was the age of scriptural glosses and homilies. The awakening of the 11th century, leading to the renaissance of the 12th century and to the great systems of the 13th century, was part of a universal return to some kind of order and security and the new forms of life, institutions, organization, and problems that flowed from them. The details must lie largely outside the scope of this chapter; but we shall have occasion to see the ways in which the changes in institutions—the renewed contact with the East, the revival of towns as the centres of society, and the tensions both within the Church and between spiritual and temporal power—all had an important bearing upon the intellectual history of these centuries, as they did on its last phase in the later Middle Ages. The period of the so-called Dark Ages was far from uniform. Although, as we have suggested, they were for the most part largely barren of originality, at their threshold stood two of the most important thinkers of the Middle Ages, St Augustine and Boethius. They, perhaps more than any others, may be regarded as the founders of the mediaeval intellectual tradition. Differently though they did so, they each gave lasting formulation to concepts that they drew from an earlier tradition: St Augustine as the last of the African Fathers of the Latin Church, Boethius as the last Roman philosopher. In their different emphases they paradoxically personify the inherent dualism between theology and philosophy that was the driving force in the development in Christian thought. Each was the product of a classical education, with its strong emphasis upon rhetoric and a knowledge of grammar, dialectic, music, geometry, astronomy, and arithmetic as the preparation for philosophy conceived as wisdom. Each, in different circumstances, witnessed the collapse of the world from which these had come. It led St Augustine to turn increasingly to the City of God and the need for God's efficacious grace; it caused Boethius, imprisoned and awaiting death, to call upon philosophy for consolation. Their ideas were to be taken up again and again.

St Augustine

St Augustine wrote with the Roman world falling about him. Although the Empire had become Christian under Constantine in 312, this had not prevented its dissolution during his lifetime. St Augustine spent his last years defending the city of Hippo, of which he was bishop, against the Vandals; and Rome, the "eternal" city, had been sacked by Alaric in 410. Meanwhile, within the Church, a succession of heresies—Manicheism (which St Augustine had once embraced), Donatism, Pelagianism, and Arianism—threatened it with schism. Accordingly, St Augustine wrote as an apologist to establish the foundations of Christian faith.

Although Christian thought had begun in the 1st century A.D., continuity with the mediaeval tradition in the West effectively starts from St Augustine. It was he who formulated the main dogmatic teachings of the Church on the Trinity, grace, merit, original sin, and predestination, while philosophically his doctrine of the soul, divine ideas, inner illumination, free will, and the relation of God to creation formed the point of departure for all subsequent Christian thinking. Every important thinker until the 14th century, with perhaps the exception of John Scotus and the neo-Platonists of Chartres, measured his outlook by reference to St Augustine, the majority as professing disciples. His influence remained largely unchallenged until the emergence of Aristotelianism in the 13th century; and it was never eclipsed.

Beyond these specific areas, however, St Augustine provided the intellectual orientation for the Middle Ages. Both expressly in *De doctrina christiana* and in his whole approach he transformed the notion of philosophical inquiry.[1] Accepting the classical meaning of philosophy as concerned with man's life and the attainment of wisdom, St Augustine set it within a Christian context. Because man's end was blessedness, Christianity itself became the true philosophy. But, unlike pagan philosophy, its truth lay in the acceptance of Christ's teachings. It was therefore qualitatively different from philosophy based upon natural reason, in beginning from authority. The failure to recognize the need for revelation was St Augustine's main criticism against neo-Platonism, which was the major influence in his own philosophical development. Such a recognition reversed the order of truth and inquiry. Belief now formed the starting-point for understanding; it gave priority to the believer, however untutored, over the "philosophers of this world," as St Paul had said before St Augustine. But unlike Paul, St Augustine regarded his earlier Platonism as a preparation for Christianity. In *De doctrina christiana* he put forward a programme for utilizing learning in the service of faith. It excluded all that was not germane to the study of the Bible, but it nevertheless gave profane knowledge a propaedeutic place in Christian education that was to be lasting, and largely underlay the preservation of the classical heritage in the succeeding centuries. Equally fundamental was his definition of belief as "to think with assent." In both his theory and his practice, St Augustine treated faith as the prerequisite for the understanding that came only with ceaseless inquiry into its meaning. "Unless you believe, you shall not understand" (Isaiah VII: 9). "The right direction for the search must start from faith."[2] This was to be the basis of all Christian thought until the 14th century. In that sense St Augustine, the last of the Fathers, was also the first scholastic in the application of natural knowledge and reason to revealed truth. The difference was that, for St Augustine, their connection was so close, and the subordination of reason to faith so complete, that he did not attempt to distinguish between them. Truth was supernatural in origin and conditional upon assent to faith, and conduct was no less defined by its orientation to God. St Augustine's ethics rested upon the distinction, originally from pagan philosophy, between enjoyment (*fruitio*) and use (*uti*): "To enjoy something is to possess it, loving it for its own sake." It was reserved for love of God. Use, on the other hand, was "for the obtaining of something that we love"[3]; it should therefore be directed to those things that help towards love of God, which is blessedness. Sin lay in the perversion of this order, leading to the love of things that should be used only for a higher end. That applied to knowledge no less than to actions; it gave a theocentric direction to both which was to be of enduring effect.

The guiding thread in St Augustine's thought was the attempt to overcome the dualism between the natural and the supernatural in terms of creature and creator. To this end he employed not only the full range of Christian doctrine, to much of which, as we have said, he gave lasting definition; he also brought to bear those concepts of neo-Platonism that supported the primacy of the spiritual and intelligible over the material and sensory. As a Christian, however, his assumptions were radically different. In contrast to the neo-Platonic tradition, for St Augustine, as for all Christian believers, God was supreme being, defined in his own words as "I am that I am" (Exodus III: 14). As such the antinomy was between the supreme being—with all his perfections of omniscience, omnipotence, goodness, wisdom, mercy, justice, and so on, as the attributes of his being—and creatures who owed their being to him. Their relation was as different kinds of being, one "unchanging yet changing all things; never old, never new," the other mutable and dependent upon a creator.

Ontologically, it contrasted with the neo-Platonic conception of the One as above all being and the multiplicity of beings outside the One. Theologically it introduced the notion of a God who was not only the immediate source of creation but whose providence extended to every aspect of it, the material as well as the spiritual. The Christian had therefore to explain the universe in its totality; he could not break off at the spiritual, treating what was corporeal, including man's body, as merely a derogation from being.

In St Augustine's case, although he broke away from neo-Platonism in defining the relation between God and creation in terms of being, his notion of being was itself neo-Platonic. With Plotinus, he regarded being as residing in the essence or the idea or form that defined it: goodness, humanity, whiteness, and so on; this in turn derived from God, whose word (which Plotinus had identified with the intellect or *nous* coming after the One) contained the archetypes of all creatures upon which he conferred being in the actual world. The divine idea in God, therefore, became the source of all created being, the means by which God, through his word, gave intelligibility and beauty to the world.[4] Moreover, again under neo-Platonist inspiration, St Augustine located man's awareness of the truth, contained in the essences or ideas of things, within man's soul; by looking within himself, and turning away from the multiplicity and flux of the world of the senses, man could become aware of the truth, which—like God, from whose word it derived—was eternal and immutable. Here, again, however, St Augustine gave a Christian stamp to this notion of truth as intelligible and non-sensory, which was to be one of the most formative elements in all subsequent Christian thought. It had three main aspects.

In the first place, he defined man as a soul using a body; the soul was a spiritual being, which, although joined with a body in this world, was independent of it, surviving it after the body's death. Not only did the soul animate the body, but it represented the true "interior man," the "I," as opposed to the "exterior man" that was the body.[5] Unlike the Aristotelian theory of cognition, which was to become widespread in the 13th century, St Augustine treated the soul as the active agent in all human knowledge. It governed the body and informed the body of what it was experiencing through the senses, as the superior acts upon the inferior. In the second place, because God had created man in his image, St Augustine regarded the soul as a trinity, of intellect, will, and memory. Because it was incorporeal, it knew not by reference to objects extended in space and in time, but through an inner awareness.

The very act of doubting is evidence that the soul exists and that it knows. "Everyone who is aware that he doubts, knows the truth and is certain of it . . . and should not doubt that he has the truth within him."[6] This was an argument Descartes was to take up; but in St Augustine's case it was designed to show the significance of inner awareness. The fact that such knowledge came from within meant that it was contained within the soul. Its indubitability was contrasted with the uncertainty of knowledge that comes through the senses. The dualism between inner intelligible knowledge and sensory knowledge that St Augustine took over from Platonism was one of his most enduring legacies to the Middle Ages. It went together with the supreme importance of memory (*memoria*). For St Augustine this was more than the mere recall of past experience; although that aspect was included, its meaning was nearer to inner discovery. By ceaseless searching and reflection the soul came upon "the multitude of principles and truths, none of them from any sense impression," by which it understood all that it experienced.[7] The ideas of number, order, justice, goodness, and so on enabled it to grasp the meaning of empirical things. Although, as a Christian, St Augustine could not accept Plato's theory of reminiscence as the soul's awareness of its once purely spiritual condition, he owed much to the idea of memory as reminiscence. The difference is that, in St Augustine's view, the truths that the soul discovered were from God.

This leads to the third feature of the soul: inner illumination. This again was the translation of a Platonic concept into Christian terms. As conceived by St Augustine it consists in the light of eternal reason, which is present to the mind and is the work of God. It comes from the mind's participation in God's word. It is therefore directly from God, independent of all external sensory experience. The truths it reveals are immutable and eternal.

In this way St Augustine traced man's relation to God through the spiritual nature of the soul. Although it gave no formal evidence of God as St Anselm was later to deduce it, it had a profound influence upon all subsequent thinking about both God and the soul. It united them through intelligible, non-sensory knowledge, which—as divine ideas in God and as essences or forms in his creatures—was to be the indispensable intermediary between the divine and the created for all mediaeval thinkers except the nominalists. It made inner illumination, whether defined as natural (which it seems to have been for St Augustine) or supernatural, the condition of higher understanding. It made the soul a spiritual being in its own right that had to renounce the senses if it was to be freed to search within for the "interior master" who was God. Knowledge of God came through knowledge of the soul, not directly but through his eternal truths by which he illuminated it.[8]

St Augustine's conception of the soul's relation to God was at once metaphysical, epistemological, and psychological. It was also moral, not only in the sense that man had to will to turn away from the world and towards God, but also because of the impediments that weighed man down and kept him away from God. Philosophically St Augustine's greatest legacy was the notion of inner illumination, but morally and ethically it was his teaching upon grace, predestination, and sin. Because these concerned matters of dogma, it could be argued that their influence was more all-pervasive, touching upon the very nature of man as an individual, from whichever aspect he was regarded. Indeed one of the hallmarks of Augustinianism was the inseparability of human actions from the moral state of those who performed them. Ethical truths were just as necessary, immutable, and eternal as those that concerned knowledge, and equally the result of divine illumination. Just as illumination enables us to grasp the idea of number, so by means of it we come to know of justice and goodness and strive to act according to their rules. Such wisdom is the common property of all who are prepared to discover it within. It makes up the natural law, and our awareness of it, gained in the "light of the virtues," is what we call conscience.[9] Knowledge of the moral order is not enough, however. Man must also want to conform to its precepts, in particular the four cardinal virtues of prudence, fortitude, temperance, and justice, in which the rules of conduct are eternally given. To do so is to accept the order decreed by God, which St Augustine saw exemplified in the identity of number and wisdom.[10] To follow this order, which was the means of sharing in God's life, could be achieved only with God's help. As the result of the Fall, man's will was no longer whole; his soul had become subject to ignorance and concupiscence, where before it had been free from the control of the passions. To overcome this bondage, free will did not suffice of itself; it needed grace to heal man's infirmity and to turn his will toward God.

The theological emphasis that he gave to man's dependence upon grace and the unreliability of free will tend to dominate St Augustine's later writings and to overshadow the metaphysical foundations of his notion of sin. There is a discrepancy in tone—at the very least—between a belief in the essential goodness of the world and all being as conceived by God, and the sinfulness of free will and man's present wretched state. Theoretically, they could be reconciled in man's betrayal of his own spiritual nature, and of God, for the world of the senses. Morally and dogmatically, however, they led to a depressed view of free will and fallen human nature that counteracted the metaphysical presuppositions of the goodness of creation. This is apparent in the Augustinian tradition, which, for all that St Augustine said to the contrary, tended to oppose free will to grace and to treat sin more positively as a punishment and guilt rather than as mere lack of righteousness. Although St Augustine stressed that free will is as indispensable to a righteous action as grace is (since there would be no grace without free will to receive it), nevertheless the role of free will was hard to reconcile with the eternity of God's predestination. St Augustine's position as enunciated in his later works, especially against Pelagius,[11] was that, although the power to choose freely (*liberum arbitrium*) enabled the will to choose evil, it was even more free in being able to choose good with God's aid. The highest freedom was to follow Christ and abjure sin. But this state could be reached and maintained only if sustained by God. Anyone who persevered in grace to the end was saved; but he could do so only if he received the grace of final perseverance, which Adam before the Fall had not needed, and which in turn was awarded to those who God foresaw would persevere to the end. That is to say, God aided those who turned towards him, but they could turn to him and renounce the love of earthly things only if he gave them the grace to do so. Who was to receive the grace of final perseverance and salvation, and who, through lack of it, was damned to perdition, was a mystery. It rested upon God's eternal decree.

The same conception informed St Augustine's teaching on human society in his *De civitate Dei*. Through the Fall, man had lost the original righteousness that had enabled Adam and Eve at first to live without fear of death or suffering. Sin had brought not only these into the world, but also coercion, slavery, and private possessions. In order to mitigate their worst effects, God had invested rulers with power to govern states. Only within the Church was there righteousness.[12] As God's saving will on earth, it embraced all Christians. They alone understood the meaning of their present life as a journey to their ultimate destination in the next. They alone, therefore, knew the meaning of happiness. Accordingly, while Christians, like other men, had to live in earthly cities, some also belonged to the heavenly city of God. The two coexisted in this world, and had done so from the beginning of time. For St Augustine, history was the progressive unfolding of God's design in the gradual formation of the heavenly city; with the end of the world it would be complete as the kingdom of the blessed.

The influence of St Augustine upon the mediaeval conception of history was scarcely less profound than upon subsequent philosophical and moral teaching. The notion of the two cities as representing the saved and the damned, and his conception of the Church as itself a city or communion of all the faithful, whatever their ultimate place at the Last Judgment, were of lasting importance for mediaeval ecclesiology. Until the middle of the 13th century they reigned unchallenged by rival interpretations, which were to appear under the influence of Aristotelianism, Joachism, and Waldensianism.

As with any figurative conception, the precise meaning of the heavenly and earthly cities is open to more than one interpretation. But it is most plausible, as well as consistent with its subsequent place in the mediaeval tradition, to see them as standing for the saved and the damned, as opposed to the Church and the state.[13] St Augustine's definition of the Church as the communion of all Christians included within it the damned as well as the saved. In this world, as the triumphant Church, it was not therefore synonymous—as Wyclif was to make it—with the heavenly city: the latter existed outside space and time. Accordingly, St Augustine's attitude toward society expressed the same dualism between the eternal and the temporal, the spiritual and the material, that informed all his thinking. Just as truth was the property of divine illumination, and goodness dependent upon grace, so the heavenly city was the true communion of God. Christians, although they had to live in this world, were not of it. They could not reject it, but neither could they accept it for itself. Society as the result of sin was at once God's punishment and God's remedy for man's fallen state.

The circumstances of the time could only confirm St Augustine's emphasis upon faith and inner experience as the source of hope and certainty. Metaphysically, God had created the best of all possible worlds; but man, through Adam's fall from grace, had failed to live up to its possibilities. Despite St Augustine's repeated invocation of man's freedom, the total effect of his outlook was a deep-seated pessimism about fallen humanity that had little use for the contrivances of this world. Death, ignorance, and desire were man's condition, which he could overcome only with God's grace. It was hardly a message of inspiration; and the main reaction to Augustine in later centuries was to be a renewed turning towards the world and the elevation of the natural order.

Such a change, however, did not occur until the late 11th century. Meanwhile, in a world where the monasteries largely replaced the towns as surviving pockets of stability and learning, St Augustine's emphases were the dominant ones, and his own teachings were of paramount importance. From the end of the 6th century, withdrawal from the world into monastic life went together with study. Their association owed much to Cassiodorus (*c.* 477–*c.* 570), who, after withdrawing from Theodoric's court, founded a monastery at Vivarium in Calabria with this intent in about 540. The second book of his *Institutiones* became a handbook of monastic learning; modelled on St Augustine's *De doctrina christiana*, it set out the main fields of knowledge in which a monk should be proficient in order to be able to understand scripture.

Boethius

St Augustine gave a direction to the intellectual life of the ensuing centuries; Boethius (*c.* 480–510) provided much of the propaedeutics that helped to form it. Philosophically his greatest contribution was the translation of, and commentary on, Aristotle's logic, which was part of his unrealized aim to do the same for all the works of Plato and Aristotle. Educationally, he defined for the Middle Ages the classification of natural knowledge into the seven liberal arts. Imaginatively, he produced *De consolatione philosophiae*, one of the most widely read allegories of the Middle Ages. He also wrote treatises on music, arithmetic, and geometry, besides his influential work on the Trinity. Boethius's writings were imbued with his absorption in philosophy: even in *De consolatione* it is Philosophy who speaks. Nevertheless, his outlook was in many ways complementary to St Augustine's. Like the latter, he believed that the highest knowledge was the most purely intellectual; as a purely intellectual intuition, its object was God. Man had an innate knowledge of God as the highest good, by which he was able to judge all that is imperfect.[14] Man's own soul no longer had the capacity for direct "intellectible" knowledge, of which God was the object, but only of intelligible knowledge, of which the object was reason. Boethius regarded the soul as an independent spiritual being, going so far as to talk of its pre-existence[15]; like St Augustine, he believe that the more man followed God, the freer was his will; the more dependent it was on the senses, the more it was enslaved.

Perhaps Boethius's greatest contribution to Christian thought was his application of his philosophical vocabulary to theological questions in his five short theological treatises (*opuscula sacra*). Here, especially in the *De trinitate* and *De hebdomadibus*, Boethius moved beyond the role of commentator to independent speculation. He took over St Augustine's definitions of God as absolutely simple being and of the Trinity as three persons subsisting in a single substance; but, unlike St Augustine, he went on to develop them philosophically. God as absolute being was also being in itself (*ipsum esse*), the condition of being in everything else. According to Boethius all other being, as dependent upon absolute being, is composite: it consists of its essence, which gives it identity, together with the particular attributes that define it as individual being. Accordingly, all created being consists of substance (*id quod est*) and the form by which it is what it is (*quo est*). Together they constitute the individual thing as it exists in time and space. Logically and ontologically, however, they remain distinct, as in the case of the soul and the body, through whose conjunction a man is a man. The forms that constitute the natures of all created things derive from their archetypes, or divine ideas, in God. In that sense, all created beings can be traced to God's absolute being, in which they participate but do not share.

Boethius's ideas here, and on the elements of being, were to be of lasting importance from the 12th century onwards. Together with his logical and educational writings, they make him one of the founders of mediaeval Christian philosophy. Where St Augustine stressed the theological and dogmatic elements, Boethius was almost exclusively concerned with their philosophical facets, but to a higher end than the mere acquisition of knowledge. Thus in his writings on the seven liberal arts he divided knowledge into four practical subjects (arithmetic, astronomy, geometry, and music) and three expository disciplines (grammar, rhetoric, and logic). He called the first group the *quadrivium*, the fourfold path to knowledge, and the second the *trivium*, the threefold path.[16] These became the basic categories of mediaeval education and continued to be employed even when the content of the two groupings became largely transformed in the 13th century.

The predominantly monastic culture of the early Middle Ages accepted this view of knowledge without on the whole attempting to extend it. The age of Isidore of Seville, Bede, Alcuin, and the Carolingian writers generally, was one of compilations and manuals. Profane knowledge, contained in the seven liberal arts, was the stepping-stone to the comprehension of Scripture. The educational reforms introduced into Charlemagne's empire by Alcuin gave institutional expression to that belief. The subjects of the *quadrivium* and the *trivium* formed the syllabus that came to be taught in all monastic and cathedral schools. They were to serve the higher end of theological knowledge. From this developed the mediaeval conception of the seven liberal arts as the handmaids of theology, which (although modified) was not overthrown for

400 years. Although, on the one hand, this gave effect to Augustine's programme of *De doctrina christiana*, on the other hand it received its impetus from the circumstances of the time. Culturally, the period from *c.* 600 to *c.* 1000 was the age of the monks. It reached its apogee in the reign of Charlemagne (768–814)—in the so-called Carolingian Renaissance—which, although short-lived, gave a permanent imprint to subsequent mediaeval intellectual development. That it should have occurred in the Frankish lands north of the Alps, where its main effects continued to be felt, was not entirely adventitious. There was greater continuity with Roman life and institutions in Italy: towns, law, and education all in some degree survived through these centuries and provided a distinctive urban and lay culture from the 11th century onwards: law and the classical Roman stress upon grammar and rhetoric as the main elements of education, which were taught in urban as opposed to cathedral schools. The latter displaced the monasteries as the centres of learning.

In north-western Europe, however, continuity with Roman times was lacking. The barbarian peoples who settled there and took over political and military authority were more easily assimilated to the one surviving institution—the Church; to it belonged such organization, literacy, and culture as existed. They were transmitted through evangelization, itself the work of monks such as Augustine of Canterbury, Wilfrid, and Boniface. Their activities largely formed the culture that emerged. To begin with, it was based upon the Benedictine monasteries from which the missionaries came. This meant that it was at once Latin and liturgical; and this in turn determined the curriculum that an understanding of both demanded: instruction in reading, writing, grammar, calligraphy, chronology, knowledge of the calendar, and Christian doctrine. At the same time the spread of Christianity imposed the need for uniformity in religious usage and observance. Hence the gradual substitution of public for private penances to be seen in the elaborate code of penalties that were prescribed for every sin, drawn up by Theodore of Canterbury and Egbert of York in the 8th century and adopted both in Anglo-Saxon England and on the Continent. The predominance of the monasteries as the foci of religion and learning meant a corresponding transformation of values. The monasteries were viable simply because they were adapted to the conditions of the time. Physically they were self-contained estates, which demanded work and individual poverty as well as prayer, meditation, and study. Their material conditions did not differ essentially from those of the populace who also lived by their labour from the land; while socially, the strength of Benedictine monachism was that it was fitted to the limitations of the average man, not the saint. The stress upon stability and obedience to the abbot gave the monasteries discipline and cohesion and sanctified the obligation to a life of work and service for God rather than for worldly success.

These were the values that now formed the dominant ethos. How successful they were can be seen in the succession of rulers—beginning with Oswald and Oswy in Northumbria and culminating in the Carolingians and Alfred and his successors in England—who accepted monastic ideals. Indeed, in one sense the monastic conception of authority was a permanent legacy to the notion of a Christian society, enshrined above all in the image of Charlemagne as the Christian emperor. It is with him that there clearly emerges the belief that a ruler was God's representative on earth. In one sense, Charlemagne's reign can be seen as its conscious application: in his massacres of the Saxons, sanctified by their forcible conversion to Christianity; in his appointment of bishops as well as counts in equal numbers to represent his authority in the localities as legates (*missi*); in his coronation as emperor by the pope, which (by design or not) gave him the aura of a Christian emperor; and above all in his own court at Aachen, which, with its palace school presided over by Alcuin, was the centre of the so-called renaissance in learning.

Here perhaps more than anywhere else we can see the fusing of the Germanic and the Christian, through the imposition of monastic values. It came from the alliance of king and Church. The close interdependence of the two is one of the features of the period until the emancipation of the Church in the 11th century, when it was strong enough to demand its own corporate independence. By then, however, the notion of a Christian society embracing all its members, lay and religious, had become firmly established. It received literary expression in the *chansons de geste*, which (although the work of the 12th and 13th centuries) translated the Germanic conception of heroism and personal loyalty into a Christian idiom of which Charlemagne was the archetype. During the reign of Charlemagne and his immediate successors it was the king who legislated for the Church, both educationally and liturgically. Through him its teachings and practices were put on a permanent footing. Alcuin encouraged Charlemagne in this theocratic role. Repeatedly he referred to Charlemagne as a second David, the chosen leader of his people, and the guardian of the Church and of Christian truth. This conception was expressed in the Carolingian coronation rite, which became that of the Anglo-Saxon kings and later of the German emperors. Although

Charlemagne, in spite of his interest in learning, remained illiterate, his grandson Charles the Bald in the middle of the 9th century actively raised theological questions for scholars to dispute, and in England a little later Alfred of Wessex was translating Boethius's *De consolatione* and Gregory the Great's *Cura pastoralis*.

Charlemagne's educational reforms were essentially an extension of monastic practices, above all at the school of York from which Alcuin had gone to Charles's court at Aachen. As established by Alcuin's master Egbert, himself the pupil of Bede, the curriculum at York covered grammar, rhetoric, law, poetry, astronomy, natural history, and music, all conceived as aids to the scriptural study in which they culminated. Little of classical science or cosmogony was then known; and the other subjects were treated as aids either, like rhetoric, to the figures of speech in the Bible or, like mathematics, to the computation of the calendar. This was *De doctrina christiana* in practice, now that there was no longer an independent lay civilization, not least in the preservation of those classical elements that were essential to Christian understanding. Alcuin's reforms under Charlemagne institutionalized this order of learning throughout the Carolingian Empire. In a series of capitularies beginning in 787 it was decreed that there should be schools in every monastery and cathedral for the purpose of educating those who were to enter the Church or monastic life. With this went a particular emphasis upon the writing of correct Latin, which for Alcuin was the foundation of reason and authority—the language at once of the Vulgate and of the Fathers. For this he chose the *Ars minor* of Donatus, suitably adapted to the needs of non-Latin speakers. Together with it went an emphasis upon computation, arithmetic, and religious instruction. Alcuin not only wrote handbooks to aid their teaching, and dialogues on rhetoric and dialectic, but also demanded the clear copying of books upon which the success of his reforms depended. The introduction of the new minuscule into calligraphy was among the lasting achievements of his educational reforms.

Their success lay in establishing a framework of elementary education, which now became the responsibility of the Church, above all in the monasteries. Despite the collapse of the Carolingian Empire in the late 9th century and the widespread disruption caused by the invasions of the Northmen, learning was preserved in communities such as Fulda (in Hesse), Corbie (near Amiens), Reichenau (on Lake Constance), and St Gall (in Switzerland). Alcuin had a worthy successor in Raban Maur (d. 836), who did for Germany what Alcuin had done for Charlemagne's lands. At the same time, at a higher level there was something like a revival of interest in classical letters among Charlemagne's circle at Aachen (including Peter of Pisa, Paul the Deacon, Theodulph of Orleans, and St Agobard of Lyon), which also carried into the next generation.

John Scotus Erigena

The effect was felt upon Christian thought as well. Although little of it was original, there was renewed interest in theological questions such as predestination and the soul. Among those involved was the Irish scholar John Scotus Erigena (*c.* 810–77), the outstanding thinker of the epoch, who was to be of great influence in the 12th century. Much of his novelty and importance derives from his knowledge of Greek and his attempt to apply the ideas of the Greek neo-Platonist tradition. Where his contemporaries sought to interpret their faith through the teachings of St Augustine, John Scotus embarked upon the construction of a new system, largely out of elements foreign to the West. These derived from the near-mystical speculation of the pseudo-Dionysius—mistaken for Dionysius the Areopagite, St Paul's disciple, but in reality belonging to the later 5th century—and from his commentator, Maximus the Confessor (*c.* 580–662).

As later developed (as we shall see) by Eckhart and the Rhineland mystics, John Scotus's system can be regarded as the third main stream making up the mediaeval outlook in addition to Augustinianism and Aristotelianism. Central to it was what is called negative theology: the problem of how to describe God when he is by definition ineffable. Since God cannot be known directly either to reason or to the senses, all our terms for him are drawn from his creatures. When we say that he is good or wise or merciful, we are therefore talking not about God but about what we—as participants in his goodness or wisdom or mercy—understand by these words. To overcome this limitation, we have to go beyond such expressions and, having said that God is good or wise or merciful, negate the terms and deny that as they stand they can be applied to God. We are then able to reconcile this second stage of negative theology with the first affirmative stage in a third term: of hyper-goodness or hyper-wisdom or hyper-mercy. By doing so we recognize God's ineffability while not totally denying ourselves any glimpse of what it means. The pseudo-Dionysius justified applying any description to God by referring to the use of such words as goodness, wisdom, mercy, and so on in the Bible. But he also showed himself in a different tradition from St Augustine by making "goodness" rather than "being" the supreme term for God. Moreover, as part of the same neo-Platonic tradition, the pseudo-Dionysius followed Proclus in seeing evil not as a corruption or negation of being, but as non-being. God therefore was not its cause. All being emanated from his goodness, although from the point of view of creation it was most appropriate to regard him as being; and all that is not God exists through participation in his being. It does so through the divine ideas that derive from his own being. Accordingly the pseudo-Dionysius tended towards the neo-Platonist distinction between the One and the manifold to describe the relation between God and his creatures. As the One, God was absolutely simple and unknowable; hence, so far as his own nature was concerned, the highest wisdom was ignorance. Accordingly, the pseudo-Dionysius introduced the antinomy between God as One, of whom nothing could be said beyond affirming his ineffability above all affirmation and negation, and as creator, who can be negatively described by reference to what he has created. In the process, the Trinity as well as the supernatural virtues tended to be passed over.

Much of this was taken over by John Scotus, especially the view of creation as God's realization of himself through his word. Every creature seeks its essence in its return to God.[17] What John Scotus added was the rational interpretation of such an outlook. He introduced four divisions into being, or "nature," as he called it: two divine and two created. All were derived from God and through participation in his being. He then postulated three levels of existence: purely spiritual beings (angels), spiritual and corporeal beings (man), and finally corporeal beings (other forms of animal life). Man therefore stood between the spiritual and the material. Each of these different levels of existence was the work of God and reflected God's own illumination. God himself, however, stood above them, a being whose own being was above being. In taking over this formula from the pseudo-Dionysius, John Scotus was in fact avoiding the pantheism of which he was so often accused and which, among some of the so-called school of Chartres and Amaury of Bène, he inspired. For if God's nature is to be a being above other beings, to say that he participates in every other being is not to merge divine and created being: it is rather a hierarchical notion of God as the transmitter of his creatures' being. Indeed, man through Adam's sin had become separated from his original spiritual nature as an idea in God. The multiplicity of the material world was the direct consequence of man's sin; it destroyed the intelligible form in which God originally conceived all being. Nevertheless all being still retained its divine imprint, especially man, who was created in God's image. Man's soul remains always turned towards God; and on death it returns to him. This applied to all men, good and evil. There was, therefore, no Hell for John Scotus: evil would disappear with the ending of the material world at the Last Judgment; the damned would suffer the punishment of eternal ignorance.

The complexity and novelty of John Scotus's thought made it a dangerous instrument for the unwary. Its main effect was to introduce a pantheistic tendency into subsequent mediaeval thought with its emphasis upon creation as a theophany. Although, in *De praedestinatione*, he gave a more orthodox interpretation of Hell, nevertheless the dominant effect of this thought was to make beatitude an intellectual process. As with the Greek Fathers, the relation between God and man was mediated through the image of God in the soul. Man's return to God reunited him with his original form or idea in God's intellect. Accordingly, although John Scotus stressed the importance of grace in bringing man to God, the soul, as a spiritual nature, naturally turned towards him. The sense of participation of the divine in the created, central to all Christian thinking, can blur (as it later did with Amaury of Bène) the distinction between the divine and the created. The divine imprint upon all created things could make the direct awareness of God individual rather than sacramental. Even the German mystic Meister Eckhart (1260–1327), in taking a similar path, did not entirely escape these consequences.

The influences of St Augustine, Boethius, and John Scotus were all, in their different ways, profound. Although that of St Augustine was by far the most important, it was reinforced rather than challenged by those of the other two. Over and above Boethius's transmission of Aristotle's logic and the impulse given by John Scotus to pantheism, they also shared with St Augustine a neo-Platonist conception of reality. Truth lay with the idea, which was to be found within the soul; all intelligibles derived from God. The contrast between God and his creatures was between absolute simplicity and multiplicity, eternity and time. Add to this the neo-Platonic notion of illumination and the hierarchical nature of creation, and the main elements of a Christian philosophy were present. To say this is not to minimize the great differences and contradictions between these and subsequent mediaeval thinkers. It is rather to stress that mediaeval thought, despite its dependence upon Aristotle, rested even more firmly upon certain fundamental tenets drawn from neo-Platonism. Without them a Christian philosophy, in the sense of combining faith and reason, would have been impossible. Intelligibility, unity, and participation, in addition to hierarchy, were the essential elements in any outlook that sought to relate the divine to the created. In some degree they remained common to most mediaeval thinking until the 14th century.

The Rise of the Schools and Universities

The 11th century saw the beginning of the transformation of mediaeval society from a series of makeshifts to a comparatively stable and coherent social order. The ending of the period of invasions and migrations made possible the development of a more cohesive life at every level. The new cultural diversity that resulted was amply expressed in the outlook of the period. We may discern two main phases in its growth, the first extending over most of the 11th and 12th centuries, and the second for the greater part of the 13th century. Together they marked the shift from knowledge mediated by revealed truth, which characterized the earlier period, to revealed truth mediated by reason and natural experience. It was a change from the predominantly monastic attitude of understanding as a meditation upon faith to the new standpoint of the professional thinker and teacher in the schools and universities and courts for whom knowledge existed in its own right. It had, no less than before, to conform with canonical truth, but there were diverse ways of reaching it and testing it.

The change was social and institutional no less than intellectual. In general it rested upon the re-emergence of towns as the foci of life, and their displacement of the monasteries as the centres of learning; it rested, specifically, upon the rise of cathedral schools north of the Alps and the urban schools in Italy. That in turn institutionalized the divergence between these regions, itself an important factor in the intellectual history of the period. The ecclesiastical ambiance of the northern cathedral schools kept them directly under the control of the Church and theologically orientated: logical and speculative thought became their hallmark, as it did of the northern universities, above all Paris and Oxford. The Italian schools and, later, universities such as Bologna and Padua were predominantly practical and non-theological in their pursuits; law and rhetoric, and in the south medicine, were the main subjects. Moreover, they were not controlled by the ecclesiastical authorities (although there was some degree of supervision of the Italian universities), and their students enjoyed the same clerical status as those in universities of north-western Europe.

The growth of the schools into universities from the middle of the 12th century onwards represented the professionalization of knowledge. This, above all, differentiates the intellectual life of the period from that of earlier centuries. The expansion of society and the emergence of new institutions and occupations led to the demand for practical knowledge and for training in a profession, especially the law and its ancillaries—

which were needed in Church and temporal affairs alike—teaching, medicine, and commerce. Literacy became increasingly a means of livelihood and a condition of advancement. Whereas the Carolingians had treated learning as the adjunct of a religious life, by the 13th century it was essentially of the world. It was in the hands of a trained body of teachers who had to profess their subject proficiently and independently of their knowledge of Scripture or their love of God. Thus, within the very domain of the Church, there grew up a body of non-theological knowledge directed for the most part by non-theologians to non-theological ends. Although this became apparent only with the appearance of the universities, it was already inherent in the renewal of letters and speculative thought which began in the 11th century and constituted the renaissance of the 12th century. It was enshrined in the division between the profane knowledge of the seven liberal arts and the higher understanding of scripture for which they were a preparation. The conflicts between the demands of the sacred and the profane started early, in the 11th century, and never really ceased throughout the Middle Ages.

The emergence of the professional teacher and a non-theological education was accompanied by far-reaching changes in the content of logic, natural philosophy, and metaphysics. The change was due principally to the translation of the main corpus of Aristotle's works, together with a large body of Greek and Arabian science and philosophy. Beginning in the first third of the 12th century, with the main centres in Spain, Sicily, and Constantinople, the translations confronted Christian thinkers of the West with a new realm of natural knowledge, which they spent the greater part of the 13th century trying to assimilate. Ultimately, it was their failure to harmonize this body of new knowledge with the received truth that effectively marked the end of the classical age of scholasticism.

The reasons for that failure were far from exclusively intellectual. They arose on the one hand from the institutional demands that Christian thinkers had to meet in upholding an orthodoxy, and on the other from their own experience. Christian thought, however abstract or dogmatic its concepts, also articulated men's response to their lives and circumstances. As these changed, so did their interests and preoccupations, not only in the ways we have indicated but also in how men evaluated their condition. The translation of Aristotle, in spite of its importance, was but one element making for a change of emphasis. The structure of society, both temporal and spiritual, changed profoundly between 1000 and 1250.

From the 11th century onwards there was a progressive coming to terms with the world that contrasts strongly with St Augustine's attitude.

It affected the Church no less than the temporal order, and was ultimately responsible for polarizing the dualism between the spiritual and the temporal inherent in the Augustinian and monastic tradition. In the 11th century it was directed towards freeing the Church from lay thrall and regulating it according to spiritual criteria. This reforming movement, which culminated under Pope Gregory VII (1073–85), revolutionized the political structure of Western Christendom; it established the independent corporate power of the Church, which continued to grow until the 13th century. But its very success turned the contrast between the spiritual and the temporal upon the Church. Whereas the great political and spiritual issues of the 11th and 12th centuries were fought out in terms of the rival claims of popes and emperors, by the 13th century they were increasingly concerned with the contradictions between ecclesiastical practice and Christian precept: between priestly privilege and wealth and the evangelical poverty in which Christ and the apostles had lived; between the sophistication of learning and apostolic simplicity; between worldliness and *contemptus mundi*. Paradoxically, by the end of the 13th century the Church had become the arena for many of the tensions that in preceding centuries had been between a religious and a secular ethic within society at large. The change helped to give rise to the new themes that were to dominate the outlook of the later Middle Ages.

As far as the 11th and 12th centuries were concerned, the predominant tendencies were away from the monastic traditions of withdrawal towards the rediscovery of the world of nature and the powers of reason. If that distinguished the intellectual life of these centuries qualitatively from the 9th and 10th centuries, there were also quantitative differences. The new developments were not confined to isolated monasteries but extended over most of western Europe, beginning in northern Italy and France and subsequently spreading to England, Germany, southern Italy and Sicily, and northern Spain. Nevertheless the debt to the Carolingian reformers should not be minimized; their work provided the foundation for what was to come. They had established the curriculum that, with all its modifications, was to be followed for over three centuries. Through the cathedral schools and especially the monasteries they had put education upon an institutional footing which became the basis of its expansion in the 11th and 12th centuries. Finally, in reforming calligraphy and the copying of books they transmitted the means of learning and culture.

Not surprisingly, the monastic schools north of the Alps, such as those at Reichenau, Fulda, and Tours, in maintaining continuity with the earlier age, formed the starting-point of the subsequent phase. In the

11th century the monks were in the forefront, and the interconnection between spiritual, political, and intellectual issues was very close. As we have mentioned, the 11th century was the first great age of religious reform, both monastic—with the abbey of Cluny as its spearhead—and more directly political, in gaining emancipation from lay control (a struggle that led in 1075 to 50 years of civil war in Germany). Many of the leading figures in intellectual life were also reformers, notably Peter Damian (1007–72), Manegold of Lautenbach (d. 1103), and Lanfranc of Canterbury (1010–89). The more extreme their conception of the supremacy of spiritual power—as in the case of Damian and Manegold— the more marked their tendency to be hostile to reason. This may have been accentuated by their own training in the liberal arts, especially in the urban schools of Lombardy, before they took up the monastic life and renounced the profane world. But it was precisely through their grounding in rhetoric and dialectic, which remained an established part of the curriculum in the monastic and cathedral schools as well as the urban schools, that the reformers conducted their arguments. Damian, in particular, as a former teacher of rhetoric, was not only one of the finest stylists but also a religious poet of a very high order.

The issue that initiated the new phase of intellectual inquiry was the place of dialectic, or logical discussion, in matters of faith.[18] In one sense this, too, was a continuation of the disputes that went back to the mid-9th century—disputes over predestination and the soul among Gottschalk, John Scotus, and Ratramnus of Corbie. At the end of the 10th century, discussion arose over the nature of Boethius's *De consolatione*. The question whether it was Christian or Platonist directly raised that of the relation of faith to reason. It developed during the 11th century into opposition between the supporters of dialectic and the anti-dialecticians. This was a division also between authority and philosophy. Out of their clash each became more firmly established. On the one hand, ecclesiastical intervention in intellectual matters became the main regulator when the argument went too far. On the other hand, dialectic, based upon Aristotle's logic, had come to stay, and as applied by Lanfranc and above all by Anselm, it was treated as complementary to faith. The search for complementarity governed the activities of the majority of Christian thinkers for the next two centuries. Characteristically, in the earlier disputes, before that position was reached, the claims made by both sides were unprecedentedly far-reaching. They culminated in the controversy over the eucharist from the 1050s to the 1080s. Berengarius, of the ancient school of St Martin of Tours, was the main protagonist of a dialectical treatment of the sacrament. Like the new professional teachers who had appeared during the century, of whom Anselm of Besate (*c.* 1050) is the prototype, he sought to apply Aristotelian logic to matters of faith. At the time, knowledge of Aristotle's logical writings was confined to the *Categories* and *De interpretatione* in Boethius's translations, together with his commentaries and Porphyry's introduction to the *Categories*, the *Isogogue*.

Berengarius bears witness to their new intense study. Although employing Aristotle's terms in an imprecise way, he attempted to define the eucharist through its categories as a substance, thereby reaching the conclusion that in retaining the accidents, or appearances, of bread and wine after consecration, it must continue to remain bread and wine. In one sense Berengarius was a pioneer in the application of dialectic to matters of doctrine. He differed not only in his confidence in reason—as the sign of God's image in man—to explain what belongs to God's revelation, but also in the then inchoate state of much of the doctrine. It is a paradox that the nature of the eucharist came to be defined only as the result of Berengarius's incursion. That took place in 1059 and again in 1079 at Roman synods; on each occasion Berengarius's own conclusions were censured but he remained unmolested and continued to teach. Moreover he was able to quote in his own defence both St Augustine and John Scotus, whose writings were later to be condemned at the Synod of Sens in 1210.

This fluidity is characteristic of what was a formative period. It went with extremes on both sides. Cardinal Humbert, the most uncompromising of all the reformers in his fight against simony, had helped to bring about Berengarius's condemnation in 1059. Damian, in reply to Berengarius's claims for reason, enunciated an extreme doctrine of divine omnipotence by which God could do anything: human reason was powerless to understand the divine mysteries. Humility, not confidence in syllogisms, should be man's attitude to faith. Manegold, writing under the impact of the eucharistic controversy, denounced the intrusion of philosophy into theology. He saw Boethius's *De consolatione*, with its Platonism, as the source of the widespread resistance to right order.

It was left to Lanfranc to attempt to harmonize faith and dialectic. He did so as the main opponent of Berengarius, whom he criticized not for employing reason in matters of faith but for taking it beyond its limits. Lanfranc, another product of Lombardy, was a Benedictine and a canon legist rather than a theologian. As a member and then abbot of the new Norman monastery at Bec, he recognized the need to safeguard the sovereignty of faith; but, trained in dialectic and law, he also recognized its value in helping to elucidate the articles of faith and to strengthen their authority. This conviction caused him to engage directly against Berengarius for bringing reason into disrepute. Although Lanfranc himself achieved little that was lasting, he inspired his pupil St Anselm (1033–1109) to do so.

St Anselm

St Anselm became a monk at Bec in 1060, just after Berengarius's first condemnation, in which Lanfranc had been involved. He therefore came at a time when his master was preoccupied in reconciling the use of dialectic with faith. It was along this path that he directed his own intellectual efforts; to that extent he followed Lanfranc. But the developments to which they led took St Anselm into a realm of pure speculation far beyond the previous landmarks. When St Anselm sent him his early treatise on the Trinity, Lanfranc seems to have questioned its exclusively intellectual approach without reference to authority. But this was not to revive Berengarius's error. Not only was St Anselm's whole outlook, as we shall mention shortly, in the line of St Augustine; he wrote as a monk for his pupils and *confrères*. His works arose from his discourses and teaching in the abbey: the problems he sought to resolve were those put to him by his companions. They were an extension of the cult of friendship that he so assiduously practised. He wrote in the form of monographs designed to answer a particular question. In keeping with the tradition of St Benedict, his purpose was to gain conviction through assent rather than through assertion of authority or victory in disputation. For that reason, and because of the supremely individual quality of his work, Anselm stands apart from the main currents of the age, profoundly important though his thinking was.

In its comprehensiveness, his thinking extended to every aspect of faith, including God, the Trinity, the Incarnation, and original sin. In its distinctiveness it renewed speculative thought in the West, which had lapsed, except for John Scotus, since St Augustine and Boethius. That is to be seen above all in St Anselm's proofs for the existence of God. He developed them in two works, the *Monologium* and the *Proslogion*.[19] They were an extension of St Augustine's arguments for evidence of God. In the *Monologium*, St Anselm began with the differing degrees of goodness and perfection in things. The fact that we can recognize one thing as better or worse than another presupposes the existence of an absolute good by which we can judge what is more or less perfect. Everything therefore must participate in this absolute goodness from which its limitations are measured. Unlike all that is relative, the absolute must be good in itself. This is what we call God, the sovereign good and the source of all other goodness. The same reasoning was applied to degrees of being and absolute being. From three such proofs for God's existence in the *Monologium*, St Anselm finally evolved the central one in the *Proslogion*: the idea of a being than which none greater can be envisaged. Such a being was by definition God, recognized by even the fool of the Psalm (XIV: 1) when he said "There is no God"; for by those words he was affirming the very truth that he denied—the existence of a being than whom no greater can be conceived. He therefore had the notion of God in his mind, although he rejected it. To exist in the mind, it must also exist outside it, because otherwise something greater than that which the mind conceives would exist outside it—which is contradictory. Whatever may be brought against the argument, its pedigree is clear: it rests upon the identification of the idea with truth, and hence with being. Since, moreover (as St Anselm showed in his reply to the monk Guanilo), it concerned faith, its truth was independent of natural experience. To know God in the mind was not the same as to know the Isles of the Blessed, lost in the ocean, by having an idea of them. The idea of God alone carried with it the necessity of his existence.[20]

St Anselm's ontological proof, as it has come to be known, displayed the limits to which a purely dialectical discussion of revealed truth could go. It is the summation of the neo-Platonic Augustinian identification of being with the intelligible within the mind. As such its influence was not confined to the Middle Ages. Although his proof was taken up by only a few scholastics, notably St Bonaventure, St Anselm pointed the direction that mediaeval Christian thought was to follow: in his own words in the *Proslogion*, "I do not seek to understand in order to believe, but I believe in order that I may understand."[21] This has often been regarded as the motto of scholasticism; and if we allow for the latitude with which "understanding" came to be interpreted through extension of the area of natural experience and speculation, it may be accepted. In Anselm's case, understanding still meant logical discussion and elucidation of revealed truth. But the search for truth lay in comprehending faith rather than existence. As he expressed it in *De veritate*, God is the only truth of all that is true.[22]

Like St Augustine, St Anselm also treated the soul as made in the image of God, with the will as the first of its faculties.[23] Because man had free choice, which St Anselm defined as reason guiding the will, man had sinned. With Adam's sin, he had lost the power of acting justly. Accordingly, original sin meant the absence of original righteousness and of the liberty to remain whole that had accompanied man's initial state. It was as if man had been plunged into darkness and could no longer follow rectitude; he still had freedom of choice, but without the inclination to choose what is right, which is the very essence of liberty. Hence St Anselm, although following St Augustine's distinction, nevertheless came to a more favourable interpretation of man's fallen estate. Man could regain his liberty only through grace, which returns to man the power to choose freely what is right; but he is still able to choose. There is not the same, almost Manichean, dichotomy between the flesh and the spirit that so dominated St Augustine's moral theology. The emphasis was less on man's impaired powers than on the loss of the righteousness that had given them liberty.

Anselm, for all his desire to say nothing that had not already been said by the Fathers, above all St Augustine,[24] marks a new point of departure in mediaeval thought. His proofs for God's existence and his treatises on the Incarnation, the Trinity, truth, and the will in its different facets, were the beginning of speculative theology. The attempt to grapple with revelation in all its aspects showed a profound confidence in the power of reason when informed by faith. In that sense, St Anselm effected the first real synthesis between them, showing that dialectic, far from undermining the tenets of belief, could bring understanding. Only a minority was capable of maintaining this equilibrium between faith and reason: St Anselm was the first, even though he relied upon logic, rather than metaphysics, to demonstrate that it could be achieved.

St Anselm's ideas had little impact. He was writing for his monastic circle at a time when all forms of intellectual and artistic life were increasingly flourishing outside the monasteries. The close connection between understanding and believing that he cultivated was not so apparent in the world of the professional teacher, the full-time student, or the princely courts and chanceries to which learning was increasingly directed.

The 12th-century Renaissance

To make too sharp a division between the 11th and 12th centuries would be artificial. In one sense the term "renaissance," usually applied to the 12th century, would be as apposite to the 11th, if it is understood in a literary sense of reviving classical models. The poetry of Hildebert of

Le Mans at the end of the 11th century still shows the classical influence that came through the Carolingian humanists. In Italy, literary culture was the direct heir to the classical tradition. The library of the great Benedictine abbey of Monte Cassino contained a rich collection of works by classical authors, including Cicero, Virgil, Ovid, Terence, Seneca, Juvencus, and Sedulius. Around its abbot, Desiderius (1058–87), gathered a group of notable men, including the poet Alphanus, Alberich (compiler of the *Dictamen*, the first manual for letter-writing), and Constantine the African (responsible for translating important medical treatises by Galen and Hippocrates). In Germany, however, learning hardly moved out of its monastic milieux until the 12th century, being largely dependent on contact with France and Italy.

At the same time, however, dialectic, as we have seen, was emerging to challenge increasingly the older stress on grammar and rhetoric for the cultivation of style. It did so not only in theological matters but also in law. During the second half of the 11th century, Bologna became the centre for the study of civil law, as it was soon to be also of canon law. Each received a new impetus from the struggle between pope and emperor in the late 11th century. With Salerno already the centre for medicine, the pattern of intellectual development had begun to emerge by the end of the 11th century. Literary values were being subordinated to the demands of theology, law, and medicine; grammar and rhetoric were being displaced by, and adapted to, dialectic. Although the cultivation of style still continued in the so-called school of Chartres until beyond the middle of the 12th century, its decline had begun long before.

The changes that accompanied the rise of dialectic were far more than those of curriculum or even milieu, important as these were. If the term "renaissance," as applied to the 12th century, means anything, it denotes a widening of the range of experience, knowledge, and expression. Much of this was due to sheer physical events, such as the renewed contact with the richer civilization of the Moslem world and Byzantium and the intellectual rediscoveries that it brought. Much of it was economic and social—such as the coming into being of courts and chanceries that offered not only professional but also cultural employment, such as those of Guilhem of Poitou, ninth duke of Aquitaine (1071–1127), or of his grand-daughter Eleanor and her daughter Marie of Champagne in the 12th century. Much of it belonged to the experience of the age: chivalry, wars, crusades, and the impact of personalities such as St Bernard, Abelard, and Frederick Barbarossa. The total effect was a new awareness of the natural order: both man and nature became studied for themselves.

The themes of philosophy and art were drawn from human experience, whether through reason or the senses. The ambiance of the schools and the court was no longer that of the cloister. Reason, love, war, and wine had a human as well as a divine connotation. It is their progressive desacralization, their treatment in profane terms, that distinguishes so much of the outlook of the 12th century. The troubadour and the goliard, the bestiary and the epic, are as much part of it as the Platonism of Chartres, or the theological systematization and exegesis of the cathedral schools of Laon and Paris, or the legal codification of Bologna. They coexist and often conflict with the religious demands of both orthodoxy and the older monastic tradition of which St Bernard (1090–1153) was the outstanding upholder in the first part of the 12th century. Although there was often a resonance between the cult of love in the lyrics of the troubadours and minnesingers and the mystical love imagery of St Bernard or Hildegard of Bingen, or the sacrament of the eucharist and the grail, or the veneration of the Virgin and the idealization of woman, it should not be pressed too far. The similarity is one of form and perhaps impulse rather than of content. The restless interest in exploring natural experience so characteristic of the 12th century, despite the borrowings of religious imagery, is of a different order from mystical and sacramental elevation above nature. There is a lack of a defined rapport between them just because one could not be readily assimilated to the other.

Intellectually and artistically, the first two thirds of the 12th century were perhaps the freest period of the Middle Ages. Reason and the senses found a new awareness without yet having to conform too closely to orthodoxy or stereotypes. Interest in the natural world was more poetic than scientific. The sense of rediscovery created a maximum of diversity with a minimum of uniformity.

Abelard

As far as Christian thought was concerned, the change is almost personi-fied in Peter Abelard (1079–1142). Although he appears within a decade of St Anselm's death, he represents another world—the world of the schools and the professional master. Not an original thinker of St Anselm's cast, Abelard was the supreme dialectician and teacher. Little that he wrote was of enduring philosophical or doctrinal influence, but he gave an impetus to Christian thinking probably unequalled until the time of Ockham. The ways in which he did so were diverse. His first notable achievement was over the problem of universals.

They were another legacy of Aristotle's *Categories* and the logical commentaries of Boethius and Porphyry. Like the previous eucharistic controversy, too, the disputes that they engendered between the nominalists and realists were no more than a phase, which had largely passed by the 1120s. This time, though, they did not impinge upon faith. Their importance is that, through Abelard's involvement, they gave a new vogue to dialectic, above all at Paris. The great following that he attracted there, as everywhere, led to the opening of schools around the mount of St Geneviève. Although for a time in the middle of the century they vanished, by the end of it the schools on the Left Bank of the Seine were to dialectic what Bologna was to law.

The problem of universals centred on the relation of genera and species to individuals. What was the status of terms such as "humanity" and "whiteness," and where were they to be found? With remorseless logic Abelard destroyed the position of both the realists (who posited the independent existence of genera and species) and the nominalists (who denied that they were more than mere words whose only physical attribute was as sounds—*flatus vocis*). His own solution was the one given by Boethius: that the mind gained its knowledge of universals through abstracting them from the individuals encountered in the senses. Hence the species man did not exist independently outside the mind, as the realists maintained; but neither did it stand for nothing, as the nominalists held. It inhered in individual things (*in re*), but could be known whole and independently only in the mind. Abelard largely resolved the problem for the rest of the Middle Ages; it never recurred in the form in which he disputed it with his former master, William of Champeaux (*c.* 1070–1121). William's defeat at the hands of his pupil led him to retire to the abbey school of St Victor, Paris; he remains, however, important in the history of biblical exegesis.

The magnetism of Abelard's personality gave a new prominence to dialectic and to the Left Bank at Paris, where he had taught before crowded audiences, as one of its main centres. But his activities extended far beyond the problem of universals. He helped to popularize the dialectical method of disputation, which became characteristic of scholasticism, by his work entitled *Sic et non*—a compilation of 158 conflicting theological statements taken from the Bible and resolved dialectically. In that sense, Abelard was grappling with the same problem of understanding faith to which St Anselm's work had been directed. The difference was that Abelard sought to make revealed truth amenable to reason alone, so that it was as valid for the infidel as for the Christian believer. He attempted to do so in his *Dialogue between a Philosopher, a Jew, and a Christian*, and in his *Theologia christiana* (Christian Theology). For Abelard, reason surpassed the barriers of creed: non-Christians who had reached the truth, as many Greek philosophers and Jews had done, were equally saved; for they too had been illuminated by the same divine wisdom and had led the same evangelical lives as Christians. Christianity to Abelard was less an exclusive body of faith than the totality of truth, which embraced all who had reached it.

The same confidence in man's natural powers is to be seen in Abelard's work on ethics, *Scito teipsum* (Know Thyself).[25] Like St Augustine, he regarded sin as a negative quality, devoid of substance; and he defined it negatively as not abstaining from what should not be done.[26] Sin entails consenting to evil, which is to shun God. It is the intention to do so that constitutes sin. Conversely, goodness resides in the intention to do good. In consequence, it is the intention, rather than the deed, that counts in assessing what is either good or bad. The act in itself has no moral value apart from the intention. Hence intention, act, and deed must be separated in any moral judgment. An action is good or bad according to the intention informing it; the deed that results, whether good or bad, is morally neutral. A good intention can result in a bad deed without impugning the morality of the action that led to it.[27]

It was over the problem of what constituted a good intention that trouble arose. Abelard recognized that its goodness lay not in being pleasing to man's will, but in conforming with God's will. In his later works he sought to define a good action as acting from a knowledge of what is right; hence pagans, ignorant of scripture, were not committing evil when they unknowingly went against Christian precepts. It was here that he fell foul of St Bernard and Christian authority, and his teaching was condemned at the Synod of Sens in 1141: in making knowledge and intention the foundation of morality, Abelard was effectively by-passing the need for grace. The illumination of reason carried a man over the barrier between natural and supernatural understanding. That in no way led Abelard to deny the dogma of original sin and predestination; but, equally with John Scotus and Eckhart, there was no automatic convergence between natural reason and revealed truth. To follow one or the other too far upset the equilibrium between them.

Abelard's naturalism in reason and ethics made him no less devout a Christian than his opponents. In his desire to understand what he believed, he, rather than they, was representative of his age.

The "School" of Chartres[28]

For all his individualism, Abelard was not a lone philosophical voice. Indeed, the home of philosophy in its purest speculative form, as opposed to mere dialectic, was at the cathedral school of Chartres during the first two thirds of the 12th century. There, through a combination of Platonism and the whole range of the liberal arts—the sciences of the *quadrivium* as well as the *trivium*—it attained a degree of freedom unsurpassed in the Middle Ages. Chartres, however, did not become a university, and it declined rapidly in the later part of the century before the coming of the Graeco-Arabian scientific and philosophical corpus changed the direction of philosophy. Its members therefore depended almost exclusively for cosmogony upon the neo-Platonic heritage. As Thierry of Chartres (d. 1156), one of its outstanding figures, wrote in his *Heptateuchon*, a handbook of the seven liberal arts: "To philosophize, two instruments are necessary: the spirit and its expression. The spirit is illuminated by the *quadrivium*; its expression, elegant, reasoned, and embellished, by the *trivium*." This book, which mentions some 45 different works used in their teaching, is not, apart from reference to recently translated Arabian astronomical tables and Ptolemy's canons, notable for its scientific texts. Boethius, genuine and pseudo, is still prominent in arithmetic and geometry. Among its most notable features is the inclusion of Aristotle's *Organon* (the so-called New Logic), the *Topics*, the *Sophistical Questions*, and the *Prior Analytics*, only the *Posterior Analytics* being omitted. The value of the *Heptateuchon* is precisely that, in spite of Thierry's interest in the *quadrivium*, the main heritage is literary rather than scientific: Priscian and Donatus, Virgil, Horace, Ovid for grammar, Cicero and Quintilian for rhetoric, and Aristotle's logic for dialectic. When to these we add the treatises and commentaries on Aristotle by Boethius and his *De consolatione*, the fragment of the *Timaeus* translated by the neo-Platonist Chalcidius, together with his commentary, Macrobius's *Dream of Scipio*, the *Quaestiones naturales* of Seneca, together with John Scotus's *Division of Nature*, the Platonic ambiance of Chartres is not far to seek. It also accounts for the diversity of Chartrain Platonism. Aristotle was still known only as a logician, not as a philosopher. Moreover, he was seen predominantly through the medium of Boethius, whose role in the philosophy of Chartres cannot be overstressed. It was he who provided a metaphysical interpretation of Aristotle's categories in his division of the different elements of being into substance (*id quod est*) and the form by which it subsists (*quo est*) and their application to the distinction between God's being as supremely simple and the composite nature of all that is created. Until his system was challenged by Aristotle's metaphysics (based upon the contrast between matter and form), which became known in the 13th century, Boethius provided the metaphysical foundation of philosophy. Moreover, in his five theological treatises, above all the *De trinitate* and *De hebdomadibus*, Boethius himself set the example of applying his categories to theology. Gilbert de la Porrée (1076–1154) directly took up Boethius's work in his commentary on those two writings as well as in his own treatise on Aristotle's *Categories*, *On the Six Principles*, which became a standard text in the arts course at Paris university and elsewhere in the 13th century. (Gilbert was carried away by his distinctions into implying that God had his own form of divinity by which he was defined. For this unwitting deviation he was duly arraigned by St Bernard before the Council of Rheims in 1148, but not condemned.)

Of all the Chartrains' Platonism, Gilbert's was the most strictly philosophical and theologically controlled: like his master Bernard of Chartres (master of the school from 1114 to 1119 and chancellor from 1119 until 1124, and its real founder), he identified universals with the forms or essences of things, which in turn derived from divine ideas. But unlike his other Chartrain contemporaries (Thierry, Bernard's brother William of Conches [1080–1145], and Bernard of Silvester) he did not attempt a Platonic cosmogony. Perhaps for that reason, Gilbert's influence was lasting.

The spectacular effects of the other elements of Platonism can be seen above all in these three thinkers. The *Timaeus* itself was the only work of Plato then known and that only partially; the *Meno* and *Phaedo*, translated in the 1150s by Henricus Aristippus, were the only others known during the Middle Ages. Of all Plato's writings the *Timaeus* was at once the least representative, and from a Christian standpoint the most suggestive of a doctrine of creation. As neo-Platonized by Chalcidius, and in the company of the rest of the neo-Platonic corpus then known to the Chartrains, it offered a new and exciting interpretation of the universe. Accepting the Christian doctrine of the six days of creation in Genesis, which formed the title of Thierry's work on the subject, they sought to explain philosophically how nature had come into being. This was revolutionary—too revolutionary to last. Although St Thomas Aquinas was later to adopt a method that also proceeded from the natural to the supernatural, he did so within a theological framework and with a clear awareness of the limitations of natural reason in demonstrating revealed truth. Thierry and his *confrères*, however, were intoxicated with the richness of nature. In an age when the world of reason and the senses was being rediscovered, they sought to understand it for itself. They did not deny God as creator;

on the contrary, that was their premise; but whereas Thierry applied mathematical reasoning (derived from a knowledge of Boethius's treatises, and probably also inspired by Macrobius's mystical use of numbers) to treat God as unity in comparison with the plurality of creation, with William and Bernard God virtually disappeared from sight. They were so keen to show the principles of order operating in nature that both come near to pantheism: in Aristotelian terminology, the search for secondary causes displaced the emphasis on the first cause.

William and Bernard were greatly influenced by a neo-Platonist syncretism. To John Scotus, in particular, they owed the pervading sense of universalism by which the world was a theophany, expressing God's creation and the eternal archetypes of all being in him, and man was the meeting-point between the divine and the created, the spiritual and the material. As such he was a microcosm of the universe, itself composed of the intelligible and the material. Where they broke with John Scotus was in carrying the sense of divine participation into the material world itself, and thereby searching for the intelligible and the eternal within the visible and the sensible. In turning to the world, instead of withdrawing from it into the soul, to find the eternal and the divine, they were at the opposite pole from mysticism. They adopted the Platonist notion of the world soul (*anima mundi*), which in the *Timaeus* acts as the demiurge or creator of the world, although subordinate to the supreme being. The neo-Platonists had established a much more precise relation between the world soul and the powers that were above it: it came third in the triad, to the One, who was supreme and stood above all being, and the *logos* or word emanating from the One and containing the intelligibles or archetypes of all being. The world soul translated these intelligibles into actual existence in the universe. In taking over this notion of the world soul the Chartrains were playing with danger from a Christian point of view; although they identified it with the Holy Spirit working in God's creatures, the need to make it part of God invited in turn the identification of the created with the divine. For the Chartrains, especially William of Conches, the world soul acted as the interior intelligence immanent in the cosmos, from which the latter received its order, goodness, truth, beauty, and the other moral virtues. The actual world was thereby united with the eternal truths in God by means of the world soul. The existence of the world soul in nature was the proof of the intelligibility and plan of the universe. To be grasped, then, it must be seen as a whole; and that is what the Chartrains attempted to do by treating it as a moral order in which every creature had a place.

In spite of its intellectualism, this was also a hymn to nature. It is not, therefore, surprising that it took the form of poetry in Bernard's *De mundi universitate sive megacosmus et microcosmus* (On the Totality of the World, or Macrocosm and Microcosm) and later in the *Planctus nature* (The Complaint of Nature) and *Anticlaudianus* of Alan of Lille (1125–1203). The theme is the same desire to find the principles of order in nature through the unfolding of its creation. In Bernard's *De mundi*, "Nature addresses a plea to Reason, that is the Providence of God, over the confusion of the first matter, and asks that the world be more beautifully fashioned. Reason, moved by her prayers, willingly agrees to the request, and separates the four elements from one another. In the first book the order of the elements is described. In the second book, entitled the *Microcosmos*, Reason speaks to nature and glorifies the beauty of the world, and promises that on its completion she will fashion man. Nature therefore forms man from the four elements." It is less the absence of God that is striking than the attention to the workings of providence in nature. It is linked in a "golden chain," through the world soul, with what lies above the stars.

Alan of Lille's poems sprang directly from Bernard's influence; but whereas Bernard was almost entirely pagan in his classicism, Alan's work is tinctured with a Christian sentiment that becomes more marked in the second of the two works. For him nature is directly "the child of God," the intermediary between God and man. The theme of the *Anticlaudianus* is something quite new: the creation of a new man, who shall be both man and God. The Christian element becomes more apparent, but, significantly, as with Bernard, this takes place through nature rather than in theological terms of redemption through Christ.

The cult of nature that reached its highest expression at Chartres extended not only to poetry: it can be seen on the capitals of the cathedrals and in the bestiaries of the period. It expressed the desire to find a place within a divine order for the natural world in all its aspects. It was superseded, in thought at least, owing to its fundamental incompatibility with an increasingly defined body of theological teaching. Only the sense of man as microcosm survived as an active force, because it could be directly reconciled with the fundamental tenet of his creation in the image of God. When, in the *Divina commedia* (*c.* 1306–21), Dante came to treat the same subject of man's renewal, he did so not in the natural terms of the *Anticlaudianus* but in the elaborate symbolism of a Christian eschatology.

Against the combined forces of Christian orthodoxy and Aristotelian and Arabian science, the Chartrain interpretation—fruitful though it was for literature and engaging for itself—could not survive. Neither Thierry's notion that the four elements could change their qualities, nor William of Conches' atomic theory that they were the first principles of being, could find room in either a Christian or an Aristotelian cosmology.

St Bernard of Clairvaux

The brake on the free play of reason, however, was inherent in the development of orthodoxy. While the Chartrains were apostrophizing nature, much of the same neo-Platonist inspiration was being put to a very different interpretation and directly contraposed to that of Chartres. The Cistercian monasteries under St Bernard (1090–1153) became the focus of a new militant spirituality. Together with his *confrère* William of St Thierry (d. 1148), he preached the renunciation of worldly vanity and natural curiosity in favour of inner illumination. St Bernard was no ordinary monk or mystic: the effective founder of the most powerful religious movement of the early and mid-12th century, he also dominated its religious life. Popes such as Eugenius III, the Second Crusade in 1147 (which he preached), heretics such as Henry of Lausanne, erring thinkers such as Abelard and Gilbert de la Porrée, all came under his surveillance. He was campaigning against the very climate of natural awareness and worldliness. Although he did not succeed in overcoming them, he helped to define their limits.

As a mystic, St Bernard gave a new meaning to the ineffable ecstasy of the soul's awareness of God. His use of the sensuous imagery of the Song of Songs and his exaltation of the Virgin are the mystical counterpart of the cult of courtly love. But for St Bernard love was at the outset divine; it was realized through God's grace. Hence it could not be compared to the divinity with which the courtly lover invested his beloved. On the other hand, the parallel cannot be denied. The current of personal ecstasy runs through both traditions in the 12th century. Richard of St Victor (*c.* 1123–73) and Hildegard of Bingen (d. 1179) both go farther in recognizing human love as a first stage to divine love, Hildegard to the point of making woman a divinely fashioned "embodiment of man's love."[29]

That said, however, there can be no denying the profoundly anti-mundane bias of St Bernard's outlook. Beyond any similarities of impulse and language, he and William of St Thierry represented the other side of the antinomy between faith and nature. Their importance is that they sought to overcome it through the subordination of the natural to the revealed, thereby accentuating their incompatibility when the natural was followed for itself.

For St Bernard the highest truth was to "know Jesus and Jesus crucified"; that could not come by way of reason.[30] To gain it we must begin from humility. Only when we had reached its highest degree in the awareness of our own wretchedness could we ascend to the next stages of charity and compassion, which in turn freed us for contemplation of the divine. This culminated in an ecstatic awareness of God. It came from emptying the soul of all created awareness and so, in a manner of speaking, detaching it from the body. St Bernard stressed that such ecstasy was essentially a personal experience by following a defined progression through humility, compassion, and contemplation. The knowledge to which it led was not of the eternal truths—number, wisdom, order, and so on—that St Augustine had taken as the signs of God illuminating the soul; rather, it was an incommunicable awareness of God himself. In retracing this path to God in the soul, through its separation from all earthly ties, St Bernard was returning to the neo-Platonist tradition. But whereas among the Greek theologians it had led to a blurring of the distinction between the image and the exemplar in inner contemplation, St Bernard followed St Augustine in stressing the role of the will and the indispensability of grace in turning it towards God. The ascent to God was inseparable from the soul's purification from sin; the higher it went, the more the will looked away from the world and towards God. Accordingly, the acme of mystical experience was not the merging of the soul with God but the uniting of man's will with God's will in sublime harmony. Their substances remained infinitely distinct: man did not become divine; his soul, created in the image of God, returned, through charity, to its maker. Here we can see St Bernard's fusion of the two streams of St Augustine's teaching with the neo-Platonism of the Greek Fathers, the pseudo-Dionysius, and perhaps John Scotus. Mystical awareness of God is the foretaste of the beatific vision. It is not a permanent state: man remains created, but God's grace has worked within him to lead him to God in a union of the two natures as two distinct beings. The importance of St Augustine's doctrine of the will and grace needs no stressing. Knowing God is dependent upon loving God; it entails rejecting sin—which is self-will and love of this world—for God. True freedom is to submit man's will to God's. In that sense, ecstasy is merely the culmination of a Christian life.

William of St Thierry was closely associated with St Bernard. He shares both his mysticism and his distrust of profane learning. Although his doctrine was similar in emphasis to St Bernard's, it was more neo-Platonic—or, perhaps more accurately, it stressed the neo-Platonic element in St Augustine's notion of memory as the innermost recess of the soul. Like St Bernard, William made love of God inherent in man's nature, which sin had impaired. The need was therefore to overcome the effects of sin and turn back again towards God. That could be achieved by looking within the soul and searching for the sign of God, which was to be discovered in memory. From this, man could then gain the understanding and will to recognize his soul as the created image of the uncreated Trinity. By such self-knowledge, and with the aid of God's grace, man could come to a fuller love and understanding of God and so closer to his own original nature.

The message of St Bernard and William of St Thierry was at once moral and theological. Mystical experience could not be transmitted, but the lesson of the need to love God above all could. It demanded a life devoted to God, which both men identified with the monastic life.

Although neither St Bernard nor William was able to withdraw from the world entirely, their views implied a monastic way of life that for a time continued to be associated with the Cistercian order.

Theology and Canon Law

The paths that were to become the main highway of Christian thought in the 13th century lay neither in Chartres nor in Clairvaux but in the theological systematizing and biblical exegesis of the northern French cathedral schools such as Rheims, Laon, and Paris, together with the abbey school of St Victor, the law schools of Bologna, and the centres of translation in Spain, Sicily, northern Italy, and Constantinople. Diffuse as they were, they provided the doctrinal and intellectual foundation of a Christian outlook. Although they offered none of the ready parallels between art and thought that could be found elsewhere, they nonetheless shared the same reliance upon reason and knowledge drawn from the world and natural experience.

Chartres was the exception among the cathedral schools, even when we recognize that its Platonism went with a humanism based upon the cultivation of style. The latter culminated in John of Salisbury (1125–80), who despite his elegance was not wholly in place in a world of either hard thought or hard facts, but its Platonism led directly to the pantheism of David of Dinant and Amaury of Bène, whose works, together with John Scotus's, were condemned as heretical at the Synod of Sens in 1210.

Meanwhile new and far-reaching methods of theological systematization were being developed—above all at Laon and Paris—of which Abelard's *Sic et non* was a flamboyant expression. They were the counterpart of similar developments in canon law, which antedated them. They appeared within a generation of each other in comparable codifications: that of canon law in the *Decretum* of Gratian (*c.* 1142), and that of theology in Peter Lombard's four books of *Sentences* in 1152. Both the *Decretum* and the *Sentences* became standard textbooks in the 13th century. They used the same method of the question treated dialectically through a resolution of the arguments *pro* and *contra* taken from authority and reason. This disputatory form—already popularized by Abelard—became the hall-mark of scholastic method. Employed in both teaching and writing, it ousted the other, freer literary forms of the 12th century. That it should have done so is indicative of the hold that this systematic approach came to exercise. It arose out of the very need to elucidate what was held on authority and to reconcile the different statements and canons found in Christian teaching and the law of the Church. In that sense its triumph was the triumph of orthodoxy. It was inseparable from the hegemony of the Church and of its control of a Christian ideology. The strength of St Bernard, for all the vigour of his advocacy, lay ultimately in the consonance of his attitude with authority and the power that it gave him to impose his interpretation, whether by crusade, by preaching, or by ecclesiastical council. Similarly, the work of systematizing theology and law was at once in support of authority and under its aegis, whether in the cathedral and abbey schools of the north or in the monasteries of Italy: Abelard was excluded as a master from Laon and Paris, and forbidden to teach, after his condemnation at Sens. In each case acceptance or rejection involved obedience to the Church, which ultimately decided who and what should be accepted, whether Gratian's *Decretum* or Lombard's doctrine of the Trinity, promulgated at the Fourth Lateran Council in 1215.

The methods of systematization in theology and law arose directly from their relation to authority. They were designed to further a proper understanding of the sacred texts upon which authority was based. This took two main forms: glosses or aids through an exposition of the text designed for teaching; and independent exegesis by means of dialectic. The first produced the standard *Glossa ordinaria* for the Bible, and the different apparatus for the body of Roman law and canon law; the second produced the *Decretum* and the *Sentences*. Theology, however, did not lend itself to the same definitiveness as law. The Bible as God's word could be read in a variety of ways. It invited not only diverse interpretations but different levels of meaning, as expressed in Hugh of St Victor's threefold division between the letter (*littera*), the sense of the words (*sensus*), and understanding (*intelligentia*). Hence, whether as theological or textual exegesis, the study of the sacred page directly impinged upon Christian doctrine. As such it lay at the centre of the mediaeval outlook.

It was at Laon at the turn of the 12th century under its master, Anselm (d. 1117), and his brother Ralph (d. 1134 or 1156) that both glossing and exegesis underwent a far-reaching development.[31] On the one hand, through what must have been a co-operative enterprise, they began a gloss of the Bible that became the standard introduction to its different books during the Middle Ages. Later known as the *Glossa ordinaria*, because it had ordered the Bible, it was produced over the first 30 or so years of the 12th century. Like the legal glosses, it consisted of both marginal and interlinear commentaries on the text; these, in turn, were glossed by later commentators. It was some time before the *Glossa ordinaria* was recognized, but eventually it displaced other similar apparatus. Among those who helped to establish it were Gilbert de la Porrée (Anselm's pupil) and Peter Lombard. Under Anselm, Laon occupied, in a smaller and more diffuse way, the focal position in theology that Paris was to have from the late 12th century onwards: many of the leading thinkers of the period, including Abelard—who characteristically denounced him—were Anselm's pupils at Laon.

Directly growing out of their exegetical work was the development of its speculative aspect. Here dialectic entered. Already, in the 11th century, Berengarius and Lanfranc, in addition to glossing the text between the lines or in the margin, had written continuous expositions. These, also, were designed for teaching, and were used as an extension of the methods of grammatical instruction when the text was analysed. Dialectic was brought in to clarify it and to resolve its meaning, and it was particularly useful in such writings as the Pauline Epistles, although as applied by Lanfranc the dialectic was more legal than philosophical.[32]

Manegold of Lautenbach seems to have gone further, and to have been among the first to introduce questions as part of an independent theological discussion. This was taken up by Anselm in his lectures at Laon, and formed the beginning of the new *sentence* collections, of which Peter Lombard's *Sentences* were the fullest development. If for a time it diverted attention from exegesis to speculation, it also gave theology a new direction. As the work of the cathedral schools, it departed from the monastic conception of theology as the study of the Bible, and came increasingly to concentrate upon those very matters that so fascinated Abelard and the Chartrains: the Psalter, the Pauline Epistles, and the Hexaemeron. But they differed in accepting the word of authority as their framework. Although lacking the spectacular quality of these others, the effect of this work was no less far-reaching. It gave rise to a new discipline, based upon the Bible and the canonical authorities, that was able to incorporate natural experience through the use of dialectic. It thereby assimilated the created to the divine: it was at once a liberation from servitude to the text and the means by which natural experience could be absorbed into a Christian outlook.

The stages by which the development of the *sentences* came about are far from clear. Whether they were initially a separate activity, or, as has been suggested, they arose out of the lectures on the Bible given to the pupils of the cathedral school, is uncertain.[33] Certainly by the late 12th century, doctrine was being taught independently; and already in the first half of the century Abelard and Hugh of St Victor (1096–1141) were giving separate lectures on theological questions. What can be said is that the *sentences* included questions that arose from study of the Bible: the *Sentences* of Peter Lombard include a number that were from his scriptural gloss. With his work, a new textbook was created: by the end of the 12th century it had become a vehicle of theological speculation, and the commentaries on it included some of the major theological works of the 13th and 14th centuries. Composed of four books, the *Sentences* treated of God, creation, the Incarnation and Redemption, the theological virtues, and the sacraments. Although largely unoriginal and relying mainly upon St Augustine, they brought together in a balanced and impersonal way all the main questions that arose from a dialectical treatment of theology. Hence their suitability as an instrument of teaching and speculation.

The *sentences* represented the speculative side of biblical study. Although this approach came to predominate in the schools, the Bible remained its foundation. Moreover, textual exegesis itself developed in response to the growth of speculation. At the very time when Abelard was popularizing the methods of Anselm and his school, Hugh at St Victor abbey in Paris was putting exegesis upon a new footing.[34] There is a certain parallel between Hugh and St Bernard. While St Bernard was recalling to men their fallen state and the need for the monastic virtues, Hugh of St Victor was attempting to bring learning back to the monastic programme of *De doctrina christiana*. He, too, was a mystic, though in a different, more intellectual way than St Bernard. He wished to make the knowledge

contained in the seven liberal arts the starting-point for theological understanding, as outlined in his guide to knowledge, the *Didascalion*.

But Hugh was more than a pedagogue, outstanding though he was in
establishing St Victor as a new centre of biblical study. He also put his
preaching into practice. In differentiating between the three senses of the
Bible he gave a new meaning to the order between them. To begin with,
he stressed the importance of the letter as the prerequisite for all higher
understanding. "The mystical sense," he wrote, "is only gathered from
what the letter says in the first place . . . subtract the letter and what is
left?"[35] This was in direct opposition to the prevailing cult of allegory,
which derived from Gregory the Great and all too often made nonsense
of the literal meaning. In Hugh's own example, "as *lion*, according to the
historical sense, means a beast, but allegorically it means Christ. Therefore *lion* means Christ."[36] In the second place, however, the literal sense
for Hugh did not mean slavish submission to the word but to the sense of
the word. Only when the word was taken for what it connoted literally
could it be construed grammatically. Without such a foundation there
could be no means of higher understanding. In the third place, and
perhaps most revolutionary, there was Hugh's identification of the literal
with the historical. Here he passed from being the mere exponent of a
return to the pre-Gregorian tradition of the unreformed Church to being
a man of his own age. From the last decade of Hugh's life there was a
growing sense of history, fostered by the changes in society and above all
by the redefinition of the position of the Church and the Empire in the
Investiture Contest. It went together with a new awareness of the sacraments as the centre of the Church's life. Hugh bears witness to both. His
De sacramentis, the forerunner of the *summa*, is theology conceived as
sacramental history. In this it is unlike the other theological works of the
period, although it bears striking affinity with the new sense of universal
history that was to culminate in the work of Joachim of Fiore (d. 1102).
Hugh traced the history of the sacraments, and thus of the Church,
through three ages: before law, under the law, and under grace. Like
Otto of Freising's *Chronicle*, it owed its inspiration to St Augustine, for
whom the history of man culminated in the Redemption and man's
salvation through the sacraments. Hugh, however, was a theologian
whose interest centred upon finding the meaning of the Bible, whereas
Otto was concerned with the City of God, which—in contradistinction
to St Augustine—he identified with the Church.

With his emphasis upon the study of the Bible as the culmination of all
knowledge, Hugh's influence in an age of increasing specialization was

231

bound to be restricted. Nevertheless, Hugh and his successors at St Victor, especially Andrew, saved biblical studies from both mere allegorizing and mere speculation. Above all, through his historical and sacramental approach, he established a new relation between the literal and the mystical senses which, through the work of three Paris masters—Peter Comestor (d. 1169), Peter the Chanter (d. 1197), and Stephen Langton (d. 1228)—gave the study of the Bible a place in the theological course of the universities. Through Hugh, the Bible, from being an object of meditation and imagination, became an intellectual structure, with its apparatus drawn from an historical foundation.

Intellectual activity until the later 12th century, then, was animated by a renewed awareness of nature, reason, and society. Although most of it was carried on in the schools under the aegis of the Church, the courts were also becoming centres of artistic and literary life. Together they led to a diffusion of knowledge and culture that in many ways makes the 12th century the richest and most diverse of the Middle Ages.

The Graeco-Arabian Translations

By the last decade of the 12th century a discontinuity in intellectual life becomes apparent. Its principal causes were the growing impact of the Graeco-Arabian translations and the rise of the universities. Together they radically altered the form and content of learning. On the one hand, the chief branches of knowledge—the liberal arts, philosophy, theology, law, and medicine—all came under the syllogistic methodology of Aristotle's logic. It accounts for a uniformity in expression and treatment that contrasts markedly with the freer and more personal style of the 11th and 12th centuries. Theology, like any other discipline, became an art and a science governed by principles and axioms from which its propositions were deducible. On the other hand, while for that reason dialectic ousted the study of grammar and rhetoric as independent university subjects, philosophical and theological speculation became predominantly metaphysical, framed in terms of the problems raised by the translations. These developments made at once for a greater cohesion and a narrowing of the focus of Christian thought. Discussion in the 13th century centred within the universities, or schools as they were called: Paris and, to a lesser degree, Oxford for theology; Bologna for law; Montpellier for medicine; Oxford for natural science and mathematics. The topics now, however, largely arose from the study of Aristotle and his Arabian and Jewish commentators: Alfarabi, Algazali, Avicenna, Averroes, Avicebron,

232

and Maimonides. Although differing in important respects among themselves, they introduced a new metaphysical and cosmological dimension. The Aristotelian and neo-Platonic conceptions that underlay this new dimension constituted a direct challenge to the Christian teaching of God as immediate creator of the universe, of a divine providence, of the spiritual nature and immortality of the individual soul. Instead, man and the sub-lunar world became threatened by subjection to the heavenly bodies, as the intermediaries between them and the first cause (the One). Necessity, eternity, and pantheism were the accompaniments of such a cosmogony, which treated God or his equivalent as an indirect first mover that did no more than put in train an eternal series of cause and effect without immediate control or involvement in its operation. To reaffirm revealed truth in face of this challenge became the central preoccupation of Christian thinkers during the 13th century. The need to take account of the Graeco-Arabian cosmology explains in large measure the difference between Christian thought in the 12th and 13th centuries.

Until the 13th century the main philosophical inspiration had been neo-Platonist. St Augustine had fashioned his outlook from largely neo-Platonic elements; John Scotus, the most original thinker of the early Middle Ages and a pervasive influence in the 12th century, had been almost a pure neo-Platonist; so, too, had the speculations of the Chartrains and St Anselm's notion of being. Far from having dominated mediaeval thought, Aristotle did not have a formative role in Christian thinking until the 13th century. It is truer to say that, until the time of St Thomas Aquinas, Aristotle supplied its mechanism rather than its principles. Down to the later 12th century his contribution was his logic and his theory of abstraction. It was when his metaphysics and natural science, together with their interpretation by Arabian and Jewish commentators, became current through translation that he became a threat to Christian values. In that sense he was both indispensable to Christian thought and alien to it in a way that neo-Platonism was not. Neo-Platonism constituted the mainstay of a Christian philosophy: it provided the means for harmonizing the created and the divine, the oneness of God and the multiplicity of creation. Aristotle, on the contrary, presented an alternative, non-Christian interpretation of reality that made no call upon a non-sensory order of reality. For that reason the translations crystallized the latent conflict between natural philosophy and revealed truth.

The reaction was correspondingly pronounced. The 100 or so years from the first decade of the 13th century were a period of almost continuous intellectual ferment. The great systems of Grosseteste, St Bonaventure,

St Thomas Aquinas, Henry of Ghent, Duns Scotus, and others, which evolved during it, were not monuments to the pre-existing harmony of faith and natural experience, but attempts to restate their relationship in the absence of harmony. Of all the outstanding thinkers of the epoch only St Thomas made the complementarity of natural and supernatural the foundation of his thinking; for this he had to suffer the attacks of the majority of his contemporaries in the theological faculties at Oxford and Paris, as well as the inclusion of some of his propositions among those condemned at both universities in 1277.

The intellectual development of the 13th and 14th centuries, then, was the product of a new and greatly increased tension between the demands of faith and the dictates of reason and natural philosophy; from the outset it took place against a background of censure and prohibition. The existence of a new intellectual climate was most strikingly apparent during the middle years of the 13th century, between 1231 and 1270, when ecclesiastical pressures eased for a while. These years represent perhaps the most constructive intellectual period of the Middle Ages; but they were also a period in which the limits beyond which natural reason could not go became most rigorously defined. There was a new awareness of the need to state the relation between theology and philosophy, which had been almost entirely absent from the speculation of the 12th century. It is equally apparent in the political and ecclesiological thinking of the 13th and 14th centuries. It arose because the natural order had come to exist in its own right. Not only the vast accession of new knowledge, but also the new forms and institutions of mediaeval civilization, including those of the Church, demanded a rethinking of the old Augustinian view of the world. It could no longer be merely subsumed under a non-sensory conception of reality; nor could society be regarded as simply the penalty and remedy for sin. The new issues to which the change gave rise dominated the intellectual life of the later Middle Ages.

It was the dependence of Christian thought—and of mediaeval culture in general—upon the classical heritage, above all upon Greek philosophy, that made the translations of Aristotle and his commentators so significant. The Moslem conquests of North Africa and Spain in the 7th and 8th centuries had effectively cut off the West from Byzantium and the East, and so from the sources of classical learning. Although contact was renewed before the end of the 10th century, the transmission of Aristotle and other writings began properly from about the first third of the 12th century. Spain and Sicily were the two main areas from which they came; Constantinople and North Africa also played a part. These had all belonged to the Arabian caliphate, whose learning and science derived directly from the Greek, and had been taken over with the territories of Syria and North Africa. The writings of Aristotle, Ptolemy, Euclid, Hippocrates, and Galen were among others translated into Arabic; they had in turn inspired the philosophical systems of the leading Arabian thinkers, such as Alfarabi, Avicenna, and Averroes, which were notable for combining philosophy with science and other branches of knowledge.

Spain in the 12th century attracted an array of translators and scholars, above all to Toledo.[37] They included native Christians, such as Dominic Gundissalinus and Hugh of Santalla; Jews, such as Petrus Alphonsi and John of Seville; and numerous Christians from other countries—Adelard of Bath, Plato of Tivoli, Gerard of Cremona, and Hermann of Carinthia, to mention only some. Originally they worked from both sides of the Pyrenees; but after about 1126 they gathered in Toledo under the patronage of Archbishop Raymond and Bishop Michael of Tarazona. The works translated were mainly on astronomy, mathematics, and astrology. Thus, in about 1126, Adelard of Bath, the first in the field, rendered into Latin Euclid's *Elements* and Arabian astronomical tables. Gerard of Cremona, the most prolific of these translators, was responsible for 71 writings, including Aristotle's *Posterior Analytics* and a work, mistakenly attributed to Aristotle, that came to be known as the *Liber de causis* (The Book of Causes—a commentary on extracts from the *Elements of Theology* of Proclus, the 5th-century neo-Platonist). Already known to Alan of Lille (*c.* 1128–1203) in Gerard's translation, under the title of *Aphorisms on the Essence of the Supreme Goodness*, this more than any other work was responsible for confusing Aristotle with neo-Platonism. Together with another pseudo-Aristotelian work, *The Theology of Aristotle*, which consisted of parts of Plotinus's *Enneads*, it led Christian thinkers to attempt to reconcile the neo-Platonist notion of being as a series of emanations, originating from and culminating in the One, with Aristotle's hierarchy of causes, beginning with the first cause. Their conjunction had the effect of spiritualizing Aristotle's cosmology: Alan of Lille, for example, the first Christian thinker to have used the *Liber de causis*, in his work *On Catholic Faith Against the Heretics*, identified God with the One or the Monad and deduced unity of being as the first theological principle. The true identity of the *Liber de causis*, and with it the pedigree of Aristotle's own outlook, was reached only when St Thomas Aquinas recognized it in his *confrère* William of Moerbeke's translation of *The Elements of Theology* in the 1260s.

At the same time the neo-Platonist element was greatly accentuated by translation not only of the writings of the pseudo-Dionysius, Apuleius, Chalcidius, and Macrobius, but also of the entirely new corpus of Arabian and Jewish thinkers. It was from here that the most formative influences upon Christian thought derived, in the sharply neo-Platonic systems of Alfarabi, Alkindi, Algazali, Avicebron, and above all Avicenna. Among the most important of their works translated into Latin by 1200 were parts of Avicenna's encyclopaedia of philosophy, *Aš-Sifa* (The Book of Healing), known to the West as the *Sufficientia*. As a paraphrase of Aristotle's philosophy it was an important influence in giving it a neo-Platonist orientation in the late 12th and early 13th centuries. The translators working in Spain during this period were often aided by Jewish interpreters, who turned the Arabic texts into Spanish for them to render into Latin. It was thus that the great body of Aristotelian and Arabian works became known in the 12th century.

Although these were at first the main intermediaries between Greek and Arabian learning and the Latin world, translation direct from the Greek was equally important. The centres here were Sicily and the Norman kingdom of southern Italy. They had both been part of the Byzantine Empire, and had retained a knowledge of Greek. Libraries of Greek writings, chiefly theological and biblical, were to be found in the monastery of St Basil in Caesaria and at Palermo. Sicily, in particular, as the meeting point of three cultures—Greek, Arabian, and Latin, with the languages of each used officially—offered a unique opportunity for translation. It was directly fostered for over a century by Sicilian kings, from Roger II in the early 12th century to Manfred, the last of the Hohenstaufen, in the mid-13th century. Under William I (1154–66) the two principal translators, Henricus Aristippus and Eugene the Emir, were both court officials. Aristippus was the first to translate Plato's *Meno* and *Phaedo*, which were, as we have said, the only two of his works, other than the fragment of the *Timaeus*, known to the Middle Ages. Aristippus's version of Aristotle's *Meteorology*, Book IV, was used until the Renaissance. Scientific works of Euclid, Proclus, and Hero of Alexandria were also translated by the Sicilian school, all directly from the Greek.

The other source of Greek translation was Latin writers, such as James of Venice, Burgundio of Pisa, and Moses of Bergamo, who had learnt their Greek at Constantinople; they were all active in the first third of the 12th century. James of Venice was responsible for rendering into Latin Aristotle's *Topics*, *Analytics*, and *Elenchi*—the "New Logic," which came to be known between 1121 and 1158. Boethius had in fact also translated them in the 5th century, and it seems to have been in his version that they re-entered the mediaeval canon. Meanwhile, north of the Alps, the works of the pseudo-Dionysius were brought to the abbey of St Denis, outside Paris, by its future abbot William. Here they were translated into Latin by, among others, John Sarrazin, one of the few Greek scholars in France in this period—although they had been known to the West since the 9th century.

By 1200 the main body of Aristotle's writings was known to the West in Latin versions. This included his Old and New Logic, a large part of his scientific writings (*libri naturales*)—translated both from the Arabic, by Gerard of Cremona, and from the Greek—part of the *Metaphysics*, and part of the *Nicomachean Ethics*, also from the Greek. Together with the commentaries of Porphyry, Boethius, and others, and with the Greek and Arabian writings already mentioned, they presented the West with a body of knowledge and thought that was to revolutionize Christian thinking.

The process of translation and diffusion was completed between about 1220 and the 1260s. It included not only the full recension of Aristotle's writings taken from the authentic Greek texts, but also those of Averroes and the translation of a number of Greek commentaries and neo-Platonist works, among them Proclus's *Elements of Theology*. Aristotle was now rendered into Latin, both through the reworking of the earlier literal versions of the 12th century, as in part of Grosseteste's first complete translation of the *Ethics* between 1240 and 1243, and through entirely new translations, above all by William of Moerbeke (1215–85). William was the first to translate the *Politics* (1260) and the *Economics* (1267). His achievement was not confined to providing his *confrère* St Thomas Aquinas with authentic texts of Aristotle: his translation of other Greek thinkers, such as Alexander of Aphrodisius and Proclus, also had an important bearing upon the philosophical and spiritual climate of the later 13th century, as indeed the *Politics* had upon political thinking. Even so, it is questionable whether any of these developments can compare in immediate importance with the advent of the works of Averroes, Aristotle's commentator *par excellence*.

Unlike the other translations, which were done largely within an academic milieu (either the universities or the *studia* of the friars) and were adjuncts to an existing corpus, Averroes represented a further alien incursion. How alien can be measured by the impact of his teaching at Paris in the 1260s and 1270s, which we shall discuss below. In the form of commentaries on Aristotle's writings by a faithful disciple, they gave a radically naturalistic—and so non-Christian—interpretation of Aristotle.

Their Latin renderings were mainly by Michael Scot, who worked first at Toledo, in the early 13th century, and then, between 1228 and 1235, at the court of Frederick II in Sicily, where he was the king's astrologer. In 1230 Frederick—among the mediaeval papacy's greatest enemies—sent some of Scot's translations to universities in Italy; they reached Paris at about the same time. During the next decade most of Averroes's writings became known to the West, other translations being by William of Luna, Master Theodoric, and Hermann the German. They were accompanied by the translation of Aristotle's works to which they were commentaries. In that way the *De caelo*, *De anima*, *Ethics*, *Rhetoric*, and *Poetics* were also translated.

The Universities

The diffusion of the new knowledge that came from the translations began in the earlier 12th century. But it was only in the 13th century that its influence in producing new problems, new alignments, and new ways of thinking became dominant. Its impact was felt above all in the universities, especially at Paris.

As we have abundantly seen, the ecclesiastical ambiance of cathedral schools north of the Alps, and more particularly in France, gave them a theological and speculative orientation. That was carried over into the universities that succeeded them: it was there, and in the schools of the new mendicant orders (the Dominicans and Franciscans) which provided an equivalent academic grounding, that the intellectual changes were registered.

The universities were the focus of intellectual life for most of the 13th and 14th centuries. They form the pendant to the translations in the intellectual history of the epoch. But whereas the Italian universities, as the centres of law and medicine, were predominantly practical in emphasis, the northern universities, especially Paris and Oxford in their concern with theology, were in large measure responsible for the tenets of faith and thereby directly answerable to the Church and to its head, the pope. This was especially true of Paris university, which was associated with the most important thinkers and issues of the 13th century. It was there that the great questions of God's providence, the eternity of the world, and the immortality of the individual soul were debated in the 1260s and 1270s. Hence, the close papal and ecclesiastical attention that it received, going back to the early years of the 13th century. The debates of the schools on the Left Bank had wide doctrinal significance. For that reason much of mediaeval intellectual history from 1200 to 1400 centres upon Paris and, to a lesser degree, upon Oxford.

The universities were, however, more than ideological forums[38]: they were independent corporations. It was this that distinguished them from cathedral, urban, and other schools. As autonomous bodies they expressed the intellectual tensions not only between faith and natural knowledge, but also between the demands of higher authority—principally papal and ecclesiastical—and their own corporate life. There was the paradox of a self-governing community being frequently judged by spiritual criteria. Unlike the earlier schools, the universities had an independent juridical standing that went back, in the case of Bologna and Salerno, to the mid-12th century. Moreover, again in contrast with the cathedral schools, learning, not the cultivation of religious understanding, was the university's purpose. In that sense the universities professionalized knowledge: they consisted predominantly of those teaching and those studying in non-theological fields. Both the organization and the content of learning were orientated to the secular world. Like any other corporation, the university was concerned with regulating rights and privileges among its members and in its relations with the outside world. Internal and external friction was scarcely ever absent, and conflict was frequent. Whatever the role of the Church in controlling their intellectual activities, in practical terms the universities depended upon the protection of the king, prince, or other lay power in whose territories they lay. Without the frequent intervention of the kings of France and England in the 13th and 14th centuries, Paris and Oxford universities would have been dispersed or destroyed long before the end of the Middle Ages. As it was, many universities, including those of Padua and Cambridge, were founded as a result of migrations from other universities. All members of a university enjoyed the legal immunity from civil jurisdiction granted to clerics ("benefit of clergy"); but upon this were superimposed grants of temporal privilege, whose enforcement by the lay power made their position tenable.

This juxtaposition of the spiritual and the temporal was characteristic of the mediaeval universities. Physically, like any other corporation, they belonged to the city, without which they could not have survived; institutionally, they were international, immune from urban control but subject to spiritual jurisdiction. Intellectually, their pursuit of learning within a framework of revealed truth set them apart from all other corporations. They dealt in an international medium that had ecumenical significance and so went beyond local regulation. The very definition of a university was a place of universal study (*studium generale*) that conferred the right to teach anywhere (*ius ubique docendi*).

By the late 13th century, universities were effectively an independent order, compared by more than one writer with other universal institutions such as the priesthood. Together with the religious orders, they had a monopoly of higher education, as opposed to learning, which still continued independently in the monasteries and cathedral schools. Increasingly, from the second half of the 13th century, the way into the higher reaches of the Church or other professions, such as teaching, medicine, or law, was through a university training. Higher learning bore the stamp of a university in the subjects, texts, topics, and disputatory mode of discussion. As a consequence, learning itself became increasingly vocational. It was directed to acquiring knowledge for a professional end; the majority of those engaged in its pursuit were, as in any modern university, governed by the demands of the syllabus.

The framework of university education, however, remained ideological, governed by the demands of orthodoxy. This affected the conception of knowledge and the structure of learning no less than it had done in the previous epoch. Since all truth was ultimately supernatural in origin, what remained to man's natural powers could be only partial and incomplete. Full comprehension lay in an illumination reserved for the blessed in the next life. That had the effect of putting the search for truth in any full sense beyond the scope of human inquiry; there continued to be little notion of building up a body of knowledge that could lead to increasing comprehension of reality. The attitude to knowledge in the strict sense remained, throughout the Middle Ages, *a priori*. It put the search for truth in the comprehension of the authoritative texts—an outlook that pervaded every branch of knowledge. Such a view made for a disregard of experiment and natural investigation. Commentary, speculation, and question were the techniques common to all mediaeval learning, including science. There was a descending hierarchy of knowledge, from theology at its apex to the experience derived from the senses, the most uncertain source of all. It was enshrined in the division between the faculties of the university. Arts—the former liberal arts, now largely dominated by Aristotle's logic, natural philosophy, and metaphysics— constituted the base. Above arts came the three higher faculties of theology, law, and medicine, which could be entered only after passing through the arts faculty. Formally, the faculty structure preserved continuity with the Carolingian educational reforms. The difference was in the content of what was now taught. In one sense the conflict between form and content underlay the main intellectual issue of the 13th and 14th centuries: the collision between the demands of knowledge as an independent and vocational pursuit and the tenets to which it had to conform ideologically. In this connection it is important to recognize that only a minority of teachers, thinkers, and students were engaged in the study of theology. The vast majority were concerned with arts, to obtain a mastership in which took at least six years. Of the relatively small number who went on to one of the higher subjects, to spend at least another five or six years in the appropriate course, law, as the most lucrative, was by far the most popular. The supreme subject, theology, probably contained the smallest numbers. Moreover, its teaching was confined to the *studia* of the religious orders and to a few universities—Paris, Oxford, and Cambridge until the 14th century—by licence from the pope.

With the universities, learning took on a new autonomy. Although they continued to need the support of the Church and the lay power, there was not the exclusive dependence upon either that existed in a cathedral school or under princely patronage. These and many other forms of culture, learning, and education continued to exist outside the universities. Nonetheless, from the 13th century the history of Christian thought revolves around the universities and the thinkers who attended them.

It began with their response to the translations,[39] which was far from clear-cut. In the first place, what belonged to Aristotle and what to his commentators was initially obscure. There was the *Liber de causis*, usually taken for Part 3 of the *Metaphysics*; there was also the pervading influence of Avicenna, through whose paraphrases of Aristotle's philosophy Aristotle's ideas were refracted during the first three decades of the 13th century. Indeed, the problem posed by Aristotle was posed equally by his Arabian and Jewish commentators. In one sense, the main phases of 13th-century thought can be seen as alternations between the influence of Avicenna, Aristotle, and Averroes. Aristotle came to be taken for himself by Albertus Magnus only in the 1240s; and it was not until St Thomas, in the 1250s, that his metaphysics were properly adapted to a Christian outlook. But St Thomas's achievement was in turn overshadowed in the 1260s and 1270s by the influence of Averroes in the arts faculty at Paris, which after 1277 led to a general revulsion against Aristotelianism, whether Greek, Arabian, or Christian.

In the second place, the university was far from homogeneous, as the history of Paris in the 13th century shows. The arts faculty was concerned with natural knowledge, for all practical purposes to the exclusion of theological considerations. Its criteria were philosophical rather than doctrinal. Hence from the outset its members were especially receptive to Aristotle. Although it was only in 1255 that the syllabus of the arts faculty revealed the full range of Aristotle's writings in use—including the *Physics, Metaphysics, De anima, De generatione, De caelo*, in addition to the Old and New Logic used from the beginning—his natural philosophy and metaphysics had been read since the end of the 12th century. This led to three separate condemnations, in 1210, 1215, and 1228, against their teaching at Paris. The condemnations point to the conflict in outlook between the ecclesiastical authorities and theologians on the one hand, and some at least in the arts faculty on the other hand. Only after 1231 did Gregory IX tacitly recognize the *libri naturales*, which had already been permitted at his newly founded university of Toulouse two years earlier. From then until the condemnations at Paris in the 1270s there was no further official action against the new philosophy.

What is striking about these early attempts to counter it is that both officially and intellectually they centred upon Paris and concerned a complex of doctrines—neo-Platonist, Arabian, and Aristotelian. Else-where, at Oxford as well as at Toulouse, there were no such bans. They had the effect of holding back the development of science and natural philosophy at Paris—in striking contrast with Oxford—and of fostering concentration upon logic and ethics, where the teaching of the relevant texts of Aristotle was permitted. There was thus a direct relation between ecclesiastical attitudes and the intellectual climate. The theological conservatism of the cathedral authorities at Paris retarded philosophical development there for a time, just as it resisted the university's institutional development.

The bans against Aristotle and his commentators pronounced in 1210 and 1215 expressed the hostility of the leading members of the theological faculty to the new ideas. It is indicative of the shift away from the unrestrained speculation of Chartres and of independent spirits such as Abelard. Although the dialectical form of Peter Lombard's *Sentences* had become generally accepted, the content of theology, as we have seen, was predominantly sacramental and moral rather than metaphysical. Most of the early-13th-century Paris theologians evince a distrust of natural profane knowledge, and a reliance upon scripture. As Stephen of Tournai, one of the most representative, put it, "The arts called liberal are of great value in sharpening the understanding of scripture . . . but the reading of pagan books darkens, not enlightens, the mind." Among this group was Robert de Courçon, a master in the theological faculty between 1204 and 1210, who as papal legate gave the university its first statutes in 1215, while at the same time repeating the ban of 1210. On both occasions the Paris theologians took a prominent part.

The decrees of 1210 were passed by the provincial synod of Sens presided over by the archbishop, Peter of Corbeil; it was held in Paris, where Corbeil had been a master of theology and canon law from 1190 to 1198. The council not only banned the teaching of Aristotle's natural philosophy and metaphysics; it also banned "the commentaries on them," almost certainly those of Avicenna. At the same time it anathematized the teachings of David of Dinant and Amaury of Bène and ordered their books to be burnt; they were both pantheists but of rather different kinds, Amaury's pantheism being a debased neo-Platonism with echoes of John Scotus. Since the natural philosophy of both Aristotle (through being mistakenly identified with the *Liber de causis*) and Avicenna (in his own right) had a strongly neo-Platonist flavour, it can be seen how closely associated neo-Platonism and Aristotelianism were at that time. The hostility was less against a particular thinker than against an outlook that seemed to fly in the face of Christian belief.

Those injunctions against this outlook, with certain additions, were repeated by Robert de Courçon in his 1215 statutes and were confirmed by Pope Gregory IX in 1228, before he changed his attitude in 1231.[40] Their repetition at papal level shows how seriously they were regarded by the authorities; it is also clear evidence that at least some of the banned works were being studied. Only their public teaching had been prohibited, and during this period there were continuing attacks upon profane philosophy by many of the theologians. These were not confined to the theological faculty: the early Dominicans in particular shared the same hostility. Indeed in 1228, the same year as that in which Pope Gregory renewed the 1210 and 1215 decrees, the Dominican order passed a statute declaring that its members "shall not study in the books of the Gentiles [i.e. the pagan philosophers]. . . . They shall not learn secular sciences nor even the arts that are called liberal, unless sometimes in certain cases the Master of the Order or the general chapter shall wish to make a dispensation; but they shall read only theological works, whether they be youths or others."[41] Despite this, it was through the work of two Dominicans, Albertus Magnus and St Thomas, that Aristotle's philosophy was subsequently harmonized with a Christian outlook.

By the late 1220s there was a growing encroachment by natural philosophy into the domain of theology. It arose in large measure from the arts faculty, so that, in the words of John of St Giles, one of the first

Dominicans to hold a chair in the theological faculty at Paris, "When such masters come to the faculty of theology, they can scarcely be detached from their knowledge, as some of them show, who, in their theology, cannot be detached from Aristotle . . . posing philosophical questions and opinions."[42] This in turn was part of a universal change, to be felt throughout the centres of learning in the West. Pope Gregory was bowing to it in 1231 by his decision to establish a commission to expurgate the errors of the *libri naturales* so that they would be fit for study. In the event the commission never completed its work, but the barriers to Graeco-Arabian philosophy had in effect been lifted. For the next 40 years the full range of accessible knowledge was explored until, by the 1270s, the limits of orthodoxy had been reached and passed. The reaction that followed began the retreat of philosophy from revealed truth.

Until the middle years of the 13th century the predominant effect of the Graeco-Arabian corpus was to accentuate the neo-Platonic elements in it. This largely centred upon the need to Christianize the succession of intelligences coming between the One and the separated active intellect, the last in the spiritual hierarchy; the illumination from the latter was in turn the source of human understanding. Such a division between the One and the active intellect could only, as we have seen, make God an indirect mover in human affairs and man himself subject to a celestial power instead of to God. From a Christian standpoint it had to be overcome; and from the late 1220s onwards an increasing number of theologians attempted to do so, among them William of Auxerre, William of Auvergne, and Philip the Chancellor.

All three were at some time members of the theological faculty at Paris. Of these William of Auvergne (*c.* 1180–1249), Bishop of Paris at the time of the university's dispersion in 1229 and remaining at Paris until his death, went furthest to assimilate the new ideas.[43]

To begin with, he was prepared to follow Aristotle "in all his statements in which he was found to be right." That these were no longer confined to matters of dialectic can be seen in two important steps that William took. One was to identify the separated, active intellect with God and thereby to treat its illumination of the human intellect as divine illumination. Here William, like the majority of his contemporaries, was drawing upon Avicenna's interpretation of Aristotle's cosmology. Avicenna and other Arabian thinkers had transformed the active intellect, conceived by Aristotle as part of the human intellect, into a separate celestial intelligence. In choosing to follow Avicenna's conception—itself in keeping with the view of Aristotle presented by the *Liber de causis*—William was at the beginning of a line of Augustinian thinkers that stretched through the 13th century. Although many of the most influential Augustinians, such as St Bonaventure, took the other alternative and treated the active intellect as the property of the individual soul, William had pointed the way to adapting the new cosmology to St Augustine's teaching. He thereby gave it a new import, above all as it concerned illumination and the soul. Like all such refinements, it went beyond the original outlook from which it derived. The Augustinianism of the mid- and late 13th century included elements and emphases not found in St Augustine. But on the essentials of illumination, the independence of the soul as a spiritual being, the dichotomy between intelligible understanding of necessary truths and sensory experience, and the primacy of essence or forms as the constituents of all being, its adherents were in the tradition of St Augustine. The additions such as the doctrine of hylomorphism—the combination of form and matter—for all beings, spiritual as well as material, and the much more defined place given to sensory knowledge, were part of the refinements that the new cosmology called forth.

William's other important step, again under the influence of Avicenna, was to treat the relation between God and creatures in terms of being. Here, too, he introduced one of the central themes of all subsequent theological speculation until the time of Duns Scotus, half a century later. For William, like Avicenna, it revolved around the distinction between essence and existence, which in turn served to distinguish divine from created beings. Among creatures, essence or nature does not of itself signify existence: to say "man" does connote the existence of an individual man, say Socrates or Plato. Until the individual man takes on an independent existence, humanity as his essence represents only possible being. In God, on the other hand, essence and existence were synonymous, because God as creator must by definition necessarily exist. He was therefore pure being. This can be seen as a metaphysical development of Boethius's division between that which is (*id quod est*) and that by which it is (*quo est*). It was a development taken up by St Thomas, and repeatedly.

In these ways William of Auvergne gave an orientation to subsequent Christian thought. Although he by no means developed them into a new integrated system, he sought to come to terms with Aristotelian concepts such as abstraction by subsuming them under Augustinian notions such as illumination. The effect was to stress the neo-Platonic elements in the new corpus and to harmonize it with St Augustine above all. St Augustine's thinking thereby itself took on a new significance.

St Bonaventure

These tendencies were taken further, particularly by the Franciscan thinkers at Paris, notably Alexander of Hales (*c.* 1186–1245), John of La Rochelle (d. 1245), and above all St Bonaventure (1221–74). Perhaps their most noteworthy development was the more complex elaboration of the operations of the soul in an ascending order from the senses, through reason and intellect, to intelligence, concerned with the supreme truth and good, which is God. At the same time, they diverged from William of Auvergne in attributing an active intellect to each individual soul. For John of La Rochelle the active intellect was the result of God's working in the soul; it was distinct from the soul's own substance, enabling it to know the intelligible nature of all that it experienced. The active intellect contrasted with the possible intellect in man, which was a *tabula rasa*, dependent upon the illumination of the active intellect for knowledge of intelligibles. This was to take over Aristotle's distinctions and to incorporate them into an Augustinian framework. It is evidence of the Christian awareness of the need to come to terms with Graeco-Arabian philosophy.

This awareness is equally apparent in the outlook of St Bonaventure. It was essentially a restatement of St Anselm's position of faith seeking understanding, but in the new scholastic form of the mid-13th century. The role of Aristotle was principally a delimiting one. The need to take account of his philosophy led St Bonaventure to marshal more systematically than perhaps any other mediaeval thinker the theological truths handed down by Augustine as they had become defined philosophically: namely, inner illumination with special emphasis upon the divine quality of light as the universal element of being; individual being as composed of a plurality of forms, including a distinctive form for matter; the soul as an independent spiritual being; and seminal reasons or tendencies inherent in matter to receive certain forms (an idea taken over by St Augustine from the Stoics). Within this framework St Bonaventure utilized a number of Aristotle's distinctions; but the context remained non-Aristotelian. St Bonaventure belonged to the tradition that put inner experience before external knowledge, making the soul the centre of awareness, and sought illumination by seeking God and following Christ. St Bonaventure was a Franciscan and, like many of his order, a mystic. He shared the mystical evocation of the Passion and the Virgin with his founder and with the Franciscan poets—of whom he was one—especially Pecham, Jacopone of Todi, and Thomas of Celano. For them all, Jesus was the central figure. For St Bonaventure, as for St Francis, nature was to be venerated not for itself but as God's work. St Bonaventure showed something of the same regard for creation as a theophany as John Scotus had expressed: in St Bonaventure's words, the whole of creation is an open book in which we read the Trinity.[44]

The foundation of St Bonaventure's outlook was that reason should follow faith as far as it could, until faith alone took over in reaching a higher awareness of God in the soul. The subject of theology was the credible; reason was used to render it intelligible.[45] The need, therefore, was to ascend from the signs, or vestiges, of God in creatures, through his image in the soul, to contemplation in love and knowledge of him. The evidence of God was correspondingly in an ascending order of importance. That offered by sensible experience was the least able to give us knowledge of him; only by turning away from the world to the soul could we begin to find the image of God. St Bonaventure took over St Anselm's onto-logical proof to demonstrate that, once aware of God's image, we cannot doubt his existence, even though we do not know him in himself. That is to say, awareness of God means by definition that he *is*.[46] Divine illumin-ation in this highest form was therefore supernatural: it came from God through his grace.

Within this distinctive spirituality St Bonaventure gave a precision to the other main Augustinian tenets of the period. The soul's inde-pendence as a spiritual being was affirmed, while Aristotle's psychology of abstraction was accepted for sensory knowledge; the distinction between man's possible and active intellects represented two phases in this process, the illumination of the active intellect enabling the possible intellect to classify the images of objects already derived from the senses. We know higher intelligible truths not through abstraction but within, through illumination in the manner described by St Augustine: by the eternal reasons in the soul, which are a reflection of the divine ideas in God. Hence all certainty lay in their light. By the same token, all beings, matter included, were composed of essences, which were prior to their existence. Because all created beings comprise both matter and form, they contained a plurality of forms: those of matter (in turn made up of the universal form of light and the forms of the four elements) and those, such as the human soul, that give it identity. Individuation is thus the combination of matter and form so far as corporeal beings are concerned. For the angels, on the other hand, it derives from their spiritual forms alone.

St Bonaventure gave a decisive stamp to Augustinianism, although he left the lecture room and the study of theology to become general of the Franciscan order in 1257, when still in his early thirties. His outlook became associated above all with the Franciscan school. As can be seen, it was a reaffirmation of Augustinianism through assimilating to it Aristotelian—and indeed Jewish—elements. It could not for that reason be called a synthesis between the old and the new. On the contrary, what is most noteworthy in the Franciscan outlook is the accentuation of the dualism between nature and grace, faith and reason, the intelligible and the sensory. The two realms were each given due recognition—in a way that neither St Augustine nor St Anselm began to approach—only to demonstrate more clearly the difference, indeed the gulf, between them. Metaphysically, the link between them lay in the all-pervasiveness of essence. As the created reflection of the archetypes of all being in God, essences or forms were the source at once of being and intelligibility; they extended to all existence, including matter itself. Existence was thereby relegated to the mere occasion of being. The practical outcome was to force attention upon the intelligible.

Science at Oxford

Not surprisingly, such an emphasis gave little encouragement to the investigation of natural phenomena in their more directly physical aspects; and the absence of experiment, which has long been recognized as the major weakness in mediaeval science, was a direct legacy of Augustinianism. At the same time, however, by turning the mind away from sensory experience to a knowledge of intelligibles, it stimulated the study of mathematics and thereby (at least in their theoretical and cosmological aspect) the natural sciences of physics and mechanics. The outstanding thinkers in these fields were to be found not at Paris, with its predominantly dialectical and speculative tradition, but at Oxford.

Two things accounted for Oxford's scientific pre-eminence in northern Europe during the 13th and 14th centuries. The first was the early appearance in the field of English translators of Arabian and Greek scientific works, such as Adelard of Bath, Daniel of Morley, and Alfred of Sareshel, who helped to generate a scientific tradition going back to the 12th century.[47] The second was the presence and influence of Robert Grosseteste (1175–1263), first chancellor of Oxford university and also first lecturer to the Franciscans, newly established in the city, from 1229 to 1231.

Doctrinally Grosseteste was in the full Augustinian tradition; theologically he added little to it. But metaphysically he provided it with a new foundation that was to produce some of the most fruitful scientific speculation of the Middle Ages and to give a new direction to Oxford thinking. This had two aspects. One was his acceptance of the Augustinian dualism between the sensory and the intelligible; the other was the Augustinian doctrine of illumination.[48] As far as the first was concerned, Grosseteste, in his Commentary on Aristotle's *Posterior Analytics*, sought to establish the basis upon which the mind could arrive at demonstrable truths. He distinguished between knowledge that was self-evident, such as the axioms of mathematics, which held without recourse to the evidence of the senses, and knowledge that could only be gained inductively, through generalizing individual occurrences. The certainty of mathematics led Grosseteste to look to it as the highest form of knowledge attainable to man in his natural state, and to employ mathematical reasoning in attempting to establish scientific propositions. The impetus that his use of mathematics gave to physical calculations and to the study of optics carried through Roger Bacon (*c.* 1214–94), his foremost pupil, to 14th-century mathematicians such as Bradwardine and the Mertonian school. It was directly related to the second aspect of his work, on light. As expressed in his treatise *On Light*, it has come to be known as the light-metaphysic. For Grosseteste, light was the universal stuff of all being. The reason lay in its substance, which was so fine as to be almost incorporeal. It therefore needed only to be diffused beyond a point (which has no magnitude) to become corporeal. Now, it is the characteristic of light to be ceaselessly diffusing itself. From its self-diffusion Grosseteste traced the physical existence of the universe. Initially created by God, light, as the first matter and form, multiplied until it had engendered the universe. It ceased when it had reached the limits of refraction, and was accordingly finite. From this, Grosseteste went on to explain the different spheres and elements. The ingenuity of his cosmology apart, Grosseteste gave a new importance to light as an object of physical and mathematical investigation. The divine illumination of God in the soul had its counterpart in the physical world, of which light was the ultimate constituent. The effect was to introduce a new dimension into mediaeval thinking: to Aristotle's logical categories and Aristotelian cosmology and metaphysics were now added mathematical inquiry, by which alone they could be properly understood, and which, with Bacon, marked the beginnings of something like experimental science. If they did not advance very far in that direction, mediaeval science and the growth of a non-Aristotelian cosmology were a positive step toward scientific development in the 16th and 17th centuries. They must be taken into account as the accompaniment of the decline of scholasticism and the product of a predominantly Augustinian tradition.

It is in the light of the latter's continuance that the thorough-going acceptance of Aristotelianism must be seen. This took two main directions: the Christian Aristotelianism of St Thomas Aquinas and the pure Aristotelianism (often but misleadingly called Latin Averroism) predominant among the arts faculty at Paris. It was only with Albertus Magnus (*c.* 1206–80) that a change towards a deliberate acceptance of Aristotelianism became apparent. Although already in evidence during the 1240s at Oxford—which had not suffered the bans on the *libri naturales*—it was another decade in making itself felt at Paris. By then Albertus had left Paris after eight years in the theological faculty from 1240 to 1248. It was at the Dominican *studium* in Cologne and with the co-operation of the general of the order, Humbert of the Romans, that he embarked upon his life work of presenting Aristotle's works to the Christian world. To achieve this aim of making "all parts of the physics, metaphysics, and mathematics [of Aristotle] intelligible to the Latins," he followed Avicenna's method of paraphrase, rather than commentary in the manner of Averroes and later of St Thomas. His cosmology was also strongly Avicennan. It was in Albertus's preparedness to take the Graeco-Arabian philosophy on its own terms for the natural order that he is important, rather than as an original thinker. Unlike that of his pupil St Thomas, his vast erudition did not result in a new synthesis. But he was the first Christian thinker of the Middle Ages to accept the independence of philosophical criteria from those of theology. Philosophy and theology were distinct activities with different objects and premises: one was governed by reason and demonstrative evidence, the other by the articles of faith. Each thereby gained a defined place. In terms of Christian thought, this was his greatest legacy, and it was taken up above all by St Thomas Aquinas (1226–74).

St Thomas Aquinas

Albertus, however, spoke as a theologian. Although reason and faith were complementary, they were not equal. For him, as for his contemporaries, all knowledge must submit to the judgment of revealed truth. It was when that was no longer accepted as axiomatic among the philosophers of the arts faculty that conflict arose. Albertus cannot be held responsible for that; it was rather a danger inherent in differentiating between philosophy and theology. That it need not occur can be seen in the different conclusions that St Bonaventure and St Thomas drew from the demarcation between faith and reason. St Bonaventure's response was to seek to transcend natural experience in a higher theological awareness, but St Thomas put natural theology upon a new philosophical foundation. He was the first to accept Aristotle's metaphysics as the means of doing so. From that standpoint his outlook was the antithesis of St Bonaventure's and different in kind from Albertus's. They had both kept Aristotelianism (and the Arabian systems) separate from the tenets of theology, at most selecting certain aspects of Aristotle's psychology to explain the soul's sensory knowledge. This was inevitable so long as the Augustinian framework of the independence of the intelligible was maintained; being was then regarded as the property of essence, which could be conceived only by a spiritual being, namely, the soul. To start from the actual existence of the sensory world as the basis of created being, as St Thomas did, and to take its modes as the explanation of being as such, was little short of revolutionary: it was to make all knowledge begin from the senses and to overcome the division between sensory and intelligible understanding. The autonomy of inner knowledge and the need for divine illumination were thereby dispensed with.

St Thomas did not credit natural experience or human reason with a greater capacity to elucidate the mysteries of faith than St Bonaventure did; but he accepted for them a less transcendental role. Man's dependence upon the senses for any higher awareness sprang from his present earthbound state. The understanding that he could gain was correspondingly restricted: it could give no demonstrable knowledge of God's nature, the Incarnation, the creation of the world in time, or other Christian tenets, which had to be held on faith. What natural reason could do was to recognize an analogy between God the creator and his creatures, of whom he is the cause.

This, like all human knowledge, was reached through abstraction. The mind by its own natural powers was able to recognize the intelligible forms and principles inhering in the individual things encountered through the senses. By isolating these universal elements the mind restored them to their state of pure intelligibility as the essences that derived from the archetypes in God. From knowledge of these elements—such as goodness, or humanity, or whiteness—judgments could be formed affirming what they were.

The most universal of such concepts was being, the first intelligible by which everything else could be known. Knowledge of it enabled us to arrive at the axioms that governed all our thinking, such as the principles of contradiction, substance, efficient causality, and so on. These could in turn be applied to our propositions about God, by definition the supreme

251

being. By means of Aristotle's categories of causality, potentiality, and actuality, St Thomas established God's existence by five proofs in terms of the distinction between a first necessary being and possible beings. He went beyond Avicenna and William of Auvergne to Aristotle's notion of being as actual existence rather than essence, to show that in God essence and existence were the same. Because only that which actually exists is being and God must be, he is pure actuality, and so self-caused. His existence must be given in his essence as God. His creatures, on the other hand, receive their being from him; hence they have to pass from potentiality to actuality before they can exist. They therefore need an efficient cause in order to be, so that their essence and existence are not synonymous.

Although the analogy between God and creatures was founded upon the Aristotelian notion of being as existence, it was made possible only by the Christian notion of God as creator. Aristotle's first uncaused cause was unconcerned with what lay outside it; St Thomas's God was first cause in virtue of freely willing to confer being upon the archetypes of all possible things eternally known to him.[49] Hence, although St Thomas rejected St Anselm's ontological proof for God's existence on the grounds that the mind can have no concept of God as infinite being, he adhered to the traditional Augustinian doctrine of divine ideas: "All things must pre-exist in the word of God before they exist in their own nature." In that sense they participated in God's being, not in sharing his being but in holding their existence from his perfections. By recognizing them in individual things we are enabled to gain a faint glimmering of God's attributes, his wisdom, omnipotence, goodness, and so on. This is attained by abstraction.

St Thomas's system was therefore Christian before it was Aristotelian. Nevertheless it diverged too deeply from the established Augustinian positions to be regarded as another variant. In addition to his rejection of divine illumination for higher necessary truths, St Thomas also made a radical departure on two other Christian fundamentals. Both arose from his adoption of the Aristotelian analysis of all created being as composed of matter and form. Matter was of itself merely potential; form was the active agent that conferred being upon the matter to which it was joined. The antinomy was therefore not between being and non-being, but between potentiality and actuality; it was resolved through the conjunction of form and matter. On the one hand, "form gives being to the thing"; on the other hand, matter became the principle of individuation.

In the context of the time, the effects were far-reaching. Matter at once lost its own form and became "the principle of diversity among individuals of the same species." It was thus inseparable from all being, itself conceived as actual existence. In turn, a single substantial form—humanity in a man, or whiteness in something white—displaced the traditional Augustinian plurality of forms.

It was as they concerned man that the full implications of St Thomas's notions are to be measured. To begin with, they meant the rejection of illumination for abstraction, because, as we have seen, man could know only through the senses. This in turn was due to the way in which the soul was joined to the body in this world. St Thomas fully upheld the spiritual nature of the soul and its immortality as a spiritual being; but where all previous Christian thinkers had conceived it as a spiritual being inhabiting a body, for St Thomas the soul was the substantial form of the body; it defined man's nature and gave him actuality as a being. In his own words: "I say that there is no other substantial form in man than the intellective soul, and as such it contains virtually all inferior forms."[50] That was at once to dethrone the two cherished Augustinian principles of the soul's autonomy and the plurality of forms within any being. Not surprisingly it aroused more opposition than any other of St Thomas's conclusions. To his opponents it appeared that St Thomas had bound the soul to the body, making it dependent upon the senses for its understanding instead of directing the body. Together with his dismissal of illumination he seemed to deny man any direct contact with intelligible reality or awareness of the divine truths within the soul.

St Thomas also departed from Augustinian tradition by assigning primacy to the intellect in moral actions. Man as an intelligent being apprehended the objects to which he inclined and so had the capacity to choose between them. Therein lay his free will; but in his natural state, although he sought the supreme good, he could not directly apprehend it. He could only seek to discover which particular good was most closely related to the supreme good. This was the ceaseless task of the intellect. Man could act virtuously only by the correct use of his reason. Its rules were binding commandments that sprang from God's eternal law regulating the whole of creation. They were accessible to man through the natural law, which bore its imprint. As man's being was a participation in God's being, so the natural law was a participation in the eternal law. In both, St Thomas saw the complementarity between the divine and the created: "Grace does not abolish nature, but perfects it."

Nevertheless, to his contemporaries among the theologians, St Thomas seemed to have withdrawn knowledge from divine understanding and to have put the soul at the disposal of the body. On one occasion in about 1270, after his return to Paris, he was confronted by more than 20 opponents of his doctrine of the oneness of the substantial form, which they "solemnly excommunicated."[51] It was not owing to his tenets alone, however, that opposition became so bitter. During the decade from 1259 to 1269, while he was teaching at the Dominican *studium* in Naples, a stream of heterodox Aristotelianism associated with Averroes was developing in the arts faculty. It made no attempt to harmonize faith with natural experience—the foundation of St Thomas's system—or to safeguard faith from a clash between them. St Thomas's absence removed any middle way between the pure Aristotelians in the arts faculty and the theologians who followed Augustine and the traditional outlook in all that concerned the tenets of faith. By the time he returned to Paris in 1269 there was no hope of mending the rift between the extremes; and before long St Thomas entered the struggle on the side of the theologians, although his own ideas were attacked, and some were to be condemned in 1277, three years after his death.

Averroism

As we have said, the tendency in the study of philosophy was to follow reason beyond the limits set by faith. Already in the 1230s there were signs of this in the arts faculty at Paris, in questions arising from the study of Aristotle's *Ethics*. But the dangers became apparent only in the late 1260s, and crystallized, paradoxically, through the attacks upon them by Albertus Magnus and St Thomas as well as by St Bonaventure. By then the study of the metaphysics and natural philosophy of Aristotle and his Arabian commentators had developed an anti-Christian cosmogony largely inspired by Averroes. It led to propositions asserting that, from the standpoint of natural reason, the world could be considered eternal; that there was a single intellect for all mankind (monopsychism); that men had no individual immortal souls; that God was no more than an indirect mover; and that in place of his providence there were the celestial spheres acting directly upon all creatures. These propositions were tantamount to a denial not only of Christian belief but of theology as demonstrable truth.

The importance of Averroes was twofold. First, he alone of the Arabian philosophers interpreted the notion of the active intellect so as to denude man of any independent spiritual faculty: man's soul was corruptible and material and would die with him; the intelligible knowledge that he gained under the influence of the active intellect left him on death. Second, Averroes, like his fellow-Arabians, was a Moslem as well as an Aristotelian, and he sought to regulate the relations between his faith and philosophy. Unlike Albertus and St Thomas, however, he was not prepared to treat them as complementary and to try to reconcile what he considered to be irreconcilable. For him the very differences between faith and reason sprang from different levels of truth; hence their divergences had to be recognized, not artificially overcome. This distinction, somewhat loosely known as the "double truth," was applied by the philosophers in the arts faculty. But there is no evidence for regarding it as a deliberate attempt to undermine the articles of faith. It is true that St Thomas, among others, accused the philosophers of affirming by reason what was contrary to faith; but certainly after 1270, when the first condemnation of 13 propositions occurred, the leading so-called Latin Averroist, Siger of Brabant (d. before 1285), tended increasingly to stress that propositions held philosophically could be wrong when taken theologically. Such a position did not amount to the double truth; on the contrary, it acknowledged that philosophical conclusions could be judged false. Even if Siger was not sincere in his professions, it was a valid qualification to make.

The real issue, however, was over the nature of the ideas to which it was applied. Here Siger and Boethius of Dacia (d. after 1283), the main figures, seem to have followed Averroes in his interpretation of Aristotle, particularly his doctrine of monopsychism. But they did so less as creators of specific philosophical systems than as commentators on Aristotelian and Arabian philosophical texts. For that reason it is difficult to distinguish their own opinions from those they were expounding. Monopsychism, as we have seen, was only one among them; although Siger seems to have renounced it after the attack upon it by St Thomas in his treatise *On the Unity of the Intellect* (1270), the philosophical movement continued.

How it arose is not known. In one sense it was the outcome of the arts faculty curriculum from 1250 onwards in making accessible for study the full Graeco-Arabian corpus. In another sense it was inherent in the need to come to terms with a body of non-Christian thought that could not be ignored. From the point of view of authority the failure to Christianize Aristotelianism made it a threat to Christian belief. The dangers from its undiluted tenets seem first to have attracted attention in the mid-1250s when Albertus Magnus, on a visit to Rome, was commissioned by Pope Alexander IV to write a treatise against Averroes's errors, which he did in his *De unitate intellectus contra Averroem*. This was the first explicit association of Averroes with the doctrine of monopsychism; a few years earlier at Oxford, Roger Bacon and Adam Buckfield had interpreted him in a contrary sense. Even at this stage Albertus was arguing against the Arabian thinkers as a whole, not against a specific school of Averroists. This development occurred a decade later, towards the end of the 1260s.

Tempier's Condemnations

The first signal of a new phase came in a series of Lenten lectures by St Bonaventure at the Franciscan convent at Paris in 1267 and 1268. There St Bonaventure directly attacked the errors of the pagan philosophers mentioned earlier, which were being propagated in the arts faculty. St Bonaventure saw their source in the pursuit of philosophy for itself. Three years later St Thomas, the supreme Christian Aristotelian, joined the battle with his treatise *On the Unity of the Intellect*, directed against monopsychism. Unlike St Bonaventure he did so not by condemning philosophy but by philosophically refuting Averroes' arguments. He had some success with Siger; but not enough either to stem the movement or to escape the opprobrium that his own use of Aristotelian ideas brought upon him. To the conservatives St Thomas, too, had taught what was "contrary to the teaching of the saints." In the same year, 1270, came the first of the two condemnations by the Bishop of Paris, Stephen Tempier, a former master in the theological faculty. Thirteen propositions on the soul, providence, the eternity of the world, creation, and free will were anathematized, and anyone holding or teaching them was to be excommunicated. They therefore extended to the main Aristotelian and Arabian positions besides monopsychism.

These remained the themes of the next phase of polemics, which culminated in Tempier's second condemnation in 1277. The failure of the first to silence the arts philosophers precipitated a new wave of attacks upon them. Once again it was St Bonaventure who in his *Collationes in hexaemeron*, delivered at Paris in 1273, set the tone: the truths of theology must be put first even if their defence involved suppression of philosophical opinions. "It is more prudent," he declared, "to say that Aristotle did not think the world was eternal, whether he himself thought so or not, for he was so great that all would follow him and affirm that he said so."[52]

Giles of Rome also wrote two treatises between 1270 and 1274; the first, *The Errors of the Philosophers*, dealt with the doctrines of Aristotle,

Avicenna, Maimonides, and others besides Averroes. He also wrote a refutation of monopsychism along the lines of St Thomas. Meanwhile, some time between 1272 and 1276, a Flemish Dominican, Giles of Lessines, sought to enlist the aging Albertus by sending him 15 questions for comment extracted from the teachings of "the masters in the arts faculty who are reputed the most important." But the reply he received was of little relevance.

Tempier's second condemnation was the culmination of over 10 years of growing tension.[53] This time nothing suspect was omitted. Its 219 articles constituted an attack upon naturalism and paganism in most of its known forms. Although the attack revolved around the previous themes, it also dealt with the treatise of Andreas Capellanus on courtly love, *De amore* (or *De arte honeste amandi*), and a number of Thomist theses on individuation, the intellect, and its relation to the will. Their conjunction, although haphazard, is not fortuitous. The second condemnation differed from the first in having been initiated by Pope John XXI, who as Peter Hispanus had taught logic in the arts faculty at Paris. The pope had written ordering Tempier to investigate reports of erroneous opinions in the arts faculty. Tempier not only gathered together all that he could find, but he went further and condemned them. The pope then ordered Siger of Brabant and Boethius of Dacia to appear before him; Siger died at the papal curia several years later, having been in confinement.

There is a striking parallel between the philosophical and the ethical propositions listed by Tempier. Although the book of Andreas Capellanus was not perhaps the most representative of the philosophy of courtly love, it was nevertheless a widely read hand-book on the art of love. For that alone it stood condemned. Moreover, it shared the widespread notion, expressed particularly in the *Roman de la rose* by Jean de Meung (Jean Clopinel), that what is natural is good, including love. Jean, indeed, had gone so far as to call the species "eternal being," to preserve which "nature has set delight in it."[54] Such views have their counterpart in Tempier's 219 propositions. Jean de Meung was a master in the arts faculty in the 1270s when he was completing* the *Roman de la rose*: he was also an opponent of the friars, and satirized their claims to evangelical perfection based upon a life of poverty and begging in both the *Roman* and a series of other poems. His anti-mendicancy is of a piece with his naturalism: to live in poverty was a denial of man's nature and could lead only to hypocrisy, the charge most commonly levelled at the friars. The papacy

* The first 4000 lines of the 22,000-line poem had been written by Guillaume de Lorris between 1225 and 1237.

had been the main support of the friars in their struggle with the rest of the university during the 1250s; it is at least possible that more than one of Jean's own opinions was included in Tempier's condemnation. Thus proposition 9 declared "that there was not a first man nor will there be a last man, but there always was and always will be generation of man by man." Similarly a series of propositions expressed a profane, indeed an amoral, attitude to sex: that continence was not necessarily a virtue (168), that perfect abstinence from sexual intercourse destroyed virtue and the species (169); that chastity was not a greater good than perfect abstinence (187); that enjoyment and lovemaking did not impair the use of the intellect (172); that humility, which consists in self-humiliation, was not a virtue (171); that happiness belonged to this life, not another (176). They went together with a devaluation of theological truths; they were founded on fables (152), and Christian law, like any other, contained myths and falsehoods (174). Men should not be content to accept as certain what was decreed by authority (150).

Philosophy and natural reason, on the other hand, were exalted. All the good of which man was capable resided in his intellectual powers (144); there was no question open to reason that the philosopher could not determine (145); he could decide what was possible and impossible (146). This was tantamount to reversing the order between the philosopher and the theologian. Only the philosophers were wise in knowing the world (154); a man rightly orientated through philosophy was in a position to gain eternal bliss (157). Conversely, the supernatural nature of ecstasies and visions was denied (33).

The challenge to Christian faith in the 219 propositions was thus no longer covert. They represented the open denial of its fundamental propositions, including God's nature as a Trinity (1), God as creator (2, 4, 5, 43, 44, 48, 49, 55), his omnipotence (25, 29), and his omniscience (42). He became a remote first cause (43, 44, 55), his power over this world annexed to the heavely spheres and separated intelligences (56, 60, 67, 71, 72, 78). It was upon these that man was dependent (73, 74). Hence, in place of God's immediate action upon his creatures, the universe became subject to astral determinism operating eternally (87, 90, 92, 94, 95, 98, 99, 107). "Philosophical reason demonstrating that the movement of the heavens is eternal is not sophistical; and it is surprising that men of understanding do not see this" (92). The main consequence of its recognition as revealed in the propositions was monopsychism and lack of personal immortality (116–22, 125–7). Because the superior intelligences impressed themselves on the inferior, man's rational or intellectual soul knew only through the active intellect to which his knowledge belonged (115). The dependence of the human intellect upon the active intellect in turn subjected man's will to his understanding. The primacy of the intellect over the will—also one of St Thomas's tenets, but from very different premises—thus became one of the great issues of the next 50 years; henceforth it was associated with the absence of free will and the power of the heavenly bodies.

The revulsion against any kind of determinism was perhaps the most lasting legacy of the condemnations. Its presence runs through the articles of 1277. "There is no freedom of action, but it is determined," declared proposition 160; this could be by reason (129, 163) or by the will's own appetites (134, 164), as well as by the celestial bodies (133, 161–2). It meant the loss of the soul's autonomy. "The soul wills only when it is moved by something else; hence it is false to say that the soul wills of itself" (190).

It would be quite artificial to see the 219 propositions as representing a coherent outlook or as the work of any defined school. They were, as we have said, a collection of all that appeared inimical to Christian belief. Compiled by theologians, they constituted an attack upon the devaluation of theological truth. As such, they cannot be regarded as impartial; no doubt many of the opinions included were distortions or based on hearsay. Yet it cannot be denied that together they stood for a naturalistic view of reality largely inspired by Graeco-Arabian philosophy, a view that came from applying natural standards to man and to the world. The absence of any transcendental conception of reality is their most striking feature. Necessity and determinism are their themes. In that sense they are at the opposite pole from the idealism of Chartres. The propositions of 1277 represent a desacralizing of nature and a despiritualizing of man. The mechanisms of the stars and the instincts govern all creation; and man's reason is to be used to recognize this. Apart from a few more flagrantly anti-ecclesiastical sentiments, the 219 propositions should be regarded less as attacking the foundations of faith than as expressing its inapplicability to natural experience. To have accepted such an attitude would have meant dethroning theology. Philosophy had therefore to withdraw from its attempts to explain reality. After 1277 it increasingly did so; but in leaving the field free for theological truth it also abandoned the attempts to give such truth metaphysical support. In short, 1277 saw the beginning of the end of the attempt to harmonize faith with natural reason, which had been the foundation of Christian thought since St Augustine.

The Aftermath of the Condemnations

Although 1277 was a turning-point, the events of that year were not alone responsible for the changed climate of the later Middle Ages. The crisis in intellectual life was part of a growing tension in religious life as a whole. Ockhamism, as the dominant outlook of the 14th century, enshrined the polarization between faith and reason; it had its spiritual accompaniment in the prevalence of mysticism, with its stress upon inner experience, while ecclesiologically there was a parallel movement for a return to apostolic simplicity and reform.

In contrast to the developments of the preceding epoch, these new developments did not receive their impulse from external events, such as the translations, or from new institutions, such as the universities, or from new religious orders. On the contrary, they arose because there was no comparable replacement of existing forms. The change that becomes apparent from about the 1280s is through the decline of these forms. This change was more revolutionary than anything before it: it was inspired by a revulsion against the existing order and a desire to return to first principles.

Much the same tension is apparent in mediaeval society generally. From the first decade or so of the 14th century there was a growing disequilibrium. It is to be seen in the universal economic recession—of population, trade, land under cultivation, towns, prosperity—and with it a loss of social stability. This was accentuated by the series of plagues of which the worst was the Black Death from 1348 to 1350, and of endemic wars in Italy and between France and England, which in turn weakened the existing political structure and helped to engender the unrest that made the 14th century, perhaps more than any other, a period of class struggles. Nor was there any counterbalance from the Church. By the end of the 13th century the papacy had irretrievably lost the universal authority of a century before; the change was symbolized in the attempt by the agents of the French king, Philip IV, to kidnap Boniface VIII in 1303. Although the Church continued to be the most pervasive power within society, its position now rested almost exclusively upon its privileges as an institution rather than upon its spiritual force. There were no new religious orders to succeed the friars. When, by the later decades of the 13th century, their reforming zeal was spent, spiritual renewal was sought outside the Church, in unofficial groupings, or in mystical experience, or in the advocacy of ecclesiastical reform.

The Church, however, remained the ideological focus of society; hence it was within its ambit that the main ideological issues continued to be debated. But now these debates increasingly centred upon the failure to harmonize Christian principles with their application. The tension between them had, as we have seen, underlain Christian thought. From about the 1280s, however, it became uppermost, extending over the whole front of awareness: intellectual, spiritual, and institutional. The recognition that the existing balance was wrong was the great new force in later mediaeval Christian thinking.

It arose from the very nature of a society in which there was a spiritual and intellectual arbiter. By the 13th century the Church was suffering from its own success as an institution. As the communion of all believers it was confronted with the problem of how to combine authority with comprehensiveness. Until the middle of the 12th century it had been at the centre of the successive movements for religious reform. Its struggle for freedom from lay oppression and the imposition of Christian standards had canalized the idealism of successive generations from Humbert and Damian to St Bernard. Yet in achieving independence it had come increasingly to take on the attributes of a privileged corporation, as had the monastic congregations—above all, the Cluniacs and Cistercians— which had originated in the desire to purge themselves of involvement with the world. The growing definition of the rights and powers of the Church and its hierarchy in canon law made their maintenance a central preoccupation. From the 12th century onwards the Church was increasingly a career open to talents. As the one truly ecumenical body it offered advancement to those who had the qualities demanded in the exercise of any kind of authority. The personnel of the papal curia and bishops' chanceries were distinguished from their secular counterparts principally by their greater learning and sophistication, rather than by different spiritual qualities. Until the later 13th century, ecclesiastical organization was far in advance of secular governments, and reached its height in the 14th century under the Avignon popes.

Inevitably, therefore, while it would be quite mistaken to speak of a moral decline, the Church came increasingly to take on the very attributes of worldliness and wealth that it was supposed to hold in contempt. Its hierarchy appeared to be one more privileged corporation. That made it vulnerable because, even if its increasingly burdensome financial demands could be justified by its spiritual functions, the Church was concerned with men's souls. It was the communion of all believers of every sort and condition. Hence it must ultimately be judged by spiritual criteria.[55]

Already in the 12th century this had led to the emergence of lay reforming groups, such as the Waldensians and the Humiliati, who had pointed to the contrast between the present life of the Church and the poverty and simplicity in which Christ and the apostles had lived. They had attempted to emulate Christ's example by preaching his gospel and living on alms. In doing so they had inevitably clashed with the clergy. A number of such movements had been banned and became heretical, foremost among them the Waldensians. The coming of the orders of friars, founded upon the same apostolic principles of poverty and preaching, had offered a new outlet for reform. But they were to be the last. In 1215 the Fourth Lateran Council had decreed—because of hostility from the local clergy—that no new religious orders were to be founded.

The consequences of this decree were to be felt throughout the rest of the Middle Ages. When spiritual renewal could no longer come through the existing forms of the Church, it sought outlets elsewhere. This was happening by the later 13th century, not only in the growth of extra-ecclesiastical movements such as the Beguines and the various apostolic groups in Italy, but also in the struggles within existing orders, above all the Franciscans. It was accentuated by 50 years of papal involvement in fighting its enemies over Sicily. This had resulted in the abuse of its spiritual and financial prerogatives, which made the very invocation of terms such as "crusade" and "excommunication" suspect; moreover the exploitation of papal dispensations and provisions to benefices left a legacy of hostility that even the much more balanced system of papal government at Avignon could not eliminate. The aggressive policy of successive 13th-century popes, from Innocent IV (1243–54) onwards, provided the central theme of subsequent reformers, even moderate ones: the demand for the Church's return to a purely spiritual role and its relinquishment of any pretensions to power (*plenitudo potestatis*) in temporal matters. The debate reached its climax at Avignon in the 14th century, after the papacy had passed its zenith; henceforward the Church no longer sought to impose its will so overtly outside its own domain. But by then the very foundations of ecclesiastical power had been called into question. The 40 years of the Great Schism, which began in 1378, and the Conciliar movement that succeeded it, effectively ended the universal authority of the Church as an institution, which had long been under ideological attack. Thus 13th-century naturalism had its counterpart in a new spirituality. But, unlike that of naturalism, its inspiration was Christian; and, although quite as subversive of the existing order, it did not reach a sudden *dénouement*, but entered into the outlook of the later Middle Ages. Indeed, in one sense it could be said to have constituted that outlook—the fideism of the Ockhamist no less than the mystic's renunciation of worldly knowledge or the reformer's denunciation of worldly power. To that extent there was a convergence between them in reaffirming the truths that came from faith. Together they represented a Christian reaction to non-Christian theory and practice, and their adherents included the most influential men of the age.

Ockhamism

Let us begin with Ockhamism. As we have seen, 1277 marked a lasting victory for theology. Like all conquests it entailed new alignments. The mere negative act of proscription was not enough: a redefinition of the relation of philosophy to theology was needed. For a time there were attempts by theologians to adopt or to reaffirm different aspects of the older Augustinianism of St Bonaventure, such as the doctrine of illumination, which was resuscitated by Matthew of Aquasparta, general of the Franciscans from 1282 to 1288. But piecemeal adaptations could not suffice: it needed a rethinking of the role of philosophy in theological speculation.

Henry of Ghent (d. 1293), one of the secular masters who had assisted Tempier in 1277, was the first to make the attempt. He was particularly influential in two respects. First, he affirmed God's omnipotence as the positive attribute to do anything. As creator, God was supremely free. This was a riposte to the Graeco-Arabian view of God as an indirect mover. It stressed the radical contingency of everything other than God and its direct dependence upon God's will. Second, Henry sought another metaphysical basis for conceiving God's being; he found it in Avicenna's notion of being as the most universal term of all and the first object of knowledge, coming before any other term such as essence or existence. Thus understood, the idea of God as being could reside in an entirely abstract notion independent of sensory images. The Scottish Franciscan Duns Scotus (1266–1308) developed these conceptions into a new system. It is frequently described as the second Augustinianism; but although Duns, like Henry, sought a return to a more traditional Christian standpoint, away from the deterministic tendencies of Aristotelianism, the outlook that emerged was a radical departure from Augustinianism. Duns went beyond Henry in dispensing with both illumination and the notion of analogy between the divine and the created. Metaphysical knowledge of God was restricted to what could be deduced from the concept of being taken in its most abstract sense—as denoting "to be," as opposed to "not being." This enabled God to be defined as infinite and necessary being. But it could not go beyond that in describing God from the aspect of creation. It was here that Duns's notion of God's will made even more tenuous the connection between natural knowledge and revealed truth. Since God was sovereignly free to do as he willed, and man could experience only the effects of his actions, there was no means of ascribing an order to them from the aspect of God. Beyond saying that God as supreme infinite being decides to act freely and eternally from the knowledge of everything possible that he possesses eternally, man could not establish a causal relation between creation and the way in which God wills. The inherent contingency of creation meant that the knowledge man gained of it naturally was contingent, not necessary. Only faith could give a firm knowledge of God: and that was to move beyond philosophy to theology.

The consequence of Duns's system lay in reducing the area of revealed truth accessible to natural reason. It introduced a discontinuity into the relations between the divine and the created through God's will, which excluded such fundamental questions from philosophical discourse as the immortality of the soul and God's providence, as well as the mode of his operations. The effect was decisive for subsequent Christian thought. Duns's exclusion of illumination and analogy left the notion of common (univocal) being as the only metaphysical link between God and man, and his stress upon God's will brought a new element of indeterminacy to its workings. It needed only the rejection of the one and the development of the other to eliminate any demonstrable arguments for Christian tenets at all. That elimination was accomplished by William of Ockham (*c.* 1300–49).

With Ockham we reach the final separation of faith from natural knowledge.[56] Destructive though he and his followers were of traditional thinking, there can be no direct comparison between Ockhamism and Aristotelianism. Unlike the latter, Ockhamism was the reaction of Christian theologians to the impasse that had been caused by pagan philosophy. It grew out of Henry of Ghent's and Duns Scotus's attempts to find a new basis for Christian thought. The difference is that Ockhamism took the final step of disengaging knowledge founded upon experience from that which could be held only on faith. Much of Ockham's thinking was formulated as a critique of Duns, from whom it took its point of departure. But that should not lead us into treating their opposition in terms of the misleading labels of realism and nominalism. Ockham rejected Duns's metaphysics and notion of common being for a theory of individual knowledge; but he also carried further Duns's stress upon God's omnipotence and the contingency of the created order. He shared the same almost obsessive awareness of the contingent finite nature of creation to which they each opposed the infinite freedom of God. Both thinkers refused to attempt to prove God's existence from laws drawn from natural experience, by either analogy or movement. Again, Ockham followed Duns in reducing the elements of natural knowledge to what could be derived from direct intuitive awareness of the individuals encountered through the senses, differently though he interpreted the status of the concepts that could be thus formulated; and he likewise allowed no place for divine illumination.

Ockham's distinctiveness is in his denial of universals and general categories as the constituents of being: natures, essences, genera, species—all lost their independent ontological status. Being was reduced to individual existence, and hence metaphysics was largely displaced by physics, mechanics, and measurement. Categories such as movement, time, and place became the attributes of objects extended in space and ceased to be independent principles. Certainty had in turn to be founded upon verifiable experience; there was no self-evident reason for affirming the relation of one thing to another that could not be actually known. The vast conceptual apparatus of more than a century of metaphysical speculation was effectively reduced to propositions that could be validly formed from verifiable experience. There was no room for any independent notion of being that, with Duns, had provided the epistemological link between creation and God.

But although Ockham removed any means of unifying being, and so of arriving at a natural theology, he did not thereby leave the natural order to itself. As the work of God it was also contingent, and subject to his will. Ockham was anything but the pure philosopher, content to discuss only what could be adduced from natural experience. Most of his speculative works, like those of all his predecessors, were theological. His main ones, the Commentary on Lombard's *Sentences* and *Quodlibeta*, directly took up the central theological issues debated over the previous 70 years. Hence, although he gave them radically different solutions, they belonged directly to a line running from St Bonaventure and St Thomas, through the post-1277 period, to his own day. Nowhere is this more apparent than in his treatment of God's omnipotence. It was at the opposite pole from the Parisian naturalism of the 1260s and 1270s, coming closer to fideism in submitting all that concerned faith and natural experience alike to God's omnipotence. He did so by taking over the distinction—made as far back as the 11th century by Peter Damian, and given renewed currency by Duns Scotus—between God's ordained power, which was his law for this world, and his absolute power, which referred to his own pure omnipotence and therefore was bound by no dispensation. Duns had used it to stress God's freedom to do directly what he normally did through secondary causes—or not to do it at all. He invoked it to show that God could, as in a miracle, supersede the ordinary laws of creation, which were contingent. It was a direct reply to the determinism condemned in 1277. Although used moderately by Duns, the concept of God's two powers became a hallmark of Ockhamism.

Initially a theological device to show God's freedom from any inexorable movement of secondary causes, it became as great a threat to the foundation of belief as Graeco-Arabian determinism had been. The challenge now came from a divine indeterminacy that, in exalting God's power as creator, made nonsense of moral theology in particular: grace and the other supernatural virtues lost intrinsic efficacy; God in his absolute power could reward the sinner or damn a man in grace, or he could allow a man to resist sin by his own powers. As conceived by the Ockhamists, free will became the beneficiary because God was rewarding its actions, not the moral state of the man who performed them. Ockhamism gave sustained application to the idea that acts are morally neutral, making God the arbiter of whether they are good or bad. It was in this respect that Ockhamism—especially among such men as Thomas Buckingham (d. 1351), Robert Holcot (d. 1349), John of Mirecourt (d. after 1347), Nicholas of Autrecourt (d. after 1346), Adam of Woodham (d. 1357)—was so disruptive of tradition. Together with its denial of any possibility of proofs for God's existence or the other articles of faith, Ockhamism represented the end of the attempt to buttress revealed truth by natural knowledge. It did so in the name of God's ineffability, not the superior wisdom of the philosophers, as in the 1270s. To invoke God's power was not to deny revealed truth but to make it the preserve of faith, passing human understanding. It was not to deny God the accepted attributes of wisdom, mercy, justice, and so on, but to acknowledge that man as a finite and contingent being could have no certain knowledge of these terms as they applied to God. Such limitations could be overcome only through belief at once in God's law and in his power to override it.

Ockhamism, however, was not merely negative and destructive. Although it destroyed the harmony between natural experience and revealed truth, it gave a new consistency to the natural order. Physical laws, no less than those regulating the theological virtues, were liable to be superseded; but in this case to the benefit of cosmology. God, it is true, could make man's knowledge illusory, enabling him to know what no longer existed; but he could also make two bodies occupy the same space concurrently, or make a form infinitely intense, or the world infinite, or more than one world.[57] Here Aristotle's fixed cosmology—eternal, finite, and unvarying—was displaced by the possibilities of an open universe, which was to become so scientifically fruitful in the 17th century. At this stage the movement toward it was still mainly speculative and lacking a firm quantitative basis. But, together with Ockham's simplification of concepts such as movement and the increasing use of mathematical formulations, it gave a new direction to philosophy and science. The constructive intellectual effort of the mid- and late 14th century went increasingly into scientific and mathematical work. If they were not as spectacular as the great theological systems of the 14th century, the treatises on proportions, movement, and kinetics, and the new methods of calculation evolved by Bradwardine, Buridan, Oresme, Dumbleton, Heytesbury, Swineshead, Albert of Saxony, Marsilius of Inghen, and others, represent a comparable creative effort. The difference is that this new intellectual wave was a product of the breakdown of Christian thought.

Although Ockham was not himself a scientific innovator, he had begun the mind's release from the mesh of abstractions in which individual experience had been held—as, for example, his revolutionarily simple explanation that movement consisted in something moving, which was taken up by Buridan in his theory of impulse (*impetus*). Moreover, whereas Aristotelianism had never been more than a minority movement, Ockhamism dominated the intellectual life of northern and central Europe in the 14th century. It did so because it gave an outlet for intellectual doubt and for distrust of the certainty of contingent knowledge, while strengthening the tendency toward fideism. In this it expressed the deep-seated antinomy in Christian thought between what could be known and doubted by experience and what should be held on faith. In that sense Ockhamism was the outcome of a development extending over 1000 years.

As time went on it became less disruptive. We can distinguish two phases in it, separated by the Black Death around 1350. The first phase, from about 1320, was when the iconoclasm of Ockham and his more extreme followers was threatening the established values in the ways we have mentioned. It was marked by a sharp division between the Ockhamists and the more traditional thinkers, of whom the most prominent were Thomas Bradwardine (before 1300–49), Walter Burley, and Gregory of Rimini (d. 1357). These latter, in reaffirming the traditional theological conceptions of God, man, and the relationship between them, tended in turn to stress their autonomy from philosophy and natural experience. In that sense, both sides were accentuating the gulf between natural and supernatural knowledge. Their debates centred especially upon the resources of free will and the extent to which its actions were affected by God's foreknowledge and predestination. These problems assumed a new importance during the 14th century: they preoccupied Wyclif and his contemporaries in the 1360s and 1370s, and we find them mentioned in Chaucer.[58] They were, as we have said, accompanied by a new interest in scientific and cosmological problems. The polarization between theology and cosmology radically reduced the traditional areas of theological speculation. That can be seen in the shrinking of the commentaries on the *Sentences* after Ockham. A number of thinkers, such as Holcot, Buckingham, Bradwardine, and Gregory of Rimini, virtually ignored most of the metaphysical issues (such as essence and existence) that had been so important in the preceding epoch.

In the earlier phase Ockhamism also inspired official action against it. In 1324 Ockham was summoned to the papal curia at Avignon to answer 51 questions extracted from his writings, mainly his Commentary on the *Sentences*. They arose from his conception of divine indeterminacy as it affected grace, free will, love of God, the divine attributes, and the suspension of physical laws. They were formally condemned by a papal commission in 1326, but by then Ockham had fled to the pope's enemy, Emperor Ludwig of Bavaria, with the leader of the Franciscan order, Michael of Cesena, as a result of the pope's rejection of the Franciscan doctrine of poverty.

During the 1340s at Paris there were three further censures.[59] The first, in 1340, was issued as a general admonition by the rector, John Buridan—himself, as we have seen, influenced by Ockham—to the arts faculty against doubting the accepted authorities. In contrast to the attacks of the 1270s, it was directed against the constraints of empiricism, not against a naturalistic ethic. The two other condemnations took place in 1346 and 1347: they concerned two widely differing sets of opinions— those of Nicholas of Autrecourt and of John of Mirecourt—which in turn differed from Ockham's teaching. Both, however, had in common a denial of natural certainty—the attitude that Buridan had censured in 1340. Autrecourt was concerned with the limits of verification, which, according to his condemned propositions, allowed no means of knowing the existence of natural substance or causality or of inferring the existence or non-existence of one thing from the existence or non-existence of another. Mirecourt, on the other hand, showed the lengths to which speculation on God's absolute power might go in moral matters. Among other things, he held that God could cause a man to sin, make a soul hate him, allow Christ to mislead his disciples, and allow Christ himself to be misled—the last two notions being bound up with the problem of God's future knowledge. Taken together, these propositions are indicative of the climate of philosophical doubt and fideism engendered by Ockhamism. The limitations upon natural knowledge, when allied to the idea of God's infinite freedom of action, made nothing intrinsically certain save that what was could be otherwise.

The year 1347 saw the last of such explosions. The reasons are not exclusively intellectual. The Black Death (1347–50) carried off many of the previous generation and broke the continuity with those who survived. Little is clearly known about the generation that followed, but Christian thought never regained its earlier impetus. There was a greater diffusion of thinkers and activities, and with it a slackening of intellectual tension. Only John Wyclif (*c.* 1320–84) and Nicholas of Cusa (1400–64) attempted syntheses on traditional lines, but they were working in an intellectual vacuum: interest had shifted to more clearly defined areas of ecclesiology, science, and a growing humanism, while theology was increasingly treated in terms of the articles of faith.

Paris was now no longer the main centre of Christian thought. The outbreak of the Hundred Years' War in 1337 impeded the interchange with Oxford that had been a feature of intellectual life for more than a century. It also helped to stimulate the founding of new universities in Germany and central Europe in the mid- and late 14th century, drawing foreign scholars such as Albert of Saxony, Henry of Langenstein, and Marsilius of Inghen, who might otherwise have gone to Paris. Meanwhile, from the third decade of the century, Oxford was at least the equal of Paris in intellectual thought and was predominant in mathematics and physics. Finally, many of the most influential thinkers of the age were involved in no university. Richard de Bury's circle in the 1330s included Holcot and Bradwardine; and Ockham, Marsilius of Padua, and John of Jandun were among other exiles at the court of Emperor Ludwig of Bavaria, as a result of their opposition to Pope John XXII. The spread of learning outside the schools among laymen, together with the decline in the standing of the Church, left scholasticism increasingly a formal pursuit by the end of the 14th century.

The two other main currents in the outlook of the time, mysticism and reform, were both more directly subversive of the existing order. In the forms in which they dominated the religious life of the later Middle Ages, they both went back to the 13th century and shared much the same impulse. Mysticism was the most pervasive spiritual force of the 14th century. Much of it was histrionic, spurious, or heretical; but, however imperfect, it involved the search for God within the soul and a turning away from the world, including the life of the Church. It introduced another dimension—of inner truth—just as the Ockhamists had done by invoking God's absolute power. But, unlike Ockhamism, or indeed any of the other elements in Christian thought that we have so far considered, mystical awareness was equally accessible to the lay, the unlettered, and the theologically untutored. Hence its heterogeneity. By the 13th century it flourished in most of Western Christendom among diverse sorts and conditions: the lay communities of the Beguines and Beghards of northern France, the Low Countries, and the Rhineland; the religious orders in which the theological symmetry of St Bonaventure's contemplation was outstanding; and the remarkable women mystics, Hadewijch (*c.* 1250) and Mathilde of Magdeburg (1207–82 or 98), whose "nuptial mysticism" derived largely from St Bernard. These and many more made up what was essentially a series of individual experiences.

The literature they could inspire was equally diverse, ranging from the expositions of William of St Thierry or Hugh of St Victor, to the account of mystical exploration couched in the imagery of heterosexual love to be found in the writings of Richard of St Victor and Hildegard of Bingen,[60] which has its echo a century later in Mathilde's dialogue between the soul and its fiancé, Christ. The *Divina commedia*, too, can be read in one sense as a mystical poem: the ascent through Hell, Purgatory, and Heaven has been likened to the three main mystical stages of purgation, illumination, and perfection,[61] culminating in the vision of the Trinity[62] (Canto XXXIII, 112–20). Moreover, St Bernard, the archetypal mystic, takes over as Dante's guide for the final and highest phase. Quite different again are Jacopone of Todi's *Laude*.

Meister Eckhart

This diversity was accentuated in the 14th century as mysticism became more widespread. Its most important new element was the speculative mysticism of the Rhineland that derived from Meister Eckhart (1260–1327). It is a paradox that the most complex of all the mystics should have exercised the greatest popular influence, especially through his disciples Suso and Tauler. Eckhart's mysticism differed from all others in its neo-Platonic inspiration—a product of the Dominican *studium* at Cologne to which Eckhart belonged and where he spent a large part of his career. Albertus Magnus, who had been head of this Dominican school for 30 years, had stressed the mystical elements in the Augustinian doctrine of illumination. This, together with the impact of Proclus's newly translated writings and the influence of the pseudo-Dionysius, had contributed to the rise of a new mystical outlook among Albertus's Dominican pupils Hugh and Ulrich of Strassburg. From this line sprang the two outstanding mystics of the era, Dietrich of Freiburg (d. *c.* 1310) and Eckhart.

Eckhart's mysticism was of a piece with his speculative theology.[63] It was distinctive in resting upon a metaphysical basis that conceived all being in terms of the essences emanating from God. Because man was created in God's image, his soul contained the divine light or spark (*Fünklein*) that united him with his creator. To rediscover this spark was the end of mystical exploration. But it could come about only through denuding the soul of all awareness, not merely of external images but of itself. This was where Eckhart gave a new conception to the notion of spiritual poverty or renunciation (*Abgeschiedenheit*). The divine element in the soul, as God's imprint, was independent of the soul's own created being. Hence the soul must renounce itself in order to allow God to enter. This meant self-oblivion in contrast to the striving to reach God characteristic of the Western tradition of St Bernard. Instead of a soul inflamed with love for God, Eckhart preached that man must cease to be in order to be reborn as God's son. The rebirth of the divine word in the soul, as he termed it, was the culmination of mystical experience; it constituted the reunion of the soul with its archetype in God.

The tendency of Eckhart's mysticism, as with all neo-Platonism, was to make the recovery of the divine image through contemplation the path to spiritual awareness, independently of the agency of the sacraments or other recognized aids. Eckhart was so concerned to stress the need to empty the soul that he frequently depreciated or ignored works and external signs. This went together with the pseudo-Dionysian stress upon God's essential unknowability. Hence the tendency was to withdraw from the known toward the unknowable.

Eckhart was also one of the supreme preachers of his time: it was through his sermons, delivered in the vernacular to unsophisticated audiences of nuns and laymen, that his outlook took hold. The inevitable simplifications that made his message so vivid and direct tended to distort the subtlety and profoundly Christian nature of his thought. When taken out of context, many of his statements sound pantheistic, especially his recurrent theme of the birth of the word or son in the soul. "The highest oneness that Christ attained with God is possible for me only if I should renounce what is individual to me for my essence of humanity." This and other sayings put the onus of salvation upon personal disposition: they were an invitation for each individual to take up the challenge to reach God. Many did so: some, like the heretical Free Spirit, in the belief that thereby the soul became divine.

The danger to faith was apparent to the authorities. Towards the end of his life Eckhart had to answer a series of articles drawn up at Cologne. Many were based on hearsay as well as on his writings. Although Eckhart was able to show his true meaning, a list of propositions was sent to Avignon and examined there by a papal commission. Eckhart may well have appeared before it. But it was not until March 1329, after his death, that 28 articles ascribed to him were condemned in the bull *In agro dominico*. They show striking affinities with the propositions of Ockhamism at this time in depreciating the intrinsic value of the created. There is a comparable divine indeterminacy and moral neutralism expressed in such propositions as that God did not recognize acts or works but only souls, and that he could will a man to sin mortally (No. 16–9); or that evil redounded to God's glory equally with the good (4); or that God would reward all those who renounced good works and inner devotions (8). There was also a pantheism not to be found in Ockhamism. Thus God was identified with nature (23 and 24); all creatures were pure nothing (26); men could be transformed into God and so become indistinguishable from him (10).

It hardly needs saying that such statements distorted the whole import of Eckhart's teachings: that they nevertheless could produce such impressions is to be seen in the heresy of the Free Spirit for whom the soul's union with God meant both pantheism and amorality. In that sense Eckhart, like Ockham, had a disturbing effect upon the spiritual climate of the later Middle Ages.

As we have said, however, later mediaeval mysticism was too diverse to be made the property of any one group or outlook. Its products were equally diverse: the quietism of Groendal and later the *Devotio moderna*; the prophecies and hectorings of Catherine of Siena or the solitariness of Richard Rolle; the Friends of God and the Free Spirit; the neo-Platonism of *The Cloud of Unknowing* and the simplicity of Julian of Norwich. Even such a non-mystical work as *Piers Plowman* was in the form of a vision, or a series of visions. Of all the outlooks of the Middle Ages, mysticism was, of its nature, the most universal.

By the same token, it was the least direct in its impact. The most overtly influential were the advocates of reform. In one sense they were even more heterogeneous than the mystics and, as a formative influence, had a longer history. However, it was only after the middle of the 13th century that a distinctive reforming outlook emerged to challenge the very notion of the Church as it then existed. Those who shared it, from whatever standpoint, may be said to have been actuated by an apostolic ideal of the Church as it had originally been. Here, too, as in mysticism, there was a convergence between orthodox and heterodox, lay and ecclesiastic, learned and popular.

Joachism

The concept of an original apostolic Church, as the model for what the Church should forever be, gradually took shape during the 13th century, principally in the Franciscan order, under the influence of the ideas of Joachim of Fiore (d. 1202), and among the Waldensians. But it found a ready response beyond them, among individuals as different as Dante, John of Paris, Ockham, Marsilius of Padua, the conciliarist Dietrich of Niem, and the heretics Wyclif and Hus. It introduced a new critical attitude to the Church by treating the Bible and Christ's example as the record of events that had occurred in time and opposing them to the present condition of the Church.

The role of Joachism in this development was central.[64] Although by the late 13th century it had taken a form that went far beyond the teachings of Joachim himself, they had provided its inspiration. Joachim had been a Cistercian monk known for his piety. In 1196, after becoming abbot of the Calabrian monastery of Curazzo, he founded a new monastic order of Fiore. Living in Calabria in the second half of the 12th century, he was close to both Byzantine and Moslem civilizations, and to the papacy; that may have accentuated the prophetic cast in his outlook. But the form it took, biblical exegesis, was common enough; so was the division of Christian history into seven ages, as we have already seen in the case of Otto of Freising. During the 12th century, the writing of universal history became an accepted genre, and Otto's Augustinian perspective was shared by other, mainly German, contemporaries, notably Anselm of Havelberg, Geroch of Reichersberg, and Rupert of

Deutz. The last also made a trinitarian division into the reigns of the Father, the Son, and the Holy Spirit. But it was left to Joachim to combine this and the seven ages of St Augustine into a new philosophy of history.

This he did in three main works written as commentaries on the Bible: *The Concord of the Old and New Testaments*, *The Exposition of the Apocalypse*, and *The Psaltery of the Ten Chords*. By means of elaborate symbolic comparisons and numerical calculations between different events, particularly those of the Book of Revelation, Joachim arrived at a new pattern of history; it went beyond previous interpretations both in positing a new future age on earth after the present order had elapsed, and in the mode of change from one age to another.

Joachim divided the whole of created time into three great overlapping and interacting eras. The first was that of the Father, and corresponded to the period of the Old Testament; the second was the age of the Son, and ran from the time of King Osias until about the middle of the 13th century (beyond the period at which Joachim was writing); it was to be followed by the third and final age of the Holy Spirit, which would last for 1000 years, until the end of the world and the Last Judgment. Each age was symbolized by a particular group of men: the age of the Father had been the age of the married men (the patriarchs); the second was the age of the clerics; and the third would be the age of spiritual monks, of whom the Benedictines were the precursors. Each age also had, or would have, three great men; but whereas those for the first two ages were actual figures drawn from the Old and New Testaments, the three for the coming third age were merely symbols that Joachim found in the Book of Daniel and the Book of Revelation. This distinction between the first two ages and the third is the dominant theme in Joachim's system: it was from the relationship between the first two that he was able to deduce the patterns of history that could be projected into the future third age. Hence his treatment of the first two ages was much fuller and more precise than for the third age; and he interpreted the transition from the second to the third age largely in terms of what had occurred in the change from the first to the second. Thus, the third age was inseparable from the first two ages not only as their outcome, but also in the way in which that outcome would occur. It was treated less for itself than as the consummation of what had gone before; it is the most unorthodox and revolutionary aspect of Joachim's teaching, and also the least substantial, providing an historical perspective rather than a defined epoch.

Now, this threefold perspective meant that, instead of the traditional two ages of the Old and the New Testaments, an additional (and higher) era was interposed between them and the Last Judgment. As envisaged by Joachim, it would mean superseding the existing forms, and their transformation into something higher. Whereas the first age had been under the law and the second was under grace, the third would have still greater grace; whereas the first age was of knowledge, and the second of partial wisdom, the third would be of full understanding; servile duty and filial duty would give place to liberty. With these and many other antitheses Joachim sought to characterize the difference between the ages and their culmination in the third age. Although Joachim never went beyond metaphor in describing the order still to come, there can be no doubt that he envisaged it as one of spiritual renewal in which, to use his own image, the spirit would triumph over the letter. What this would mean in practice he did not say, except that it would not entail a new faith or a new Church, but rather their expression at a new and higher level.

It was precisely at this point that Joachim's thinking was most betrayed by those who claimed to be his disciples. His own symbolic terms, such as a new "spiritual Church" and "spiritual men," and his frequent references to the displacement of the outward "figures" of the sacraments by their inner spiritual import, came to take on an independent meaning and to be contraposed to their present visible forms. By the end of the 13th century, among some of the "Spirituals"—the extreme wing of the Franciscan order, who adhered most rigorously to St Francis's conception of poverty—and their followers in Provence and Italy, the "spiritual Church" had come to mean a new congregation of "spiritual men," themselves, as opposed to the carnal church of Rome under the pope, which they condemned as the Whore of Babylon and the congregation of Antichrist. They were the bearers of a new gospel and possessed a true spiritual insight. Not only was the terminology taken over from Joachim's apocalyptic language, but so also was the framework in which the change from the second to the third age would occur.

It is here that Joachim's division of the first two ages into seven phases or epochs was significant. From the parallels between them he sought to show the way in which each phase was succeeded by the next. In particular, he emphasized, first, what amounts to a dialectical interplay between one epoch and the next, so that the new was germinating within the old and finally emerged only through the supersession of the old. Thus the "spiritual men" who were to typify the third age of the Holy Spirit had their harbingers in St Benedict's order of monks, which had been founded in the fourth phase of the second age. Joachim computed that the age of the Son would end in about the year 1260, so that this meant that the bearers of the new age had coexisted with the old for over 600 years. They were the agents by which the dualism between the flesh and the spirit, which characterized the age of the Son, would be overcome in the triumph of the Spirit in the third age. This transformation would not come about imperceptibly or gradually, but by means of a struggle between the new and the old. Joachim distinguished between phases of quiescence and phases of disturbance in each of the first two ages. As each age drew to its close, the latent antagonism between the forces of the old order and the forces of the future came to a head, and a period of conflict between them ensued before the new age could finally emerge. Joachim placed this struggle in the sixth and penultimate phase of the expiring age: just as Christ and his disciples had been persecuted by the synagogue, and he had been crucified before his message had finally prevailed, so Christ's successors, the new spiritual monks, would have to suffer the attacks of Antichrist before they, too, emerged to inaugurate a new golden age on earth, in the seventh and last phase of the second age. Accordingly, the pattern that Joachim presented was of an underlying continuity by means of discontinuity; of a series of consummations, or (as he called them) "sabbatical periods," preceded by periods of violent struggle; until, some time after the middle of the 13th century, a new and final era of sabbatical peace would reign.

Now, it was in the transition from the second to the third age that Joachim's teaching had such relevance for the 13th century and beyond: by his own computation the present age of the Son was due to end about 1260 at the completion of the 42nd generation from the birth of Christ (counting each generation as 30 years). Thus, the beginning of the 13th century marked the beginning of the sixth phase, when the struggle between the old and the new would reach its climax. For the generations immediately succeeding Joachim's, they appeared to be in the very vortex of the upheaval. Hence the immediacy of his message to those who, like the Franciscan "Spirituals" and many others, were suffering either persecution or the effects of the devastating wars between the imperial and papal armies in Italy. Their miseries found a vindication in Joachim's predictions and his emphasis upon the coming tribulations that would precede the age of the Spirit. He foretold that the years from 1200 to 1260 would be worse than the preceding centuries of the second age put together; they would be filled with the evil doings of Antichrist. The sixth phase would witness great persecutions, culminating in the seventh phase with the appearance of the first Antichrist (the second would appear at the end of the third age, before the final end of the world and the Last Judgment). The sixth phase, however, would also see the harbingers of a new spiritual understanding of the Old and New Testaments, which would be consummated in final victory over the forces of Antichrist. It would be followed by a second incarnation of Christ and the period of sabbatical calm that would inaugurate the third great age of peace on earth and the rule of the Spirit.

Here, then, was an interpretation that offered not just an explanation of the present ills of the world but also hope and justification in suffering. It gave a cosmic setting to the struggles of the various reforming and apostolic groups: they were enacting the final struggle between the forces of Christ and Antichrist, of Jerusalem and Babylon. Moreover, the effect was not confined initially to those in opposition to the Church and the existing dispensation. Thinkers such as Robert Grosseteste, Adam Marsh, William of St Amour, St Bonaventure, and John of Pecham, to mention only a few, took up the theme of imminent apocalyptic change; many members of the new orders of friars identified themselves with Joachim's prophecy of a new order of spiritual monks; at least one 13th-century pope—John XXI—was sympathetic to Joachite ideas. Nevertheless, by the middle of the 13th century, as the time allotted for the close of the second age approached, Joachism became increasingly a vehicle for dissent and apocalyptic prophecy. The extent to which it had become transformed into a doctrine of subversion was first revealed in the affair of the Eternal Gospel at Paris in 1254.[65] A young Franciscan, Gerard of Borgo San Donnino, published an Introduction to the Eternal Gospel in which he substituted Joachim's own three main writings for the Bible: they had become the everlasting gospel in about 1200, with the coming of the sixth phase of the age of the Son. Gerard went on to translate Joachim's images of a new spiritual order into contemporary historical terms, with St Francis and the Franciscans true to him as the new order of spiritual monks and the renewers of Christ's teachings. The Roman Church became the carnal Church, the Whore of Babylon, whose persecution of those who upheld St Francis's ideal of absolute poverty represented the struggle between the forces of Christ and Antichrist. The year 1260 would see the beginning of the end of the present age with the appearance of Antichrist. After terrible ravages and destruction, Christendom would be reunited and a new era would begin.

The direct challenge represented by Gerard's interpretation of Joachim led to the condemnation of his Introduction and his own imprisonment. Although he was strongly criticized by others who were adherents of

Joachim, Gerard, in providing his own *dramatis personae* for Joachim's scheme, helped to make it into a vehicle, if not of revolution, at least of opposition to the present order. The Church was now being challenged as an institution: it was to be superseded, not merely renewed from within. Although Joachism was not yet discredited, and Joachim's own writings never as such condemned, Gerard had shown them in another light. The first outbreak of the Flagellant movement in 1260, the year of Joachist prophecy, the emergence of the heretical semi-Joachist sect of the False Apostles (condemned in 1274), and above all the growth of prophecy within the Franciscan order in Provence and Italy, all helped to set the seal upon its subversive tendencies.

What Gerard did, in transposing Joachim's doctrine into Franciscan terms as an apologia for poverty, was to be repeated again and again during the next century both by Franciscans, such as Peter John Olivi, Angelo of Clareno, and Ubertino of Casale, and also by numerous others.[66] It became incorporated into quite other outlooks, such as the prevalent belief in the coming of a last world emperor and a line of angelic popes; and all the time it continued to influence individuals and groups who could in no way be considered subversive. It is significant that Joachim's works were among the first to be printed in Venice in the early 16th century; and a series of scurrilous portraits of popes, falsely attributed to Joachim and originating in the late 13th century, continued to circulate in new up-to-date versions down to the 17th century. In all these ways Joachist prophecy, even when shorn of all Joachim's nuances and qualifications, was an important element in the outlook of the late Middle Ages and beyond. Few movements of protest were not to some degree influenced by it, and the sense of impending change and of an end to the present order was widespread.

The Apostolic Ideal

At the same time there grew up independently of it—especially in the lay ambiance of popular piety—a new veneration of the Bible as the direct source of truth: to preach and practise its precepts, on the model of Christ and his apostles, was the criterion of Christian life. This ideal was carried through the 13th and 14th centuries, above all by the Waldensians. Having been excommunicated during the late 12th century, the Waldensians framed their beliefs as a direct challenge to the Church; they claimed theirs to be the one true apostolic Church, which the Roman Church had betrayed when it had been recognized and endowed by Emperor

Constantine in the 4th century. The so-called Donation of Constantine came to be treated as a turning-point in Christian history, the beginning of its decline. Such a view, although not held by Joachim, was not confined to the Waldensians. By the middle of the 13th century it had entered into common currency, particularly in Italy, which had most direct experience of the devastating wars between papal and imperial armies. It occupied a central place in Dante's *De monarchia* and recurs in the *Divina commedia* (*Inf.* XIX, 115), where denunciation of the Church's departure from apostolic simplicity and the religious orders' loss of their evangelical mission reaches a climax in the *Paradiso*.

The *Divina commedia*, the meeting-point of so many streams—the courtly and the mystical, the classical and the symbolic, the speculative and the revealed—is perhaps the most complete rendering of a society's outlook ever achieved, artistically or otherwise. Its genius lies in imaginatively fusing the experiences of an epoch. There is a place for Siger of Brabant as the representative of philosophy as well as for Joachim among the 12 souls in the circle of lights. That did not make Dante either an Averroist or a Joachist; but each expressed truths appropriate to their sphere. If Siger's truths were invidious for faith, they were also as "logic taught him":[67] a view of the autonomy of philosophy when confined to natural experience that is consistent with Dante's earlier demarcation between philosophy and theology and the earthly and the heavenly paradises in *De monarchia*. Joachim similarly was a "prophet spirit-fired and true,"[68] although Dante expressly dissociated himself from the Franciscan Spirituals, whom he rebuked for playing "now fast, now loose with rule and discipline."[69] It is precisely among these 12 lights, the founders of the outlook of the Middle Ages, that Dante singles out the betrayal of the ideals of St Francis and St Dominic—"the two champions" who had renewed Christ's gospel—in tones not far removed from the apocalyptic note of Joachim's followers. Much of Canto XI is a paean in praise of poverty; and, in place of an emperor, to whom Dante had looked in *De monarchia* to restore order to the world, are the prophecies of vengeance that follow St Peter's denunciation of Boniface VIII in Paradise.[70] The late 13th century was the great age of poverty and prophecy, and no one reading the *Divina commedia* can fail to recognize their importance for Dante. It marks a shift from his earlier attention to the empire to his preoccupation with the Church and its reform:

> Henceforth say this: The Church of Rome doth fall
> Into the mire, and striving to combine
> Two powers into one, fouls self, load, and all.[71]

If Dante looked to Providence, which "will swift lend aid" for remedy, others—such as Marsilius of Padua (*c.* 1275-1342)—sought it in the intervention of the lay power. Marsilius, in his *Defensor pacis* (1324), was the first to develop the apostolic ideal into a historical critique of papal supremacy. Treating the Bible as historical evidence and conflating its events with the accounts of chronicles, he sought to show that Christ had never conferred headship of the Church upon Peter, and that Rome had never had primacy among the churches. He explained its rise to supremacy through the Donation of Constantine, which had made a purely customary precedence binding. The Church had thereby departed from the apostolic path. Christ's Church had been without possessions or coercive power, for Christ had come to minister spiritually to mankind. Before Pilate he had declared that his kingdom was not of this world. Moreover, in the early Church no hierarchy had existed, only the two orders of priests and deacons.

The comparison between the Church then and in his own time led Marsilius to deny virtually all the existing prerogatives of the hierarchy and to demand its dissolution as an independent corporation. Like the Franciscan Spirituals, the Waldensians, and Dante, he made loyalty to Christ mean renunciation of all such privileges of property, rights of litigation, and intervention in temporal affairs.

In Marsilius's hands, then, and repeatedly after him, the Bible became a weapon against the Church in its corporate state. He opposed its testimony to the current decrees and practices of the Church. What was contained in scripture, or necessarily followed from it, must be believed to the exclusion of anything that contradicted it in canon law—a position adopted by Ockham and Wyclif, who expressed with Dante the widespread detestation of the canon legists for creating the contrary conception of papal supremacy and of the Church as a corporation. Although Marsilius, and later Wyclif, went furthest in advocating the total submission of the Church to the lay power, they were only applying the full logic of the apostolic ideal. To have followed it would not only have taken the Church back to Christ; it would also have meant its dissolution as an independent order. As such, it challenged the very existence of the Church. Not surprisingly, the *Defensor pacis* was banned and Marsilius condemned as a heretic, as Wyclif was to be at the end of the century; and both Marsilius and Ockham, as we have seen, needed the protection of Ludwig of Bavaria.

The apostolic ideal added a new critical and historical dimension to Christian thinking. It conceived the Church no longer in its undifferentiated divine aspect, timelessly, but according to its different historical phases; these represented not just the progressive unfolding of its divine mission as God's saving will on earth, but also its qualitative developments —for evil as well as for good. Its present state was one of decline from its apostolic past: it must therefore be reformed. Because the criterion for doing so was contained in scripture, this was in turn to give a new role to the Bible as a vehicle of criticism and reform. That was not the same as a doctrine of sole reliance on the Bible; but it inevitably exalted the Bible at the expense of all other forms of canonical truth, and it culminated in Wyclif's condemnation of all that was not scriptural. In that sense the Bible was made into the single most destructive arm of the attack upon the existing Church. It went with a new stress upon Christ's historical example.

It is one more paradox of the period that the image of Christ as a man became the main threat to the divine sanction of the Church as a body. The events of Christ's life on earth were made the touchstone of ecclesiastical practice. Christ and the apostles, possessionless and humble, meant a Church without dominion or jurisdiction. The Church, as Christ's mystical body, could not be a privileged corporation; its only identity was as the spiritual communion of all true believers in Christ. That was the doctrinal import, given with greater or less explicitness, of the apostolic ideal. Whether it engendered prophecy, poverty, withdrawal, or secular action, it was essentially a Christian response to the conflict between precept and practice that could no longer be contained within the existing framework. Although it led to a new order in which the spiritual and the temporal, faith and knowledge, became progressively separated, the change came from within a society where the old forms could no longer operate.

References

1. For what follows, see the chapters on St Augustine by R. A. Markus in *The Cambridge History of Later Greek and Early Mediaeval Philosophy* (Cambridge 1967), especially pp. 344 ff., to which I am particularly indebted.
2. *De trinitate* IX, 1, 1 (*Patrologia latina* [Paris 1844–64], Vol. 42, col. 961).
3. *De doctrina christiana* I, 4, 4 (*Patr. lat.*, Vol. 34, col. 20).
4. *Confessions* I, 4, 4.
5. *ibid.*, X, 6, 9.

6. *De trin.* X, 10, 13–6.
7. *ibid.*, 24; *Conf.* X, 12, 19.
8. *De magistro* 32; *De libero arbitrio* II, 2–12.
9. *De lib. arb.* I, 6, 15; *Sermo* 341, 6, 8; *In Johannis evangelium* IX, 5, 12.
10. *De lib. arb.* II, 11.
11. For example, *De spiritu et littera, De natura et gratia, De perfectione justitiae hominis, De gratia et libero arbitrio, De gratia Christi et peccatio originali, Contra Julianum, De correptione et gratia, De praedestinatione, De dono perseverantiae.*
12. *De civitate Dei*, especially Bk XIX, Ch. 21 ff.
13. E.g., *ibid.*, XIV, Ch. 2, 28.
14. *De consolatione philosophiae*, Pros. 11.
15. *De arithmetica* (*Patr. lat.*, Vol. 63, cols 1079 and 1082); *In Porphyrium dialogi* (*Patr. lat.*, Vol. 64, cols 11–2).
16. Contained in *De divinis nominibus* and *De mystica theologia.*
17. Contained in his main work, *De divisione naturae.*
18. For what follows, see H. LIEBESCHÜTZ, "Western Christian Thought from Boethius to Anselm," in *The Cambridge History of Later Greek and Early Mediaeval Philosophy* (Cambridge 1967), Ch. 37.
19. The standard critical edition of St Anselm's work is F. S. SCHMITT, *Sancti Anselmi opera omnia*, 5 vols (Edinburgh/London 1938–51); see also his separate editions of the *Monologium, Proslogion*, and *Cur Deus homo.*
20. *Liber apologeticus contra Gaunilem.*
21. *Proslogion*, Ch. 1.
22. *De veritate*, Ch. 2.
23. For what follows, see especially *De lib. arb.*
24. *Monologium*, Prologue.
25. Translated by J. R. McCallum as *Abailard's Ethics* (Oxford 1935).
26. *ibid.*, pp. 17 ff.
27. *ibid.*, pp. 42 ff.
28. On the Platonism of Chartres, see especially M.-D. CHENU, *La théologie au douzième siècle* (Paris 1966), Pt I, Ch. 1, 5, 6, and 7. Since this chapter was written, R. W. SOUTHERN, *Medieval Humanism* (London 1970), has sought to disprove the existence of the "school" of Chartres; be that as it may, I have continued to treat the thinkers traditionally associated with Chartres as holding a common outlook.
29. Quoted in P. DRONKE, *Mediaeval Latin and the Rise of the European Love-Lyric* (Oxford 1965), Vol. 1, pp. 63–9.
30. See St Bernard's *De diligendo Deo*, trans. by E. Gardiner (London 1915), and *Sermons on the Canticles.*
31. For what follows, see B. SMALLEY, *The Study of the Bible in the Middle Ages*, 2nd edn (Oxford 1952), pp. 66 ff.
32. *ibid.*, p. 71.
33. *ibid.*, pp. 75 ff.
34. *ibid.*, pp. 83 ff.
35. *ibid.*, p. 93.
36. *ibid.*

37. For what follows, see C. H. HASKINS, *Studies in Mediaeval Culture* (New York 1960), and *Studies in the History of Mediaeval Science* (New York 1960); also G. LEFF, *Paris and Oxford Universities in the Thirteenth and Fourteenth Centuries* (New York 1968), pp. 127–37.

38. See LEFF, *op. cit.*

39. For the theological reaction to Aristotle, *ibid.*, pp. 188 ff.

40. *ibid.*, pp. 193 ff.

41. *ibid.*, p. 201.

42. *ibid.*, p. 199.

43. *ibid.*, pp. 211 ff.

44. *Iterarium mentis in Deum.*

45. *Commentary on the Sentences*, Prologue, q. 5.

46. *De mysterio trinitatis* I, 1329.

47. LEFF, *op. cit.*, pp. 129 ff.

48. For what follows, see A. C. CROMBIE, *Robert Grosseteste and the Origins of Experimental Science* (Oxford 1952).

49. *Summa theologie* I^a, q. 75, 1, 2, 3, and 6.

50. *ibid.*, q. 75, a. 6.

51. A. CALLEBAUT, "Jean Pecham et l'Augustinisme," *Archivum Franciscanum Historicum* 18 (Florence 1925), p. 448.

52. *Collationes in hexaemeron*, ed. by F. Delorme (Quaracchi 1934), p. 92.

53. Articles in H. DENIFLE and A. CHATELAIN, *Chartularium Universitatis Parisiensis* I (Paris 1889), pp. 543–58; see also LEFF, *op. cit.*, pp. 229–40.

54. *Roman de la rose*, lines 4403–20. For this, see DRONKE, *op. cit.*, Vol. I, pp. 81 ff. I am indebted to this work for much that follows.

55. For what follows to the end of the chapter, see especially G. LEFF, *Heresy in the Later Middle Ages*, 2 vols. (Manchester 1967).

56. *ibid.*, Vol. I, and G. LEFF, *Bradwardine and the Pelagians* (Cambridge 1957), Pt II.

57. G. LEFF, *Gregory of Rimini* (Manchester 1961), Ch. 4.

58. "The Nun's Priest's Tale," line 422.

59. LEFF, *Heresy in the Later Middle Ages*, Vol. I, pp. 296–9.

60. DRONKE, *op. cit.*, Vol. I, 167.

61. J. LECLERQ, F. VANDENBROUCKE, and F. BOUYER, *La spiritualité du moyen âge* (Paris 1961), p. 439.

62. *Paradiso*, Canto XXXIII, lines 112–20.

63. LEFF, *Heresy in the Later Middle Ages*, Vol. I, pp. 260 ff.

64. *ibid.*, pp. 68 ff.

65. *ibid.*

66. *ibid.*, pp. 100 ff.

67. *Paradiso*, Canto X, lines 133–8.

68. *ibid.*, line 141.

69. *ibid.*, line 124.

70. *ibid.*, Canto XXVII, lines 19–27.

71. *Purgatorio*, Canto XVI, lines 127–9.

Bibliography

The following works are recommended in addition to those cited in the References.

R. R. BOLGAR, *The Classical Heritage and Its Beneficiaries* (Cambridge 1954).

E. R. CURTIUS, *European Literature and the Latin Middle Ages* (New York 1966).

C. DAWSON, *Religion and the Rise of Mediaeval Culture* (London 1950).

J. DE GHELLINCK, *L'essor de la littérature latine au XIIIᵉ siècle* (Brussels 1954).

E. GILSON, *History of Christian Philosophy in the Middle Ages* (London 1955); includes a comprehensive bibliography for the period covered by this chapter.

C. H. HASKINS, *The Renaissance of the Twelfth Century* (Cambridge, Mass. 1953).

D. KNOWLES, *The English Mystical Tradition* (London 1961).

G. LADNER, *The Idea of Reform* (Cambridge, Mass. 1959).

G. LEFF, *Mediaeval Thought* (paperback: Harmondsworth 1968).

G. PARÉ, A. BRUNET, and P. TREMBLAY, *La renaissance du XIIᵉ siècle* (Paris 1933).

E. PORTALIÉ, *A Guide to the Thought of St Augustine* (London 1960).

CHAPTER 8

Mediaeval Ideas of History[1]

Maurice Keen[*]

I

It may reasonably be asked why a book about mediaeval literature should include a chapter about mediaeval ideas of history. The objects of the historian and the creative writer are not the same, and the rules of their crafts are different. Nevertheless, there are ways in which the historian and the writer do not stand so very far apart. The writer's imagination is fed by the circumstances of the world around him, which will one day be history, and his view of the way that men act in the present is coloured by his view of how they have acted in the past, which is history already. The historian's business is largely to supply the writer—and others too— with just such a view: his object is not simply to record facts, but to sift and select them, so as to ensure that those he passes on are not merely true, but significant also—facts that will help men to understand more about what has made them as they are. This is really very little different from what the writer does, except that, where he embodies his views about the world into the structure of his story, the historian states his moral more prosaically, as a conclusion from evidence. This is why it is useful for the student of literature to know something of the ideas that a past age has entertained about history. Its historians will tell the student what well-informed men thought was interesting and significant about things that, they believed, had actually happened: this can help him toward an understanding of how and why the imaginative range of writers of the period, and their methods of presentation, differ from those of other ages.

The Middle Ages have left behind a host of chronicles, so numerous and so diverse in quality that it is not easy to generalize about the historical attitudes that they reflect. The task may be a little simpler if

* Fellow of Balliol College, Oxford.

we draw a broad distinction between those chroniclers who considered history from a universal standpoint, and those who wrote from a local point of view or with a local bias of interest. The latter are more numerous and, for the purposes of the historian whose object is to reconstruct the shape of past events, usually more valuable. For this purpose the kind of qualities that mark such histories as, for example, the *Gesta novella* of William of Malmesbury (*c.* 1090–1143) or the *Chronicle* of Giovanni Villani of Florence (*c.* 1275–1348)—a first-hand knowledge both of contemporary people and events and of their local historical background—will always be prized most highly. From the point of view of a literary scholar, on the other hand, the universal histories of the Middle Ages have a greater interest. In them, certain qualities of approach, such as a quite different standard of historical significance from that of the 20th century, and a different idea of causation, appear more clearly than they do in the local histories. In them, broad attitudes toward the meaning of the human past are more obvious, because they are not obscured by a wealth of local and personal detail. That is why, in this chapter, it is on the great universal historians of the Middle Ages that attention will chiefly be focussed: not because they wrote better history than others, but because prevalent historical attitudes stand out more clearly from their work.

Before we proceed to examine the work of individual authors, two preliminary points need to be mentioned. First, we must remember that history, in the Middle Ages, was never studied formally and for itself in the schools. The great names in the intellectual history of the period from A.D. 600 to the Italian renaissance were those of the theologians and Christian philosophers, and the study of history was not then thought to be more than ancillary to these higher pursuits. This helps to explain why the compilation of universal histories was more fashionable in the Middle Ages than it is now. Because history's highest object was to be handmaid to the purposes of thinkers interested in truths whose validity was not circumscribed by time or place, the best history was that which was not circumscribed by time or place either. Second, we must remember that, for most of the Middle Ages, Christian churchmen had a near monopoly of education, especially of the higher education that led students forward to the consideration of general problems of theology and philosophy. This is why the Bible, the inspired book that then provided the framework for these higher studies, was also for the Middle Ages the most significant historical work that ever had been, or ever could be, written.

II

The Bible, to the Middle Ages, was central to the study of history, as it was to all other studies. The particular history recorded in Scripture was therefore studied, and in detail, by every aspiring scholar, with the aid of an armoury of patristic comment, both literal and allegorical. The Fathers—and in particular Jerome, whose Vulgate translation of the Bible was their authoritative text—taught scholars to search Old Testament history for signs that foreshadowed the events of the Gospel story. Some commentary—for instance, Jerome's exposition of Daniel's prophecy concerning four kingdoms, the last of which he identified as the Empire of Rome—taught them to look to Scripture for matter that could illuminate post-scriptural history, and that might perhaps even throw light on events still in the future. The direct influence of this sort of biblical study is, in fact, stamped clearly on the work of the first two authors through whose writings I shall hope to illustrate some important features of mediaeval ideas about history: Joachim of Fiore and Vincent of Beauvais. Neither was a particularly wise or discriminating historian, it should be said, but this may be all the better for the purpose of illustrating prevalent attitudes.

Abbot Joachim of Fiore was born about 1145, in Calabria, and died in 1202. His ascetic bent drew him into a Cistercian cloister, but his true leanings were toward a more eremitic life, to the solitary vigils and meditations of the desert fathers. His long thoughts in the remote mountains of southern Italy bore fruit finally in three works: the *Psalterium decem chordarum* (Psaltery of the Ten Chords), the *Expositio in apocalypsim* (Exposition of the Apocalypse), and, most important of all, the *Concordia novi ac veteris testamenti* (Concord of the Old and New Testaments).[2] Their titles give a hint of their matter and object. As Joachim ruminated on the divine history recorded in the Bible he was seeking always to pierce through the letter to the fuller truth hidden beneath it. It was the prophetic books that he searched most diligently: above all, the writings ascribed to the apostle John, the fourth gospel and the Book of Revelation. In the end Joachim believed he had found the key that would turn the obscurity of their mystical allegory into the clarity of historical prophecy, and this is what his *Concordia* is about. It is a demonstration and exposition, astonishing in its range and multiplicity of detail, of the "concords" or parallels between the Old Testament and the New (with the subsequent history of the Church added to it), which reveal the regular, cyclic pattern of history growing like a plant that throws out from its stem the same number of leaves at regular intervals. The key to this pattern he found in the story in Revelation of the book sealed with seven seals, the breaking of each seal marking the dawn of a new period in history, with seven periods in the Old Testament echoing and presaging seven periods in the new dispensation after Christ's coming.[3] This "concord" of periods within two great epochs was but one in a great series of subordinate concords that Joachim worked out meticulously. Thus he found there were 12 patriarchs in the Old Testament, 12 apostles in the New: 12 tribes of Israel, and 12 churches. Five of the 12 tribes entered on their inheritance before the others: five churches of the New Testament, those of St Peter, had already received the primacy, so he concluded that the seven churches of Asia, mentioned in Revelation, would be those that would hold it in due course.[4] The pattern of the wars, persecutions, and tribulations of the past similarly, for Joachim, repeated themselves. His imagination was pictorial: he visualized the complex working of his concords as trees producing branches in parallel growth. These trees he drew, and they were put together to make a fourth book, a companion volume to his other works, called the *Liber figurarum* (Book of Figures).[5]

The beautifully drawn trees of this book delineate a theory of history as the working of a divine plan, the perfection of whose symmetry is revealed when one peers behind the confusing surface of events. The process of reducing history to figures encouraged Joachim to entertain many remarkable and individual ideas, for the drawings suggested further possibilities of interpretation that words, by themselves, might never have revealed. The span of Joachim's first age, from Adam's creation to the coming of Christ, has indeed nothing out of the way about it; but he rooted his second age, which was its "concord," in the first, overlapping it and running from the time of Osias until the second advent.[6] This latter event Joachim believed to be not far distant from his own time; comparing the generations of the first age, from Adam to Christ, with those of the second, he calculated that a new generation, the last but one in the series, had begun in the year 1200.[7] The world and the Church that he knew had therefore only a short span left, and would pass away in the dawn of the third age, of the Holy Spirit, whose foundations were already laid in the age of the Son (the New Testament), as those of the age of the Son had been laid in the age of the Father (the Old Testament). In this coming age of the Holy Spirit, the human spirit would achieve its fullest fruition, just as it had achieved a fuller fruition in the second age than in the first. Joachim's idea of history was

288

thus more than simply repetitive: it contained an idea of growth toward the more perfect expression of the will of the Creator.

Thus the driving force in history, to Joachim, was the active and progressive fulfilment of God's design. The point may be better illustrated in detail by one of his own trees, which is intended to explain the spiritual development of the Church.[8] The Church grows out of the order of patriarchs; its trunk grows then among the Gentile peoples, then among the Latin peoples among the Gentiles, then among the monks among the Latins. At each stage this tree of the Church develops branches— the Jewish people, the Greeks, the order of Christian priests, the order of monks of Cluny—each of which bears richer spiritual fruit than the last, because it branches from the trunk at a higher point of growth. As this tree also illustrates, although Joachim's historical system was founded in a framework based entirely on the Bible, it created room for the whole history of man, not just for biblical history; the Greeks, the Latins, even orders of monks that had arisen in living memory (such as the Cistercians), found their allotted place and purpose in his scheme of events. He had worked carefully over the history of the post-scriptural ages, consulting such famous authorities as Eusebius for the story of the early Church, and the best chronicles for more recent times; and he carefully noted the concords between the history he found in these books and that of the Old Testament.[9] He thus drew out of Scripture a whole universal scheme of history and of time.

With his figures, Joachim made of history almost a spurious science. His imaginings were individual and ill-disciplined, however, and his ideas, although they had a wide influence for many years (especially among the Franciscan Spirituals), were never accepted as orthodox.[10] What look like echoes of them appear from time to time in purely historical writings: for instance, Honoré Bonet in the 14th century prefaced his account of the history of the ancient world and the Church with an introduction in which he explained that Revelation, in its story of seven angels and their trumpets, presaged the seven ages through which the Church would live and endure tribulations. It is not Joachim's specific views, however, but his general approach that is significant for our purposes. This will become apparent if we compare his work with the *Speculum historiale*, the great universal history of Vincent of Beauvais (*c.* 1190–1264), who lived a generation later.

Vincent's book has little trace of the stranger sort of fancy that Joachim toyed with. Vincent was not an erratic and individual genius, as the Abbot of Fiore was: he was a Dominican who rose to be a tutor in the

T

royal household of St Louis, and whose reputation was made as an encyclopaedist. His three books, the *Speculum doctrinale*, the *Speculum naturale*, and the *Speculum historiale*, were intended as companion volumes in a compendium of all useful knowledge. In particular, he was interested in the ideas of the great sages of the past, and took care to record examples of their writings wherever he could come by them, so that his extracts from the works of such diverse writers as Plato, Cicero, Augustine, Jerome, and Bernard of Clairvaux give his book the status of a mediaeval history of thought, as well as a record of events.[11] These sages, it must be admitted, do not seem to have taught him a very critical approach to the verisimilitude of events that he found recorded in the numerous histories he read. His book is a great repertory of marvels, in which stories of Arthur's sword, of the trees of the sun and moon that spoke to Alexander in India, of Charlemagne's gigantic strength (which was such that he could lift an armed knight standing on the open palm of his hand), are interwoven with sober history.[12] The basic framework of the book is nevertheless soberly historical, a chronological account of world history from its beginnings to Vincent's own day, and this is what makes it a work different in kind from the works of Joachim, and one that it is interesting to compare with them.

Notwithstanding the great differences between their work and its nature, there is a distinct family resemblance between Vincent's idea of history and Joachim's. Both men were indifferent to problems of historical causation. Joachim saw cause entirely in supernatural terms, and could find no room for purely human agency in his theories: Vincent, it seems, simply assumed that causes were not human, and did not bother with theories about them. The structure of Vincent's chronology, like Joachim's, was founded firmly on Holy Writ. Like Joachim, he viewed human history as a single whole, whose events, both triumphant and disastrous, fitted into the symmetry of divine foresight. What the working of history showed, Vincent declared, was

> how those evils, which the faithful suffer at the hands of evil men, are of profit to themselves, whether for the purging of their sins, or to exercise and try their righteousness, or to teach them how miserable this world is: for God has so geared things together for the good of his chosen ones, that if any of them sin, he turns it to his profit to make him more humble and serviceable.[13]

Like Joachim again, Vincent found in the biblical past the key to future as well as present events. He believed that he was writing in the sixth age of the world's history,[14] the last age of the world as it had been known, which would end with Christ's second coming. This is where the affinity between Vincent and Joachim is most obvious. When Vincent had brought his history of the world down to his own age, he turned to consider in the last chapters of his book "the death and end of things" in the future, the coming of Antichrist, and the Last Judgment. Here he quoted Abbot Joachim directly as an authority on the signs that would herald the approach of the end of the world.

Vincent's divisions of history, like Joachim's, were based on the Bible. The divisions that Vincent observed, however, were not, like most of those that Joachim explored, individual to his own book, but were the commonplaces of historical writing in his age. He believed that there would be seven ages,[15] the last following the second advent; the first five had ended respectively with the Flood, with the death of Abraham, with the death of David, with the captivity of Israel in Babylon, and with the Nativity.[16] He identified four great empires mentioned in the prophecy of Daniel with the four great empires known to men—those of Persia, Babylon, Macedon, and Rome—the last of which, the prophet's words seemed to imply, must be destined to endure to the end of time. That the Roman Empire still survived in his own day, Vincent did not question. Neither he nor any of his contemporaries thought of the invasions of the barbarians as having ended its sway in Europe; they could not do so, once they accepted the currently authoritative interpretation of Daniel's prophecy.[17] Here once more we are reminded that Vincent and Joachim were of the same school of historians, to whom history, prophecy, and the study of time were one science.

I have said that Vincent presents the history of the human race, in spite of its division into epochs, as a single whole: the key to his manner of presentation here is the chronological structure of his work. This was based on the Bible, and the generations mentioned therein, as far as they could take him. His starting-point was the Creation, which was the starting-point for all who essayed the writing of universal history in the Middle Ages, such as Peter Comestor, Otto of Freising, Matthew Paris, and Antoninus of Florence, to mention just a few. Into the framework of dating that the biblical generations provided for the period from the Creation to the coming of Christ, Vincent incorporated the whole history of classical and pre-classical antiquity. Thus he dated the rise of the Argive kingdom in the time of Jacob, and that of the kingdom of Crete in Moses' day; while Jephthah judged Israel, he wrote, "Menelaus was ruling in Lacedaemon, Agamemnon in Mycenae, and Hercules died."[18] This chronological scheme, which derives ultimately from Eusebius, was common to most writers about universal history, for instance Peter Comestor, whose *Historia scolastica* (*c.* 1170) Vincent certainly used. Comestor, however, stuck much more closely to the biblical story than Vincent did, discussing scriptural events in detail, and usually simply adding to his chapters a list of contemporary incidents in classical history. Vincent went much further in running the two together into a single story—witness the remarkable heading to the 73rd chapter of his sixth book: "The suicide of Cato and the conception of John the Baptist."

Vincent had to be selective about the facts that he chose to retail about the classical past, because he had so much ground to cover. It is worth asking what his principle of selection was, where the Bible could not serve him as a guide. Very largely, it is clear, his selection was dictated by the sources he used, such as Eusebius, Augustine, Orosius, and Josephus: often he followed them word for word. Thus he referred to Eusebius for his analysis of the "causes" of the Trojan war;[19] and he took from Augustine the account of Ulysses' wanderings and his misfortunes at the hands of Circe, incorporating the saint's curious ruminations about the credibility of the metamorphosis of Ulysses' companions into pigs.[20] But it would be unfair to suggest that Vincent was a mere copyist. No one, in his day, would have thought that a contemporary could improve on the words or thoughts of such inspired masters as these great Christian Fathers. Besides, as his history approached his own times, he found no such masters as Augustine and Eusebius to follow. It is true that he borrowed, and very freely, from such masters fo universal history as his contemporary Helinandus (Hélinand de Froidmont) and Sigebert of Gembloux (*c.* 1030–1112), but these could not have been his only guides. The medley of events that he threw together is witness to a very considerable breadth of reading, and a real effort of research.

It is therefore in the later parts of his book that his selection of events and his divisions of period are most interesting. It was natural, no doubt, that Vincent should treat the age of the persecutions of the Church under the Roman emperors as a period of special interest within the sixth "age," and start a new book on the eve of Constantine's conversion in 312,[21] which harnessed the administrative authority of the Roman Empire to Christian purposes. This was a commonplace division, and its significance to a consciously Christian historian is obvious. Another of his books starts with the reign of Heraclius, the 7th-century Christian Greek emperor who reconquered Jerusalem from the Sassanians of Persia and was later regarded in the West as the first crusader; and the book closes with the translation of the "Roman" Empire from Constantinople to the

West in 800 when the Pope crowned Charlemagne.[22] This was a crucial date to men of Vincent's age, because the story explained how Roman rule, which Daniel prophesied would last till the end of time, was still (through a kind of imperial apostolic succession) an active force in Latin Christendom. Each division of Vincent's work thus had a specific Christian significance, which helped to bring into relief the pattern of God's purpose in history, and to show how its course had conformed to biblical prophecy.

To illustrate the medley of events that Vincent singled out for mention, the contents of the book that covers the period from Heraclius to Charlemagne may furnish an example. Here are thrown together the stories of Æthelfrith of Northumbria's wars against the Scots and Picts, of the rise of Mahomet, of the descent of the Irish visionary Fursey into Hell, and of Amis and Amiloun (the basis of a French romance).[23] As was said earlier, Vincent was not very selective among his authorities. Always there are hints of a kind of process of selection, however, as Vincent fixed on those events that seemed to him to indicate the working of a divine purpose. This is why he was always concerned to mention those phenomena that foreshadowed future events, and not just those in the Bible: witness the story of the fire in the sky and the blood that ran from bread broken at a feast in Tarentum, which presaged the civil wars in which the Roman republic foundered.[24] This is why his history of the pagan Roman Empire is more a list of martyrs and their miracles than a real history. This is also why he has much more to say about St Bernard of Clairvaux (1090–1153), the great Cistercian preacher, than about either the crusades or the struggles of the empire and the papacy. A spiritual "event," for Vincent, was much more important than anything that happened at the political or social level. He was so interested in wonders in all ages and places—those of classical myth as well as those of Jewish and Christian history—because wonders were to him manifest signs of God's power and intent. The interest that he could show in a secular society (for instance, the Roman Empire) was not that of a secular historian, but again "spiritual." He felt that he ought to know about it, because the empire, like the Jewish nation in early days, had become a chosen vessel for the achievement of God's purpose.

When all is said and done, one cannot claim for Vincent that he was a historian of much acumen or discrimination. Obviously, this is equally true of Joachim, although one might perhaps claim that he was not so much a historian as the eccentric protagonist of a prophetic theory of history. If their work, and the similarities of outlook that they share,

are to be seen in perspective, it may therefore be wise to set alongside them a brief consideration of the work of a mediaeval historian of acknowledged merit. The most illuminating basis for comparison, clearly, will be the work of one of those historians whom we mentioned at the beginning of this chapter, whose best historical qualities appear when they are considering history with a local bias. This will enable us, at the same time as we draw comparisons, to see also how the kind of attitudes that seem typical of the universal historians can be reflected in the work of another kind of author. No better example for our purposes can be found than the Venerable Bede (*c.* 672–735), whose *Historia ecclesiastica gentis anglorum* (Ecclesiastical History of the English Nation) has been hailed for its almost modern standard of accuracy, and is still for historians the main authority for a knowledge of events in England in the period from 597, when the first missionaries arrived from Rome, to 731, when Bede completed his book.

In spite of the immeasurably superior quality of Bede's book as a record, and although he lived 400 years before Joachim was born, we shall find that he clearly belonged to the same "family" among historians as did Vincent and Joachim. His approach to history, like theirs, was founded on the study of the Bible.[25] It was indeed as a biblical and patristic scholar that his reputation was first founded, and it was these studies that taught him the painstaking regard for accuracy that, in his history, has made him impressive to subsequent ages. The best years of his life at the monastery of Jarrow in Northumberland were spent in putting together commentaries on the Scriptures; and when one looks at what he had to say about the allegorical significance of such books as the Song of Songs or of the Temple of Solomon, and at his attempts to juggle numbers in Scripture into mystical significance, one must recognize that, for all Bede's discrimination as a textual scholar, he and Joachim had something in common as interpreters.[26] Bede also compiled a martyrology, based on a very wide reading of early hagiographical sources, and wrote a life of St Cuthbert of Lindisfarne: the miracles that he retails so often in these works and in the *Historia ecclesiastica* show that he saw in wonders the same sort of significance that Vincent did, as evidence of God's power and purpose.[27] Moreover, though the work for which he is chiefly remembered is a local history, Bede's first attempts at historical writing were, like Vincent's great book, in the universal mould. They are the short lists of the principal events in the world's history that he appended to two of his earlier works, the *De temporibus*, completed in 705, and the *De temporum ratione*, finished in 725, when he was already gathering facts for the *Historia ecclesiastica*.

These two works on chronology are important to an understanding of Bede's outlook as a historian. History for him meant what had happened in time: its events were witnesses to the harmony of a divine plan, just as, in a different way, were the regular movements of the heavenly bodies that mark the passing of time in days and months and years. For Bede, as for Joachim and Vincent, time was not something endless, but a limited thing, a fixed period from the creation to the second coming. Bede had already learnt, we find, of the same seven ages of history that Vincent was to know, and he knew that he was writing in the sixth age, the last of the world as it has been known.[28] His principal source here was St Augustine, who in his *De civitate Dei* (The City of God) had explained how the six days of creation foreshadowed the six ages of history, and the seventh day of rest that lay beyond it at the end of time, "the most great sabbath, having no evening."[29] Bede had also, as his *Commentary on the Apocalypse* shows, glimpsed something of the prophetic implications for the historian of the description in Revelation of the opening of the book with seven seals, which to Joachim later would seem to offer the key to the pattern of history.

Bede's musings on history in its universal aspect had a direct effect on the way in which he recorded the story of the English, his own people. Because he believed that history's shape was fixed before it began, he was, like Vincent, not much concerned with causation in human terms. History for him was a significant study not because it could teach one why men act, but because it could show how their actions were rewarded according to their worth:

> If it records good things of good men, the good religious reader is encouraged to imitate what is good: if it records evil of wicked men, the good religious listener is encouraged to avoid all that is sinful and perverse, and to follow what he knows to be good and pleasing to God.[30]

It is worth stressing that Bede, although he was always inclined to emphasize the blessings that attend the righteous in this world (such as the victories of English Christian kings over pagan rivals), did not suppose that they would always receive their reward here below. "I know that he will be taken from us, for this nation is not worthy of such a king," said Bishop Aidan of the noble Oswin, foreseeing his betrayal and murder at the hands of the followers of Oswy of Northumbria.[31] It was on the extra-terrestrial significance of events that Bede's attention was most firmly focussed. This is why he was so careful to record the miracles wrought by the relics of such English martyrs as St Oswald[32] (who died in battle against the pagans), for these miracles were signs both of the blessed state that was the martyr's reward in heaven, and of the way in which even the death and defeat of his saints served God's purpose.

Bede's treatment of such saints, the heroes of his book, has a further interest for us. It shows how, in spite of a theory of causation that was almost entirely supernatural, the lives that the great and holy men of the past led as individuals had a direct importance in Bede's eye, because it was through their efforts and endurance that God's purpose had been fulfilled. This recognition of the significance of individual lives and efforts was, of course, common ground to Bede, Vincent, and Joachim, but it does not emerge so clearly in the work of the other two writers, because Vincent had none of Bede's skill as a narrator, and Joachim was not a narrator at all. Bede brings the point home in a way that they do not, because he was fired with a pride in the stories of the great men of his own nation, and in the heritage they had left; in the sanctity and learning of priests such as Aidan and his own abbot Ceolfrid; and in the valour and victories of Christian kings such as Oswald and Edwin of Northumbria. Thus he shows us how a providential theory of history, which did not allow to the interplay of human motives and actions any determining power of their own, could still allow a crucial role to individuals in the story of humanity. This is an important point to remember when assessing the kind of world-view that emerges from a reading of the works of historians who belong to the same general school of history as Bede did.

We are now in a position to summarize some of the aspects that identify Bede, Joachim of Fiore, and Vincent of Beauvais as belonging to a single broad tradition of historical thinking. History, for all three of them, is to be seen as the unfolding of God's providential scheme for his creation. It repeats itself not so much because human nature and motives are constant, as because of the symmetry of the creator's design. The outlines of God's plan are discernible, partly because of the essential similarities of one period to another, but chiefly because they have been revealed through the inspired word of prophets and apostles in the Bible. Thus the study of history is linked to the study of prophecy and of time, whose origins are described in the Bible story of the creation and whose end is prophetically forecast in Holy Writ. In consequence, chronology is structured around the Bible story. The theory of causation of this school of history is a consequence of assuming that the connected stories of the Old and New Testaments indicate the structure of historical progress. The evidence about what decrees the rise and fall of empires is not understood in terms of human events and material factors: the laws of history are made not in this world but in another. To the determining authority of that other world, miraculous incidents, defying explanation in human terms, bear witness; and they are, in consequence, the most important events for any historian worthy of the name to record. The definition of the miraculous is, moreover, broadened to meet the requirements of this sort of attitude, so that divine power is seen as directly decisive in, for instance, victories and defeats that we might be tempted to attribute to human agency. To our minds, these set attitudes of the historians of the Middle Ages must seem very jejune. Nevertheless they were common ground to most historians, not just to the three that we have considered, for a period of more than 1000 years. Their longevity poses three questions. How were these attitudes first formed? Why were they so little questioned? Lastly, how did their currency affect those whose writing was creative, and so not circumscribed by the historian's duty to record what actually happened?

III

The first two of these questions are so closely connected that an answer has to be sought to both of them together. In a brief chapter, obviously a total explanation will be out of the question: but the outlines of their solution seem to be found in terms of the essentially derivative nature of much mediaeval culture. One of the most striking features of the intellectual history of the Middle Ages is the importance of their progressive rediscovery of the cultural heritage to which classical antiquity made them heirs. Theology apart, the two fields in which their highest intellectual achievements were recorded were those of philosophy and jurisprudence. Yet Thomas Aquinas (*c.* 1225–74) could never have written his *Summa theologica* but for the new vistas in philosophy opened by the rediscovery of large parts of the corpus of Aristotle's writing, hitherto unknown in the West, in the late 12th and early 13th centuries. Similarly, the development of juristic thought in these two centuries and after would have been impossible without the "rediscovery," by the lawyers of Bologna in the 12th century, of the text of Justinian's *Digesta* (or *Pandectae*). It was not until much later, however, until the great revival of interest in profane classical literature at the end of the Middle Ages, that scholars found their attention drawn to historical writings whose approach seriously challenged their own preconceived ideas. These ideas were themselves an inheritance, but from the age of the Christian Fathers, not that of pagan antiquity. The Fathers of the Church had forged them in the course of the controversy that arose out of the challenge they threw down in the early days to the assumed superiority of pagan culture and the traditions of the Roman Empire over anything that had its origins in Jewry. The Christian historical arguments, by means of which the Fathers trounced their opponents, set the pattern for historical thinking for the whole Middle Ages.[33]

The historical presentation of the Christian message had posed a problem for the Church from the moment that the apostles decided that their message was not for the Jews only but for the whole world. The significance of the New Testament story could (and indeed still can) be clear only against the background of the history and prophecies of the Old Testament, which prepared for it and foretold it. The pagan world of the Roman Empire knew nothing of the Old Testament, however, and had no reason to regard it as of any special import. Thus, as Professor Momigliano has put it, for the new Christians of the Gentile world, conversion "meant literally the discovery of a new history from Adam and Eve to contemporary events."[34] It therefore became a matter of urgency for the early Fathers to show that this new history was not just of an equal but of a higher status, in terms of antiquity and reliability, than the more familiar and famous histories of pagan nations, and that it was of immeasurably greater significance. Justin Martyr in the 2nd century laid down the main lines that argument was to follow:[35] Tatian, Theophilus, Tertullian, Clement of Alexandria, Julius Africanus, and a host of others carried it further and into greater detail.[36] In the later patristic period the work of two men, Eusebius of Caesarea and Augustine of Hippo, served to give the ideas of their predecessors the definitive shape and form in which they were transmitted to the Middle Ages.

The history of the Old Testament, the Fathers claimed, was older and more accurate than anything to be found in pagan annals: the culture of the pagan world was not as old as that of the Jews, and was essentially derivative. "If you have ever heard of a certain Moses," wrote Tertullian, "he goes before the fall of Troy by a thousand years: our other prophets, even the last of them, are not later than your first philosophers and law givers and historians."[37] The laws of Numa Pompilius of Rome, claimed Clement of Alexandria, derived their precepts ultimately from those of Moses: for men such as Clement it was not difficult to see in the Mithraic mysteries distortions of the prophecies of Daniel and Isaiah, or to believe that Plato's ideas were shaped by his contact with Hebrew traditions surviving in Egypt.[38] One great strength of the case presented by the Christian Fathers was that it presented a single, positive interpretation of the whole of history, which could find room in its framework for the story of pagan peoples as well as for that of the Jews; another strength was the impressive record of the fulfilment of biblical prophecy in world history to which the Fathers pointed. To assess their arguments critically would be a long process, and here it must suffice to say that they triumphed in the end. What their triumph meant was summed up well by Professor Coopland as "a gigantic reshuffling, a shifting of the centre of gravity of world-history,"[39] by which the history of the classical world, including its cultural as well as its political achievements, was incorporated in a subordinate role into a Judaeo-Christian framework. The foundation of this achievement was a new chronology based on the generations of the Bible, into which the Fathers assimilated the history of all the Gentile peoples, and which had the tremendous advantage of uniformity.

This Christian reorientation of history profoundly modified men's views of both the scriptural and the classical past. Of necessity, it prised the significance of the Old Testament story away from a strictly racial context. The Christian message was for all men, not for one race only. On this earth the chosen people, for the Fathers, were not the Jews, but rather the subjects of the Roman Empire, the world power under whose sway the Christians lived, and by which, as Irenaeus put it, "the world hath peace, and we walk in the ways without fear, and sail wheresoever we will."[40] The authority of the empire came to them to seem providential: "In the emperors we reverence the judgment of God who has set them over the nations," wrote Tertullian.[41] Eusebius made it clear that the Roman Empire had been foreseen in Scripture: "When Christ was come, concerning whom it had been foretold by the prophet that in his day righteousness should flourish and abundance of peace . . . then did events correspond to the voice of prophecy,"[42] in that Augustus's victories had ended the civil wars of Rome and restored peace to the whole Roman world. Here we can plainly see ideas taking shape that were to appear later, more simply formulated, in the writing of such men as Vincent of Beauvais and Otto of Freising. It is worth noting, too, that already in the age of the Fathers there was careful note being made of prophecies other than scriptural ones that conformed to the scriptural pattern of prognosis. Eusebius himself heard the Emperor Constantine identify Virgil's vision (4th *Eclogue*) of a coming golden age and a miraculous birth as a foreshadowing of Christ's coming.[43] For the Fathers, Scripture was not by any means the only witness to the truths to which it testified. The history of the pagan nations, even in the Old Testament period, pointed the same way, though not so clearly, and pagan philosophers had glimpses of the truth, though not of the whole truth. As has been said, one of the reasons for the Fathers' success as controversialists was their ability to assimilate into a Judaeo-Christian framework things that originally had nothing to do with Judaism or Christianity.

The special contribution of Eusebius of Caesarea (263–339)[44] toward a definition of the general historical thesis of the Fathers was in the matter of chronology. His work in the field was not original, and he owed a great debt to Julius Africanus in particular; but he was more systematic than any of his predecessors. The book that is called his *Chronicle* records an immense effort to sort out the chronologies of all the various kingdoms and nations of the classical and oriental past, and to correlate them in tabular form, so that, arranged in parallel columns, the relations of the histories presented could be taken in at a glance. The master-keys to his system were, of course, the dates of scriptural history, calculated by means of the generations recorded in the Bible. Translated into Latin by St Jerome (the Greek original has not survived), this work furnished the basic chronological structure for all subsequent Christian histories. It provided the framework that Bede and Vincent of Beauvais and all the other great historians of the Middle Ages used, when dealing with the early periods of history.

Eusebius is now better remembered for another work, his *Ecclesiastical History* (the *Ecclesiasticae historiae libri decem*, usually read in the Middle Ages in the translation of Rufinus of Aquileia). This book was much studied in the Middle Ages and was the chief source for the early history of the Church for writers such as Bede and Vincent. Its manner of interpretation also had an important influence. The history of the Church was a subject rather different from ordinary history, which described the fortunes of a people or nation, because the Church was not an ordinary people or nation. Nevertheless, Eusebius, like his forerunners, spoke of the Church of Christ as a "nation," though a nation different from others because of its transcendental nature and purposes.[45] He treated it thus in a manner very similar to that in which Scripture treats Jewish history, which is again the history of a race or nation that has a special, transcendental significance. This manner of treating the history of the Church within the Roman Empire, an originally pagan institution, was one that naturally tended to blur for subsequent readers any sharp distinction of tone between classical and biblical history.

The idea of the Church as the "nation" of the Christians was central also to the great book by St Augustine of Hippo, *De civitate Dei*, the book that, after the Bible, probably exercised a wider influence than any other single work on the West in the Middle Ages. This book, as it happened, was also the last chapter in the controversy of the Fathers with the pagans.[46] When Augustine wrote, the Roman Empire had already begun to crumble under the impact of barbarian invasions. In the year 410, Alaric the Visigoth had sacked Rome. Augustine took up his pen in order to frame a reply, then urgently needed, to the arguments of those pagans who, forging a providential history of their own, laid the blame for Rome's disasters on the Christians, who had taught the Romans to abandon their ancestral gods. On this task Augustine brought to bear not only a mastery of Christian teaching but also a knowledge of profane history, philosophy, and literature whose range no pagan scholar of his age could rival.

For Augustine (354–430), two things about past history stood out clearly: its events arranged themselves according to a pattern prophetically foretold; and these events, if divorced from a transcendental context, degenerated into a story without significance. The two points were directly connected: "The centuries of past history would have rolled by like empty jars, if the coming of Christ had not been foretold by them."[47] Much history by his standard remained confused and pointless, because it foreshadowed and signified too little: "Why are but two of Japheth's eight sons' progenies known by name, three of Ham's four, two of Shem's six? Had the others no children? No, we may not argue that, but they did not grow up into nations worth recording, as the others did."[48] This did not mean that Augustine regarded histories other than Jewish and Christian as irrelevant. (For the benefit of those who blamed the Christians for contemporary disasters, he was careful to point out that worse disasters had befallen Rome in the days of the republic, and that the old gods had then proved utterly vain to prevent them.[49]) It did, however, mean that for him the strand of prophetic insight running through historical events was the key to their significance. Here he was framing the outline of a general interpretation of history that subsequent generations accepted, very largely on his authority.

Augustine was too subtle an apologist of the Christian cause to seek to belittle the achievements of the Roman past, as many of his predecessors had done. He was quick to point out occasions when pagan history directly echoed that of Scripture: "concords," as Joachim would have called them. Thus the story of Cain and Abel was, according to Augustine, reflected and repeated in Roman history in the story of Romulus and Remus.[50] But there was a difference for him between the two stories, and a crucial one. The story of Romulus and Remus was a story of strife in this world, that of Cain and Abel a story of the tension between the values of this world and the values *in this world* of another. The fixed and eternal values of the other world, the heavenly city, should be the determining factors in judging all events, past, present, and future. The fulfilment of prophecy in history was simply the witness and proof of their eternal validity. Those who blamed the Christians for the sack of Rome were thus for Augustine missing the point: they were falling into the easy error of considering achievement in human terms only, and were blind to the transcendental values to which history itself bore testimony. History was not just about human lives, but also about their spiritual worth: "Let the virtue that serves human glory be never so much extolled, it is not comparable with the beginning of the saint's virtues, whose assured hope stands fixed in the grace and mercy of the true God."[51] Here Augustine proposed a standard of historical judgment that, backed with the authority of his erudition, was to last a millennium. In effect, the standard he proposed was that which would come into play at the Last Judgment—an event that, as we have seen, the historians of the Middle Ages never had far from their minds. It is no accident that when Bishop Otto of Freising (*c.* 1115–58) came to compile his universal history, he called it the *Chronicon de duabus civitatibus* (History of the Two Cities), of which Cain and Abel were respectively the first citizens, and in its eighth book gave an account of what would happen at the end of the world's history.[52] The whole structure of historical thought as he knew it was coloured by the teaching of Augustine.

There is one other writer of the last age of classical Rome whose work must be considered in any assessment of the historiographical heritage of the Middle Ages, although his contribution was of a rather different order from those of Eusebius and Augustine. This is the polemist Orosius (*fl. c.* 400). His *Historia adversus paganos libri VII* (History in Seven Books against the Pagans) was in fact written at Augustine's direct instance, and its object was to prove in detail what Augustine had himself suggested—that worse disasters had befallen the Romans in the days of paganism than anything that threatened them contemporarily. Five of its seven books were for this reason taken up with the history of the Republic, the heroic age of Roman history, and the one that furnished the Roman citizens of Orosius's day with their most familiar and honoured national memories. The argument and method of this ponderous work are merely cumulative.[53] It is a gloomy catalogue of tales of war, defeat, and crimes, and of such natural disasters as famines, storms, and earthquakes. Orosius went to special pains to belittle the individual acts of heroism of the great Romans of the past, and to remind his readers that when Romans had been victorious, the price of victory had been paid in the blood of other nations. In terms of causation his approach was wholly unsubtle, and virtually reduced the whole history of the classical, non-Christian past to the level, in terms of cause and effect, of the books of Kings in the Bible. Nevertheless, in its own way the book was impressive. Although he was concerned largely with the accidentals of history, and entirely uninterested in the growth and structure of society, Orosius ranged so far in his quest for material that few after him saw much need to search further. His book taught the historians of the Middle Ages most of what they ever came to know of Livy and Caesar, and indeed it is still the chief source for what we know of the lost books of Livy. It became, in fact, an accepted and authoritative guide to the history of antiquity.

It is not clear that Orosius himself was fully convinced by his own arguments. He viewed the barbarian invaders of the Western Empire with fear and loathing; but it was part of his avowed purpose to minimize the disastrous nature of their invasions, and he very largely succeeded in doing so.[54] There were crumbs of comfort for his Roman readers in his story of the Visigothic King Athaulf, who, despairing of his original plan of replacing the Roman Empire with a Gothic one, resolved to use the arms of the Goths to restore the name and power of Rome.[55] More importantly, this attitude of Orosius's helped to make his history acceptable to the barbarians, who within 100 years of his death had made themselves rulers of most of Western Europe. Encomiasts of the early barbarian rulers were among the first historical writers who are known to have used his book.[56] At the end of that 100 years, moreover, there were very few men in the West capable of subjecting its plan and method to sophisticated criticism. Together with the unassailable orthodoxy of its standpoint, its encyclopaedic quality made it appear not jejune but authoritatively impressive.

The period following the collapse of imperial administration in Western Europe was the one in which the historical attitudes that were to prevail throughout the Middle Ages became fixed. Somewhere about the year 500 an unidentified cleric, working probably in Gaul, produced a list of books authorized as profitable reading for all Christians, which purported to be a decree of Pope Gelasius (492–6). The list mentions only two historians: Orosius and Eusebius. Augustine is also included, of course, as are many other Fathers, but this author rightly thought of their work as important in a wider reference than that of history only. This spurious decree was, much later, incorporated into Gratian's *Decretum* (the *Concordantia discordantium canonum, c.* 1140), and so became part of the accepted canon law of the mediaeval Church.[57] It was quoted by Vincent of Beauvais himself, in defence of the attention he paid to secular authors: he was, he claimed, only following the example of the great Orosius. By indicating which authorities were to be regarded as most reliable and useful, this decree helped to stereotype the historical orthodoxy of the Middle Ages. At the time when it was forged, the age of polemic was already effectively over: the outlines of a Christian interpretation of history and a Christian standard of significance for assessing historical events had been set by authorities whose stature put their conclusions beyond question.

If one seeks a direct tribute to the impact of the late patristic period on the historical writers of the Middle Ages, perhaps the words that John of Salisbury, the great 12th-century scholar, wrote in the prologue to his *Historia pontificalis* (Memoirs of the Papal Court) are as good as any. The memoirs, written from personal experience and constantly dealing with men and events that John knew at first hand, are one of the most sophisticated and humane efforts in historical writing that his age has bequeathed us. Yet John did not think of himself as making an essentially individual contribution to the record, only as fitting a part of the history of his own time into a framework already provided. The foundation of this framework was the Bible, read alongside the commentaries of the Fathers, in particular of Jerome. After the evangelists and Luke, John wrote, Eusebius of Caesarea had carried on their sacred tradition and "told the story of the Church in its youth." He had found successors in Orosius, Cassiodorus, Isidore, and Bede. It was in their steps that John's immediate predecessors, Hugh of St Victor and Sigebert of Gembloux, trod. But John could not find that anyone had taken up the story of the Church after Sigebert, so he took his own pen in hand to continue the tradition that the Bible and the Fathers had founded:

> For all these chroniclers have had a single purpose: to relate noteworthy matters, so that the invisible things of God may be clearly seen by the things that are done, and men may by examples of reward or punishment be made more zealous in the fear of God and the pursuit of Justice.[58]

IV

Two of the questions that were put earlier in this chapter have now
been considered. We have learnt something of how ideas that historians
of the Middle Ages took on trust were formed, and why they remained
unqueried. There remains the third question: how did the currency of
these ideas affect creative writers, who were not concerned merely with
the historical record? In tackling so broad a question as this, we cannot
hope to do more than make a few suggestions. It is fortunate, therefore,
that the writer whose work will most readily show how the ideas that we
have been examining could be important outside the field of historiography is also one whom many would regard as the greatest poet of the
Middle Ages: Dante (1265–1321).

The Christian providential view of history is central to the structure of
Dante's *Divina commedia* (*c.* 1306–21).[59] Just as the measure of its cosmo-
graphy is the whole universe as Dante believed it to be, so its human
compass is the whole of history. When he began to write the *Commedia*,
Dante's imagination had already been fired by the Roman imperial
past; and his passions, we know, had long been roused by the miseries
of the Italy of his own day, torn with internal wars. The providential
view of history supplied the connection between these themes. It was
no more an accident in Dante's eye than it had seemed to the Fathers
that Christ was born when the dominion of Rome was world-wide:

> Since at His coming into the world it was meet that not only the
> heavens but also the earth should be in their best frame, and since
> earth is in her best frame . . . when the whole earth has one prince
> [to ensure universal peace], divine providence ordained the people
> and the city that should fulfil this condition, namely, glorious
> Rome.[60]

The desperate conditions of Dante's own day had arisen, he believed,
because men, in their covetousness, had torn apart the "seamless garment" of empire, and denied its universal authority, which was willed
by God.[61] The chief cause of trouble had been the dowering of the
Church with earthly riches, which in the end had led the popes to
challenge the temporal authority of the empire.[62] So, by denying what
was willed by God, they had plunged Italy into a new age of tribulation
and persecution.

Thus, for Dante, the troubles of his own time appeared as a historical
punishment for a historical transgression against the will of God. His
outlook here was perfectly in tune with the teaching of the Fathers and

U

of contemporary historians, and it is worth noticing how well his handling of the past, too, conformed to their approach. At first sight it may not appear to do so: the object of the Fathers of the Church was to prove Jewish Scripture superior to the culture of pagan Rome, and Dante's reverence for the imperial past sometimes went so far as to seem almost to reverse the process. He believed the citizens who founded and guarded Rome's fortunes in the days of the republic to have been divinely inspired: and he carefully listed in his *Convivio* (*c.* 1304) the miracles that showed that the finger of God had pointed Rome to her high destiny.[63] In the *Commedia* he found a place for Trajan in Paradise, and cast Brutus and Cassius, who betrayed Caesar, alone among men (except for Judas Iscariot) into the uttermost pit of Hell.[64] Notwithstanding all this, Dante's views prove on closer inspection to be true to the traditional teaching that the Fathers bequeathed to his age. It was they, after all, who had first taught that Rome had a providential part to play in the history of man. For him as for them, there was one decisive dividing line in history, and one only—the Incarnation; and for him as for them, it was from this event that all history, previous and subsequent, derived its significance. In spite of Dante's admiration for the ancient world, he consigns Virgil and all the other great pagans who had lived before the days of Christ to Limbo because "they did not worship God aright."[65] When Christ harrowed Hell, those who were delivered were not the famous Romans, but those who had had a part in shaping a more important destiny: Adam, Abel, Noah, Abraham the patriarch, Moses, and King David.[66] Dante's history was the same as that which the Fathers taught: he saw it as a single whole, whose significance was transcendental; Holy Writ was the key to its theme, the fulfilment of God's foreordained purposes.

Faithful to the teaching of the Fathers, Dante found historical events interesting not primarily for themselves, but for what they taught man about God's designs, and hence about man's place in the universe. For Dante, history was thus in itself an allegory, with an inner meaning of far deeper significance than the external passage of events. This inner meaning was what St Augustine, in the past, had expressly taught men to look for in historical events. In taking the injunction seriously Dante was typical, as we have seen earlier from the example of Joachim, who worked this inner meaning up into a prophetic structure that would foretell the future of history, as well as explaining its past. This is why we find Dante setting out on the same road as Joachim, and searching his chronology for "concords" that would bring the significance of events into truer perspective—jubilant to find, for example, that the birth of David, from whose line the mother of God sprang, seemed to coincide with the arrival in Italy of Aeneas, the father of the Roman people.

> Thus the divine choice of the Roman Empire is sufficiently proved by the birth of the Holy City, which was contemporaneous with the root of the family of Mary.[67]

Here is a point of direct relevance to the literary scholar. It is hardly surprising that allegory, as a literary genre, had a special fascination for people in the Middle Ages, or that their writers were masters of its conventions: to them allegory was, almost literally, the stuff of life. This is also, conversely, the reason why most historians of the Middle Ages were not very good at distinguishing myth from history, as we can see in the host of fabulous marvels that found their way into Vincent's *Speculum historiale*. Myth could teach a genuine moral allegorically, quite as effectively as the historical record could. It thus becomes very difficult, in Dante's *Inferno*, for instance, to decide whether he regarded the stories of the giants as telling of a race of monsters that, by his own day, had become extinct, or whether he saw them as mere fables. What he did know, from careful study, was the accepted allegorical significance of such stories, whether fabulous or otherwise.[68]

Dante's poem is a complex allegory into which many levels of meaning are woven. This is why, for all his sense of the gradual unfolding of God's designs for men through passing ages, he found the chronological framework of history too cramping in this his greatest work. The arrangement of human events and lives in tiers and grades of significance lent itself far better to his purposes than the historian's terms of years that succeed one another. It made possible a far more dramatic presentation of what, for Dante, was the central theme of history—the achievement of divine justice. By wresting history loose from the context of time, he could show God's judgment at work through all the ages simultaneously. In the spheres of Heaven and circles of Hell, he allotted a place for the reward or punishment of every human virtue and vice in its degree. To show what these virtues and vices meant in human terms, he furnished at each point a series of glimpses of the lives of men and women from all ages in the world's history, which had been made or marred by them. Thus at the same time as he demonstrated the meaning of God's justice, he could demonstrate what for him was significant in the lives of men living in the world about him and his readers—or indeed, in any human context.

307

It is clear that, in Dante's judgment, it is not what men achieve that matters, but how they achieve it. This is a transcendental standard: the concern is with how men surmount or fail the moral tests that life puts in their path. Dante sorted men out not according to the age in which they lived or the station that they occupied, but according to whether they were covetous, or vengeful, or licentious, or negligent of their vows; or showed the virtues that are the converse of these vices. This is not the way in which a modern historian would attempt to classify individuals, but it is entirely in accord with Augustine's injunction to the Christian historian: "In our discipline, we do not ask whether a pious soul is angry, but why: not whether he is sad, but for what reason."[69] It is of course true that Dante's judgments were not historical judgments, and that it did not affect his purpose if some of the subjects of the *Commedia* did not really commit the sins he ascribed to them. In fact, many of his opinions about contemporaries were distorted by his own partisan bitterness, and his erudition shows nowadays much more clearly in his mastery of the theological and philosophical implications of the good and evil influences that he describes than in his knowledge of the past. What is important, however, is that in judging individuals and the significance of their lives he used the same standards as a historian would—standards that the Founding Fathers of historical writing in the Middle Ages had considered most appropriate. The way in which he handled the lives of the individuals in his poem is thus an indication of the way in which the notion of history current in his time could influence the approach and outlook of a writer who was not a historian at all.

V

Two further points seem to be worth making here, by way of a conclusion, about the sort of way of looking at men's lives that, by Dante's time, was common to historians and to most other writers. The first is this. If one assumes—as did Dante and all the historians we have considered in this chapter—that history is a single whole with a pattern fixed upon it from outside by the will of God, and that the focal thread of interest in its course is the conformity, or otherwise, of men's actions with God's justice, then lines of demarcation in history inevitably tend to become blurred. For example, although men may value different kinds of wealth in different epochs, it is not easy to see how avarice, the over-mastering desire for wealth, differs from one age to another. This is one of the reasons why Dante was insensitive to differences of quality in the kind of lives people led in classical antiquity, in biblical times, and in his own day. Among the spirits of the incontinent, he could place alongside one another Dido, Cleopatra, Semiramis, Paris, Tristan, and Paolo and Francesca, without seeming to be aware of any difference between the worlds in which they lived.[70] This is a typical insensitivity, which Dante shared with most other men of this time. The mediaeval historical approach taught men to look for similarities in all ages, not for differences. This made it easy for someone such as Dante to believe that, in the past, men had been better morally; and he was fervent in his admiration for a golden age that was gone. But he and his contemporaries could not think of the past as a foreign country where people did things differently. This was one of the reasons why the authors of mediaeval romance were so successful in handling stories that they deliberately located in a remote age, such as that of Arthur. They did not feel a need to make the actors old-fashioned to suit their setting, and so they could write about them with a natural ease.

The preoccupation of mediaeval authors with moral values that do not vary much from epoch to epoch had a second, very important, consequence. It is one that is not very obvious in the *Divina commedia* because the poem is set outside a chronological framework; but it becomes clear if one tries to picture what sort of story Dante's material would grow into, if the life of one of his subjects, as he handles it, were put into a chronological setting. What one would get would be the tale of a man or woman encountering in the course of life a series of problems posed by external events, in which the interest would centre on whether the way in which he or she tackled these conformed to a high or low moral standard. The skill in presenting this story would therefore not arise from the way in which one event was made to stem naturally from another, but from the subtlety and complexity of the moral problems at issue, or perhaps from their unusual and dramatic context. In other words, the story of the central character would be fitted into a context not of human relations but of moral significance. This is in fact the way in which (as we saw earlier in this chapter) historians such as Bede approached the problem of presenting the contribution of individuals in history. It is also, as it happens, the way in which most authors of romances approached the problem of structuring narrative. The moral context of their stories was not always, of course, the same broad and eternal framework in terms of which both Bede and Dante considered human behaviour. The ethos of courtly love, or of knightly honour and fidelity, is more likely to be the moral context in which the episodic history of a romantic hero has to be seen. In broad terms, however, one manner of structuring narrative was common to the historian and the romantic author; and romantic authors showed the same indifference to human causation, and the same concern that events should be related to values that they believed significant, as historians such as Bede did. The author of the English romance of *Sir Gawain and the Green Knight* (*c.* 1380) did not feel any need to explain why the Green Knight came to Arthur's court; but he did feel the need to make the outcome of his story fit precisely the degree of knightly punctiliousness that Gawain showed, once he had taken up the Green Knight's challenge.

Judged by modern critical standards, many mediaeval romances seem episodic almost to the point of formlessness: just as most mediaeval histories, judged by modern historiographical standards, seem indifferent to causation to the point of naivety. There is more here than naivety, however: in the background, in each case, is a different set of ideas from our own about the way in which things happen, and about the methods by which human behaviour needs to be assessed. This does not mean that most authors of the Middle Ages were steeped in contemporary historical literature (though some of them were); only that, of necessity, the way in which they wrote reflected current assumptions about the record of events. These assumptions, in the mediaeval period, were for a long time constant: and that is why their clear formulation in the writing of historians should be of interest to the literary scholar. They go a long way toward explaining certain features of mediaeval creative writing that seem also to be constant: the love of allegory, the fascination with the marvellous, the appetite for prophetic insights, and the facility for viewing the past in terms of the present—all familiar to anyone who has walked in what W. P. Ker called the "secret orchards" of mediaeval romance. They also help to explain why mediaeval authors were insensitive to the dogma that in narrative the accidental is an offence to artistry, and why they seldom thought about the tragic interplay of human strength and weakness in the manner of Shakespeare and the best Greek dramatists. These are important matters; and their importance will perhaps justify this glance at mediaeval ideas of history in a book about mediaeval literature.

References

1. This chapter was written in 1968. Since then a number of important works have appeared that bear directly on topics and authors that are discussed in it. Notable among these are M. E. REEVES, *The Influence of Prophecy in the Later Middle Ages* (Oxford 1969), and the articles by Dr R. W. Southern, under the general title of "Aspects of the European Tradition of Historical Writing," in *Transactions of the Royal Historical Society*: "The Classical Tradition from Einhard to Geoffrey of Monmouth," *Trans. R. Hist. Soc.* 20 (London 1970) pp. 173–96; "Hugh of St Victor and the Idea of Historical Development," *ibid.*, 21 (1971), pp. 159–79; and "History as Prophecy," *ibid.*, 22 (1972), pp. 159–80. Without rewriting the chapter I could not do justice to their findings, and I have done no more than revise some passages. In this process of revision I have been greatly helped by the advice and criticism of Mr C. P. Wormald of All Souls College, Oxford.

2. There is a very interesting chapter on Joachim of Fiore in E. GEBHARDT, *Mystics and Heretics in Italy*, trans. by E. M. Hulme (London 1922). Among important recent works in English is M. E. REEVES, "The *Liber figurarum* of Joachim of Fiore," in *Mediaeval and Renaissance Studies* II (London 1950), pp. 57–81, on which much that I have said here depends.

3. *Expositio in apocalypsim*, Intro. 6. For the Old Testament the first seal represents the period from Jacob to Moses, the second from Moses to Samuel, the third from David to Elias, the fourth from Elias to Isaiah, the fifth from Isaiah to the Captivity, the sixth from the Captivity to Malachi, the seventh from Malachi to Zacharias (the father of John the Baptist). For the New Testament, the first seal represents the period from the Resurrection to the death of St John the Evangelist, the second from St John to Constantine the Great, the third from Constantine to Justinian, the fourth from Justinian to Charlemagne, the fifth from Charlemagne to Joachim's day; the sixth is *nuper initiata* (recently begun).

4. *ibid.*, I, 1, comment on the words "Joannes septem ecclesiis."

5. The *Liber figurarum* is independent of the three works of Joachim so far mentioned and illustrates ideas that run through all of them. The ascription of its model to Joachim himself has been doubted, but is convincingly defended in REEVES, "The *Liber figurarum* . . . ," pp. 65–9.

6. *Concordia novi ac veteris testamenti* II, i, 4 and 9; *Expos. in apoc.*, Intro. 5.

7. See REEVES, "The *Liber figurarum* . . . ," pp. 69–70, and the references given there.

8. This tree is drawn in the manuscript of the *Liber figurarum* at Corpus Christi College (Oxford), MS. 255 A, folio 13r; reproduced in REEVES, "The *Liber figurarum* . . . ," pl. III.

9. Thus, in *Concordia* IV, 5, Joachim makes the division of Israel into two kingdoms, Israel and Judah, in the time of Rehoboam a concord of the schism of the Greek and Latin churches, and strikes a concord (IV, 17 ff.) between the disasters that overtook Jerusalem in Josaiah's reign and those of Rome during the 11th-century papal-imperial contest.

10. For Joachim's influence on the Franciscan Spirituals, see DECIMA L. DOUIE, *The Nature and the Effect of the Heresy of the Fraticelli* (Manchester 1932), Ch. II, and REEVES, *The Influence of Prophecy* . . . , Pt II. His influence was still felt as late as the 16th century: see M. E. REEVES, "The Abbot Joachim and the Society of Jesus," *Mediaeval and Renaissance Studies* V (London 1961), pp. 163 ff.

11. Vincent probably copies the format from his contemporary Helinandus (Hélinand de Froidmont), whose *Chronicon universale* is lost: see E. BOUTARIC, "Vincent de Beauvais et la connaissance de l'antiquité classique," in *Revue des Questions Historiques* XVII (Paris 1875), p. 13.

12. For Arthur, see *Speculum historiale* XX, 56: for the trees of the sun and moon, IV, 56–7; for Charlemagne's feats, XXIV, 1. Vincent's account of Charlemagne, however, is not inaccurate in those parts where the ultimate authority is Einhard's contemporary biography, the *Vita Caroli Magni,* and not (as here) Pseudo-Turpin's later and spurious *Historia Karoli Magna et Rotholandi.*

13. *ibid.,* I, 6. Vincent's point here is to remind his readers that historical disasters are not evidence that God is the author of evil.

14. *ibid.,* XXXI, 105.

15. *Speculum naturale* XXXII, 26. This idea of seven ages, an echo or concord of the seven days of creation, was first clearly formulated by St Augustine in *De civitate Dei* XXII, 30; it makes its first appearance in a purely historical work in the *Chronicon de sex aetatibus* of St Isidore of Seville (*c.* 570–636).

16. *Spec. hist.* VI, 88.

17. The decay of the empire's authority, which by the 13th century was obvious, posed a problem for this interpretation. Vincent mentions the facts (*Spec. hist.* XVI, 1) but does not elaborate. A way out of the difficulty was to regard Roman authority as now vested finally in the Roman Church as a result of Constantine's Donation, which is discussed with care (XIII, 56–7). Dante (as we shall see) found a very different way out of the difficulty.

18. *Spec. hist.* I, 109 (origin of Argives); II, 53 (origin of Crete); II, 59 (Menelaus and Agamemnon).

19. *ibid.,* II, 60.

20. *ibid.,* II, 64–5; cf. St Augustine, *De civ. Dei* XVIII, 18.

21. *ibid.,* XIII.

22. *ibid.,* XXIII.

23. *ibid.,* XXIII, 8 (for Æthelfrith); XXIII, 39 ff. (Mahomet); XXIII, 81–3 (Fursey); XXIII, 162–6 (Amis and Amiloun).

24. *ibid.,* V, 96.

25. J. CAMPBELL, "Bede," in T. A. DOREY (ed.), *Latin Historians* (London 1966), is a masterly introduction to Bede's work as a historian. The best general account of his life and writings is A. HAMILTON THOMPSON (ed.), *Bede, His Life, Times, and Writings* (Oxford 1935).

26. See CLAUDE JENKINS, "Bede as Exegete and Theologian," in HAMILTON THOMPSON, *op. cit.*, Ch. VI, especially pp. 173 ff.

27. On Bede's handling of the miraculous, see BERTRAM COLGRAVE, "Bede's Miracle Stories," in HAMILTON THOMPSON, *op. cit.*, Ch. VII; and C. G. LOOMIS, "The Miracle Traditions of the Venerable Bede," *Speculum* XXI (Cambridge, Mass. 1946), pp. 404 ff.

28. *De temporum ratione* 10 and 66; see also *De temporibus* 16. It is interesting that Vincent, in *Specularum naturale*, immediately follows his discussion of the seven ages with a succinct chronicle of world events, just as Bede does in *De temporum ratione*, which Vincent certainly knew.

29. *De civ. Dei* XXII, 30.

30. *Historia ecclesiastica gentis Anglorum*, Preface.

31. *ibid.*, III, 14.

32. *ibid.*, III, 9–13.

33. For what follows I have relied extensively on A. MOMIGLIANO, "Pagan and Christian Historiography in the Fourth Century," in A. MOMIGLIANO (ed.), *The Conflict between Paganism and Christianity in the Fourth Century* (Oxford 1963); also on G. W. COOPLAND, "The Medieval View of World History," a masterly essay in his edition (Liverpool 1949) of *The Tree of Battles* of Honoré Bonet (*c.* 1345–1406).

34. MOMIGLIANO, *op. cit.*, p. 83.

35. See especially *Apologia* I, 54 and 59 ff.; *Ad Graecos cohortatio* 9.

36. An excellent synopsis of the most important passages in these and other authors in this context is in COOPLAND, *op. cit.*, Appendix III, p. 304. I have used this extensively.

37. *Apologeticum* 19.

38. *Miscellanea (Stromateis)* I, 15; II, 5. It is useful to compare Clement's remarks about Moses and Plato with the earlier comments of Justin Martyr in *Ad Graec.* 20 and the later ones of Eusebius in *Praeparatio evangelica* IX, 6.

39. COOPLAND, *op. cit.*, p. 41.

40. *Adversus haereses* IV, 30, Section 3.

41. *Apologeticum* 32.

42. *Praep. evangel.* I, 4.

43. Constantine, *Oratio ad sanctorum coetum* 19, appendix to Eusebius's *De vita Constantini*. The question of the authorship of this oration has aroused endless controversy; for a brief review, see N. H. BAYNES, "Constantine and the Christian Church," in *Proceedings of the British Academy* XV (London 1929), pp. 388–94.

44. For a recent and scholarly examination of Eusebius's work, see D. S. WALLACE HADRILL, *Eusebius of Caesarea* (London 1960). I have found Ch. VIII and IX particularly useful.

45. This point is developed in MOMIGLIANO, *op. cit.*, pp. 90–1.
46. For what follows I have relied extensively on the recent outstanding biography, PETER BROWN, *Augustine of Hippo* (London 1967), Ch. 25–7.
47. *Tractatus in Johannis Evangelium* 9, Section 6. The translation of these words is by Peter Brown and cannot, I think, be bettered.
48. *De civ. Dei* XVI, 3.
49. *ibid.*, III, *passim*.
50. *ibid.*, XV, 5.
51. *ibid.*, V, 19.
52. *Chronicon de duabus civitatibus*, trans. by C. C. Mierow (New York 1928), has an illuminating introduction by the translator.
53. For what is said here about Orosius, I am largely indebted to my colleague Mr. J. F. Matthews, of Corpus Christi College, Oxford, who very kindly lent me his unpublished paper "Orosius and the History of Rome."
54. See, for instance, *Historia adversus paganos* II, 19, where Orosius compares the sack of Rome by the Gauls under Brennus in 390 B.C. with its sack by the Goths in his own day; at every point the former occasion is shown to be more severe and more disastrous.
55. *ibid.*, VII, 43.
56. Mr Matthews (see Note 51 above) mentions in particular Cassiodorus in his *Historia Gothorum*, written in honour of the house of Theodoric; hence Jordanes (from whose *De rebus Getica* of *c.* 550 Cassiodorus's history is known) also came to use Orosius.
57. *Concordantia discordantium canonum*, Pt. I, XV, 3. On this canon see G. BARDY, "Gélase (Décret de)," in L. PIROT (ed.), *Dictionnaire de la Bible: Supplément*, Tome III (Paris 1938), cols. 579–90.
58. *The Historia Pontificalis of John of Salisbury*, ed. and trans. by M. Chibnall (London 1956), pp. 1–3.
59. In what follows I must acknowledge my debt to W. H. V. READE, "Dante's Vision of History," in *Proc. Brit. Acad.* XXV (London 1939), pp. 187–216.
60. *Convivio* IV, 5.
61. *De monarchia* I, 16.
62. See in particular *Purgatorio* XVI, 103–29; and the speech of St Peter in *Paradiso* XXVII, 40–54.
63. *Conv.* IV, 5; *De mon.* II, 4.
64. For Trajan, see *Par.* XX, 43–8, and *Purg.* X, 73–81; for Brutus and Cassius, see *Inferno* XXXIV, 64–9.
65. *Inf.* IV, 34–42.
66. *ibid.*, IV, 52–63.
67. *Conv.* IV, 5.
68. For a most interesting discussion of Dante's treatment of the giants, see E. F. JACOB, "The Giants (*Inferno* XXXI)," in *Medieval Miscellany*, ed. by F. Whitehead, A. H. Diverres, and F. E. Sutcliffe (Manchester 1965), pp. 167–85.
69. *De civ. Dei* IX, 5.
70. *Inf.* V, 52 ff.

CHAPTER 9

Mediaeval Rhetoric

Peter Dronke[*]

I

In terms of history, Plato has been defeated.[1]

The reasons why rhetoric—the art of effective speech and composition—
became an important subject of study in the Middle Ages are complex
and lie far back in time. In Greece in the 4th century B.C. one can observe
a philosophical ideal of culture being supplanted by a rhetorical one:
Plato's concept of education stood no chance against that of the wealthy
and successful orator Isocrates.[2] Education became first and foremost a
training for public life; the arts of judicial, political, and panegyric oratory
became central to the curriculum of the majority; the role of other
subjects diminished, stressed chiefly with a view to equipping the "public
man." In these respects the Roman education system copied the Greek
faithfully. And even with the diminution of political and judicial freedom
under the Empire, the orator's patterns lived on in the schools, for mock-
trials, mock-declamations, and mock-debates. Panegyrical rhetoric flowed
ever more copiously, and the system of rules that had originally been
devised for the orator became adapted to every aspect of literary
composition, including poetry and drama.

The Christians, inevitably, had to work out their attitude towards an
education in which rhetoric played a dominant part. Their religion, like
that of the Jews, centred on a Book: they could not forfeit the ideal of
literacy without endangering their religion's survival. They came to terms
with rhetoric in the first instance because in the late Roman world it was
virtually the only training towards literacy available. Even those Church
Fathers, such as Tertullian (*c.* 150–*c.* 230), who most vehemently condemned the notion that a committed Christian could take pleasure in
pagan authors *for their own sake*, could not deny that the rhetorical

* Fellow of Clare Hall, Cambridge, and University Lecturer in Mediaeval Latin.

315

education, which drew its illustrations from pagan literature and pagan myths and compelled its pupils to copy these, was a practical necessity. It was necessary to "plunder the Egyptians so as to enrich the Hebrews," as a favourite Patristic phrase expresses it—that is, to take up the literature and education of the pagans in order to furnish the Christian with an armour of educated speech and writing, articulateness in argument, and literary comprehension of his own sacred texts. Even when, with Constantine (*c.* 280–337), Christianity became the official religion, there was no attempt at an "educational reform": the young continued to receive essentially the same pagan-oriented literary training they had received for centuries. Some of the works used—such as Cicero's *De inventione* and the pseudo-Ciceronian *Rhetorica ad Herennium*, with their strong emphasis on forensic eloquence—continued to be studied many centuries more, surviving as textbooks through the Middle Ages. With rare exceptions in the East, there was no attempt to establish "denominational" schools, no attempt to replace the traditional texts by Christian ones.

It may at first seem more surprising that, after the fall of Rome and the invaders' destruction of the schools in many parts of the Empire, vestiges of the ancient rhetorical tradition should still be perpetuated and renewed in the West. This was due, at least in part, to individuals of exceptional influence: to St Augustine (354–430), who determined a new and specific role for rhetoric in a Christian education, and to Cassiodorus (*c.* 490–*c.* 583), who established its place in his plan of monastic studies. Only in Byzantium did the traditional Hellenistic type of school continue virtually unchanged; in Gaul and Spain it disappeared in the course of the 5th century, in Italy in the 6th, not long after the Indian summer of learning in Theodoric's reign. Among the ruins of the ancient schools, new types of school arose: in the monastery and the convent, attached to the bishop's court or cathedral, and, most modest of all, in the house of the local parish priest, who would give the young at least a rudimentary education, chiefly to ensure a succession of clergy in his region. A "court school" in the palace of a ruler or great nobleman was exceptional before Charlemagne.

What was taught in the various schools and countries at different periods throughout the Middle Ages is so complex a question that to generalize would be almost meaningless. What is certain is that, however modest a school was, it tried to give some instruction in "grammar" (i.e. in the reading, understanding, and imitation of the older authors, both pagan and Christian) and in rhetoric (i.e. in the art of prose and verse composition with the help of rules). This was done in the belief that such composition could become more artistic and more effective if the student first approached problems of style methodically, mastering a number of verbal patterns and procedures of discourse, which would give him a greater range, and hence greater freedom, of expression. Though we are often told that grammar and rhetoric were distinct subjects in the mediaeval *trivium*, it is clear that from late antiquity the boundaries between them were fluid (nor is dialectic, the third element in the *trivium*, fully separate from these two). It is always some measure of grammar and rhetoric combined, however the proportions and ingredients vary, that forms the basis of mediaeval literary study.

To convey at least a little of the outlook, quality, and achievement of such study, I should now like to take some specific soundings, in particular to outline some outstanding contributions to this study made at four different moments in the Middle Ages. This specific approach is necessary because the most prevalent conceptions of mediaeval rhetoric tend to present a generalized system that appears homogeneous, lacking in original insight, and (at least in comparison with the finest approaches to literature since Lessing or Coleridge) trivial. Thus J. M. Manly, in an influential paper on "Chaucer and the Rhetoricians" (1926), was able to write:

> Fortunately for our inquiry, the Middle Ages knew only one rhetorical system and drew its precepts from few and well-known sources. Moreover, there was little development of the doctrines or variety in the mode of presentation.[3]

And even in a book first published in 1958, an outstanding mediaevalist such as the late Erich Auerbach was able to suggest that

> All the theoretical statements of the period show that elevation of style was equated with wealth of ornament . . . the truly rhetorical style was regarded as ornamental and profane.[4]

That such an equation of the rhetorical and the ornamental *was* made at times in the Middle Ages is undeniable: there can scarcely be an age in which no one hankers after affectation, scarcely a place without its Holofernes or Polonius, its Osric or its Dogberry. But from the evidence to be cited and discussed it will be seen that this conception must not be generalized—that at the heart of the mediaeval rhetorical tradition, in some of its central texts, there existed a profoundly functional approach to artistic expression, a refusal to see the problem of style divorced from that of meaning, an unequivocal condemnation of verbal ornament and display for their own sakes. Nor is the tradition boringly homogeneous: while St Augustine's statement of these basic principles served as a landmark for the following centuries, at the height of the mediaeval literary flowering, from the 11th century to the 14th, these principles were refined and further developed in original directions by some admirable teachers of the art of style, whose achievement has not yet, I think, been seen at its full value.

II

Thanne was þere a wiȝte · with two brode eyen,
Boke hiȝte þat beupere · a bolde man of speche.
"By godes body," quod þis boke · "I wil bere witnesse . . ."[5]

(Then appeared a fellow with two wide eyes; Book was that reverend's name, a man of bold speech. "By God's body," said this Book, "I will bear witness . . .").

St Augustine's treatise on Christian teaching (*De doctrina christiana*)—especially the fourth book, which deals with problems of style and discourse—is seminal for the later discussion of rhetoric in mediaeval Europe. The first three books, treating aspects of the *matter* of Christian teaching—of understanding Scripture through love, of elucidating its difficulties by a study of biblical language, with the help of logic, history, and the sciences, and of illuminating its enigmas by figural interpretation—were composed in 396–7, soon after Augustine had become Bishop of Hippo. The fourth book, treating of the *manner* of Christian teaching, was added in 426, four years before his death. Here Augustine, who in his years as professor of rhetoric had absorbed and transmitted much that was second-hand and second-rate in the Roman tradition, was able to work out an attitude of remarkable vigour and vivacity, lending his authority to an acceptance, however qualified, of some of Cicero's finest principles and setting these in a new perspective: a manifesto affirming what excellence of writing and eloquence can mean in a Christian context. From this manifesto it became possible to derive an educational programme, not only in matters of literary judgment and expression, but also in the question of what role these should play in the educated Christian's total commitment. The most influential Christian didactic programmes of later centuries—that of Cassiodorus in the 6th, of Rabanus Maurus in the 9th, and of Hugh of St Victor in the 12th, to mention only three that are famous—drew their inspiration to a large extent from Augustine's passionately argued recommendations.

Near the opening of *De doctrina* IV the tone of the apologist is upper-most. Augustine warns his readers: "Don't expect a treatise on rhetoric from me," but at the same time justifies the use of rhetoric by Christians: do not they, the champions of truth, need to speak and write as tellingly as possible? How can they leave the weapons of effective discourse to their enemies, who propagate evil and falsehood?[6] When he argues that nonetheless rhetoric should play only a brief and minor role in a Christian education, it is still the bishop rather than the savant who speaks; but the reasons Augustine gives for this view take him straight into some profound insights into the nature of rhetoric itself. Essentially it is not a body of rules that can be learnt by rote, but rather a dynamic presence pervading discourse that is itself worthwhile. The writer who has truly mastered the art of rhetoric does not write to rule; he writes freely, because he has made his expressive art second nature. Some writers indeed can have an intuitive mastery that surpasses all that the rhetoricians can teach and yet owes nothing to them:

> For if there is an acute and ardent imagination, eloquence will come more readily to those who read and hear the eloquent than to those who pursue rules for eloquence. . . . But if such imagination is lacking, not even those rules will be mastered, nor are they any use if they are mastered to some small degree only after great toil. . . . And yet in the discourses and oratory of the eloquent the rules of eloquence are found to be fulfilled, rules that they did not have in mind in order to be eloquent or while they were being so, and whether they had learnt those rules or had not even met with them. They fulfil them because they *are* eloquent; they do not employ them in order to be eloquent. . . . For we know many who, without the rules of rhetoric, are more eloquent than many who have studied them.[7]

For Augustine, then, there must be no dichotomy between rhetorical techniques and the writer's total intention. Throughout the treatise he concedes that matter is essentially more important than manner, and that an empty "gift of the gab" is a worthless thing: for this he enlists Cicero's support, citing Cicero's dictum that while "wisdom without eloquence is of little benefit to the state, eloquence without wisdom is often most harmful and never of use." Like Cicero, Augustine sets up an ideal of *sapientia* and *eloquentia* perfectly conjoined.[8] It is this same double ideal that, in the 8th century, Alcuin propounds to Charlemagne in their (largely Ciceronian) dialogue on rhetoric, that is invoked in the 12th century by Thierry, head of the school of Chartres, and is prefixed by William of Conches to his *Philosophia mundi*.[9]

Augustine shows that this unity of *sapientia* and *eloquentia* is exemplified in the Bible. Once more his tone is somewhat defensive: though he does not mention it here, he must have remembered only too well his own earlier distaste for the scriptural language and style, so modest that "it seemed to me unworthy to compare with Cicero's splendour."[10] This, he felt, was the arrogant blindness to which his rhetorical training had led him. Among Augustine's contemporaries there were a number of educated Christians who still felt about this as he had done. His stylistic defence of the biblical authors is subtle and penetrating: their eloquence has a truly functional excellence: what they say could not have been said in any other way. They speak with the eloquence appropriate to themselves and to what they are trying to express. In addition to the eloquence they share with pagan authors, they have a distinctive quality, an eloquence not conspicuous by presence or absence, but completely subservient to their subject-matter, so that the words seem right *velut sponte* (as if spontaneously). *Sapientia* is the mistress of their house, but *Eloquentia* is her inseparable maid-servant, who follows her even when she is not called.[11]

When Augustine discusses the aims of discourse, he again takes a Ciceronian formulation as his starting-point: *ut doceat, ut delectet, ut flectat*[12] (to teach, to delight, to move). All three, as he will show in detail, are relevant to Christian discourse. With this formulation he combines another, by which Cicero had linked the teaching of the "three styles" (unassuming, temperate, and grand) with three ranges of subject (small matters, moderate, and great). Augustine is still reflecting Cicero's own thoughts when he goes on to link the aim of teaching with the unassuming exposition of *parva*, the aim of delighting with the temperate expression of *modica* (making them memorable by the grace with which they are expressed), and the aim of moving with the highest, most passionate utterance of *grandia* (in order to sway men's minds and hearts).[13]

Cicero had both the stylistic aim and the degree of importance of the subject in view, but for Augustine's purposes the first is more relevant than the second. Still making a consciously Ciceronian distinction in terms of function and context, he argues that gradations by subject are appropriate in the treating of legal matters, but not of religious ones. All that the Christian speaker or writer as Christian will want to express will relate to realities that are eternal and so cannot but be *grandia*. Even the "cup of cold water" offered in Christ's name has a meaning that is great, because divine. This is not to say that the Christian must always express himself in a high style or disregard the question of stylistic differences, but that in the religious context questions of style should be determined wholly by the writer's purpose: the most unassuming style will be used for all that is factual and didactic; a more emotional and artistically wrought style for showing the importance or beauty of a subject, for praising or censuring; and the highest style when what is at stake is to win one's audience over completely, to carry them from reading or hearing to participation.

One might suppose that what in effect distinguished the "high style" from the other two would be an extravagantly rich use of oratorical devices and verbal mannerism. But this is not at all what Augustine has in mind. When he goes on to give extensive illustrations of the uses of each of the three styles in the Bible* (as well as in Church Fathers such as Ambrose and Cyprian), he deliberately stresses that stylistic devices are not an essential attribute of the high style:

> But the high style differs from the temperate most of all in this, that it is not so much enriched by stylistic devices as deeply stirred by the emotions of the spirit. For it too can contain almost all those devices, but if it does not have them, it does not need them. It is borne along by its own impulse [*fertur impetu suo*], and snatches beauty of expression, if it should occur, out of the subject's own power [*vi rerum*]; it does not take up such beauty for the sake of ornament.[14]

Of the examples Augustine gives, one especially brings this out vividly— St Paul addressing the Galatians:

> I am afraid of you, lest perhaps I have worked among you in vain. Be like me, for I too am like you. My brothers, I implore you. You have not injured me at all.[15]

The diction and syntax are starkly plain; the grandeur lies in the *vis rerum*, in the language that *fertur impetu suo*. I do not know how Augustine's literary judgment here can be improved.

It is necessary to use all three styles, Augustine argues, *quantum congrue fieri potest*[16] (in so far as this can be done functionally). It is not merely a matter of achieving stylistic variety, but that the writer's intention will normally be more complex than any one stylistic pattern can adequately reflect. One realizes that Augustine himself must have been acutely conscious of this problem in writing his *Confessions*, where the innumerable contrasts and transitions in thought and mood are so sensitively mirrored in the texture of the language itself.

In the concluding chapters of *De doctrina*, Augustine further refines and

---

* Note that St Augustine (IV, xx, 39–44) explicitly demonstrates all three styles from Scripture. Auerbach's exposition of Augustine—"the style of the Scriptures throughout is *humilis* . . . , the lowly, or humble style is the only medium in which such sublime mysteries can be brought within the reach of men"—is seriously misleading on this point (see AUERBACH, *Literatursprache* . . . , p. 42).

qualifies his conception of the three styles. Where before he had written as if each style had an exclusive characteristic (to express oneself lucidly in the unassuming style, or attractively in the temperate, or with over-whelming conviction in the high style), he now asks, should not each of the three share something of all these qualities? Here his ideas come closest to those of Quintilian[17] (*c.* 40–*c.* 100), who had explicitly set aside the familiar demarcations of the styles, to envisage, as it were, a spectrum of style in the service of an indefinably many-sided range of intention and content. Augustine reverts to the temperate style, where he sees the greatest danger of festooning what is said with extrinsic ornament:

> What the temperate style urges, that is, that eloquence itself should give delight, must not be usurped for its own sake. . . . Let those seek [the goal of pretty ornament] who glory in their language and vaunt themselves in panegyrics and suchlike, where there is no question of imparting knowledge to the listener, nor of moving him to action, but only of entertaining him. As for us, let us order this goal of entertainment towards a further goal.[18]

In the ideal that Augustine here envisages, the perfect rhetorician's integrity of style and the perfect Christian's integrity of subject coincide. The final emphasis is on the *truth* of what the writer or speaker has to say: this is the only possible foundation for any authentic style, and for the Ciceronian goal, *sapientia-eloquentia*:

> Even in his language let him choose to delight by the content rather than the words; let him not think anything better said unless it be more truly said. . . . What is it, then, to speak not only eloquently but wisely? Is it not to bring adequate words in the unassuming style, sparkling ones in the temperate, passionate ones in the high style, to matter that is true and must be heard?[19]

With this treatise, Augustine not only introduced the whole question of literary standards into the Christian tradition, he put his finger on what remained most valuable in the half-decayed tradition in which he himself had grown up. He taught the Middle Ages how to approach the problem of the relations between rhetoric and meaning in an unpretentious, functional way, a way that need not lead to over-simplification, as his subtle "practical criticism" of biblical and patristic passages showed. Above all, the importance of his work was that it encouraged the study of the arts of writing and speaking to continue even in the centuries when the original framework from which they had drawn their life and meaning had collapsed.

III

... the harsh and thorny writings of that monk Alberic, unfathomable
except by the monstrous Sphinx. . . .[20]

The following five centuries have left no discussion of the nature of
rhetoric comparable in stature to St Augustine's. They are centuries in
which fragments of the rhetorical heritage were preserved, laboriously
and often against great odds, rather than renewed creatively. The most
widespread attitude, deriving from Augustine, allowed rhetoric only a
minor place in a Christian universe: as a "liberal art," rhetoric was one
of seven recognized means toward *Sapientia*; the justification of the seven
arts lay not in themselves but in their providing indispensable instruments
for the understanding of divine (that is, primarily scriptural) Wisdom.
This is the "philosophy of study" that underlies Cassiodorus's *Institutiones*,
and again Alcuin's *Disputatio de vera philosophia*.[21] From having been, in a
secular context, the bridesmaids of *Philologia*,* the seven liberal arts
become the pillars of the house built by *Sapientia* (Cassiodorus, Alcuin),
the seven steps leading up to the height of her dwelling (Alcuin), and,
from the 9th century onwards, they are personified once more, as
Sapientia's seven daughters.

When Bede composed a small treatise on figurative expressions (*De
schematibus et tropis*), his innovation is understandable in the light of this
philosophy of study: Bede decides to draw his examples exclusively from
Scripture and not from ancient literature. For although "the Greeks
indeed vaunt themselves as the inventors of such figures or tropes ... holy
Scripture surpasses all other writings not only in authority (since it is
divine) and in utility (since it leads to eternal life), but also in antiquity
and in the very mode of expression."[22] So, too, Alcuin concludes the
dialogue known as *The Rhetoric of Alcuin and Charlemagne*[23] (794), most of
which is a compilation from Cicero and the 4th-century rhetorician Julius
Victor, by resolving the discussion of the four virtues—which Cicero had
treated in relation to rhetorical invention—into explicitly Christian
doctrine. When in 984 Walter of Speyer, in his *Libellus scolasticus*, tells of
his education at the cathedral school, the emphasis is in the last resort
the same. Walter spends eight years studying: two on elementary reading
and writing, and learning to sing psalms; four on *grammatica*, studying the
poets Virgil, Lucan, Statius, Horace, Persius, and Juvenal, as well as the
Latin adaptation of the *Iliad*; and two on the other liberal arts (largely
with the help of Boethius and Martianus Capella). Walter would have

* In MARTIANUS CAPELLA (*fl. c.* 420), *De nuptiis Philologiae et Mercurii*.

323

had longer for these, but his bishop intervened: the bishop and the young scholar agree that eight years is quite long enough for "sterile secular pursuits" (*steriles mundi . . . labores*)—now it is time to "run to the sacred banquet."[24]

New approaches and new developments in rhetoric can be seen in the second half of the 11th century. First in Italy. The art of controversy is demonstrated by Anselm of Besate in his *Rhetorimachia*[25] (*c.* 1050), a feigned rhetorical polemic against his nephew Rotiland, in a flamboyant, protean fashion that is unlike anything that went before. Alberic of Monte Cassino writes comprehensive rhetorical textbooks for the first time since late antiquity. Then, in early 12th-century Bologna, a group of rhetoricians (of whom the first, Adalbertus Samaritanus, writes in scornful reaction to Alberic's work) elaborate a substantially new genre: a system of instruction in the art of letter-writing, along with illustrative collections of model letters. Adalbertus taught at an influential city school (a type that may never have quite died out in northern Italy in the early Middle Ages), educating a largely lay student population for the professions.[26] His attack on Alberic shows not only the secular teaching asserting itself against the monastic, but a utilitarian and specialist view of learning pitted against a more literary one: it is more important to teach young men to draft documents and letters than to waste years on the subtler stylistic points in the ancient authors. Here it is the monk, and not the city professor, who is the humanist. Again, in the great new flowering of the cathedral schools, especially in France, from the later 11th century onwards, substantial works came to be composed on the art of poetry. All these are symptoms of that new surge of interest in humane culture which is often called "the Renaissance of the 12th century," but which can assuredly be traced back at least two generations before 1100. From the 12th century, too, concepts of classical rhetoric and dialectic come to be adapted for instruction in preaching, and a range of *artes praedicandi* emerges. Among the earliest examples, one that became extremely popular was composed by Alan of Lille, poet and *doctor universalis*.

To focus on some specific achievements in this unprecedented wealth of rhetorical instruction, it seems best to select one of the most fertile of the new fields, that of poetics. I shall signal particular contributions that fall approximately at the turn of three centuries—1100, 1200, 1300—and compass the most vigorous age of mediaeval rhetoric.

That Alberic of Monte Cassino was a pioneer, who must be regarded as a major figure in the history of rhetoric, seems certain. It is not yet possible to assess the full significance of his work, since the greater part of

324

his most substantial treatise, the *Breviarium de dictamine* (Compendium of Composition), is still unpublished.[27] But his smaller treatise, *Flores rhetorici*, at least allows us to glimpse a mind of unusual freshness and acumen. Near the opening of the *Flores*, for instance, comes a series of observations particularly pertinent to narrative. One can see, Alberic argues, from the prelude of Boethius's *De consolatione philosophiae* or from the beginning of the *Aeneid*, that the poets have succeeded *quasi quibusdam matris visceribus ex ipsa materia trahatur prologus*[28] (in drawing their opening forth from the matter itself as if from the womb of its mother). If the opening is thus intrinsically related to the principal theme, it can fore-shadow the development of the entire narrative: "You see that such an opening can be brought forth from what follows, so that authors can, by giving a foretaste, prepare the mind in advance for the story that is to come." There is an art of a different kind, however, in opening with an apparently—but only apparently—unrelated prelude:

> For some things can occur that are in a sense remote from the principal intention, and yet are necessary for shedding light on that intention itself. Here, lest the style should be burdened by the fault of obscurity, or a digression should interrupt the work at a later stage, a prelude is prefixed in such a way as to prepare illumination for what follows. This is the form of expression chosen by Sallust both in his *Catiline* and in his *Jugurtha*.[29]

The narrative itself must be a harmony: "you will avoid an abrupt transition, you will not bark out a story stitched with shreds and patches" (Alberic's deliberate mixed metaphor wittily reinforces his point). Incongruity is a kind of dishonesty: *sinceritatem operis quasi quibusdam inficit maculis* (it stains the sincerity of the work). Alberic develops this concept of the inner unity of narrative in a series of sexual metaphors:

> Let meaning proceed content with her own body, not torn by foul, adulterous copulation: her own inner beauty will be enough to make her radiant. Narrative indeed has such a nature that you can lay her full length well enough while keeping her integrity. So do not abandon innocence![30]

Another range of Alberic's notes that is of special interest concerns the cognitive function of metaphor. Metaphor must cast *radios honestatis* (beams of integrity) on the writing.

> But it is characteristic of metaphor as it were to twist the mode of expression away from its own nature, and by that twisting in a sense to renew it, and in renewing to cover it as with a wedding-dress, and having covered it, as it were to sell it honourably.[31]

What does Alberic wish to say with this tantalizing flow of images? By the transference of language, expression is made new—but to what purpose? For a new marriage of expression and meaning? Or simply to be able to "sell" one's matter better (however honourably)? For a moment it looks as if Alberic will reach the fully organic conception of metaphor that Geoffrey of Vinsauf was to develop more than a century later, but at the last moment he retreats from it to the older notion of metaphor as an "embellishment." In the next paragraph, however, one senses that he is still not satisfied: he invents a new sub-species of metaphor, which he calls "light-beam," whose direct function of illuminating—as against adorning—is unmistakable:

> Subjoined to metaphor is a figure that I call "light-beam"—it is indeed a beam that with its light as it were penetrates, uncovers, irradiates whatever is dark in metaphor. You will see its power if you take not any metaphor, but one that is in a sense remote from the nature of the matter or unaccustomed, and uncover it with this expository beam of light.[32]

A perfect illustration for Alberic's concept can be found in a German stanza composed only a generation after he was writing, in the early-12th-century "Song to Mary" from the monastery of Melk:

> Ein angelsnuor geflohtin ist,
> dannen dû geborn bist:
> daz was diu dîn chunnescaft.
> der angel was diu gotes chraft,
> dâ der tôt wart ane irworgen:
> der von dir wart verborgen,
>   Sancta Maria.[33]

> (A fishing-line was woven,
> Out of which you were born:
> That was your ancestry;
> The hook was the divine energy
> On which Death was choked:
> Through you he was revoked,
>   Sancta Maria.)

The first, obscure metaphor (the line of David as a fishing-line) and the second, traditional one (of the cross as the hook Christ placed in Leviathan's jaw) are at the same time expounded, illuminated, and enriched.

326

IV

> Could a rule be given from without, poetry would cease to be poetry,
> and sink into a mechanical art. It would be *morphôsis*, not *poiêsis*. The
> rules of the Imagination are themselves the very powers of growth
> and production. The words to which they are reducible, present only
> the outlines and external appearance of the fruit.[34]

The most perceptive and original of the "new" rhetoricians of the 12th
and 13th centuries was the Englishman Geoffrey of Vinsauf. "Vinsauf"
has been thought to be his nickname, deriving from *De vino salvo*, a
treatise on preserving wines that is reputedly his work. This attractive
suggestion is far from certain, however. All that we know of Geoffrey
with certainty is that he travelled to Rome and there dedicated his "new
poetics," his *Poetria nova*,* composed between 1208 and 1213, to Pope
Innocent III. Some notion of its influence can be gauged from the fact
that more than 80 manuscripts of it have been noted.

While much of the framework as well as of the detail of the *Poetria nova*
is traditional, it contains a number of insights that go well beyond earlier
mediaeval tradition, and that are of interest and value in a far more than
antiquarian way. Underlying these insights is Geoffrey's remarkable
leit-motiv: his insistence on the organic nature of a work of art, on the need
for every aspect of the work to be functional, to bear an intrinsic relation
to the whole. This motif looms so large in the treatise that I believe it is
in no way anachronistic to see it, and all the critical and practical insights
that flow from it, as central to Geoffrey's purpose, and to see the traditional
detailed lore about "your termes, your colours, and youre figures," which
he also carries, as secondary. It is with this emphasis that I should like to
approach the ideas in the *Poetria nova*.

After a witty dedication, sparkling with word-play, to Pope Innocent III,
Geoffrey opens the discussion with a statement fundamental to an understanding of the intentions of his work, and fundamental to much that is
most precious in more recent critical theory:

> Si quis habet fundare domum, non currit ad actum
> Impetuosa manus: intrinseca linea cordis
> Praemetitur opus, seriemque sub ordine certo
> Interior praescribit homo, totamque figurat

---

* CURTIUS, *Zeitschrift* . . . , p. 25, affirms that "the title *Poetria nova*, which Geoffrey of Vinsauf
gave his work, . . . means only that the author wanted to add a supplement to Horace's *Ars
poetica*." I know no evidence for this affirmation (nor indeed for the assumption that the title is
Geoffrey's own). If the title *is* Geoffrey's, I suspect it launches a more ambitious claim than to
be only a supplement—the "supplement," incidentally, being almost five times as long as
Horace's poem.

> Ante manus cordis quam corporis; et status eius
> Est prius archetypus quam sensilis. Ipsa poesis
> Spectet in hoc speculo quae lex sit danda poetis.[35]*

(If a man has to build a house, his hand does not rush to the task impetuously: the heart's intrinsic measure first compasses the work, the inner man prescribes the design, ordering its unfolding with sureness, the hand of the heart forms the whole before the physical hand does so. The work exists first as an archetype, then as a physical reality. Let poetry see in this image what rule must be given to poets.)

Geoffrey has often in the past been counted among those foolish rhetoricians who thought that writing poetry consisted in mechanical devices and verbal tricks. But, as this opening shows, such a view is incompatible with his philosophy of art. Like the architect, the writer must begin with an "idea" (in Plato's sense), with the imaginative conception or essence of the work as his mind envisages it. It is this "idea" in the mind and heart of the writer that must order and be the measure of his modes of expression. The rules for poetry must not be extrinsic, for then they would be arbitrary: they must be determined by the "archetype," the wholly organized imaginative conception of the work. Thus for Geoffrey the all-important thing is not the means but the end: not the tools of expression but what the artist is trying to convey. Being a good teacher, he does not try to indoctrinate in this. What he is saying in effect is: "You must have something to say first of all, I cannot give you that; and it is what you have to say that must dictate your style, down to the last detail. Where I can help you as a teacher is on a lower level, by showing you various techniques for expressing what you want to say more effectively." It follows from this—and Geoffrey stresses it several

---

* The opening of this passage was beautifully translated by Chaucer (*Troilus and Criseyde* I, 1065-9):

> For everi wight that hath an hous to founde
> Ne renneth naught the werk for to bygynne
> With rakel hond, but he wol bide a stounde,
> And sende his hertes line out from withinne
> Aldirfirst his purpos for to wynne.

The precision of Chaucer's rendering, especially in his first four lines, will be evident from comparison with the Latin. Recently, however, J. J. MURPHY, *Review of English Studies* (N.S.) XV (Oxford 1964), pp. 1–20, wishing to cast doubt on Chaucer's direct knowledge of the *Poetria nova*, suggested that this thought (which he summarizes as "a builder must plan his house") is "a commonplace *sententia* found in Scripture (Luke XIV: 28–30) and numerous other places" (*op. cit.*, p. 15). But in the absence of any other *equally precise* analogue to Chaucer's lines—and Murphy has given no indication that such exists—it seems to me unreasonable to question that Chaucer was using the *Poetria nova* here. Moreover, it will I think become apparent from the following discussion that if any mediaeval poet was capable of understanding and of carrying out the profoundest principles of Geoffrey's poetic, it was Chaucer.

times throughout the work—that in themselves the techniques are value-less; to use them for their own sake is to write "falsely," as a mere exhibitionist.

A sentence that follows soon after may seem at first glance to contradict this view:

> Mentis in arcano cum rem digesserit ordo,
> Materiam verbis veniat vestire poesis.[36]

> (When order has disposed the subject in the mind's recesses, then let poetry come to clothe the matter in words.)

Does this not suggest that the form is no more than a garment, the poetry an adornment, a way of "dressing up" what the poet is saying? I think not: the thought behind *vestire* is not that of a dress that can be put on or taken off at will. The only way we can perceive an artist's "idea" at all is in its "dress"—its words, shapes, colours, or notes. Only the "dress" can incarnate an imaginative reality in a physical mode. As Rosemond Tuve has acutely remarked in another context, the thought underlying the "garment" metaphor is rather that of the flesh as the soul's garment.[37] And, as Geoffrey goes on to add a moment later, it is not a question of choosing one dress rather than another: it is a matter of finding *the* dress that belongs to the idea, it must be a perfect fit:

> Quando tamen servire venit, se praeparet aptam
> Obsequio dominae. . . .
>   pars si qua sedebit inepte,
> Tota trahet series ex illa parte pudorem.[38]

> (But when poetry comes to serve, let her make herself ready and apt for the service of her mistress [the *materia*]. . . . If any part should fit badly, the whole ordered conception will be shamed by that part.)

All poetic accomplishment, that is, must be subservient to the organized whole; every expressive aspect of the work must be there for the sake of its vital contribution to the whole.

After a discussion of techniques of beginning and ending a work (traditional material on the "disposition" of one's subject-matter), Geoffrey goes on to discuss techniques of developing one's themes or of making them more succinct. But again he reminds the reader that the technical advice he can give must be controlled and impelled by the artist's own imagination (*ingenium*): the poet's matter is a substance like wax; if it is heated by his imagination, then it becomes ductile and follows imagination's hand wherever it is bidden. It is this "hand of the inner man" that must be the guide and show the poet where he should develop his theme and where make it succinct.[39]

Among the various means of developing or expanding subject-matter, Geoffrey's discussion of two seems to me of outstanding interest. One is that of comparison, the other of digression. Comparison can be open or hidden (*collatio aperta* or *collatio occulta*). This pair of terms does not quite correspond to the modern "simile" and "metaphor": the first, to which Geoffrey alludes only briefly, involves juxtapositions of "more than, greater than, less than," as well as of likeness or equivalence. The second extends more widely than metaphor (which Geoffrey considers separately later), to all that would today be called poetic imagery—all, that is, save explicit comparisons, for it is the hidden comparison that has "more art":

> Quae fit in occulto, nullo venit indice signo:
> Non venit in vultu proprio, sed dissimulato,
> Et quasi non sit ibi collatio, sed nova quaedam
> Insita mirifice transsumptio, res ubi caute
> Sic sedet in serie quasi sit de themate nata:
> Sumpta tamen res est aliunde, sed esse videtur
> Inde; foris res est, nec ibi comparet; et intus
> Apparet, sed ibi non est; sic fluctuat intus
> Et foris, hic et ibi, procul et prope: distat et astat.
> Hoc genus est plantae, quod si plantetur in horto
> Materiae, tractatus erit iocundior; hic est
> Rivus fontis, ubi currit fons purior; hic est
> Formula subtilis iuncturae, res ubi iunctae
> Sic coeunt et sic se contingunt quasi non sint
> Contiguae, sic continuae quasi non manus artis
> Iunxerit, immo manus Naturae.[40]

(The hidden comparison comes with no signal of indication; it comes not in its own aspect, but dissembling, as if there were no comparing there, only as it were a new, wondrously ingrafted transplantation, where something assumes its place so surely in the design as if it were born of the theme itself—yet it is taken from elsewhere, though it seems to be from there: it is without, makes no appearance there, but within it does appear, yet is not there; thus it wavers, in and out, here and there, far and near: it is absent, and present. It is a kind of plant that, if planted in the garden of one's matter, the treatment will be more felicitous; it is a brook in which the source flows purer; it is a form subtly conjoined, where the things joined so unite and touch as if they were not touching, as continuous as if Natura's hand, not that of art, had joined them.)

Here Geoffrey illuminates the relation between the poet's imagery and his theme. It is a paradoxical relation: at first it seems that, no matter how intimately image and theme can be conjoined or unified, this can never result in a complete fusion. There is always an element of "dissembling";

even words such as *insita mirifice transsumptio* remind us that, however great the poetic miracle, what was ingrafted was once alien, what is taken over must have been taken over from without. In Coleridge's words, to which this passage bears striking affinities, the Imagination

> reveals itself in the balance or reconcilement of opposite or discordant qualities: of sameness with difference; of the general with the concrete; of the idea with the image . . . and while it blends and harmonizes the natural and the artificial, still subordinates art to nature, the manner to the matter.[41]

The very notion of the balance or reconcilement of discordants would seem to preclude that of their full identification. This is still Geoffrey's thought when he speaks of images as plants in the garden of the poet's matter. But with the expressions that follow he goes further. It is the theme itself, the source (*fons*), that is channelled into and becomes the brook of imagery (*rivus fontis*). Source passes over completely into brook, and the brook contains nothing which is not the source, distilled. Here it is possible for the theme to be embodied in the imagery more "purely" than it could be in any other way; here art can imitate "great creating Nature," and almost match the perfect fusion of matter and form that she achieves in her creations. So too Coleridge, in the same well-known passage, uses expressions that go beyond balance and reconcilement: Imagination is that "synthetic and magical power" which "blends and (as it were) *fuses*, each into each."

Beside the technique of "hidden comparison," which Geoffrey singles out for special praise, he sets a number of familiar ways of developing poetic themes: by expressing statements in a variety of ways (*expolitio*), by circumlocution, by apostrophizing the person or thing of which you speak, by personifying inanimate objects and making them speak, by extended description (as of looks or dress), or by a series of contrasts and negations. The luxuriant illustrations—which, here as throughout, are Geoffrey's own—include a lament for the death of Richard Coeur-de-Lion, containing among its apostrophes an outcry against the Friday on which Richard was fatally wounded; this later was deftly parodied by Chaucer in his "Nun's Priest's Tale."[42] It is important to understand the purpose of these demonstration-pieces, as well as the nature of Chaucer's humour, and in this neither to disparage Geoffrey of Vinsauf nor to imagine that Chaucer was doing so. The lament for Richard is indeed too *pathétique* to be taken very seriously as an elegy, but this is not the reason for its presence in the work: first and foremost, what Geoffrey requires is a virtuoso illustration of techniques of apostrophe, so that in a brief space he can give six kinds of example. It is a little like one of those test records that are produced expressly to demonstrate the range of performance of record-players. It cannot aptly be compared with other elegies, any more than the test record can be compared with records of particular quartets or symphonies. The point of Chaucer's parody lies in his deliberate, mischievous misapplication of a poetic technique; he is not, as is sometimes thought, laughing at mediaeval poetic techniques as such, or taking a "modern" stand against an older conception of rhetoric.

Geoffrey's view of digression (527 ff.) again shows the paradox, within and without, far and near. It is a question of leaping away from the principal theme, but in such a way that the seemingly far is still near, that an effortless transition back to the first theme is always possible. He illustrates with a brief love-poem, depicting the parting of two lovers in spring. The transitions are from their grieving farewells to the spring world around them, then back to the lovers once more:

> Estque doloris
> Calcar amor viresque dolor testatur amoris.
> Veri cedit hiems. Nebulas diffibulat aer
> Et caelum blanditur humo. Lascivit in illam
> Humidus et calidus; et quod sit masculus aer
> Femina sentit humus. . . .
> Haec temporis hora,
> Quos nondum divisit amor, divisit amantes.

(Love is the spur of pain, and pain bears witness to love's force. Winter yields to spring. The air unbuckles his clouds and sky caresses earth. Hot and moist he dallies with her, and the womanly earth feels air's virility. . . . It was this moment of the year that divided the lovers, still undivided in their love.)

Every image in the spring digression, carrying associations of love, furthers the love-theme though seeming to digress from it; the images are chosen in such a way that each can lead back to the love-theme.

Going on to discuss the question of poetic succinctness, Geoffrey begins by swiftly mentioning a number of technical devices, but a moment later he shows that these must depend for their use on an underlying imaginative act, an effort towards concentration and unity that must draw its strength from what the poet is trying to convey. The lucidity must first be grounded in the poet's "idea," the devices can only "concur" in helping him to achieve it in its expression:

> Vel manus artificis multas ita conflet in unam,
> Mentis ut intuitu multae videantur in una.
> Hac brevitate potes longum succingere thema,

Hac cymba transire fretum. Narratio facti
Eligit hanc formam verbi, quae facta modeste
Non superinfundat nubem, sed nube remota
Inducet solem. Concurrant ergo, sed apte,
Emphasis, articulus, casus sine remige liber . . .[43]

(Let the artist's hand fuse many [clauses] into one, so that with the
mind's eye many may be seen in one. With such succinctness you can
compass a long theme, with such a skiff you can cross the ocean.
Straight narrative chooses this form of expression, which, being
unobtrusive, should not becloud, but clear the clouds away and
bring forth the sun. So let the devices collaborate in this, but aptly:
innuendo, omission of connectives, ablative absolute . . .)

Geoffrey's next topic, that of *ornatus* (adornment) and of the "colours"
of rhetoric, is one that has often, since the Romantic period, given rise to
misunderstandings. The very terms would seem to suggest a non-
functional approach to poetic diction: simple language to be "orna-
mented" to make it more "poetic," plain language to be more highly
"coloured." Perhaps even in Geoffrey's day some of his contemporaries
suspected just such a sham ideal behind the teaching of rhetoricians. At
all events, the first thing he does is to forestall these objections:

Sit brevis aut longus, se semper sermo coloret
Intus et exterius, sed discernendo colorem
Ordine discreto. Verbi prius inspice mentem
Et demum faciem, cuius ne crede colori:
Se nisi conformet color intimus exteriori,
Sordet ibi ratio: faciem depingere verbi
Est pictura luti, res est falsaria, ficta
Forma, dealbatus paries et hypocrita verbum
Se simulans aliquid, cum sit nihil.[44]

(Whether short or long, let expression always be coloured within and
without, but with determining of the colour from the poetic design
that has been determined. First look at the mind of your word, then
at its face—don't trust the face's colour! Unless the inmost colour is
at one with the external, meaning there grows base. To paint a word's
face is to paint scum, it is a falsification, a pretence at form, a whited
wall, a hypocrite word, pretending to be something though it is
nothing.)

The "colouring" and "adorning" of language, then, for Geoffrey, is
simply a question of manifesting meaning as perfectly as possible. Any
use of poetic language for display alone, any use that does not reflect and
enhance poetic meaning, is dishonest writing, and worthless. Once more,
the choice of expression must be intimately related to the *ordo discretus*—
to the imaginatively organized design of the whole work. What is said and

how it is said must be matched so completely that it becomes meaningful to speak of inward colours, of the minds of words. In the same years as Geoffrey was writing, one of the greatest vernacular poets, Gottfried von Strassburg, formulated similar thoughts still more memorably in his *Tristan*, when commending another narrative poet, Hartmann von Aue:

> ·Ahî, wie der diu maere
> beid' ûzen unde innen
> mit worten und mit sinnen
> durchvärwet und durchzieret!
> wie er mit rede figieret
> der âventiure meine!
> wie lûter und wie reine
> sîn kristallîniu wortelîn
> beidiu sint und iemer müezen sîn![45]

> (How he through-colours and through-adorns his narratives, both without and within, words and meanings! How his expressions transfix the meaning of the story! How clear and pure his crystalline words are and must forever be!)

Each of the successive metaphors—words and meaning pervaded through and through by the same shared colour, words piercing meaning's target, and words wholly transparent to the meaning that shines through them—adds a nuance to this profound view of poetic diction.

The specific discussion of *ornatus* in the *Poetria nova* begins with techniques of metaphor (*transsumere verba*—transference of expressions). Again Geoffrey takes up his notion of the reconcilement of opposites: each metaphor must contain something "heavy" and something "light" (*est gravis estque levis*)[46]: it must have an element that is serious (so that the metaphor is not capricious or trivial) and an element that is graceful (so that the metaphor is not pretentious or obscure). For Geoffrey, the delight in the act of recognition plays an essential role in the function of metaphor. In the tempering of the heavy and light aspects of metaphor, the poet achieves a "harmony of discordants" (*concors discordia*). This emerges particularly where metaphors work by deliberate contrasts, a practice that Geoffrey specially commends:

> *Ante Dei faciem devota silentia clamant.*
> Consule res alias et idem mireris in illis:
> Litibus alternis quando bellantur amantes,
> Crescit in hoc bello linguarum pax animorum;
> Hoc odio conditur amor. Sic est et in istis:
> Se voces introrsus amant licet exteriores
> Sint inimicitiae. Lis est in vocibus ipsis;
> Sed litem totam sedat sententia vocum.[47]

("Before the face of God rapt silence shouts." Look at other situations, and you will see the same [concord through opposition] there: when lovers fight in quarrels with each other, their peace of spirit grows through that war of words, love is spiced by that hate. So too in these metaphors: inwardly the words love each other, though on the outside there are enmities. Among the words themselves there is conflict, but the meaning calms all conflict in the words.)

Alongside metaphor are treated devices such as metonymy and synecdoche, hyperbole and catachresis. And yet again the reminder comes that all these figures are there in order to serve meaning:

Quae clausum reserent animum sunt verba reperta,
Ut quaedam claves animi.[48]

(The expressions are found in order to unlock the sealed spirit: they are, as it were, the keys of the spirit.)

So far Geoffrey has been dealing with the *ornatus* traditionally called "difficult"—difficult because it is meaningful only in relation to the writer's total intention, and presupposes that this intention is of value. Now he passes to "easy" *ornatus*—the figures to which the term "colours" was often confined. In the tradition these were further divided into figures of speech and figures of thought: that is, a series of devices to vary and modify expression (e.g. repetition, inversion, rhetorical questions, exclamations), and a series of devices to vary and modify meaning (e.g. by argument, appeal, illustration and description, by ambiguity or innuendo). It is notorious that figures of these kinds were endlessly classified under learned names; mediaeval rhetoric is often supposed to consist in little more than learning excruciating lists of such figures. Geoffrey at least attaches little importance to this rigmarole: while he alludes to some of the traditional figures, he mentions scarcely any by a technical name; for the most part he is happiest to take "colouring" in his stride by showing it at play in his profuse illustrations. It is his modern editor, Faral, who (admittedly basing himself on Geoffrey's mediaeval glossators) has filled the margins of his poem with hundreds of technical names: for Geoffrey, it is the figures in operation that matter, not the labelling.* He sums up the import of the devices by returning to his *leit-motiv*, this time under a new metaphor:

Verborum flores et rerum confer in unum,
Area sermonis ut floreat his speciebus
Florum. Surget enim quidam concursus odorum
Et redolet plene permixtus uterque colorum.[49]

* Nonetheless it is worth noting that, with an art concealing art, Geoffrey illustrates the figures in the precise order in which they had been discussed in the *Rhetorica ad Herennium* (IV, xiii, 19 ff.).

> (Unify the flowers of expression and meaning, so that language's plot
> of ground may flower with flowers of these kinds. For thus a blend of
> perfumes will arise, and each of the two colours, wholly mingled, gives
> its scent.)

The fusion of idea and image that was sketched earlier is here extended
to the whole relation between words and objects, expression and meaning.
When the "two colours," inner and outer, are united as perfectly as can
be, then their "perfume"—their artistic effect—is likewise a harmony.
And it is only through this harmonious growth of the twofold flowers that
the garden of language can blossom: wherever language is used artistically,
the oneness of artistic means of expression with imaginative content is
fundamental.

Even in the final section of the treatise, which is on performance,
Geoffrey's principal guide-lines re-emerge remarkably: the performer,
like the poet, must set all his art in the service of the work he performs;
there must be no element of virtuoso self-display. The voice must be so
trained that it is not in disaccord with the reality it has to express
(2036–7); the voice must become, as it were, an image of that reality (*vox
quaedam sit imago rei*). The movements of voice and gesture must reflect
an inner imaginative apprehension of the work or the character performed:

> . . . interiorem
> Exterior sequitur motus, pariterque moventur
> Unus et alter homo.
>
> (The outward movement follows the inward one, and the inner and
> outer man move together.)

Yet here, in the question of performance as in that of creation, we return
to Geoffrey's paradox: like the poet making "hidden comparisons," the
performer too in a sense is "far and near, absent and present." There is an
element of identification with what he performs (to achieve authenticity),
but also an element of detachment (which cannot be wholly forfeited if
artistic control is to be preserved): the performer is advised:

> Veros imitare furores,
> Non tamen esto furens: partim movearis ut ille,
> Non penitus.[50]
>
> (Imitate real passions, yet do not be carried away by passion; be
> moved in part like the passionate man, but not to his depths.)*

---

* There is a strikingly similar observation in Bertolt Brecht's theatre criticism: "Even portraying
the possessed, he himself must not appear to be possessed; otherwise, how could the spectator
discover what possesses the possessed?" (*Kleines Organon für das Theater*, Section 47; *Gesammelte
Werke* [Frankfurt a.M. 1967], Vol. XVI, p. 683).

336

Thus Geoffrey's central perceptions extend to every aspect of the work of art: every aspect is there not for its own sake but for the sake of that "idea" with which the artist began. Every technique has value only in so far as it helps to serve and to realize the "idea" in a physical mode. Between the "idea" and its artistic expression, in the work or in the performance, there is a tension that can never be resolved into complete identity. But it is a fruitful tension, and the aspiration towards that identity is the artist's perpetual challenge.

V

When the critics are themselves poets, it may be suspected that they have formed their critical statements with a view to justifying their poetic practice.[51]

The 13th century sees the growth of a vernacular reading public. Now for the first time treatises giving poetic, rhetorical, and grammatical instruction were composed in and for the Romance vernaculars. The earliest surviving is a brief essay, *Reglas de trobar*, written by a Catalan troubadour, Raimon Vidal, about 1200.[52] But none of the 13th-century treatises can compare in breadth of conception and wealth of insight with the most remarkable of the "arts of vernacular discourse," Dante's *De vulgari eloquentia*, composed in 1303–4; none seriously challenges Dante's claim, in his opening sentence, that he can "find no one before me who has discussed the teaching of vernacular stylistic art in any way."[53]

Dante's incomplete treatise contains material of three kinds. First, there are his views on the origin, nature, development, and characteristics of languages. These are primarily of historical interest, and I shall not dwell on them here. Second, there are his normative prescriptions regarding poetic styles and subjects, the choice of diction, form, and construction. These are often remarkable, both in their formulation and in the ways by which Dante arrives at them. But the unique contribution of this treatise seems to me to lie in its third element: in its specific critical observations, in attempting a certain amount of descriptive and evaluative criticism of poetry for the first time since "Longinus" in the 1st century A.D.

This criticism is intimately related to the second, normative element in the work; to illustrate its force, therefore, it may be best to begin with a swift indication of some of the prescriptions. For the highest kind of poetry in his own vernacular, Dante seeks an "ideal" Italian—a language that draws on what is finest in particular Italian dialects, but transcends whatever is crude or ugly or specifically regional in any of them. Such a language has been attained intuitively by the finest vernacular poets hitherto, but with this treatise Dante intends that the means to it should be made accessible in systematic form. Having a lofty and severe ideal of the absolute oneness of form and content, he hedges the use of his purified vernacular with formidable restrictions: this illustrious language demands men who excel in both imagination and knowledge (*excellentes ingenio et scientia querit*); it will accord only with the greatest poetic conceptions (*optimis conceptionibus optima loquela conveniet*); for to make beautiful is to add what is congruent (*est enim exornatio alicuius convenientis additio*).[54] Only the subjects intrinsically of greatest worth are fit for expression in this language; Dante argues that there are three: prowess of arms, the kindling of love, and the directing of the will towards virtue (*armorum probitas, amoris accensio, et directio voluntatis*).[55]

Poetry is an imaginative conception expressed in verse in accordance with rhetorical and melodic art (*fictio rhetorica musicaque poita*).[56] What distinguished the great poets of antiquity was a sense of order and form in their poetic language and art; till now, vernacular poets have had no guidance of the kind the ancients had. Dante intended to fill this gap for the whole range of vernacular poetic; in the part he completed, however, he was able to treat only of the highest style (which, following a mediaeval Latin terminology, he also called the tragic style), with specific reference to lyric, of which he thought the highest form to be the *canzone*.

Once more Dante's demands are awe-inspiring. In this supreme style four ingredients—thought, musicality, structure, and diction—must harmonize perfectly and each be at the highest level.[57] This presupposes intense imagination, technical accomplishment, and mastery of the sciences: the finest kind of poet, that is, must be not only a genius and a virtuoso, but also in a profound sense an intellectual.

Now Dante goes on to a detailed discussion of the splendour (*superbia*) of versification, and of excellence in construction and vocabulary, and here the most important range of his specific critical insights begins.[58] Among vernacular verses the 11-syllable line (to which Dante also assimilates the Provençal and French one of 10 syllables) is the most splendid: it has a greater capacity for holding thought, construction, and words than the rest. Dante gives illustrations from Provençal and French lyric, as well as from Italian, to bring this out. At the same time, he says, a special quality is achieved, setting off the 11-syllable lines with even greater distinction, by interweaving them with occasional lines of 7 syllables. Dante's own *canzoni* always follow this procedure, except on the few occasions when they are composed wholly of 11-syllable lines.

These observations lead him at a later stage to a remarkable judgment of three *canzoni*, including one by his revered "father" in the art of lyric, Guido Guinizelli (*c.* 1230–76), where 7-syllable lines open the stanza and predominate. This, Dante argues, has a less exalted poetic effect, which has implications for both style and thought:

> But if we want to enter subtly into the meaning of these canzoni, it will be seen that here the high ["tragic"] style has come forth not without a certain shadow of the elegiac.[59]

For Dante, elegiac content fits a lowly style: it is right for the lamenter to come as a suppliant. Thus the perception of technique is here inseparable from that of content, and both inseparable from an evaluation. The 7-syllabled opening establishes as it were a minor key; it is congruent with the lover's complaint, not with the celebration of love; the poetry of the lamenting lover can never be the highest type of love-lyric, which, however it may explore love's states, is composed out of the fullness of love; there the technique too must be different: the stanzas will open with the strongest, most confident type of line, and this type will be preponderant.

Dante's chapter on construction[60] is a high point in the treatise. Dante has in mind not only the way in which words and phrases are related to each other within a sentence, but the relations of the sentences within a stanza, and of the stanzas within the whole *canzone*. Giving brief instances, at first by way of Latin sentences, he argues that the most excellent construction must have savour and grace and loftiness (*sapidus et venustus et excelsus*). That is, first, it must be unusual or striking enough (*sapidus*) not to be insipid. At the same time, the unusual or striking could also become the overstrained, so Dante adds *venustus*: that is, the construction must also be harmonious and effortless enough not to seem precious or stilted. But the harmonious, effortless construction might also dwindle into a uniformity that could be banal, so Dante adds *excelsus*: the constructions of sentence, stanza, and poem are not the pedestrian ones of everyday usage. The finest poetry must employ a "heightened" syntax and structure.

Here the choice of *canzoni*—again Provençal, French, and Italian—that exemplify this threefold quality of construction reveals a judgment of extraordinary subtlety and penetration. Consider one of the examples Dante adduces, that of his friend Guido Cavalcanti. It is one of the rare *canzoni* complete in a single stanza:

> Poi che di doglia cor conven ch'i' porti
> e senta di piacere ardente foco
> e di virtù mi traggi' a sì vil loco,
> dirò com' ho perduto ogni valore.

E dico che' miei spiriti son morti,
e 'l cor che tanto ha guerra e vita poco;
e se non fosse che 'l morir m'è gioco,
fare'ne di pietà pianger Amore.
    Ma, per lo folle tempo che m'ha giunto,
mi cangio di mia ferma oppinïone
in altrui condizione,
sì ch'io non mostro quant'io sento affanno:
là 'nd'eo ricevo inganno,
ché dentro da lo cor mi pass' Amanza,
che se ne porta tutta mia possanza.[61]

(Since I must have a heart of grief
And feel the ardent fire of delight
And trail from honour to despondency,
I'll tell how I have lost all excellence.
    And I say that my mind's impulses are dead,
And the heart holds such great war and little life;
And were it not a joy for me to die,
I would make Love lament with pity for it.
    But, given the foolishness that's come upon me,
I act as if my constant state had passed
Into what other men would have it be,
So that I do not show what ache I feel:
Through this I have grown impaired,
For the state of loving penetrates my heart,
And carries with it all my faculties.)

It is at first glance an inconspicuous *canzone*: it is quite devoid of rhetorical fireworks. Later Dante twice mentions Guido's most spectacular song, "Donna me prega" (A lady asks me), both for its versification and for its rhyme technique; but significantly he does not include it here, among the most illustriously constructed ones. This strongly suggests that it is an inner "contexture" rather than outward splendour that he is concerned with here. (So too, in his consideration of the troubadour Arnaut Daniel, Dante mentions Arnaut's most brilliant stylistic exercise, "L'aur' amara" [The bitter air], only for its content, whereas for its "most excellent degree of construction" he chooses the seemingly plain "Sols sui qui sai" [I alone know]: the *miglior fabbro* is not the Arnaut who carries off a form and rhyme-scheme no one else could emulate, but the Arnaut who achieves an unobtrusive, flawless marriage of words and meaning.)

In this *canzone* Guido portrays a state that comprehends not only the lover's physical and emotional being, his mind and his will, but the serene exterior he puts on for the outer world. The structure of the *canzone* is a perfect mirror of this complexity, in the smallest parts as in the whole.

The lucid conjunction of opposites in the two opening lines conveys the tension of the inner paradox; the simple concatenation within the first eight lines by "and" brings out that everything is adding to a single, unbroken statement of the lover's condition. It is "savoury" and "graceful" to achieve a subtle evocation by such limpid means. But Guido achieves more: he extends the pattern of thought and language over a further six lines, making that pattern comprehensive enough to include, beyond the inner conflict, the world's view of the lover and the mask he wears for the world, and finally the destructive effect of that mask on the wearer. Here, I think, we approach the secret of a construction that is *excelsus*. The *canzone* has been woven entirely in one piece, just as the many-sided thought is essentially one thought carried through. It could be printed as a single sentence: in unravelling the tangle of the lover's state, Guido has not dropped one thread; unerringly, he has set all in order.

The chapter on diction[62] is again largely prescriptive, but the prescriptions give rise to fascinating illustrations. In the highest style, Dante argues, the choice of diction must be rigorous: virile (as against childish or womanish), elegant (as against countrified). And even then the selection must be narrowed further, the criterion being the texture of the words themselves: developing in original fashion a metaphor that was hinted at in 12th-century Latin poetics, Dante envisages the poet's diction as a fabric in which a certain range of textures can and must be achieved. In the highest style this fabric must be woven of words combed out like the finest wool (*pexa*), and of a more robust but rougher tweed (*yrsuta*); it must avoid words that are too slippery (*lubrica*), that would make the fabric satiny, and words that are too bristly (*reburra*), that would make it more like sackcloth. It is a diction, we might say, that must strive to be sweet without being over-sensual, and strong without being coarse. Dante's examples show that sometimes when he thinks of texture he has also the connotations of the word in mind (thus *donna* belongs to the *pexa*, *femina* to the *lubrica*), sometimes the sound alone (thus monosyllables, or words with double consonants, such as *speranza*, are *yrsuta*), sometimes both (*corpo* belongs to the *reburra* for its earthy connotations as for its harsh sound). Dante promises detailed poetic examples of the interweaving of *pexa* and *yrsuta* at a later stage, but unfortunately he did not carry this out in the completed part of the essay.

Will not such a daunting range of requirements and restrictions as Dante lays down for the highest achievements in lyric stifle originality and weigh down the poet of genius? The thought seems to have crossed Dante's mind as, near the close of the work, he catches himself out for having broken one of his own rules (not to use the same rhyme to excess): he had written a *canzone* (sometimes known as his "double sestina") in which only 5 rhyme-words are repeated in a virtuoso pattern over 66 lines. His self-justification is delightful: indeed the poet must not hammer on the same rhyme too much,

> . . . unless perhaps he thereby claims for himself something new and untried in his art; like a day of chivalric initiation that disdains to run its course without some unique exploit; and this is what I tried to do there, with "Amor, tu vedi ben che questa donna" [Love, you see well that this lady]. . . .[63]

Ideally, to comprehend the force of Dante's judgments in the art of lyric, we should have to consider each example that he cites together with him, thinking it through in terms of his own problematic. But perhaps even these brief glimpses will indicate the freshness of his critical approach to poetry, an approach that both in its expertise and in its commitment is inseparable from thought about his own poetic art. He is the first of the modern poets who reflect consciously and deeply on their craft: the line continues with Boccaccio, Petrarch, and Chaucer.

References

1. MARROU, *Histoire* . . . , Ch. X.
2. *ibid.*, pp. 292 ff. In my remarks on education in the Greek and Roman world I have been guided by Marrou's admirable synthesis.
3. *Proceedings of the British Academy* XII (London 1926), p. 99.
4. AUERBACH, *Literatursprache* . . . , p. 148.
5. WILLIAM LANGLAND, *Piers Plowman*, Passus XVIII.
6. *De doctrina christiana*, ed. by H. J. Vogels (Bonn 1930), IV, i, 2; ii, 3.
7. *ibid.*, IV, iii, 4–5.
8. *ibid.*, IV, v, 7.
9. Cf. GREGORY, *Anima mundi*, pp. 247 ff.
10. *Confessions* III, v, 9.
11. *De doctrina christiana* IV, vi, 10.
12. *ibid.*, IV, xii, 27.
13. *ibid.*, IV, xvii, 34.
14. *ibid.*, IV, xx, 42.
15. *ibid.*, IV, xx, 44.
16. *ibid.*, IV, xxii, 51.
17. Cf. *De institutione oratoria* XII, x, 67.
18. *De doctr.* IV, xxv, 55.
19. *ibid.*, IV, xxviii, 61.

20. ADALBERTUS SAMARITANUS, *Praecepta dictaminum,* ed. by F.-J. Schmale (Weimar 1961), p. 51.
21. *Cassiodori Senatoris Institutiones,* ed. by R. A. B. Mynors, 2nd impr. (Oxford 1961); ALCUIN, *Disputatio de vera philosophia,* in *Patrologia latina* (Paris 1844–64) CI, where it is printed as part of his grammatical treatise.
22. *De schematibus et tropis,* in *Rhetores latini minores,* ed. by C. Halm (Leipzig 1863), p. 607.
23. Ed. and trans. by W. S. Howell (Princeton 1941).
24. P. VOSSEN (ed.), *Der Libellus scolasticus des Walther von Speyer* (Berlin 1962), p. 43.
25. Ed. by K. Manitius in *Monumenta germaniae historica: Quellen zur Geistesgeschichte des Mittelalters,* II (Weimar 1958).
26. ADALBERTUS, *op. cit.,* especially pp. 8 ff.
27. Extracts have been published in ROCKINGER, *Briefsteller . . . ,* pp. 29–46, and recently by H. H. DAVIS in *Mediaeval Studies* XXVIII (Toronto 1966), pp. 198–227. Dr Davis has promised a critical edition of the entire *Breviarium (ibid.,* p. 200).
28. *Flores rhetorici,* ed. by D. M. Inguañez and H. M. Willard, *Miscellanea Cassinese* 14 (Monte Cassino 1938), pp. 33–4. Alberic here applies his discussion to prose as well as to poetry, and even to didactic writing.
29. *Flor. rhet.,* p. 35.
30. *ibid.,* p. 36.
31. *ibid.,* p. 45.
32. *ibid.,* p. 46.
33. F. MAURER (ed.), *Die religiösen Dichtungen des 11. und 12. Jahrhunderts* (Tübingen 1964–5), Vol. I, p. 361.
34. SAMUEL TAYLOR COLERIDGE, *Biographia Literaria* (1817), Ch. XVIII.
35. *Poetria nova* 43–9, in FARAL, *Les arts poétiques . . . ,* pp. 197–262.
36. *ibid.,* 60–1.
37. ROSEMOND TUVE, *Elizabethan and Metaphysical Imagery* (Chicago 1947), p. 61.
38. *Poetria nova* 62–7.
39. *ibid.,* 213–8.
40. *ibid.,* 247–62.
41. COLERIDGE, *op. cit.,* Ch. XIV *ad fin.*
42. *Poetria nova* 368 ff.; cf. *Canterbury Tales* VII, 3338 ff.
43. *Poetria nova* 700–7.
44. *ibid.,* 737–45.
45. *Tristan* 4620–8.
46. *Poetria nova* 833 ff.
47. *ibid.,* 878–85.
48. *ibid.,* 1065–6.
49. *ibid.,* 1584–7.
50. *ibid.,* 2048–50.
51. T. S. ELIOT, *The Use of Poetry and the Use of Criticism* (London 1933), p. 29.

52. In P. MEYER (ed.), "Traités catalans de grammaire et de poétique," *Romania* VI (Paris 1877), pp. 344–53.
53. *De vulgari eloquentia*, ed. and trans. by A. Marigo, 3rd edn (Florence 1957), I, i, 1.
54. *ibid.*, II, i, 5; II, i, 8; II, i, 10.
55. *ibid.*, II, ii, 8.
56. *ibid.*, II, iv, 2.
57. *ibid.*, II, iv, 7.
58. *ibid.*, II, v, 1 ff.
59. *ibid.*, II, xii, 6.
60. *ibid.*, II, vi.
61. G. CONTINI (ed.), *Poeti del Duecento* (Milan and Naples 1960), Vol. II, p. 504. I have followed the interpretations suggested by Contini in his notes.
62. *De vulg.* II, vii.
63. *ibid.*, II, xiii, 12.

Bibliography

Primary sources are cited in the References; the works listed here contain the discussions and documentation I have found most valuable.

Since the present essay was completed (Spring 1968), a number of important books in this field have appeared. I would signal especially H. CAPLAN, *Of Eloquence: Studies in Ancient and Medieval Rhetoric* (Ithaca/ London 1970); P. BOYDE, *Dante's Style in his Lyric Poetry* (Cambridge 1971); E. GALLO, *The Poetria Nova and its Sources in Early Rhetorical Doctrine* (The Hague/Paris 1971); and *Three Medieval Rhetorical Arts*, ed. by J. J. Murphy (Berkeley/Los Angeles/London 1971), translations of Anonymous of Bologna, Geoffrey of Vinsauf, and Robert of Basevorn. Further references to very recent work can be found in MURPHY, *Medieval Rhetoric* (below).

M.-TH. D'ALVERNY, "La Sagesse et ses sept filles," *Mélanges Felix Grat* (Paris 1946), Vol. I, pp. 245–78.

L. ARBUSOW, *Colores Rhetorici*, 2nd edn (Göttingen 1963).

E. AUERBACH, *Literatursprache und Publikum in der lateinischen Spätantike und im Mittelalter* (Berne 1958). English edn: *Literary Language and its Public in Late Latin Antiquity and in the Middle Ages*, trans. by R. Manheim (London 1965).

F. BRUNHÖLZL, "Der Bildungsauftrag der Hofschule," *Karl der Grosse, Lebenswerk und Nachleben*, Vol. II: *Das geistige Leben*, ed. by B. Bischoff (Düsseldorf 1965), pp. 28–41.

E. DE BRUYNE, *Geschiedenis van de Aesthetica*: Vol. III, *De Christelijke Oudheid* (Antwerp-Amsterdam 1954); Vol. IV, *De Middeleeuwen* (Antwerp-Amsterdam 1955).

H. CAPLAN, "Classical Rhetoric and Medieval Theory of Preaching," *Classical Philology* XXVIII (Cambridge, Mass. 1933), pp. 73–96.

A. K. COOMARASWAMY, "Meister Eckhart's View of Art," *The Transformation of Nature in Art*, 3rd edn (New York 1956); "The Mediaeval Theory of Beauty," *Figures of Speech and Figures of Thought* (London 1946).

E. R. CURTIUS, *Europäische Literatur und lateinisches Mittelalter*, 2nd edn (Berne 1954) (English trans. of 1st edn: *European Literature and the Latin Middle Ages*, trans. by W. Trask [London 1953]); "Dichtung und Rhetorik im Mittelalter," *Deutsche Vierteljahrsschrift* XVI (Stuttgart 1938), pp. 435–75; "Die Lehre von den drei Stilen in Altertum und Mittelalter," *Romanische Forschungen* LXIV (Cologne 1952), pp. 57–70; "Zur Literarästhetik des Mittelalters," *Zeitschrift für romanische Philologie* LVIII (Halle 1938), pp. 1–50, 129–232, and 433–79.

E. FARAL, *Les arts poétiques du XIIᵉ et du XIIIᵉ siècle* (Paris 1924).

E. GARIN, *Geschichte und Dokumente der abendländischen Pädagogik*: Vol. I, *Mittelalter* (Hamburg 1964).

T. GREGORY, *Anima Mundi* (Florence 1955), Ch. V.

R. W. HUNT, "Studies in Priscian in the Eleventh and Twelfth Centuries," *Medieval and Renaissance Studies* I (London 1941), pp. 194–231; II (London 1950), pp. 1–56.

H.-I. MARROU, *Histoire de l'éducation dans l'antiquité*, 6th edn (Paris 1965) (English trans. of 3rd edn: *A History of Education in Antiquity*, trans. by G. Lamb [London 1956]); *Saint Augustin et la fin de la culture antique*, 4th edn (Paris 1958).

J. J. MURPHY, "The Arts of Discourse, 1050–1400," *Mediaeval Studies* XXIII (Toronto 1961), pp. 194–205; *Medieval Rhetoric: a Select Bibliography* (Toronto 1971).

J. P. RICHÉ, *Éducation et culture dans l'occident barbare* (Paris 1962).

L. ROCKINGER, *Briefsteller und Formelbücher des elften bis vierzehnten Jahrhunderts* (Munich 1863).

F.-J. SCHMALE (ed.), *Adalbertus Samaritanus, Praecepta dictaminum*, in *Monumenta germaniae historica: Quellen zur Geistesgeschichte des Mittelalters* III (Weimar 1961).

CHAPTER 10

Bards, Minstrels, and Men of Letters

J. A. Burrow[*]

I

In the Middle Ages, as in antiquity, verse was a normal medium for the recounting of past and contemporary events. If a person was telling a story and wished, for whatever reason, to tell it in what we should now call "literary" form, he would as likely as not turn it into octosyllabic couplets, or alliterative verses, or assonantal stanzas, or *ottava rima*. It would make very little difference whether he regarded the story as history or as fiction (supposing him to have been aware of that distinction). History and fictional story alike went naturally into verse; and the response of the audience was not constrained by our modern sense that a story-teller who chooses verse as his medium must have had some uncommonly pressing reason for doing so.

Relatively little has survived of the narrative verse produced in the European vernaculars during the early Middle Ages (up to about 1100). There are a few biggish clusters, such as the Anglo-Saxon poems dating from the 8th and 9th centuries (*Beowulf*, the Bible poems of the Junius manuscript, the poems of Cynewulf, and so on); but these are not large by the standards of the later period. In the 12th, 13th, and 14th centuries, on the other hand, the bulk of material in the manuscripts becomes enormous—so enormous that we must reckon these centuries as the heyday (on surviving evidence) of the narrative poem in Europe. It is true that in this same period we can already trace the origins of the modern decline of verse as a medium of narrative. There is a movement away from the verse-narrative in France, dating from as early as 1200, which seems to have been more than an eddy of fashionable taste. During the

[*] Fellow of Jesus College, Oxford, and University Lecturer in English.

347

13th century in France, a considerable number of narrative poems dating from the previous century (romances as well as *chansons de geste*) were turned into prose by a dismantling process known as *dérimage* (de-rhyming); and by the 14th century, French poets (occupied with *ballades*, dream-allegories, and the like) were no longer interested in narrative. Yet the 14th century was also the age of Juan Ruíz in Spain, of Chaucer, Gower, and the *Gawain*-poet in England, and of the Boccaccio of the *Filostrato* and the *Teseida* in Italy. These poets, working in a less stratified literary culture, did not follow their French contemporaries in neglecting narrative. The audiences for whom they worked were not self-consciously and exclusively courtly, in the French fashion. They had appetites too robust to be satisfied with fricassees from the *Roman de la rose*. They still wanted stories. In England, the earliest monument to the spirit of *dérimage* comes as late as the 15th century, in the work of Sir Thomas Malory. Malory imitated the French prose romances of the 13th century and, in his "Tale of King Arthur and the Emperor Lucius," turned an English alliterative poem into prose very much in the French manner. Such narrative prose in the late mediaeval vernaculars does, no doubt, point forward to developments in the modern period; but it does not mean that verse had yet given up its ancient function of recording events.

Most of the poems mentioned in the present chapter, then, will belong to the period after 1100. But in order to keep a broad view of the whole period, I have divided the material into three loosely chronological categories that take us, if only sketchily, to the extreme limits of the Middle Ages. I distinguish the poetry of "bards," the poetry of "minstrels," and the poetry of "men of letters." These categories raise a multitude of issues, many of which I shall have to ignore. My chief concern here will be with a factor critical for the development of narrative verse: the gradual growth, throughout the mediaeval period, of the habits of reading and writing.

II

The old runic and ogham scripts used by Germanic and Celtic peoples in early times were restricted to very specialized functions (magic and memorial); and it was only with the coming of the Roman alphabet that vernacular poetry began to enjoy a chance of survival. The chance was at first a remote one, because the production of manuscript books remained for centuries a virtual monopoly of the Church, and in particular of the monks; but from time to time the scriptoria did devote some of their resources to the production of vernacular manuscripts, such as the four volumes[1] on which the greater part of our knowledge of Anglo-Saxon poetry depends; and in these scattered documents we can get some glimpses of the ancient vernacular art of narrative verse as it was practised by the bards.

"Bard" is a Celtic word that properly designates the Celtic equivalent of the Teutonic *scop*; but I shall use the word more generally, for lack of a better, to designate the most ancient of the three kinds of narrative poet. He is the poet—Celtic or otherwise—whose work represents the oral stage of a European literature. Now it is obvious that no manuscript can survive from an age innocent of writing; and it follows that no text preserved in a manuscript can be entirely free from the suspicion that writing and the habit of writing have contributed not merely to its preservation, but also to its formation and character. It must also be said that romantic mediaevalists have sometimes yielded too readily to the temptation to see the old purely oral art, the art of the bard, in this or that early mediaeval text; and recent scholarship has been right to react against these excesses. Yet there are some poems that do seem to represent, more or less perfectly, an art older and in some ways nobler than that of the high Middle Ages. And because this art can be shown to have its roots in the period when reading and writing did not enter in to the composition and transmission of poetry, it is a matter of indifference that the authors of the texts we have can never be entirely cleared of the suspicion of literacy. Even scholars who hold the extreme view that *Beowulf* (one of the earliest and most important of these texts) is a literary imitation, standing to the true oral art as Virgil stands to Homer, would admit that something can be learnt from it about the objects of its imitation.

In the first volume of their massive and still somewhat neglected work,[2] H. M. and N. K. Chadwick demonstrate that the ancient literature of Europe is to be found, outside Greece, chiefly in what they call "the island literatures," i.e. the oldest records from the British Isles (Wales, Ireland, and Anglo-Saxon England) and from Iceland. As far as strictly narrative poetry is concerned, the extant evidence from England and (to a slightly lesser extent) from Iceland is more substantial than that from the Celtic countries. It is therefore appropriate to take a passage from *Beowulf* as our text in considering the work of the bards.

After Beowulf's defeat of Grendel, some of the warriors go out to see the mere into which the dying monster plunged. On their way back to the great hall of Heorot, they amuse themselves as follows:

> Hwilum heaþorofe · hleapan leton,
> on geflit faran · fealwe mearas,
> ðær him foldwegas · fægere þuhton,
> cystum cuðe. · Hwilum cyninges þegn,
> guma gilphlæden, · gidda gemyndig,
> se ðe ealfela · ealdgesegena
> worn gemunde · —word oþer fand
> soðe gebunden— · secg eft ongan
> sið Beowulfes · snyttrum styrian,
> ond on sped wrecan · spel gerade,
> wordum wrixlan.[3]

> (At one time, the brave warriors let their bay mares gallop and run in rivalry, wherever the tracks seemed good to them or were known for their excellence. At another time, one of the king's followers, a man of reputation who remembered lays and knew a great many old tales—one word found another, linked correctly—this man undertook then to speak wisely of Beowulf's adventure and effectively recited an apt tale, varying his words.)

A poet improvising on horseback ·about a very recent event seems unfavourably placed for any but the most unpremeditated results; yet this passage is most striking precisely for the high value that it puts upon the *scop*'s art. He himself is a person of consequence (*cyninges þegn, guma gilphlæden*); and we are told that his poetic version of Beowulf's adventure is apt, effective, and even wise (*snyttru* means "wisdom"). He draws on his extensive knowledge of old songs and stories (the stories of Sigemund and Heremod are introduced in what follows), and he is as skilful in the handling of words—in the arts of verbal variation (*wordum wrixlan*) and correct alliteration (*soðe gebunden*)—as the horsemen are in handling their horses. The linking of the recitation of narrative verse with riding and racing (*hwilum . . . hwilum*) shows how the bard's art entered into the life of the community. His performances were not confined to the great feasts with which we most often associate them. Like any other highly skilled man, he would be called upon to practise his art whenever the occasion seemed to require it. He would perform whenever his companions felt the need for celebration.

This picture of the high status of the traditional bard and of his art could be supported from other Anglo-Saxon poems (*Widsith*, *Deor*), not to speak of the Celtic evidence discussed by the Chadwicks in Chapter XIX of their book. Not all vernacular poets, of course, enjoyed such a status; but the essential point is that it was possible for them to do so, because they had, so far as their special skills were concerned, no rivals. The historian and the literary man, as we understand those types today, are creatures of reading and writing, and in particular of the Roman book-culture that literacy made available to the European peoples. The bard, as portrayed by the author of *Beowulf*, belongs to a world in which these bookish experts have not yet appeared. If he does not remember the *ealdgesegen* (the old tradition), no one will; if he cannot manipulate words, no one can.

We should not take it for granted that *Beowulf* was itself the work of such a man. Some recent scholars, such as A. B. Lord,[4] have argued, chiefly on stylistic grounds, that it was. They hold that its author must have worked under conditions essentially the same as those that he represents within the (admittedly historical) fiction of his poem, and was most probably a quite unlettered man, who would have had to dictate his poem to a scribe. It is a matter of controversy at present whether these conclusions can safely be drawn from the evidence, given the possibility that oral features may survive the conditions that produced them, at least for a time. But the biographical question about the education of poets such as the author of *Beowulf* is a relatively minor one, after all, if we are ready to allow that their art has been shown to have its main roots in an age without books.

The cardinal stylistic feature of the oral, or in my terminology "bardic," narrative poem is the *formula*. This is customarily defined as "a group of words which is regularly employed under the same metrical conditions to express a given essential idea."[5] The formula differs from the tags and stereotyped expressions found in the poetry of the minstrels, and still more from the echo-phrases characteristic of literary poetry, in that it forms part of an intricately organized conventional mode of expression without which the poet (composing originally without books and in the presence of his audience) would not be able to express himself at all, or not correctly. The workings of this formulaic mode of composition in our example of bardic poetry, Anglo-Saxon alliterative verse, may be explained briefly as follows. A "given essential idea" (a ruler's virtue, the striking of a blow, embarkation on a voyage, and so on) would be associated in the poet's mind with a conventional mode of expression. This would be either adapted or adaptable to the particular metrical conditions under which the poet wished to use it. In Anglo-Saxon verse, where the "line" consists of two two-stress half-lines linked by alliteration, a formula might be adapted to the second half-line and further be adaptable, usually in a specific way, so as to alliterate correctly with whatever first half-line the context might require, alliteration being the chief metrical condition in this species of verse. Three lines will illustrate the point:

gestrudan gestreona · under stanhliðum

(they plundered possessions under the rocky slopes)

ða com of more · under misthleoþum

(then he came from the moor under the misty slopes)

feorhseoc fleon · under fenhleoðu[6]

(to flee mortally wounded under the fen slopes).

In each of these cases, the second half-line takes the form *under x-hleoþu(m)*, with the first stressed syllable (the first part of the compound) varied in order to alliterate, as Anglo-Saxon rules required, with the first half-line. We can perhaps get some idea of what it felt like to compose verse in this fashion from the *Beowulf*-poet's description: "One word found another, linked correctly." So, in the second of the three lines quoted above (*Beowulf* 710), the word "moor," dictated by the context, found the word "mist" for the poet: it is not easy to think of any other word that would have been both metrically correct and contextually as acceptable (Grendel is attacking Heorot at night).

This mode of composition—which is characteristic of ancient, or bardic, narrative poetry (it was first studied in the Homeric poems)— is fairly called mechanical; and it is not impossible that quite correct Anglo-Saxon verse will some day be produced by a computer. Yet the chief impression left by the oldest mediaeval texts (Icelandic and Continental, as well as Anglo-Saxon) is of a cultivated and much-prized human skill. This impression is reinforced by the only surviving treatise on the art of poetry that can be taken to reflect (though imperfectly) the ancient art of the European bard: the so-called *Prose Edda* of the Icelander Snorri Sturluson, which dates from about 1220.[7] Snorri treats the art of the *scald* (a later and in some ways peculiarly Scandinavian development of the Germanic *scop*) under three heads: the knowledge of old tales, the handling of metres, and the mastery of poetic language. For him, as for the *Beowulf*-poet, these three skills constitute an art worthy of a king's thane. There is no suggestion in his work that the scaldic art, being vernacular, lay, and independent of books, is therefore an easy or inferior one. The scaldic poems themselves are, in fact, extremely complex and difficult, with their allusive treatment of old stories, their subtle metres, and their three-piled poetic diction. Although the narrative poetry of the bardic period is not always so demanding, it does generally display an archaic formality and intricacy of texture that reminds one of the style of the carvings and manuscripts of the period. It is this highly wrought archaic style that most sharply distinguishes the verse of the older "island litera-tures" from the more rapid, open-textured, and easy verse of the narra-tive poets of the high Middle Ages.

III

A superior written style is the development of generations. When a tradition or an individual goes from oral to written, he, or it, goes from an adult, mature style of one kind to a faltering and embryonic style of another sort.[8]

This generalization comes from a professed champion of oral poetry; but it is worth bearing in mind as we turn from the predominantly oral ancient phase of European narrative verse to its second and more charac-teristically mediaeval phase—the period, starting in the 11th and 12th centuries and ending in the 14th, of the minstrel.

"Minstrel," like "bard," is a vague and highly coloured term; but there does not seem to be a better, for present purposes, in English. I shall use it here as the equivalent of the more exact French term *jongleur*, to designate that class of entertainer who, among other forms of amuse-ment, recited tales in verse. Such minstrels were not usually poets in their own right. Most commonly, no doubt, they performed (more or less accurately) the works of others; and in such cases the original author may or may not have been himself a minstrel by profession. Yet the minstrel seems to represent better than any other the special conditions of the time, so far as they affected narrative verse; and it is the minstrel's repertoire of *chansons de geste*, romances, lays, and *fabliaux* that forms the core of the huge mass of material that survives from these centuries. If this is indeed a period that, in the harsh words of a great mediaevalist, "no longer possesses the power of collective creation and does not yet have the idea of art,"[9] then the minstrel is its truest representative. He no longer commands either the art or the prestige of the bard; but he is not yet a man of letters. The works that form his stock-in-trade are generally composed in writing (the line between the "clerk" and the minstrel-author is very hard to draw in this period), and they are frequently distributed in unpretentious written form; but they rarely if ever invite judgment, by the highest standards, as works of literary art. They are intended for the entertainment or edification of a listening audience that, whether "courtly" or not, accepted something less than the very best from its poets. The ever-growing dominance of the international Latin-borne book-culture, which had so early obliterated (at least from our sight)

z

most of the mature native poetic traditions, gave currency to ideals of poetic art that the vernaculars were, for the time being, ill-equipped to achieve. At the very highest level, it was only the Latin poets of the time who attempted to meet the ancients on equal terms. The answer of the 12th century to Virgil was not the *Roman d'Eneas* but Joseph of Exeter's *De bello Troiano*, a work that lies outside the limits of our subject.

It is possible to distinguish, in this period, three grades of narrative verse, all of which derive something of their character from the prevailing minstrel conditions, though differing greatly in skill and sophistication. The first grade, which shows perhaps the most skill and certainly the most sophistication, is best represented by the large body of courtly narrative produced in French, on both sides of the Channel, mostly during the second half of the 12th century. This group of poems is of the first importance in the literary history of the Middle Ages. It includes the "romances of antiquity" (of Thebes, of Aeneas, and of Troy) that were produced between 1150 and 1165; Wace's version of Geoffrey of Monmouth's history of the British kings; and the *lais* of Marie de France. But its chief representative is Chrétien de Troyes, the author (among other pieces) of *Le chevalier de la charrette* (otherwise known as *Lancelot*), *Le chevalier au lion* (*Yvain*), and *Le conte du graal* (*Perceval*), all composed in the years around 1180.[10]

Chrétien can hardly count as a minstrel, in the ordinary English sense of that word. When French critics call him a *ménestrel*, they mean that he was a poet attached to the households of the great (*ministerialis* originally denoted anyone with a position in a household); and this places him in the very highest class of *jongleur*, at the point where the *jongleur* shades off into the household "clerk." He is perhaps best thought of as a clerkly companion, or learned confidant, especially of the great ladies who played such a prominent part in the cultural life of the day. He himself says that Marie, Countess of Champagne, suggested both the *matière* (subject-matter) and the *sen* (signification) of *Le chevalier de la charrette*; and this autobiographical detail matches the blend of learning ("clergy") and elegance ("courtesy") that marks his work. Bédier's condemnation of the age as "not having the idea of art" cannot apply to Chrétien. His stories are cunningly, if sometimes oddly, constructed so as to express the particular *sen* that he saw in them; he can convey subtle shades of motive and feeling; his handling of the octosyllabic couplet (a form common to nearly all courtly narrative in his age) is correct and graceful; and his language reflects both the ease of the courtly vernacular and the artfulness of Latin rhetoric. A short passage (to which Frappier

calls attention) from *Le chevalier au lion* will illustrate some of these characteristics. A maiden is travelling in search of the hero, Yvain:

> Et cele erra au lonc del jor
> Tote sole grant anbleüre,
> Tant que vint a la nuit oscure,
> Si li enuia mout la nuiz.
> Et de ce dobla li enuiz,
> Qu'il plovoit a si grant desroi,
> Con Damedés avoit de quoi,
> Et fu el bois mout an parfont.
> Et la nuiz et li bois li font
> Grant enui, mes plus li enuie,
> Que li bois ne la nuiz, la pluie.[11]

> (And she rode all day long, alone and at a quick pace, until dark
> night came; and the night troubled her much. And her trouble was
> the greater because it was raining as hard as the Lord God could
> make it; and she was very deep into the wood. And the night and
> the wood troubled her much; but the rain troubled her more than
> either the wood or the night.)

Frappier points out two key rhetorical devices in this passage: the chias-
mus of *la nuiz et li bois . . . li bois ne la nuiz*, and the *annominatio*, or varied
repetition, of *nuiz* and *enui* and *enuier*. We may add that the musical
effect created by these repetitions is completed by the introduction of a
new *-ui-* word, *pluie*. The idea of rain has already been introduced in a
word of different sound (*il plovoit*); but the word *pluie* itself is held in
suspense, with the help of a mannered inversion (*plus li enuie . . . la pluie*),
until the very end of the passage, where it makes its appearance, in rhyme,
with exquisite effect.

This style of narrative verse has great merits. Chrétien's poems were
admirably suited to being read aloud (as was clearly his intention) to a
group of connoisseurs in a great household; and even today they are
among the most readable of narrative poems. And yet, if we recall that
they represent, by common agreement, the finest flower of vernacular
narrative in the high Middle Ages, we are forced to recognize a limitation
as well as an achievement. Chrétien's limitations have been well described
by Erich Auerbach:

> The rapid but easygoing rhymed octosyllable embraces all these
> themes and levels of feeling [he has been speaking of the opening of
> *Le conte du graal*]; it can be broadly descriptive or moralistic or
> didactic, it can be moving and vibrant with feeling or ironic and
> almost flippant, but it never attains to the tragic and sublime. For
> that it is too naive and short-winded; it never rises above the
> pleasing.[12]

355

These observations may be applied to our passage from *Le chevalier au lion*. The description of the lost and bewildered girl is "easygoing", "vibrant with feeling" (perhaps), and certainly "pleasing"; but is it not also "naive," or at least *faux-naïf*? The repeated co-ordinating *et*, the phrase *Con Damedés avoit de quoi*, and even the musical repetition of *nuiz* contribute to produce an effect of charming simplicity. In this particular case there is no call for more than that; indeed, tragic or sublime effects might have been out of place. But Auerbach is right when he says that Chrétien never rises above this level, not even in passages (such as the description of the Grail in the Castle of the Fisher King) where sublime effects might seem to be almost impossible to miss.

I suggest that these limitations, which are more apparent in the other courtly narrative poets than in Chrétien himself, are related to the "minstrel" conditions prevailing at the time. Unlike, for example, the authors of the *chansons de geste*, these poets had no inheritance (so far as we can tell) from earlier vernacular poetry. They were complete moderns, catering for the new courtly and romantic tastes of their age in a new style and a new metre. To them the "ancients" would have meant not the old bards, but Virgil, Ovid, Statius, and the rest. Their art is a written art, and its origins lie in books—in the old Latin poets and in the rhetoricians, especially. Learning and chivalry, says Chrétien in the prologue to *Cligès*, once migrated from Greece to Rome, and have now migrated once more, from Rome to France. Yet when historians speak of a renaissance in the 12th century, we do not feel that the term is altogether applicable to vernacular narrative verse, even at its most learned and artful; nor does it seem quite appropriate to call Chrétien a man of letters or a humanist. Perhaps it is that Chrétien's art, unlike that of the humanist (or the bard, for that matter), has so much the air of knowing its place. It follows the classics, but at a respectful distance. It is, above all, an easy art, in every sense of the word: it is relaxed, civilized, and not difficult (for the right people) to appreciate or understand. For Chrétien, just as much as the humbler minstrel, wrote for the ear of an audience; and, although his audience was more sophisticated and perhaps more intelligent than most, it was weak where the audience of the bards had been strong: in the knowledge of the old tales, and in trained appreciation of the language and metres of vernacular verse. Hence the very explicit style of narrative, the absence of poetic diction, and the persistent use of the octosyllabic couplet—a metrical form that, by comparison either with the old Germanic alliterative line or with the Virgilian hexameter, appears sadly lacking in subtleties.

But not all narrative verse in the age of the minstrels was so completely cut off from the older oral traditions of the vernaculars. The *chanson de geste*, which bulked large in the repertoire of the French *jongleur* up to and beyond the time of Chrétien, is certainly more archaic in character than the courtly romance; and some recent critics have argued that its style is basically a formulaic one, after the manner of oral poetry.[13] Much the same archaic character distinguishes the Old Spanish *cantar de gesta* (e.g. the *Poema de mio Cid*). In England, we find a still more remarkable anachronism: a large body of narrative verse dating from as late as the 14th and 15th centuries and composed in the ancient alliterative way. The existence of this body of verse side by side with Anglo-Saxon alliterative poetry (most of it composed some 600 years earlier) provides unusual opportunities for comparing the later with the earlier age. With this comparison in mind, let us now look briefly at the best-known of the Middle English alliterative story-poems: the 14th-century Arthurian romance *Sir Gawain and the Green Knight*.

Nothing is known of the author of this poem, except that he was a contemporary of Chaucer and used the English of the North-West Midlands. He may have been a clerk of some kind, attached to one of the baronial households in this region, in which case he could be counted as a provincial English equivalent of Chrétien de Troyes. His poem was certainly intended, like Chrétien's, for recitation to a listening audience; and occasionally (particularly at the end of a section or "fitt") he addresses his audience directly, in the minstrel fashion:

> And ȝe wyl a whyle be stylle
> I schal telle yow how þay wroȝt.[14]

> (If you will keep quiet for just a little, I shall tell you what happened to them.)

On the other hand, there is no question here of oral composition in the ancient alliterative manner. Despite the presence in the text of poetic formulas that may have originated in a time of oral composition, this poem was certainly written. The *Gawain*-poet, in short, belongs to the phase that can be called neither oral nor bookish, the minstrel period whose transitional character is well suggested by the phrasing (so unidiomatic in Modern English) of one of his own allusions to his source:

> Mony wylsum way he rode,
> Þe bok as I herde say.[15]

> (He followed many a bewildering path, as I heard the book say.)

357

The *Gawain*-poet was a more conscientious exponent of the techniques of alliterative verse than most of his contemporaries; but if we compare his poem with *Beowulf*, we are forced to conclude that, so far as technique is concerned, the alliterative tradition had declined since the Anglo-Saxon period. The craft is less subtle; it demands less both of poet and of audience. For example, the two two-stress parts of the Anglo-Saxon "classical" line were linked by alliteration that fell on either or both of the stressed syllables in the first half-line together with the first, and only the first, stressed syllable in the second half-line:

> on geflít fáran · féalwe méaras,
> ðær him fóldwégas · fǽgere þúhton.[16]

The rule preventing the last stress from participating in a line's alliteration was relaxed in Middle English; and double alliteration in the first half-line also becomes much more common. This general increase in alliteration is one index of the growing taste of audiences for more obvious effects. Here is one (admittedly rather extreme) example from *Sir Gawain and the Green Knight*:

> Þay boȝen bi bonkkez · þer boȝez ar bare,
> Þay clomben bi clyffez · þer clengez þe colde.
> Þe heuen watz vphalt, · bot vgly þer-vnder;
> Mist muged on þe mor, · malt on þe mountez,
> Vch hille hade a hatte, · a myst-hakel huge.[17]

> (They went by hills where the boughs were bare; they climbed past cliffs where the frost still lay. The clouds were high, but it looked ugly under them. Mist lay damp on the moor and settled on the hills: every hill had a hat, a huge cloak of mist.)

This passage illustrates another point of metrical form, besides heavy alliteration. Anglo-Saxon poets tended to avoid sequences of half-lines with the same basic rhythm. Their art required variety in the placing of the stresses in the half-line, thus:

> on geflít fáran · féalwe méaras,
> ðær him fóldwégas · fǽgere þúhton.

The first four half-lines in the passage quoted from *Sir Gawain*, on the other hand, all approximate to the same rhythmic type, the prevailing "rising-falling" type, di-dum-di-di-dum-di; and the result, although more familiar to modern ears than the shifting rhythms of *Beowulf*, is distinctly less subtle:

Þay bóȝen bi bónkkez · þer bóȝez ar báre,
Þay clómben bi clýffez · þer cléngez þe cólde.

The repeated rhythms and heavy alliteration underline the syntactic parallel between the two lines; and that is intended, rhetorically, to convey a sense of journey. The effect is plainly a calculated one; but, like so many other rhythmical and rhetorical effects in the poetry of the period, it is somewhat overdone. It would be unjust to call the *Gawain*-poet's style "faltering and embryonic"; but it is a less adult and mature style than that of the *Beowulf*-poet, and it implies a less well-trained and less exigent audience.

But there is gain as well as loss. The more informal relationship existing between poet and audience in the age of the minstrels found expression in flexible, easy, and even sometimes intimate tones that many modern readers prefer to the stately, hieratic manner of the older period. When the *Gawain*-poet writes *Vch hille hade a hatte, a myst-hakel huge*, the two images of the hat and the cloak, both popular in character, crowd in on each other in a way that suggests the eagerness of spoken description, so that we are ready to refer even the rare compound *myst-hakel* to colloquial rather than poetic usage. The *Gawain*-poet does, in fact, have a hoard of poetic words inherited from the alliterative tradition; but these elements are absorbed into the relaxed "middle style" that he shares with so many of his contemporaries. In some ways this style is a better medium for narrative, dialogue, and description than older, higher styles. It favours an easy flow in narrative, a lively variety of tone in dialogue, and a vividness and particularity in description. One does not often find these characteristics in the poetry of the bardic period; but they are almost commonplace in the age of the minstrels. Chrétien de Troyes and the *Gawain*-poet have them; and so, at a much lower level of art, have the minstrels proper.

The true minstrel poetry of the 12th, 13th, and 14th centuries (my third and lowest "grade") forms a huge and ill-defined mass of material that can only be touched on here. It includes popular narrative verse of every description: saints' lives and Bible stories as well as funny stories and romances. Verse-forms vary from country to country. In 14th-century Italy, the *cantari* (romances) recited in the city piazza were composed in *ottava rima* (stanzas rhyming a b a b a b c c); in England at the same time, popular poets used the tail-rhyme stanza, together with the international octosyllabic couplet. We should not expect too much of this kind of poetry, which is eminently characteristic of circles that no longer possessed the power of collective creation and did not yet have the idea of art. The popular minstrel is disciplined neither (like the *Gawain*-poet) by the remains of an old poetic craft, nor (like Chrétien) by the demands of a new sophisticated audience. He thinks little of himself and less of what he produces. His highest claim is that he makes available to unlettered folk the old stories that "clerks" have written in their books. He is no longer himself the sole custodian of these stories, as was the Anglo-Saxon or Celtic bard. Books have deprived him of his old function, without providing him with the basis of a new literary art. Although minstrel poems were normally composed in writing, the extent of textual variation in pieces that survive in more than one copy suggests that the idea of a fixed text had gained little currency in minstrel circles. Hence the delicacy of true literary art, as well as that of true oral art, is absent from the minstrel poem.

Perhaps the most characteristic feature of minstrel style is the "tag." In the bardic phase, repetitions of pairs or groups of words occur as an inevitable consequence of the oral-formulaic mode of composition. In purely written literature, on the other hand, such repetitions are cultivated for their meaning or their music, as when one passage or line "echoes" another. In this matter, as in others, the minstrel is closer to the bard than to the man of letters; but there is still a great difference between his tags and the old formulas. Consider the following example from the English tail-rhyme lay, *Sir Launfal:*

> Þey wer ywedded, as y you say,
> Vpon a Wytsonday,
>   Before princes of moch pryde;
> Noman ne may telle yn tale
> What folk þer was at þat bredale,
>   Of countreys fer & wyde.
> No noþer man was yn halle ysette
> But he wer prelat oþer baronette
>   (In herte ys naȝt to hyde);
> Yf þey satte noȝt all ylyke,
> Har seruyse was good & ryche,
>   Certeyn, yn ech a syde.[18]

Tail-rhyme is not a very difficult verse-form; but a poet such as this makes us painfully aware of his efforts to reconcile the demands of metre and sense. The need to find four rhyme words in the short line forces him into one completely pointless line—*In herte ys naȝt to hyde*—and another very weak one. The asseveration *as y you say,* very typical of minstrel poetry, also lacks force here. Such tags are found even in the very best poetry of the age; but in poems such as *Sir Launfal* they serve as a reminder that verse could be a workaday and quite sub-literary medium for story-telling. In such cases one must assume that it was enough that the minstrel should keep going, making the points that his story required without breaking the metre, or not too frequently. If there was such poetry in ancient Europe, it has not survived.

IV

The habit of reading and writing, largely confined in the earlier Middle Ages to centres of religious life such as monasteries and cathedrals, spread quite rapidly from the 11th century on. Three factors in particular contributed to this spread: the growth of the universities; the growth of administration, especially the royal administration or civil service; and the growth of towns and of the merchant class. Academics, administrators, and businessmen all needed written documents in order to carry on their affairs. Texts, papers, deeds, and bills formed part of their daily life in a way that would have seemed strange in the earlier Middle Ages. These men were not themselves usually much interested in vernacular literature (the academics least of all, perhaps); but they created circles in which a new kind of vernacular literature could eventually grow—circles more deeply penetrated by the habits of literacy than had existed before, at least in the Middle Ages. It was in such circles that there appeared for the first time writers in the vernacular who could truly be called "men of letters." Chief among these were, in Italy, Giovanni Boccaccio, and in England, Geoffrey Chaucer.

Boccaccio, like Chaucer, was the son of a city merchant. His father was associated with the great banking house of the Bardi. After spending his early years in Florence, he was sent by his father to Naples to work in a bank. It was in Naples that he composed, while still in his twenties, his two chief narrative poems: the *Filostrato* (*c.* 1335) and the *Teseida* (*c.* 1340). These works derive their verse-form, the *ottava rima*, together with many points of style and diction, from the minstrel tradition of the *cantari*.[19] But they have other sources of a quite different kind. The *Filostrato* draws on the *Roman de Troie* of Benoît de Sainte-Maure for its story, on classical literature (chiefly Virgil and Ovid) for decorative detail, and on the poets of the *dolce stil novo* for its love-poetry. The *Teseida* is the more ambitious and, for our present purposes, the more significant. It is, as W. P. Ker wrote, different from all the narrative poems hitherto published . . . . The *Teseida* is meant to compete with Virgil and Statius. It is a modern epic poem, in twelve books, with everything that an epic poem ought to have: gods and goddesses (technically called the machinery in later times), catalogues of the forces, similes, combats, funeral games—everything, except the visit to the infernal regions, for which there appears to have been no room.[20]

The strongly literary flavour of the *Teseida* can be caught from its opening stanzas, in which Boccaccio invokes the Muses:

> O sorelle castalie, che nel monte
> Elicona contente dimorate,
> dintorno al sacro gorgoneo fonte,
> sottesso l'ombra delle frondi amate
> da Febo, delle quali ancor la fronte
> spero d'ornarmi, sol che 'l concediate:
> le sante orecchi a' miei prieghi porgete
> e quelli udite come voi dovete.

> E' m'è venuto in voglia con pietosa
> rima di scrivere una istoria antica,
> tanto negli anni riposta e nascosa
> che latino autor non par ne dica,
> per quel ch'io senta, in libro alcuna cosa;
> dunque sì fate che la mia fatica
> sia graziosa a chi ne fia lettore
> o in altra maniera ascoltatore.[21]

(O Castalian sisters, who dwell happy on the mount of Helicon, around the sacred Gorgonean fount and in the shade of Phoebus's beloved leaves, with which I yet hope, if you permit, to adorn my brow; open your holy ears to my prayers and pay due attention to them. I have determined to write in piteous rhyme an ancient tale, a tale so lost in the years that no Latin author seems to tell anything of it in a book, so far as I can find; so bring it about that my labours may be pleasing both to him who reads and to him who hears in other fashion.)

In one of the learned notes that he so characteristically provided for the poem, Boccaccio claims that this invocation of the Muses follows the custom of classical antiquity (*l'antico costume de' componitori*). Such invocations were indeed foreign even to such learned predecessors in vernacular poetry as Chrétien de Troyes (though not, of course, to Dante); and the manner of Boccaccio's invocation confirms our impression that the poem is "meant to compete with Virgil and Statius." The reader notices especially the sustained syntax and artful word-order in both stanzas, and, in the first, the employment of learned, if rather elementary, periphrases: *sorelle castalie* for "Muses," *frondi amate da Febo* for "laurel leaves." It is by such devices that Boccaccio aspires to win the crown of laurel, that apotheosis of the neo-classical man of letters.

Boccaccio's words at the end of the second stanza quoted above suggest that he wrote chiefly for the private reader (*lettore*); and this conclusion is confirmed by various features of the poem, most of which we hardly notice because they imply ordinary modern conditions that we take for granted. These features include the presence of footnotes, the division of the poem (for the first time in Italian) into books (*libri*), and (most significant of all, perhaps) the reference to a previous event as having been narrated not "before" but "above" (*come su si detta*, [IV, 56]). Yet we should notice that Boccaccio refers in his invocation to "him who hears in other fashion" as well as to "him who reads." This shows that he expected listeners as well as readers; and it also seems to imply that private reading was for him, as for the *Gawain*-poet, a kind of listening. So we should not identify him too completely with ordinary modern conditions, although he and Dante come closer to them than any other vernacular writers of the time. He belongs to a phase in the evolution of the modern man of letters at which mediaeval minstrel conditions have not yet been altogether left behind.

It is not difficult to trace the consequences of this uneasy situation in Boccaccio's poem. The *Teseida* is far from being an unqualified success. It suffers, for one thing, from what Branca calls *incertezza di stile*. On the one hand, as we have seen, Boccaccio sedulously cultivates a lofty neo-classical style, modelled on *l'antico costume de' componitori*. On the other hand, his poem bears many of the marks of the popular *cantare* tradition from which its stanza-form was borrowed. There are, for example, cantaresque rhymes and rhyme-tags that remind us of English poems such as *Sir Launfal*. It is not altogether surprising that, according to the so-called *Cantare dei cantari*, the *Teseida* came to be included in the repertoire of an Italian minstrel.[22]

A similar uncertainty affects the substance of the poem. Having decided to write an epic, Boccaccio was faced with the peculiar difficulty of the literary man: what should he write an epic about? One thinks of Milton listing possible subjects in his notebook, or of Wordsworth brooding hopefully over Mithridates and Wallace. There is one passage from Wordsworth's account of his own uncertainties in *The Prelude* that exactly defines the central weakness of the *Teseida*:

> Sometimes it suits me better to shape out
> Some Tale from my own heart, more near akın
> To my own passions and habitual thoughts,
> Some variegated story, in the main
> Lofty, with interchange of gentler things.
> But deadening admonitions will succeed
> And the whole beauteous Fabric seems to lack
> Foundation, and, withal, appears throughout
> Shadowy and unsubstantial.[23]

Boccaccio, so far as we know, invented his romantic tale of the rivalry of Palemone and Arcita for Emilia. It is a story in the French courtly manner, akin, no doubt, to his own passions and habitual thoughts. It also gives him the opportunity of blending two of the three lofty subjects mentioned by Dante in his *De vulgari eloquentia* (*c.* 1305): love and arms. Yet the result is unsatisfactory, "shadowy and unsubstantial." Palemone and Arcita move about in the epic world of Thebes and Athens, and rub shoulders with Theseus and Hercules, without our ever really crediting their existence. W. P. Ker's general comment on the imitative or artificial epic applies to this case: "The suspicion is aroused that the author does not believe what he is telling. One feels as if trying to dream when not really asleep."[24]

The *Teseida* is a marvellous experiment; but it is crippled, as a narrative poem, by this "unsubstantiality" in its story. It lacks a necessary virtue which, one realizes, is not often lacking in the work of bards or minstrels, even when they are dull or incompetent. This virtue is simply conviction, about the people in the story and the things they do. The right note is struck in the opening lines of *Beowulf:*

> Hwæt, we Gar-Dena · in geardagum,
> Þeodcyninga · þrym gefrunon . . .

> (Lo, we have heard of the might of the kings of the people of the Spear-Danes in days gone by . . .).

Here the poet shares with his audience knowledge of, and belief in, the deeds of the old Danish kings. The assurance of his tone contrasts with the embarrassed manner in which Boccaccio explains that his *istoria antica* (recorded, as he claims in a note, in Greek) appears somehow to have escaped the Latin authors. However one takes this apology—whether as a real attempt to claim authority for his tale, or as some kind of donnish joke—it points to a weakness in Boccaccio's position. He is not custodian of the old traditions and tales of Florence and Naples; so what is he? In his prefatory letter, addressed to Fiammetta, he suggests that the whole thing is designed to represent, in the person of a Theban lover, his own sufferings in love; but this bold attempt to identify his own role as that of the lyric-poet-in-love fails, simply because there is so much in the poem (especially the extended epic battle-scenes) that it quite fails to account for.

Flaws such as these prevent the modern reader from responding to the *Teseida* as a living classic: Boccaccio is, of course, chiefly remembered as a story-teller in prose. But the *Teseida* deeply impressed his contemporaries and successors. It represented, so far as vernacular writing was concerned, a thing unattempted yet in prose or rhyme; and among its admirers was the English poet Chaucer. Not only is the *Teseida* the source of Chaucer's "Knight's Tale"; it is also, in many respects, the inspiration of his greatest work, *Troilus and Criseyde*.

Geoffrey Chaucer was the son of a wealthy London wine-merchant, and he became (after studying, possibly, at the law school of the Inner Temple) a civil servant. These circumstances together imply an unusual degree of familiarity with writing and written documents[25]; and we have Chaucer's own word for it (admittedly in a passage of some comic exaggeration) that when not at work on his official books in the Customs House, he read for his own pleasure. This is what the Eagle says to "Geoffrey" in *The House of Fame* (c. 1379):

> . . . when thy labour doon al ys,
> And hast mad alle thy rekenynges,
> In stede of reste and newe thynges,
> Thou goost hom to thy hous anoon;
> And, also domb as any stoon,
> Thou sittest at another book
> Tyl fully daswed ys thy look.[26]

The phrase *domb as any stoon* is particularly notable, since even private reading, in the Middle Ages, was usually accompanied by a whispered or muttered vocalization of the text. If Chaucer did indeed read quite silently to himself in his mansion over Aldgate, then he was as advanced in habits of literacy as any Florentine. Yet his circumstances as a poet were not entirely in keeping with these habits. There is no doubt that he did write partly in order to be read, privately if not silently, by men of his own stamp: lawyers, civil servants, businessmen, and gentlemen of intellectual tastes. Perhaps it was this audience that he most cared about. Yet he also, just as certainly, intended many of his works to be read aloud to a listening audience. The most influential listening audience was provided by the court circles attached to Edward III and, particularly, to Richard II.

This situation is reflected in the text of *Troilus and Criseyde*. Here is a poem designed, we might say, to go out on two channels. Some passages are definitely shaped to fit the circumstances of recitation to a courtly audience in a chamber. An example is the last stanza of Book II:

> But now to yow, ye loveres that ben here,
> Was Troilus nought in a kankedort,
> That lay, and myghte whisprynge of hem here,
> And thoughte, "O Lord, right now renneth my sort
> Fully to deye, or han anon comfort!"
> And was the firste tyme he shulde hire preye
> Of love; O myghty God, what shal he seye?[27]

This agrees with a picture found in one of the early manuscripts of *Troilus*, which shows Chaucer reading the poem aloud to a circle of aristocratic listeners. The appeal to *ye loveres* to judge of Troilus's predicament reminds one of Chrétien's relationship with his courtly audience; but the manner of the appeal (in particular, the question *what shal he seye?*) has more of the minstrel about it than is common in Chrétien. Chaucer, like the *Gawain*-poet, was not above appealing directly, at a pause in his story, to the curiosity of his audience. However, there are other passages in *Troilus* that suggest a quite different kind of audience, notably the lines at the very end of the poem:

> O moral Gower, this book I directe
> To the and to the, philosophical Strode,
> To vouchen sauf, ther nede is, to correcte,
> Of youre benignites and zeles goode.[28]

Gower and Strode seem both to have been legal men. Strode was probably also a former Fellow of Merton College, Oxford; and Gower was, of course, himself a poet (in Latin and French as well as in English). The "directing" of an English poem to such readers (and they would certainly be readers) would attract no particular comment in the age of Spenser or Milton; but in the 14th century it is a remarkable anticipation of things to come.

Like Boccaccio, then, Chaucer had to reckon with both the *lettore* and the *ascoltatore;* and his *Troilus* combines minstrel features with literary ones, like the *Teseida*, though much more harmoniously. As for the literary features, Strode and Gower would not have had far to look.

Chaucer, like Boccaccio, is the first to divide a poem in his vernacular into "books." The five-book structure of *Troilus* (modelled, probably, on the five-book structure of Boethius's *De consolatione philosophiae*) marks out a carefully balanced narrative. During the first two books Fortune raises the hero to a felicity that he enjoys in the third book and loses in the last two. Such symmetry is rare in earlier vernacular narrative (though we find something like it in *Sir Gawain and the Green Knight*). The book-division also brings with it the usual invocations and proems, expressed in a lofty literary language, just as in Boccaccio. Another feature of similar effect is the "heightened time-description," also imitated from the *Teseida*.[29] This is a form of amplification very familiar in later literature, already mastered here by Chaucer:

> In May, that moder is of monthes glade,
> That fresshe floures, blew and white and rede,
> Ben quike agayn, that wynter dede made,
> And ful of bawme is fletyng every mede;
> Whan Phebus doth his bryghte bemes sprede,
> Right in the white Bole, it so bitidde,
> As I shal synge, on Mayes day the thrydde.[30]

Chaucer also has the elaborate literary simile, as in this very beautiful example:

> And as the newe abaysed nyghtyngale,
> That stynteth first whan she bygynneth to synge,
> Whan that she hereth any herde tale,
> Or in the hegges any wyght stirynge,
> And after siker doth hire vois out rynge,
> Right so Criseyde, whan hire drede stente,
> Opned hire herte, and tolde hym hire entente.[31]

The very familiarity of such features to any reader of post-mediaeval European poetry is a measure of Chaucer's modernity. Yet these things coexist in his work with features characteristic of older minstrel poetry, and in a fashion somehow harmonious. There is a mystery here. Chaucer's attitude to the story-telling minstrels (whom he would have called *gestours*) is expressed clearly enough in the tale that he represents himself as telling on the Canterbury pilgrimage, the tale of "Sir Thopas." This satirical imitation of popular tail-rhyme romances places Chaucer firmly in the *literary* tradition. It is the work of a fastidious writer, whose ear was offended by the bad rhymes, vacuous tags, and motley diction of

367

the minstrels. Yet if we attempt to analyse the satire in any detail, we find that it is not at all easy to draw a clear line around the absurd minstrel features. There are, it is true, words, phrases, forms, and rhymes that plainly make part of the joke, because they occur in the popular romances but do not occur elsewhere in Chaucer's work (or only in contexts themselves suspect, such as "The Miller's Tale"). But there is also a considerable penumbra of features that seem ridiculous in "Sir Thopas" but occur elsewhere in normal Chaucerian contexts too:

> An elf-queene wol I love, ywis,
> For in this world no womman is
> Worthy to be my make. . . . [32]

Ywis is a very common rhyme-tag in such objects of Chaucer's ridicule as the early-14th-century *Guy of Warwick;* and we may well laugh at it here. Yet Chaucer himself rhymes on it 29 times in *Troilus and Criseyde.* Similar considerations apply to other fillers that occur in "Sir Thopas," such as *also moote I thee* and *in good certayn,* and to such minstrelisms as the following:

> And so bifel upon a day,
> For sothe, as I yow telle may,
> Sire Thopas wolde out ride. [33]

Is this so very different from what we find in the quite serious tale of the Physician?

> And so bifel soone after, on a day,
> This false juge, as telleth us the storie,
> As he was wont, sat in his consistorie. . . . [34]

Yet Chaucer's poetry does not convey that sense of stylistic *incertezza* that Branca finds in the *Teseida:* it is various, but not uncertain. What made this achievement possible? The answers lie too deep for the present inquiry, in the society of 14th-century England, and in Chaucer's own ironical and self-dramatizing personality.

But Chaucer's achievement may suggest one final reflection. For him and for Boccaccio, narrative poetry was a difficult art; but for their successors it was to become impossible. Under increasingly "literary" conditions, verse shed its true narrative function, and poets such as Tasso, Spenser, and William Morris were left "trying to dream when not really asleep." Like the *Teseida*, but to a greater degree, their work is curiously deficient as narrative, for all its many literary virtues. It lacks that

368

essential quality of conviction, which Chaucer shared with the much despised minstrel story-tellers, and which we find even in the ridiculous "Sir Thopas":

> And so bifel upon a day,
> For sothe, as I yow telle may,
>   Sire Thopas wolde out ride.

References

Editorial note: Medial points have been inserted to separate half-lines of alliterative verse quoted; they are, however, absent from the various editions of works of alliterative poetry cited below.

1. These are: manuscript Cotton Vitellius A.xv (including *Beowulf* and *Judith*) in the British Museum; Bishop Leofric's Exeter Book (including *Christ, Juliana, Deor, The Wanderer, The Seafarer,* and *Widsith*) in Exeter Cathedral Library; manuscript Junius XI (containing *Genesis, Exodus, Daniel,* and *Christ and Satan*) in the Bodleian Library, Oxford; and the Vercelli Book (containing *Andreas, The Dream of the Rood, Elene,* and *The Fates of the Apostles*) in the cathedral library at Vercelli in north-western Italy.
2. H. M. and N. K. CHADWICK, *The Growth of Literature* (Cambridge 1932).
3. *Beowulf,* ed. by F. Klaeber, 3rd edn (New York 1950), 864-74.
4. A. B. LORD, *The Singer of Tales* (Cambridge, Mass. 1960).
5. A. PARRY (ed.), *The Making of Homeric Verse: The Collected Papers of Milman Parry* (Oxford 1971), p. 272.
6. *Daniel* 61, in *The Junius Manuscript,* ed. by G. P. Krapp (New York 1932); *Beowulf* 710 and 820.
7. See *The Prose Edda,* trans. by A. G. Brodeur (New York 1916), which contains English versions of the sections on mythology and diction.
8. LORD, *op. cit.,* p. 134.
9. J. BÉDIER, *Les fabliaux,* 5th edn (Paris 1925), p. 432.
10. See J. FRAPPIER, *Chrétien de Troyes* (Paris 1957).
11. *Yvain,* ed. by T. B. W. Reid (Manchester 1942), 4836-46.
12. E. AUERBACH, *Literary Language and Its Public in Late Latin Antiquity and in the Middle Ages,* trans. by R. Manheim (London 1965), p. 218.
13. See LORD, *op. cit.,* pp. 202-7, and J. RYCHNER, *La chanson de geste* (Paris and Lille 1955).
14. *Sir Gawain and the Green Knight,* ed. by J. R. R. Tolkien and E. V. Gordon, rev. by N. Davis (Oxford 1967), 1996-7.
15. *ibid.,* 689-90.
16. *Beowulf* 865-6.
17. *Sir Gawain and the Green Knight* 2077-81.

18. THOMAS CHESTRE, *Sir Launfal*, ed. by A. J. Bliss (London 1960), 49–60.
19. See V. BRANCA, *Il cantare trecentesco e il Boccaccio del Filostrato e del Teseida* (Florence 1936).
20. W. P. KER, *Form and Style in Poetry*, ed. by R. W. Chambers, with Introd. by J. Buxton (London 1966), p. 70.
21. *Teseida*, Bk I, 1–2, ed. by A. Limentani, in *Tutte le opere di Giovanni Boccaccio*, ed. by V. Branca, Vol. II (Milan 1964).
22. The *Cantare dei cantari* is a poem in which a minstrel is represented as displaying his wares, with a list of all the stories and songs he knows.
23. *The Prelude*, ed. by E. de Selincourt (Oxford 1926), Bk I, 220–8.
24. KER, *op. cit.*, p. 282.
25. On merchants in Chaucer's day, see S. L. THRUPP, *The Merchant Class of Medieval London* (East Lansing, Mich. 1948); on civil servants, see T. F. TOUT, "Literature and Learning in the English Civil Service in the Fourteenth Century," *Speculum* IV (Cambridge, Mass. 1929), pp. 365–89.
26. *The House of Fame* 652–8, in *The Works of Geoffrey Chaucer*, ed. by F. N. Robinson, 2nd edn (London 1957).
27. *Troilus and Criseyde*, Bk II, 1751–7.
28. *ibid.*, Bk V, 1856–9.
29. The most useful study of the influence of the *Teseida* upon Chaucer is R. A. PRATT, "Chaucer's Use of the *Teseida*," *Publications of the Modern Language Association of America* 62 (New York 1947), pp 598–621.
30. *Troilus and Criseyde*, Bk II, 50–6.
31. *ibid.*, Bk III, 1233–9.
32. *The Canterbury Tales* VII, 790–2.
33. *ibid.*, 748–50.
34. *ibid.*, VI, 160–2.

Bibliography

E. AUERBACH, *Literary Language and Its Public in Late Latin Antiquity and in the Middle Ages*, trans. by R. Manheim (London 1965).

H. M. and N. K. CHADWICK, *The Growth of Literature*, Vol. I: *The Ancient Literatures of Europe* (Cambridge 1932).

H. J. CHAYTOR, *From Script to Print: An Introduction to Medieval Vernacular Literature* (Cambridge 1945).

E. R. CURTIUS, *European Literature and the Latin Middle Ages*, trans. by W. R. Trask (New York 1953).

E. FARAL, *Les jongleurs en France au moyen âge* (Paris 1910).

W. P. KER, *Form and Style in Poetry*, ed. by R. W. Chambers, with Introd. by J. Buxton (London 1966); *Essays on Mediaeval Literature* (London 1905).

A. B. LORD, *The Singer of Tales* (Cambridge, Mass. 1960).

CHAPTER 11

The Story and its Setting

Derek Pearsall*

Epic and Romance (1897) is the title of W. P. Ker's great book on mediaeval narrative literature, and some discussion of these two terms will be useful to begin with, although it must be recognized that only broad distinctions can be made at this stage, and that each national literature—each piece of narrative writing, in fact—has its own identity in which these distinctions will become blurred. The term "epic" itself may be rather misleading for much of this literature, if it implies any association with the sophisticated and politically orientated myth of national emergence, such as the *Aeneid,* and perhaps it will be better to use the term "heroic," which identifies a type of relationship between literature and society but does not stipulate a mode of literary treatment. Heroic literature is the celebration of the values of a heroic age, usually past: it is historical, quasi-historical, or has the air of history, and assumes that its events and persons are real as well as important. It is the literature of a society in a state of dynamic activity, on the edge of either disintegration or stabilization, in which survival is difficult, but not all-important. The literature of survival alone can only be comic. In heroic narrative, loyalty to one's kin or one's leader, the ethic of revenge, above all the overwhelming pressure to assert self, status, and reputation, transcend the fear of death, and provide both the glory and the tragic horror. The actions are meaningful in themselves, concerning power, possession, and revenge, and it is characteristic of the heroic lay to concentrate on a moment of strong dramatic crisis in which the heroic concept of life is exposed and put to the final test: the defence of the narrow place against odds, whether it is Maldon, Roncesvalles, or Gunnar's farm at Hliðarendi, is the most perfect demonstration of heroic values in action. There is no theory of conduct, and characters act for the most

* Reader in English, University of York.

part without explicit recognition of what upholds them; they come before us fully formed, behave sensibly and realistically as individuals, and there is no exploration of inner consciousness or sensibility, although sometimes there are laconic hints that they have one.

Heroic literature passes away some time later, usually, than the age it remembers, although its values and techniques can be resurrected when conditions are suitable, as for instance in *The Battle of Maldon* (*c.* 993) and perhaps the ancestors of the legends of *Horn* and *Havelok*, when the Viking invasions temporarily reproduced the anarchy of the Age of Migrations and a return to its values. The coming of Christianity plays a large part in the decline of heroic literature, and it is characteristic of the West Germanic area that the consolidation of Christianity comes at just the period when the body of Germanic heroic legend was being committed to writing, so that the heroic impulse was to a large extent deflected and transferred, as in *Beowulf* and, more particularly, in the Christian heroic poetry. The heroic treatment of the Christian story—as in the Old Saxon *Heliand* or the Old English *Genesis, Exodus,* or *Andreas*—cannot disguise the fact that Christian and heroic values are incompatible, because the former refers human behaviour to a series of universals that transcend and outlast the human event, whereas it is fundamental to heroic literature that the human event is meaningful in and for itself. Political centralization and stability also assist in the decline of heroic literature, by limiting the possible scope for heroic action, so that the history of the present, having already become the legend of the past, is in turn mythologized and romanticized.

The energies of mimesis (the imitation of human action in stories) are now taken up in various ways—in biblical narrative and saints' lives, in history and chronicle, even in comedy, all with some tincture of heroic motif and method—and above all in romance, which is the characteristic literature of the chivalric age, of Christian feudal society. Romance deals in adventure, not survival: the hero is not defending desperately, but chooses to go out from a secure bastion of wealth and privilege to seek adventures, in which the values of chivalry and service to ladies that he explicitly upholds are to be formally submitted to testing. There is still room for heroic action (courage and loyalty are always good currency) but it is now heroic action in the service of an ideal or transcendental code of values—Christian, chivalric, or erotic, and sometimes all three together. The demands made of the hero in the service of this ideal may deliberately contradict older heroic values, such as the humiliation and loss of face that Lancelot chooses to suffer by riding in the cart, because Guenevere has asked him to. The action is no longer "real," nor more than cursorily historical, and the element of the marvellous and supernatural, which in heroic literature could be accommodated because it was credible, is now deliberately exaggerated so as to be incredible. The character of the hero is idealized into a symbol, raised above heroic status so that he is superior not only to other men but also to his environment.[1]

With these distinctions made, it must now be said that the isolation of heroic literature as a type is, with one exception—that of Icelandic saga—an operation that demands some surgery, for in the literature that has come down to us from the West Germanic peoples of the early Middle Ages it is blended inextricably with other forms, and almost invariably suffused with Christian sentiment. The one or two pieces that we can point to where heroic motifs appear in their "pure" form are short and comparatively insignificant. The Germanic peoples carried with them a store of heroic materials from the age of the *Völkerwanderung* and later— stylized versions of episodes in Frankish or Burgundian or Danish history—and the fragments that survive, such as the Old High German *Hildebrandslied* (c. 780) and the Old English *Waldere* and *The Fight at Finnsburg*, suggest that these were in the form of lays: fairly short, as the recital of the Finnsburg story as part of the evening's entertainment at Hrothgar's court would indicate,[2] and concentrating on the crucial moment of a complex action, particularly on the high peaks of passionate character-drama. The short fragment of the *Hildebrandslied* is connected with the legends of Theodoric (Dietrich), king of the Ostrogoths, and concentrates on a moment of typically heroic crisis in the invasion of Italy: the fight of Hildebrand, Dietrich's champion, against Hadubrand, whom he discovers to be his son. This highly charged dramatic situation is handled in a characteristically laconic manner. *Waldere* consists of two short fragments of a lay on Walter of Aquitaine, probably analogous with that used by Ekkehard of St Gall (d. 973) as a source for his Latin *Waltharius*: the theme is the defence of a narrow place, Wasgenstein in the Vosges, and the material is drawn from the Frankish-Burgundian-Hunnish store of heroic tradition, like the saga of the Völsungs (or Nibelungs). *The Fight at Finnsburg*, from Danish-Frisian history, is again a fragment, and the tangled web of vengeance to which it alludes needs the Finn episode in *Beowulf* to make it intelligible to us: the episode shows a typical concentration of the narrative into two peaks, the wrong and the vengeance, with powerful evocation of the drama of character, conflicting loyalties, and passion.

There are one or two pieces that have reference to heroic tradition, but that are not heroic in themselves. *Deor* is cryptic, and difficult to interpret, but it looks like a court-poem of the 8th century, lamenting the *scop* Deor's fall from favour, and demonstrating by its compact range of allusion that he deserves better: a begging-poem, in fact. *Widsith* is early, parts of it perhaps earlier than any other Germanic poetry, but it is only on the fringes of the heroic tradition, and its encyclopaedic nature, in which it anticipates some of the mythical lays of the Icelandic *Poetic Edda* (e.g. *Vafþrúðnismál, Grímnismál*), suggests that it is a kind of mnemonic for that tradition. This, maybe, is why it survived the pruning of successive generations of monastic culture, which could always accommodate a good encyclopaedia, even a pagan one. The author of *Beowulf* used, and profited by, a similar indulgence.

We can take it that the heroic lays were well known and widely disseminated late into Anglo-Saxon times, as the highly compressed nature of the allusions in *Beowulf* would suggest, but once the literary culture had been established by Latin Christianity there was little chance of their being written down, at least in their pure heroic form. It is a characteristic accident of Anglo-Saxon history that, at a time when more settled conditions and an emergent sense of nationhood might have been expected to give rise to a great flowering of heroic literature, the major literary monument should have been Bede's *Historia ecclesiastica gentis anglorum* (*c.* 731). The decay of Latin culture in the 9th century, as a result of the Viking invasions, created the conditions for the rise of the written vernacular, but Alfred's renaissance was primarily directed toward the preservation in English of Christian-Latin culture, not of the heroic tradition. Christianity had taken deep root. The *Anglo-Saxon Chronicle* (890 ff.) is the nearest that the age has to a national epic, and parts of that—such as the episode of Cynewulf and Cyneheard, presumably itself derived from a lay[3]—present high dramatic action in characteristically denuded heroic form. But these again are accidents of transmission, and on the whole the *Chronicle* is too historical to be heroic—dry, factual, annalistic, proof that Bede had done his work well. The wars of Alfred against the Danes provide material, again and again, for authentic heroic treatment, but the monastic compilers are too closely tied to their facts to shape the material freely. The clear mark of the character of the *Chronicle* is that, when the pressure to celebrate some heroic deed of arms becomes irresistible, it takes the form, as in the *Battle of Brunanburh*, of a poem, an artificial and slightly spurious anthology of heroic motifs and phrases, which is quite detachable from its context.

374

Icelandic saga, by contrast, weaves its own free heroic dramas from the authentically historical verses embedded in it.

The pressure of heroic themes and techniques remained strong throughout the Anglo-Saxon period, however, and *Beowulf* is an attempt to accommodate them to a Christian ethic. The poem is of cloistered provenance, but probably does not misrepresent the mixed nature of Anglo-Saxon society, in which blood-feuds, for instance, still provided a strong motive for action (as in the Icelandic sagas), but in which the Church and the law-givers strove to substitute the *wergild* (compounding for money). The author, recognizing that much of the traditional heroic material is morally dubious, or at least intractable to a Christian interpretation, has chosen to elevate a comparatively insignificant figure from heroic tradition, has possibly even invented him—just as Chrétien de Troyes (*fl.c.* 1170–80) was to elevate a new hero, Lancelot, when he needed the vehicle for a new *sen* (inner meaning) in Arthurian story—and has assigned to him three adventures that are at once heroic and morally clear-cut. No vengeance motive, no greed for money or possession of a woman, such as are almost universal in heroic lays, attaches to Beowulf's killing of Grendel, Grendel's mother, or the dragon. What he does is for the protection of an allied people (although he is eager for fame too) and then for the safety of his own people. His enemies present fierce and increasing physical problems, but they do not involve the hero in any character drama, any crisis in which heroic values are exposed in a moment of conflict. The Finn episode—with its concentration on the conflict of loyalties in the minds of Hildeburh and of Hnæf's followers, the irreconcilable demands of kinship and marriage, of revenge and the sworn oath—has more of critical heroic action in it than the whole of the rest of *Beowulf*. At the end of it, heroic values have been upheld at terrible cost and order has been restored, but there is no sense that society has been cleansed. Finn and his Frisians are part of that society, and have just as much right to do what they do as Hengest and the Danes. In the rest of *Beowulf*, on the other hand, the enemy is identified as the enemy of God and of mankind, not of a person or of a people: Grendel is *feond mancynnes* (enemy of mankind), *helle hæft* (hell's captive): he "bears God's anger," and (like his mother) is specifically related to the race of Cain.

The dragon is not quite so simple. One of the author's problems is that even these comparatively simple stories of monster-slaying come to him trailing some kind of intrinsic "meaning," and in adapting the story of the slaying of the dragon that guards the treasure he involves himself in certain difficulties. The account that he gives of the origins of the treasure—the last survivor of the race guarding its heirlooms, his death, and the taking over of the guardianship of the treasure by the dragon—includes the dragon, however arbitrarily, in some sort of ordered pattern of existence, and gives him the right, therefore, when the hoard is violated by the exile, to take his revenge on the surrounding country-side. Beowulf's first reaction to the news is one of guilt and self-questioning,[4] as if it must be some fault in him, the king, that has caused such a monstrous disturbance in nature—a piece of analysis as unexpected in a heroic poem as Hrothgar's warning against pride, with its Pauline imagery of the armour of the soul being pierced

> wom wundorbebodum · wergan gastes[5]
>
> (by the crafty, evil commands of the ill spirit).[6]

It may be that Beowulf is guilty of pride, or at least of complacency; it is certainly true that, after his first gloomy gesture of self-sacrifice in going out against the dragon, he comes to seem far more interested in the dragon's treasure than he ought to be. A whole series of references attributes greed for gold to him as a motive, and his prayer to God on accomplishing the battle is one of thanks for being allowed to lay his eyes on the treasure.[7] It seems unlikely that the poet intends any extended psychological analysis of the hero; it is simply that the heroic motif of the accursed dragon-guarded treasure is too powerful to resist, and is allowed to bring the hero to his doom.

There are other ambiguities, too, thrown up by the blending of heroic and Christian values. The poet makes frequent reference to God's controlling providence, more than once with the suggestion that God intervenes on the side of the brave and virtuous, as in the finding of the *ealdsweord eotenisc* (old sword of giants) in the underwater cave.[8] On one occasion, however, he extends this eschatology to the heroic concept of fate,

> Wyrd oft nereð
> unfægne eorl · þonne his ellen deah[9]
>
> (Fate often succours the undoomed warrior when his valour is strong),

which of course makes nonsense of fatalism, and of heroism too. There is also the famous passage where he speaks of the paganism of the Danes —*Metod hie ne cuþon* (they knew not the Lord)—as the explanation of their failure to cleanse Heorot, which is a strange comment, coming as it does just after the song in praise of the Creation sung by the *scop* in Heorot.[10] But such contradictions may reflect a real ambiguity in early Christian society, when men might easily relapse into heathen practice in times of stress. Certainly the Christian colouring cannot be referred to an interpolator: it is inherent in the choice and disposition of the subject, in the sententious tone and elegiac sense of the transitoriness of the world, and in the very language, where specifically Christian periphrases, such as *Godes leoht geceas*[11] (chose God's light) for "died," have become fossilized in quite casual contexts.

The central preoccupations of *Beowulf* are with the hero as symbol, with the fight of good against evil. Beowulf is precariously perched on the edge of romantic idealization, as in the eulogy at the end of the poem, which celebrates some markedly unheroic qualities—

Manna mildust · ond monðwærust[12]

(The mildest of men and most kindly)

—and in his approximation to the type of hero who is superior to his environment, for instance in his underwater swimming feats. But the adventures in which Beowulf is engaged are so enmeshed in "history," so enriched with allusion to heroic traditions, that they take some of their colouring from that history. Historical circumstance surrounds and enfolds the action, and is introduced so casually and elusively as to convince us of its authenticity. The allusions of the first part of the poem, to the dynastic traditions of the Danes, create an aura of grandeur, but those of the second part are particularly closely related to Beowulf because they deal in detail with the wars of the Geats and the Swedes and the uneasy peace that Beowulf has maintained, and they provide an ominous sense of the dire consequences of Beowulf's death. The effect is to guarantee Beowulf's "reality" by associating him with known heroic actions, such as Hygelac's raid on the Franks, where he escapes by swimming (again!) to safety. To criticize *Beowulf* for putting the unimportant material (the monster-slayings) at the centre, and the important (history) at the edges, is to misrepresent the mixed nature of the genre. The author is using the heroic traditions of Germanic history, for which he and his audience have great respect, to authenticate stories that in themselves he believes to have greater moral significance. There are even moments when he passes judgment on the heroes of Germanic history, such as Heremod, as if to compare them unfavourably with Beowulf—quite explicitly in one case—and there is no doubt that the continuous theme of greed, betrayal, and vengeance in the allusions comes to have a sharp contrasting relevance to the unsullied self-sacrifice of Beowulf. It is doubtful whether they were chosen for this purpose: it is rather that heroic action, once deprived of its own values, can easily come to seem a bloody saga of meaningless violence. These values are not questioned in the poem, but they come close to being undermined by the idealization of Beowulf. Against this we have to set the admiration for heroic life that sustains the poem, the solemn courtly etiquette of Beowulf's reception in Denmark, the strong sense of loyalty in Beowulf's relation to Hygelac, or Wiglaf's to Beowulf, and the majestic funeral obsequies at beginning and end. The mixed and richly ambiguous nature of the poem is the result not of imperfect grafting but of a genuine admiration for heroic society.

It is not only through its history that the poem is given heroic stature, but also through its manner, which is consistently lofty and grand. The complex network of allusion is matched by an equal complexity of style, all directed to the celebration of heroic society, as if the author, having once ensured that it need not be pagan, felt free to evoke all its glories. The narrative, particularly in bravura passages such as the setting forth of Beowulf for Denmark or the arrival at Heorot, is infinitely slow and measured, rich in texture, heavily brocaded, with the circuitous and allusive method of narration reflected in techniques of style such as variation and circumlocution. There is a strong liturgical element of celebration, with parenthesis—*þæt is soð Metod*[13] (that is the true Lord)—functioning as a kind of *Alleluia*. Elaborately sought-out periphrasis concentrates on the nominal element, so that a static, compositional effect is built up, in which action has an ordained quality: "he killed the sea-monster" becomes

> heaþoræs fornam
> mihtig meredeor · þurh mine hand.[14]

(The rush of battle carried off the mighty sea monster by my hand).

There is little interest in the sequence of events, or in suspense. We often know the results of actions before the actions themselves, and we always know their meaning. Heroic action and heroic society are presented as a formal design, all the parts of which press upon our apprehension at the same time: the building of Heorot is balanced by an allusion to its destruction, the description of the celebrations at Hrothgar's court by foreshadowing of the treachery that is soon to disrupt its harmony. These are all techniques of heightening style and grandeur, but they contribute also to another impression of *Beowulf*, perhaps the dominant one. The taut and sinewy narrative of Icelandic saga is artful in its own way, but only in arrangement: the events speak for themselves, positively, in their own terms. Behind the narrative in *Beowulf*, however, there is always the pressure of other potential meanings—meanings that transcend the world it speaks of and bring a sense of its inexorable pastness.

II

In one literature of Western Europe, however, the heroic strain, so blurred in Old English, stands forth clear and unmistakable, as a reflection of a society that re-created, by a unique series of historical coincidences, many of the preconditions of heroic literature, and that acted not only to sustain and preserve but also to renew it. Iceland was settled between about 870 and 930 by Norwegian nobles and yeomen who resented Harald Finehair imposing his sovereignty on the whole of Norway, and who had courage and independence enough not to submit, and wealth enough to seek an alternative. The physical barriers to communication within the island made every settlement virtually independent, but a strong instinct for law, especially for the intricacies of legal manoeuvring, led to the establishment in 930 of the Althing, the Icelandic assembly to which every man of substance would ride yearly. There was no executive, however, and the enforcement of law rested ultimately on private vengeance: that is, on the sanction of the violence of a heroic society. The aristocratic oligarchy of families proud of their ancestry and jealous of their cultural heritage was ideally suited to preserve and foster heroic traditions, and the development of a large national literature was encouraged by other factors: there was no royal court, and therefore no elite culture separating itself from the body of society, such as lies behind romance; no royal dynasty, on which celebration of the past would tend to concentrate; no need for myth-making, because the origins of the nation and of every man in it were known to all; no rigid class system, because even chieftains were farmers; and no large cultural communities, only homesteads that had to be culturally self-supporting and that therefore encouraged the development of oral narrative tradition. The country as a whole was geographically remote from Europe, and free from fear of aggression, but it was no more cut off than it wanted to be, and Icelanders, with their taste for journeying and with a language that was understood over much of Northern Europe, could bring back all they needed of intellectual stimulation from the mainland. All the court poets of Norway from the 10th century onward were Icelandic.

Above all, Iceland survived its conversion to Christianity more or less unchanged. The settlers brought the worship of the old Northern gods—principally Thor—with them, but the practice of the religion was pragmatic and undemanding, and when Óláf Tryggvason showed himself prepared to press hard for Christianity, and sent firebrand missionaries to stir up converts, the Icelanders acquiesced at the Althing of the year 1000, and Christianity became the religion of the commonwealth. The acceptance of Christianity is described in *Brennu-Njáls saga* as an act of deliberate policy, to prevent division within the country,[15] and reveals an extraordinary political sophistication and instinct for national survival. Things went on probably much as before, with Christianity practised publicly and heathen rites performed in private, as described in *Grettis saga Ásmundarsonar*.[16] In another respect, however, the coming of Christianity had an essential part to play in the development of Icelandic literature, because it introduced the Roman alphabet and the practice of writing on parchment, for which the native runic script never seems to have been used. The first results of this were translations of Latin homilies and lives of saints, but the powerful historical sense of the Icelanders soon asserted itself, especially through Ari Þorgilsson (d. 1148), whose *Íslendingabók* (Book of the Icelanders)—a factual, annalistic account of Icelandic history, flowering into eloquence for the Conversion—is the foundation of Icelandic historiography and the oldest example of narrative prose in any Scandinavian language. Ari had much influence on the *Landnámabók* (Book of Settlements), written soon afterwards, a detailed account of the early settlers, with genealogies that were used in all subsequent family sagas. The extraordinary preoccupation of the Icelanders with their own national history—for which the only English equivalent is the *Anglo-Saxon Chronicle*—is further demonstrated in ecclesiastical works such as the *Kristni saga* (the story of the Conversion) and the sagas of the bishops, written from 1130 onward; in the sagas of contemporary history, many of them compiled in the *Sturlunga saga* of Sturla Thorðarson (d. 1284); and in the historical sagas of the kings of Norway, culminating in the superb *Heimskringla* of Snorri Sturluson (1179–1241). It achieves its ultimate literary expression in the family sagas, or sagas of the Icelanders, which are essentially a heroic interpretation of Icelandic history, written just at the moment when the society that they celebrated was collapsing into civil war and Norwegian domination.

380

The Icelandic renaissance of the 12th and 13th centuries did not, however, confine itself to native material, nor to prose: it is from Iceland, too, that there comes the most significant body of heroic poetry on the traditional Germanic themes of the Age of Migrations. It is in the form of short lays, mostly to be found in the late-13th-century Codex Regius known as the *Poetic Edda* or *Elder Edda*, copied in the early 13th century from manuscripts no longer extant; the poems themselves may date from anywhere between 800 and 1200. The material of the heroic lays is that with which we are familiar from allusions in Old English poetry, principally Burgundian-Frankish history of the 4th–6th centuries, so hammered to the heroic shape that virtually all historical reference is lost. As usual in heroic narrative, political history is "personified" into family quarrels, the defeat of the Burgundians by the Huns in 437, for instance, being represented in the blood-feud of Gunnar (Gundicarius) and Atli (Attila). Historical time is collapsed so as to bring together in a strong dramatic sequence characters as far apart as Jǫrmunrekkr (Ermanaric, d. 375) and Brynhild (the Frankish queen Brunehild, d. 613). The lays, at their best, present heroic action in starkly concentrated form: the actual narrative is cryptic and allusive, the focus being on the drama of character, with much direct speech. Often events are shaped to a pattern of action and reaction, as in the barbaric *Vǫlundarkviða* (Lay of Wayland—who is also mentioned in the Old English *Deor*) or in the great *Atlakviða* (Lay of Attila), which is unusually explicit in its celebration of the heroic ideals of steadfastness, loyalty, and stoic endurance in the face of death.[17] Another set of lays, such as those of Guðrun, concentrates the action even further, to a dramatic outburst by one of the characters, in which a complete knowledge of the story is assumed, and the poet develops the emotion aroused at the high peak of the action in a principal character. Others build up the action towards some famous paradox or dilemma of heroic behaviour, such as Sigrun's curse on her brother Dag when he comes to tell her that he has slain her lover Helgi (who himself slew their father), in the second lay of Helgi Hundingsbana. The tendency of all is to expose for us the complex intricacies of heroic motive and behaviour at a moment of naked truth.

The very starkness of these lays means that they exist in a kind of void, and the compiler of the *Poetic Edda* shows his awareness of this in the prose patchwork with which he tries to link them. There are other signs of syncretism, too, such as the linking of the lays of Helgi with the *Völsung* cycle by making Helgi a son of Sigmundr. We can recognize in this the attempt to subdue the heroic fragments to a larger and more

coherent narrative pattern. The later lays (in so far as they can be dated)
also include some pot-boilers—such as the *Guðrúnarhvǫt*, a catalogue of
Guðrun's causes of lamentation after she had lost her two sons by yet
a third husband—and some rather desperate psychological analysis of
motive, as in *Brynhildar Helreið*.

These poems are worth mentioning, but they are like fragments of noble
statuary compared with the living heroic spirit of the family sagas.
The growth of these from historical writing has already been suggested:
they drew from written sources, such as genealogies, skaldic verses, the
Landnámabók, and the writings of Ari, as well as from oral tradition.
Most of the characters in the sagas, and many of the events, are undeniably
historical—a cowshed *was* burnt at Bergþórshvoll—and the networks
of cross-reference built up through the genealogies with which each
character is introduced give a powerful air of historicity to all the sagas.
But they are not confined by history, and the best of them shape the
material to larger artistic purposes in the manner of a realistic historical
novel. They are all set in the period 930–1030, the so-called Saga Age,
when the conditions of Icelandic society reproduced most nearly the
conditions of heroic society—a period near enough to be real, because it
dealt with the actual ancestors of the writer and his audience, but far
enough away to be tractable to the artist's shaping hand. Within the
frame of historicity, the writer can manoeuvre freely so as to enact his
purposes through narrative. Grettir, for instance, was a historical outlaw
who died about 1040, but the accumulation of material about him is
largely legendary: the traditional anecdotes are expanded, new ones
invented, and motifs of great antiquity attached to him, such as the
fights with the troll-wife and with the giant in the cave under the waterfall
(both *Beowulf* analogues). There is even some influence from romance,
in the incongruous final episode of Lady Spes in Constantinople, which
we may attribute to the late date of *Grettis saga* (it was written in the early
14th century, and is the last of the authentic family sagas). But the
multiplication of adventures is not wanton, because all have their part
to play in tracing the course of Grettir's heroic, luckless, and sardonic
outlawry to the last unforgettable fight on the island of Drangey. Nor
can the marvels undermine our sense of the authenticity of the narrative,
the close-grained texture of realism that is built up in a thousand details
of setting, of farm and homestead, of Icelandic nights and winters,
of landscape, such as the casual mention of the "frozen thatch" as Glámr
and Grettir tumble struggling out of the door (Ch. 35), or the equally
casual sense of shared knowledge of a familiar and real place:

There is some marsh-land stretching away from the ridge with much grass-
land, where Thorbjorn had made a quantity of hay which was just dry.[18]

Other sagas also draw material from traditional legend: the *Laxdœla
saga* is a deliberate reworking of the Sigurðr-Brynhild-Gunnar story,
not out of antiquarianism, but as a tribute to its efficacy for demonstrating
the ethos of heroic society in action. The same saga can also take up
events from contemporary history and work them into the artistic pattern,
as the story of Ásbjǫrn wiping his sword on the clothes of Vigdís (whose
husband he has just slain) in the *Sturlunga saga* is repeated at the slaying
of Bolli, by Helgi and Guðrun.

The historicity of the narrative is on the whole less important than
the authentic *air* of historicity that is undeniably conveyed: the best
sagas are not always the ones that are truest to the details of history.
Eyrbyggja saga, for instance, is probably as near to historical fact as any
of them, dealing as it does with a variety of events in the life of a whole
district, but its authenticity is shapeless, and it is manifestly less successful
as a saga than *Hrafnkels saga Freysgoða*, which is beautifully shaped to its
purpose and yet has little basis in fact, some of the leading characters
never having existed. The issue is presented in its most crucial form
in the saga of Egil Skallagrímsson, which is plausibly attributed to
Snorri Sturluson himself, and which is the most grandly "historical"
of all the sagas, with famous scenes at the courts of King Athelstan, and
of Eirik Blood-Axe in York, where Egil, a skaldic poet, gets out of a
tricky situation with the poem *Hǫfuðlausn* (Head-ransom). Moreover, the
treatment Skallagrím receives at the hands of Harald Finehair, and his
decision to leave for Iceland, are an accurate explanation, in condensed
form, of the whole settlement of Iceland; and no saga gives a more reliable
picture of the Viking ethic, as in the forays in Kurland and Frisland, with
the gratuitous slaying of stock and aristocratic contempt for the
villagers.[19] But *Egils saga Skallagrímssonar* is harsh and unsatisfying as a
whole, and the explanation must be that there is too much history in it,
and non-Icelandic history at that. Snorri wove his saga from a quantity
of authentic verse by Egil, and from other sources, which provided him
with plenty of saga material, but he had to provide his own motives, and
although the avarice he ascribes to Egil is of heroic dimensions, it is too
mean a motive to satisfy us. The scenes where Egil sits and sulks after
the battle of Vínheiðr because Athelstan has not rewarded him as he
deserves,[20] or struggles from his death-bed to bury his treasure so that his
family shall not get it,[21] are in the end merely comic. *Egils saga* has facts,
but dubious truth, where other sagas have truth, but dubious facts.

The method of narration in the sagas is objective, impersonal, and cool. There is little overt comment, and action and speech alone reveal character. When a character is introduced, his genealogy is given, so as to ensure his historical placement, but rarely any sketch of his character. Dialogue is restrained, even to a stylized cultivation of laconic understatement:

> Ulf the Unwashed saw this and said, "That was a heavy blow, Hrut; you have much to thank Queen Gunnhild for."
> "I have the feeling that these will be your last words," said Hrut.
> At that very moment Atli noticed a gap in Ulf's defence and hurled a spear that went right through him.[22]

The reticence of the narrator creates an extraordinary tension: the spring is wound in silence, and the outburst of passion, when it comes, is overwhelming, like Bolli's reply to Guðrun's taunts after the murder of Kjartan.[23] The eye of the narrator is firmly fixed on the scene before him: there are no vertical levels of meaning, no idealism, no sentiment, no irony, no didacticism. The audience is rarely told the significance of an event. It is up to them, for instance, to recognize in Thorkell's repeated question about Auðr's reaction to her brother's death his desire to see her suffer for having first unwittingly been an agent in arousing his jealousy.[24] The texture of the narrative is so seemingly transparent that we are given the sense of things happening as we watch. What is left unspoken comes to have tremendous weight and pregnancy, and perhaps it is a mark of the slight romantic tendency in the *Laxdæla saga* that it succumbs in the end to the temptation to allow Guðrun to speak her mind:

> Then said [her son] Bolli, ". . . You have not told me yet whom you loved best. . . ." Then Gudrun said, "To him I was worst whom I loved best."[25]

The objectivity of the narration does not, of course, imply any canons of naturalism. Events are left to speak for themselves, but they are so shaped and ordered that they can speak in only one way. It is not to any larger scheme of values that they are made to refer: Christianity, as we have seen, is mostly irrelevant in the sagas, and it is only a late work such as *Grettis saga* that ends on a note of pious penitence, reminiscent of *Guy of Warwick* or the *Mort Artu*, and even there it concerns Thorstein, not Grettir. The conversion to Christianity described in the middle of *Njáls saga* has no issue in the narrative: it is part of a series of legal and political manoeuvres, followed by a return to business as usual—the complex processes, legal and otherwise, of vengeance—with God now as a convenient ally:

> Said Ámundi the Blind, "May God judge between us." He walked out of the booth. At the door he turned once more, and at that moment his eyes opened.
> "Praise be to the Lord my God," he said. "His will is revealed."
> He ran back into the booth right up to Lyting, and sank his axe up to the haft into Lyting's head.[26]

If there is any transcendental significance to events, it is in the operations of fate that the sagas (like the lays) find it, and all the sagas use dreams, omens, prophecies, and curses to foreshadow the course of events. Sometimes it is on a small scale, like the episode in *Njáls saga* when Sæunn is found cudgelling the pile of chickweed that is later to be used as kindling in the burning of the house;[27] sometimes it provides the whole frame of the story, as in *Grettis saga*, in the terrible curse of Glámr's ghost.[28] The most elaborately fatalistic of the sagas is *Gísla saga Súrssonar*, where the narrative is skilfully contrived to display the behaviour of the hero as if in the hands of an impersonal fate, represented through his dreams.

But for the most part the allusions to fate are not an explanation of events but a device to impress on us the inevitability of action as it issues from character. Every saga traces a course of events whose logic is inviolable once it is set in motion. Nothing is arbitrary, except where character is shown at its most convincing in acting arbitrarily, as in the marvellous scene of Gunnar's sudden decision to remain in Iceland and defy the sentence of exile:

> "How lovely the slopes are," he said, "more lovely than they have ever seemed to me before, golden cornfields and new-mown hay. I am going back home, and I will not go away."[29]

The motivation of the action, the basis of the conflicts, is that with which all men are familiar in their daily lives—love, property, status—and the men of the sagas fight in the midst of their daily lives: Gunnar is ridden down by Otkel as he goes out to sow his seed, and Flosi and his followers delay their vengeance until they have been home from the Althing to see to the haymaking.[30] But it is the characteristic nature of heroic society to raise the actions of a man in these conflicts to a higher, more crucially exacting level not only by insisting upon the need for a man to maintain the honour and integrity of himself and his family, but by at the same time denying him any resource to do so except his own courage. The public vindication of reputation is essential, and the law, with its elaborate apparatus of compensation and reconciliation, can act as a forum in lesser matters. The Althing, like the United Nations Assembly, was valuable because it brought some pressure to bear on a man to behave so as to gain credit in public opinion. But ultimately every man was his own law-man, as in the heroic society of the modern Western, and the code of violence and personal vengeance was the only resort. Every saga has as its recurrent theme and as its high peaks the readiness of a man to die fighting rather than to surrender the integrity that resides in his honour or loyalty.

This is simple, but there is more to it than this, for there is a code of restraint as well as a code of violence. It is essential not only that a man should die fighting, but that he should face death with equanimity: whence the elevation of the "death-quip" into a stylized feature of the saga, as in Bolli's words when he is pinned to the wall of his dairy by a spear:

> Then spoke Bolli, "Now it is safe, brothers, to come nearer than hitherto you have done."[31]

A man must choose to die in the way that is fitting, as Kjartan does by riding on to the ambush with a depleted company of followers:

> "Thorolf the thief," he said, "shall not have that matter to laugh at that
> I dare not ride on my way with few men."[32]

And he does it again by throwing aside his sword when he sees that it is Bolli who intends his death. So too does Skarp-Heðinn, in accepting Njál's advice to stay in the house, against his own better judgment:

> ". . . I do not mind pleasing my father by burning in the house with him,
> for I am not afraid of dying."[33]

The death of Njál, composing himself as if for sleep with his wife, with their small grandson between them, has a tincture of martyrdom about it, but it is unbearably moving not because of this but because it is so fitting that the old man should die in this way:

> Now the main beams fell down from the roof. Skarp-Heðinn said, "My father must be dead now, and not a groan or a cough has been heard from him."[34]

These are the great moments of saga, the moments when its values are displayed for us at their loftiest, but they are not the only ones in which nobility of action—what they themselves called *drengskapr* (lack of meanness)—tempers violence. Not to slay an enemy asleep or unarmed, not to scorn a brave adversary, and to offer one's hospitality to a mortal foe (as Flosi does to Kári at the end of *Njáls saga*)—these are the marks of *drengskapr*, and it is found too among Eyjólfr's band of cut-throats when they are thwarted in their search for Gisli by his wife Auðr, who throws the bribe-money in Eyjólfr's face:

> Then Eyjolfr said: "Seize the bitch and kill her, woman or not!" Havard has something to say: "This errand has been poor enough, without this coward's work. Stand up, men, and do not let him get his way in this."[35]

These values lie for the most part beneath the surface of the sagas, which are solidly realistic and often comic. The characters are individuals, not types or symbols, and they have an identity—Skarp-Heðinn above all—that is the stronger for never being discussed or commented on, but revealed only in word and action. They have that strongest of all claims to reality, the capacity for the unexpected, such as Bjǫrn the White, who has all the makings of a traditional coward, but who fights well from behind Kári's back.[36] Only occasionally, as in Kjartan, does idealization threaten this reality. Women play a large part in the action, especially as instigators of revenge—the *hvǫt*, or inciting, is a traditional saga motif—and they too have their own individuality. Love is a major motive for action, but there is no discussion of its nature, and one can see, in the ease of marriage and divorce as described in the sagas, why idealized codes of love took no root in Icelandic literature.

The density of the portrayal of historical and real life should not disguise from us the sophisticated and stylized art of these narratives. They have a characteristic structure, beginning with a complexly co-ordinated series of events and a web of genealogies, out of which are drawn the major characters and their relationships, essential to the motivation of the action that follows; the pace then quickens, as the theme of conflict is announced, and the action concentrates into a series of waves, of wrong and vengeance, action and reaction (as in the heroic lays), lengthening in violence, with pauses of peace between, to the final climax, which is preceded by a deliberate slowing-down of tempo and more elaborate staging. Journeys abroad provide relief and variety, but they are never digressions, and the narrative at its best has both perfect unity and perfect economy. There is a degree of stylization, as in the use of foreshadowing devices, or in techniques of symmetrical structure (especially in the *Gísla saga Súrssonar*), all of them designed to bind the narrative to its central theme and purpose, and the theme is usually concluded with some stylized and memorable act of heroism.

The literary conventions of saga are strong, and they had their influence on the writing of history, just as they themselves used history. Snorri saw history as a series of kings' sagas, and his brilliance as a historian is a literary brilliance, in which he shapes and orders political events to themes of personal conflict of the saga type. In the early history of the Battle of Stiklestad, for instance, Kalf Arnason is just a name, a traitor: in *Óláfs saga Helga*, Snorri supplies him with a motive for revenge in the king's slaying of his stepson Thorir, and presents the conflict in vivid detail, all invented. In the saga of King Óláf Tryggvason, there is the same raising of pitch when history offers saga material of honour, bravery, and vengeance, as in the story of the capture of the Jomsburg Vikings,[37] or the death of Jarl Hákon after a waking-match with the thrall Kark.[38] In the saga of King Harald (part of *Heimskringla*), events are selected and dramatized to reveal character in action, and there is even use of the stylized conventions of symmetry and foreshadowing.[39] Many of the historical facts that can be checked are inaccurate, and it is this literary attitude to history that makes the "Vinland sagas," incidentally, such a teasing problem in interpretation.

The later mythical and romantic sagas represent a sad decline. Under the influence of the Norwegian translations of French romance that were becoming known from the mid-13th century onward, a work such as the *Völsunga saga*, for instance, loses the human in the superhuman, history in marvels, and the heroic spirit in mere heroics. *Hrólfs saga Kraka* finds it difficult even to take itself seriously, and pads out the decayed myths of the Skjǫldung dynasty with stock romance motifs—father-daughter incest, an elfin mistress, the sword in the stone—and ludicrous embroidery such as the episode where Bothvar props up the monster he has killed so that his friend Hjalti can claim credit for killing it.[40] The sagas that are frankly comic, the so-called "lying sagas," are more successful: in these the element of phantasy and violent comedy that is present in some of the family sagas is elevated to a pitch of wild absurdity, and at the same time is given, in the best saga manner, an "authentic" historical setting. It is recognizably the same literary art as in the family sagas—the sense of character, the use of dialogue to advance action, the symmetry of structure—but the authors have stopped taking it seriously. It is essential to heroic literature that it should take itself seriously:

romance and religion evaporate the seriousness of the heroic and create in its place another *sen*, equally serious, but comedy simply stands it on its head.

III

Like Icelandic saga, the Old French epic appears in written form when the society it celebrates is on the point of disintegration. Most of the best *chansons de geste* were written in the 12th and early 13th centuries, but the events on which they are based are mostly from the 9th and 10th centuries. The historical tradition, however, was much less strong than in Iceland, and from the first the *chanson de geste* is a mixed form, with Christianity, comedy, and the marvellous, as well as heroic action, and with a wider and more complex range of material than the saga. An added complication is that the processes of transmission, which in Iceland are fairly simple, are affected by the heroic martyrologies that grew up along the pilgrim routes; furthermore, extant *chansons de geste* are themselves often *remaniements* of earlier written versions, with a strong and spurious element of syncretism at work in the grouping of the many *chansons* into three or four great cycles. The best of the French epics, by no accident, is the earliest, the *Chanson de Roland* (*c.* 1080), which is based on earlier lays—as the evidence of the Spanish *Nota emilianense* (*c.* 1050) suggests—but which is in itself a work of superb assurance and panache. The events it describes have a historical nucleus in the destruction of Charlemagne's rearguard at Roncesvalles in 778, but they have been shaped to a more decisive pattern. Roland has emerged from the shadowy mention of history as the hero, Charlemagne (who was 38 at the time) has taken on patriarchal status, and the battle—which in fact was of no historical significance, being an ambush by marauding Basques as Charlemagne was returning from Spain, where he had been fighting battles in alliance with one group of Saracen princes against another group—has becomes a crucial event in the wars of Christendom against the Infidel, a matter of survival. In this it reflects the pressures of later history, just as the large-scale mobilizations and cross-country marches at the end of *Njáls saga* reflect the turbulent history of Iceland in the 13th century: the Saracen menace was becoming formidable in the 11th century, as the kingdoms of Aragon and Navarre knew to their cost, and the First Crusade was preached in 1095. The theme of the *Chanson de Roland* is elevated, but not fundamentally changed, by being made part of this holy war. The mixture of heroic and Christian is quite different from *Beowulf*, with its ambiguity of motive and settled melancholy, for the material is much more single-mindedly heroic, dealing with the defence of the land, the *tere major*, and of a narrow place, against the invader. The fact that "we" are Christians and "they" are Saracens is a happy coincidence, as it is with the Vikings in *The Battle of Maldon*, and does not affect the essential interpretation of the material. It is only when the warfare is displaced to an alien territory—when Charlemagne goes on his spurious crusades, for instance, in the *Pèlerinage de Charlemagne à Jerusalem*—that the heroic atmosphere evaporates, and the authors have to make up for the loss of reality with sensations, marvels, and buffoonery.

There is a good deal of Christian ceremony and paraphernalia in the *Chanson de Roland*—masses are frequently attended, and the warriors recognize the convenience of having Archbishop Turpin at hand to shrive them before they go into battle—but it does not affect the behaviour of the characters. The archbishop fights like the rest of them, and Roland puts the religious motive briskly in its place in his famous speech before the battle, as an accessory *casus belli* to proper heroic action:

> Ben devuns ci estre pur nostre rei:
> Pur sun seignor deit hom susfrir destreiz
> E endurer e granz chalz e granz freiz,
> Si'n deit hom perdre e del quir e del peil . . . .
> Paien unt tort e chrestïens unt dreit. . . .[41]

> (Here we must stand to serve the king:
> A man must suffer great hardship for his lord's sake,
> Endure great heat and cold,
> Lose his skin and hide, if need be . . . .
> Paynims are wrong and Christians are right . . . .)

The idol-smashing and forcible baptism that follow the later battle are simply an extension of the fighting. Religion is never investigated, simply taken for granted, as a guarantee, or stamp of approval, for actions that proceed from more fundamental motives: defence of the land, honour, loyalty, and the spoils of war. Christianity comes more into prominence in death-scenes, such as that of Roland, with its sensational piety, and in the later part of the poem in connection with Charlemagne, as part of the apparatus that elevates him to near-divine status. Not only is he ageless and prescient, but he seems also to have a special relationship with God, which enables him to bid the sun stay still to give him time to catch the Saracens, or to fight against the emir Baligant under the direct supervision of God, who sends Gabriel to remind him of the fact when he is momentarily shaken.

Roland is affected by none of this. His behaviour is that of the authentic hero: he welcomes the assignment to the rearguard *because* it is suicidal, and refuses more men (he has 20,000, but it is the same basic situation, on a much more grandiose scale, as Kjartan riding on with two followers, or Beowulf asking to cleanse Heorot without the aid of the Danes). He refuses to blow his horn to summon help, and thirsts the more for battle because the odds are so great. He has a superbly boyish, clean-cut, unquestioning heroism, like Shakespeare's Hotspur, and rides forth to battle *le vis cler e riant*[42] (with a clear and laughing face). He also has character, conveyed not through commentary, which is of the brevity typical in heroic literature—*Rollant est proz e Oliver est sage*[43] (Roland is brave and Oliver is wise)—but through speech and action. He can realize his mistake in not summoning help, he can be spoken to and reproached by Oliver, and his gentleness when struck by Oliver is as much part of his characteristic identity as the overweening pride that makes him spend his last strength trying to break his sword so that it shall not pass into anyone else's hand. Roland may not have much history, but he has reality, and so has Ganelon, who is far from being a mere villain. He is portrayed with deliberate nobility, especially on his embassy to the Saracens, tough and brave, setting his life on a gamble, and the scene where his hatred and jealousy are provoked by Roland's casual insolence is a marvellously economical revelation of motive. His plan is directed personally against Roland, not against Charlemagne or Christendom: he makes this his defence, and is answered with equal juridical realism by Thierry, who argues that offence against a king's officer is just as much treason as offence against the king. Even the Saracens have a proper respect paid to them. They are admired as fighters, and although huge numbers of them are thrown into battle they are not degraded to ludicrous sub-human monsters, as in some later *chansons de geste*.

The assurance, the confidence in its own values, of the *Chanson de Roland* is nowhere better displayed than in the beautifully muted ending, where Charlemagne receives Gabriel's call to go to war again with weary resignation. Unlike the hero of romance, he can afford to be tired and dispirited, because he has been engaged in real events. Nevertheless, *Roland*, though invulnerably heroic itself, prepares the way for the intrusion of other elements and the mixing of the genre. Roland's lady is spoken of once, and does nothing but die on hearing of his death; but she is there, whereas she would be unthinkable in *Beowulf*. The earth shakes as Roland's death draws near: events are beginning to assume the kind of supernatural significance that will eventually absorb their heroic and human reality altogether. Battle description is detailed, but extravagant and stylized, and the jousts of romance are anticipated in the etiquette of ordeal by battle, between Pinadel and Thierry, at the end of the poem.

The earlier *chansons de geste* preserve something of the heroic simplicity of *Roland*. *Gormont et Isembart*, for instance, deals with the battle of Saucourt (881), when a Viking army ravaging Normandy was defeated by Louis III. In the battle, the Viking Gormont is assisted by the exiled Frankish Isembart, who thus fights against his own kinsmen, even at one point his father—a *locus classicus* for the demonstration of heroic values in conflict—and dies. The *Chanson de Guillaume* is unhistorical, but it has authenticity enough to deal at length with a defeat of the French at the hands of the Saracens, the battle of L'Archamp, and the death of the noble hero Vivien. Guillaume himself, although he fights on, has something of the weariness of Charlemagne at the end of the *Chanson de Roland*. The comedy of the giant scullion Reneward, in the latter half of the *Guillaume*, is probably a later addition: it is quite different from the comedy of the cowardly Tedbald, which is by no means alien to heroic tradition. In *Aymeri de Narbonne*, however, *chanson de geste* is shown in its later, more mixed and sophisticated form. It begins as a sequel to *Roland*, portraying Charlemagne burdened with remorse at the death of the *douze pairs*, and seizing on the chance of besieging Saracen-held Narbonne as a way of revenge. But his warriors are tired, dispirited, and want to go home; only the young Aymeri, son of Ernaut de Beaulande, has the spirit of aggression, and he takes the city. This exaltation of youth over age is characteristic of the new growth of the *chanson de geste*, almost a symbolic rejection of the old, and is expressed in extreme form in *Gui de Bourgogne*, where the young warriors treat Charlemagne's veterans with disdain, and seize a city in defiance of their king. *Aymeri de Narbonne* displays the same detachment of the hero from the majesty of the king and the land's defence: Aymeri fights for himself; he is essentially embarked on a quest for honour, through the winning of a woman as well as victory in battle. Crusading, for him, has become a gesture, not a necessity for an expression of the noble life. Aymeri has all the makings of a romance hero.

Another, earlier generation of epics deals not with defence against the Saracens but—like many Icelandic sagas—with the internal disputes of a heroic society, in this case the early feudal society of 10th-century France. This was an age of comparative anarchy, when the claims of duty and allegiance, like those of law in Iceland, counted for nothing unless backed up by personal power, and by the bands of armoured horsemen that were the instruments of such power. It was a society permanently geared for warfare, its values those of loyal vassalage and comradeship in arms. Heroic legends grew up around historical or quasi-historical figures of the age, and they were often attached to Carolingian epic: for instance, Geoffroi Grisegonelle, the founder of Anjou, is made Charlemagne's standard-bearer in the *Chanson de Roland*. In this way, *chansons de geste* such as *Raoul de Cambrai*, *Renaud de Montauban*, and *Girard de Roussillon* could interpret 10th-century history in 12th-century terms as a stylized heroic version of the strains in society as kings brought their nobles under firmer control. The expression of this conflict in *Raoul de Cambrai*, in the hero's unjust, cruel, and barbarous attempts to recover his just rights, is characteristically authentic. *Huon de Bordeaux* starts from problems and conflicts that are equally real—Charlemagne's right to exile Huon for having killed his son Charlot, and Huon's right to defend himself in an ambush—and the court scene is detailed and realistic, but the story escapes from this into a phantasy-world where Aubiron (Oberon) solves the problems, and even appears at the end to save the hero, like a fairy in a pantomime. The epic background is there, although Charlemagne has declined into a treacherous and malicious tyrant, but it soon gives way to a romantic quest, which itself is a rich conglomeration of Celtic, oriental, and folk-loristic motifs, and by turns romantic, heroic, burlesque, satiric, and sentimental. Its very richness makes an evolutionary view of *chanson de geste*, in which purity is the norm, difficult to sustain after the *Chanson de Roland*. What we have is the adaptation of the form, in competition with (and imitation of) the *roman courtois*, to a more aristocratic and varied taste. In addition to marvels, women come to play a larger part, and there is a good deal of courtship, with the trappings of *amour courtois*, though not its ethos: sometimes the women, like Rigmel in *Horn*, make the advances. A special feature is made of the rustic *vilain*, such as Gautier in *Gaydon*, who fights in rusty armour on an old mule and has no knowledge of orthodox methods of warfare: this is a form of class-comedy designed to identify and reassure the audience. Finally, *chanson de geste*, like most mediaeval forms of narrative, is made the vehicle for Christian didactic themes, as in *Ami et Amile*.

The transition from epic to romance is demonstrated partly in this gradual adaptation of heroic forms. Transplantation—in historical terms, the substitution of crusades for wars of survival—is a major factor in this adaptation. When the "Matter of France" is transplanted to Britain, for instance, it loses its heroic potential, until, in one or two later pieces, the English adaptors can make the transition from "we (French)" to "we (Christians)," and produce—in *Rowlande and Ottuell* and the *Sege of Melayne*—heroic battle-poetry of some power and authenticity, though of an unsophisticated kind. The "Matter of Britain" suffers a similar sea-change in crossing the Channel. Arthur at home, or at least in English, is a heroic figure, and in Laȝamon's *Brut* (*c.* 1220) is portrayed as such. Geoffrey of Monmouth and Wace, from whom Laȝamon derives his material, are both historians or pseudo-historians, and Geoffrey's interest is certainly more in inventing stories than in developing themes through them. But Laȝamon is a poet, a shaper of history, and he expands the role of Arthur to produce a poem that is near to epic. His influence carried down to the "alliterative revival" of the 14th century, and to the great alliterative *Morte Arthure*, in which heroic and tragic themes are blended. Arthur is portrayed as a great national hero, brought to his downfall by *hubris*. Malory embedded a paraphrase of this northern English poem in his vast prose compilation of Arthurian legend, *Le Morte Darthur* (*c.* 1470), but he dissipated its heroic mood, deprived it of its ending, and was on the whole concerned with quite different themes. In France, however, Arthur was from the start a "romantic" figure, king of a never-never land on the Celtic fringes, and his court was useful chiefly as a starting-point for romantic adventures or as a linking device. Heroes of Arthurian romance have a duty to their own hearts rather than to Arthur or to the group. They seek the enemy by going out alone from the city, not by defending it, and the court has meaning only as a base from which various individuals make periodic flights into the wilderness, or go on "quests," where chivalric values can be tested *in extremis*.

> The series of adventures is thus raised to the status of a fated and graduated test of election; it becomes the basis of a doctrine of personal perfection....[44]

The "Matter of Antiquity" had little opportunity to be heroic, in any Western literature. The Alexander story, for instance, was mostly an excuse for the accumulation of sensational and exotic adventures, and as a moral against pride; and the story of Troy, the greatest of the mediaeval stories of antiquity, was derived not from Homer but from crude Latin prose epitomes, in which the material had already been boiled down to bare facts, as if waiting to be clothed in the garb of romance—which is what they received in Benoît de Sainte-Maure's

Roman de Troie (1154–73). Even the legends of Trojan ancestry—which most western European nations cultivated, following Virgil—could do nothing to elevate the Troy story to heroic level. Benoît is frankly romantic, developing the stories of Medea, Cressida, and Polyxena, whereas the dominant tone in Guido delle Colonne, his 13th-century Latin adaptor, is moralistic, scientific, and antiquarian.

Degenerate epics, however, do not represent what is best in mediaeval romance, which is a new growth, not a mere adaptation. Its germs are in Celtic legend (which provides a whole new corpus of unsullied story-material, devoid of *sen*, and waiting to be infused with one), Arabic philosophy (which offers the basis for an idealized view of love), and changes in society (which provide the opportunity for these new interests to be exercised). Heroic literature rests on heroic violence, anarchy, and wars of survival; but these are not the conditions of the 12th century. The stabilization of Europe's boundaries, in which the menacing ring of barbaric tribes of the 10th century became well-established Christian kingdoms in the 12th; the growth of political order and of effective centralized administrations in the hands of university-trained men; the acceleration of economic activity, especially through the rapidly expanding luxury trade with the East—all these were factors in creating the conditions for a more leisured and self-regarding literature. It was an age of ideals, and of codes of ideals. The growth of the institution of knighthood, which had little to do with property or government, is an example of this idealism; knighthood came to have a strong religious colouring, and was a potent influence in literature, where it helped in the creation of concepts of social conduct and of refinement of feelings and manners. The concern of romance with the minutiae of codes of behaviour is reflected in the development of elaborate legal systems based on canon law to replace older methods (such as the ordeal) based on an appeal to the supernatural, and in the development of systematized rules of monastic life. It is in the monasteries also that we find a concentration, corresponding to that of romance, on the individual, on self-knowledge and introspection, on the value of feeling. St Bernard and Chrétien de Troyes are two sides of the same coin: both recognize a new intensity of inner life in the striving after perfection.

Endurance, staying and protecting what he has, have now become less important to the hero than questing, in accord with an idealistic code. It is not his business to protect his people from the Saracens, but to venture in search of the Grail. Naked courage is important, but subsumed in obedience to a set code, of chivalry and the higher erotic sensibility, and it is to the demonstration of this code in action that mediaeval romance, at its best, is dedicated. It is the literature of a self-conscious and sophisticated elite, and its aim is not to reproduce the behaviour of aristocratic society as it really is, but to provide a series of "machines" in which the ideals of that society can be proved and tested. Marvels and magic are the stock-in-trade of romance, partly (in popular romance, wholly) because they are interesting and exciting in themselves, but partly because they are as good material as any for the proving of the romantic hero. What the hero does is still important—he must still be brave and loyal in his actions—but what he thinks and feels is more important, and aristocratic romance spends much of its time in the minute dissection of sensibility to demonstrate these thoughts and feelings at work, and above all to demonstrate their value.

Northern France in the late 12th century is the focus for the development of the new forms of literature, particularly the courts of Eleanor of Aquitaine and Marie de Champagne. Society here—ordered, leisured, wealthy, sophisticated, woman-orientated, culturally ambitious—provides the conditions for the rapid emergence of romance in the precise and identifiable form that it has from the start in the work of Chrétien de Troyes (*fl.c.* 1180). The Arthurian world of *Erec*, *Lancelot*, and *Yvain*— and (to a lesser extent) of *Cligès*—is an unreal world. Its geographical location and boundaries are vague; the names of real places are occasionally mentioned but they serve only to enhance the general atmosphere of unreality. Castles spring as if from the ground, and the landscape throws up features—a forest, a tower by the sea, a river—only in order to provide opportunities for adventures. Time is equally unreal. Calogrenant, in *Yvain*, waits seven years to tell the story of his adventure by the spring, but we are not told why, or what happened in those seven years, or given any sense of time as a continuum. The action, above all, is "romantic" in its essence. The knight is not impelled by dynastic or territorial ambitions, nor by the need of defence: he chooses to go out from a place of safety to seek adventures because it is only through adventures that he can prove the values by which he lives—can prove his reality, in fact. Trial through adventure, the process of self-realization, is thus the central feature of romance, and it takes the form of feats of arms, often arbitrary and meaningless in themselves, rather than war. Action exists in a void, without exterior motivation or consequence. There is no *reason* for the knight, Laudine's husband, to defend the spring, nor for Arthur to ravage the country if the spring is undefended. Reality, when it is convenient, is simply evaded: wounds can always be healed with magical ointments, life protected with magical talismans. In heroic literature the hero's death is the most perfect moment of his life, the proof and demonstration of the value of his life: in romance, with its sense of the educative possibilities of life, death is irrelevant.

Combined with the romantic unreality of setting and action there is, in Chrétien and in mediaeval romance in general, a mass of explicit detail on the exterior forms of life, the rituals of welcoming and departing, washing and eating. The dress that Guenevere gives to Enide, the festivities at Erec's wedding or his coronation, the trappings of Enide's horse (right down to the story of Aeneas carved on the saddle-bows), are all elaborately described, in a manner that recognizably refers to contemporary reality, though in a heightened and idealized form. Such descriptions serve to illustrate the function of romance as a celebration of chivalric society in its ideal state, as well as a confirmation of its values, although in later romance, particularly popular romance, they tend to degenerate into more or less fantastic imitations of supposed "high life."

The material of Chrétien's romances, chiefly from Celtic sources, is turned with considerable skill to illustrate the knight's search for perfect self-realization through adherence to a code of chivalry and courtesy. The arbitrariness of the legends, with their frequent outcroppings of symbolism, is thus given a new significance in the exploration of the interior man and his growth toward a "civilization of the heart." The narrative tends to concentrate on crucial situations, on problems of conscience and right conduct posed by the conflict of love, morality, and knightly honour. *Erec et Enide*, for instance, sets the necessity of loving against the necessity of sustaining the life of honourable action, and the hero achieves through adventure an understanding of the balance between the two, which is then underlined in the episode of Mabonagrain, and the all-absorbing, stultifying nature of the love-relationship there. In *Yvain*, the hero's boyish zest for battle, by contrast, makes him completely forget his promise to his wife, and he must be tempered in adversity through a graduated series of generous and selfless acts. *Lancelot* is simpler, for it takes as its axiom that love is supreme among the knightly values, and then presents in extreme form the dilemmas of the lover in the cultivation of this self-transcending sensibility. The ultimate proof of Lancelot is that he is prepared to sacrifice even honour to his love: he rides in a cart, like a common criminal, when he is unhorsed in pursuit of Guenevere—though even here Guenevere later reproaches him for hesitating; and when Guenevere bids him to do so, he strives a whole day in tournament to do his worst and show himself a coward, declaring his submission to her will in quasi-religious terms.[45] There is something oddly comic, though, in the episode where he fights with backhand blows because he cannot take his eyes off Guenevere, and the romance as a whole has a theorem-like quality, as if it were organized simply to demonstrate, in the most extravagant possible situations, the supremacy of love. *Lancelot* is true, in its way, to the type of romance, and the hero to the type of the romantic hero; but its views on love should not be taken as authoritative in the romance tradition, particularly on the necessity of adultery. Not much is made of Arthur, nor of the fact of adultery, and Chrétien could hardly have foreseen the heart-ache he would cause to writers (such as Malory) who took Arthur seriously, or the heaven-sent opportunity that the liaison would give to those who wished to moralize upon the fall of the Round Table.

In Chrétien's other romances, love is the prime but not the sole motive, and it is usually marital love. Sophisticated flirting is distinguished from love, as in Laudine's behaviour to Arthur's knights, and love is specifically associated with marriage in Guenevere's advice to Alexander and Soredamors in *Cligès*.[46] The romances are full of theorizing about the nature of love, and of long introspective soliloquys in which characters analyse their feelings and engage in fastidious debates about fine points of conduct: Laudine on whether she can love the slayer of her husband (yes, because he is therefore the better man); Soredamors on how she should address Alexander. There is a strong quasi-didactic element in the way details of the code of love are introduced, like laws, and some elaborate exercises in the metaphysics of love, on how two hearts can become one, for instance, or on the strange paradoxes of joy and grief in the malady of love.[47] Chrétien provides an impeccable pedigree for *roman courtois*, and presents the new form with a distinctive sense of its identity, but he suggests already the limitations of romance, the thinness of its stylized view of reality. The narratives are wonderfully contrived to their purpose as exemplars of the action of a recognized code of values, but not to much else, and the analysis of thought and feeling is satisfying chiefly as a formal display of rhetorical skills. To talk of it in the same terms as the psychological analysis in a modern novel is to mistake its nature utterly.

Within the limits set for it by Chrétien, the *roman courtois* continues as the dominant form of fictional narrative, though with shifts of emphasis within these limits, and produces its greatest masterpiece in the Middle High German *Tristan* of Gottfried von Strassburg (*fl.* 1210). Gottfried based his work (which is unfinished) on the *Tristan* of the Anglo-Norman

Thomas (*fl.* 1160–70), a poem of which only fragments survive, but sufficient to suggest a psychology of passion more subtle and more powerful than Chrétien's. Gottfried carries this skill in analysis of motive and sentiment into his own poem, but transforms the story by investing it with religious and mystical overtones, as in the paradisal idyll of the Cave of Lovers. The Prologue speaks of love as a faith that can be proved only in sorrow, and of the story of Tristan and Isolde as a martyrdom that will create such faith:

> Ir leben, ir tôt sint unser brôt.
> sus lebet ir leben, sus lebet ir tôt.
> sus lebent si noch und sint doch tôt
> und ist ir tôt der lebenden brôt.[48]

> (Their life, their death are our bread. Thus lives their life, thus lives their death. Thus they live still and yet are dead, and their death is the bread of the living.)[49]

The freedom of allusion to the Eucharist is typical of Gottfried's remarkable blend of the sensual and the spiritual, which enables him to see passionate love as the highest expression of the "noble heart." He was freer to do this in *Tristan* than anywhere else because the immorality—indeed, criminality—of the passion, of which Chrétien spoke more than once, reflected the workings of fate through the love-potion, not the nature of the lovers. There is much psychological analysis in *Tristan*, but it is limited in scope, and the train of motivation, of cause and effect, always works back to the irrationality of the potion. This sophisticated development of a primitive story motif is typical of Gottfried, who handles the narrative with immense skill, subtlety, ingenuity, and learning, but rarely makes any attempt to reshape it. Where the narrative defies interpretation, as in the episode of the ordeal of Isolde or the attempted murder of Brangane, he withdraws into irony and self-conscious manipulation of the narrative point of view, so that the story is at once magnificently moving and also complexly layered in interpretation. It is the only other work of mediaeval fiction that matches Chaucer in sophistication.

It is interesting that *Tristan* should have been written at almost the same time as the *Nibelungenlied*, the last great flowering of the heroic legends of the Germanic peoples. This poem bears the mark of its origins in an age of romance, in the first part especially, with its opulence of setting (especially detail of dress), conventional love motifs, and taste for the marvellous. Siegfried is idealized out of existence—it is poor heroic stuff when the enemy stop fighting as soon as they recognize the hero[50]—

and Brunhild is a mere cipher once she has shed her Amazonian background; Siegfried's magic cloak is enough to make nonsense of the games at Brunhild's court, and even the marriage substitution scene is faintly ridiculous. The crudities of the professional entertainer are much in evidence. But in the second part of the poem, which is derived from a different source,[51] the narrative rises to its theme of Kriemhild's revenge.[52] Although there is still some exaggeration (as of numbers), the romantic paraphernalia are discarded, and the poet concentrates on the heroic defence of the hall by the Burgundians against the attacks of the Huns, treacherously instigated by Kriemhild. Hagen and Volker take on an authentic heroic identity, something of the barbaric nonchalance of Skarp-Heðinn, and the conflict of motive in the attackers—particularly Rudiger, who is placed on a knife-edge of contradictory loyalties—is well developed. It is perhaps overdone and long-winded by Icelandic standards, but the emergence of such a powerful heroic theme out of such rubbish is something of a miracle for its time.

In France, meanwhile, the glorification of erotic sentiment reaches its dizzy apotheosis amid the phantasies of Renaut de Beaujeu's *Le bel inconnu*, at the same time that other romances, such as *La chastelaine de Vergi*, develop themes of conflict within the code of courtly values, with more realistic settings and analysis of motive. There is a vogue for romances such as *Guillaume de Dole* and *Le tournoi de Chauvency*, which are little more than idealized *reportage* of courtly tournaments and fetes. Such writings suggest not growing realism, but a growing tendency of life to imitate the literature to which it had been exposed for so long. A wealth of new story material was adapted to the prevailing conventions of the *roman courtois*, as in *Floire e Blancheflor* or the *Cléomadès* of Adenet le Roi, with their strong infusion of oriental motifs. The purity of the form is constantly compromised, and there is a continual tendency, especially under the pressure of popularization, for the adventures to lose their *sen* as a means of testing and proving chivalric values, and to be multiplied and sensationalized for their own sake.

A particular development is that of the Breton *lai*. These *lais*—the best of which are attributed to Marie de France, who was more or less a contemporary of Chrétien's—are more "romantic," in the modern sense, than any other mediaeval writing. They tell little of battles or the exercise of prowess, but concentrate on the expression of a fine and tender sentiment of love, and a delicate evocation of the magical and the supernatural. They are lyrically expressive and sentimental in a way that makes Chrétien look hard, direct, and masculine, and some, such as

Le chèvrefeuille, are close to the sung *lais* (concentrating on the moment of emotional crisis) in which the form is said to have had its origin. The Breton *lais* have a marked fondness for magical machinery—elfin mistresses (*Lanval*, *Graelent*), steerless ships (*Guigemar*), shape-changing (*Yonec*)—and for touching romantic incident—love-tokens (*Guigemar*), foundlings (*Le fresne*), the magical revival of the dead (*Eliduc*), the swan as messenger (*Milon*). *Lanval* is a tightly constructed narrative, with some strong dramatic motivation and a keen and accurate interest in the intricacies of the law, but the quality of most of the *lais* is a suffused melancholy and enchanting irrationality, which is not entirely brought about by the displacement of themes from their original context.

At the opposite extreme, and far more influential, is the spiritualization of romance. It can be seen that romance presents, in its pure form, a kind of transposed Christian idealism. Romances are the saints' legends of secular chivalry, and Lancelot, in Chrétien's poem, offers himself—that is, his honour—as a martyr to a self-transcending love. The quest is close to the pilgrimage, and once Chrétien had popularized the theme of the Grail in *Perceval*, it was not difficult for later writers to invest it with a powerful spiritual significance. Out of this movement grew the prose *Perlesvaus*, the *Parzival* of Wolfram von Eschenbach (*fl.* 1200–20), and the great prose romances of the 13th-century Vulgate cycle, above all the *Lancelot* trilogy (*Lancelot*, the *Queste del saint Graal*, and the *Mort Artu*). Secular chivalry and love are transcended in spiritual chivalry and love, Galahad replaces Lancelot as the ideal knight, and the Grail story becomes the climax of the whole history of the Round Table, and the source of its downfall. The penetration and annexation of the *roman courtois*, as of courtesy and knighthood itself, by monastic and spiritual concepts was easy, given the essentially idealistic nature of romance and its establishment of a validity for human experience in codes and ideals that lie beyond the world of reality. As we have seen, heroic literature, with its assumption that events are real and important in themselves, is much more resistant to transcendental interpretations.

The secular idealism of love and chivalry is meanwhile transferred to allegory, where it finds its most fruitful and influential expression in the *Roman de la rose* (1225–37 and *c*. 1275). The analysis of sensibility in Chrétien had always threatened to become detached from character as a formal debate—for instance, in the dialectic of love and hate in the heart of Yvain before the fight with Gauvain—and character itself often verged on the exemplary, so that it needed only a slight shift of technique to isolate these features from narrative and to redispose them according to the characteristic manner of allegory. Relieved of the need to maintain a fiction and to pay attention, even in the most rudimentary fashion, to consistency of character and the logic of events, the poet could now evolve a much richer kind of psychological analysis, in which the formal structure, inorganic and encyclopaedic, reflected the idealized structure of the mind. The conflicts created by the love-code could be accurately represented through the deployment of personified abstractions in the psychomachia of love, just as its paradoxes could be expressed through formal features such as the traditional oxymoron of love's pain and joy. This kind of allegory of love-experience, in its turn, is adapted to the expression of religious experience with a didactic purpose, typically in the *Pèlerinages* of Guillaume de Deguilleville.

Romance suffered from these successive erosions, and it is in a sterile form, emptied of its significant content as the embodiment in narrative form of the ideal values of chivalry, courtesy, and love, that romance reaches England—or expression in English, rather, because French romance had been cultivated in England as long as in France. It is the historical accident of the depressed status of English in the 13th and early 14th centuries that accounts in large part for the debased state of most Middle English romance. By the time a literate English audience was available, contemporary French romance was a degenerate form—endless catalogues of sensational and pointless adventures, little different from later *chansons de geste*. It was these that were translated to satisfy the tastes of the new audience. *Guy of Warwick* and *Bevis of Hamtoun* (both *c.* 1300) are the type of this first development of romance and *chanson de geste*, respectively, in English, and the Auchinleck manuscript—a collection of mostly inferior romances of about 1330 (Advocates' Library, Edinburgh, MS. 19, 2, 1)—represents the tastes of the rising bourgeoisie for which they were written. Even where the English professional romancers were working on earlier and more authentic French source material, they could convey little of their sophistication of analysis and idealism, and in simplifying them they destroyed their essential nature. *Ywain and Gawain*, the English adaptation of Chrétien's *Yvain*, keeps the story more or less intact and is not incompetently done, but the treatment assumes that the audience will take little interest in matters of the heart, or in analysis of conflict and motive, and the characteristic identity of romance is thus dissipated into a mere string of adventures. In all these adaptations of French romance—and the great bulk of English romance is drawn from French originals, extant or inferred—the tendency is the same: the love-interest is suppressed, and women are portrayed as explosive objects, best avoided; the niceties of the chivalric code are coarsened into bravado; the marvellous is greeted with open-mouthed wonder; and the principle of structure is that if one fight with a giant is good, two are better, with perhaps a dragon thrown in for good measure. A few romances are exempt from these strictures—*Havelok*, for instance, is the nearest that English has to a genuine folk-epic, and the treatment of the French originals in *Floris and Blauncheflour* and *Sir Orfeo* shows some delicacy—but the level of the whole is that of popular entertainment.

Certain particular tendencies manifest themselves in English romance. There is none of the Cistercian spiritualization of the French *graal* romances, but there is a marked strain of more homely piety and morality, in which romance blends with pious tale and exemplum, and an equally marked reluctance to indulge the erotic streak of elite French romance. These are probably class-conditioned reflexes. More significant in its consequences is the growth of realism, of a more substantial content, in English romance. In part it is genre realism: that is, it has to do with lowly settings, as in certain scenes in *Octovian* or *Isumbras*. But there is also a growing tendency to invest the characters of romance, having deprived them of their ideal *raison d'être*, with real existence and realistic motives. Nothing could illustrate this development more clearly than *Sir Degrevaunt*, where the action is set in motion by the legal technicalities of trespass and the hero's first action is to send a letter of complaint to his offending neighbour. The trappings of romance are soon reassumed, but the shift of ground is quite fundamental, and it seems to be general to English. It is found on a low literary level, as in Thomas Chestre's version of *Launfal*, where the early poverty of the hero, which Marie de France merely hinted at, is given extended realistic and dramatic treatment; and it is also found on the very highest level, in Chaucer, the *Gawain*-poet, and Malory. All three were under powerful imaginative pressure to give new interpretations to the traditional material of romance, and all worked with a freedom that was impossible in other, elite-dominated cultures. Chaucer, in so doing, almost breaks the old moulds: in giving a philosophical dimension to "The Knight's Tale," for instance, he involves himself in a contemplation of human suffering that the romance form will hardly bear; and in "The Franklin's Tale" he gives a dramatic reality to the situation of a woman whose husband goes off on "adventures" (the situation of Laudine in *Yvain*) that almost persuades us to think of Arveragus as a dedicated prig. Only some dextrous manoeuvring returns us to the charmed world of romance. In *Troilus and Criseyde*, above all, Chaucer invests the romance of love with a human substantiality, a sense

403

of character and drama, as well as a powerful philosophical undertow, which makes it by far the richest of mediaeval narratives.

Sir Gawain and the Green Knight (*c.* 1380) shows similar pressures at work. In its form and accessories, the poem is the very archetype of romance: the riding forth of the knight to an essentially unreal adventure, the celebration of chivalric values, the heightened picture of chivalric society. But the narrative introduces a second test, of which the hero is unaware, and weaves around him a complex web of dilemmas, so that in the end—human nature being what it is—he fails. It is the attention to human nature as it is that is so extraordinary and so liberating in *Sir Gawain*—traditionally, romance is concerned with no such thing— and the failure of the hero finally breaks the association of romance with saint's legend, and forges a new one with realistic "low-mimetic" fiction.

Malory shows no such certainty of touch. He is overwhelmed by the multifarious nature of his sources, by their palimpsest-like and often contradictory layers of *sen*. But when he is able to work with clear direction, as in the last three books of *Le Morte Darthur*, he is drawn towards a humane and tragic view of the narrative. He rejects the transcendental interpretation of his Vulgate sources, and refuses to accept that secular chivalry, having failed in the quest of the Grail, is worthless and doomed. Instead, he places the responsibility for the fall of the Round Table squarely on a human conflict of loyalties, and traces in Lancelot— tentatively at first, but with growing conviction—the lineaments of a genuine tragic hero.

The development in Chaucer, the *Gawain*-poet, and Malory is towards a concept of narrative in which the fiction is self-validating: in which, that is, the "truth" of the sense is to be found not in the reference of the narrative to some external scheme of values, but in the events themselves and their reference to human behaviour. Romance as a type of narrative is exemplary in a way that all other types of mediaeval narrative before Chaucer—saint's legend, pious tale, exemplum, fable, allegory—are exemplary. Even *fabliau*, which is often referred to as a type of realistic fiction, is realistic only in its accidentals, in its genre-scenes of bourgeois life. Its realism is governed and limited by the rhetorical doctrine of the decorum of styles. In its essence, however, *fabliau* is as "idealistic" as romance—is, in fact, the antitype of romance, or anti-romance. Romance is sustained by an ideal of self-transcendence and super-humanity: *fabliau* is sustained by an ideal of self-debasement and sub-humanity. Romance celebrates courtesy, loyalty, generosity, and self-denying love: *fabliau* celebrates avarice, cunning, and lust. It would be hard to say that one is more "realistic" than the other. *Fabliau* has its myths, one of the most powerful being that lust in the young is comprehensive and unquenchable; it also has its own rigid social etiquette, as in the duping of the bourgeois and the violation of his wife by some errant member of the classless intellectual elite, such as a scholar or a cleric. The picture of bourgeois life is realistic only in so far as it is designed to provoke an amused response on the part of an aristocratic audience— for it must be emphasized that *fabliaux* are designed for elite audiences, not for the bourgeoisie that they so mercilessly ridicule. The taste of the middle classes is for romances of high society, for escapist entertainment, not for unflattering pictures of their own marital inadequacies. Despite their scandalous inventiveness and occasional wit, the *fabliaux* are a limited diet. It is a final tribute to Chaucer's greatness as a narrative poet—certainly the finest that the Middle Ages produced—that he was able to release into even this stereotyped narrative form the complex world of reality, and to explore in it, in "The Merchant's Tale," even the possible borderlands of disgust and pity. Chaucer, with his complexly layered narrative personality and elusive point of view, carried mediaeval narrative far beyond the limits that it had set for itself, into territories where we have only just begun to catch up with him.

References

Editorial note: Medial points have been inserted to separate half-lines of alliterative verse quoted; they are, however, absent from the various editions of works of alliterative poetry cited below.

1. See NORTHROP FRYE, "Theory of Modes," *Anatomy of Criticism* (Princeton 1957), p. 33.
2. *Beowulf* 1063–1159; a fuller analogue to the independent but fragmentary *Fight at Finnsburg*.
3. Or prose saga: see C. E. WRIGHT, *The Cultivation of Saga in Anglo-Saxon England* (Edinburgh 1939), p. 80.
4. *Beowulf* 2329–32.
5. *ibid.*, 1747.
6. Translation in R. K. GORDON, *Anglo-Saxon Poetry* (London 1926).
7. *Beowulf* 2794–8.
8. *ibid.*, 1558; cf. 706.
9. *ibid.*, 572–3.
10. *ibid.*,180; cf. 92.
11. *ibid.*, 2469.
12. *ibid.*, 3181.

13. *ibid.*, 1611.
14. *ibid.*, 557–8.
15. *Njáls saga*, Ch. 105.
16. *Grettis saga Ásmundarsonar*, Ch. 78.
17. *Atlakviða*, stanzas 21 and 34.
18. *Grettis saga Ásmundarsonar*, Ch. 48: trans. by G. A. Hight, *The Saga of Grettir the Strong* (London 1965), p. 127.
19. *Egils saga Skallagrímssonar*, Ch. 46 and 69.
20. *ibid.*, Ch. 55.
21. *ibid.*, Ch. 85.
22. *Njáls saga*, Ch. 5: trans. by M. Magnusson and H. Pálsson (paperback: Harmondsworth 1960).
23. *Laxdæla saga*, Ch. 49.
24. *Gísla saga Súrssonar*, Ch. 14.
25. *Laxdæla saga*, Ch. 78: trans. by Muriel Press, *The Laxdæla Saga*, (London 1964).
26. *Njáls saga*, Ch. 106.
27. *ibid.*, Ch. 124.
28. *Grettis saga Ásmundarsonar*, Ch. 35.
29. *Njáls saga*, Ch. 75.
30. *ibid.*, Ch. 53 and 124.
31. *Laxdæla saga*, Ch. 55.
32. *ibid.*, Ch. 48.
33. *Njáls saga*, Ch. 128.
34. *ibid.*, Ch. 129.
35. *Gísla saga Súrssonar*, Ch. 32: trans. by G. Johnston, *The Saga of Gisli* (Toronto 1963), p. 51.
36. *Njáls saga*, Ch. 150.
37. *Óláfs saga Helga*, Ch. 46.
38. *ibid.*, Ch. 55.
39. See, for instance, Ch. 4, 27, and 80–2.
40. *Hrólfs saga Kraka*, Ch. 58.
41. *Le chanson de Roland* 1009–15.
42. *ibid.*, 1159.
43. *ibid.*, 1093.
44. E. AUERBACH, *Mimesis*, trans. by W. Trask (paperback: New York 1957), p. 118.
45. *Lancelot* 5910–3.
46. See, for instance, *Yvain* 2457, and *Cligès* 2302.
47. *Cligès* 2830 and 3076.
48. *Tristan* 237–40.
49. Translation by A. T. Hatto (paperback: Harmondsworth 1960).
50. *Nibelungenlied*, stanza 216.
51. Known to scholars as *Diu nôt*: it exists only by hypothesis.
52. Kriemhild is the Guðrun of Icelandic legend.

CHAPTER 12

Courts and Courtly Love

Elizabeth Salter[*]

When Geoffrey of Monmouth, in 1137, gave to the floating stories of the British hero Arthur a form that the Middle Ages could accept as history, he shaped the king and his court in an image already becoming familiar in his century. For it was, indeed, a century of great kings, whose territories and influences ranged almost as widely as those of the half-legendary Arthur, and whose courts were far more brilliant than Camelot. It was, significantly, a century of expansion; the frontiers of Western Europe were enlarging rapidly, and new contacts with other cultures were enriching Western art, literature, and life.

The gradual reconquest of Spain from the Arabs, in the late 11th and early 12th centuries, opened up to the Spanish princes of Aragon and Castile the splendours of Moslem civilization. From then on, in a wealthy mixture of elements—Spanish, Moslem, Jewish, and southern French—the courts of Aragon and Castile were held to be the most colourful in all the Christian world. On a state visit to Castile, Louis VII of France declared that "like magnificence was not to be found in all the world—he had never seen a display equal to it."[1] Alfonso II of Aragon (1162–98) was a lavish patron of music and literature; to his court came artists from all countries: "I have never," said the troubadour Arnaut Daniel, "left the court of Aragon without wishing to return next day, in one single leap."[2]

The same tide of wealth that had washed over the Spanish courts reached the south of France as well: the courts of Poitou, Toulouse, and Provence exploited the new-found benefits of commercial treaties with Spain, Syria, and Italy. Out of material luxury and aristocratic leisure, poetry of sensibility and passion grew; we shall have occasion to say more of the ladies of southern France and the poets of their courtly

* Professor of Mediaeval Literature and Director of the Centre for Mediaeval Studies, University of York.

households: Eleanor of Poitou and Aquitaine, Beatrice Countess of Die, Azelaïs of Ventadorn.

The Norman conquest of Sicily in the 11th century paved the way for the achievements of the 12th, with the great kings Roger II (1105–54) and William I and II (1154–89). Under their rule, the intellectual and substantial wealth of the eastern world was gathered for the service of the West. Twelfth-century scholars were drawn to Sicily for its learning and piety. Twelfth-century travellers were astounded by the symbols of magnificence that met them: the royal brocades of rose and gold, the churches of Palermo with walls of "sheet of gold . . . panels of coloured marble . . . all inlaid with gold mosaic, and garlanded with leaf-forms in green mosaic. . . ." The glove worn by the Sicilian kings at coronation still spells dominion in its pearl-encrusted state.[3]

To the north, at the court of Duke Henry and Marie of Champagne, theologians and writers of lyric and romance found encouragement and patronage: the function of the great secular court as a centre of learning, literature, and art was vigorously demonstrated. The Angevin Henry II of England ruled from Scotland to the Pyrenees: to his Christmas feasts came vassals more powerful than any whom Arthur commanded in the pages of chronicle or romance. His queen, Eleanor of Aquitaine, as famous as Iseult or Guinevere, was celebrated in four languages for her beauty and her wit.

Movement between these courts, between countries, and even between continents, was free in the 12th century. Although it was not yet true that a man might know the streets of Pekin as well as those of Venice or London, scholars, diplomats, soldiers, merchants, and men of religion travelled extensively. Journeying was urged by the voice of a Crusading Church, which pictured the Holy Land in the language of a fairy-tale, a land filled with silver and gold and precious stones, rich in corn and flowing with wine and oil. It was urged by the promise of recovering ancient wisdom and learning: the English mathematician Adelard of Bath searched Syria and Greece in the early years of the century for texts to bring back to the West. John of Salisbury, servant and friend of Henry II, moved untrammelled among countries and literatures, both pagan and Christian. The explorations of Franciscans such as John de Plano Carpini, and those of Marco Polo, still lay ahead, but stories of distant Asian lands were already tempting the imagination of Europe: the kingdom of Cathay, and beyond that, the terrestrial Paradise. It is typical of the 12th century that it produced the legend of Prester John, whose dazzling accounts of his eastern Empire persuaded the pope to send a letter and emissary in reply. Both letter and man vanished over the horizon in 1177.[4]

The results of this easy communication between nations and cultures were rich and varied: eastern peacocks and griffins on the silk copes of English bishops; French saints as stiffly set into gold leaf on the manuscript page as in a Byzantine mosaic; English Madonnas with the long, mournful, and compelling eyes of Spanish ivories; legends that poets, painters, and preachers tirelessly searched for hidden meanings (for example, the legends of the phoenix and the unicorn); exotic heresies, of religion and of love, washed up on the shores of Provence, and fostered in its warm cultural climate; and, indeed, the whole legacy of ancient science and philosophy.

The dynastic ties of the noble patrons of Europe are vital parts of this network. The Norman invasions of Sicily and England in the 11th century were parallel enterprises. In the 12th century, Joan, daughter of Henry II, married William II of Sicily; another daughter, Eleanor, married Alfonso VIII of Castile; a third, Matilda, married Henry, Duke of Saxony, the chief vassal of the German crown. Marie of Champagne was the daughter of Eleanor of Aquitaine and her first husband, Louis VII of France. The counts of Toulouse and Provence were more closely connected by marriage and treaty with the kings of Castile and Aragon than they were with the king of France: Alfonso II of Aragon took the title of Count of Provence; Alfonso VII of Castile received the homage of the counts of Toulouse and Gascony.

The easy passage of scholars, poets, ecclesiastics, and diplomats between these courts had important cultural implications. The rapid spread of romance themes—especially those associated with the Arthurian legend—may have been helped by the marriages of the Angevin princesses. The Anglo-French *Tristan* verse romance was probably written for their mother, Eleanor of England.[5] By 1210, the German poet Gottfried von Strassburg was making his own more complex version of the Tristan story: "their life, their death, their joy, their sorrow."[6] By the end of the 12th century, legends of Arthur were as familiar in Sicily as in Wales: the Isle of Avalon was frequently identified as Sicily, and Arthur was said to have lived in the fortress of Mongibel, or Mount Etna.[7] By 1170, the knights of the Round Table were celebrated in Catalonia: Guiraut III of Cabrera prescribes a list of them as suitable subjects for his *jongleurs*: Tristan, Iseut, Erec, Artus.[8] These phenomena may be partly explained by the lands and movements of the Angevin royal house. Earlier in the 12th century the troubadours of Provence made familiar reference to

Arthur and Tristan, and it is significant that in many such cases the poetry is connected with Eleanor of Aquitaine, or with her father, Guilhem, 10th duke of Aquitaine.[9] Even by the mid-12th century, the court of Poitou was probably a disseminating centre for romance materials.

It is possible that Henry II shared some of the literary interests of his wife and daughters. For him, Chrétien de Troyes may have written his earliest romance, *Erec*; the *Lancelot*, beyond doubt, was made for his step-daughter, Marie of Champagne. Walter Map, clerk and courtier of Henry II, visited Henry of Champagne, and discussed with him "the proper limits of generosity"[10]; from his knowledge of northern European court life comes his major work, *De nugis curialium*—a satire, as its title states, of "the follies of courtiers." The troubadour poets of southern France were as much at home at the Spanish courts as they were in Provence: "It might be said far more truly than in the time of Louis XIV that the Pyrenees did not exist."[11] The very first known troubadour, Guilhem of Poitou, ninth duke of Aquitaine (1071–1127), married the widow of the king of Aragon: the influence of Hispano-Arabic poetry and music upon that of southern France is a serious probability. Aristocratic society on all levels was involved: the marriage of Joan of England to William of Sicily, in 1177, encouraged a provincial poet and his patron from Wales to undertake a romance with a Sicilian setting.[12] The pattern of courtly patronage spanned the Mediterranean and the fringes of the Nordic world: it is true of this century, as perhaps never again, that "what counted for more than the quality or nationality of the writer was the taste, power and riches of the patron."[13] And the patrons for whom many of the great works of the time were undertaken were travelled, sophisticated, and cosmopolitan.

In such a context, it is quite natural that Sicilian architecture of the 12th century should be a triumphant fusion of Norman and eastern-Mediterranean features, and that in the *lais* of Marie de France— probably the half-sister of Henry II, and later Abbess of Shaftesbury— the older stories of Celtic tradition should be touched with the romantic sensibility of 12th-century courtly society. Her *lais* were dedicated to a king: like many writers and artists of her time, she composed for aristocratic patrons on both sides of the Channel. Nor is it surprising that the great English Bibles of the 12th century, sumptuously decorated by monastic artists, should be reminiscent of the glittering mosaics in the Sicilian cathedrals of Cefalù and Monreale. In monastic schools and in the courts of archbishops, the same rich compounding of elements took place: professors from Salerno came to teach and to consult; Byzantine workmen visited England; Byzantine copybooks were available to English artists. The Bury and Dover bibles[14] are splendid examples of the co-operation of native and eastern-Christian art-forms in monastic ateliers of Canterbury and East Anglia, made, no doubt, for ecclesiastical patrons whose tastes were no less refined and sophisticated than those of kings. The households of Theobald, Archbishop of Canterbury (1139–62), and later that of Thomas à Becket, rivalled any secular courts for the learning and literary talents of the men connected with them; John of Salisbury, Walter Map, and Gerald de Barri, philosophers, humanists, satirists, and historians belonged to such circles.[15] Students as well as men of the world, they are as much a product of mediaeval court society as Chrétien de Troyes.

This age of movable boundaries, geographical and cultural, raised few barriers between religious and secular domains. The strong centripetal force exerted by courts and courtly patrons did not result in art and literature of an unmixed, secular kind. Just as 12th-century illuminated manuscripts, made for ritual use in the abbeys and priories of England, sometimes allow subjects taken from contemporary life (bear-baiting and cookery are examples) into the dazzling hieratic designs of their initials,[16] and just as 12th-century capitals in southern European cathedrals draw upon classical and oriental sources for human and animal forms of violent life but of essentially non-religious significance,[17] so the literature born of courtly society often admitted what a later age might judge paradoxical interests in patrons and writers. At the court of Henry and Marie of Champagne, for instance, aristocratic romance and what appears to be a philosophy of adulterous love developed in a setting of erudition and piety. Henry took more than a layman's interest in the theological debates of his day, and Marie's interests seem to have been served equally by works of spiritual edification and by treatises on the rituals of love. Eleanor of Aquitaine was well known as a patroness of courtly lyric, but at least one long semi-historical poem was dedicated to her, the *Roman de Brut* (*c.* 1155) of the Norman clerk Wace. The context in which secular literary forms such as the courtly romance came to full growth was by no means entirely secular. The ardour with which the knight dedicated himself to service in love was often not so far removed in intensity from the ardour of spiritual dedication: the sufferings of the hero in Chrétien de Troyes' *Lancelot* are sometimes phrased in language that calls to mind the anguish of the religious life. The closeness of the secular and the religious quest in this century is pointed for us, on a historical level, by the crusades:

411

it is symbolized finally by the Grail legend, in which primitive adventure and high spiritual endeavour are compounded.

The richness and fluidity of the European scene in the 12th century could hardly be better illustrated than by Sicily. This island was the meeting-point of east and west, of Latin and Byzantine Christendom, of the ancient and the mediaeval world. Its history is many-layered: for long a part of the Byzantine Empire, it had been under Arab rule for two centuries before the Normans made it the centre of their southern Italian kingdom. Under a Norman dynasty, it maintained the widest, most varied contacts, both commercial and cultural. In Monreale cathedral (begun in 1174) carved capitals of northern French inspiration contrast with interlaced arcading reminiscent of Islamic styles. Byzantine craftsmen were imported to work with textile and with mosaic; and the Palatine Chapel (1132–40), at Palermo, which was built as part of the Norman royal palace, has a European plan, Byzantine mosaics, and Moorish vaulting. If the setting was exotic, the atmosphere was enlightened: Muslim and Christian countries sent their scholars to Palermo, and no religious obstacles were set against either. Arab, Greek, and European co-operated in the service of kings whose yearning for knowledge was limitless. At the court of Roger II, for example, scribes were at work on New Testament manuscripts; here the Arabic geographer Edrisi composed his greatest treatise, and Roger also requested that a large silver map of the world be made. The reigns of William I (1154–66) and William II (1166–89) record even wider intellectual activity—in particular, the effort to make accessible to the Western world the science, mathematics, and philosophy of the Greeks. The first translations into Latin of Euclid, Plato, and Aristotle were made during these years in Sicily. There was, indeed, "no other region where east and west met in such constant and fruitful intercourse."[18]

The connections between England and Sicily were close and significant. English clerks and ecclesiastics were prominent at Palermo: as early as the reign of Roger II, the king's chancellor was a Yorkshireman, Robert of Selby. Two English brothers, Walter and Bartholomew, were successively archbishops of Palermo, and Walter had previously been tutor to the king's children. Richard Palmer, later Bishop of Syracuse, was only one of a large number of English clerks who came to the court of William I, drawn by its reputation for learning. Men such as Gervase of Tilbury served both Henry II of England and William II of Sicily. The long struggle between Henry and Thomas à Becket that ended in Becket's murder in 1170 was fought out at the Sicilian as well as at the English court. Indeed, the marriage of William of Sicily and Joan of England in 1177 was, in some senses, the outcome of those years of busy negotiation between the conflicting parties.

In such circumstances, it would be surprising if we could not find particular, even *personal*, witnesses to the alliance of England and Sicily in fields other than intellectual or diplomatic. For Sicily had untold riches to offer England: not, it is true, the precious bones of Virgil demanded by one visiting Englishman, but artistic riches. The magnificence of 12th-century Byzantine art can still be seen more clearly in Sicilian mosaic than in anything comparable at Constantinople: English travellers to Sicily between 1131 and 1190 must have watched stages in the gradual completion of the decorative mosaic schemes in the Palatine Chapel at Palermo and in the cathedrals at Cefalù and Monreale. And although the shimmering art of mosaic was never attempted in western or northern Europe, it worked potently upon the imagination of European painters. English book-painting of the 12th century, especially in the great Bibles, is often strikingly reminiscent of the mosaics at Palermo: solid, monumental figures; sweeping drapery; deep, rich colours; and lavish use of gold. Wall-painting at Canterbury, using the awesome eastern-Christian imagery of Christ the Judge, probably draws directly for theme and style upon Sicilian mosaic.[19]

The route between Canterbury and Palermo was well used in the 12th century, and it is easy to see how manuscript illumination and fresco might record this. The route between the Welsh border and Sicily must have seen fewer travellers, and it is all the more surprising that the marriage of an English princess to a Sicilian king in 1177 should have roused an obscure Norman-Welsh clerk to write a romance set in Calabria and Sicily. Hue de Rotelande, the poet of *Ipomedon*, and his patron Gilbert Fitz-Baderon, Lord of Monmouth, knew enough, perhaps, of the historical Sicily—even if at one or two removes—to enjoy a phantasy woven around a few familiar places. Ipomedon, heir to the kingdom of Apulia, loves La Fière, Duchess of Calabria, and is aided by the queen of Sicily. The classical past of the Mediterranean world is briefly evoked by names such as Jason, nephew of La Fière, and Medea, queen of Sicily. If *Ipomedon* seems an unlikely product of the Welsh border country, we might recall that contemporary sculpture in some small Herefordshire churches drew on equally varied and far-away sources. The profuse carvings on the doorway at Kilpeck range from older Nordic animal motifs to zodiacal signs of distant classical origin; the figures of evangelists on the chancel arch have no known English prototypes, and their melancholy faces, with high cheekbones, large expressive eyes, and drooping moustaches, have stronger affinities with romanesque sculpture in southern France: from Moissac in Languedoc, for instance, or from churches in Aquitaine.[20] It would be a mistake to assume that those who wrote, designed, and built in the remoter parts of the English countryside lived narrow, circumscribed lives, or were uninformed about the grander worlds of the 12th century. According to the poet Hue, Gilbert of Monmouth had a large library, and we know that the lavish decoration of one Herefordshire church, Shobdon, reflects the travels of its patron to Spain and to southern France on pilgrimage.[21]

But in spite of all its intellectual and artistic treasures, it was not the court of Sicily that had the most immediate and far-reaching influence upon the vernacular literatures of Europe. We know very little of what may have been written in the vernacular at the Sicilian courts of the 12th century. The spoken language was apparently northern French: official documents used Latin, Greek, or Arabic, according to need. The names that survive from those brilliant years are those of scientists, philosophers, theologians, translators: Edrisi, Henricus Aristippus, Eugene the Emir, and so on. It may be, of course, that vernacular literature existed but has been lost. It is hard to believe that the accomplished Sicilian poetry of the 13th century could have been written without precedent from the 12th: at the court of Frederick II (1194–1250) a group of poets—aristocratic and learned courtiers of professional status—composed lyrics in Italian, dealing with human love in a wide variety of modes and forms.[22] But individual though their voices and their skills appear to be (to Jacopo da Lentini, notary at the royal court, we owe the first examples of the sonnet), they turn us more toward the known poetry of the troubadours of southern France in the 12th century than to the unknown court poetry of their predecessors in Sicily.

For, whether we are considering the vernacular poetry of northern French courts in the late 12th and 13th centuries, or that of English and Sicilian court society, we must recognize the vital part played in the shaping of such poetry by the philosophies and art-forms of the troubadours of the courts of Provence, Toulouse, and Poitou. Having said this, we are also committed to recognizing the linked importance of literary activity at the courts of Aragon and Castile, where the troubadours found encouragement and patronage. The literary and political fortunes of Spain and southern France during the 12th century can hardly be separated; it is a great irony that the political union of southern and northern France, achieved in the 13th century by means of the savage

Albigensian crusade, was also the death of the poetry and the civilization of the south.

But before this death much had been achieved and passed on. It is important that the first troubadour poet of southern France whose work has come down to us was Guilhem of Poitou, ninth duke of Aquitaine. For although the troubadours who succeeded him were drawn from many levels of society—some, such as Peire Vidal (*fl.* 1180–1205), were sons of merchants; others, such as Bertran de Born (*c.* 1140–*c.*1215), were of the minor aristocracy; and others still, such as Bernart de Ventadorn (*fl.c.* 1145–80), were sons of tradesmen to the aristocracy—they can all be characterized as "courtly poets." Their verses catered for the refined literary tastes developed at the seigneurial courts of the Midi, and they lasted only as long as did those courts. Although we must not define their work too narrowly—they were highly individual poets, ranging over moral, satirical, martial, and amatory themes—they were most remarkable for their exposition and exploration of one particular kind of love: *amour courtois*, or, as it has usually been translated, "courtly love." This term has the advantage of reminding us that the first extensive formulation of such love in a European vernacular was in the courtly poetry of southern France, but a better term would be that used by the troubadours themselves, *fin'amors*, which expresses the central concept of "purity" and "refinement" in this love, and its rejection of gross sensuality in favour of exquisite emotional experience. This experience might imply both pleasure and pain: if it did not always imply physical fulfilment in love, it invariably implied the desire for such fulfilment.

Without devaluing particular, personal variations among the troubadours on the theme of *fin'amors*, it is possible to find in their verses fundamental agreement on the nature of this love. They present us with an ideology of love, drawing upon the widest range of source materials, and proclaiming a self-justifying system of moral standards with its own precise terminology. This ideology was to influence all succeeding love-poetry in the West, whether it was accepted whole or in part, or was opposed.

More often than not, the love celebrated by the troubadours was an adulterous love, because marriage, based customarily upon material considerations, could not be considered a fruitful ground for the exercise of the finer emotions. The ladies—real or imagined—to whom the poets addressed their verses were noble and married. Hence, this love was secret, and hedged about with difficult conditions: the jealous husband, slandering courtiers, and the preservation of the lady's reputation. It is important to take account of the atmosphere of constant danger and unrest that surrounded the love-relationship; joys were perilously snatched from wastelands of public coldness and indifference. Suffering was an inevitable part of *fin'amors*; it was to be accepted as a kind of discipline that both heightened brief moments of happiness and qualified the lover to progress further toward the goal of his desire. The basic tensions of his state are deliberately increased by the poet-lover, as he imagines and describes, in language both erotic and delicate, the beauty of his lady and their amorous exchanges. Critics have traditionally disagreed about the extent to which the code of *fin'amors*, as expressed in the poetry of the troubadours, admits that total possession of the beloved is the ultimate end of love. In one (perhaps cynical) sense it would be logical to suppose that such possession would be the death of love, as it would be the death of stress and aspiration. In another sense, it would be illogical to ignore what is very evident in Provençal poetry: that physical desire is an integral part of the poet's homage to his lady. If every vestige of hope of final recompense were taken away from him, his court to her would be pointless. One of the most recent studies of *fin'amors* declares quite simply:

> the *fin'amors* of the troubadours was precisely that total love, of heart and body, which was realised in the state of *joie, in totius personae concessione finitur* [it is completed in the yielding-up of the whole person].[23]

Whatever the truth of this, a reading of troubadour poetry makes it clear that erotic delight is celebrated as an essentially ennobling experience, in a total context of generous virtues and considerations. It was therefore easy for the later troubadours of the 13th century, such as Guilhem Montanhagol (*fl.* 1233–58) and Peire Vidal, to deepen the concept of *fin'amors*, recommending it as a compound of virtues—pity, moderation, wisdom, charity—and even as absolute virtue itself.

Fin'amors had its own vocabulary in which to express its special concepts of moral behaviour: the three most important terms were *cortesia*, *mesura*, and *joven*. *Cortesia*, inadequately translated as "courtesy," covered all those qualities that, in the mediaeval feudal contract, made a man a "verray parfit gentil knyght," and that, in the life of *fin'amors*, made him an observant and deserving lover: discretion, generosity, humility, and fidelity. *Mesura*, a blend of patience, reason, and good sense, constituted the inner discipline of the lover in his long trials of fortitude. *Joven* is difficult to define: the reverse of meanness in thought or action, it was used sometimes to signify generosity, sometimes magnanimity. It is easy to see that the possession of both *mesura* and *joven* must immediately involve the lover (and his lady) in complex adjustments of behaviour toward each other and toward the rest of the world. But no one in the mediaeval period seriously supposed that the life of *fin'amors* was an easy one: at the end of the 14th century Geoffrey Chaucer, with mingled fear and pleasure, was writing in his *Parliament of Fowls* of

> The lyf so short, the craft so long to lerne,
> Th'assay so sharp, so hard the conquering,
> The dredful joy, alwey that slit so yerne,*
> All this mene I be love. . . .[24]

The expression of this love-philosophy in the lyrics of the troubadours is as varied as are the personalities and skills of the poets, but certain concepts and conventions are unvarying. Even the poetry of the first acknowledged troubadour, Guilhem of Poitou—who was more often direct and vigorous than subtle in his verbal dealings with love[25]—pays respect to the idea that the lover mutely suffers, fearful of approaching, let alone courting, his lady:

> Ren per autruy non l'aus mandar,
> Tal paor ay qu'ades s'azir,
> No ieu mezeys, tan tem falhir,
> No l'aus m'amor fort assemblar. . . .[26]

> (I dare not send her messages by another,
> So do I fear to anger her:
> Nor do I dare, for fear of doing wrong,
> To show my love. . . .)

His love, in this particular lyric, is a kind of illness beyond his means to control:

> Pus sap qu'ab lieys ai a guerir. . . .

> (For she knows that she alone can cure me. . . .)

The dramatic symptoms of love are already established; we shall meet them again in every succeeding century:

> Per aquesta fri e tremble. . . .[27]

> (For her I shake and tremble. . . .)

* ". . . that always slips away so rapidly" [slit="slideth"].

Guilhem presents a rather enigmatic image as a courtly lover, appearing sometimes to accept and sometimes to mock those finely drawn rituals of adoration:

> Amigu' ai ieu, no sai qui s'es,
> Qu'anc non la vi, si m'ajut fes. . . .[28]
>
> (I have a love; I don't know who she is,
> For, in all truth, I've never seen her. . . .)

A much more consistent and developed version of *fin'amors* comes from the poetry of Jaufre Rudel of Blaye (*fl.* 1147); indeed, if we are to believe the old Provençal biography, it comes from his life too. His seven extant poems tell of an *amour lointain*, a "distant love"; some of these clearly refer to a lady of some standing in France: "all the Poitevin, and all Anjou and Guienne and Brittany, should rejoice in her. . . ." She is married, and aristocratic:

> Luenh es lo castelhs e la tors
> ont elha jay e sos maritz. . . .[29]
>
> (Far away are the castle and tower
> Where she and her husband live. . . .)

Jaufre is by turns despairing and hopeful; he sees nothing but death for himself

> s'alqun joy no.n ai en breumen. . .[30]
>
> (if I do not soon receive some joy. . .).

His consolations come in day-dreams and reveries, but he dreams of substantial and passionate rewards: of taking his love "into a garden, or into a room," of secret night visits, when the lady assures him *tro qu'abduy en siam jauzen* (we two may possess each other).[31]

It is, however, in the account of Jaufre's love for another noblewoman, the Countess of Tripoli, that life seems to strive to fulfil the pattern of *fin'amors* most exactly. According to the Provençal source,[32] Jaufre fell in love with the Countess without having seen her, having been moved by reports of her from pilgrims to Antioch. Setting sail to visit her, he became ill, and reached Tripoli just in time to die in her arms: *et enaissi el mori entre sos bratz* (and so he died in her arms). The Countess took the veil *per la dolor qu'ella n'ac de la mort de lui* (because of her sorrow for his death).

Scholars are sceptical, but the legend—if legend it is—has been built on some facts of history. Tripoli was conquered by the Crusaders in 1109, and given to the Lords of Toulouse, who ruled it until 1200. The connections between the noble houses of Tripoli and Provençal poets could, reasonably, have been close. Several of Jaufre's poems seem to be describing a situation not unlike that of the old story: here is *fin'amors* at its most exquisite—a complex of joy and pain, resolve and despair, a yearning of body and spirit for the unattainable, a life that is tangential to death. Guilhem of Poitou might almost have been thinking of verses such as these when he wrote his parody of *fin'amors*:

> Let no man think it strange that I
> Love one whom I shall ne'er behold.
> No other love as dear I hold
> Save her on whom ne'er looked my eye.
> Who's never told me truth or lie.
> Nor know I if 'twill e'er be told. . . .
>
> She strikes a blow of joy that kills,
> A wound of love that steals my heart. . . .
>
> No man with such sweet ills
> E'er died, rejoicing, from love's dart.[33]

In the lyric "Lanqand li jorn son lonc en mai" (When the days are long in May),[34] the poet contemplates his departure:

> Iratz e gauzens m'en partrai
> qan veirei cest amor de loing,
> mas non sais coras la.m veirai
> car trop son nostras terras loing.
> Assatz i a portz e camis!
> E, per aisso, non sui devis . . .
> Mas tot sai cum a Dieu platz!
>
> (Despairing, rejoicing will I go
> That I may see my distant love,
> But I know not how that may be—
> Our countries are so far apart.
> Countless are the ports and roads!
> And therefore, I cannot forecast. . .
> But all will happen as God wills!)

The rapid fluctuation of feelings (hope, desolation, resolve, resignation), and the acceptance of the essentially paradoxical nature of love (*iratz e gauzens*), make this a classic expression of *fin'amors*. For Jaufre Rudel, as for the 17th-century English poet Andrew Marvell, love is indeed "begotten of despair upon impossibility."[35]

More of the joy of love occupies the lyrics of Bernart de Ventadorn. Of lowly birth, with parents in the service of the Viscount Ebles II of Ventadorn, he enjoyed the patronage of Ebles and of his son Ebles III. At their courts, he learned the craft of poetry: Ebles II, called "lo Cantador," was himself one of the earliest troubadours. Bernart's love for the Viscountess Azelaïs of Ventadorn is part of Provençal tradition:

> mout duret lor amors longa sason enans qe.l vescoms, sos maritz,
> s'en aperceubes.[36]

> (their love lasted a long time before the Viscount, her husband, noticed it.)

Forced to leave Ventadorn, Bernart travelled north to the court of the Duke and Duchess of Normandy; the rest of his love-poetry seems to have been written for the Duchess, Eleanor of Aquitaine, who in 1154 went to England with her husband Henry II and was crowned queen. The interweaving of life and literature in the work of Bernart is therefore very complex, and if we are tempted to see *fin'amors* as a purely aesthetic sentiment existing in words alone, Bernart's story should make us pause. His poetry is agile and passionate: the spring-song of love becomes vibrant in his hands:

> Can l'erba fresch' e.lh folha par
> e la flors boton' el verjan
> e.l rossinhols autet e clar
> leva sa votz e mou so chan,
> joi ai de lui, e joi ai de la flor
> e joi de me e de midons major;
> daus totas partz sui de joi claus e sens,
> mas sel es jois que totz autres jois vens.[37]

> (When the new grass and leaves appear,
> And the flowers bud in the gardens,
> And the nightingale, loud and clear,
> Raises its voice and sings its song,
> I've joy in bird, and joy in flower,
> Joy in myself, and in my lady more;
> On every side by joy I am constrained,
> But she's the joy from which all others flow.)

His desires find dramatic expression:

> e baizera.lh la bocha en totz sens,
> si que d'un mes i paregra lo sens.[38]

(And I would imprint her mouth with kisses
So that the marks would be seen a whole month.)

Through the elaborate modes of language and sentiment, personality and feeling run strongly; Bernart's lyrics often sound the same notes as the earlier Latin lyric, "Karissima, noli tardare!" (Beloved, delay not!)

Per Deu, domna, pauc esplecham d'amor!
Vai s'en lo tems, e perdem lo melhor![39]

(By God, lady, little use we make of love!
Time flies, and we waste the best part.)

Among the lyrics addressed to Eleanor of England and Aquitaine are lyrics of sadness in separation, when the lady went to join her husband in England, and Bernart remained in France; their situation is likened to that of Tristan and Iseult:

Plus trac pena d'amor
de Tristan l'amador,
que.n sofri manhta dolor
per Izeut la blonda. [40]

(More pain of love I feel
Than Tristan, that lover
Who suffered much agony
For the fair-haired Iseult.)

It is interesting that some of the first references in French literature to the Tristan story should be found in this context: whatever the nature of the relationship between Eleanor and Bernart, the poet clearly felt it appropriate and powerful to offer the queen homage out of an old, tragic story. More than one man would write of the Tristan legend for Eleanor; but Bernart de Ventadorn pictured her as a character in that legend.

The sense that this poetry of southern France was, in its content and in its style, the work of an elite is confirmed most dramatically by the lyrics of Arnaut Daniel (*fl.* 1180–1210). A *gentils homs*, who, so it was said, loved a lady of Gascony but was not loved in return,[41] he wrote of his longings and frustrations in language that is part frank display, part veiled enigma. Elliptical, self-mocking—

I am Arnaud who loves the wind,
Who hunts the hare with oxen,
And swims against the tide.[42]

—wry, sensual (even if often in dream, rather than in reality), he turns mood after mood of love into new and brilliant texture of rhythm and meaning:

> L'aur' amara
> fa.ls bruoills brancutz
> clarzir
> qe.l dous'espeis'ab fuoills,
> e.ls letz
> becs
> dels auzels ramencs
> ten balps e mutz,
> pars
> e non pars;
> per q'eu m'esfortz
> de far e dir
> plazers
> a mains, per liei
> que m'a virat bas d'aut,
> don tem morir
> si l'afans no m'asoma.[43]

> (The biting wind
> Strips the branchy woods,
> Which the soft breeze
> Once clothed in leaves;
> Turns halt and mute
> The chattering beaks
> Of birds on bough,
> Paired and unpaired.
> Why do I strive
> In act and speech
> To please so many?
> For her sake, who
> Now sets me low.
> Time then for death
> If this pain spares me.)

No one has ever questioned the profound influence of troubadour love-poetry upon all succeeding European traditions. Minor lyric and romance were indebted to it, as was the work of major mediaeval writers such as Dante, Petrarch, and Chaucer. But the questioning of the origins of their love-philosophies has been continuous. As we have seen, conditions at the courts of southern France and neighbouring Spain in the late 11th and early 12th centuries were favourable to the development of extravagant art-forms, as they were to all forms of extravagant living and thought. It is not difficult to account for the flowering of troubadour poetry at this time; the richness and elaboration of the verse are natural counterparts to the lavish manners of society. Gestures of ostentation such as that of

Bertram de Raimbaux, who, at an assembly of Aragonese and Toulousian nobility in 1174, had 30,000 sous sown into a ploughed field,[44] can be paralleled by gestures of ostentation in the sentiment and verbal patterning of troubadour poetry. But something more exact must be said of the origins of the *idéologie amoureuse* at the heart of Provençal *fin'amors*. In the normal mediaeval context, some of the features of this ideology are startling, even alien; it is easy to see how the articulation of *fin'amors* in southern French lyric verse could once have been called "a revolution," compared with which "the Renaissance is a mere ripple on the surface of literature."[45]

More recently, critics have been doubtful about the term "revolution," pointing out that love-poetry similar in many respects to troubadour poetry can be found in Egypt, Byzantium, Georgia, Islam, and Greek Italy prior to, and contemporary with, Provençal compositions.[46] Certainly it is true that *amour courtois*, seen basically as refined and passionate love-worship, was pre-dated by Latin lyric of the 10th and 11th centuries. Some of the so-called *Cambridge Songs*, copied by an Englishman about 1050 into a large miscellany of Christian-Latin poetry, could indeed be described as courtly love-poetry:

> Tu saltim, Veris gratia,
> exaudi et considera
> frondes, flores et gramina;
> nam mea languet anima.[47]
>
> (Do thou, O spring most fair,
> Squander thy care
> On flower and leaf and grain.
> Leave me alone with pain!)

And so, too, could many of the Latin lyrics of the even more famous *Codex Buranus*,[48] written over the 12th and 13th centuries:

> Noblis, mei
> miserere precor,
> tua facies
> ensis est quo necor,
> nam medullitus
> amat meum te cor,
> subveni!
> Amor improbus
> omnia superat,
> subveni![49]
>
> (Noblest, I pray thee,
> Have pity upon me;
> Thy face is a sword,

> And behold, I am slain.
> From the core of my heart
> I have loved thee.
> Aid, oh aid!
> Love the deceiver,
> Love the all-conquering,
> Come to my aid!)

But although there are good grounds for allowing that love-poetry in many languages may be "courtly" by reason of its milieu, its type of sensibility, its style of approach, there are also grounds for insisting that the love-poetry of the southern French troubadours is a unique version of "courtly experience," and that its exposition of what it defined as *fin'amors* is also unique.

We cannot ignore the fact that the love-ideology of the troubadours was elaborately constructed upon a principle quite irreconcilable with the teachings of the mediaeval Church: that of the possibility, and indeed the desirability, of a passionate but at the same time virtuous love outside the marriage contract. The orthodox views of the Church were sufficiently clear to rule out any valid relationship between "virtue" and "passion" even in married love; nothing but wholesale condemnation of adulterous liaisons could be expected, however "courtly" and "ideal" they might be. It is not, of course, that love-poetry had never been addressed to married women before the time of the troubadours: Ovid immediately comes to mind. Rather, the troubadours were the first to formalize non-marital love into a poetic ritual of adoration that could comprehend both ardour and delicacy of feeling, and could respond, morally and aesthetically, to the rich, aristocratic, and intelligent court society of the south. Social, geographical, and political factors account for the timing and the shaping of the troubadour love-ethic. Feudal life, especially as developed in the wealthy provinces of southern France—great princes with vast lands and numerous vassals, at the head of hierarchical structures of government—must have provided the general background. It may even have provided some of the poetic vocabulary; the troubadours often spoke of the lady as *midons* (my lord). The geographical and political closeness of southern France to Spain was of specific as well as general importance. It was probably through contacts with the courts of Aragon and Castile, through inter-marriage such as that of Guilhem of Poitou with Philippa of Aragon in 1094, and through political dealings, that knowledge of Hispano-Arabic love-philosophies and love-poetry of the 10th and 11th centuries came to the courts and poets of the Midi. The most striking comparisons are possible between troubadour love-poetry and the treatises and verses of Arabic Spain. They are not identical in their attitudes and expression: no troubadour poet, for instance, ever took the sublimation of passion to the lengths of the Hispano-Arabic poet Ibn-Darrach (*d.* 976):

> The love that consumes me is as pure as the
> Visages of the elect. . . .
> I laid my face against the ground that it
> Might be as a footstool to my lady.
>   She said:
> Rejoice, for you may set your lips upon my veil!
> But my heart would not consent: for she
> Entrusted to the nobility of my feelings
> The care of her honour. . . .[50]

Moreover, Hispano-Arabic treatises on love are strongly influenced by mystical doctrines of the East, by those of Plato and the neo-Platonists; and by those of the Sufis, who assimilated divine to profane love, and made use of an erotic, symbolic language. The stress in these treatises and poems of Moorish Spain is more frequently than in the poetry of the troubadours upon a spiritualizing of passionate love. "The union of the spirit is more beautiful than the union of the body . . ."; "love is a reunion of souls in the original sphere of their higher world": these quotations are taken from a treatise on love, the *Tawq al-Hamamaw*[51] (The Dove's Neck Ring), written in 1022 by the Andalusian religious philosopher Ibn-Hazm (994–1064); their ultimate source in Platonic theory is clear. But the idealizing tendencies in the love-poetry of the troubadours may be a pale reflection of such ideas; certainly the Muslim work suggests that it, or other similar treatises, played some part in the troubadour formulation of *amour courtois*. The sovereignty of love, the conception of love as a longed-for malady, the association of love with sleeplessness and lamentations, the necessity of secrecy and faithful service, and the almost blasphemous nature of faithlessness are features common to the doctrine of Ibn Hazm and the troubadours; all agree that, to love properly, the virtues of magnanimity, self-discipline, loyalty, and courage are necessary.

All these are familiar and respected virtues in the Christian ethical code; it is their operation in a context fundamentally unacceptable to Christianity—that of passionate and extra-marital love—that requires comment and explanation. We may find satisfaction in the theory that some of the basic ideas and themes of the troubadours were borrowed from traditions foreign to Christianity; we have then to inquire how they could have been developed and codified in mediaeval courts that were, in name at least, Christian. It has been suggested that once again we may

425

look to the Arabic world for a solution, and more particularly to Muslim Spain of the late 11th and 12th centuries. There, in the writings of Averroes (1126–78), could be found a persuasive account of what has often been called "double truth": the co-existence of truths valid separately for philosophy and religion.[52] The influence of Averroist thought upon the 12th and early 13th centuries was pervasive; this attempt to "delimit the respective areas of faith and reason"[53] helped Aquinas, later, to make his own resolution of the problem. The distinctive feature of Averroes' doctrine was its denial of the ultimate harmony of faith and reason: what was irreconcilable could nevertheless be admitted as "true," but at different levels of operation. It may, at first, sound unlikely that Arabic philosophy should have provided not only some of the concepts and forms of troubadour love-poetry but also an ideological structure within which it could safely exist. The fact remains that the "double truths" of Christian and courtly love, basically irreconcilable, were held in conjunction in southern French courtly society. We can, at this date, only speculate how such a balance or juxtaposition was possible, not neglecting any evidence that may throw light upon a difficult subject. No art historian finds it surprising that early-12th-century sculpted columns at Moissac, in Languedoc, are strongly reminiscent of Arabic models[54]: literary historians cannot afford to be entirely sceptical.

In the hands of the troubadours of the 12th and early 13th centuries, *fin'amors* can hardly be said to change and develop; it seems to have been protected from sociological influences by the court civilization that had first produced it. Only some deepening of original concepts can be detected: no radical alteration. But the same cannot be said of *fin'amors* outside the particular troubadour context. After 1150, its influence upon the literature of the aristocratic courts of the north of France begins to be evident: what is also evident is the way in which it is adapted in response to different cultural conditions and literary tastes. From now on, the history of *fin'amors* in western vernacular writings will be highly complicated; each country, each set of authors, will work important changes upon its doctrines and forms. And we might reasonably mark the point of departure by substituting for the term *fin'amors*, with its power to suggest the exclusive quality of the troubadour synthesis, the term *amour courtois*. If it has less to recommend it in authentic mediaeval usage, it has the advantage of a wide usage in descriptive and critical writings from the late 19th century to the present day, covering not only Provençal love-poetry, but all its varied derivatives in northern France, Germany, Italy, and England.[55]

The passage of Provençal *fin'amors* into the *amour courtois* of northern European writers was no doubt aided by royal patronesses such as Eleanor of Aquitaine and her daughter Marie, Countess of Champagne. Theirs has been called a decisive role. But when we turn to consider their courts, and the literature of *amour courtois* written there, a sense of the continuity of Provençal tradition is crossed and disturbed. An important general point to make is the predominantly narrative character of northern French literature compared with the lyrical character of that of the south. The characteristic vernacular genre of the north had been the *chanson de geste*; indeed it retained its popularity well into the 12th century, overlapping with the *lai* and the *roman* as favourite entertainment for laity and clerics alike. Although there is evidence that lyric did exist, it was not a greatly admired literary form until late in the 12th century. Even then, the best of northern French lyrics are written in a semi-narrative form, the so-called *chanson de toile*, which is often closer in approach and temper to ballad than to troubadour *canzo*. *Amour courtois*, as it appears first in northern European poetry, is given a narrative setting. The consequences of this are more than formal: once extended from lyric into narrative, the Provençal love ideology is subjected to new pressures, and is required to adapt to new literary situations. It becomes, in fact, much more a method of treatment for stories already in existence than a philosophy of experience, valuable in itself. And it could not therefore be expected to preserve a strong, consistent identity; *amour courtois* in the romances of Chrétien de Troyes, in the *lais* of Marie de France, in the *Roman de la rose* of Guillaume de Lorris, and in Geoffrey Chaucer's *Troilus and Criseyde* is almost as variable as the authors and the audiences for whom such works were written.

Authorship, too, must be taken into account. The writers of Provençal lyric were either aristocratic by birth, or closely connected with the seigneurial life; they were all laymen. The writers of northern French romance, chronicle, and allegory, however, were predominantly clerks of various kinds and degrees. With the growing prosperity of the schools after 1150, their numbers had increased; many of them were willing to put their knowledge of literature at the disposal of courtly patrons, and to compose for them. The clerks of northern Europe, from the late 12th century onward, were often a curious blend: part men of letters, part men of the Church. Well-read in the ancient authors, and especially in Ovid, trained in the arts of rhetoric, and familiar with theological argument and debate, they go a long way toward explaining the diverse ideological tendencies in the love-literature of the 12th century. They

427

may also be able to explain particular changes in the literary presentation of *amour courtois*: the partial loss of what has been called the *densité érotique* of troubadour *fin'amors*, its close, almost obsessive preoccupation with a limited range of emotions; the decreased emphasis upon extramarital love-relationships, except in certain of the Arthurian stories; and the greater degree of realism in the handling of love-themes (where Ovid was no doubt very influential).

In 1154, Eleanor of Aquitaine came to England to be crowned with her Angevin husband, Henry II. We know that the troubadour poet Bernart de Ventadorn wrote despairing lyrics after her: that despair was entirely justified, because Eleanor was henceforward to move in a sphere of power far more exalted than that she had occupied as Duchess of Aquitaine, or even as Queen of France. Yoking her fortunes to those of the energetic Henry of Anjou, she shared with him a court life that was restless but immensely rich and influential. It was, essentially, a European, rather than a narrowly English, court-life; both king and queen travelled extensively between their domains in France and England. And the character of the works produced for them is anything but narrow. We might at first be tempted to distinguish very simply between Henry and Eleanor as literary patrons; to Henry, we could assign the learned literature of science, government, law, and history, predominantly in Latin, to Eleanor, the lyric poetry and romance in the vernacular. We gather from Peter of Blois, who was familiar with both the English and the Sicilian courts, that Henry was a better scholar than William of Sicily:

> . . . with the king of England there is school every day, constant conversation of the best scholars and discussion of questions. . . .[56]

Adelard of Bath dedicated to Henry his treatise *On the Astrolabe*; and Henry commissioned Lawrence, Abbot of Westminster, to write a life of Edward the Confessor. The *Chronicle* of Jordan Fantosme, written between 1174 and 1183, is one of the few vernacular works presented to him.

But Eleanor cannot be totally relegated to more frivolous cultural matters: she is described by one learned clerk as a lady *en cui tote sc̈ience abonde*[57] (in whom all learning is plentiful). There seems to be no doubt but that she could read Latin and that her tastes in literature ranged impressively over historical and moral areas. Her connections with clerks seem to have been closer and more numerous than her connections with troubadour poets; the same Jordan Fantosme who wrote his *Chronicle* for Henry is mentioned by a contemporary as *clericus reginae Alienorae*[58] (Queen Eleanor's clerk). In fact, the list of clerkly compositions associated

with Eleanor is very interesting; although they are in the French vernacular, they are by no means only light entertainment. They satisfy, from
a variety of sources in classical and earlier mediaeval literature, an appetite
that was clearly as much historical as romantic. Thus, the unknown
author of the *Roman d'Eneas* (*c.* 1160), writing for the Plantagenet court,
adapts the *Aeneid* and draws upon Ovid for a lengthy treatment of the
love of Aeneas and Lavinia, full of complaints and monologues: twin
interests, in stories of the past and in the rhetoric of passionate love, are
indulged. The *Roman de Troie* by Benoît de Sainte-Maure (*fl. c.* 1160), one
of the most substantial versions of the Troy legend made in the Middle
Ages, pays only thinly disguised homage to Eleanor for her learning,
beauty, and virtue: *riche dame de riche rei....*[59] An early-13th-century writer
assures us that the *Roman de Brut*, the long poem on the history of the
Britons by the Norman clerk Wace, was offered to Eleanor. Wace certainly wrote movingly of her in his *Roman de Rou* (1160–74), a history of
the dukes of Normandy:

> Franche est Alienor et de bon aire et sage.[60]
>
> (Generous is Eleanor, gracious and wise.)

The *Brut* may be, by later standards, popular history—part chronicle, part
romance—but it does remind us that the duchess who began as *midons* of
the troubadours developed into the queen of formidable political talents.
History was as important to Eleanor, with her own feudal responsibilities
and ambitions, as it was to Henry.

It is in this setting that we should view the composition (*c.* 1154–8) of the
Anglo-French poem *Tristan* by a clerk whom we know only by the name of
Thomas. Experts now agree that this highly sophisticated working of a
tragic story was produced for the English court, and most probably for
the queen herself. At about this time, Bernart de Ventadorn was likening
his separation from Eleanor to that of Tristan from Iseult; could the
description by Thomas of Iseult singing be a description of Eleanor too?
It is as delicate as 12th-century ivory carvings from England and
France:

> La reine chante dulcement,
> La voiz acorde a l'estrument.
> Les mainz sunt bele, li lais bons,
> Dulz la voiz, e bas li tons.[61]
>
> (The queen sings softly,
> Her voice in tune with the instrument.

> Her hands are graceful, the lay good:
> Sweet the voice, and the key low.)

Tristan is a poem of courtly sentiment; it presents the old story of sad, illicit love with sympathy and grace. Yet we are in a different world from that of the troubadours of Provence; the clerkly poet Thomas, writing in London for a queen who came from far south, warns in his conclusion:

> Pur essemple l'ai issi fait. . .
> Aveir em poissent grant confort. . .
> Encuntre tuiz engins d'Amur.[62]
>
> (I have written this as an example. . .
> May they be fortified by it. . .
> Against the wiles of love.)

A touch of frost lies upon passionate love; the critical eye of orthodox religion is turned upon it. We shall find other northern European examples of these sterner conclusions; the clerks intend that such love should be made to acknowledge its responsibilities in the wider context of Christian morals.

But whether it appears as a sudden retraction of approval or as a subtle adaptation of concept, change is everywhere present in the literature of *amour courtois*. This is not all due to clerical authors. The most attractive set of poems associated with the court of Henry and Eleanor was written by a noblewoman. Sometime after 1160, a certain Marie, naming herself "de France," offered twelve *lais*, or shorter narrative poems, to a "noble and courteous king." If indeed she was Henry's half-sister, the dedication to the king, rather than to the queen, can probably be seen as a matter of family prestige. Marie's poems are moving and dramatic tales of devoted love in situations of great adversity: Tristan and Iseult meeting briefly in the forest, and lovers parted by cruel parents, or menaced by jealous queens. Love is refined, faithful, passionate, generous; we recognize its lineage. It is frequently presented in adulterous settings: that of Tristan and Iseult, in the *Lay of the Honeysuckle* (*Chèvre-feuille*), is paralleled by others in the *Lay of the Nightingale* (*Laüstic*) and in the *Lay of Yonec*. Both of the last-mentioned *lais* treat the jealous husband as the villain of the piece; the *Lay of Yonec* has the dead lover avenged by his illegitimate son, who kills the husband:

> when the son saw that his mother lay dead upon her lover's grave, he raised his father's sword and smote the head of that ancient traitor from his shoulders.[63]

But this love is modulated very variously by Marie de France for the purpose of her narratives; its central qualities are always those of *amour courtois*, but we grasp immediately that it is a simplified version—less analytical, less idealizing. The ladies are not distant; they respond frankly to their lovers:

> . . . the maiden hastened to embrace her lover. He got him nimbly
> from his horse, and taking her softly between his arms, kissed her
> with more kisses than I can tell.[64]

An intrigue between a married woman and her lover may just as easily end in savage retribution as in a compassionate recital of their sufferings. The *Lay of Equitan*, in which two lovers of courtly stereotype perish wretchedly, having plotted the husband's death, contrasts starkly with the *Lay of the Honeysuckle*, in which the fleeting delight of Tristan and the queen is its own great good. And *amour courtois* can appear as a ritual of courtship, preliminary to marriage; Marie is quite explicit about this in the *Lay of the Thorn:*

> It begins well, and endeth better, for these kisses find their fruit in
> marriage.[65]

We need not, therefore, be surprised that Marie was also responsible for a collection of beast fables in French verse, *Ysopet*, dedicated to a certain *cunte Willime*, whom she describes as *flurs de chevalerie, d'enseignement, de curteisie*. For this man—perhaps William Longsword, Earl of Salisbury, or William Marshal, Earl of Pembroke—she provided a series of decorous *exempla*, with morals neatly enforced: a work of maximum usefulness to a magnate in the exercise of his seigneurial duties.

Marie's work is designed for court society; her poems describe life from an aristocratic viewpoint: the characters are of noble birth, their settings are rich and fashionable. The abandoned child of the *Lay of the Ash Tree* is wrapped in

> a piece of sanguine silk, brought from a bazaar in Constantinople . . .
> with a silken lace they bound a great ring to the child's arm . . . the
> ring was of fine gold, set with garnets. . . .[66]

The hero of the *Lay of Sir Launfal* is served by a maiden carrying "a basin of pure gold, cunningly wrought by some crafty smith. . . ."[67] Sir Guigemar, in the *lai* of his name, finds himself on a deserted ship, lit by gold candlesticks, "decked with jewels worth a lord's ransom. . .": he comes to a castle by the sea, in which the queen's chamber is lavishly painted:

431

> . . . on one wall might be seen Dame Venus, the Goddess of love,
> sweetly flushed, as when she walked the water . . . on another, the
> Goddess threw Ovid's book upon a fire of coals. . . .[68]

The decorative arts of the 12th century and the expensive tastes of the
noble classes are vividly recorded for us in these lais, and refinement is
present in more than just the settings of the *lais*. The *Lay of the Honeysuckle*
is the best example of her fastidious art, with its acute dramatic sense and
its controlled emotion. It is extremely short, only one episode in the
melancholy story of Tristan and Iseult. But into it Marie has distilled the
essence of "this love which passed all other love, of love from whence came
strange sorrow, and whereof they died together on the same day."
Tristan, hiding in Cornwall, hears that Iseult will ride out on her way to
Tintagel, and he lies in wait, to catch a glimpse of her. They meet in the
forest for one hour, and part again. The poem lights up a few moments in
a dark, long-drawn tragedy: its effectiveness lies partly in the economy
of its telling, and partly in the reflective power of the one image it uses
for the lovers—the intertwined honeysuckle and hazel tree in the forest:

> so sweetly laced and taken were they in one close embrace, that
> thus they might remain while life endured. But should rough hands
> part so fond a clasp. . . .[69]

Most effective of all is the simplicity and strength of the poetry when it
comes to expressing the Tristan theme:

> Bele amie, si est de nus,
> Ne vus sanz mei, ne jeo sanz vus.[70]
>
> (Sweet love, thus it is with us:
> Not you without me, not I without you.)

In such an idyll, *amour courtois* creates its own standards and fulfils its own
special nature. But taken as a whole, Marie's poetry shows us that Angevin
court society had needs and tastes less exclusive than those of southern
French court society. Her third work was a translation of *St Patrick's
Purgatory*: she presented this saint's legend to *seigneurs*, but also to *la simple
gent* (ordinary people). Whoever her "ordinary people" were, it is clear
that she looked beyond the immediate boundaries of the court, or, perhaps,
that she knew those boundaries to be flexible.

We receive the same impression of literature written in wide contexts
and to varied demands when we turn to the court of Eleanor's daughter
Marie and of her husband Henry, "the liberal," of Champagne—a court

that was active from roughly 1160 to Marie's death in 1198. Both the Angevin house and that of Champagne were responsible for the encouragement of secular literary forms against a background of traditional learning and devotion.[71] Associated with Marie and Henry were scholars and theologians (Nicholas of Clairvaux, Peter of Celle), clerks of all kinds (the "chaplain" Andreas), clerkly poets (Chrétien de Troyes, Evrat), and aristocratic authors (Gace Brulé, Gautier d'Arras). Henry of Champagne was a competent latinist, with a strong liking for religious and classical literature. He commissioned a Latin poem dealing with the Trojan war, and maintained a lively correspondence with learned Englishmen such as John of Salisbury and Herbert of Bosham on points of biblical scholarship. Again, it would be tempting to contrast the interests of husband and wife, characterizing those of Marie as secular and romantic, catered for in French rather than in Latin. Her appearance in a lyric by Gace Brulé—one of the most prolific knightly poets of northern France in the late 12th century—suggests that she was desirable and imperious, commanding him to sing, but turning aside his suit of love with the brusque inquiry, *"Cant ireis vos outre mer?"* (When are you going abroad?). This is not out of keeping with the image of "my Lady of Champagne," who ordered Chrétien de Troyes to write the romance *Lancelot*, dictating not only the material but also the treatment of that famous document of *amour courtois*:

> the Countess is worth as many queens as a gem is worth of pearls and sards. . . .[72]

Nor is it out of keeping with the citation of her views upon love in the treatise *De amore*, by Andreas Capellanus (*c.* 1190). Andreas, who has been thought, upon slender evidence, to be her chaplain, quotes a letter, supposedly written by Marie in 1174, declaring that love cannot exist between married people. This reference to Marie's idealization of adultery—*amorem non posse suas inter duos iugales extendere vires* (love cannot flourish between two married persons)—has encouraged many to visualize her as the most powerful advocate of *amour courtois* in 12th-century northern Europe, and her court at Troyes as the main centre of influence for its doctrines.

But the real woman and her court were obviously more complex than this, as was also the presentation of *amour courtois* in texts connected, however remotely, with her. *La gentis contesse* requested not only *Lancelot*, but a verse translation of Genesis, with full glossing. The poet Evrat pictures Marie for us, not singing or listening to romances, or giving judgments of love, but reading his fruitful lines:

> Lo peut en son armaire eslire. . . .[73]

> (she can read them in her library. . . .)

Needless to say, both Evrat and the anonymous poet who wrote a paraphrase of Psalm 43, "Eructavit cor meum," for Marie take an entirely orthodox mediaeval view of human love; the tragic, romantic, and illicit passion that enslaved Lancelot to Guenevere and Tristan to Iseult is nowhere countenanced. Evrat sums up the matter:

> Hom doit avoir et sens et force;
> N'est pas hom cant femme l'esforce.[74]

> (A man should possess both common-sense and strength:
> He is no man at all when a woman enthralls him.)

This is indeed a far cry from Chrétien de Troyes' *Lancelot*, in which the hero is made to suffer painfully for a moment's hesitation before obeying the uncompromising commands of love; when he leaves Guenevere's bed, "he bows and acts precisely as if he were before a shrine. . . ."[75] It would, however, be a mistake to underline this too dramatically. *Lancelot* is not a simple work: its author was probably of clerical training, and was certainly a skilled literary artist. The impression given by a careful reading of the romance is entirely different from that given by a reading of troubadour poetry. There are suggestions of a humorous attitude to the gestures and poses of *amour courtois*, as when Lancelot fights backwards for Guenevere: "he did not turn or take his eyes and face from her, defending himself with backhand blows."[76] The description of Lancelot's love for Guenevere is much more often concerned with ritual than with passion: finding her comb, stranded with her hair,

> he begins to adore those tresses . . . a hundred thousand times he raises
> them to his eyes and mouth . . . he would not exchange them for a
> cartload of emeralds and carbuncles . . . he holds in contempt essence
> of pearl, treacle, and the cure for pleurisy; even for St Martin and St
> James he has no need. . . .[77]

The tone of such passages is extremely difficult to gauge; it is delicately positioned between sympathy and irony. Even the account of the lovers at last brought to bed is reticent compared with the generous imaginings

434

of the troubadours: "in truth such a marvellous joy comes over them as was never heard or known. But their joy will not be revealed by me, *for in a story it has no place.*"[78] The literary and the moral setting of *amour courtois* has indeed changed; its presentation in *Lancelot* is meticulous, but cerebral. Chrétien is more interested in the processes of his hero's inner reasonings than in the nature of his absorbing desire. It is also clear that his material sometimes constrains him; he would sometimes like to say more on ethical matters than the story allows:

> For prowess cannot accomplish so much as wickedness and sloth can do: it is true beyond a doubt that it is possible to do more evil than good. I could say more on these two heads if it did not cause me to delay. But now I must turn to something else and resume my subject. . . .[79]

Taken as a whole, however, the romances of Chrétien mirror the outward forms, the varied preoccupations and ideals, of his high-born world. It is very likely that he knew both the Angevin court and that of Champagne; he provides for them a series of dazzling pictures of princely life:

> The mantle was very rich and fine; laid about the neck were two sable-skins, and in the tassels there was more than an ounce of gold: on one a hyacinth, and on the other a ruby flashed more bright than burning candle. . . .
>
> . . . the saddle bows were of ivory, on which was carved the story of how Aeneas came from Troy . . . cunning was the workmanship . . . all decorated with fine gold. . . .[80]

He tells us, more often than Marie de France, of the great pageants of the age: a royal wedding, a coronation. He relishes the symbolic splendours of throne and sceptre (". . . all of one solid emerald, fully as large as your fist . . .") and of censers and crosses. At the coronation mass in *Erec et Enide*, crowns, mitres, and croziers are gathered into a glittering field:

> . . . the procession came out of the church with relics and treasures to meet them . . . crosses and prayer-books and censers and reliquaries . . . were all brought out . . . nor was there any lack of chants made. Never were seen so many kings, counts, dukes and nobles together. . . .[81]

It is of course natural that "no low-born man could enter there, but only ladies and knights. . . ."

When the bustle of everyday life can be heard, it is still the life of the court:

> within the town there was great joy of knights and ladies, of whom there were many and fair. Some were feeding their sparrow-hawks in the streets . . . others play at dice . . . some at chess . . . the grooms in front of the stables are rubbing down and currying the horses . . . the ladies are bedecking themselves in their boudoirs. . . .[82]

Sometimes we catch a glimpse of peasant existence, but in deep, receding perspective, as if seen distantly, through an opened window:

> a squire met them in a little valley, accompanied by two fellows, who were carrying cakes and wine and some rich autumn cheeses to those who were mowing the hay in the meadows belonging to Count Galoain. . . .[83]

The wide range of literary activity sponsored by both courts is confirmed by Chrétien's work. Willingly turning his hand to fashionable poetic subjects and modes—*Lancelot* is one instance—he shows himself to be nevertheless a man of learning, with a deep respect for the literature of the past. His knowledge of the classical poets, and his debt to them for themes and images, was considerable. The opening of *Cligès*, his second romance, tells us proudly how learning and chivalry have passed from Greece and Rome to the France of his day, and indeed, he must have observed exactly that alliance of book and sword in Henry of Champagne, his patron. He was trained in methods of composition taught by the schools of northern France, perhaps those of Troyes itself. He was a skilled rhetorician, and allowed his characters to analyse their emotions with the precision of a school exercise; Soredamors, in *Cligès*, falls in love with painful finesse:

> One cannot love with the eyes alone. What crime, then, have my eyes committed, if their glance but follows my desire? What is their fault, and what their sin? Ought I to blame them, then? Nay verily. Who, then, should be blamed? Surely myself, who have them in control. . . .[84]

Even when, as in *Lancelot*, his subject-matter is the force of love, there is much in his presentation to appeal to intellectual taste: the problem, as well as the passion, absorbed him.

His romances take up widely differing stances on human love. *Erec et Enide* celebrates a marriage in which love is a compound of wifely obedience and knightly courtesy: *Lancelot* describes a relationship that has no social or religious sanction, but that asks its hero to dedicate himself quite as uncompromisingly as a saint or a disciple. Although the love is a sin, it teaches virtue. The contrast between *Erec* and *Lancelot* is

436

strong, but it is no more problematic than the contrast between Marie's request for *Lancelot* and her request for Evrat's paraphrase of Genesis, with its stern warning:

> N'est pas hom cant femme l'esforce.

> (He is no man at all when a woman enthralls him.)

Indeed, it would be sensible to attribute to Marie, to Eleanor, and certainly to their court writers, a whole spectrum of interested attitudes toward the human condition: some of these attitudes, no doubt, had a more vital connection with their literature than with their lives.

With this proviso, we may look again at the most enigmatic of all the works associated with Marie of Champagne and *amour courtois*, the *De amore* of Andreas Capellanus.[85] Although Marie is referred to, and quoted, in the treatise, we do not know if she knew the author, or even if she read what he wrote. All the other works dedicated to her are in French, not Latin: the obvious audience for Andreas would have been clerics or well-educated laymen, and this becomes even more likely when we consider the content of *De amore*. Its first two books describe various kinds of love, but in particular *amour courtois*, with which Andreas deals systematically in terms of Provençal *fin'amors* and which he defines as extravagant, illicit, secret, ennobling, and passionate. But in the third book, "De reprobatione amoris," he attacks it, and expounds the traditional teaching of the Church on love and morality. This is a *volte-face* of no mean order; its significance is not, and probably never will be, entirely clear. An elaborate and learned joke for a group of clerical friends; a daring excursion into a secular, forbidden world, followed by a devout retraction of interest; an assertion of the Averroist "double truth"; a reflection of the 12th-century divorce between the social needs of the aristocratic classes and the traditional needs of Christianity: all these explanations have been proposed and all contain some element of truth. But it is worth reminding ourselves that, although we cannot be certain of the intent or the public of *De amore*, we may plausibly regard it as representing, in a highly dramatic form, the insistence of northern European writers upon a wider, more varied setting for *amour courtois*. We have already seen something of this in Thomas's *Tristan*, written for Eleanor of Aquitaine, in the *lais* of Marie de France, and even in the romances of Chrétien de Troyes. *Amour courtois* now had to encounter the many realities of mediaeval life, in social, devotional, and philosophic spheres. Moving out of the courts of Provence, it became part of European tradition. Henceforward, its history is part of the general history of European sentiment, and cannot be charted without reference to innumerable religious and philosophic issues and literary fashions.

After 1200, the connection of *amour courtois* and court society is no longer vital; its development is still rapid, but it is dispersive. It provided English religious writers, such as the author of the *Ancrene Riwle* (c. 1200), with an allegory of Christ and the soul: Christ the adoring courtly lover petitioning his distant love, the human soul. It also inspired French clerks of the 13th century to codify it in stiff allegory, and to use it for anti-feminist Christian moralizing. Thus, the *Roman de la rose*, begun by Guillaume de Lorris in 1237 and completed about 1275 by Jean de Meung, unites within one poem the adoration and the condemnation of women. Adopted into the mainstream of European vernacular love-lyric, *amour courtois* often appears as a decorative ritual of courtship rather than as an "idealization of adultery." Still powerful enough to engage the lyrical and rhetorical energies of a learned poet such as Petrarch (1304–74), whose verses to his real or imagined Laura made Italy one of the richest sources of *amour courtois* for later centuries, it also attracted the attention of Italian poets whose purposes were rarer by far. In Dante's *Divina commedia* (c. 1306–21), for instance, courtly love and spiritual vision are fused: Beatrice, the idealized lady of his earthly devotion, the wife of another man, becomes wisdom, philosophy, and guide to the mysteries of God's purpose.

Its original social exclusiveness is replaced by that of the *cuore gentile* (noble hearts), who, by education and by natural virtue of character, are fitted—whatever their social origin—to share in and to understand its torments and raptures. In Gottfried von Strassburg's *Tristan* (c. 1210), courtly society at large is not appealed to; this cultured and subtle poet, who was probably a member of the urban aristocracy and of clerkly training, directs his tale of love and despair to an elite of the spirit, not of class. Here *amour courtois*, although remaining fully passionate, is introduced in the language of the mystics; Gottfried offers his poem as nourishment for the initiate, in the very terms used by St Bernard of Clairvaux (1090–1153), giving his sermons on the Song of Songs only to those who are fit to receive them:

> This is bread to all noble hearts. With this their death lives on. We read their life, we read their death, and to us it is as sweet as bread.
> Their life, their death are our bread. Thus lives their life, thus lives their death. Thus they live and yet are dead, and their death is the bread of the living.[86]

But the uncertain, sometimes precarious, existence of the concept of *amour courtois* in a changing mediaeval world that had already begun to idealize marriage itself is best seen in English courtly poetry of the late 14th century. Geoffrey Chaucer's *Troilus and Criseyde* takes a situation that preserves in part, at least, the old pattern of secret, irresistible, passionate, unmarried love, with its heightened raptures and sufferings. Its hero, Troilus, acts out with grace and energy, in both marital and romantic contexts, the role of one who is "moost subgit unto love."[87] His dedication to it is seen not only in the faithful performance of all the rituals of *amour courtois*—his acts of worship, his gestures of despair—but also in the gradual refinement of his character under the influence of this love:

> For he bicom the frendlieste wight,
> The gentilest, and ek the mooste fre,
> The thriftiest and oon the beste knyght,
> That in his tyme was or myghte be.
> Dede were his japes and his cruelte. . . .[88]

Amour courtois is still able to provide its own impressive code of ethics. But as the poem proceeds, Chaucer's conception of the nature and significance of the love between Troilus and Criseyde becomes richly ambiguous. Their union is set against a background of pagan and Christian mythology; their devotion is associated with God's love for man and man's for God:

> God loveth, and to love wol nought werne;
> And in this world no lyves creature
> Withouten love is worth, or may endure.[89]

Troilus praises love in terms of orthodox Christian philosophy:

> So wolde God, that auctour is of kynde,
> That with his bond love of his vertu liste
> To cerclen hertes alle, and faste bynde. . . .[90]

The dominant impression left with the reader is of a fully sanctioned love—

> Benigne Love, thou holy bond of thinges[91]

—even though its circumstances are still those of the old illicit passion. Chaucer's transmutation of *amour courtois* in this poem has been described as the bringing of "the old romance of adultery to the very frontiers of the modern . . . romance of marriage."[92] Although the bitter ending of

439

Troilus and Criseyde, with Criseyde unfaithful, Troilus dead, and the poet lashing "the blynde lust, the which that may nat laste,"[93] makes such a statement debatable, we can turn to one of the later *Canterbury Tales*, "The Franklin's Tale," in which a relationship between husband and wife is modelled upon *amour courtois*, but takes advantage of the stability of an acknowledged social and domestic structure.

Chaucer wrote for the court of Richard II; in one manuscript miniature he is pictured reading *Troilus and Criseyde* to Richard and his family and friends.[94] The formal park setting, the burnished sky, the jewel-colours of the listeners' robes spread like gaudy wings about the figure of the absorbed poet—all serve to remind us that this was a court of international prestige, of exquisite artistic and literary taste, of flamboyant gesture. Richard's dress ("a white satin doublet embroidered with golden orange-trees bearing a hundred silver-gilt oranges . . ."[95]), the glittering manuscripts made for him and for members of his retinue, the *Wilton Diptych*, the splendid examples of the goldsmith's art commissioned by the king or by powerful princes such as John of Gaunt, Duke of Lancaster, are all products or manifestations of a courtly society that might be expected also to demand literature of fine sentiment.[96] Both French and English artists catered for that society, composing in two vernaculars. But it would not be proper to visualize Richard's court as a small, exclusive world of its own, bent only on supplying its delicate aesthetic sense with new objects for contemplation. It was interpenetrated with men of learning and religion, and with men of business—the *haute bourgeoisie*, who served the king, often opposing him but just as often lending him money to finance his extravagant tastes. An English court audience of the late 14th century—outside the convention of manuscript painting—was probably very mixed: courtiers, minor gentry, clerks, high ecclesiastics, and business men were all likely components. The literature produced for them is as varied as we might expect. Thomas Usk, member of the city government and eventually made Under-Sheriff of London at Richard's request, wrote his prose *Testament of Love*[97]* for the court; his treatise on "blisse of two hertes in ful love knitte" is courtly in ways familiar to the student of *amour courtois*. But the object of his love, Margaret, is much more than a woman; with a display of encyclopaedic learning, Usk allegorizes her as God's wisdom, and as Holy Church. Serious, too, is the *Confessio amantis*,[98] the poem on love that the Kentish John Gower dedicated first to Richard and then to his successor. Here is an autumnal view of *amour courtois*: the poet remembers amorous youth, useless jealousies, faithful service. At the

*See Ch. 19, "*Piers Plowman* and the Ricardian Age in Literature."

440

end, he sees himself as he is, old and fragile; his tempestuous heart is quietened, and he takes from Venus a rosary of black and gold, inscribed *por reposer* (to rest).

Into this society Chaucer—of merchant origin, first esquire and soldier, then important government servant—fits without difficulty. We may imagine that his poetry, ranging over elaborate lyric compliment, romance narrative, pious tale, and ribald *fabliau*, fairly gauged the mixed needs and the mixed nature of his courtly audience. *Troilus and Criseyde*, with its movement from a precise and traditional observation of *amour courtois* to a deepened study of human love as part of universal Christian law, and, further, to a rejection of all mundane affections in favour of heavenly love, casts a wide but not impossibly wide net. "The Franklin's Tale," with its explicit attempt to domesticate *amour courtois*, is also credible in terms of English court history; Chaucer's sister-in-law, Katherine Swynford, for many years mistress of John of Gaunt, eventually became the Duke's third wife. The words of Marie de France, in her *Lay of the Thorn*, come again to mind:

> It begins well, and endeth better, for these kisses find their fruit in marriage.

For some, the lasting value of *amour courtois* must lie in its gradual absorption into an ideal of marriage; the poetry of Edmund Spenser (1552–99) completes what the later Middle Ages had begun. For others, it must rest upon the special imaginative appeal of the original stories of secret, unlimited passion. Sir Thomas Malory, whose vast Arthurian compilation *Le Morte Darthur*[99] (c. 1470) was made almost at the close of the mediaeval period and whose inclinations were all toward stability and orthodoxy, was moved to write with pity and admiration of the love of Lancelot and Guinevere. It is their parting, rather than the death of King Arthur, that we find memorable:

> And Sir Lancelot awoke, and went and took his horse, and rode all that day and night in a forest, weeping.

References

1. Quoted in R. S. BRIFFAULT, *The Troubadours* (Bloomington, Ind. 1965), p. 69.
2. *ibid.*, p. 70.
3. See F. HEER, *The Mediaeval World* (London 1961), pl. 82.
4. See R. W. SOUTHERN, *The Making of the Middle Ages* (London 1953), pp. 71–2.

5. M. DOMINICA LEGGE, *Anglo-Norman Literature and its Background* (Oxford 1963), pp. 49–50.
6. GOTTFRIED VON STRASSBURG, *Tristan*, trans. by A. T. Hatto (paperback: Harmondsworth 1967), p. 44; see also R. S. LOOMIS (ed.), *Arthurian Literature in the Middle Ages* (Oxford 1959), pp. 145 ff.
7. LOOMIS (ed.), *op. cit.*, pp. 61 and 67.
8. *ibid.*, p. 394.
9. *ibid.*, pp. 396–7.
10. J. F. BENTON, "The Court of Champagne as a Literary Center," *Speculum* XXXVI (Cambridge, Mass. 1961), p. 576.
11. BRIFFAULT, *op. cit.*, p. 59.
12. LEGGE, *op. cit.*, p. 86.
13. *ibid.*, p. 364.
14. Corpus Christi College (Cambridge) manuscripts 2 and 3–4.
15. See F. J. E. RABY, *Christian Latin Poetry* (Oxford 1953), p. 334.
16. See, for instance, initial 'N' of the Prologue to Isaiah in the Bury Bible.
17. See *Larousse Encyclopaedia of Byzantine and Mediaeval Art*, ed. by R. Huyghe (London 1963), p. 231 (pl. 470–2).
18. C. H. HASKINS, *The Renaissance of the Twelfth Century* (New York 1957), p. 293.
19. See M. JAMIESON, "The Alliance of England and Sicily in the Second Half of the Twelfth Century," *England and the Mediterranean Tradition* (Oxford 1945), pp. 20–32; also OTTO DEMUS, *The Mosaics of Norman Sicily* (London 1949), pp. 448 ff.
20. T. S. R. BOASE, *English Art, 1100–1216* (Oxford 1953), pl. 22a.
21. *ibid.*, pp. 78–9.
22. See P. DRONKE, *The Medieval Lyric* (London 1968), pp. 151 ff.
23. M. M. LAZAR, *Amour courtois et fin'amors dans le littérature du XIIᵉ siècle* (Paris 1964), p. 278; passage translated by the author.
24. *The Parliament of Fowls*, ed. by D. S. Brewer (London 1960), lines 1–4.
25. DRONKE, *op. cit.*, pp. 109–12.
26. A. JEANROY (ed.), *Les chansons de Guillaume IX*, 2nd edn (Paris 1927), No. IX.
27. *ibid.*, VIII.
28. *ibid.*, IV.
29. Text in F. R. HAMLIN, P. T. RICKETTS, and J. HATHAWAY, *Introduction à l'étude de l'ancien provençal* (Geneva 1967), No. 18.
30. *ibid.*
31. *ibid.*
32. *ibid.*, p. 87.
33. Trans. by B. Smythe in *Troubadour Poets* (London/New York 1911), p. 20.
34. Text in HAMLIN, RICKETTS, and HATHAWAY, *op. cit.*, No. 17.
35. ANDREW MARVELL, "The Definition of Love."
36. HAMLIN, RICKETTS, and HATHAWAY, *op. cit.*, p. 96.
37. *ibid.*, No. 22.

38. *ibid.*
39. *ibid.*
40. *ibid.*, No. 24.
41. See the Provençal Biography in HAMLIN, RICKETTS, and HATHAWAY, *op. cit.*, p. 188.
42. *ibid.*
43. *ibid.*, No. 57.
44. BRIFFAULT, *op. cit.*, pp. 84–5.
45. C. S. LEWIS, *The Allegory of Love* (Oxford 1936), p. 4.
46. See P. DRONKE, *Medieval Latin and the Rise of the European Love Lyric* (Oxford 1965), Vol. I, Ch. I.
47. Original and translation in H. WADDELL, *Mediaeval Latin Lyrics* (London 1933), pp. 156–7. For the *Cambridge Songs*, see DRONKE, *The Medieval Lyric*, pp. 29–30 and 92–4, and *Medieval Latin . . .*, pp. 271–7.
48. See DRONKE, *The Medieval Lyric*, pp. 192–4, and *Medieval Latin . . .*, pp. 300–18.
49. Original and translation in WADDELL, *op. cit.*, pp. 246–7.
50. Quoted in BRIFFAULT, *op. cit.*, pp. 29–30.
51. *The Dove's Neck Ring*, trans. by A. R. Nykl (Paris 1931).
52. See A. DENOMY, *The Heresy of Courtly Love* (New York 1947).
53. G. LEFF, *Mediaeval Thought* (paperback: Harmondsworth 1958), p. 156.
54. See *Larousse Encyclopaedia of Byzantine and Mediaeval Art*, pl. 604.
55. See E. T. DONALDSON, "The Myth of Courtly Love," *Ventures* V, No. 2 (Yale 1965), pp. 16–23.
56. See C. H. HASKINS, "Henry II as a Patron of Literature," *Essays in Mediaeval History Presented to T. F. Tout* (Manchester 1925), p. 72.
57. BENOÎT DE SAINTE-MAURE, *Roman de Troie*, line 13,465; quoted in R. LEJEUNE, "Le rôle littéraire d'Alienor d'Aquitaine et de sa famille," *Cahiers de Civilization Médiévale* I (Poitiers 1958), p. 22.
58. LEJEUNE, *op. cit.*, p. 27.
59. *ibid.*, pp. 22–3.
60. *ibid.*, pp. 25–6.
61. LEGGE, *op cit.*, p. 53; ed. by J. Bédier (S.A.T.F., 1902, 1905), lines 843–6.
62. *ibid.*, p. 57; lines 3136, 3141, 3144.
63. *French Medieval Romances from the Lays of Marie de France*, trans. by E. Mason (London: 'Everyman' edn, undated), p. 136. The originals are in J. RYCHNER (ed.), *Les lais de Marie de France* (Paris 1969).
64. *French Medieval Romances . . .*, p. 143: *The Lay of the Thorn (Lai d'espine)*.
65. *ibid.*, p. 147.
66. *ibid.*, p. 93.
67. *ibid.*, p. 62.
68. *ibid.*, pp. 7–8.
69. *ibid.*, p. 103.
70. RYCHNER (ed.), *op. cit.*, *The Lay of the Honeysuckle*, lines 77–8.
71. BENTON, *op. cit.*, pp. 551 ff.
72. *Arthurian Romances: Chrétien de Troyes*, trans. by W. C. Comfort (London 1913), p. 270.

73. BENTON, *op. cit.*, p. 564.
74. *ibid.*; the quotation is from Evrat's verse translation of Genesis.
75. *Arthurian Romances: Chrétien de Troyes*, p. 329.
76. *ibid.*, p. 316.
77. *ibid.*, p. 289.
78. *ibid.*, p. 329.
79. *ibid.*, p. 310.
80. *ibid.*, pp. 21 and 69 (*Erec et Enide*).
81. *ibid.*, p. 89.
82. *ibid.*, p. 5.
83. *ibid.*, p. 41.
84. *ibid.*, p. 97 (*Cligès*).
85. ANDREAS CAPELLANUS, *The Art of Courtly Love*, trans. by J. J. Parry
86. (New York 1941).
87. GOTTFRIED VON STRASSBURG, *op. cit.*, p. 44.
    Troilus and Criseyde I, 231. The edition cited here and below is in *The Works of Geoffrey Chaucer*, ed. by F. N. Robinson, 2nd edn (London 1957).
88. *ibid.*, I, 1079–83.
89. *ibid.*, III, 12–4.
90. *ibid.*, 1765–7.
91. *ibid.*, 1261.
92. LEWIS, *op. cit.*, p. 197.
93. *Troilus and Criseyde* V, 1824.
94. Corpus Christi College (Cambridge) manuscript 61, folio1[b].
95. J. EVANS, *English Art, 1307–1461* (Oxford 1949), p. 84.
96. See GERVASE MATHEW, *The Court of Richard II* (London 1968).
97. W. W. SKEAT (ed.), *Chaucerian and Other Pieces* (Oxford 1935), pp. 1–101.
98. JOHN GOWER, *Confessio amantis*, ed. by R. A. Peck (New York 1968); see also the translation by T. Tiller (paperback: Harmondsworth 1963).
99. See E. VINAVER (ed.), *The Works of Sir Thomas Malory*, 3 vols. (Oxford 1967).

CHAPTER 13

The Mediaeval Lyric

Elizabeth Salter[*]

Nothing better illustrates the originality and resourcefulness of the mediaeval centuries than lyric poetry. As it is the most various of all their art-forms, constantly taking new shapes, accepting new resolutions, so it is the most richly venerable—its roots in a classical and oriental past, in traditions of song both learned and popular. Its themes span countries and cultures; it refuses to acknowledge strict linguistic boundaries; it is the servant of the simplest priest, instructing his country folk, and it is the splendid ambassador of prelate, king, and countess in their suits to earthly or heavenly lovers. To describe the mediaeval lyric is, in a very real sense, to describe mediaeval life—thought, sensation, and sight—for no other genre is so comprehensive in range and appeal. The world of the mediaeval lyric is the world of Celtic hermit and French courtier, Castilian monarch and Icelandic farmer, English civil servant, German aristocrat, and Italian friar. Its languages are those vernaculars of the brawling, expanding nations of Europe, as well as Latin, the international tongue of learning and sensibility.

Among all the remarkable features of its history, perhaps the most remarkable is its power to draw upon a multiplicity of sources—from the literature of the past, and from that of contemporary and neighbouring cultures—and to work constant, creative transmutations upon these materials. Consequently, there is no simple way of tracing out a steady progress from unformed beginnings, through trial and experiment, to maturity in one fortunate century. And this is true, whether we are concentrating upon the Latin or upon the vernacular lyric, in French, English, or German. Indeed, it would be disappointing if there were. We have long agreed that the development of mediaeval Western art, from early Christian mosaics and catacomb paintings to the late splendours of Gothic

[*] Professor of Mediaeval Literature and Director of the Centre for Mediaeval Studies, University of York.

445

cathedrals, is a series of encounters of old with new, East with West, Nordic with Mediterranean traditions. There is no century or country from which we can take the supreme and definitive examples of mediaeval art; each century solved afresh the problem of how best to spend its increasingly rich inheritance upon the needs of its people; each country contributed uniquely and recognizably.

So, before the "renaissance" in 14th-century Italy, came other mediaeval "renaissances": the Carolingian of 8th- and 9th-century France, the Ottonian of the 10th century under the Saxon emperors of Germany, and that of the 12th century, which was internationally active, from England to Sicily and beyond. No one could say that these great flowerings of mediaeval art, long before the days of Giotto, the van Eycks, and Donatello, were "preparations," either for each other or for that last renaissance of the 16th century. They present their own particular versions of a wealthy situation, in which the art and literature of the ancient world, available to varying degrees and in varying forms over the whole period, inspired new creative action. And each time, art-forms were produced that were complete and secure in themselves: there is nothing hesitant about the vibrant restless energy of a Carolingian line-drawing, or about the sumptuous colour of Ottonian painting. Twelfth-century Romanesque architecture and illumination, with their clear reminiscences of a Roman and a Nordic past and their acknowledgments of a Byzantine present, are full and assured statements. The free and intimate graces of high Gothic succeed these, supplementing other styles as expressions of mediaeval thought and devotion, but never replacing them.

Looking over the whole range of mediaeval art, and over that of the mediaeval lyric, we are bound to be impressed by this continuous freedom of inventiveness. Dealing with their source-materials, however august, in a spirit of lively admiration rather than obedient respect, mediaeval painters, sculptors, and poets adapt, rather than imitate. The precise imitation of classical form belongs to the renaissance of the 16th century, and it is a mark of its separation from the past. To the mediaeval artist, the past, whether immediate or distant, is an integral part of his history and his life; it is to be used for new and original conquests in words, stone, or paint.

At the outset, then, two observations. The sources of the mediaeval lyric, like those of mediaeval art, are deep and wide. To account for the origins of the earliest lyrics would be to deal with only a small part of the problem; later lyrics draw upon earlier ones—as Ottonian manuscript painters drew upon Carolingian, and 12th-century painters upon both—

in an exuberant plundering of source-materials. Moreover, no one century or country has the exclusive right to provide us with a dominant concept of the mediaeval lyric. Irish hermit poetry from the 9th century, Latin spring songs and Scandinavian skaldic verse from the 10th, English religious lyrics from late-13th-century Herefordshire, courtly ballads from 14th-century northern France, the hymns of the Latin Church and their simpler vernacular counterparts—all are "representative." But if complete coverage of this vast body of verse is not practicable, we can at least recognize its scope and variety.

One way of limiting the size of the problem is to make an early decision about treating the lyric from a poetic rather than a musical point of view. This, of necessity, means some sacrifice of truth as well as subtlety of presentation, but there are grounds for such a decision that are not altogether those of expediency. It must first be said that the relationship of words and music in the Middle Ages is a vital one. We know that Germanic, Celtic, and Roman peoples had musical traditions that contributed to the shaping of mediaeval song. The established range of Roman instrumental accompaniment, the constant and almost sacred association of Germanic court poetry and the harp, and the ancient connection between dance and music in the popular songs of the people, all played a part in the texts and music that have come down to us from the Middle Ages. In the finest of all the Anglo-Saxon heroic poems, *Beowulf*, the sound of the harp at the feast in hall represents the culture and civilization against which the forces of darkness enviously press:

> the harp-music, and clear song of a poet relating the creation of the world. . . .[1]

The Anglo-Saxon lay *Widsith* tells of the great poetic repertoire of the Germanic world: "loud to the harp the words sounded in harmony."[2]

It was natural for the Christian world to perpetuate these associations. True, the early Church Fathers had mixed feelings about the universal human liking for song. St John Chrysostom (345-407) sees that music is a natural accompaniment of the activities of daily life, but condemns "songs and dances of Satan," and the playing of professional musicians. Nevertheless, the church generally recognized the role of music in acts of worship: St Augustine speaks of being moved to tears by hymns and canticles, "when the sweet sound of the music of Thy Church thrilled my soul. . . ."[3] The legitimate co-operation of music and sacred words was strongly affirmed by St Ambrose (340-97), whose hymns were meant for the instruction of, and for use by, an unlearned congregation; he defined the

447

hymn as "song with praise of the Lord."[4] The Ambrosian hymns, with their uncomplicated quatrain form, their admirable blend of enthusiasm and dignity, and their simple melodies, were the foundation of Christian lyric. The hymn tradition of the Middle Ages was based upon such poetry; although metrical and musical changes would be wrought in succeeding centuries, the principles of Catholic hymnody had been set down.

But apart from this official recognition that religious song could be fully approved of in the hymn, as in liturgical ritual generally, it was also realized, especially in countries newly converted to Christianity, that existing local poetic forms with musical accompaniment could be used for sacred ends. The well-known story of Aldhelm, Bishop of Sherborne (639-709), attracting an audience for religious instruction by singing secular songs on a bridge at Malmesbury, gives some idea of the Church's tolerance of native traditions, provided they could be put to religious use. This remained a constant characteristic: we shall have many opportunities to notice the adaptation of secular modes for religious purposes—and, indeed, the reverse—in the mediaeval lyric. The early history of the sequence will show that this was a most complex business. The sequence was, after the hymn, the most important lyrical form of the Christian Church. Here, we have been told, the connection between words and music was fundamental: the lengthy melodic prolongation of the final *a* of the *Alleluia* in the Gradual of the Mass induced writers, for mnemonic reasons, to add words.[5] Words were found that fitted the strophic and repetitious arrangements of the melodies, and a poetic form emerged, built up of pairs of lines of parallel structure. Thus, in a very basic sense, music gave birth to words: even in the later stages of the development of the sequence, when it seems to have achieved independent poetic status, it can still, at times, be distinguished from the hymn in that its melody is changed for each pair of verses.[6]

But there are a few intrusive elements in what looks, at first, like a purely religious pattern. Some of the sequences of the 9th and 10th centuries seem to have borrowed well-known secular melodies for their words, and it has been suggested that the origins of the sequence lie as much in secular and vernacular song as in the Latin liturgy.[7] If there were "earlier, secular songs composed in the demanding sequence mode,"[8] none has survived: we find them first only in the late 10th century. But clearly we cannot afford to ignore the possibility that the creation of the sequence, verbally and musically, may have involved the progressive repetitions of both dance-song and liturgy.

The significant correlation of words and music in mediaeval secular lyric is most vehemently spoken for and illustrated in the works of the troubadour poets of southern France: "a verse without music is a mill without water," stated Folquet of Marseilles (d. 1231). Only about one tenth of the original settings of troubadour lyrics has come down to us; a larger proportion has been preserved in the case of the *trouvère* lyrics of northern France. On the evidence we have, it is possible to see that words and melody co-operated rewardingly:

> . . . the genius of the 12th and 13th centuries, which constructed architectural marvels in stone, achieved delicately balanced and infinitely varied forms in tone also . . . the forms of the troubadour and trouvère melodies anticipate practically all later song-forms.[9]

If, as is at least possible, the troubadours and *trouvères* were strongly influenced by religious music, by the hymns and sequences of the Church, they used what they borrowed in fresh and interesting ways. No other vernacular lyric literature of the high Middle Ages can rival that of northern and southern France for the verbal and musical dexterity expressed in a substantial number of pieces. The mediaeval lyric of France, therefore, would persuade us that we lose a great deal by considering words without music. To experience the total effect of an *alba* such as "Glorious king who heaven and earth did make," by the troubadour Guiraut de Bornelh, with its nostalgic refrain *Et ades sera l'alba* (And soon will come the morning), we need to have some sense of its complex and beautiful melody.[10]

The mediaeval lyric of England, however, allows for a great flexibility of attitude. Apart from the 15th-century carol, which was almost always intended to be sung, the religious lyric seems to have been primarily a literary form. Only about 30 of the large number left to us have musical settings. The very early English hymns of St Godric, hermit of Finchale, who died in 1170, show the influence of liturgical music in their settings,[11] and this represents a fairly general situation. If the poems of the troubadours and *trouvères* were known in England—and we have good reason to believe that they were—their music did not inspire any similar composition. The metres of some of the early-14th-century lyrics in the important Harleian collection (manuscript 2253) may suggest troubadour influence, but musically the connection seems to have been unimportant. Rather more 13th- than 14th-century lyrics have musical settings: it seems as if the circumstances that so notably widened the range of the English religious lyric in the 14th century also narrowed the function of music as a useful part of this religious verse. Many lyrics of the 14th century have specific jobs to do as devotional literature; manuscript rubrics make it clear that they were often intended as prayer or meditation.[12] The "song" with which the early-14th-century mystic Richard Rolle expressed his love of Christ—

> My sang es in syghyng, whil I dwel in þis way;
> My lyfe es in langyng, þat byndes me nyght & day[13]
>
> (Sighing is all my song, while I linger in this way;
> Longing is all my life, it binds me night and day)

—is a spiritual and poetic act, complete in itself: song symbolizes meditative fervour, and the melodies are "spirit ditties of no tone."

Some attractive settings of secular lyrics come down to us from both the 13th and the 14th centuries (the famous "Sumer is icumen in," from about 1320, needs no introduction[14]). But it is important to notice that Chaucer's lyrics are nearly all elaborate, literary productions, and that, for the roundel that closes his early dream-poem *The Parliament of Fowls*, he refers to a "French tune":

> The note, y trowe, ymaked was in Fraunce. . . .

It was, indeed, to France that Chaucer and courtly poets like him looked, for both literary and musical models, in the 14th century. Examples could be found in the works of Guillaume de Machaut (1300-77), who played a double role as musician and poet with the greatest skill and inventiveness. Not until the 15th century, with the compositions of John Dunstable (d. 1453) and the meteoric rise to popularity of the carol as a melodic and poetic form, did England really come into its own as a creative force in European music.

Situations such as these, in which exists an extensive lyric literature only partly linked with music, give us grounds for a predominantly non-musical approach. One other factor should weigh with us. The intimate fusion of words and music that often occurs in the Elizabethan madrigal, or in the songs of Schubert—the melody and accompaniment sensitively expressive of the nuances of the poetry—is not generally characteristic of the mediaeval lyric and its music. The melody can complement the words, co-operate with them, decorate them, or even clash with them. Always it maintains an independent existence, however, and is not intended to draw out the sense of the text by tonal or rhythmical subtleties. Consequently, the literary qualities of a mediaeval lyric can perfectly well be analysed and discussed, even when its music is ignored. The poem, like the music, can stand alone, and although we may miss a complex pattern

450

of words and music, we shall not often miss an interpretation of the words in the melody. A good example of this is the gloomy 13th-century lyric "Man mei longe him lives wene" (Man may expect his life to be long), which ends with the trenchant advice, "Man, before you drop from your bench, root out your sin." The music for this sad little piece is quite unsuited to its sentiments, and is probably a dance-tune in origin.[15] The music here acts as a counterpoint to the words rather than as a reinforcement. It is also interesting that two of the lyrics contained in Harley 2253 have musical settings in other manuscripts. The fact that the Harley scribe chose to present all the lyrics without music is surely some indication that in their own century these poems were regarded as self-sufficient literary productions, and that we shall not injure them if we also treat them as such.

Another procedure that might at first recommend itself as economical and reasonable would be the separation of the Latin and the vernacular lyric. But here at once we set up an entirely artificial, and perhaps dangerous, barrier. Not only do poets composing in the vernacular draw strongly and constantly upon Latin for their themes and lyric forms, but the writers of Latin lyric often preserve, as if in amber, refrains from some of the long-lost vernacular songs of Europe. If we isolate the Latin or the vernacular lyric, we are doing what no mediaeval poet ever did. It is not simply a question of translation, although the importance of this can be demonstrated from the religious verse of all the vernacular literatures of Europe. The mediaeval English religious lyric of the 14th century—

> Þe kynges baneres beth forth y-lad,
> Þe rode tokne is nou to-sprad,
> Whar he þat wrouth havet al monkunne,
> An-honged was vor oure sunne.[16]

> (The King's banners are led forth,
> The cross is now stretched out,
> Upon which He, who made mankind,
> Was hung, for our sins.)

—turns the celebrative pageant of the great processional hymn by Venantius Fortunatus (530-603), "Vexilla regis prodeunt," into a personal witness of triumph.

But the relationship of Latin and vernacular lyric is more subtle and complex than this might suggest. The influence of Latin words and rhythms is often pervasive and evocative. Behind one of the finest of early English lyrics of the Passion—

> Nou goþ sonne under wod—
> Me reweþ, marie, þi faire Rode.
> Nou goþ sonne under tre—
> Me reweþ, marie, þi sone and þe[17]
>
> (Now sinks the sun behind the wood—
> I pity, Mary, thy fair face.
> Now sinks the sun behind the tree—
> I pity, Mary, thy Son and thee)

—lies traditional imagery from Latin hymns. The Latin concept of a double eclipse of the sun at the Crucifixion, in the dying God and the dying sun,

> Sol eclypsum patitur
> dum sol verus moritur
>
> (The sun suffered an eclipse
> While the true sun died. . .)

is localized and dramatized: a particular sunset, in an English wood, and a particular moment, with the poet looking compassionately upon the grief-stained face of Mary: "Me reweþ, marie, þi faire Rode." The elaboration of a Latin theme is at once delicate and bold.

On the other hand, Latin lyrics are rich with suggestions of vernacular songs from the earliest centuries of the mediaeval West. A dawn-song in a 10th-century manuscript, with a refrain in Provençal, speaks of a cultural situation in which the languages of scholarship and love are interchangeable: it also speaks, provocatively, of a poem just beyond our reach:

> Dawn over the dark sea brings on the sun;
> She leans across the hilltop: see, the light.[18]

The close and entirely natural association of Latin and Provençal in this poem makes us wonder how many Latin lyrics of the 10th and 11th centuries draw upon such elusive vernacular love-poems. There was a strong tradition of love-poetry as early as the 9th century in Europe, as we know from the *Capitulary of Charlemagne*, which in 789 laid down that no abbess should allow her nuns to compose or send *wini-leodas* (love-songs). It is more than likely that such *leodas* were in the vernacular languages, as well as in Latin. From the *Codex Exoniensis*, written in the west of England in the 10th century, we have the fragmentary love-lament *Wulf and Eadwacer*, a woman's intense expression of desire for her outlawed lover:

Wulf, my Wulf, my longings for you
Have made me faint: your rare visits,
My sad heart, no hunger for food.[19]

With its refrain "Ungelic is us" (Our lots are different), its brief but telling references to sadness in a wintry landscape, and its dramatic fluctuation of rhythms—

I longed for my Wulf on his wide wanderings,
When it was rainy weather, and I sat desolate:
When he put his strong arms about me,
I was happy, but I was also sad.
Wulf, my Wulf

—it bends the long alliterative line of Germanic tradition to its passionate purposes.

Miscellanies of Latin poetry—such as the one that belonged to the monastery of St Augustine at Canterbury in the 11th century, and that is now in Cambridge—probably represent the gathering of riches from all known kinds of verse, Latin and vernacular. Among the half-dozen love poems of this manuscript are the incomparable "Levis exsurgit zephirus" (Lightly stirs the west wind) and "Iam, dulcis amica, venito" (Now come, my sweet love). Their place in *The Cambridge Songs*,[20] among fragments of classical verse, Church sequences, *fabliaux*, and laments for emperors and kings, is only at first surprising. In spite of the official complaints of the Church about secular song, a monastery (no less than a secular school or an ecclesiastical or royal court) acted as a magnet for literary compositions of all kinds. It was in a legal manuscript (Vatican Reg. 1462) that the first bilingual *alba* was written down; and it was in a "useful" monastic miscellany that the first of many European invitations to love was recorded:

Iam, dulcis amica, venito
quam sicut cor meum diligo;
intra in cubiculum meum,
ornamentis cunctis onustum.

(Now come, my sweet love,
Whom I love as my heart;
Come to my room,
Filled with delights for you.)

But this and its melancholy companion, the spring-song "Levis exsurgit zephirus," are not simple poems; they are elaborate complications, carrying their burdens of classical and biblical reminiscence with graceful confidence. Ovid and the Song of Songs are two of the sources: others, no doubt, lie in the dancing rhythms of vernacular lyric. A fragment on the last folio of the manuscript is a Latin dance-song: the origins of this little poem, which is a woman's frank offer of love, are probably older than the manuscript and its Latin words. A clue may lie in the refrain, which is little more than a pattern of sound, a guide for hands and dancing feet:

> Veni, dilectissime,
> et a et o,
> gratam me invisere,
> et a et o et a et o![21]

> (Come to me, my dearest love,
> With ah! and oh!
> Visit me—what joys you'll have!
> With ah! and oh! and ah! and oh!)

It has been thought that poems such as these are Latin versions of songs against which Church councils from the 6th to the 9th century set themselves. Snatches of these *puellarum cantica* (women's love-songs) have been preserved in the *ḫarǧas* of Moslem Spain—verses in romance dialect, often strikingly similar in theme and tone.[22]

The Latin lyric, therefore, is not safely regarded as "the scholar's lyric"—a witty, graceful, often imaginative and sensuous poetic form, of different context and aim from the vernacular songs of its time. The most recent study of its history and nature stresses that

> it is not possible even to aim at an assessment of what the Latin lyric lends or borrows. The Latin lyric is omnipresent and everywhere contemporaneous with the vernacular. Often they enrich each other—it is scarcely possible to say more.[23]

When we find expressions and attitudes common to Latin, English, French, and German poetry, it is only necessary to remember that the contacts between various classes of mediaeval poets and singers were lively and continuous. Minstrel, cleric, and courtier met naturally at ecclesiastical or royal court, at cathedral school or university.

Although it is important to remember the easy commerce between Latin and vernacular lyric poetry, it is even more important to allow for the interchange of lyric forms and conventions among all the vernacular literatures of Europe. We need not go into elaborate examination of metrical and verbal formulas to prove this: it is difficult (and not always rewarding) to establish precise patterns of indebtedness. Certain statements have already been made about the relationship of Latin religious verse with that of the vernacular. It is more than likely, also, that Latin secular lyric influenced southern French troubadour poetry of the 12th century and German *Minnesang* of the 13th and 14th centuries in a variety of ways. But, as we have seen, vernacular lyric forms pre-date, and coexist with, Latin: only in the case of the most exact translation can we ever be sure that the flow of influence is one way, not two. What has been described as a "total situation . . . shared by 'chevalier et clerc et lai' "[24] embraces all kinds of composition. This total situation is European in the widest sense: similarities in stanza forms and types of sentiment can be discovered between the Arabic love poetry of mediaeval Spain and that of Provence. French *rondeaux* and *virelais* also seem to resemble the Arabic *zajal* stanza. In turn, the Italian *canzone* is an adaptation of the Provençal *canso*. The *laude* poems of the 13th-century Italian Jacopone da Todi use verse structures reminiscent of French dance-songs. It is probably a misrepresentation of the facts to say that any one vernacular poetry was ever, at any one time, dependent upon, and wholly imitative of, another: each body of mediaeval vernacular lyric must have been built upon an indigenous tradition of song.

But the passage of influences was easily made. In Spain and in Sicily, for instance, there were courts such as those of Alfonso of Castile (1221-84) and Frederick II (1194-1250), to which came Moslems, Christians, and Jews, scholars, musicians, and poets of all nationalities. In multilingual centres such as these, the exchange of ideas and forms would have been constant. We know that much of the philosophy and science of the ancient world was transmitted to the West through Moslem Spain and Sicily, and we may suppose that poetic themes and forms were transmitted too. As long as our observations about likenesses—between Islamic and Romance poetry, between troubadour lyrics and popular verse of Arabic Spain, between Italian love-songs written in Sicily and French love-songs written in Provence—are not turned into rigid theories of origins, there can be nothing more rewarding than the sense of a many-levelled and international community of lyric poetry during the mediaeval period. We may not want to prove that the measures and some of the materials of the first recognizable troubadour poet, Guilhem of Poitou, ninth duke of Aquitaine (1071-1127), were derived from the poetry of Moslem Spain. But it is interesting that he married a Spanish princess, who no doubt had bilingual minstrels at her court. However sceptically we may regard the more romantic stories of his grand-daughter Eleanor of Aquitaine and her "courts of love," it is significant for the general development of secular English lyric that the queen of England in the 12th century was patroness of many famous French poets.

Europe, in these centuries, is webbed by lines of communication, routes along which traders, diplomats, pilgrims, courtiers, scientists, and scholars take their business. Moreover, in spite of the crusades and a Holy War against the Moslem "infidels," the frontiers between the East and the West were not closed to mercantile and cultural exchange. Up to the mid-13th century, the mediaeval Western world was an open and expanding world, receptive and forthgoing. When we read of the "tribute that Islamic, Byzantine, and border people paid to Western merchants and conquerors"[25] during these years, it is tempting to see the richness of the mediaeval lyric, Latin and vernacular, as one of the results of that tribute.

Demarcation between languages and countries is a crude way of dealing with a complex subject: demarcation between religious and secular areas in lyric composition is almost as unsatisfactory. True, certain bold contrasts are possible: the tender meditations upon Christ's harsh death—

> Whyte was his naked breste, & rede his blody syde[26]

—compared with vigorous songs of peasant life by the German poet, Neidhart von Reuenthal (1180-1250), or the gay and rueful little narratives of casual love-encounters from the English 15th century:

> Hey noyney, I wyll love our ser Iohn and I love eny.[27]

Contrasts are possible because the mediaeval lyric covers all parts of mediaeval life: it is devout and bitterly satirical, coarse and refined, simple and learned. Its writers are professors, civil servants, aristocrats, monks, and minor clergy. A performer could rise to become a renowned poet, as did Martin Codax in 13th-century Portugal; a diplomat or civil servant in imperial service could assume the literary role of vagabond, to produce the most "bohemian" poem of the Latin Middle Ages, the *Confessio* of the "Archpoet":

> Via lata gradior
> more inventutis,
> implico me vitiis
> inmemor virtutis,
> voluptatis avidus
> magis quam salutis,
> mortuus in anima
> curam gero cutis.[28]

(Down the broad way do I go,
Young and unregretting,
Wrap me in my vices up,
Virtue all forgetting,
Greedier for all delight
Than heaven to enter in:
Since the soul in me is dead,
Better save the skin.)

By the very nature of their composers, their materials, and their social contexts, mediaeval lyrics can, within their span, provide us with contrasts, paradoxes, and reversals of expectation of a most dramatic kind. But the easy contrast between devout and secular poetry, frequently urged upon us by voices from the Middle Ages—Church councils, preachers, monastic chroniclers—does not tell us much more than we already know: that lyric served all classes and needs in this period. It gives us a quantitative, not a qualitative, pattern for the whole wide field before us.

Some of the most significant—possibly unique—qualities of the mediaeval lyric could have come into being only in a situation that allowed great freedom of movement between secular and devout worlds. We owe the preservation of many of the finest of secular love-lyrics to their inclusion in religious manuscripts: it is more important that love-poems were first admitted to the 11th-century collection from St Augustine's, Canterbury, than that they were later scratched over by the knife of a disapproving scribe. Manuscripts from the monastery of St Martial, in Limoges, show that, as early as the 9th century, its stock of muscial items included heroic verse, laments upon Frankish leaders, and personal and philosophic lyrics. By the 10th century it had "Iam, dulcis amica, venito"— in a shortened form—in its repertoire. And by the 12th century, one of its manuscripts contained the moving, nostalgic "De ramis cadunt folia" (Down from the branches fall the leaves), one of the most imaginative of Latin lyrics, a celebration of love in winter-time and a lament for unsatisfied desire:

Down from the branches fall the leaves,
A wanness comes on all the trees,
The summer's done;
And into his last house in heaven
Now goes the sun.[29]

The finest collection of Latin secular lyrics remaining to us, the 13th-century *Codex Buranus*, came from the monastery of Benedictbeuern, in Upper Bavaria. In this manuscript the proportion of secular to religious pieces is uniquely high: love-lyrics, some of them bilingual, in Latin and German, fill more than half the pages. Yet it is even more significant that such a compilation could have been associated, however unofficially, with a monastery. Its best lyrics, the *Carmina Burana*, blend argument, passion, and metaphor in a way unrivalled by any other of the whole period.[30]

This secular-religious conjunction applied to England too: Harleian 2253, which preserves a large number of secular lyrics from the 13th and early 14th centuries, was probably connected with one or other of the many religious foundations in mediaeval Herefordshire. In the variety of its contents, it resembles some of the earlier manuscript collections: saints' lives, *fabliaux*, political songs and satires, extracts from theological works, and religious paraphrases are accompanied by lyrics both secular and religious. In its bilingual (even trilingual) range, it carries much further the tendencies already noticeable in the *Codex Buranus*: Latin, Anglo-French, and English are used for its prose and verse. The quality of the secular lyrics in English is very high indeed; they range from elaborate rituals of adoration to delicate spring-songs of supplication. Their imagery is rich and their verse-forms expertly managed. Reading these poems in the context of their manuscript, we must find them a familiar blend of sophistication and sensuousness; their writers can manipulate language and ideas already well-tried in Latin and continental lyrics. The presence of the trilingual "Dum ludis floribus" (While you play amidst the flowers) is symptomatic: the manuscript takes for granted a cultured milieu, in touch with courtly and devout literature, both Latin and vernacular, as well as with more popular teaching literature of the Church:

> Scripsi hec carmina in tabulis;
> mon ostel est en mi la vile de Paris;
> may y sugge namore, so wel me is;
> ʒef hi deʒe for love of hire, duel hit ys.[31]

> (I have written down my songs in a book;
> My lodging is in the city of Paris;
> I cannot say more, for the life of me;
> If I should die for love of her, it would be a sad thing.)

But the easy company kept by secular lyric poetry in religious miscellanies is not by any means the only reason for refusing to separate the two areas of composition. Certainly it seems true that compilers of manuscripts, in monastery or cathedral priory, were able to draw upon an impressive variety of sources for their materials. It also seems true that the contacts of religious and secular lyrics were close and mutually beneficial. That a lyric could, in fact, be shared by religious and secular worlds is abundantly clear from the "double" version of "Iam, dulcis amica, venito." Without its last two ardent verses—"Karissima, noli tardere; studeamus nos nunc amare . . ." (Beloved, do not delay: let us turn now to love . . .)—it occurs as a sacred song in one of the early St Martial of Limoges manuscripts; complete, it comes from the St Augustine of Canterbury manuscript. And, in many ways, the flexible use made of it is legitimate: as we have said, it is indebted alike to Ovid and the Song of Songs:

> Already snow and ice are melting,
> Leaves and plants spring:
> The nightingale sings on high—
> Love burns deep in the heart.

When mediaeval poets had to hand a biblical expression of love such as the Song of Songs—which, in spite of thorough allegorization by the Church Fathers, retained all its original power as an erotic celebration of beauty—the overlapping of the vocabulary of religious and secular hymns of love was inevitable.

> Your breasts
> Are scented as wine,
> Their pallor finer than milk or lillies,
> Their perfume sweeter than flowers and spices.[32]

The lady of these lines is the Virgin Mary, but her traditional attributes could just as easily be applied to a mortal girl:

> Ave, formosissima,
> gemma pretiosa,
> ave decus virginum,
> virgo gloriosa.[33]
>
> (Hail, most beautiful one,
> Most precious jewel,
> Hail, glory of virgins,
> Virgin most renowned.)

So, with the growth of a particularly personal devotion to Christ and his mother, from the late 10th century onward, the naturalness and the desirability of re-interpreting the most secular of spring and love conventions in spiritual contexts would have seemed unquestionable. All

459

must be lavished upon Christ and Mary, instead of upon a mortal lover: the shift of emphasis in itself is an act of worship. Consequently, much lies behind the "paired" lyrics in Harley 2253, which describe Christ's love and woman's love in identical stanza forms and with some parallelisms of language—"Crist, þin ore!", "Ledy, þin ore!" (Christ, have mercy! Lady, have mercy!)[34] And much, too, lies behind those lyrics that preface a meditation upon Christ's passion or a prayer to Mary with a seasonal motif—of autumn, for instance:

> Nou skrinkeþ rose ant lylie-flour
> þat whilen ber þat suete savour
> in somer, þat suete tyde.[35]

> (Now rose and lily fade away,
> Which once gave forth such sweet scent,
> In the happy summer season.)

Or of spring:

> When y se blosmes springe
> ant here foules song,
> a suete love-longynge
> myn herte þourhout stong.[36]

> (When I see flowers spread,
> And hear bird-song,
> A sweet desire for love
> Pierces right through my heart.)

In the Canterbury collection of Latin lyrics, the poem "Vestiunt silvae" (The woods are clothed) prefaces one stanza of pious allegory with five that rehearse how, in the thick woodland, "all birds, everywhere, sing of summer."[37]

More difficult to define, but equally important if we are to understand the subtler ranges of the mediaeval lyric, is the mixture of religious and secular language and concepts within a single poem. Nothing could better prepare us for the splendid certainties of the presentation of human love in Dante's *Divina commedia* (c. 1306–21), or for the equally splendid ambiguities of its presentation in Chaucer's *Troilus and Criseyde* (c. 1385), than a 10th-century Latin song from a theological manuscript, "Deus amet puellam" (May God love my girl). The most recent study of the Latin lyric has brought to notice the extraordinary qualities of this poem,[38] which occurs in its manuscript between theological writings. The refrain of "Deus amet puellam" links the idea of salvation with that of the beauty of the beloved: through adoration of her perfect and blessed beauty, all men can come to God:

> Hail, now, for ever!
> And may Christ be with you.
> May God love my girl.
>
> Let all say "Amen"
> Who seek repose in heaven!
> May God love my girl.[39]

Although this appears to be the most audacious example of its kind, love-poetry of the Middle Ages does sometimes dare to involve religious belief with human passion—not in order to contrast and evaluate, but to enrich. The whole of Book III of Chaucer's *Troilus and Criseyde*, with its concrete and passionate praise of love, is built upon a religious and philosophical foundation. When Troilus acknowledges "Benigne love, thow holy bond of thinges" (III, 1261), he sees the human dedication and contract as one way of confirming the divine coherence of creation. This occurs in a narrative poem. In a slighter but still significant way, English vernacular lyrics bring human love within the compass of God's approbation: the lady of the ornate lyric "Annot and John"[40] is praised in a wide range of images, some of which have distinct religious connotations:

> trewe triacle ytold wiþ tonges in trone
>
> (the finest remedy heaven could describe).

She is also "blithe yblessed of Crist" (joyfully blessed by Christ) when she grants her lover's requests. Of another lady of "Rybbesdale," in Yorkshire, the poet assures us,

> He myhte sayen þat Crist hym seʒe
> That myhte nyhtes neh hyre leʒe,
> Hevene he hevede here.[41]
>
> (He could say that Christ favoured him
> Who might lie beside her of a night:
> His heaven would be here.)

It is in Italian lyrics of the 13th century, however, that the confrontation of divine and human issues is most movingly expressed. The Florentine poet Guido Guinizelli (1235–76), challenged by God that he has sought him in a vain love, through a mere "semblance," replies that

461

his lady had the appearance of an angel—it was no sin if he set his love in her:

> . . . Tenne d'angel sembianza
> Che fosse del tuo regno:
> Non mi fu fallo, s'in le posi amanza.[42]
>
> (She had the appearance of an angel coming from your kingdom:
> it was not wrong if I set my love in her.)

The object of his love is crowned in Heaven, his hope of Paradise; to think of her is to enter into a state of holiness:

> La vostra Donna ch'e'n ciel coronata,
> ond'e la vostra speme in paradiso,
> e tutta santa ormai vostra memoria
> contemplando.[43]
>
> (Your lady, who is crowned in Heaven and is your hope of Paradise—
> in contemplation of her your remembrance becomes, at last, all
> blessed.)

Such poetry culminates naturally in Dante's vision of Beatrice, *Donna di virtu,* "through whom alone mankind excels all that is contained within the Heaven."[44]

More easily than other kinds of poetry, the mediaeval lyric passed barriers of country, language, class, and belief. Like the portable art of the Middle Ages—the reliquaries, caskets, manuscripts, fabrics, and ritual objects—its convenient form enabled it to travel light and to exert an influence quite out of proportion to its size. If we consider it as a European, and not as a narrowly national, poetic genre, it touched most experiences, intellectual, imaginative, and emotional, and spoke to most people. Faced with such wealth of material, we must select certain areas for closer scrutiny.

Early Irish Lyric

It is to Irish Christian poets of the 8th and 9th centuries that we must look for some of the most exciting innovations in Latin hymn writing and (by extension) in lyric writing generally. Their rich, almost eccentric, use of rhyme, combined with assonance and alliteration, produced a verse of thick and elaborate substance, comparable to the ornately patterned carvings and manuscript pages of the Irish Church during these centuries. But we should miss something quite unique in mediaeval lyric if we attended only to this Irish Latin poetry and ignored what was being composed at the same time in the vernacular, in a variety of stanza forms, with rhyme and alliteration.

In many fields, the Latin and vernacular verse of early Ireland is complementary: the same Christian Church that, from the 6th century onward, established itself in monastic communities and in the solitary cells of anchorites all over Ireland,[45] used both languages to express its satisfaction and its delight in the religious life:

> domus deliciis plena,
>   super petram constructa,
> necnon vinea vera,
>   ex Aegypto transducta.[46]

> (a house full of delights,
>   set upon a rock,
> indeed, the true vineyard,
>   brought out of Egypt.)

> I have a hut in the wood,
> none knows it but my lord;
> an ash tree this side, a hazel beyond,
> a great tree on a mound enfolds it. . . .

> The voice of the wind against its branchy wood,
> grey with cloud;
> cascades of the river, the swan's song,
> lovely music.[47]

The quality that distinguishes these Irish verses from their Latin counterparts is clear in the second stanza of the hermit poem, quoted above. Not only do these poets feel strongly for the changing aspects and moods of the natural world, but they have also a power of selection, a vision, that is both brooding and sharp. The description of an ideal hermit existence, attributed in the manuscript to Manchin of Lomanaghan (d. 655), picks out significant details: the purity to be found in a life

> praying through the long ages
> to the king who moves the sun. . .[48]

is focussed, brilliantly, in the "very blue shallow well" beside the cell, and in the "bright candles over the holy white scriptures." In another brief poem, the lark rising in song is likened to the solitary man, singing psalms to God; the analogy is not unusual, but the poet makes it a highly personal piece of observation by stressing the particular moment when the lark called, and he remembered its wide-mouthed song:

> The skilled lark calls,
> I go outside to watch it
> That I may see its gaping beak
> Above against the dappled cloudy sky.[49]

Everything in this poetry is lucid and disciplined, without being severe. It has the power to concentrate and re-express a whole range of emotions in a single, vividly presented image:

> Sweet little bell
> That is struck in the windy night,
> I had liefer go to a tryst with thee
> Than to a tryst with a foolish woman.[50]

This stanza, from the margin of an Irish manuscript, is of a piece with another marginal comment from a manuscript of Cassiodorus on the Psalms: "Pleasant is the sunlight today upon these margins, because it flickers so." The bell and the dancing sunlight swiftly and economically recreate an earlier world: the life of the recluse, secure in the heart of solitude, and content in renunciation: the life of the busy scribe, momentarily dazzled by natural beauty.

Not all this poetry is religious. But throughout, whether it is cast in elegiac, gnomic, or descriptive mould, it displays an intense and personal feeling for the sensuous realities of the outside world. This may be expressed in a sinister and dramatic context—as, for example, a welcoming of rough seas as a reprieve against Viking attacks:

> Bitter is the wind tonight—
> It tosses the ocean's white hair;
> Tonight I fear not the fierce warriors of Norway,
> Coursing on the Irish seas.[51]

Or it may simply inform a commentary upon the nature of the seasons. Particularly acute are the winter poems: the seasonal omens are registered with keen and delicate precision:

> I have tidings for you;
> the stag bells,
> winter snows,
> summer has gone.

464

Crimson the bracken,
it has lost its shape;
the wild goose has raised
its accustomed cry.[52]

Lyrics that preface their main themes—of human love, of Christ's passion, or of Mary's compassion—with descriptions of summer and winter are, of course, abundant in Latin and continental vernacular verse by the 11th and 12th centuries. But some of these Irish lyrics date from the 9th century. The stanzas immediately above, telling how "summer has gone," are fully four centuries older than "Estas in exilium"[53] (Summer's now in exile) in the *Carmina Burana*. A May-day song, attributed to the legendary hero Finn McCool, predates the "Levis exsurgit zephirus" by two centuries:

Cétemain cain cucht,
rée rosáir rann;
canait luin laid láin
dia lai grian gai ngann.
Seinnid caille céol;
con-greinn séol sid slán;
síatair denn do dinn,
dé do loch linn lán.[54]

(May-day, fair aspect, perfect season; blackbirds sing a full lay when the sun casts a meagre beam. Woodland music plays; melody provides perfect peace; dust is blown from dwelling-place, and haze from lake full of water.)

The origins of this Irish season poetry are obscure; pagan folk-festivals, the practical need of a peasant society to work by the signs of weather and bird-song, and a knowledge of Latin calendars have been suggested. All may be involved. The fact remains that there is a robust beauty about early Irish lyric that makes continental verse of the 12th and 13th centuries seem, by comparison, mere exercises in graceful description:

It is rough, black, dark, misty,
dogs are vicious in cracking bones;
the iron pot is put upon the fire
after the dark black day. . . .

Raw and chilly is icy spring,
cold will arise in the wind:
the ducks of the watery pool are crying. . . .

> A good season is peaceful summer;
> eddies swirl in the stream;
> good is the warmth in the turf.[55]

This direct, highly individual note is struck in humorous poetry too: the scribe Colum Cille, viewing his output with half-amused, half-weary detachment, makes the monotonous job of copying into an imaginative adventure:

> My hand is weary with writing,
> My sharp quill is not steady.
> My slender-beaked pen pours forth
> A draught of shining dark-blue ink.
>
> My little dripping pen travels
> Across the plain of shining books
> Without ceasing, for the wealth of the great,
> Whence my hand is weary with writing.[56]

The dexterity of this little poem, its neat conciseness, not excluding but containing phantasy, compare interestingly with an Anglo-Saxon poem of roughly the same date. The Anglo-Saxon verse line—with its length and weight, reinforced by emphatic alliteration, and rarely set into any stanzaic pattern—was not susceptible to compact, deft treatment. There is little in that great body of verse that could properly be called "lyric," with perhaps the exception of the *Wulf and Eadwacer* poem quoted above. The most informal kind of verse-composition from pre-Conquest England is the riddle. In one of these a poet takes the same general theme as his Irish neighbour—the labours of the scribe—but the result is quite different. The Anglo-Saxon riddle of the pen and fingers is deliberately enigmatic, mysterious. The situation is martial, even sinister—the "struggling warrior" of the arm directs the "four strange creatures," thumb, fingers, and pen, over their course:

> I saw four strange creatures
> Journeying together: their tracks were dark,
> Their path very black: swift did it move,
> Faster than birds, it flew in the air,
> Dived under the wave. Restlessly laboured
> The struggling warrior who pointed their way,
> All four of them, over inlaid gold.[57]

Lastly, we must single out the 8th- or 9th-century Irish lyric on the monk and his mousing cat, "White Pangur," as an example of humanity that never becomes sentimental, of humour that never becomes whimsical:

> I and my cat, White Pangur,
> Have each his special art:
> His mind is set upon hunting mice,
> Mine is upon my special craft.
>
> He rejoices with quick leaps
> When in his sharp claws sticks a mouse:
> I, too, rejoice when I have grasped
> A problem difficult, and dearly loved.
>
> Though we are thus at all times,
> Neither hinders the other,
> Each of us, pleased with his own art,
> Amuses himself alone.[58]

It is not, perhaps, a coincidence that the magnificent sacred monogram from the most famous of all Irish Christian manuscripts, the 8th-century *Book of Kells*,[59] contains, folded secretly into the dense spirals of its decoration, two cats and four mice. Two of the mice are impertinently nibbling cheese. Yet the humour of this subject is not allowed to disturb the mazy and sacred design of the whole page: it is controlled, as the humour of the "White Pangur" poem is controlled.

French Secular Lyric of the 12th and 13th Centuries

In spite of its individuality and beauty, Irish vernacular lyric had little influence outside the Celtic world—the lands that lay around that much-travelled "Celtic pond," the Irish Sea. In this it is similar to another form of early vernacular lyric, Scandinavian skaldic verse, which was brought to a high degree of sophistication in Iceland in the 11th century,[60] but whose circulation was limited to Norse countries and settlements. (Although we can assume, from the stories we have of Icelandic skalds or poets visiting the courts of English kings, that their poetry was understood in England, there is no evidence that it had any influence on English composition.)

The same cannot be said of French lyric verse, which came into full maturity in the 12th century and influenced the form and content of almost all other vernacular lyric on the continent, and completely redirected the course of English poetry. If we include the troubadour verse of southern France as well as the northern French lyric of the *trouvères*,[61] we are faced with the finest range of vernacular song from any country in the Middle Ages. Every kind of lyric writing is there, in all its metrical variations: like the French romances of the same period, the French lyric was rightly famous throughout the Western mediaeval world.

The first known southern-French poet using lyric forms, composing on secular themes, and exclusively concerned with the vernacular is Guilhem of Poitou (1071–1126), grandfather of Eleanor of Aquitaine, who was to become queen of France and of England and patroness of many poets. We have only to look at some of the circumstances of the life of Guilhem to realize how complex is the make-up of this southern-French lyric, which, in the hands of the troubadours of the 12th century, seems to have developed from very modest beginnings into the most admired of verse traditions. The key word here may be "seems," for the 10th-century Latin poem with its Provençal refrain probably gives us a glimpse of lyric now vanished from record, but well known to the poetic innovators of the early 12th century. Although there remains a silence between that *alba* and the love-poetry of Guilhem, we can make some guesses as to what may have existed, and what may have strengthened and enriched native resources in the 11th and 12th centuries.

The period spanned by Guilhem's life saw the establishment of a period of splendid culture in southern France and in the neighbouring lands of Castile and Aragon. These are the years of the reconquest of most of Spain from Moorish rule; begun in the reign of Ferdinand of Castile (1037–65), the recovery of Spanish territories proceeded steadily: Toledo fell to Alfonso VI of León in 1085, and Saragossa to Alfonso I of Aragon in 1118. Thus not only was Spanish dominion confirmed, but the wealth of the Moslem civilization of Spain was released to the Spaniards:

> . . . the Spanish princess . . . blossomed into Oriental splendour. The courts of Castile and Aragon were thereafter accounted the most brilliant in Christendom. They were the Mecca of the poets . . . .[62]

And this wealth, this luxury, also extended to southern France. It is worth stressing that the ties of the lands of southern France, whose language was *langue d'oc*, were traditionally with Spain rather than with northern France. The lords of Castile, Aragon, Toulouse, and Provence were linked by marriage and by political and cultural interests: the lands of Provence remained dependent territories of the kingdom of Aragon until the brutal Albigensian Crusade (1209–44) finally subjugated southern France and linked it to northern France. Contacts were strong between poets and princes of these countries. But so, too, were the links of southern France, at this time, with the world to the east; trading agreements were concluded with Italy and with Syria, and the complex of lands known conveniently by the language they spoke, Languedoc, was at the centre of a vast commercial and cultural region stretching from Portugal to Syria and beyond.

Guilhem, "a prince more powerful than the King of France,"[63] was well placed to give the vernacular lyric an aristocratic status and (although his own verses were not over-elaborate) to point the way for others to attempt more elaborate variations on models from Latin and from other vernacular languages. His marriage in 1095 to the young widow of the king of Aragon strengthened the existing bonds between the nobility of Poitiers, Aquitaine, Castile, and Aragon. His military activities in Spain, as an ally of the king of Aragon, also underline his familiarity with Spanish life and culture. It has been suggested that similarities between some of his verse-forms and those of the poets of Moorish Spain may be explained in this way. And it is certainly probable that his wife, Philippa of Aragon, had minstrels in her train who were accustomed to performing the Hispano-Moorish songs that had reached such a high level of achievement by the 11th century. During its centuries of domination, Moslem Spain had become bilingual: in addition to Arabic, a Romance dialect was spoken. Arabic poetry, especially of the more popular kind, contained a good deal of Romance vocabulary, and communication between Spaniard and Moslem had become simple and habitual. Metrical structures and even themes could easily have been passed from Hispano-Arabic poetry, through the media of the courts of Aragon and Castile, to the poets of southern France.[64]

But Guilhem had other traditions to draw upon. Within his territories lay the monastery of St Martial at Limoges. We have already noted some of its manuscript collections of religious lyrics; since the 10th century it had been recognized as one of the finest musical centres in Europe. At least one of Guilhem's lyrics is based upon a Latin hymn, in metre and melody, and the accomplished technique of his verse, as well as the clear knowledge—sometimes a contemptuous knowledge—it shows of a range of elaborate attitudes towards idealized love, makes it very likely that he was familiar not only with Hispano-Arabic but also with Latin panegyric poetry. At least three kinds of verse tradition may have contributed to the small but very important output of Guilhem, the first troubadour, for we must not forget the incalculable but very real influence of the vernacular song that momentarily breaks into Latin lyric of the 10th century and then disappears.

Only 11 poems by Guilhem remain to us, but they impress upon us one fact: that the troubadour verse of southern France is not remarkable only for its expression of courtly, idealized love in graceful and varied conventions of language and attitude.* Some of Guilhem's songs are direct and earthy, advertising his prowess in a love-making that has nothing tentative or refined about it; he is known, he says, as "maiestre certa" (acknowledged master) in that "olde daunce":

> Never did my love have me at night
> Without her wanting me next day.

His spring song "Ab la dolchor del temps novel" (In the sweetness of the new season), in a more serious vein, commemorates a day of love with a mixture of thoughtfulness and frank desire that reminds us of the best of Latin love lyrics, or of later English lyrics of the Tudor period:

> Enquer me membra d'un mati
> que nos fezem de guerra fi,
> e que. m donet un don tan gran,
> sa drudari'e son anel;
> enquer me lais Dieus viure tan
> c'aia mas mans soz so mantel![65]

> (I remember still one morning
> When we put an end to warfare,
> And she bestowed a gift so precious—
> The right to court her, and a ring;
> May it please Lord God to keep me
> Till I touch her, once again.)

Individuality is, indeed, the defining characteristic of the poetry of Guilhem and of the poets of southern France who followed him. Nothing could be further from the accepted view of refined troubadour compliment than the savage verse of Bertran de Born (1140–c. 1215), whose life was a turbulent record of political intrigue and military campaigns, ending in a Cistercian monastery. Ezra Pound's versions of his poetry give some idea of the vigour and the harsh glamour of his hymns to battle:

> Hell grant soon we hear again the swords clash!
> And the shrill neighs of destriers in battle rejoicing,
> Spiked breast to spiked breast opposing!
> Better one hour's stour than a year's peace
> With fat boards, bawds, wine and frail music![66]

* See Ch. 12, "Courts and Courtly Love."

By contrast Bertran's *planh* (lament) for the death of the young Henry
Plantagenet is stately and mournful:

> Reis dels cortes e dels pros emperaire
> foratz, senher, si acsetz mais viscut,
> quar "reis joves" avaitz nom agut
> e de joven eratz vos guitz e paire.[67]

> (Courteous king and valorous emperor
> You would have been, seigneur, had you but lived;
> You would have earned the name of "generous lord,"
> As generous was your father and your guide.)

The troubadour Marcabrun (*fl.* 1131–48)* wrote predominantly realistic
verse: complaints against corrupt society, against the betrayal of love,
and songs of the crusades, both in praise and in sadness. Many of his
poems are skilful commentaries upon political situations, upon the tense
patterns of ambition and rivalry that prevented the Christian princes of
Spain from complete victory against the Moors. His invective can be
powerful, but his best writing is in a strain of compassionate irony: the
girl who weeps for her lover away on crusade, and who doubts God's
benevolence. His poetry often begins serenely enough, and turns into
bitterness: innocent lines—

> A la fontana del vergier,
> on l'erb'es vertz josta.l gravier,
> a l'ombra d'un fust domesgier . . .

> (Down by a fountain in a garden,
> Where the green grass borders the gravel path,
> Beneath the shade of a fruit-tree . . .)

—give way to those of experience:

> . . . little he cares for me
> Who is so far away.[68]

It is true to the spirit of this great lyrical poetry of the south of France—
passionate, indignant, satirical, but above all deeply and personally
committed to the "art and craft" of composition and to the creative
freedom of the poet—that some of its last utterances should be moving
outcries against the genocide practised in the name of the mediaeval
Church—the Albigensian Crusade, which effectively destroyed the
culture of the south. That culture, reflected in poetry, religion, the way
of life, was rich, idiosyncratic, and extravagant. As we have seen,

* See Ch. 14, "Marcabrun and the Origins of *Trobar clus.*"

Languedoc was the natural receiving area for literary, philosophical, and material commodities from Spain and from the East. It also received, and fostered, spiritual commodities: "skeptical Provence was the natural refuge of all heretics. . . ."[69] The particular heresy that at last gave the temporal lords of central and northern France, aided by the Anglo-French Simon de Montfort, an excuse to seize (with Papal blessing) the wealth they had so long coveted, was Catharism. As Catharism was wiped out, so was the civilization of Provence; in the midst of unbelievable atrocities, the voices of the troubadours, not those of the Church, are the voices of humanity: from the Bishop of Cîteaux, "Kill, kill! God will know his own"[70]; from the poet Guillaume de Beziers, a lament for his patron, Roger de Trancavel, nephew of the Count of Toulouse, who was treacherously captured and killed by de Montfort:

> Mort l'an, e anc tan gran otrage
> no vi hom, ni tan gran error
> mais far, ni tan gran estranhatge
> de Dieu et a nostre Senhor.[71]

> (They have killed him, and so great a wrong
> Was never seen, nor was so great a crime,
> So great a deed of infamy,
> Done against God and Our Lord.)

The legacy of the troubadour tradition was shared by all the lyrical poetry of Europe. But the use made of it by Italians was particularly thorough, and particularly original. It was thorough in that the language of Provençal verse, as well as its themes and attitudes, was adopted. Italian poets of the 13th century often composed in Provençal, and it was some time before the question of a dominant literary vernacular was settled. Provençal, French, and Tuscan Italian were all possible choices during the later 13th and early 14th centuries: many poets wrote in two languages; Dante himself was much preoccupied with the idea of a supreme Italian vernacular. But Italian lyric was original in that, in the hands of the finest poets—Guinizelli, Cavalcanti, and Dante—the amatory themes of the troubadours were transformed, by new learning and a new spirituality, into themes of universal, not simply personal, significance.*

The influence of troubadour verse upon English poetry is less easily documented. Troubadours certainly visited England in the 12th century: Marcabrun, according to the *Roman de Joufroy*, was well known to Henry I,

* See Ch. 12, "Courts and Courtly Love."

and welcome at his court.[72] Bernart de Ventadorn (*fl. c.* 1145–80) composed one of his songs in London, and addressed several to Eleanor, wife of Henry II. The metres used in English lyrics of the late 13th and 14th century bear some resemblance to Provençal metres: critics have pointed out that two of the Harley 2253 collection use a stanza similar to one of Marcabrun's.[73]

If we compare not only the metres but also the themes and conventions of verse written in England before the 12th century with those of verse of the succeeding centuries, it becomes clear that much must be attributed to the prestige and wide dissemination of southern French poetry throughout Europe. But, in the case of England, another kind of French influence has to be taken into account. It may be generally true that the lyric poets of northern France were deeply in debt to the troubadours. Nevertheless, it was probably through their agency that many southern French forms and ideas reached English poets. In any case, it is not quite fair to label this verse derivative only. Although it is simpler in metrical structures and in language than some troubadour poetry, the northern lyric can, on occasion, show to great advantage; moreover, during the 13th century, it developed in areas unexplored by the troubadours.

The earliest of northern French songs are the *chansons d'istoire* of the mid-12th century. Those little dramatic lyrics, telling of love, disappointment, or imprisonment (by husband or mother) from the woman's point of view, are quite unrivalled except by the English ballads of a later date. It is impossible to think that they could be derived from the poetry of Provence, with its strongly masculine self-consciousness and its tendency to highly sensual or highly idealized love. The *chansons d'istoire* treat of love in a narrative setting; although they are less intense than the poems of Languedoc, they have a power of simple suggestiveness that is quite unique. Here the lover of "bele Yolanz" comes into her room:

> "Ma douce dame, mis m'avez en obli."
> cele l'entent, se li geta un ris,
> en sospirant ses bels bras li tendi;
> tant doucement a acoler l'a pris.
> "dex, tant est douz li nons d'amors:
> ja n'en cuidai sentir dolors."
>
> Li siens amis entre ses braz la prent,
> en un biau lit s'asient seulement:
> bele Yolanz lo baise estroitement,
> a tor francois en mi lo lit l'estent.
> "dex, tant est douz li nons d'amors:
> ja n'en cuidai sentir dolors."[74]

> ("My sweet lady, you have forgotten me!'
> She heard him, laughed towards him,
> sighing, she offered him her slender arms;
> tenderly, he took her to him.
> "God, how sweet is the name of love!
> I never thought I'd suffer for it."
>
> Her lover folds her in his arms,
> in a fine bed they lie together:
> fair Yolande kisses him passionately,
> bedded, they take to French sport.
> "God, how sweet is the name of love!
> I never thought I'd suffer for it!")

The women of these lyrics are forthright: even if their situations are piteous, their spirit is not broken:

> Jai ne lair ai por mon mari ne die:
> li miens amins jeut a neut aveuckes moi.
> Je li dis biens, ainz qu'il m'eust plevie,
> s'il me batoit me faisoit vilonie,
> il seroit cous et si lou comparoit.[75]
>
> (For my husband's sake I will not fear to speak:
> My own dear lover lies at night with me.
> I told him plain, ere handfasted were we,
> An he beat me, did me his knavery,
> He should be cuckolded, such his wage should be.)

We are nearer to Chaucer's Wife of Bath in these poems than in any poems by the troubadours.

The courtly poets of the north of France—Conon de Béthune (*c.* 1150– *c.* 1219), Gace Brulé (*fl.* 1180–1200), and Gui, Chatelain de Coucy (d. 1203)—are on the whole content to imitate the Provençal conventions. It was left to the anonymous poets, who may have been writing for courtly patrons but who show strong sympathies for a more robust kind of existence, to develop, rather than simply to imitate, such conventions. The *pastourelle* form, in which a knight or poet or clerk encounters rustic life and has some kind of adventure, idyllic or disillusioning, is especially well handled by northern French poets, and their work was a model for countless English equivalents. The tone of these *pastourelles* varies. Sometimes it exhibits an aristocratic shamelessness and condescension:

> Quant vi que proiere ne m'i vant noient,
> couchai la a terre tout maintenant,
> levai li le chainse,
> si vit la char si blanche,

tant fui je plus ardant;
fis li la folie,
el nel contredist mie,
ainz le vout bonement.[76]

(When I saw my prayer was no avail,
I laid her on the ground right speedily,
Lifted her dress,
Saw her white flesh,
And longed the more;
Taught her love's play—
She did not resist me,
But happily received me.)

Often it shows a zestful delight in real "country pleasures":

A lai follie a Donmartin
a l'entree dous tens nouvel
s'asamblerent par un matin
pastorelle et pastorel:
roi ont fait don plus bel
mantel ot de kamelin
et cote de burel.
s'ont le museour mande
et Tieris son bordon
a destoupe,
ke disoit "bon bon bon bon bon,
sa de la rire dural dure lire dure."[77]

(To Donmartin's merry-making
When Spring was freshly clad,
Together in the morning
Came shepherd lass and lad.
For king they chose the handsomest,
A goatskin cloak he wore,
And rough serge were his garments.
Music they shouted for
And Tieris his bagpipe
Ready got,
That skirled out "bon bon bon bon bon,
Sa de la rire dural dure lire dure.")

The 13th century sees the rise in France of a vigorous literature catering for, and sometimes springing from, the more prosperous of the middle classes. Colin Muset (*fl.* 1250), poet of sense and good cheer, can stand for these people; like the energetic pictures of real life that at this time begin to invade the borders and initials of mediaeval religious manuscripts, his lyrics are full of substantial joys and discomforts: the muddy roads of northern Europe, the fur-lined cloak against the cold,

475

the good French sauces, the warm chimney-corner in January. The French lyric is at last beginning to bear the weight of that preoccupation with realism that in the later Middle Ages was to characterize most European art and literature. In Colin Muset's lyrics there are intimations of Chaucer, Langland, and Villon:

> Quant je voi yver retorner
> lors me voudroie sejorner,
> se je pooie oste trover
> large, qui ne vousist conter,
> qu'eüst porc et beuf et mouton,
> maslarz, faisanz et venoison,
> grasses gelines et chapons
> et bons fromages en glaon . . .
> ne seroie pas envious
> de chevauchier toz boons
> apres mauvais prince angoissoux.[78]

> (When I feel winter coming on,
> Then I like to stay indoors,
> If I can find a generous host.
> Who will not count the cost:
> Who will provide pork, beef, and lamb,
> Wild duck, pheasant, and venison,
> Plump chickens and capons,
> And good cheeses in baskets . . .
> I am not anxious
> To ride mud-spattered
> Behind a bad-tempered, arrogant prince.)

The Mediaeval English Religious Lyric

With the mediaeval English lyric, our search for sources and influences takes in the vernacular lyric of 12th- and 13th-century France: but we must also look beyond it. It is not only the accident of chance survival that makes this body of poetry far more remarkable for its religious than for its secular achievements. In the secular field, English poetry (and prose) had suffered tremendous disturbance after 1066, with the coming of William of Normandy and the imposition of first a Norman and then an Angevin dynasty in England. The rapid growth of French vernacular literature during the 12th century—lyric, romance, drama, chronicle—and its spreading fame, meant that the ruling classes of England and those who wrote for them naturally favoured continental texts, or those written in imitation of them in Anglo-French. The 12th and 13th centuries in England are predominantly centuries of French or Anglo-French literature, at least in the secular field. It was probably not until well into the

13th century that any need was felt for the courtly lyric in English: until then French had sufficed. The elaborate and beautiful secular poems of the Harley 2253 collection are the first substantial group of English lyrics that bear comparison with those of the Continent.

But the religious lyric was in a different position. Latin hymn-writing had been well represented in England since the early days of Christian civilization. Aldhelm, Bishop of Sherborne (650–709), is credited with rhythmical compositions similar to those of the Irish Christian Church of that time. The Anglo-Saxon scholar Bede (673–735) wrote hymns in rhyming quatrains on the Saints and the Holy Innocents. By the 10th century, Wulfstan of Winchester was rhyming even more elaborately in praise of St Augustine of Canterbury:

> aveto, placidis praesul amabilis,
> aveto, celebri laude notabilis,
> aveto, salubri luce capabilis,
> Augustine placabilis.
>
> (Hail peaceful and lovable protector,
> Hail, o thou, famous in splendid praise,
> Hail, o thou bringer of healing light,
> Gentle Augustine.)

Not only was the hymn form familiar in England, but the Latin sequence too. The gradual regularization of the sequence form, during the 11th and 12th centuries, had produced a standard metrical type, usually consisting of a couplet or a triplet followed by a shorter line, and rhyming aab or aaab. The quatrain form of the Latin hymn, and the sequence form set into various stanzaic patterns, were widely influential upon vernacular religious lyric. During the 12th century, someone (probably Simon Langton, Archbishop of Canterbury) composed one of the most famous of all Latin sequences, the "Veni, Sancte Spiritus."[79]

There was no reason why the Norman Conquest should have cut across the writing of Latin verses; nor was there any reason why translations of Latin hymns and sequences, when they were first attempted in 13th-century England, should not have been made into English rather than into French. Such translations were intended not for the court but for an amorphous public—ranging from illiterate congregations to country priests and to the less-well-educated of conventual communities—who needed the doctrines and meditations of the Church in a convenient and accessible form. This public was quickly extended, over the 14th century, to the middle- and even upper-class lay devout.

The close relationship between the English and the Latin religious lyric, turning upon its vital function as part of the didactic and meditative equipment of the mediaeval Church, is vitally important. St Godric, the hermit of Finchale, composed his English poems in the 12th century in a simple quatrain form; so, too, did the author of the famous "Sunset on Calvary," in the early 14th century.[80] Several versions of the *Stabat Mater* sequence—that quintessence of Franciscan devotion to the crucified Christ and his mother—were made in England during the late 13th century. They all follow the form of the Latin precisely, combining the basic sequence triplet into a six-line stanza. This stanza was to become one of the most popular of all lyric stanzas in England, for both religious and secular themes:

> Iesu cristes milde moder
> stud, biheld hire sone o rode
> þat he was ipined on;
> þe sone heng, þe moder stud,
> and biheld hire childes blud,
> wu it of hise wundes ran.[81]

> (The gentle mother of Jesus Christ
> Stood, gazed at her Son on the cross,
> The cross upon which he was tortured.
> The Son hung, the mother stood
> And watched her Child's blood,
> How it streamed from His wounds.)

The institutional context of many of these lyrics is made clear by the manuscripts in which they appear: quite frequently, the Latin precedes the English translation. We know that English verses were often used within sermons, to vivify or expand a point of doctrine: a Latin sermon of about 1300 quotes lines from a well-known English verse dialogue between Christ and the Virgin: "As it is put in a certain song."[82] Song and sermon were intimately linked: for confirmation of this we need look at only one particular class of people, the Friars. Franciscans first came to England in 1224, and rapidly made their mark on the English religious scene. Popularization of the great devotional themes of the mediaeval Church was one of their strongest practical intentions: they achieved this mainly through the connected genres of vernacular sermon, lyric, and drama. In all they strove to enliven, to dramatize, and to instruct. Many of the richest miscellanies of mediaeval lyric verse are friars' miscellanies: they have been called the "Golden Treasuries or Oxford Books of Verse" of the 13th century.[83] Many of the identifiable authors of mediaeval lyrics are friars: John Audelay, William Herebert, William of Shoreham, Thomas of Hales.[84]

But when we stress the functional importance of the mediaeval English religious lyric, we are not necessarily committed to making special pleas in excuse of its poetic quality. It is true that it sometimes excels in the hymn mode—in that quiet expression of communal faith that has always had a vital socio-religious part to play in the organization of the Christian Church. Here it shares with Latin hymns (and with some of George Herbert's verse) a grave and appropriate beauty, inseparable from Church ritual and prayer:

> Swete ihesu, king of blisse,
> min herte love, min herte lisse,
> þou art swete mid I-wisse,
> wo is him þat þe shal misse.[85]

> (Sweet Jesu, king of bliss,
> The love and peace of my heart,
> Indeed thou art sweet;
> Sad is he who is bereft of thee.)

It is also true that because the demands made upon it need be no more than religious in the simplest sense, it can sink to the level of mere versified precept. But there is no doubt that it draws great power and confidence from its established position as an instrument of the Church. Its vast coverage and its range of experimentation with themes and forms could not have been achieved otherwise. Confidence ensures that where it is closest to a Latin source it often becomes most successful as an independent composition. The 13th-century lines on mortality—

> When the turf is thi tour,
> & thi pit is thi bour,
> Thi wel and thi white throte
> Shalen wormes to note.
> What helpit the thenne
> All the worlde wynne?[86]

> (When the turf is thy tower,
> And the grave is thy bower,
> Thy beauty and thy white throat
> Shall be meat for worms.
> What use to thee, then,
> All the joy in the world?)

—follow their Latin directly and fairly accurately on the manuscript page. But the closeness of Latin and English only serves to dramatize the different effects made by the poems: the Latin solemn, stately, and brooding; the English terse, concrete, its message rapped out in alliterative hammer-strokes.

We cannot expect of this lyric the tortured self-questionings, the vivid re-creations of spiritual crises, that make the English lyric of the 17th century so compelling to read: this is a poetry of service, not of self-expression, in which private experience is used, not exploited. But thoughtfulness is not excluded, whether it centres upon the paradoxes and mysteries of the Christian faith—

> A God and yet a man?
> A mayde and yet a mother?
> Witt wonders what witt can
> Conceave this or the other.
>
> A god, and can he die?
> A dead man, can he live?
> What witt can well replie?
> What reason reason give?[87]

—or upon the paradox of man's equal willingness and reluctance to respond to God—

> Louerd, þu clepedest me,
> an ich nagt ne ansuarede þe
> bute wordes scloe and sclepie:
> "þole yet! þole a litel!"
> Bute "yiet" and "yiet" was endelis,
> and "þole a litel" a long wey is.[88]
>
> (Lord, you called me,
> And I gave you no answer
> Except slow, sleepy words:
> "Be patient still! be patient a little longer!"
> But there was no end to "still,"
> And "be patient" can last for ever.)

Perhaps the most impressive quality of the English mediaeval lyric, especially in the late 14th and 15th centuries, is its keen dramatic sense. The personal emotion that could not be easily or constantly exploited in an art-form that had such universal responsibilities was diverted to the imaginative resetting of biblical events. Into the lullaby lyrics, the dialogues at the Crucifixion, the laments and meditations upon the Passion of Christ and the Compassion of Mary, goes all that raw feeling that in a later age would have found an outlet in private and idiosyncratic modes of poetry. And similarly with the themes of man's life and death:

there is no room for John Donne's whispered admission: "I have a sin of fear. . . ."[89] Instead, human pride, panic, and remorse are lifted out of the small context of one man's experience and presented in terms of a drama, no less moving because its end is foreseen in its beginning. The splendid 15th-century lyric "Farewell, this World is but a Cherry Fair"[90] passes from the terror of the moment of summons—

> Today I sat full ryall in a cheyere,
> Tyll sotell deth knokyd at my gate,
> And, on-avysed, he seyd to me "chek-mate!"
>
> (Today I sat in royal array on a throne,
> Until that moment when cunning death knocked at my gate,
> And, unannounced, he said to me "Checkmate!")

—to the deep silences of the grave—

> Speke softe, ye folk, for I am leyd aslepe!
> I have my dreme . . .

—and on to the certainties of judgment and eternity—

> When I have endid all myn adversite,
> Graunte me in paradise to have a mancyon,
> That shed his blode for my redempcion.
>
> (When I have endured all my punishment,
> Grant that I may have a dwelling in paradise,
> O Thou who shed blood for my redemption.)

—with an imaginative and spiritual confidence that belongs only to the lyric of an age of faith.

References

1. *Beowulf*, trans. by D. Wright (paperback: Harmondsworth 1957), p. 29.
2. *Widsith*, trans. by R. K. Gordon (London 1957).
3. See F. J. E. RABY, *Christian Latin Poetry* (Oxford 1953), p. 33.
4. See GUSTAVE REESE, *Music in the Middle Ages* (London 1941), p. 104.

5. See RABY, *op. cit.*, pp. 210 ff.
6. See REESE, *op. cit.*, p. 188, on the 12th-century sequences of Adam of St Victor.
7. See PETER DRONKE, *The Medieval Lyric* (London 1968), p. 38, No. 1, and p. 39.
8. *ibid.*, p. 38.
9. REESE, *op. cit.*, p. 217.
10. *ibid.*, p. 215.
11. *ibid.*, pp. 241 f.
12. See R. H. ROBBINS, *Secular Lyrics of the XIVth and XVth Centuries* (Oxford 1961), p. xxiii.
13. CARLETON BROWN (ed.), *Religious Lyrics of the XIVth Century* (Oxford 1952), No. 83.
14. See discussion in REESE, *op. cit.*, pp. 243 ff. and 396 ff.
15. Text and music in REESE, *op. cit.*, p. 243.
16. BROWN, *op. cit.*, No. 13.
17. CARLETON BROWN (ed.), *English Lyrics of the XIIIth Century* (Oxford 1950), No. 1.
18. HELEN WADDELL, *Mediaeval Latin Lyrics* (London 1930), pp. 138 f., contains original and translation. An amended text is translated in DRONKE, *op. cit.*, p. 170.
19. Old English text is in W. F. BOLTON, *An Old English Anthology* (London 1963), pp. 33 f.
20. The name commonly used for this manuscript in editions such as those of K. Breul (Cambridge 1915) and K. Strecker (Berlin 1926). Originals and translations of both lyrics in WADDELL, *op. cit.*, pp. 144 f. and 156 f.
21. Latin text in PETER DRONKE, *Medieval Latin and the Rise of the European Love-Lyric* (Oxford 1965), p. 274; translation in DRONKE, *The Medieval Lyric*, p. 190.
22. See DRONKE, *Medieval Latin . . .*, pp. 26 ff.
23. *ibid.*, p. 285.
24. *ibid.*, p. 56.
25. A. R. LEWIS, "The Closing of the Mediaeval Frontier, 1250–1350," *Speculum* XXXIII (Cambridge, Mass. 1958), p. 477.
26. BROWN, *English Religious Lyrics of the XIVth Century*, No. 83.
27. ROBBINS, *op. cit.*, No. 26.
28. Original and translation in WADDELL, *op. cit.*, pp. 170–7.
29. *ibid.*, pp. 274 f.
30. *ibid.*, pp. 184 ff.
31. G. L. BROOK (ed.), *The Harley Lyrics: the Middle English Lyrics of MS. Harley* 2253 (Manchester 1948), No. 19.
32. Original in RABY, *op. cit.*, p. 365.
33. *ibid.*, p. 295.
34. BROOK (ed.), *op. cit.*, No. 31 and 32.
35. *ibid.*, No. 23.
36. *ibid.*, No. 18.

37. See WADDELL, *op. cit.*, pp. 142 f.
38. DRONKE, *Medieval Latin ...*, pp. 264 ff.
39. *ibid.*, p. 265, contains Latin original.
40. BROOK (ed.), *op. cit.*, No. 3.
41. *ibid.*, No. 7.
42. L. VALERIANI (ed.), "Rime antiche," in *Poeti del primo secolo della lingua italiana*, Vol. I (Florence 1816), p. 93.
43. *ibid.*, p. 90.
44. *Inferno* II, 76 ff.
45. See R. FLOWER, *The Irish Tradition* (Oxford 1947), Ch. II.
46. RABY, *op. cit.*, p. 136: the verse dates from the 8th century.
47. Translation in K. JACKSON, *Early Celtic Nature Poetry* (Cambridge 1935), No. 5: the verse dates from the 10th century but describes events in the 7th.
48. *ibid.*, No. 3.
49. *ibid.*, No. 4.
50. Translation in KUNO MEYER, *Selections from Ancient Irish History* (London 1911), p. 101
51. *ibid.*, p. 101.
52. JACKSON, *op. cit.*, No. 27; original in KUNO MEYER, *Four Old Irish Songs of Summer and Winter* (London 1903), p. 14.
53. Original and translation in WADDELL, *op. cit.*, pp. 272 f.
54. Text and translation in G. MURPHY, *Early Irish Lyrics* (Oxford 1970), pp. 156–7.
55. JACKSON, *op. cit.*, No. 31 b–d.
56. MEYER, *Selections ...*, pp. 87.
57. *Anglo-Saxon Riddles*, trans. by P. F. Baum (Durham, N. C. 1963).
58. MEYER, *Selections ...*, pp. 81–2.
59. Reproduced in A. GRABAR and C. NORDENFALK, *Early Mediaeval Painting* (Geneva 1957), p. 115.
60. See L. M. HOLLANDER, *The Skalds* (Princeton 1945).
61. The terms "troubadour" and "*trouvère*" distinguish the poets of southern and northern France, respectively, in mediaeval as well as in modern usage; both express the concept of the poet as "maker, inventor."
62. R. BRIFFAULT, *The Troubadours* (Bloomington, Ind. 1965), p. 67.
63. *ibid.*, p. 53.
64. *ibid.*, Ch. II.
65. HAMLIN, RICKETTS, and HATHAWAY (ed.), *Introduction à l'étude de l'ancien provençal* (Geneva 1967), pp. 54 f.
66. EZRA POUND, *Selected Poems* (London 1928), p. 27.
67. HAMLIN, RICKETTS, and HATHAWAY (ed.), *op. cit.*, p. 81.
68. Provençal original, *ibid.*, pp. 65 f.
69. BRIFFAULT, *op. cit.*, p. 137.
70. Arnaud of Cîteaux; recorded in *Caesarii Heisterbacensis chronicon* (Cologne 1851), Bk V, Ch. xxi.
71. BRIFFAULT, *op. cit.*, p. 141.

72. *ibid.*, p. 4, No. 3.
73. *ibid.*, p. 38 and No. 40; see also H. J. CHAYTOR, *The Troubadours and England* (Cambridge 1923), Ch. III.
74. Original in C. C. ABBOTT, *Early Mediaeval French Lyrics* (London 1932), No. 5.
75. Original and translation, *ibid.*, No. 24.
76. Original, *ibid.*, No. 55.
77. Original and translation, *ibid.*, No. 49.
78. Original, *ibid.*, No. 86.
79. Original in RABY, *op. cit.*, pp. 343 f.
80. *ibid.*, pp. 16 f.
81. BROWN, *English Lyrics of the XIIIth Century*, No. 47.
82. *ibid.*, p. 204.
83. See ROBBINS, *op. cit.*, p. xvii.
84. See R. WOOLF, *The English Religious Lyric in the Middle Ages* (Oxford 1968), Appendix B, "Authorship."
85. BROWN, *English Lyrics of the XIIIth Century*, No. 50.
86. *ibid.*, No. 30; the spelling has been slightly modernized. The Latin original is on p. 191.
87. CARLETON BROWN (ed.), *Religious Lyrics of the XVth Century* (Oxford 1939), No. 120.
88. BROWN, *Religious Lyrics of the XIVth Century*, No. 5.
89. *A Hymne to God the Father.*
90. BROWN, *Religious Lyrics of the XVth Century*, No. 149.

CHAPTER 14

Marcabrun and the Origins of "Trobar clus"

Lynne Lawner[*]

Among the troubadours, there was a cult of a difficult-obscure style commonly called *trobar clus* (closed writing) that had an extremely important influence on the troubadour tradition itself and on the Italian, French, Spanish, and English poets writing several centuries later. Yet this style and the tradition to which it gave rise have been little studied by scholars, partly because the very nature of this hermetic poetry is obscure, and often impenetrable, but also because hardly anyone has recognized the continuity of the *clus* tradition, which extends past Dante and Petrarch to Scève, Donne, Góngora, and even Mallarmé. This tradition cannot be traced through direct influence, but it can be followed in relation both to certain techniques of "closing" form and to certain key concepts and symbols. I believe that it would not be an exaggeration to say that the basic paradoxes and devices of so-called metaphysical poetry and the refinements of *cultismo* and *conceptismo* originate in this early poetry in the vernacular, which is in general far more intellectual, cultured, and subtle than is usually thought. Indeed, in future years we may come to see how most Provençal poetry is immensely different from the simple, limpid love poetry it is ordinarily accounted to be. Not even the work of the great singer Bernart de Ventadorn (*c.* 1145–80) is exempt from occasional ambiguities and a certain complication of style. Judged from the perspective of what follows, *trobar clus* can, in a sense, be considered the mainstream of Provençal poetry and not, as scholars have consistently claimed, a deviation or aberration from it, nor a grotesque or perverse exaggeration of certain stylistic tendencies.

The origins of *trobar clus*, in the sense of a possible derivation from

[*] Fellow of Radcliffe Institute, Harvard University, and member of Gruppo di Ricerca "Officina Romanica" of the Institute of Romance Philology, University of Rome.

earlier literary-philosophical traditions, are even more difficult to root out than the origins of Provençal poetry itself—one of the great perplexing knots of Romance philology and of literary history in general. An analogous series of debates (though less in number) has taken place in the last few years about whether *clus* derives from mediaeval Latin traditions such as the *oratio glossematica* and *elocutio contorta* and the stylistic categories of *ornatus facilis* and *ornatus difficilis*; the tradition of scriptural exegesis; or techniques of Arabic poetry such as the *qufl*, a kind of refrain; or whether it represents instead an autonomous development deriving from minor poets such as Peire d'Alvernhe, Bernart Marti, and Allegret, who first speak about writing in a "closed," obscure style. Surely Viscardi[1] in the 1930s was correct in relating phenomena such as *entrebescamen* (the weaving together of words, sometimes in an intricate and hence obscure manner) to the *tragica coniugatio* of the *grande genus dicendi* (cf. Dante's *gradus constructionis excelsus*) and the classical *ligare* and *contexere*, as well as *motz brus e teintz* (darkly coloured words) to *oratio glossematica* and *verba abstrusa* (although rare, difficult words are not always the same thing as "dark" ones). At the same time, these connections have offered no help whatsoever in understanding either the motivation behind *clus* or the particular forms that it takes. Nor is any help to be found in the stylistic divisions of the *artes dictamini* of the end of the 12th and beginning of the 13th century, except, perhaps, for the categories of "allegory" and "enigma" under the heading of the "difficult style." In my opinion, there is still much to be said about the exegetical tradition, but specifically in relation to the Song of Songs and less in relation (as has been suggested) to interpretations such as that of Gregory the Great of the Book of Job.[2] As for Arabic poetry, the problems presented by the *ḫarǧas*—those multilingual postscripts to the *muwaššah* form containing elements similar to the Provençal *gap* (vaunt, jest) practised already by Guilhem of Poitou (1071–1126) and by Marcabrun (*fl. c.* 1131–48)—remain fascinating and pertinent, which is not to say that the cult of the obscure style necessarily derives exclusively from this source. Certainly, the first manifestations of *trobar clus* among the troubadours were influenced by the *docta obscuritas* of the entire mediaeval Latin tradition. Examples include not only the early "hisperic" writers in the British Isles and the deliberately tangled styles of Abbone of Saint Germain, Hincmar of Laon, Attone of Vercelli, and Ratherius of Verona, but also, and more importantly, great intellectuals such as Boethius (*c.* 480–524) and John of Salisbury (*c.* 1115–80), who gave an intellectual, indeed a theological, foundation to the theory and practice of an obscure style.[3]

The necessity of veiling meaning when speaking of "higher" things not assimilable by the common, vulgar mind, together with the will to communicate with a social or spiritual elite, are motives certainly not extraneous to at least three of the *clus* poets: Marcabrun, Peire d'Alvernhe, and Gevaudan. However, there are numerous other reasons for withholding meaning, for baffling, confounding, entangling, and even for rendering one's art so dense and opaque an object that no one in the world can penetrate it. The inspiration for writing "closed poetry" in this period is a very particular one, manifesting itself first in the world of the most obscure poet of them all, Marcabrun. It is only by examining his *œuvre* of 44 poems that we can come to understand something of this inspiration and poetical necessity. At the end, we may be driven to conclude that, paradoxically, it was the historical context in which he wrote that, more than any other factor, led to the creation of this new poetic style.

Very little is known about Marcabrun, a poet of the second generation of troubadours, whose output spans the period 1131–48. His *vida*, which, like so many other "lives of the poets" based on this period, has the air of being entirely fictive and drawn from information in the poems themselves, states that the poet was an orphan left on the doorstep of a noble house. But everything about Marcabrun is contradictory and problematic. Even his name is mysterious, being a nickname meaning "he who writes darkly and obscurely." His poems are overlaid with allusions to current political events and personages, most of which elude the modern reader and many of which must have eluded his contemporaries as well. He writes in the most jongleuresque form of all, the *gap*, in a language plebeian and obscene; but at the same time he styles himself an Old Testament prophet, fills his poems with learned allusions, paraphrases of the Scriptures, and faint echoes of classical poets such as Virgil, and buries his deepest meanings in those very same *gap* forms. There is no denying his clerical background (for example, his use of musical terms is more technical than that of any other troubadour); and recent studies have gone on to show a direct relation, in his work, to the imagery and style of Guillaume of St Thierry and the Cistercian writers.[4] At the same time, his moralizing is not what it seems to be on the surface; it is not directly related to either the misogyny of the clerks or the contemplative mysticism of intellectuals such as Guillaume or St Bernard. Nor is his polemical attitude toward the newly formed cult of courtly love entirely free from ambivalences and ambiguities. Marcabrun's bitter satire is directed toward a special kind of object and therefore has a special meaning and original colouring. Finally, and despite some appearances to the contrary, his poetry can be seen to be more socio-political than religious, and perhaps more artistic than anything else; for his goal is the creation of a central image and symbol, a poetic world to which he can escape from the negativeness of this one.

Marcabrun is a poet of *transformation*, a poet who notes, registers, and renders artistically a world in transformation that he sees around him—a process that he in part intuits. This is not to say that he writes in terms of an Ovidian metamorphosis: his perception of the world and his artistic means are, in this sense, much more primitive. Yet there is an original power in Marcabrun's vision of a world in perennial mutation, a kind of ballet in which everyone, on every level of life, goes to Hell:

> Cill son fals jutg' e raubador,
> Fals molherat e jurador,
> Fals home tenh e lauzengier,
> Lengua-loguat, creba-mostier,
> Et aissellas putas ardens
> Qui son d'autrui maritz cossens;
> Cyst auran guazanh ifernau.
>
> Homicidi e traïdor,
> Simoniaic, encantador,
> Luxurios e renovier,
> Que vivon d'enujos mestier,
> E cill que fan faitilhamens,
> E las faitileiras pudens,
> Seran el fuec arden engau.
>   [XL, 15–28][5]

> (Such are the false judges and thieves,
> False husbands and false witnesses,
> Men who wear masks and liars,
> Impostors, monastery-wreckers,
> And those burning whores
> Lusting after other people's husbands:
> All these will go to Hell.
>
> Homicides and traitors,
> Simoniacs, magicians,
> Luxurious ones and usurers
> Who ply a hideous trade,
> And those who cast spells,
> The stinking fortune-tellers
> Will all be together in the hot flames.)

The *terribilità* of this vision is all the more striking to us today for the fact that it was created in the vernacular two centuries before Dante's *Inferno* at the initial, budding point of Provençal poetry (still commonly thought

to be all springtime landscapes of roses, nightingales, and courtly lovers).
Marcabrun's poetry depicts a world of falsehood, duplicity, and change,
where nothing is the way that it was and where no one is any longer
himself (in a sense, he "is" and "is not" himself at the same time). But
where are the roots of this radical vision of life? What world is Marcabrun
describing?

We might also ask—and the question is extremely pertinent—what
were the primary characteristics of European society in the first half of the
12th century? At that time, society was undergoing a profound process
of transformation that was to affect all its basic structures. With the end
of the Ottonian dynasty, there was an accelerated mutation of feudal
structures under the pressure of a series of interrelated socio-political
factors. These factors included the crusades; the papal-imperial crisis;
the consolidation of unitarian (national) tendencies in France, Spain,
England, and, to some extent, Italy; the transcending of the manorial
economy through the opening-up of new markets in the East and the
expansion of artisan and industrial activity and the intensification of
trade; the birth of cities; and the rapid renewal of customs. All these were
part of a vast process affecting both the individual and the collectivity—
courts, monasteries, and villages. The principals in these events were no
longer only the seigneur and the peasant: new social groups deriving from
the nobility and the peasantry were complicating the fabric of society.
At the base of this process lay a fundamental transformation of the
economic structure. In the course of a century and a half, under the
pressure of dynastic and political changes, the great Carolingian estates—
a fiduciary concession of the emperor to his vassals—had become split
into progressively smaller units. The greater the fragmentation of land
ownership, the less immediate and direct was the influence of the supreme
source of property and power, the Holy Roman Emperor. Equally, if not
more, significant was the internal transformation of the feudal estate
itself. The great period of development of the manorial economy was
950–1100. After this time, the concentration and multiplication of needs
within this limited circle and the necessity of maintaining the unity of the
estate through the system of primogeniture led to increased productive
activity and an accelerated division of labour, resulting finally in the
creation of new social strata and the evolution of an economic system
based on monetary exchange.

In the first half of the 12th century, we are in the very heart of this
process, complicated in southern France and northern Italy by the
conflict between feudal structures and *latifundia* (the great estates deriving

ultimately from Roman times). When Marcabrun began to compose his poems, this new economic system was entirely interwoven with the old manorial system, and new social formations overlapped older ones. By Dante's time (the late 13th century), the old skin of society would be completely shed and the new one, though not fully grown, would already be in evidence. But in Marcabrun's day the new and old skins coexisted and were intimately enmeshed. Marcabrun could have viewed this situation only from the "inside"; it would have been impossible for him to have grasped the exact direction in which history would move, especially because the process of the formation of the bourgeoisie was slower in Gascony and south-western France in general than, for example, in northern Italy. Hence, what Marcabrun was most aware of was the *way* in which the old society was being transformed, was actually becoming "old." Because the part of France and northern Spain where he lived still lay under the rule of large-scale feudalism—the great feudal seigneury and its monarch were of direct feudal derivation—Marcabrun necessarily attempted to understand this process by looking behind him rather than ahead. But the sense of transformation is inevitably keener in one who sees directly in front of him the vestiges of the past than in one who lives surrounded by the new, already fully realized.

Transformation is thus the great historical theme of the first half of the 12th century—the transformation of every aspect of life from family to language, love, and social relationships in general—and literature in the vernacular offers the natural medium for its expression. The ineluctable beginnings of this process can be perceived even in the poems of the first known troubadour, Guilhem of Poitou, ninth duke of Aquitaine, who gazes with ironic nostalgia on a reality that seems already to have passed away. Even poets as seemingly remote as Jaufre Rudel of Blaye (*fl.* mid-12th century) are affected by this crisis, but it is Marcabrun who registers in the most far-reaching, though enigmatic, way the first tremors of the earthquake that was to prove shattering to the world in which he lived.

The world of Marcabrun's poetry is already, in fact, a vast wasteland, a desolate landscape of degeneration and destruction, containing the remains of a flourishing garden or orchard that evil forces have laid low. A mysterious tree whose roots are elsewhere has grown up in this orchard, spreading its malign influence into every nook and corner. In this world, undermined both physically and morally, spring is perennially aborted into an arid, fruitless season; all persons and objects have lost their primary essences and become their contraries; society is shot through with conflicting forces, which wrestle endlessly for its soul. Occasionally, there is the fleeting vision of a paradisiacal place where the spirit can live and contemplate itself in perfect harmony, but this image is submerged in dark shadows illuminated only by the flickering of hellish flames. Indeed, this image, the opposite of the wasted garden, flits through Marcabrun's sombre world like a hallucination or mirage, the memory of something lost, the dream of a future restoration.

In more than one poem of Marcabrun's we are called upon to witness this very process of degeneration. An early poem of considerable virtuosity, "Al departir del brau tempier" (When the dark season ends), opens ingenuously with the typical springtime *exordium* of Provençal love poetry: a description of the renewal of organic life that awakens the desire to compose:

> Al departir del brau tempier,
> Quan per la branca pueja.l sucs
> Don reviu le genest'e.l brucs
> E floreysson li presseguier
> E la rana chant'el vivier,
> E brota.l sauzes e.l saucs,
> Contra.l termini, qu'es yssucs,
> Suy d'un vers far en cossirier.
> [III, 1–8]

> (When the dark season ends
> And sap courses through the branches,
> Awakening heather and broom,
> And the peach-tree flowers,
> And the frog sings in the fish-pond
> And the willow and elder bud,
> As the dry season approaches
> I contemplate writing a poem.)

But almost immediately the poem reveals itself to be something other than what it seems: the idyllic landscape is contaminated by the presence of low, common trees such as the peach, elder, and willow; and euphony is broken by extremely harsh sounds, particularly in rhyme. Of what is the poet dreaming? In the next stanza he explains that he is dreaming of a huge orchard planted with lovely trees; but when the true nature of that orchard emerges, the dream becomes a nightmare:

> Cossiros suy d'un gran vergier
> Ont a de belhs planôs mans lucs;
> Gent sont l'empeut, e.l frugs bacucs:
> Selh qu'esser degron sordegier,
> Fuelhs e flors, paron de pomier,
> Son al fruchar sautz e saucs,
> E pus lo caps es badalucs,
> Dolen son li membr'estremier.
> [*ibid.*, 9–16]

(I dream of a huge orchard
With thick groves of fine saplings,
The grafted limbs large but the fruit empty:
The lesser part [leaves and flowers]
Makes these seem apple-trees,
Yet the fruit's that of willow and elder.
The extremities suffer
Because the head is inane.)

Although the leaves and flowers had seemed to be those of apple-trees, the fruit is that of the sterile willow and elder. Why has this happened? Using the traditional equation of the human body with society, Marcabrun relates that the "head" fails to function properly, hence causing the members to suffer. The whole of society has degenerated or is in danger of degenerating. The fault does not lie with the original "good" trees, but rather with these new scions:

Mort son li bon arbre primier
E.l viu son ramils e festucs;
Dels fortz assays los vey damnucs,
Mas de bordir son fazendier;
De promessas son bobansier,
Al rendre sauzes e saucs;
Don los claman flacs e bauducs
Ieu e tug l'autre soudadier.

[*ibid.*, 17–24]

(The first, the good trees are dead,
Only twiglets and straw remain;
Bold deeds are negated to them,
But I see they are experts at horsing around
And making great promises
That are sterile as willow and elder:
Thus I and the other salaried ones
Proclaim them slack and dull.)

The great trees—kings of brave actions and generous spirit—have disappeared, leaving behind "twiglets and straw"—vain, boisterous, avaricious princes who seem to be of an entirely different species from their fathers. Marcabrun names them contemptuously (Sir Constant, Sir Hughes, Sir Esteves—literary or proverbial and hence symbolic names) and declares that if no superior, outside force comes to aid these miserable offshoots of men who were like laurel and olive, they will soon find themselves landless and "on the road." In particular, these rascally heirs, said to be no better than common porters, are the enemies of the *soudadier*, the class of hirelings in the princes' retinues with whom

Marcabrun constantly identifies himself and in whose name he often speaks.

The theme of degeneration is conveyed by a style that deliberately deforms sounds for expressive purposes. The vitality of organic renewal—*sucs* (sap)—is distorted and degraded into *saucs* (willow) used as a rhyme-refrain throughout the poem. There are many mocking sounds (e.g. *frugs ... bacucs; sauzes ... saucs*) and a continuous harsh hissing produced by sibilance and the velar-spirant nexus, *-ucs, -aucs*. The rhyme-scheme of *coblas unissonans*,[6] through the accumulation of cumbersome rhymes, produces a monotonous, progressively irritating effect. The whole poem seems to grow out organically, like the nasty twigs of which it speaks, from a single root and trunk: to be derivative, that is, of the same perception of evil.

The symbolism of the evil tree, deriving from both Christian and Islamic traditions, becomes even more sinister and is magnified to cosmic dimensions in another poem, "Pois l'inverns d'ogan es anatz" (Since winter has given way), which similarly corrupts the positive evocation of a spring landscape—

> Pois l'inverns d'ogan es anatz
> E.l douz temps floritz es vengutz . . .
> > [XXXIX, 1–2]

> (Since winter has given way
> To the mild, flowered season . . .)

—into a negative, nightmarish vision, in this case of a monstrous tree that has filled every corner of the world:

> Totz lo segles es encombratz
> Per un albre que.i es nascutz,
> Autz e grans, brancutz e foillatz,
> Et a meravilla cregutz,
> Et a si tot lo mon perpres
> Que vas neguna part no.m vir,
> No.n veia dels rams dos o tres.

> Empero aissi es levatz,
> E vas totas partz espandutz
> Que lai d'outra.ls portz es passatz
> En Franss' et en Peitau vengutz;
> Qu'ieu sai qu'el es en tal defes,
> E dic ver, segon mon albir,
> Qu'en tenra sa verdor jasses.
> > [*ibid.*, 8–21]

> (The whole earth is encumbered by a tree
> Tall and wide, many-branched and leafy,
> So marvellously grown,
> Extending into every part of the world,
> That nowhere can I turn without encountering
> Two or three of its limbs.
>
> This tree has grown so high,
> Pushing in every direction,
> That there, beyond the mountain passes,
> It has gone into France and Poitou;
> The place where it stands is so well defended
> That I believe it will always be green.)

There are valuable indications here of the physical location of the evil that is invading the Western world. Evidently its source is in Spain, for it has passed the Pyrenees and invaded southern France; in particular it rises in a closed place (*ental defes*) that will form a kind of foil for another closed place that we will examine in a moment. Marcabrun also provides us with a hallucinating—one might almost say Villonesque—vision of Christian potentates hanged on the evil tree, the noose of avarice around their necks:

> Meravill me de poestatz
> On a tans joves e canutz,
> Comtes e reis, et amiratz
> E princes en l'albre pendutz;
> Mas lo latz escarsetatz es.
>
> [*ibid.*, 29–33]

> (It amazes me how many potentates,
> Both young and old,
> Counts and kings, admirals
> And princes, are hanged on this tree:
> Avarice is the noose around their necks.)

But after this striking vision, there is a kind of descent, a movement characteristic of much of Marcabrun's poetry—a concretization and apparent diminution of theme. The second half of the poem is dedicated to the criticism of two different kinds of personages that appear ubiquitously in Marcabrun's poetry: the licentious husband and the parasitic guardian of women. Here the tone changes, the focus narrows, and prophecy becomes bitter polemic bordering on court gossip. What is Marcabrun's complaint against the husbands?

> Non puosc sofrir qu.als moilleratz
> Non digs lor forfaitz saubutz;
> Non sai la cals auctoritatz
> Lor mostra c'om los apel drutz.
>
> [*ibid.*, 50–3]

(I am compelled to talk to the husbands
About their notorious misdeeds;
I cannot imagine what authority they invoke
For having themselves called "lovers.")

Adultery is the sin, and its implications are nearly cosmic. Because these husbands (obviously the reference is to noble husbands) have become carnal lovers of other men's wives, there has been a flourishing of whoredom in society:

Drudari' es trassaillida
E creis Putia s'onor,
E.il moillerat l'ant sazida
E soi.is fait dompnejador.
[XXXVI, 25–8]

(Courtship has gotten out of hand
And Whoredom waxes more powerful:
Married men have appropriated it,
Now turning themselves into lovers.)

Marcabrun never tires of explaining the mechanism of the process whereby the husbands set in motion a vicious cycle: the noblewomen do not hesitate to follow their husbands' example (betrayed, they betray), and a law of reciprocity begins to function not unlike the biblical "an eye for an eye and a tooth for a tooth":

Car qui l'autrui con capusa
Lo sieu tramet al mazel.
[XLII, 17–8]

(Whoever pushes head-on into the cunt of another
Sends his own to slaughter.)

But most significant of all is the fact that this vicious cycle leads to the production of bastards whom the noble husbands do not recognize, or are deceived into thinking are their own:

Moillerat, ab sen cabri,
Atal paratz lo coissi
Don lo cons esdeven laire;
Que tals ditz: "Mos fills me ri"
Que anc ren no.i ac a faire:
Gardatz sen ben bedoi.
[XVII, 31–6]

(Husbands with the instincts of a billy goat,
You set up the pillow in such a way
That the cunt grows thievish.
A man says, "My son smiles at me,"
Who never had anything to do with it.*
Look how foolish they are!)

* i.e. the son's conception.

The theme of bastardy lies at the very heart of Marcabrun's polemic and provides an essential key to the various poetic techniques he develops. It is highly important in this respect to examine the archetypal situation— the primitive narrative frame—in which Marcabrun imagines the production of bastards taking place within the closed circle of the aristocratic class; for it is this original process that offers the poet the basis for his symbolic notions of what is "opened" or "closed":

> D'autra maniera cogossos,
> Hi a rics homes e baros
> Qui las enserron dinz maios
> Qu'estrains non i posca intrar
> E tenon guirbautz als tisos
> Cui las comandon a gardar.
>
> E segon que ditz Salamos,
> Non podon cill pejors lairos
> Acuillir d'aquels compaignos
> Qui fant la noirim cogular,
> Et aplanon los guirbaudos
> E cujon lor fills piadar.
> [XXIX, 19–30]

> (Here's how rich men and barons
> Are cuckolded:
> They lock their wives at home
> So that no stranger may enter,
> While they keep young knaves near the fire,
> Ordering them to guard them.
>
> According to Salomon,
> One could not find worse thieves
> Than these men to invite in
> Who bastardize the brood.
> The masters, caressing the knavish kids,
> Believe they are fondling their own.)

This passage clearly reveals that one definite source of evil is the fact that barons and other rich men lock their wives up in castles, placing them under the protection of parasitical *gardador* who cuckold the race by fathering bastards whom the husbands assume to be their own sons. In this manner, three essential closed, guarded things are violated: the castle, woman's sex, and intact lineage.

Who are these strange *gardador* who appear everywhere in Marcabrun? In the poem about the ruined orchard, they are described as sitting around the hearth all evening, carrying on (presumably sexually) at night, and bragging about their exploits the next day "in the shade of willows." In the poem about the evil tree, the *acropitz penchenatz* (well-groomed crouchers—i.e. by the fire) and *gastaus fumos* (smoky butlers) are said to sit around all day awaiting greetings and to be false and deceptive. In the poetry of Guilhem of Poitou, the *gardador* are similarly accused of seducing the noblewomen entrusted to them; there, too, they seem to be a traditional figure of abuse, a *topos*, much like the *raqib*, or guardians of women, of Arab poetry (but the *raqib*, of course, were eunuchs[7]).

In Marcabrun, the *gardador* are described in colourful, expressionistic terms that also give us a glimpse of real life within the castle: they are always sooty and smoky, for example, because they lounge by the fire or stand in the kitchen begging for supper. A sense of promiscuity surrounds them, for they seem to be everywhere, mixing with everyone. It is also obvious that, like the degenerate heirs of the orchard poem (into which class they blur through the process of bastardization of the aristocratic line), they are the enemies of the *soudadier*, who, it is implied, actively work for a living, give wise counsel to kings, and respectfully court the same women whom these scoundrels seduce. The *gardador* are probably enemies in another sense, for they seem to be fused in Marcabrun's imagination with rival poets, the court poets who hypocritically praise a sublime love, masking the real adulterous intrigues that are leading society to its downfall. The *gardador* thus seem to represent an indeterminate but very real evil penetrating the interstices of society, a kind of classless, rootless group of men still in the shadows, not yet emerged in their true colours to reveal their true function. Marcabrun feels their infiltration, notes the menace to traditional values, but can express his fear and contempt only in terms almost of caricature and by reducing the reality of these men to a purely verbal level. Indeed, the neologistic compound nouns he uses to describe them—e.g. *corna-vi* (drunkards), *coita-disnar* (rushers-to-dinner), *bufa-tizo* (blowers-on-coals), *crup-en-cami* (stoopers by the roadside), and so on—constitute one of the most original aspects of Marcabrun's style. The *gardador* are a kind of cipher in Marcabrun's poetry, and it would be futile to try to identify them with one class or sub-class in society; on the other hand, they seem to represent a very real tendency of society, perhaps the process whereby hereditary fiefs came to be bestowed, in this period, on the personal servants (in a sense, the *ministeriales* of Carolingian origin) of the seigneur, which influenced the further disintegration of ancient feudal structures and, in some cases, the gradual formation of the bourgeoisie. But whatever social class or group the *gardador* may correspond to in Marcabrun's mind, it is patently clear that copulation between *gardador* and noblewomen has already begun to produce a new hybrid class of *nouveaux riches*:

> Domna non sap d'amor fina
> C'ama girbaut de maiso;
> Sa voluntatz la mastina
> Cum fai lebrieir' ab gosso;
>   Ai!
> D'aqui naisso.ill ric savai
> Que no fant conduit ni pai.
>   [XXXI, 46–52]

> (A lady who loves a household knave
> Knows naught of true love.
> Her lust mongrelizes her
> Like a greyhound bitch coupling with a cur.
>   Alas!
> From these unions spring those sluggish rich ones
> Who never give money away and never throw parties.)

Thus we see how a sexual sin becomes, for Marcabrun, the basis for a virtual revolution within the class structure of feudal society, an alteration of its divine and natural order. How concerned Marcabrun is with a rigid caste system, the confines of which must not under any circumstance be trespassed, is revealed by the following speech, which is significantly placed in the mouth of a wise shepherdess in a *pastorela*:

> —"Don oc; mas segon dreitura
> Cerca fols sa follatura,
> Cortes cortez' aventura,
> E.il vilans ab la vilana;
> En tal loc fai sens fraitura
> On hom non garda mezura,
> So ditz la gens anciana."
>   [XXX, 78–84]

> (—"Yes, Sir, but right reason commands
> That the foolish seek out folly,
> The courteous courteous adventures,
> And that the peasant stick to a peasant woman.
> 'There where measure is not kept
> Wisdom cannot abide,'
> Men said in olden times.")

The crime about which the poet is most concerned is a crime against the present structure of society. Far stronger than his horror at the notion of adultery *per se* is his disgust at the thought of promiscuity between different social levels. Marcabrun's concern is the maintenance of the purity of aristocratic lineage in order to safeguard the integrity of the feudal estate and to guarantee its direct transmission through primogeniture. The interruption of blood-lines, the juridic basis for the transmission of personal property, meant the risk of destroying the nature of society as it had evolved to that point. The acquisition of subsequently hereditary shares of land by functionaries of the castle (undoubtedly one of the socio-economic phenomena outraging Marcabrun) was only one aspect of the larger movement opening society, increasing its stratification, interrelating its structures, and setting up new dependencies between town and country, with a concomitant new distribution of wealth and power. The rise of the communes, the gradual liberation of the serfs, and the formation of new mercantile strata would, in a century and a half, endanger the classical feudal economy inherited from Carolingian times. In an intellectual of that age, this sense of crisis could be no more than a poetic intuition; yet Marcabrun's perception of imminent change, of a situation ineluctably slipping out of control, is keen:

> Cel prophetizet ben e mau
> Que ditz c'om iri' en becill,
> Seigner sers e sers seignorau.
> > [XXXIII, 37–9]

> (He prophesied good and bad things
> Who said the world would be reversed:
> The master slave and the slave master.)

These lines, which make one think of the parables of master and slave in Hegel, Marx, and Tolstoy, and which are most likely of biblical and proverbial derivation, appear in a poem that seems to reflect the tumultuous and potentially "revolutionary" movements of that time—in this case a revolt of Angevin barons, aided by certain vassals of Guilhem X of Aquitaine (Marcabrun's patron in the 1130s) against the young son whom Fulk V had left behind when he went to the Holy Land in 1129. Naturally, Marcabrun views this situation from the Poitevin side, blaming "the stupid buzzards from Anjou" (whom he calls cockroaches and associates with excrement in another poem) and praising his patron; but it is the fact of insurrection itself that disturbs him, because of the threat it poses to the precise, well-ordered, compact aristocratic world of 50 years earlier. Lay vassals, however, are not the only forces undermining that system. We have seen how Marcabrun does not hesitate to range "false abbots" and "false abbesses" alongside whores, ruffians, and other criminals in his imaginary hell. Not even the two great mediaeval powers, emperor and pope, are safe from his barbs if he judges them to be destroyers of the "old" values: when Emperor Lothair and Innocent II engage in a vulgar reciprocal sell-out after the defeat of the anti-pope Anaclet II—a situation in which the rumblings can already be heard of a far graver schism two centuries later—Marcabrun damns "venal Rome" and calls the emperor "a filthy rogue who got himself elected through money." Marcabrun's reformism looks to the past; the reformation that he has in mind is not so much reform of the Church as the restoration and continuation of a particular historical-political moment.

Although his loyalties necessarily shifted from one feudal monarchy to another, Marcabrun never lost sight of his vision of a united West led by an indissoluble aristocratic class and inspired by the chivalric-religious ideals of the First Crusade. It was, in fact, mainly his crusade songs that made Marcabrun famous among his contemporaries. Even when he was serving his first patron, Guilhem X, a new crusade to the East was his dream, but this dream was dashed to pieces by the death of Guilhem on a pilgrimage to Compostella in the spring of 1137. At that time, the poet seems to have joined the retinue of Guilhem's daughter, Eleanor of Aquitaine, and Louis VII, to whom he also preached the subject of the crusades, but in vain. After various sojourns at the courts of seigneurs of south-western France (Toulouse, Gascony, and so on) and of the prince of Portugal, Marcabrun went to the court of Alfonso VII of Castile, who was then becoming the dominant personality of the *Reconquista* in the first half of the 12th century. Already in Marcabrun's Lavador song (which may well be datable to 1137—a decade later than is usually thought), the need for a crusade in Spain is seen to be far more urgent than the defence of the Frankish kingdoms to the east: "I am summoning you to the 'washing-place' here at hand," the poet warns in the first stanza, claiming, further on, that the French kings are "unnatural" if they do not heed this call. Here and in the equally well-known *pastorela* where the young shepherdess, perhaps speaking allegorically in the name of all Spain, mourns the fact that King Louis has sent her love "much too far away," Marcabrun may be participating—if indirectly—in the polemic of the mid-1140s after the fall of Edessa (1144), about whether it was wise, politically or in any other sense, for the French monarch to leave on a second crusade to the East. Great ecclesiastical figures such as Suger were vainly opposing this movement, which was to prove disastrous both at home and abroad. On the other hand, the *Reconquista* seemed to be moving dramatically forward in those years in Spain: Alfonso arrived at the gates of Cordova in 1147. In 1132, he had named himself "Emperor" to demonstrate his claim over the entire peninsula (Marcabrun takes great satisfaction in continually addressing him as such). After the inertia of the 1120s and 1130s, deriving in part from dynastic quarrels between the queen of Castile and the king of Aragon, Alfonso's reign seemed to hold out the possibility of a Castilian renaissance. It is in this context that the shift of emphasis in Marcabrun's attitude toward the crusades must be seen. Although Alfonso proved a disappointment to the poet as a patron, his leadership must have seemed uniquely to point to that consolidation of power and land and maintenance of ideological unity in the Christian West to which Marcabrun aspired. It is this luminous hope that produces, almost as a kind of counter-image, the dark, tangled world of Marcabrun's vision of hell on earth.

In reality, "the enemies" are those who fail to leave on the crusade: hence, the abuse of the shadowy *gardador* that occupies two whole stanzas of the Lavador song, in which they are described (among other things) as "descendants of Cain's line," and the equally harsh abuse, in that same poem and elsewhere, of the fallen nobles for whom chivalric virtues and ideals have no more meaning. All these men have turned away from the "natural" course of their lives—the service of *fin'amors* (true love) and the crusades; for it is precisely those who refuse to go to battle who seduce the wives of the seigneurs, thus producing the race of bastards (the new class). Only by recognizing this bond between the erotic and political planes of Marcabrun's discourse can we understand the poet's obsession with one set of images, the *putas ardens* (burning whores) and the symbol and emblem of their physical and moral reality, the *con* (cunt). Only by keeping in mind the poet's obsession with the themes of purity and integrity and the need to return to an original wholeness, can we understand his fanatical condemnation of the *cons frait* (broken cunt) that has forever replaced the *cons entier* (whole cunt):

> Greu sai remnra conz entiers
> A crebar ni a meich partir.
>   [XLI, 35–6]

> (There will hardly be an intact cunt left
> To break open or divide in half.)

remarks the poet bitterly in a poem that significantly opens with a piece of Marcabrun's prophetic rhetoric: "Now that spring has come . . . my mind dwells intensely on those things . . . that the whole populace is murmuring about." We shall see how Marcabrun, the social critic and defender of the old feudal monarchies and the ideals of "the people" (we have already noted the populism of his various *pastorelas*), fastens onto the very particular symbolism of the feminine sex in an almost fetishistic way and becomes primarily a chastiser of women, certain to encompass in this way all the ills of society, all the negative forces operating around him in this world, "rising and falling" as if in one massive act of copulation.

Thus the transformed object *par excellence* is, for Marcabrun, woman and the feminine sex, and his most vicious attacks are aimed at the "burning whores." "Never since the time when the serpent lowered the branch," declares Marcabrun, have there been so many treacherous women in the world. All the figures of women, from Eve and Delilah to those of the present day, are negative, except for the shepherdess, who is a kind of counter-figure to the whore and who, as we have seen, vindicates a popular ideology coinciding with that of the great nobility. Misogyny is the quintessence of his work, a fact that led one biographer to feel that it was enough simply to say that Marcabrun "said bad things about women and love" in order to describe his life and work. It is interesting, in light of the poet's obsession with whoredom and bastardy, to note that he himself (and his biographers) recounts that he was a whore's son[8] in a stanza that subsequently became famous and lines of which were used as a kind of refrain on which to make variations:

> Marcabrus, fills Marcabruna,
> Fo engenratz en tal luna
> Qu'el sap d'Amor cum degruna,
>   —Escoutatz!—
> Quez anc non amet neguna,
> Ni d'autra non fo amatz.
>   [XVIII, 67–72]

> (Marcabrun, son of Marcabrune,
> Born under an unlucky star,
> Knows how Love runs out.
>   —Listen!—
> Never did he love anyone,
> Nor was he ever loved.)

The poem that this stanza ends is a kind of bitterly playful anti-hymn to the God of Love, in which love is called tyrant, assassin, devouring fire, and disease; a double, false, ambiguous, crooked, hypocritical, lustful, mercenary force in league with the devil. Typically, much of the weight is on the rhymes, which are pounded out monotonously (aaabab) with, in the middle of every stanza, the rhyme-refrain *"Escoutatz!"* Marcabrun especially delights in making his lines move in a serpentine, two-faced manner:

502

De sai guarda, de lai guigna,
Sai baiza, de lai rechigna.
                    [*ibid.*, 20–1]

([Love] looks one way but gestures in the other,
On one side kisses, on the other frowns.)

Yet we should not take Marcabrun too literally here, for his tone is malicious and ironic, rather than pathetic. His stance against women and love is an intellectual one, and he bolsters it with a self-abasing account of his birth and with rhetorical syntheses that serve as a kind of password for his disciples.

Marcabrun the woman-hater emerges in his finest colours in a diatribe against fallen courtesans addressed to his fellow companions-in-arms, the *soudadier*. In one sense, the poem "Soudadier, per cui es Jovens" (Hirelings, who maintain Youth) is a soldier's piece of complacent cursing of the *puta*; but it is also a showplace for the poet's erudition, rich as it is in strange images and proverbial expressions. We have already seen women compared to greyhounds coupling with common curs. Here Marcabrun carries the metamorphosis in animal terms one step further. In this poem where women are progressively reduced to *metriz, pecairitz trichairitz,* and *trairitz* (mercenary, deceptive sinners, and traitors), woman undergoes a visual transformation into a monster:

De Guimerra porta semblan
Qu'es serps detras, leos denan,
Bous en miei loc, que.l fai trian
De caval bai e d'aurifan.
                    [XLIV, 17–20][9]

(She has the appearance of a Chimaera:
A serpent in back, lion up front,
Steer in the middle, which distinguishes her
From a bay horse or an elephant.)

Here Marcabrun is something more than a mere *maldizens* (evil-sayer) of women. Against the Circe-Siren figure he weaves a hypnotic, active, diabolical spell that has an exorcizing force. Creating a verbal hell, producing nightmarish phenomena, transforming words just as he sees the reality around him transformed, Marcabrun creates a kind of magic poetry and performs an act of corruption that liberates him.

Marcabrun does not spare the depraved courtesan in this poem, who is portrayed as mercenary and opportunistic, unable to distinguish intrinsic worth, reeking like rotten meat, always sniffing her way into the kitchen, and producing bastard fledglings whom she hides away from their rightful father; but she is treated even more savagely, in a way, in the two *estornel* (starling) poems, which are mocking versions of the love poem in the form of a *salut* (message) conveyed by a gentle bird to the lady. Many of the *topoi* of traditional courtly love poetry already appear here, but slightly twisted into something vulgar and unsavoury. It was usual, for example, for the poet to declare that he wanted to be "tied and bound" (embraced) by his lady (*lassar* and *liar* are technical terms to express a sensual but limited contact between lovers as well as, in certain cases, the binding-together of the poem itself), but not to state explicitly that he wants her "flattened out underneath" him! The scope of the starling—plebeian substitute for the nightingale—is to fix a time and place for the act of copulation, and in this he easily succeeds. An interesting image in terms of the closed place is that of the *cambra . . . de cel guarnida* (room . . . decorated with the sky), signifying a garden or open field: it is here that the mistress will meet her lover. In both poems Marcabrun plays on the ambiguity of the bird metaphor: for example, in the second poem the woman "opens the door" and the bird flies straight in. In the companion poem, after having remarked that the woman is the mistress of thousands of men, Marcabrun states in his own voice that the "door" is not "closed," again using the key term *clus*:

> Marcabrus
> Ditz que l'us
> Non es clus.
>   [XXV, 60–2

> (Marcabrun
> Says that the door
> Is not closed.)

This reference to the female sex organ is part of a vast net of concrete and symbolical references obsessively woven around this object; for the corrupt hole is always, for Marcabrun, the antithesis and negation of the virginal and intact to which his mind aspires. The *con* is, in short, the non-place of love, the debasement and reduction of existence, the nothingness against which his poetry insistently beats. How many times Marcabrun harps on this theme! It seems to appear everywhere in his work, and the poet enjoys a kind of bitter satisfaction in naming the object over and over again:

> E son acaminat li con . . .

> (And the cunts have taken to the road . . .)

Maritz qui l'autrui con grata . . .

(Husbands who scratch other men's cunts . . .)

Don lo cons esdeven laire . . .

(Hence the cunt becomes thievish . . .)

Aquist con son deziron e raubador . . .

(These cunts are lustful and stealthy . . .)

Car qui l'autrui con capusa . . .

(Whoever pushes head-on into the cunt of another . . .).

Significantly, Marcabrun can use such terms as adjectives as well: a cuckold wears a *capel cornut conin* (horned cuntish cap), and adulterers participate in a *joc coni* (cuntish game).

But this emblematic, disparaging use of the word for the feminine sex organ and other words with obscene connotations did not originate with Marcabrun, even if he developed it more organically in relation to the themes of his poetry as a whole. The poems of Guilhem of Poitou (to say nothing of the long tradition of clerical misogyny in Latin literature of the Middle Ages) are full of abuse for the *puta* and *con*.[10] Three of Guilhem's poems compare women unflatteringly with horses. These are, in a way, highly intellectual poems, one of them perhaps having philosophical implications. Another poem is constructed around the idea of, and word for, the feminine sex organ, which is cynically punned on and then made the object of a mock law:

Pero dirai vos de con cal, es sa lei
Com sel hom que mal n'a fait e peitz n'a pres
Si c[om] autra res en merma qui.n pana, e cons en creis.[11]

(I'm now going to tell you the law of the cunt
Since I'm one who mistreated it and got treated even worse:
Other things diminish with use, but the cunt grows larger.)

By being named over and over, the female sex organ takes on a kind of absurd but powerful reality in this very obscure poem, which Guilhem calls a *casteis* (chastising poem); significantly, Marcabrun calls himself a *castiador* and the Marcabrunians spoke of their function as *castiar*. This is not the place to discuss it, but I believe that there is a tradition in Provençal poetry of the "negative" woman—negative both as a symbol of material reality and as being *de lonh* (distant).[12] The mysterious "Amigua" of Guilhem's famous riddle about "nothing at all" may well represent the first formulation in troubadour poetry of the mercenary, stand-offish, entirely negative courtesan who is finally immortalized as Dante's *donna di pietra* (note also Shakespeare's "Those who have power to hurt and will do none"). A somewhat later riddle by Raimbaut de Vaqueiras (*c.* 1200), constructed around the paradox of sexual intercourse in which the feminine sex—essentially "nothing"—vanquishes the seemingly more powerful male, goes even further, and seems to anticipate metaphysical poems such as Donne's "The Canonization" and "Farewell to Love" in its expression of the nothingness of love and the absolute negativeness of coitus.[13] In an important but neglected debate between Aimeric de Peguilhan and Albert de Sisteron that was also influenced by Guilhem's riddle, the nothingness of courtly love (its aspiration to an ideal Platonic form) is also seen as producing nothing: the nothingness, the non-being, of the poetry that embodies it. In this mock-scholastic debate about the reality of universals, the dice are heavily loaded in favour of what we might call a poetic nominalism, the vision of the poet as Narcissus, whose creation, inferior to that of the *logos,* can be no more than the echoing reflection of his own words.[14]

Is there, in Marcabrun, a kind of perverse satisfaction in pronouncing—indeed, drumming out—*flatus vocis* such as *puta* and *con,* things reduced to a merely nominal and hence futile reality? Certainly, in the various self-portraits that he offers, Marcabrun reveals that he is quite conscious of being constrained to write about "nothing"; and he draws a subtly connecting thread between his negative subjects (social evils, prostitutes, the female sex organ) and the nature of the poem itself and his function as a poet. He realizes that the mimesis of this material inevitably produces something sterile, unproductive, obscure. His most essential definition of this situation is a portrait of himself as one who sins in the very naming of sins:

> E ieu sui del dich pechaire . . .
> De nien sui chastaire
> E de foudat sermonaire.
>> [V, 30–2]

> (And I am a sinner in saying [these things] . . .
> A chastiser of nothing,
> And a preacher of folly.)

A *jongleur* styling himself an Old Testament prophet, Marcabrun thus complains that his destiny is to wander, seeding his criticism on barren soil.

> Semenan vau mos castiers
> De sobre.ls naturals rochiers
> Que no vey granar ni florir.
>> [XLI, 28–30]

(I go seeding my chastising [songs]
Over natural rocks
Where no grain nor flower springs up.)

Similarly, his disciple Peire d'Alvernhe was also to complain that he was
del castiar raucx (hoarse from reproving—i.e. in vain). But though there
may be a sense of humiliating impotence in the fact of not communicating
and not being able to make words efficacious so that they "flower" in the
soul of the listener, both poets take pride in the fact that the uninitiated
can have no access to their meaning. Marcabrun maliciously tells us that
not only do few understand his words; he himself sometimes has difficulty
in deciphering obscure texts:

> Per savi.l tenc ses doptanssa
> Cel qui de mon chant devina
> So que chascus motz declina,
> Si cum la razos despleia,
> Qu'ieu mezeis sui en erranssa
> D'esclarzir paraul' escura.
>   [XXXVII, 1–6]

(I certainly think him wise
Who guesses what each word means
As the argument of my song proceeds;
For I myself find it
Difficult to clarify
Dark language.)

A similarly ironic self-criticism appears in a passage by Peire where the
poet says of himself that he would be a fine poet if only he clarified his
words a bit, because hardly anyone understands them.

It is important to note that there are two kinds of obscurity for
Marcabrun: his positive obscurity is, in part, a reaction against the
negative obscurity of the poetasters who "quarrelsomely tangle their lines"
and weave broken morals into their verse. (*Entrebescar*—to weave lines
into a poem—is an ambivalent term that was to take on an alternately
positive and negative meaning; in the case of the poetasters, it is said that
they *entrebesquill* [tangle] their lines.) Marcabrun explains more than
once that his obscurity is a means of defending himself, because speaking
out is both useless and dangerous:

> E s'ieu cug anar castian
> La lor folhia, quier mon dan;
> Pueys s'es pauc prezat si.m n'azir . . .
>   [XLI, 25–7]

(And if I think to go around chastising
Their folly, I seek only to hurt myself,
Since they don't care if I get angry or not . . .).

Pois no m'en aus esclarzir
Ni mon talan ademplir,
An puois co.is pot, Dieus m'en vailla!
[XLII, 33–5]

(Since I don't dare to make myself clearer
Nor to do what I want to do,
May things go as they will and God help me!)

In this world in which the poet is forced to defend himself, to use poetry
as a kind of antidote or weapon, he must veil his meaning but, at the same
time, strive to trip up his enemies with their very own instruments. This
is, in fact, the key to Marcabrun's hermeticism, or at least to one stage of
it. If love entangles, the ingenious poet must disentangle; but what
tangled lines this thought is couched in!

Qu'amors adoncx entrebesca
Enginhos desentrebesc. [XIV, 35–6]

(What love thus entangles
An ingenious man disentangles.)

This is a kind of verbal skirmishing that appears in an odd love poem,
which is all saying and not-saying or, rather, saying one thing and
meaning another. Fighting fire with fire means, in this situation, com-
bating the tangled behaviour of others with a tangled poem:

Mos talans e sa semblansa
So e no so d'un entalh,
Pueys del talent nays semblans
E pueys ab son dig l'entalha,
Quar si l'us trai ab mal vesc
Lo brico, l'autre l'envesca. [*ibid.*, 13–8]

(My desire and its semblance
Are and are not of the same cut,
Since from desire springs semblance
Which shapes desire with its words—
For if one thing drags down the fool with an evil glue,
The other will truly englue him.)

It is not by chance that the almost impenetrable poem in which this
stanza appears is the poem of Marcabrun's that develops the *caras rimas*[15]
style furthest. Here there are at least three different, superimposed kinds

of rhyme-scheme, as well as the use of emphatic, harsh-sounding grammatical rhymes (e.g. *descrec, encresca*; *azesca, azesc*; *enguasalh, guasalh*; and
so on).[16] This poem is a kind of intricate war-dance against the enemies
of true love, but it is clear that the battle can only be one of words,
because words are the poet's sole weapon. It is Marcabrun's wit and
multi-levelled meanings that must save him, as he indicates in another
gap that is extremely important for our present discussion of the *con* in
relation to Marcabrun's conception of himself as a poet.

The *gap* "D'aisso laus Dieu" (I praise God for this) is a poem in which
the poet seems to brag about committing adultery and producing
bastards—things that are clearly condemned in all his other poems;
therefore, it has been considered to be simply a parody of his enemies'
style.[17] However, a much more complicated poetic process is involved in
Marcabrun's virulent polemic and daring imitation of the vices of others
in order to flay them. When the poet brags

> De gignos sens
> Sui si manens
> Que mout sui greus ad escarnir;
> Lo pan del fol
> Caudet e mol
> Manduc, e lais lo mieu frezir.
>
> [XVI, 13–8]

> (I am so well provided
> With ingenious reasoning
> That it is almost impossible to make fun of me;
> I eat the fool's
> Warm, soft bread
> And let my own bread cool.)

is he not bragging in his own voice about his ingenious meanings and his
ability to resist others' scorn and to take advantage of them? Is this
stanza not, perhaps, an answer to the spiteful accusation of being
"Breadless"?[18] As so many times in Marcabrun's poetry, we find the
learned and the jongleuresque combined, as in the following insistence
on his prestidigitatious use of multiple levels (the "rhetorical colours"
codified in the Latin *ars poetica* of the 13th century?), as well as his ability
to know just when and how to strike out or to hold his tongue:

> Del plus torz fens
> Sui ples e prens
> De cent colors per mieills chauzir;
> Fog porti sai
> Et aigua lai,
> Ab que sai la flam' escantir.
>
> [*ibid.*, 49–54]

> (I am full of
> Manifold meanings,[19]
> A hundred colours to choose from;
> I carry fire here
> And water there
> And know how to put out the fire with it.)

Skill in this art is truly a question of life or death for this troubadour, who—if his biographer is reporting fact—was assassinated by the chatelains of Guienne for being an "evil sayer"!

> Chascuns si gart,
> C'ab aital art
> M'er a viure o a morir.
>> [*ibid.*, 55–7]

> (May everyone beware!
> For these skills
> Are a matter of life or death to me.)

And what better description of his own poetry could there be than the following vivid portrait of the artist-soldier involved in violent single combat, perhaps one against many?

> D'estoc breto
> Ni de basto
> No sap om plus ni d'escrimir:
> Qu'ieu fier autrui
> E.m gart de lui
> E no.is sap del mieu colp cobrir.
>> [*ibid.*, 31–6]

> (No one is better than me
> At striking
> With a Breton rapier or a pole, or at fencing:
> While hitting my opponent,
> I defend myself—
> He doesn't know how to ward off the blows.)

It is, in fact, poetry that Marcabrun is talking about all through the poem. If the perverted love-song was an original contribution to Provençal poetry, here the process is far more complex, being theorized, as it were, in the heart of the poetry itself. What Marcabrun is doing here is essentially appropriating the substance of his adversaries—their verbal bread—and turning it into something else. He takes the forms and formulas of real life and makes them into an image of the poetic process. More precisely, he does in his poems what his enemies do in real life. In

510

this case, Marcabrun employs a violent, obscene metaphor to describe this imitative aggressiveness characterizing his *gap* style:

> En l'autrui broill
> Chatz cora.m voill
> E fatz mos dos canetz glatir,
> E.l tertz sahus
> Eis de rahus
> Bautz e aficatz [senes mentir].
> > [*ibid.*, 37–42]

> (I hunt whenever I wish
> In other men's preserves,
> And make my two small dogs bark;
> The third hound points,
> Then boldly and firmly
> Leaps to strike its prey.)

Surely we are not meant to think that Marcabrun actually threatens to have sexual intercourse with other men's wives, a notion that would seem to contradict the whole thrust of his other poems. The meaning of this passage cannot be a literal one. What he is saying in this very rhetorical poem (or poem about rhetoric) is that his words form an infallible instrument for attacking the poets who sing the praises of adulterous love. The very graphic tripartite phallic metaphor is purely ironic: a kind of answer, in poetic terms, to the *con* that has expanded evilly to fill the entire world. The poet must penetrate that reality in order to destroy it, hence his intellectual activity is like a sexual violence, a verbal rape. In the enigmatic finale—

> Qu'ieu sui l'auzels
> C'als estornels
> Fatz los mieus auzellos noirir.
> > [*ibid.*, 58–60]
> (For I'm the bird
> Who makes starlings
> Bring up his fledglings.)

—where Marcabrun seems to have returned to the theme of bastardy, there may well be a reference to the two *estornel* poems, the meaning being that the poet lets his poems (the little birds) grow up in a perverted, bastardized form—in effect, be "bastard poems"—because they necessarily correspond to the reality that produced them and that they reflect.

But there is one stanza that, above all, seems a quintessence of Marcabrun's notion of his art and provides a clue to his secret meaning. We are encouraged to interpret this passage on several levels precisely because the poet has warned us about his "manifold meanings" and "hundred colours":

> Mos alos es
> En tal deves
> Res mas ieu non s'en pot jauzir:
> Aissi l'ai claus
> De pens navaus
> Que nuills no lo.m pot envazir.
>
> [ibid., 43–8]
>
> (My private property [*allodium*]
> Is so well defended
> That no one but me can enjoy it.
> I've so closed it round
> With a chastity belt
> That no one can force his way in.)

What is this mysterious place or space that no other man may enter or enjoy, and that the poet has closed off from the world? Recalling other examples of refrain-like lines expressing the same idea as *Que nuills no lo.m pot envazir* (That no one can force his way in) already examined, we can conclude that, at least on one level, the closed place is the sex of the woman: his woman, her chastity, and hence the dialectical opposite of the negative *con*. It is also like the castle or mansion that no one may enter without risk of contaminating aristocratic lineage and thus leading feudal society to its downfall; hence it could be considered an ideal vision of society in the mind of the poet. At the same time—and this is the most striking aspect of the passage—this closed place is defined in terms of a specific economic entity within the feudal structure: the *allodium*, or "entire property" held in absolute or near-absolute ownership—that is, only nominally in fee from another. Suddenly we are removed from a battlefield to a rural, agrarian world.

What might the *allodium* have signified to a highly politicized intellectual of the time such as Marcabrun? It is difficult to say. On the one hand, many of the oldest estates were allodial; on the other hand, one of the symptoms (and causes) of the disintegration of the great seigneurial estates was a move toward "private property," characterized by increased allodization of the soil. One thing is certain: Marcabrun speaks of his *alos* with great pride, almost as though his ownership of it constituted a kind of vengeance on society; for behind the jocularity and provocation of this *gap* lies a ferocious desperation. Marcabrun owned no land: his *alos*, his metaphorical plot of ground, is all that the poet can cling to in this overturned world, and thus constitutes a point of anchorage in a life of vagabondage and material uncertainty, of forced travel among the often chaotic and warring kingdoms of northern Spain and the Midi. Surely the *alos* is the poem itself, the space that the poet creates and holds to be inviolable (whereas he can, instead, violate the metaphorical structures of others, because they are built on fragile moral scaffolding). Thus the woods of others are like a common property where Marcabrun can hunt whenever he pleases, but his own reserve is a virgin enclosure that belongs to him alone.

Significantly, the same imagery of the closed place, with the same ambivalent erotic-social meanings, appears in a key poem by Peire d'Alvernhe—an extremely obscure poem that is obviously an act of homage to (and variation on) Marcabrun's poetry, because it has the same rhyme-scheme and stanza as the *gap* examined a moment ago and quotes, in slightly altered form, Marcabrun's epithetic valediction to terrestrial love:

> Qu'ieu non am re
> Ni autre me
> E cug me totz d'amor lonhar.
> > [VIII, 40–2][20]
>
> (For I love no one
> And no one loves me,
> And I think I will distance myself from love.)

In addition, the poem calls itself a *casteis* and circles around the symbol of the closed, guarded place:

> Mais am un ort
> Serrat e fort
> Qu'hom ren no m'en puesca emblar
> Que cent parras
> Sus en puegz plas:
> Qu'autre las tenh'ez ieu las guar.
> > [*ibid.*, 25–30]
>
> (But I love a plot of ground
> Tightly, securely shut in
> So that no man can steal anything from me
> More than a hundred palaces
> Situated on high plains:
> May others own these and I only look on!)

There is even less doubt here that the closed place is, first of all, the sex of the woman; for Peire speaks soon after of a woman who concentrates all his thoughts and desires:

> Qu'ieu ai un cor
> Et un demor
> Et un talan et un pessar
> Et un amic
> Vas cui m'abric
> Et a cuy me vuelh autreyar.
> > [*ibid.*, 49–54]

> (For I have a heart
> And a dwelling-place
> And a desire and a thoughtfulness
> And a friend
> Toward whom I turn [for protection]
> And to whom I wish to dedicate myself.)

This person is further characterized as a *car amiga* (dear woman-friend) and *amor de lonh* (distant love). But there is another important element that makes explicit something that was implicit in Marcabrun's poetry—namely, that both poets write in the *clus* style; for Peire's poem contains the first direct application of that term to poetic technique:

> Be m'es plazen
> E cossezen
> Que om s'ayzina de chantar
> *Ab motz alqus*
> *Serratz e clus*
> Qu'om no.ls tem ja de vergonhar.[21]
> > [*ibid.*, 1–6]

> (It's pleasant
> And appropriate
> That a man sing
> Drawn-tight,
> Closed words
> Of which he need never be ashamed.)

One important conclusion that must be drawn from this confrontation of the two poems by Marcabrun and Peire is that not only was the concept of a *clus* style already consciously present in Marcabrun, but the techniques for "closing in" a poem were undoubtedly progressively generated by the theme, idea, and image of the closed place.

Interestingly, Peire uses an even humbler term than Marcabrun to describe the closed space that is the poem; for here the *alos*, a territory of indeterminate measure, is reduced to an *ort*, a mere garden-plot. In Peire's lines, the plight of the poor landless clerical-bourgeois poet emerges more clearly than in Marcabrun: here, the poet frankly admits that he has no alternative but to turn away from the material palaces that he cannot have and to construct a dwelling-place out of love itself. Whereas in Marcabrun the polemic against the fallen nobles and newly landed (non-noble) property-owners dominated, in Peire one perceives most the pathetic aspects of being *caminier* (on the road): one is also led to understand how the impossibility of possession becomes the principal theme of the *amor de lonh* poets in the 12th century. Although these poets do not all—

514

or always—consciously practice the obscure style (the argument *clus* versus *leu*, the obscure versus the light, clear, easy style, was to be enriched by an important debate between Raimbaut d'Aurenga and Guiraut de Bornelh, *c.* 1170), the notion of enclosing a small, rounded space, an ideal realm free from all material contingencies, an autonomous world in which the poet can dwell forever in absolute privacy contemplating his most sacred images, is always present in their minds and evident in their poetry.

Peire's poem is important also for the way in which it associates *trobar clus* and *amor de lonh*. For what is *amor de lonh* if not the perpetual desire to be elsewhere, in a place where one is not? The outstanding feature of this poetry based on and dedicated to the cult of a distant love is precisely an adverbial anxiety created by the contrast between where the subject is and where he would like to be but cannot be. Jaufre Rudel, Bernart Marti, Raimbaut d'Aurenga, Bernart de Ventadorn, Arnaut Daniel, Arnaut de Maruelh, and many others perceive the object as constantly elsewhere, thus forcing the poet to send his spirit out to dwell in an imaginary place often described through periphrases such as "there where she is."[22] In particular, it is the *cambra* (room) and *jardi* (garden), often coupled together in expressions that become rhetorical formulas, that symbolize the ideal location of a continuously postponed union, and that thus obsess the poet and take on an unnatural reality in his poems. The poet can be alternately tormented and consoled by the fact that he is always paradoxically *pres e lonh* (near and far). The play on the concepts of proximity and distance are endless, particularly in poets such as Raimbaut d'Aurenga and Bernart de Ventadorn. In the frequent quasi-technical use of the words *aizi* and *aizimen*[23] (signifying at the same time adjacency and ease), the poets express their longing for a place where they can be at home with the world and themselves, at ease in a space that is like an internal nearness. This continuous litany of place-words—this adverbial anxiety—produces an intensification of the poet's emotional life, enabling him to "live" in joy. Through a concentration of his energies on one single point in time and space, the closed place of the imagination becomes a palace, as Jaufre Rudel tells us in a significant passage, each line of which contains key words and the whole of which accomplishes the positive transformation of a negative reality:

> Qu'ieu vega sest'amor de lonh
> Verayamen, en tals aizis
> Si que la cambra e.l jardis
> Mi resembles tos temps palatz![24]

> (May I see this distant love
> Truly and with such ease [*or* in such a place]
> That the room and the garden
> Seem constantly to be a palace!)

Love can turn the humblest reality into the most exalted form. This is the same kind of transforming power that will miraculously reverse nature, as in a poem by Raimbaut d'Aurenga in which hills become plains, cold turns to heat, thunder changes into birdsong, and so on, and in an imitation of it by Bernart de Ventadorn, in which frost becomes flowers; the technique of *adynata* and *impossibilia* reappears in poems by Arnaut Daniel, Dante, and Petrarch, significantly in the sestina form. Sometimes the palace can be seen to emerge from a much more concrete reality, as in a passage of Bernart Marti's that has never been satisfactorily interpreted:

> Que d'als non es mos cors entiers,
> Ni autre tresaur non amas,
> Ni autra ricor non deman:
> Que qui.s haia tor ni castel,
> Eu.m ai mon bel palais el forn.
>
> (My heart is not made whole by anything else,
> I gather no other treasure
> And seek no wealth but this;
> May they keep their towers and castles!—
> My beautiful palace is in an oven.)

Rather than the poet's having built his palace in "a modest place," as the editor of his work surmised, I believe that Bernart means specifically that he has built his palace in the female sex (in the Marcabrunian tradition, *forn* [stove, furnace] is synonymous with *con*). The poet has constructed his ideal world out of the idea or figure of woman, who is essentially "nothing," negative material reality, but at the same time the goal of his desire and inspiration of his poetic phantasy:

> Molt estaria volontiers
> Lonc lo seu cors dolgat e gras.[25]
>
> (I would most willingly linger
> By her delicate, plump form.)

More delicately (although by the 1180s these things will have become near-clichés), Arnaut Daniel called his lady "the tower, the chamber, and the palace of love."

But already in Marcabrun a rich set of meanings radiates from this central symbol. In addition to the *alos* of the *gap*, the closed place appears in "Al son desviat" (On a wandering tune), a bitter satire about licentious wives, sinful husbands, and all kinds of cuckolding, the poem in which Marcabrun complains wearily that he is forced to be a "chastiser of nothing" and a "preacher of folly." After a passage of archaic mechanical Marcabrunian allegory describing the abuse of Prowess, daughter of Youth and Love (who, in another poem, is pictured besieged in her tower by Maliciousness), there is an extraordinary stanza that lifts the poem forcibly out of the world of low passions and the poet's "conditioned" attack on them. It is as if *fals'amors* (false love) had dialectically produced its opposite, *fin'amors* (true love), and as if society's dark wasteland had nostalgically evoked a luminous enclosed garden:

> L'amors don ieu sui mostraire
> Nasquet en un gentil aire,
> E.l luocs on ill es creguda
> Es claus de rama branchuda
> E de chaut e de gelada,
> Qu'estrains no l'en puosca traire.
> > [V, 49–54]

> (The love of which I am speaking
> Was born in a noble atmosphere,
> The place where it grew up
> Closed round with leafy boughs
> And protected from heat and cold
> So that no stranger could steal it.)

We have seen how the closed place, in Marcabrun's poetry, can be the woman's sex, intact lineage, and the economic measure of private property. Here, it is described in terms of an eternal, inviolate nature. The nature contained in this image is a highly symbolic one, drawing on several pagan-classical, biblical-theological traditions that are, in turn, absorbed into a higher synthesis and given new meaning. First, the *topos* of the *locus amoenus*, associated with the Golden Age, influenced the topology of this fabulous garden sheltered all round by leafy branches, knowing no change of seasons, and penetrated by no alien forces. The *locus amoenus* was inevitably associated in the Middle Ages with the earthly paradise, the Garden of Eden, a recurrent image for the nostalgia of the soul and its future hope. But the Garden of Eden did not always appear intact in its Old Testament garb; often it was fused with another biblical image—the garden of the Song of Songs—and both of these with the *hortus conclusus* of Christian theology, symbol for Mary's virginity, which in turn is used to symbolize society, and thus Jerusalem, and the Church conceived of as a sacred community.[26] By the first half of the 12th century, the *hortus conclusus* was heavily impregnated with the erotic-mystical overtones of the Song of Songs as it had been interpreted by early Fathers of the Church and contemporary theologians such as Hugh of St Victor, Guillaume de St Thierry, and St Bernard. But already by the 5th and 6th centuries Jewish authorities had attributed a secret meaning to the Song of Songs, calling it "the holy of holies" and interpreting the closed garden as the place of absolute knowledge, absolute pleasure, and union with the beloved (God). A long tradition translated spiritual ecstasy in terms of the raptures of betrothal, marriage, and conjugal love in language often surprisingly sensual and concrete. Christian authors followed this tradition in the main but interpreted the lovers as the human soul and Christ, or sometimes as the Virgin Mary (considered as both Bride and Mother) and Christ. In the biblical text there are direct references to virginity and chastity ("A garden inclosed is my sister, my spouse: a spring shut up, a fountain sealed" [Song of Songs IV: 12]), so that it was natural to identify that garden with the *hortus conclusus* and to see both as symbols for the soul.

Thus, although the *locus* that is *clus* in Marcabrun is, on one level and originally, the woman's sex (the most material point of existence even in the most Platonic *amor de lonh* poets, the object of real, if postponed, desire), it is at the same time the symbol for the exact opposite—that is to say, for the soul purified of every earthly appendage. What we have here is a kind of identification of the mind with its object (the woman) and the transposition of the mystical attributes of the *hortus conclusus* to the self-consciousness of the human spirit. In other words, the closed place—that unique, integral property—becomes a symbol for the virginal sanctum of the soul, imagined by subsequent poets as the inner "chamber" of the heart (Dante) or the "paradise within" of 17th-century English religious poets, where the soul is mystically fused with its ideal. Paradoxically, it is by secluding himself in the innermost cloister of himself that the poet achieves the relationship that he seeks with the external world, a harmony with nature and the cosmos perfectly expressed in the symbol of the garden that is at once earthly paradise and *locus amoenus*, a place where leaves never lose their green, where love springs eternal, and where sin, mutability, and death can have no sway. This harmony, which the poet possesses only in the closed space of his innermost being, is a truly musical one, for it is this secret accord with the cosmos (one is tempted to say with the Pythagorean spheres) that nourishes his spiritual life and inspires him to sing. Just as *mezura* can be found only in the disciplined and hence joyous inner life, so the "whole" song (the song that is *entier* and not *frait*) must devolve from an inner spring and vision, the central point of the microcosm.

But the closed place is not only the soul of the poet in its mystical self-contemplation; it is also the world conceived of as an ideal world, society seen as static, resistant to change (compare Dante's "garden of the Empire," his nostalgic evocation of an Italy that "was"). The expression *gentil aire* (a noble atmosphere) would lead one to think that Marcabrun is saying that *fin'amors* can issue exclusively from the aristocratic class guarding its pure lineage and maintaining its ancient customs. There is an attractive theory that the closed place in this particular poem may be a transposition, on a figurative plane, of the geographical reality of Navarre at the time of the engagement of Sanche III of Castile to Blanche of Navarre, great-granddaughter of the Cid, in October 1140.[27] However, it is not necessary to restrict this vision of society to any particular dynasty, occasion, or place. The last line of the stanza (*Qu'estrains no l'en puosca traire* [So that no stranger could steal it]), a *leit-motiv* throughout Marcabrun's poetry, serves to link this passage to the generic, archetypal situation we have already examined, of castle and chatelaine that must not, under any circumstances, be violated. Hence, the closed place would seem to be a general symbol for a socio-historical reality of his time that the poet would like to preserve, halting the process of change already in motion. He could not have foreseen how the crusades would help to contribute to further divisions in the West and the new organization of power in the form of nations, as well as a fatal shattering of East-West Christian union. Nor could he have imagined that another crusade, only 60 years after— a logical continuation of the political and economic realities of the preceding ones—would wipe out most traces of Provençal culture and life, including its poetry. Yet Marcabrun felt the imminence of a storm and sensed that wherever he set his feet down he was nowhere, in a kind of non-place. Hence, it was not only his "sociological" condition that gave Marcabrun the sense of a world shifting, splintering, and disappearing around him, but also an intuition of a larger process taking place in the long historical period.

References

1. See ANTONIO VISCARDI, *Le origini*, 2nd edn (Milan 1950), pp. 636–9.
2. See LEO POLLMANN, "Trobar clus," *Bibelexegese und hispano-arabische Literatur* (Münster-Westfalen 1965), pp. 45–54.

3. See, for example, the opening passages of Boethius's *De trinitate* and John of Salisbury's *Entheticus* (*Patrologia latina* [Paris 1844–64], CXCIX, col. 969).
4. The most recent study of this subject is AURELIO RONCAGLIA, " 'Trobar clus': discussione aperta," *Cultura Neolatina* XXIX (Rome 1969), pp. 5–55. This article opens a debate on Marcabrun's poetry to which, so far, only Eric Köhler has responded. Köhler's writings include "Zum *trobar clus* der Trobadors," in *Trobadorlyrik und höfischer Roman* (Berlin 1962).
5. The quotations from Marcabrun, and the numbering of the poems, are taken from J. M. L. DEJEANNE, *Poésies complètes du troubadour Marcabru* (Toulouse 1909). Roncaglia is in process of preparing a new edition, and has already published individual poems in the following articles: "I due sirventesi di Marcabruno ad Alfonso VII," *Cultura Neolatina* X (Rome 1950), pp. 157–83; "Il 'gap' di Marcabruno," *Studi Medievali* XVII (Spoleto 1951), pp. 46–70; "Marcabruno: 'Lo vers comens quan vei del fau'," *Cultura Neolatina* XI (Rome 1951), pp. 25–48; "Marcabruno: 'Al departir del brau tempier'," *ibid.*, XIII (1953), pp. 5–33; "Marcabruno: 'Aujatz de chan'," *ibid.*, XVII (1957), pp. 20–48; " 'Cortesamen vueill comensar': studi in onore di Alfredo Schiaffini," *Rivista di Cultura Classica e Medioevale* VII (Rome 1965), II, pp. 948–61; "La tenzone tra Ugo Catola e Marcabruno," *Linguistica e Filologia: omaggio a Benvenuto Terracini* (Milan 1968), pp. 203–54. I have used Roncaglia's text for Nos. III and XVI.
6. A scheme in which the rhymes of the first stanza are repeated in all subsequent stanzas of the poem and in the same order.
7. This was pointed out in CARL APPEL, "Zu Marcabru," *Zeitschrift für romanische Philologie* XLIII (Halle 1923), pp. 403–69.
8. The *vida* (short biography) is clearly based in part (if not wholly) on this poem by Marcabrun, just as the description therein of how the poet was found on the doorstep of a rich man's house probably derives from a pair of poems forming a mock debate between Marcabrun and "Sir Audric" in which the supposed patron calls the *jongleur* "Breadless." The fact that "Sir Audric" speaks in the same low, plebeian manner as his interlocutor, together with other internal evidence, suggests that the debate was an invention of Marcabrun's.
9. Cf. a strikingly similar passage in *King Lear* (Act IV, Scene 6), which generally shares with Marcabrun's poetry the sense of cosmic sex-sickness, the perception of something monstrously unnatural in the social world. It is also interesting that *King Lear* is dominated by the theme of bastardy:

> The fitchew, nor the soiled horse, goes to't
> With a more riotous appetite.
> Down from the waist they are Centaurs,
> Though women all above:
> But to the girdle do the gods inherit,

Beneath is all the fiends';
There's hell, there's darkness, there's the sulphurous pit,
Burning, scalding, stench, consumption. . . .

10. It is interesting to note a poem by Marcabrun's contemporary, Marbode of Rennes (1035–1123), whose *De meretrice (Patrologia latina* [Paris 1844–64], CLXXI, col. 1698–9), contains the comparison of woman to a chimaera, as in the poem we have examined.

11. These lines are from No. III (10–2) in ALFRED JEANROY, *Les chansons de Guillaume IX*, 2nd edn (Paris 1927). I have corrected the text in accordance with a new edition of the poem in NICOLÒ PASERO, "'Companho, tant ai agutz d'avols conres' di Guglielmo IX d'Aquitania e il tema dell'amore invincibile," *Cultura Neolatina* XXVII (Rome 1967), pp. 19–29.

12. For a discussion of *amor de lonh*, see Reference 21, below.

13. See LYNNE LAWNER, "The Riddle of the Dead Man (Raimbaut de Vaqueiras, 'Las frevols venson lo plus fort')," *Cultura Neolatina* XXVII (Rome 1967), pp. 30–9.

14. See LYNNE LAWNER, "'Tot es niens'," *ibid.*, XXXI, dedicated to Jean Frappier (Rome 1971), pp. 155–70.

15. *Caras rimas*—the use of rare, precious words, particularly in rhymes— is a very important tradition in Provençal poetry. The term is nearly synonymous with what scholars call *trobar ric*; both imply elaborate rhyme-schemes. The poets themselves frequently use these terms (e.g. Raimbaut d'Aurenga: *Cars, bruns e tenhz motz entrebesc* [I interweave rare, dark, obscure words]). Poetry can seldom be *car* without being *clus*, so that one finds *caras rimas* and *trobar clus* over-lapping time and again.

16. Rhymes are enchained by means of: (a) an elementary *retrogradatio*— first stanza abcdef, second stanza badcfe, and so on; (b) the semi-rhyming of derivative rhymes within the stanza—*ansa, alh, ans, alhe, esc, esca*—which can be represented as ababcc, with a division into *frons* and *cauda* (head and tail), the technical division of Provençal song-stanza; and (c) the alternation of feminine and masculine rhymes according to the scheme abbaba.

   Roncaglia has suggested to me that Marcabrun's use of derivative rhyme may stem from the same kind of thinking that appears in a passage by Bernard of Chartres, quoted by John of Salisbury in *Metalogicon* (III, 2), where it is implied that the noun contains the real substance, the adjective and verb being subsequent attenuations of that substance through conmixture with accidental elements such as the "person." This is most significant in light of the fact that the sestina form—the culmination, in my view, of both *trobar ric* and *trobar clus*—seems to derive from evolving experiments in the use of derivative rhyme. Marcabrun would thus be the first innovator along these lines of whom we have any evidence. It is important, perhaps, to point out that it is Raimbaut d'Aurenga (*fl. c.* 1175)—a much underrated poet who is more interesting than Arnaut Daniel and whose work was for long influenced by Marcabrun's—who becomes the inventor and champion of a new hybrid kind of *trobar clus* love-poetry employing the complex devices of *caras rimas*; it is Raimbaut who creates a new form that is the direct predecessor of the sestina and is formally even more complex than the latter.

17. See RONCAGLIA, "Il 'gap' di Marcabruno," Reference 5, above.

18. See Reference 8, above.

19. My translation has been influenced by another reading of line 49 (manuscripts CE): *De pluzor sens*. Roncaglia's reconstruction of the AIK version means more or less the same: "I am full of the most complicated simulations."

20. ALBERTO DEL MONTE, *Peire d'Alvernha: Liriche* (Turin 1955).

21. The italics are mine. Since ULRICH MÖLK, *Trobar Clus—Trobar Leu: Studien zur Dichtungstheorie der Trobadors* (Munich 1968), dates Peire's earliest poem to 1158, he suggests that one cannot speak of *trobar clus* being practised before that date. I hope to prove conclusively in this essay that it began earlier in the century, permeating most, if not all, of Marcabrun's work.

22. The necessity of sending the spirit "out there," where the body cannot go, derives from the practical-material situation of courtly love as it was originally conceived: an adulterous love through which the true lover, even if he cannot possess the body, can possess the soul of his beloved. Jaufre Rudel reminds us sadly: *Luenh es lo castelhs e la tors/on elha jay e sos maritz* (Far away are the castle and the tower/where she and her husband lie together): see ALFRED JEANROY (ed.), *Les chansons de Jaufre Rudel* (Paris 1965), No. III, 17–8. Every student of Provençal literature knows how Jaufre employs the word *lonh* as a rhyme-refrain in his famous "Lanquan li jorn son lonc en may" (When the days grow long in May), repeating it 14 times in the whole poem. If the *amor de lonh* is, as I believe, a much more diffuse phenomenon in troubadour poetry than even Leo Spitzer thought, its origins still remain obscure. A "distant love" or "love from a distance" can be found in Virgil, Propertius, Catullus, the Greek romances, the Tristan legend, the Platonizing Latin poetry of the Loire school, and Arabic poetry of the 9th, 10th, and 11th centuries, as well as in the *haraǧāt* (envois in Romance dialect mixed with Arabic and tacked onto Hebrew and Arabic poems from the 9th to the 12th century).

Like courtly love in general, *amor de lonh* contains a reversal of feudal hierarchy: an erotic-literary fiction permitting the woman to be *dominus* over the man, who is considered vassal, private fief entirely in her power. *Amor de lonh* was temporal as well as spatial: it was about postponement as much as it was about physical distance. An ambivalent mystical language was often used to characterize the ardour of this love intensified by its being *in absentia*, and the poets often speak of a spiritual conversion that involves the maintenance of joy and hope for their own sakes. Thus the sensation of wanting exactly what they never can have, never have had, never will have, is deliberately cultivated by these poets, who live in the no-man's land of *non-poder* (not having power), a halfway stage between knowing and not knowing, sleeping and waking, living and dying—a malaise of suspense, uncertainty, and unease, that is the perpetuation of anxiety and its exploitation for poetic purposes. The poet must make something absolute, certain, and positive out of something insubstantial, shadowy, and negative: he must create, as we have seen, a place out of a non-place.

23. See R. DRAGONETTI, "'Aizi' et 'aizimen'," *Mélanges de linguistique romane et de philologie médiévale* (Gembloux 1964), pp. 127–53.

24. This is No. V, 39–42 in JEANROY (ed.), *Les chansons de Jaufre Rudel*.

25. ERNEST HOEPFFNER (ed.), *Les poésies de Bernart Marti* (Paris 1929), No. VIII, 10–4.

26. As the Tree of Life grows in the Garden of Eden, so the Tree of Jesse associated with it grows in the mystical Christian garden. The Tree of Jesse, symbolizing the perfect continuity of lineage from King David to Christ, is often used to represent the miraculous regeneration that took place through Mary, conceived of as a life-giving, resurrecting "branch." A passage in a poem by Bernart Marti (HOEPFFNER, *op. cit.*, No. IV, 50–6), who was a follower of Marcabrun, typically uses this sacred imagery to speak of profane love (note that *verga* is a key word in the Marcabrunian tradition, and appears as a rhyme-word in Arnaut Daniel's sestina):

> Eu n'aurai la senhoria
>   En Pascor,
> Quan so.l ram carguat de flor.
> Tals pot esser l'escaria
> Qu'encaras reverdiria
>   La raïtz
> E.l verguans estes floritz.

> (I will have the dominion
>   At Easter-time,
> When the trees are heavy with blossoms.
> Such may be my fate
> That the root
>   Again flourish
> And all the branches bloom.)

27. See RONCAGLIA, " 'Trobar clus': discussione aperta," pp. 21–2, Reference 4, above.

CHAPTER 15

Mediaeval Religious Drama

A. C. Spearing*

I

The story of the origins of mediaeval religious drama has often been told, and need be repeated only briefly here. There is no firm evidence of any link between the drama of the Middle Ages and that of classical antiquity, and it appears that drama was re-born, after a lapse of many centuries, in western Europe in about the 9th century. It developed then out of the liturgy, when the practice grew up of interpolating into it tropes—that is, short poems acting as commentaries upon it. One of these, the *Quem quaeritis* (Whom seek ye?) trope, took the form of a dialogue between the Marys approaching the tomb of the risen Christ and the angels guarding it. At first it was inserted into the Introit of the Mass at Easter; later, it was transferred to Matins and there, freed from the constraint of its original position, it developed into something like a genuine little drama, in which cantors or half-choirs impersonated the two groups of characters.

In the course of time, this scene became popular in churches (over 400 manuscripts of it survive), and it gradually acquired extra scenes that extended the story in both directions. There were added an *unguentarius*, selling spices for anointing Christ; bragging Roman soldiers sent to guard the tomb; an episode in which Peter and John also approached the tomb; Christ's appearance to Mary Magdalene; and later his appearance on the way to Emmaus. Thus the story of Easter week was gradually transformed into drama, but into a drama still closely attached to the liturgy, performed by clerics inside the church, and spoken and sung in Latin. Meanwhile, on the model of this Easter drama, there grew up a Christmas drama. This also originated in a trope, in which the shepherds met the angels at the stable, just as the Marys met the angels at the sepulchre; and it too was transferred from the Introit of the Mass to Matins. Once

---

* University Lecturer in English, Cambridge, and Fellow of Queens' College.

more, there appeared a tendency toward expansion. This simple *Officium pastorum* (Rite of the Shepherds) became attached to an *Officium stellae* (Rite of the Star), in which the Magi see and follow the star, and into which Herod was soon introduced—the first villain in mediaeval drama. The way was then open to add a further episode, that of the Slaughter of the Innocents. A third point of growth in the liturgical drama was the sermon *Contra judaeos, paganos, et arianos*, attributed to St Augustine, which was read in Advent, and in which the Jewish prophets from Isaiah to John the Baptist, together with three "prophets" of the gentiles (Virgil, Nebuchadnezzar, and the Erythraean Sybil), speak those prophecies that the Church saw as fulfilled in the coming of Christ. This sermon became a *Processus prophetarum* (Procession of the Prophets), in which the prophets appeared separately to speak their prophecies. This was of great importance for the future development of religious drama: it supplied the principle of prophecy and fulfilment as a basis for a cyclic structure that would link the Old and New Testaments. The title it was given at Rouen, *Processio asinorum* (Procession of the Asses), suggests that it may also have helped to diversify the drama in other ways. Balaam with his talking ass was one of the prophets of the play (though not of the sermon), and the Rouen title suggests that the comic possibilities of the ass may have assumed a larger importance than one would expect in the *processus* as a whole.

There is of course no reason to suppose that the development of liturgical drama was as smooth as this summary implies. It was no doubt fitful and haphazard, and the development of new types of drama did not render the old types obsolete; but, once clerics and their congregations had become used to impersonation as an adjunct to ritual—and to impersonation of the horrible, the comic, and the spectacular—there were many opportunities for its further extension. Certain Old Testament stories lent themselves to dramatization: those of Daniel and Joseph were favourites; and episodes from the New Testament, such as the raising of Lazarus and the conversion of St Paul, were also seen to have dramatic potential. Material from outside the Bible and Apocrypha also came to be treated dramatically in church: the famous Fleury manuscript (an important collection, dating from the 12th or 13th century, written at the monastery of Fleury but now at Orleans), for example, contains, alongside six biblical plays, four about miracles of St Nicholas.

From the very beginnings of mediaeval religious drama, a double tendency was at work. On the one hand, the purpose of this drama—manifested in the very transition from liturgy to drama—was to make sacred events *real* to lay congregations; and this meant presenting them not as historical events but as everyday events, conceived in terms of people's real lives. On the other hand, the drama shows a tendency to bring separate events together to form a coherent structure displaying the divine purpose that gives the separate events their full meaning. These two tendencies, sometimes in co-operation, sometimes in conflict, underlie the whole course of mediaeval religious drama, until, in countries influenced by the Reformation, the attempt to present sacred events was abandoned. In the liturgical drama, a natural consequence of the desire to make sacred history real, shown already in the introduction of such characters as the *unguentarius* and (in the *Officium pastorum*) the *obstetrices* (midwives), was to move from Latin, the language of the Church, into the vernacular, the language of everyday life. This step was taken gradually and no doubt sporadically, and a Latin liturgical drama continued in existence down to the 16th century. But the vernacular seems to have been introduced in France in the late 11th or 12th century, in the plays of Hilarius and in the Beauvais *Daniel*, and, more extensively, in the St Martial play of the Wise and Foolish Virgins. French is also used in the drama in England in the 12th century, notably in the *Mystère d'Adam*, which has only a few insertions in Latin. But the first signs of the use of English in England are not found until the "Shrewsbury Fragments" in a 14th-century manuscript.

II

The English of these fragments does no more than translate from the Latin; but in the *Mystère d'Adam* the vernacular is used in a more creative way. The play as it stands in its single manuscript contains three scenes: the Creation and Fall of Adam and Eve; Cain and Abel; and an incomplete *Processus prophetarum*. Unlike the liturgical drama proper, it was performed outside the church, using the area in front of the building as a stage, and the building itself as a symbolic structure and a dressing-room. There can be no doubt of its clerical authorship, and it continued to use the church choir for singing; but it was clearly intended to make sacred history meaningful to a lay audience, and it therefore presents its vernacular scenes not with liturgical grandeur and remoteness, but with human immediacy and contemporaneity. We feel this particularly with the first and longest scene. At no point is there any doubt about the dramatic illusion, or any need felt for the audience to suspend their disbelief: in

527

creating Adam and Eve, God also creates the illusion of which they are a part (and indeed illusion is an anachronistic word: the mediaeval audience is being shown what is simply "true"). Moreover, the play presents eternal truths in the form of the accepted social ideals of the 12th century, and this fact must contribute largely to the appealing confidence of its language. The instructions that God gives to his creatures require no justification, because their ethical assumptions are those of the mediaeval present. Eve must obey Adam in everything, *car ço est dreiz de mariage*[1] (for that is the law of marriage). Adam in turn must obey God, for, as God later says, *"tu es mon serf, e jo ton sire"*[2] (you are my servant, I am your lord); and Adam agrees that if he eats the forbidden fruit he will deserve to be punished, for

> Jugiez deit estre a lei de traïtor
> Qui se parjure e traïst son seignor.[3]

> (He who breaks his oath and betrays his lord must be judged as a traitor.)

Here everything reflects the static assumptions of feudalism, where every man has his lord and the ultimate wrong is to betray one's lord. The Devil, however, suggests new social ideals, which no doubt belong to the new urban communities of the early Middle Ages, in which social mobility became once more possible. Has God created Adam solely to be his gardener, he asks? *"Ne munteras ja mes plus halt?"*[4] (Will you never rise higher?). And even—horrifying idea—*"porras estre senz seignor"*[5] (you could be without a lord). Adam is firm in sticking to the traditional ideals, and condemns the Devil as treacherous and faithless; but Eve becomes the victim of a different kind of attack. The Devil's aim is not to provoke but to seduce her, and his language is an exquisitely apt parody of 12th-century courtly poetry. He might be some young squire attempting to persuade a married lady to become his mistress:

> Tu es fieblette e tendre chose,
> E es plus fresche que n'est rose;
> Tu es plus blanche que cristal,
> Que neif que chiet sor glace en val;
> Mal cuple em fist li criator:
> Tu es trop tendre e il trop dur.[6]

> (You are a delicate and tender creature,
> And you are fresher than a rose;
> You are whiter than crystal,
> Or than snow which falls on ice in a valley.
> The Creator made you a bad match;
> You are too tender and he [Adam] is too harsh.)

The note of refined eroticism is beautifully caught, and the psychological insight and verbal dexterity, with their obvious debt to the secular romance, are unsurpassed in later mediaeval drama. An equal understanding of the human situation in contemporary social terms is shown when Adam questions Eve about her association with the Devil. As Auerbach remarks, he

> calls his wife to account as a French farmer or burgher might have done when, upon returning home, he saw something that he did not like: his wife talking to a fellow with whom he has already had unpleasant experiences and with whom he does not want her to have anything to do.[7]

But in spite of this, Eve succumbs, and so in turn does Adam when she presents the one argument that no ordinary man could resist from a woman: *"Del demorer fais tu que las"*[8] (You act like a coward in hesitating). The whole situation of the Fall is seen in terms of an intimate mediaeval humanity: naively perhaps, but with a naivety that is capable, at moments of heightened emotion, of its own dignity. In the shorter Cain and Abel scene, Cain is allowed an attractively sharp edge to his tongue and his intelligence. The sacrifice of one tenth of his produce is seen as identical with the mediaeval tithe, and Cain's comment on Abel's doctrine of tithes is *"En poi de jorz avra poi que doner"*[9] (In a short time he will be short of things to give). Of Abel's moralizing in general he drily remarks *"Icest sermon as bien escrit"*[10] (Your sermon was well composed). Such remarks, though coming from the first murderer, would no doubt find a sympathetic echo in the bosoms of mediaeval laymen; and, once again, they turn a remote historical event into a familiar part of people's daily lives.

But besides this "realizing" tendency, the other tendency we have mentioned is also at work in the *Mystère d'Adam*. In spite of the immediacy and contemporaneity of the two scenes from Genesis, they take on their full meaning only as part of a larger structure of promise and fulfilment that is expressed in the third scene, the incomplete *Processus prophetarum*. The stories of the Fall of man and of the first murder are not *simply* stories from contemporary secular life: each ends with the protagonists being carried off to Hell by devils, and requires for its completion the fulfilment of a divine purpose that stands outside any present moment. The prophets foretell in increasing detail an event that will release Adam from Hell and *salvera les filz Evain*[11] (will save the sons of Eve)—sons including themselves, for they too are carried off to Hell when they have repeated their prophecies. A natural continuation and conclusion for the *Mystère* would be to show the coming of Christ and above all the Resurrection and

Harrowing of Hell. Only in the context of the whole of this great cycle would the meaning of any single part of it be completely understood. Hence we are made to see Adam and Eve in an odd double perspective: they exist in the 12th-century present and yet have prophetic intimations of a future for which the 12th century is already a distant past. Thus, even in the immediate anguish of his Fall, Adam looks forward with precision to the possibility of his Redemption by a second Eve:

> Ne me ferat ja nul aïe,
> For le filz qu'istra de Marie.[12]

> (He [God] will never give me any help, except the son who will be born of Mary.)

And he already knows that his sin will be written in history. Moreover, just as the concreteness of a mediaevalized Genesis is interpenetrated by these hints of an eternal divine purpose, so the symbolic formality of the *Processus prophetarum* is enriched with mediaeval concreteness, when Isaiah is interrupted by a mediaeval Jew, who derisively asks, "*Est ço fable u prophecie?*"[13] (Is that story-telling or prophecy?), and tells him, "*Tu me sembles viel redoté*"[14] (You seem an old dotard to me). The symbolic cycle of divine purpose and the separate concrete episodes of contemporary life cannot be complete without one another.

III

The vernacular religious drama of the late Middle Ages shows a considerable increase in scale and scope over such works as the *Mystère d'Adam*. On the Continent, the characteristic form taken by the religious drama in the 14th and 15th centuries is the Passion play, covering usually the whole life of Jesus, of immense length, taking several days to perform, and normally performed in the open air at Whitsun or Corpus Christi. Of this kind are the French *Passion du Palatinus*, *Passion d'Arras*, and, most famous of all, the *Mystère de la Passion* (c. 1420) of Arnoul Greban. Hitherto, the Passion had scarcely been treated in the liturgical drama. This was partly perhaps because "the liturgy of Passion Week is so moving in itself as scarcely to require, or even profit by, dramatic treatment,"[15] but a more important reason for the change was surely that the drama responded to new movements in mediaeval devotion generally. As the Middle Ages proceeded, devotion came more and more to concentrate on the Humanity of Christ, on his human sufferings, and on the share of the Virgin Mary in those sufferings. There are also signs in the Continental drama of a continuation of the impulse toward the creation of historical cycles. The early-15th-century *Passion de Semur* included much Old Testament material, and ran from the Creation to the Resurrection. As early as 1303 there is a record of the performance, at Cividale in Italy, of a more complete cycle, running from the Creation to Doomsday; and from the 15th century there are records of similar cycles at Eger and Künzelau.

But it was in England that this impulse reached its culmination, for there the cycle dealing with the whole of human history, from the beginning of the world to its end, seems to have been the normal form taken by late mediaeval drama. Four such cycles survive, dating from the late 14th century onward: those from Chester and York, the Towneley cycle—named after the Lancastrian John Towneley (1731–1813), who owned the original manuscript—from Wakefield, and the *Ludus Coventriae* (probably from Lincoln). There are also fragments of other cycles. In all of them the Passion is the central event, treated at great length, but only as part of a larger structure. Because the European field is so large, we shall concentrate on these English cycles, as being the fullest embodiments of the idea of late mediaeval religious drama.

They embody this idea most fully, too, in their social context. The liturgical drama was performed in church; the *Mystère d'Adam* took place in front of the church; and the late mediaeval drama was taken over by lay civic associations and was performed in a civic setting, whether indoor or outdoor. It became an expression of the growing importance and independence of urban communities in the late Middle Ages. In France, the organization of the performances was often in the hands of associations, such as the Parisian Confrérie de la Passion, which, although they included laymen, were still essentially religious. In England, however, this role was taken over by the craft gilds, which were essentially secular, and each gild was made responsible for one episode in the cycle. In some places, such as York, the separate episodes were performed at several places in the city in succession, being moved about on wagons (called "pageants"); at others, such as the home of the *Ludus Coventriae*, they were acted in a single open space, with more elaborate stages, or *loca*, around it.

Both in England and on the Continent, the annual performance of the cycle was a genuine expression of communal feeling and communal talent. This is particularly noticeable in England, where we cannot identify any Greban, Michel, or Mercadé as the author of a cycle: each English cycle is a multi-layered structure, built up over many years by many authors. We can sometimes distinguish the work of particularly talented, though anonymous, playwrights, such as the "Wakefield Master" or the "York Realist," but the talent of individuals was put at the service of the civic community. The motives were partly commercial: a famous play would draw an audience from the surrounding country, and they would spend money in the town. But the cycle also expressed the pride and solidarity of the craft gilds themselves, and there are many signs of this in the English plays. Something of the craftsman's delight in his skill is attributed to God himself, as he creates the world:*

> Moo sutyll werkys asse-say I sall,
> For to be set in service sere.[16]

> (I shall attempt more skilful works, to be set to various uses.)

More specifically, an individual pageant was often assigned to the gild that could best use it to display the products of its craft. Thus at York the building of Noah's ark was performed by the Shipwrights. Noah knows nothing of "shippe-craft," and so God, as master-craftsman, gives him expert instructions, and he proves an apt apprentice, who is proud of his skill:

> Thus sall y wyrke it both more and mynne,
> Thurgh techyng of God, maister myne.
> More suttelly can no man sewe,
> It sall be cleyngked ever-ilka dele,
> With nayles that are both noble and newe. . . .
> This werke I warand both gud and trewe,
> Full trewe it is who will take tente.[17]

> (Thus shall I handle it in every respect, by the instruction of God, my master. No one could fix it more skilfully; it shall be clenched everywhere with new nails of the finest quality. . . . I shall guarantee that this work is good and reliable; anyone who looks will see how reliable it is.)

In the pageant of the Flood, performed by the Fishers and Mariners, although years pass in minutes, there is still a workman-like concern for practical details: Noah reminds his sons to feed the cattle, and his daughters to feed the poultry every day. The world enacted is a familiar and solid world, not the phantasy-world of aristocratic romance, but the real world of bourgeois life, in which, despite the frequent intervention of the supernatural, material details must not be forgotten. In several towns

---

* In this and the other Middle English texts quoted I have replaced the ȝ (yogh) and þ (thorn) characters, regularized the use of *u/v* and *i/j*, and modified the punctuation where appropriate.

the Goldsmiths performed the Magi and the Bakers the Last Supper, and both gilds no doubt used the opportunity to display their wares. At Wakefield the Tanners performed the Creation because they were best able to supply the close-fitting leather garments worn by Adam and Eve.

The emphasis on craftsmanship, being morally neutral, can also have its sinister side. Skilful work is the same whether the ark is to be built or Christ to be crucified—and the same "nayles that are both noble and newe" may serve both purposes. At York, "Christ led up to Calvary" was performed by the Shearmen, and the soldiers discuss the instruments of Christ's death with a chilling professional pride:

> Be-holde howe it is boorede
> Full even at ilke an ende;
> This werke will wele accorde,
> It may not be amende. . . .
> I warand all redy
> Oure tooles both lesse and more.[18]

> (See how it is bored just equally at each end; this work will do very well, it cannot be improved on. . . . I'm sure that every one of our tools is ready.)

In the next pageant, performed by the Pinners, the Crucifixion itself is seen as a job to be done with the greatest possible skill:

> Thanne to this werke us muste take heede,
> So that oure wirkyng be noght wronge.[19]

> (Now we must take care with this work, so that we don't do it faultily.)

It would be a complete mistake, however, to see this laicization of the late mediaeval drama as involving a secularization of its fundamental *meaning*. The craft gilds served religious as well as commercial ideals, and their dramatic cycles were an expression not only of civic pride and civic prosperity but also, like the great parish churches of the later Middle Ages, of civic piety. They were usually performed to celebrate the feast of Corpus Christi, and in their Creation-to-Doomsday structure they continued to express the great symbolic cycle of divine purpose that we find in the *Mystère d'Adam*. The selection of material was governed not by the gilds' desire to advertise their skills, but by an overall symbolic meaning. In the Chester cycle there is an Expositor to expound this meaning. He makes it clear that the Abraham and Isaac episode is chosen for dramatization not simply because it is a good story, or in order to advertise the

Barbers who performed it, but because it stands in a figural relationship
to the sacrifice of Christ:

> This deed you se done in this place,
> In example of Jhesu done yt was,
> That for to wyn mankinde grace
> Was sacrifised on the rode.[20]

All the Old Testament material in the cycles was selected not just for its
direct human meaning, but for its typological significance, the New Law
being not only openly prophesied in the days of the Old, but also hinted
at in the actual events of the Old Testament by "signes and shadows."
Thus, in the Chester "Last Supper," Christ is able to say,

> . . . know you now, the tyme is come
> That signes and shadows be all done;
> Therfore make hast, that we may soone
> All figurs cleane reject.[21]

But the Old Testament prophesies not only the First Coming of Christ,
but also his Second Coming, without which the cycle is incomplete. Thus
at Chester there is a separate episode, "Prophets and Antichrist," in which
the Expositor expounds the prophecies of Ezekiel, Zachariah, Daniel, and
John the Evangelist; then follow the pageants of Antichrist and the Last
Judgment. The same structure underlies other cycles, where there is no
Expositor to lay it bare. Always the same framework of biblical and
apocryphal material is used, to manifest the same divine meaning in world
history. At the end of the York cycle God tells the audience,

> All that evere I saide schulde be
> Is nowe fulfillid thurgh prophicie;
> Ther-fore nowe is it tyme to me
> To make endyng of mannes folie.[22]

And in the Wakefield cycle God explains his purpose in sending his son as
the necessary second Adam:

> I wyll that my son manhede take,
> For reson wyll that ther be thre,
> A man, a madyn, and a tre:
> Man for man, tre for tre,
> Madyn for madyn; thus shal it be.[23]

Besides these formal statements of the cyclic purpose, the individual
pageants contain innumerable references back and forward, acknowledg-
ing the unified meaning that underlies their diversity.

IV

The diversity is real and important. In the English cycles, just as in the *Mystère d'Adam* and in the liturgical drama, we find a double tendency: on the one hand toward cyclic structure, on the other toward development of the concreteness of separate episodes. This latter tendency has perhaps a special appropriateness in a drama celebrating Corpus Christi—the physical presence of God in the sacrament—and it is in any case part of the concentration on the Humanity of Christ that characterized later mediaeval devotion. This devotion encouraged the habit of imaginative "realization" of Christ's life and sufferings that must have been one of the most powerful impulses toward the development of drama itself. The 14th-century mystic Richard Rolle wrote of the crucified Christ:

> Ah, Lord! the pitiful sight I now see! As thou art stretched out, thy wounds are drawn out so wide, and thy limbs and thy nails are so tender, that thou liest raw and red extended on the cross, with the sharp crown on thy head, which is so painful to wear; thy face, which was formerly so beautiful, is so swollen; thy sinews and thy bones stand out so sharply that thy bones may be counted; the streams of thy red blood flow like the Flood*; thy wounds are covered with bleeding and hideous to see; the grief of thy Mother increases thy sufferings.[24]

Rolle is not describing an actual Passion play, but what had to be "seen" with the eyes of the mind and the heart before the Corpus Christi drama could come into existence. In that drama, the same "realizing" imagination is applied to other scenes from the Bible besides the life of Christ; and they are sometimes seen with so powerfully humanizing a vision that their symbolic function is obscured or even contradicted. A brief comparison of two versions of the Abraham and Isaac episode may make this clear.

We have seen that the story of Abraham and Isaac was included as a prefiguration of the sacrifice of Christ, with Abraham representing God the Father and Isaac representing God the Son. Nevertheless, the bare narrative of Genesis implies a dramatic and pathetic *human* situation that, quite apart from its symbolic meaning, is capable of expansion in terms of bourgeois realism. This opportunity is fully taken in the Chester cycle. Abraham speaks to Isaac with the intimate affection of any father for his son, desperately trying to make the extraordinary task seem natural for as long as possible:

> Make thee ready, my derling,
> For we must doe a lyttle thing.[25]

---

* Even here, just as in the drama, the Flood simile suggests a typological parallel within the engrossing physicality of the event.

And Isaac, when told he must be killed, again sees the situation in a touchingly human light:

> If I have trespassed in any degree,
> With a yard you maye beate me.[26]

The whole setting is conceived as domestic, seen from within a familial structure. Isaac cries:

> Wold God my mother were here with me!
> She wolde knele upon her knee,
> Praying you, father, if it might be,
> For to save my life.[27]

But it is eventually Isaac who urges Abraham to perform God's bidding, and not to tell his mother, and again he evokes a family setting:

> Father, greete well my brethren yonge,
> And praye my mother of her blessinge;
> I come no more under her winge.[28]

There are many details in the scene that can be related to its typological significance: Isaac's eventual willingness to be sacrificed is appropriate to Christ, and his references to his mother may remind us of the sufferings of the Virgin Mary at her son's death. But the scene as a whole is deliberately drawn out to produce as much tension and pathos, on a purely human level, as possible. The feeling is obviously sincere—if excessive by modern standards—and it is expressed without any damaging pretentiousness. Yet one cannot feel that all this is relevant to the scene's typological meaning: the more it is humanized, the less appropriate it is as an analogy of the relation between God the Father and God the Son. The author of the York episode of Abraham and Isaac takes a different line. Instead of making Isaac a pathetic little boy, who could not without loss of naturalness express Christ's understanding of and resignation to his sacrifice, he follows a different mediaeval tradition, and makes him a grown man of "Thyrty yere and more"[29]—the age of Christ when he was crucified. Thus the typological meaning of the story is integrated into its meaning as a human document. An adult Isaac can convincingly accept God's command that he should be killed, from the very moment when it is broken to him. The situation remains pathetic; Isaac suggests that Abraham should bind him before killing him, because

> I am ferde that ye sall fynde
> My force youre forward to withstande.[30]

> (I am afraid that you will find my strength resisting your promise.)

This legitimately hints at a conflict between the perfection of Christ's divine nature and the fears of his human nature. Like the Chester Isaac,

536

the York Isaac begs his father not to delay in striking his blow: delay is deliberately used to create tension and pathos, but at York these are less excessive and more dignified, and therefore more in keeping with the episode's place within the cycle. There is enough pathos to make clear the conflict between God's command and human instinct, but it stops short of the melodrama in the Chester episode. The springs of feeling are no longer merely domestic: in keeping with its place in the cyclic pattern, the York pageant has a certain social grace, found for example in Abraham's elegant apology to his servants at the end:

> My barnes, yee ar noght to blame
> Yeff ye thynke lang that we her lende;
> Gedir same oure gere, in Goddis name,
> And go we hame agayne,
> Even unto Barsabe.
> God that is most of mayne
> Us wisse and with you be.[31]

> (My lads, you are not to blame if you think we have tarried here a
> long time; gather our things together, in God's name, and let us go
> home again to Beersheba. God, who is greatest in power, guide us and
> be with you.)

The human and the typological meaning are thus in harmony at York, both in the pageant's content and in its style; at Chester they are at odds, and that is why the Expositor is needed, to wrench the scene away from its human significance and toward its divine significance.*

V

Having considered two possible relationships between "realization" and typology, we must consider in more detail the nature of the "realization" itself. It is the characteristic means by which the Corpus Christi drama expands biblical narratives, and, because it directly expresses the social context of the drama, it is of particular importance for our purposes. First it must be said that there is no attempt at a historical presentation of the drama's subject-matter. It is true that this subject-matter is universal history, from the beginning of the world to its end; and it is also true that the one period of history *not* dealt with is the mediaeval present-day, or indeed any of the period between the immediate aftermath of Christ's human life and the approach of Doomsday. The Bible and the

* A different view of the comparative success of these two versions of Abraham and Isaac is given by Rosemary Woolf in her admirable article, "The Effect of Typology on the English Medieval Plays of Abraham and Isaac," *Speculum* XXXII (Cambridge, Mass. 1957), pp. 805–25.

biblical Apocrypha, naturally enough, do not deal with this period; it is treated in saints' plays, such as Jean Bodel's *Jeu de saint Nicholas* (*c*.1200), or in other works such as the Croxton *Play of the Sacrament*, but these do not form part of the great cycles. But it is possible for the present to be absent from these cycles without loss, because they treat the whole of history in terms of the mediaeval present. The English cycles must have functioned not as representations of what had already happened once for all, but as annual re-enactments of what was felt to be as present to man as to God. We cannot grasp the significance of the cycles to the communities in which they were performed unless we see that they were re-acting *as present* the myth that defined their relationship to ultimate reality, and indeed defined their own nature as members of Christendom. We have found something of this presentness in the *Mystère d'Adam*, and it is characteristic of mediaeval art in general. In painting, scenes from the past are always represented in contemporary dress, with a detail and elaboration that were to be intensified in the later Middle Ages.

The same intensification is found in the Corpus Christi cycles. Thus, to take a single example, the shepherds to whom the star and angels appear are shepherds of late mediaeval England, and indeed of the particular area to which their cycle belongs. The Wakefield shepherds refer familiarly to such local place-names as Goodybower, Healey, and Horbury. They complain about the tyranny over husbandmen of "men that ar lord-fest" (bound to a lord), who can do what they like without fear of opposition, "thrugh mantenance/Of men that are gretter"[32] (through the support of greater men)—a reference to the late mediaeval system of indentured retainers. Moreover, although Christ has not yet been born, they swear by "Chrystys holy name"[33] and by various saints. They are in every respect Wakefield men of the 15th century; and yet it is to them that Christ's coming is announced for the first time. Christ's second coming is also located in 15-century Wakefield. The devil Tutivillus is a "master Lollar"[34] (lollard): he finds the damned in 15th-century fashions; and in general the social situation by which the devil recognizes the imminence of Doomsday is the same as that described by the shepherds—the mediaeval present:

> 2 DEMON: The poore pepyll must pay · if oght be in hande;
> The drede of God is away · and law out of lande.
> 1 DEMON: By that wist I that Domysday · was nere hande
> In seson.[35]

(If anything is to be done, it's the poor who must pay; the fear of God has departed and law has left the country. // I knew by that that the time was nearly ripe for Doomsday.)

538

Every episode, in the same way, belongs not to the past but to the present day on which it is performed and to the civic place in which it is performed. There is no enclosed and magical theatre space to stimulate imagination and illusion, nor even the sanctified setting of the liturgical drama; there is simply a neutral area within a mediaeval town, surrounded perhaps by structures indicating Jerusalem, Pilate's palace, or whatever, but essentially belonging to a familiar time and place. Again, although there are indications of the beginning of professionalism among the actors of major parts, and although the costumes were often lavish and the special effects ingenious, the actors of the plays were usually members of the gilds. They were not stars shining in a different sphere from their audiences, like the Alleyns and Burbages of the Elizabethan theatre: the audiences were the actors' fellow-citizens; and it was the audiences that formed the crowds (usually of Jews) so often required in the plays. It is the men of Wakefield, Chester, or York who are ordered to silence by Herod and Pilate, who demand the release of Barabbas, and who are voluntary spectators at the crucifixion of their God. In a real sense, they are participants in the drama, and in England (though not always on the Continent) it is they themselves, rather than some separate group of hated Jews, who are felt to be responsible for Christ's Passion. If we recognize this, we shall not see the persistent anachronism of the cycles as mere naivety. It originated, of course, in something naive—the mediaeval lack of historical imagination—but it was elaborated into a system, and one that served a definite religious and dramatic purpose.

It did so partly by engaging with the existing solidarities and rivalries of the communities that produced it: the solidarities, for example, of locality, of class, and of sex. The Towneley shepherds make us aware not just that they are northerners from Wakefield, but that they are *not* from the south, and are glad of it. It is the villainous Mak who pretends to be a "yoman . . . of the king," and to support this pretence he speaks in an imitation of southern dialect; at which his fellow-shepherds tell him contemptuously,

> Now take outt that sothren tothe,
> And sett in a torde![36]

> (Now take out that southern tooth, and put a turd in its place!)

Here already local feeling begins to merge into class feeling, in much the same way as between north and south in modern England. Class feeling is of great importance throughout the cycles. The gilds were essentially middle-class groups, organizations of master craftsmen, not of common labourers. This is a distinction made even among the Wakefield shepherds, where Daw classes himself with the "servandys" who "ar oft weytt and wery/when master-men wynkys [sleep]."[37] But the gilds claimed responsibility for such journeymen too, and the cycles regularly take the side of the poor against the rich. In the York "Exodus," when Pharaoh says of the plague that killed the cattle, "Ther-of no man harme has/Halfe so mekill as I" (No one suffers from that half as much as I do), one of his officers is quick to retort, "Yis, lorde, poure men has mekill woo"[38] (On the contrary, my lord, poor men suffer a great deal). Indeed, a strong vein of anti-aristocratic feeling runs through these plays, directed particularly against the magnates and rulers, the "men of cowrte" to whom the Towneley Pilate admits he belongs:

> For I am he that may · make or mar a man,
> My self if I it say · as men of cowrte now can—
> Supporte a man to day · to-morn agans hym than,
> On both parties thus I play · and fenys me to ordan
>   The right.[39]

> (For, even though I say it myself, I am the one who can make a man or mar him, as court-men can nowadays—support a man today, turn against him tomorrow. Thus I play on both sides, while pretending to judge truly.)

"Men of cowrte" seems to mean both lawyers and courtiers, and the cycles tend to lump together all those who hold power—secular lords, great ecclesiastics, lawyers, princes—as equally corrupt, proud, and contemptible. In part this attitude derives from the New Testament, for Christ was indeed brought to his death by the secular and ecclesiastical powers of his time; but it is extended far beyond this from the experience of the bourgeois creators of the drama. A modern critic has written: "It is hard to discover a good ruler in the cycles,"[40] and he excepts only the Magi, who are not shown as ruling. It is invariably assumed that men in positions of authority are corruptible by bribery and nepotism. In the *Ludus Coventriae* "Trial of Joseph and Mary," the setting is a mediaeval ecclesiastical court, presided over by a bishop, who has a Summoner to call in the accused. The Summoner makes no secret of the openness to bribery that belongs to his profession:

> Gold or sylvyr I wol not forsake,
> But evyn as all somnorys doth.[41]

> (I will not give up gold or silver, but act just as all summoners do.)

The bishop is related to Mary, and an onlooker sarcastically remarks:

> Becawse she is your cosyn yynge,
> I pray yow, sere, lete here nevyr fare the wers.[42]

> (I beg you, sir, just because she is your young cousin, don't let her receive worse treatment.)

The obvious implication is that no mediaeval accused was ever likely to fare the worse for being a bishop's cousin.

VI

The cycles satirize not only the corruption and brutality of great men, but also the absurdity of their courtly manners. We find this particularly in the York cycle's treatment of Pilate and Herod. They are, of course, boasters and enemies of Christ; but they are also affected and effeminate in their behaviour. The whole milieu of Pilate, in particular, is treated as a parody of courtly life and literature. He has a wife with whom he exchanges lengthy compliments, they have a ridiculous "after you" act when drinking wine, and their farewells are so drawn out that from the moment when Pilate's Beadle suggests that his wife should go home because night is falling, it takes 70 lines actually to get her off the stage. Even the Beadle is affected by the courtly atmosphere, and turns his warning that it is getting dark into a delightful parody of the *circumlocutio* of courtly rhetoric:

> My seniour, will ye see nowe the sonne in youre sight,
> For his stately strengh he stemmys in his stremys,
> Behalde ovir youre hede how he holdis fro hight
> And glydis to the grounde with his glitterand glemys.[43]

> (Sire, will you now turn your eyes toward the sun, for he is reducing the stately strength of his rays; behold above your head, how he is steering away from the meridian, and is gliding with his glittering beams to the ground.)

Chaucer himself has no sharper parody of "high style." There are a number of jokes concerning diffuseness of language in scenes in which Pilate appears. Both Pilate and Herod are put to bed on the stage with a great deal of fuss and exaggerated concern for their comfort, and then have to be roused from this luxury in order to question Jesus. It is an important part of the conception of the York cycle that Jesus is persecuted and killed by a corrupt and self-indulgent aristocracy. In all this it is clear that the class feeling of the mediaeval bourgeoisie plays at least as important a part as the anti-establishment feelings built into Christianity itself.

Equally notable among the social solidarities and rivalries activated are those of the sexes. Both misogyny and gyniolatry are characteristic of mediaeval Christianity, centring respectively in Eve and in the "second Eve," Mary. These currents of feeling are naturally found in the Corpus Christi cycles, but less in any theologically defined form than as traditional popular prejudices. The moment after Eve has been created from his rib, and long before she has sinned, the Chester Adam makes a time-honoured etymological joke at her expense:

> Therfore shall she be called, I wis,
> Virago—nothing amisse,
> For out of man taken she is. [44]

> (And so she shall indeed be called virago—and rightly so, because she is taken out of man.)

After her sin, Adam can make her the justification for traditional masculine prejudices: "Nowe God late never man aftir me/triste woman tale"[45] (Now may God never permit any man after me to trust what a woman says). Noah's wife is regularly made a type of disobedience to rightful authority, truly a daughter of Eve, who mocks at her husband for his obsession with the coming Flood and the need for an ark, and at first declines to enter it when it is built. The Chester Noah appeals to the prejudices of the men in his audience to confirm his view of her:

> Lord, that women be crabbed aye,
> And never are meke, that dare I saye.
> This is well sene by me to daye,
> In witnes of yow each one. [46]

At Wakefield, Noah similarly identifies his experience with that of men in general, and gives the men in his audience good advice:

> Yee men that has wifis · whyls they ar yong,
> If ye luf youre lifis · chastice thare tong:
> Me thynk my hert ryfis · both levyr and long,
> To se sich stryfis · wedmen among:
> > Bot I,
> As have I blys,
> Shall chastyse this. [47]

> (You men who have wives, while they are still young, chastise their tongues if you value your lives. My heart feels like breaking—and my liver and lungs too—to see such quarrels among married people. But I, as I hope for heaven, shall chastise *this* one.)

542

But the Towneley Mrs Noah can play at that game too: as Noah identifies his experience with that of married men in general, so does she hers with that of wives in general, speaking of "we women," and addressing the wives of Wakefield thus:

> Lord, I were at ese · and hertely full hoylle,
> Might I onys have a messe · of wedows coyll;
> For thi saull, without lese · shuld I dele penny doyll,
> So wold mo, no frese · that I se on this sole
>   Of wifis that ar here,
> For the life that thay leyd
> Wold thare husbandis were dede.[48]

> (Lord, I would be at ease and content at heart, if only I might be a widow [lit. "have a meal of widow's soup"]. I would willingly pay the mass-penny for your soul; and so, without doubt, would many more of the wives that I see in this place, who, because of the lives they lead, wish their husbands were dead.)

In the Towneley Second Shepherds' play, Mak's wife similarly invokes the traditional solidarity of her sex against her husband's complaints of her idleness. Exactly the same traditional rivalries can be found in settings that one would think far less suitable. Joseph is usually presented as seeing Mary as just another daughter of Eve, when he finds that she is pregnant. The familiar wisdom about the dangers to an old man of marrying a young woman is unrolled; and the Towneley Joseph remarks, with weary tolerance,

> I blame the not, so God me save,
> Woman maners if that thou have.[49]

Others too are ready to see Mary as a sinner, an extreme example being found in the *Ludus Coventriae* "Trial of Joseph and Mary" (see below). It becomes clear that, however great the honour paid to the Virgin Mary (and both the York and *Ludus Coventriae* cycles have pageants devoted solely to honouring her), no great change has occurred in masculine attitudes toward her sex. At York, when Peter is accused by a woman of being an associate of Jesus, he answers in words that exactly repeat those of the Chester Noah: "women are crabbed/—that comes them of kynde"[50] (women are awkward—it comes to them by nature). Even at the Last Judgment, one Wakefield devil eagerly asks another, "Has thou oght writen there · of the femynyn gendere?" to receive the answer, "Yei, mo then I may bere · of rolles forto render"[51] (Yes, I have more rolls [i.e. documents] to hand in than I can carry). The whole of God's plan is fulfilled for the mediaeval audience in an entirely familiar world that exactly reproduces the contours of their daily experience.

It is for this reason that, at their best, the Corpus Christi cycles are capable of a wonderfully touching human realism, unself-conscious yet by no means naive. We have seen something of this (although there it is pulling against the typological meaning) in the Chester episode of Abraham and Isaac, but it is also to be found in many other places. At York, for example, the dramatists enter with particular tenderness and intimacy into the domestic world of Joseph and Mary. Joseph, as usual, is quite unable to believe that Mary's expected child comes from God rather than man. He is an ordinary husband, not an elevated figure in a divine pattern. When she repeats that the child is "Youres, sir, and the Kyngis of blisse," he caustically answers, "Ye, and hoo than?"[52] (Oh yes? and who else is its father?). But he is humane too, and adds,

> Yhitt for myn awne I wolde it fede,
> Might all be still.[53]
>
> (I would still bring it up as my own, if everything could be hushed up.)

He decides that he can do nothing but leave Mary, goes out into the wilderness, falls asleep, and shows an amusing irritation at being woken up by an angel sent to tell him to return to her:

> We! now es this a farly fare,
> For to be cached bathe here and thare,
>   And nowhere may have rest.[54]
>
> (Well, this is an extraordinary thing, to be chased up and down, and not allowed to rest anywhere.)

He is to get little rest henceforward. In a later pageant he is once more awakened from sleep by an angel, to embark on the flight into Egypt, and, though willing, he is made understandably nervous by the emergency. When Mary asks where Egypt is, he answers somewhat tetchily, "What wate I?/I wote not where it standis"[55] (How should I know? I don't know where it is). Mary indeed is being rather a nuisance, lamenting instead of helping, and with a mixture of concern and exasperation he tells her, "Leve Mary, leve thy grete!"[56] (Dear Mary, *do* stop crying!). He offers to carry the baby, she anxiously tells him to take great care of it, and he sharply answers, "Late me and hym allone."[57] The whole husband-wife-child situation is captured in the dialogue with a naturalness as apparent now as it must have been in the Middle Ages: the pressure of the emergency makes Mary over-anxious and Joseph over-sharp, but the undercurrent of affection between them is never lost. In a still later pageant, another emergency brings out the same intimate understanding of family relationships. Joseph and Mary have lost their son. They are

544

astonished to find him disputing with the Doctors in the Temple, and Mary urges her husband to intervene. He is shy of doing so—"When I come there what schall I saye?"[58]—and Mary eventually agrees that they will go forward together. But he pushes her ahead:

> Gange on, Marie, and telle thy tale firste,
> Thy sone to the will take goode heede;
> Wende fourth, Marie, and do thy beste;
> I come be-hynde, als God me spede.[59]

> (Go on, Mary, and have your say first: your son will pay attention to you. Go forward, Mary, and do your best; I, with God's help, am coming behind.)

The realism of this drama, then, produces tenderness in the treatment of human relationships; but it also produces, as necessary concomitants, cruelty and a kind of derisive irreverence. These are necessary because the realism of mediaeval drama is one of truth to human nature as the dramatists saw it in their own world; and human nature did and does include cruelty and irreverence, even among the participants in the most sacred of stories. The cruelty, of course, is an essential part of the story of Christ, and it is found most strongly in the scenes dealing with the Passion. Not only are Christ's sufferings conveyed in great detail (as in the passage from Rolle), but those who cause them are also presented in great detail. His enemies, whether judges or executioners, occupy the centre of the stage for long periods, and speak nearly all the dialogue, Christ's part being largely one of silence and passivity; in general they make the play of the Passion *their* play at least as much as his. All the dramatic energy in these scenes is on the side of evil, and it is a terrifyingly powerful energy with which, in the York "Crucifixion," the soldiers gloat over Christ's pain or mock at his prayer for their forgiveness:

> 1 MILES: We! harke! he jangelis like a jay.
> 2 MILES: Me thynke he patris like a py.[60]

> (Hey, listen! he's jabbering like a jay. // It seems to me he's chattering like a magpie.)

A similar energy is shown by Caiaphas in the Towneley *Coliphizacio* ("Buffetting"):

> CAIAPHAS: Bot I gif hym a blaw · my hart will brist.
> ANNAS: Abyde to ye his purpose knaw.
> CAIAPHAS: Nay, bot I shall out thrist
>   Both his een on a raw.[61]

> (My heart will burst if I don't give him a blow. // Wait till you know his intention. // No, but I will jab out both his eyes, one after the other.)

By such energy the audience is drawn into a certain complicity with Christ's enemies. At York, one of the soldiers calls on the audience to

> ... helpe me holly, all that are here,
> This kaitiffe care to encrees.[62]

> (Give me full help, all who are here, to increase the suffering of this wretch.)

At Wakefield, Christ's enemies work hard in their speeches to establish a "we" that will include the spectators, and in the "Buffetting" one of them confidently asserts,

> Ther is none in this towne · I trow, be ill payde
>   Of his sorow,
> Bot the fader that hym gate.[63]

> (There is no one in this town, I am sure, who is displeased at his sorrow, except for the father who begot him.)

"This towne" means at once Jerusalem and Wakefield, and the speaker does not know that the criminal's father is God.

On this point it is important to avoid misunderstanding. No one would wish to suggest that this supposedly Christian drama was really anti-Christian. But it was a drama that appealed not just to the "religious" side but to the whole of human nature, and allowed expression to impulses of cruelty as well as of pity and reverence. In this respect it was important that it was played in the town, not in the church. In a neutral setting, it was possible for people to allow their own cruelty and hatred to be activated without censorship, internal or external; though, no doubt, even as these baser impulses were aroused, they produced an awareness of their own nature, and a corresponding horrified reaction. To be present at a mediaeval Corpus Christi play was, beyond question, a genuinely religious experience; but it was all the more religious for being deeply cathartic, in a way that no subsequent religious drama has dared to be.

These remarks about cruelty apply also to comic irreverence, a component equally important and equally puzzling to modern readers. Much of the comedy of mediaeval drama, which to modern readers may seem irreverent and out of place, was not intended as a mere relief from more serious material. It was an essential part of the plays' religious meaning; this is so, for example, with the comic Mrs Noah, who, as we have seen, is a type of disobedience, paralleling Eve and contrasting with her husband. In other cases, what may seem to be irreverence in fact bears witness to a faith in spiritual mysteries so unshakeable that it did not fear to bring them into contact with the grossly material. "Doubting Thomas" is a frequent pageant in the cycles, but his doubt is presented for rebuke, not for justification. Similar doubt is often felt about the virgin birth. We have noted the incredulity of Joseph; in the Chester cycle this is taken a stage further by two midwives (derived from the liturgical drama), one of whom declines to believe that Mary is a virgin, feels her in order to find out, and is punished with a withered hand. Thus a normally coarse human response is allowed its place, but also its chastisement, in the very midst of the joining of God and man. Doubt about the virgin birth is taken to its extreme in the *Ludus Coventriae* "Trial of Joseph and Mary," where two *detractores* put the view of worldly doubt at great length and with great plausibility. It is the plausibility that is disturbing: the backbiters speak with an insinuating familiarity that can almost make us *want* to adopt their attitudes even though we know them to be false. One suggests that Joseph is the child's father, but the second replies:

> A, nay, nay, wel wers: she hath hym payd.
> Sum fresch yonge galaunt she loveth wel more,
> That his leggys to here hath leyd,
> And that doth greve the old man sore.[64]

> (Oh, no, no, much worse than that: she has paid him out. She has much more love for some lively young gallant who has laid his legs to her; and that greatly distresses the old man.)

And when the Summoner comes for Mary his language has the vigour and the plausibility of the proverbial:

> My lorde the buschop hath for yow sent.
> It is hym told that in thin house
> A cuckoldis bowe is ech nyght bent.
> He that shett the bolt is lyke to be shent.
> Fayre mayde, that tale ye can best telle:
> Now be youre trowth telle your entente—
> Dede not the archere plese yow ryght well?[65]

> (My lord the bishop has sent for you. He is informed that a cuckold's bow is bent in your house each night. He who shot the arrow is likely to be punished. Fair maid, you can best explain about that: now, on your honour, say what you think—the archer pleased you very well, didn't he?)

Comic irreverence is taken furthest in the form of blasphemous parody of the sacred. A place where this might not be unexpected is the pageant of Antichrist, which at Chester precedes the Last Judgment. The very idea of Antichrist involves blasphemous parody, and in this pageant a parody of Christ's Resurrection is enacted with horrifying solemnity. In

547

dramatic terms, Antichrist's miracles are as genuine as Christ's, and he is even given a poetry as valid as God's when he claims to have created

> . . . all thinge that is on earth growinge,
> Flowers fresh that fayre can springe;
> Also I made all other thinge,
> The starrs that be so bright.[66]

Antichrist at least had an accepted place in mediaeval eschatology; such parody can be even more disturbing when it occurs outside any traditional sanction. This is the case in the Towneley cycle, where the first half of the Second Shepherds' play is devoted to a detailed parody of the sacred event that follows, the birth of the Lamb of God. The rascally Mak steals a sheep, and then, to prevent the other shepherds from discovering it, he hides it in the cradle in his cottage, and pretends that it is a baby boy newly born to his wife. The other shepherds are suspicious, and Mak and his wife swear oaths that elaborate the blasphemy by speaking of eating the child, as God's body is eaten in the sacrament (a thought appropriate to Corpus Christi):

> I pray to God so mylde,
> If ever I you begyld,
> That I ete this chylde
>   That lygys in this credyll.[67]

> (I pray to merciful God, if I ever deceived you, may I eat this child that lies in this cradle.)

The shepherds leave the cottage baffled, then think of giving the child presents (as they later give them to the real Lamb), and call him "lytyll day-starne"[68] (little morning-star), a traditional epithet that they later apply to Christ. It is only now that they notice the child's "long snowte" and discover the deception; and only after Mak has been tossed in a blanket as punishment that the angels sing their *Gloria* (which the shepherds try to imitate, with hilarious incompetence). Eventually the shepherds make their offerings at the stable, in what seems little more than an afterthought.

It is not really an afterthought, of course; and indeed all these examples of irreverence serve religious purposes. The great achievement of the Corpus Christi drama is to exclude nothing, to shut out no possible human response to sacred events. It is at the opposite pole from the aristocratic form of neo-classical drama, which ruthlessly cuts away feelings that are conceived to be irrelevant and directs emotion into a narrow but fiercely flowing channel. Mediaeval drama allows nothing to be irrelevant that is in human nature, because its central subject is a God who took on human nature. Hence its extension into innumerable episodes, to be played over several days; hence its open structure, and its inclusion of the coarse, the comic, and the irreverent. Its aim is to make reverence confront and absorb irreverence, rather than to shut it out and pretend it does not exist. This is an enormous ambition, and it is not always achieved. Sometimes mediaeval drama is merely crude (as with the Chester midwives); sometimes it gives the spirit of diabolism too free a rein (as in the Towneley "Cain and Abel," where Cain is so wildly energetic a figure that he drives God off the stage with a "We! who was that that piped so small?").[69] But the ambition is achieved surprisingly often. The *Ludus Coventriae* "Trial of Joseph and Mary" and the Towneley Second Shepherds' play both end, after all their lively derision, with an utterly secure reverence, safe against any irony, because the voices of denial have already been allowed their say. There are few moments in drama more moving than when the Wakefield shepherds at last arrive at the stable and offer the Christ-child their simple gifts.

VIII

Mediaeval drama—like drama in any period, of course—was not only a matter of words. Gesture, movement, costume, spectacle, and music all had their parts to play in the total dramatic effect. But in drama, if words are used at all, their quality is of crucial importance. Something of the varying literary qualities of mediaeval drama may have been suggested by the quotations in this chapter. Broadly speaking, the Corpus Christi plays are successful as poetry in two modes: that of everyday realism, and that of satire directed against all that lies outside the bounds of this realism. Again and again, the plays catch the very note of everyday conversation and transmute it into verse (sometimes into poetry) in such a way that we do not suspect that any heightening has been applied exter-nally, but rather that the underlying rhythmic and dramatic qualities of colloquial speech have been seized and crystallized. Thus the Wakefield Abraham falls naturally into imaginary dialogue as he wonders what he shall say to Sarah to explain Isaac's disappearance:

> What shal I to his moder say?
>   For "Where is he?" tyte will she spyr;
> If I tell hir, "Ron away,"
>   Hir answere bese belife, "Nay, sir!"[70]

(What shall I say to his mother? For she will quickly ask, "Where is he?" If I tell her, "Run away," she will answer at once, "No, sir!")

Or again, in the York "Trial Before Herod," Herod shows his incredulity at the miracle of the loaves and fishes through requests for repetition that have a rhetorical force taken directly from everyday habits of speech:

> 2 DUX: Fyve thousand folke faire gon he feede,
>   With fyve looffis and two fisshis to fange.
> HEROD: Howe fele folke sais thou he fedde?
> 2 DUX: Fyve thousand, lorde, that come to his call.
> HEROD: Ya, boye, howe mekill brede he them bedde?
> 1 DUX: But fyve looffis, dare I wele wedde.
> HEROD: Nowe, be the bloode that Mahounde bledde,
>   What! this was a wondir at all.[71]

(He easily fed five thousand people, with only five loaves and two fishes available. // How many people do you say he fed? // Five thousand, my lord, who came to his summons. // What, boy, how much bread did he give them? // Only five loaves, I dare swear. // Now, by the blood Mahomet shed, well, this was a miracle indeed!)

The dialogue is so natural and seemingly spontaneous that we scarcely notice the elaborate alliteration and rhyming that give it a forcefulness beyond that of most real-life conversations. Even when the Wakefield Master is at work with his complicated stanza and elaborate invective (as we have seen in the quotations from "Noah"), both the rhythmical units and the metaphorical inventiveness ("measse of wedows coyll") come from the spoken English of his district. The Wakefield Master heightens this spoken English; other dramatists deliberately subdue it, to produce a language of moving restraint—moving because we feel the force of all that is excluded. Thus at York John the Baptist addresses Jesus:

> What riche man gose from dore to dore
> To begge at hym that has right noght?
> Lorde, thou arte riche and I am full poure,
> Thou may blisse all, sen thou all wrought.
>   Fro heven come all
> That helpes in erthe, yf soth be sought,
>   Fro erthe but small.[72]

(What rich man goes from door to door to beg from him who has nothing at all? Lord, you are rich and I am very poor; you may bless all things, for you created all things. Everything that is of value on earth came from heaven, to tell the truth; little indeed from earth itself.)

So much for the everyday realism of the plays' language: for satire of what goes beyond this, a reference back to the York cycle's parodic treatment of Pilate will have to suffice. But it is of great significance that what goes beyond the humble, the bourgeois, and the commonplace tends to be treated in these cycles as the object of satire. The great limitation on their language is that it has no reliable means of dealing seriously with what transcends everyday reality: no means, for example, of displaying God in his divine nature and in the power by which he brings about the patternings of world history displayed by the cycles. One need only read the opening speeches of God the creator in these cycles to recognize how inadequate was the dignity of the verse available for such a subject. This literary limitation undoubtedly issues from the social limitation noted earlier. This drama, of bourgeois origin, despised the courtly way of life: but the "high style" of mediaeval literature derived not only from translation and imitation of Latin authors, but also from that very way of life—from courtly modes of feeling and the grace and dignity they can confer. This high style (found, for example, in Chaucer's religious poetry) is lacking in mediaeval English drama, and no equivalent means of conferring dignity was discovered. The exclusion of a high style based on secular classical literature may well have been deliberate, the consequence of an insight such as Auerbach finds among the Fathers of the Church into

> the true and distinctive greatness of Holy Scripture, namely that it had created an entirely new kind of sublimity, in which the everyday and the low were included, not excluded, so that, in style as in content, it directly connected the lowest with the highest.[73]

But, despite experiments with alliterative and aureate language, no equivalent to this *humilitatis sublimitas* is found in the treatment of God in the Corpus Christi cycles (as it is found, for example, in *Piers Plowman*); and in general their style, although it is often touching or forceful, is almost never capable of a sublimity to match their structure.

Once the religious drama had reached the goal of a cycle covering the whole of human history, it could develop no further. Various kinds of elaboration and extension were of course possible: for example, additional scenes from the life of the Virgin Mary (as in the York cycle) and of Judas (as in the Towneley cycle). But the cycle could go no further back than the Creation, and no further forward than the Last Judgment. The only large gap left was the Christian era itself—the period to which the present belonged. And that gap was not filled in the cycles because, for them, all events were seen as present. It was filled eventually by the Morality play, and that in turn gave way to the secular drama of the Renaissance; but these lie outside the scope of the present chapter. The Morality takes as its central figure not Christ but the Christian, and as its structure not world history but the history of the individual life: the

551

story of temptation, repentance, death, and salvation. This type of drama was readily capable of secularization, and in England, for example, we find on the one hand *Everyman* (*c.* 1510), a purely religious Morality, and on the other John Skelton's *Magnificence* (1515), whose hero is a prince, and whose central question concerns the right use of earthly riches. It used to be argued that the Corpus Christi plays fell into disuse owing to the demand for secular entertainments; recent research indicates that, on the contrary, they continued to flourish in England into the 16th century, and were eventually neither secularized nor simply abandoned, but deliberately suppressed by the religious authorities for religious reasons. In a Protestant country, their image-making and their free treatment of Scripture came to seem blasphemous. The *word* was all-important: the *image* could only mislead. It is striking that in England (unlike France) none of the cycles was ever disseminated by the printing press, that great broadcaster of the word. The secular drama of Shakespeare and his contemporaries made a greater contribution than the Corpus Christi cycles to world literature; but the social role of the cycles as an imaginative and religious focus of civic communities has never since been filled.

References

1. *Le mystère d'Adam*, ed. by P. Studer (Manchester 1918), line 38.
2. *ibid.*, 405.
3. *ibid.*, 111–2.
4. *ibid.*, 180.
5. *ibid.*, 189.
6. *ibid.*, 227–32.
7. E. AUERBACH, *Mimesis*, trans. by W. Trask (paperback: New York 1957), p. 127–8.
8. *Le mystère d'Adam*, 298.
9. *ibid.*, 614.
10. *ibid.*, 640.
11. *ibid.*, 788.
12. *ibid.*, 381–2.
13. *ibid.*, 884.
14. *ibid.*, 895.
15. ARNOLD WILLIAMS, *The Drama of Medieval England* (Michigan 1961), p. 28.
16. *The York Plays*, ed. by Lucy Toulmin Smith (London 1885; New York 1963), play II, line 27. This edition is referred to below as *York*.
17. *York* VIII, 103–7 and 111–2.

18. *ibid.*, XXXIV, 83–6 and 297–8.
19. *ibid.*, XXXV, 25–6.
20. *The Chester Plays*, ed. by H. Deimling and J. Matthews, Early English Text Society, e.s. 62 and 115 (London 1892 and 1916), play IV, lines 465–8. This edition is referred to below as *Chester*.
21. *Chester* XV, 69–72.
22. *York* XLVIII, 53–6.
23. *The Towneley Plays*, ed. by G. England and A. Pollard, Early English Text Society, e.s. 71 (London 1897), play X, lines 30–4. This edition is referred to below as *Towneley*.
24. Translated from *Meditations on the Passion*, text I, in *English Writings of Richard Rolle*, ed. by Hope Emily Allen (Oxford 1931), p. 24.
25. *Chester* IV, 229–30.
26. *ibid.*, 289–90.
27. *ibid.*, 297–300.
28. *ibid.*, 369–71.
29. *York* X, 82.
30. *ibid.*, 211–2.
31. *ibid.*, 374–80.
32. *Towneley* XIII, 20 and 35–6.
33. *ibid.*, 378.
34. *ibid.*, XXX, 213.
35. *ibid.*, 189–92.
36. *ibid.*, XIII, 201 and 215–6.
37. *ibid.*, 154 and 156.
38. *York* XI, 299–301.
39. *Towneley* XX, 19–23.
40. WILLIAMS, *op. cit.*, p. 130.
41. *Ludus Coventriae*, ed. by K. Block, Early English Text Society, e.s. 120 (London 1922), "Trial of Joseph and Mary," lines 125–6. The play in this edition is referred to below as *Ludus*, "Trial."
42. *Ludus*, "Trial" 167–8.
43. *York* XXX, 73–6.
44. *Chester* II, 149–51.
45. *York* VI, 149–50.
46. *Chester* III, 105–8.
47. *Towneley* III, 397–403.
48. *ibid.*, 388–94.
49. *Towneley* X, 209–10.
50. *York* XXIX, 130.
51. *Towneley* XXX, 161–2.
52. *York* XIII, 159–60.
53. *ibid.*, 186–7.
54. *ibid.*, XIII, 254–6.
55. *ibid.*, XVIII, 179–80.
56. *ibid.*, 192.
57. *ibid.*, 204.

58. *ibid.*, XX, 237.
59. *ibid.*, 245–8.
60. *ibid.*, XXXV, 265–6.
61. *Towneley* XXI, 191–3.
62. *York* XXXIV, 14–5.
63. *Towneley* XXI, 364–6.
64. *Ludus*, "Trial" 53–6.
65. *ibid.*, 130–6.
66. *Chester* XXIII, 461–4.
67. *Towneley* XIII, 535–8.
68. *ibid.*, 577.
69. *ibid.*, II, 298.
70. *ibid.*, IV, 225–8.
71. *York* XXXI, 198–205.
72. *ibid.*, XXI, 120–6.
73. AUERBACH, *op. cit.*, p. 134.

Bibliography

E. AUERBACH, *Mimesis*, trans. by W. Trask (Princeton 1953).
E. K. CHAMBERS, *The Mediaeval Stage* (Oxford 1903).
G. COHEN, *Le théâtre en France au moyen âge*, Vol. I (Paris 1928).
H. CRAIG, *English Religious Drama of the Middle Ages* (Oxford 1955).
G. FRANK, *The Medieval French Drama*, 2nd edn (Oxford 1960).
E. HARTL, *Das Theater des Mittelalters* (Leipzig 1937).
V. A. KOLVE, *The Play Called Corpus Christi* (London 1966).
K. MANTZIUS, *A History of Theatrical Art*, trans. by L. von Cossel (London 1903–21).
A. P. ROSSITER, *English Drama from Early Times to the Elizabethans* (London 1950).
F. M. SALTER, *Mediaeval Drama in Chester* (Toronto 1955).
J. SPEIRS, *Medieval English Poetry: the Non-Chaucerian Tradition* (London 1957), Pt V.
G. WICKHAM, *Early English Stages, 1300 to 1660*, 2nd edn, Vol. I (London 1963).
A. WILLIAMS, *The Drama of Medieval England* (Michigan 1961).
K. YOUNG, *The Drama of the Medieval Church* (Oxford 1933).

CHAPTER 16

The Literacy of the Laity[1]

M. B. Parkes[*]

In the Middle Ages the term *literatus* was applied only to those who possessed a knowledge of Latin. Sometimes it seems to indicate not only the ability to read that language but also some learning: for example, Matthew Paris (d. 1259) refers to a lay judge as *miles et literatus*. These uses of the term are too restricted to be profitable in an investigation into an age that is characterized by the emergence of written vernacular literature. In order to assess the extent and development of literacy among the laity, and its significance for the student of literature, it is necessary to include the ability to read and write in the vernacular. Moreover, I propose to distinguish between three kinds of literacy: that of the professional reader, which is the literacy of the scholar or the professional man of letters; that of the cultivated reader, which is the literacy of recreation; and that of the pragmatic reader, which is the literacy of one who has to read or write in the course of transacting any kind of business.

Throughout the greater part of the Middle Ages the professional reader was usually in holy orders, and so this category is, strictly, outside the scope of this chapter. But from the 6th to the 12th century the ability to read and write was more or less confined to the professional reader, or at least to the professed: the educational reforms of Charlemagne on the continent, and perhaps of Alfred in England, seem in the long run to have produced a better-educated clergy rather than a literate laity.[2] Books were written, copied, preserved, and read mainly in monasteries. A few literate laymen were to be found among the reigning families and in their courts: Charlemagne's entourage included laymen such as the poets Einhard (his biographer), Angilbert, and Neithard. Moreover, there are a few instances of lay patronage of ecclesiastical writers, such as the patron for whom Bishop Jonas of Orleans wrote the *De institucione laicale*,[3] or Ealdorman Æthelweard, to whom Ælfric sent a copy of his *Catholic*

* Fellow of Keble College and Lecturer in Palaeography in the University of Oxford.

Homilies.[4] But it is far from certain that all such people were actually literate. Even as late as the 12th century there is the cautionary example of Count Baldwin II of Guines, who was extremely learned and possessed a splendid library, but who never learned to read: he had his books read to him by his *clerici et magistri*.[5] Apart from the ecclesiastical prose produced in England in the 10th or at the beginning of the 11th century, the written literature of this early period was in Latin: the learned literature of a closed circle of scholars and savants. The cultivated laity turned to the minstrel or the *scop* for their recreation, and vernacular literature (apart from sermons) was transmitted orally by professional singers who were probably illiterate. When in this period vernacular poetic texts were committed to writing, they were set down by monks who had acquired an interest in them, and extant manuscripts, such as the Exeter Book of Old English poetry, survived in monastic libraries.*

The turning-point in the history of lay literacy came in the 12th century. It is among the Anglo-Norman nobility that we find the first indications of a more extensive cultivated literacy.[6] It is accompanied by a steady increase in the number of surviving manuscripts of vernacular texts: the earliest extant manuscripts of two French poems, the *Vie de saint Alexis* and the *Chanson de Roland*, were written in England.[7] Growing literacy brought vernacular literature onto the written page. Earlier texts were written down, and alongside the renaissance of learning and of Latin literature— which reached a climax in the time of Henry II[8]—there was a growing written French literature commissioned by the more cultured members of this aristocratic society.[9]

We hear of groups of connoisseurs who owned books, lent them to each other, and commissioned works in the vernacular. From the epilogue to Gaimar's *Estorie des Engleis* we learn that at some time between 1135 and 1139 Walter Espec of Helmsley lent a copy of Geoffrey of Monmouth's *Historia regum Britanniae* to Ralph Fitz-Gilbert, who passed it on to his wife Constance. She gave it to Gaimar to work on.[10] Philippe de Thaon wrote his bestiary for Henry I's second wife, Adeliza of Louvain, and Sanson de Nantuil translated the Book of Proverbs for Alice de Condet.[11] In 1185 Gilbert Fitz-Baderon, Lord of Monmouth, had a library of books in both Latin and French.[12] In the 13th century Matthew Paris, the St

---

* The Exeter Book was probably preserved because of the documents recorded in it relating to Leofric's foundation of the cathedral. For a survey of the surviving manuscripts containing Old High German texts, which provides an account of the kinds of situations in which copies of vernacular texts were produced in this period and the conditions that affected their survival, see B. BISCHOFF, "Paläographische Fragen deutscher Denkmäler de Karolingerzeit," *Frühmittel-alterliche Studien* V (Berlin 1971), pp. 101-34.

Albans chronicler, circulated illustrated copies of his translations of saints' lives among a group of aristocratic ladies.[13] The 12th and 13th centuries also witnessed the composition of the ancestral or household romances, probably commissioned by the great families that they commemorate: *Waldef* is a romance of the Bigods, *Boeve de Haumtone* of the D'Albinis, and *Gui de Warewic* was probably written (*c.* 1232–42) by a canon of Oseney to flatter Thomas, Earl of Warwick.[14] In 1315, one of Thomas's successors, Guy of Beauchamp, left a collection of books containing histories and romances to Bordesley Abbey.[15]

Moreover there is clear evidence that these aristocrats read the books they possessed. Constance Fitz-Gilbert owned a manuscript of a poem on Henry I, which she read in her room.[16] From the 12th century onward there were didactic treatises addressed to women. One of them, written in the early 14th century, discusses whether it is proper that a woman should learn to read.[17] Such a discussion would be pointless if by that time reading had not already become something of a habit. This evidence is supported in the literature itself. In Chrétien de Troyes's *Yvain* (line 5366) the 16-year-old daughter of a knight reads a *roman* to her parents in the garden; in *Yonec* Marie de France mentions a woman capable of reading; and in *Floire e Blancheflor* the author describes aristocratic children reading what must be copies of Ovid.[18]

This pattern of cultivated literacy, which we see here in the activities of the Anglo-Norman nobility, persisted among the more cultured members of the aristocracy throughout Europe during the rest of the Middle Ages. As magnates, they had the wealth to patronize authors and scribes and the influence to publicize a work by bringing it to the attention of their circle of friends and acquaintances. This was recognized by the authors. Wace (*c.* 1100–84) declared that he wrote for those

> Ki unt les rentes e le argent
> Kar pur eus sunt li liure fait.[19]
>
> (who have the incomes and the cash, because for them are books made.)

The literate recreations of the cultured nobility had a profound effect upon the development of a literary public. They set a secular example of literate culture that other laymen sought to emulate.

From the 12th century onward, however, the history of lay literacy is dominated by the steady growth of literacy among the expanding middle class. As the transaction of business grew more complex, there was an increasing reliance upon the written record. Pragmatic literacy is implicit in the mass of documents that survives from all aspects of mediaeval administration. By accident, the best collection of records in northern Europe survives in England, where also the evidence for pragmatic literacy can be linked with other evidence that shows the pragmatic reader becoming progressively more cultivated. This is especially true in three spheres of indisputably lay activity: commerce, the administration of the estates of the magnates, and the rising legal profession.

The evidence for pragmatic literacy in the commercial world is the most difficult to find. Once a transaction had been completed, the documents involved ceased to be important. They come to light only if the transaction ended in a law suit, or if the property of the merchant was sequestered to the crown. In such cases the documents found their way into the archives of the king's courts. One of the earliest documents to survive is an original bond, made some time in 1159, recording the promise of Richard, Sheriff of Hampshire, to repay a debt to William Cade, a moneylender. The document is particularly interesting because it purports to be in Richard's own handwriting.[20] Some idea of the extent of the "paper work" involved in transactions between an individual and his bankers is given in Dr Fryde's account of the deposits of Hugh Despenser with the Bardi in the early 14th century.[21] There were bonds, or letters obligatory, acquittances, vouchers, and warrants for payment. The documents take the form both of sealed letters patent and of more informal bills written by the client, the bankers, or their representatives. After accounting had been completed, the two parties delivered to each other all documents in their possession, and an indenture was drawn up recording this, and mutually acquitting them of all debts and liabilities up to that day. From the 15th century a greater number as well as a greater variety of documents survive, including bills from tradesmen. Among the Stonor papers there are bills for cloth supplied in 1380 and 1478–9, a mercer's account for 1482, and a shoemaker's bill for 1478–9.[22] Moreover the Stonor papers contain correspondence between William Stonor and his apprentices, and letters from his commercial partner Thomas Betson.

In addition to the ephemeral documents, some more permanent records survive. The Public Record Office's manuscript E 101/509/19 is a volume in which a London merchant, Gilbert Maghfeld, kept his accounts between the years 1390 and 1395,* together with a memorandum of outstanding debts carried over into this period from another book covering the year 1372.[23] The British Museum manuscript Harley 3988 is a late 14th-century collection of model business letters, mainly in

* Compare the description of the merchant in Chaucer's "Shipman's Tale" (*The Canterbury Tales*, Fragment vii, line 82):
  His bookes and his bagges many oon. . . .

French. From the end of the 12th century onward, commercial administration depended more and more heavily upon the written record, and the surviving records tend to include a higher proportion of less-formal documents as time goes on.[24]

During the 13th century, a new system of accountable management came into existence on the estates of the magnates and the monasteries.[25] This new system depended for its senior personnel upon literate laymen. Even on monastic lands the appointment of lay stewards and bailiffs was common, encouraged by Archbishop Peckham's injunctions that were aimed at preventing monks from living outside their monasteries.[26]

Of the local officers who rendered accounts under the new system, the senior was the bailiff, the direct representative of the lord and usually a salaried administrator. The other officer, the reeve, was almost always a servile tenant, fundamentally one of the local peasantry, the obligation to act as reeve being commonly included among the *servitia* owed to the lord. A comparison of accounts in the Dean and Chapter of Durham records for different manors for one year in the 14th century shows that they were all written by different hands. These are the first accounts produced by the reeve before the audit, and the different hands suggest that the accounts were actually written by the reeves themselves. The accounts were subsequently altered by the auditors, who added their totals in different hands and different inks.

Although it is not surprising that the bailiff should have been sufficiently literate to draw up accounts, it is surprising that the reeve should have been. Yet, from the early 13th century, treatises were drawn up for the instruction of reeves.[27] These take the form of model accounts, formularies designed to inculcate proper accounting methods by example. There can have been no point in such treatises unless some degree of literacy was expected of such officers. Although at this stage all accounts were drawn up in Latin, the ability to draw up an account would not necessarily require a knowledge of the Latin language as such. It would require only a knowledge of formulae. Latin terms found in the accounts could probably be regarded as the jargon of the trade.* Instructions to such

---

*¶ Compare Chaucer's account of the Somonour's use of Latin terms (*The Canterbury Tales*, General Prologue, lines 637–44):

> A fewe termes hadde he, two or thre,
> That he had lerned out of som decree—
> No wonder is, he herde it al the day;
> And eek ye knowen wel how that a jay
> Kan clepen "Watte" as wel as kan the pope.
> But whoso koude in oother thyng hym grope,
> Thanne hadde he spent al his philosophie;
> Ay "Questio quid iuris" wolde he crie.

officers from the central administration were usually written in French and later in English.* Thus, even if they could not construe Latin, they could at least read their instructions in the vernacular.

Lest this suggestion of the extent of pragmatic literacy among the peasantry be regarded as too fanciful, there is the following statement by Walter Map, writing toward the end of the 12th century:

> . . . the high-born of our country disdain letters or delay to apply their children to them, although to their children only is it rightly permitted to study the arts, . . . Slaves, on the other hand (the which we call peasants), are eager to nourish their base-born and degenerate children in the arts unfitted to their station, not that they may rise from their rudeness, but that they may revel in riches. . . .[28]

This sneer reflects the attitude of the courtier to the pretensions of his social inferiors, and also the condescension of the scholar toward the pragmatic reader. But the importance of this remark lies in the suggestion that some degree of pragmatic literacy was more extensive than the paucity of other evidence would lead us to suppose.

The English legal profession emerged during the course of the 13th century: laymen who made their living as pleaders, narrators, and attorneys, by representing clients before the king's courts and giving legal advice. The exemption of such pleaders from the law relating to maintenance indicates that they were a distinct professional class.[29] In the latter part of the reign of Henry III, the rise of this class is reflected in the tendency to recruit the bench of judges from the lay bar. Thomas Multon and Roger Thurkelby are examples of laymen who acquired a reputation as learned judges.[30] By 1292 "the great litigation of the realm . . . is conducted by a small group of men . . . one (or other) of whom will be engaged in almost every case."[31] Recruitment to the profession was by apprenticeship. Apprentices had to learn by sitting in the courts and hearing their seniors plead the cases. In 1292, pleaders, attorneys, and apprentices became subject to fixed rules, and the arrangements for legal education became more systematic.[32] During the next two centuries the legal profession organized itself and obtained the monopoly of legal business. By the time Sir John Fortescue wrote his *De laudibus legum angliae*, toward the end of the 15th century, the profession was organized under the general control of the serjeants and judges, with beneath them

---

* See B. F. HARVEY, *Documents Illustrating the Rule of Walter of Wenlok, Abbot of Westminster 1283-1307*, Camden Society, 4th series, II (London 1965). When the abbot writes to reeves and bailiffs he usually writes in French, but when he writes to the receivers or the stewards of the household he writes in Latin.

the various grades of barrister and apprentice grouped together in the Inns of Court and the Inns of Chancery.[33]

From the mid-13th century onward we find numerous books that must have been the reference books and memoranda of these administrators and lawyers. These are compilations of practical treatises, collections of precedents, and similar material, the majority of which were written in the cursive handwriting used for drafting or enrolling documents. The most important source of information for the common lawyer was the Year Books. In the words of Professor Holdsworth, they "give an account of the doings of the King's Courts which is either compiled by eye-witnesses, or from the narrative of eye-witnesses."[34] They are roughly the equivalent of the modern law reports, but the interest of the compilers clearly lies in the legal arguments rather than in the judgments. The reporting begins toward the end of the 13th century, and numerous copies of the Year Books were produced in the 14th. There are also numerous collections of statutes, pleadings, and forms of writs, as well as treatises on the law. One such lawyer's compilation in Cambridge University Library (manuscript Dd. 7.6) is a collection of statutes and treatises on the law such as those of Bracton and Britton. It was owned, glossed, and annotated by Sir John de Longueville, an early-14th-century lawyer who represented the borough of Northampton in parliament, and who on at least one occasion acted as a justice of assize.[35]

Turning to the mediaeval treatises on estate management, there are 33 copies dating from the late 13th and early 14th centuries. The majority of these are in compilations that also contain treatises on husbandry and accountancy, legal texts, statutes, treatises on conveyancing, and definitions of technical terms. Dr Oschinsky, who has studied them, concluded that such manuscripts "were more than . . . estate lawyers' text books: they were the reference books of experienced estate stewards who probably acted as teachers in their profession."[36] All these manuscripts contain not only copies of texts, but texts that have been excerpted, adapted, or enlarged, and thus demonstrate that the compilers had taken that intelligent and intimate interest in the subject-matter that we should expect of the practitioner.

Thus in commerce, seignorial administration, and the law we find that the practitioners were not only using written instruments in the course of their professional activities but also that many of them had acquired the habit of having at their elbows a book to which they could refer for information. The problem is not whether there were literate laymen, but how far they used this literacy outside their professional activities.

The emergence of this rising middle class as a class of cultivated readers is best evidenced, first, by some of the material to be found in their books, and, second, by new developments in the handwriting used for books.

Alongside the statutes, precedents, and treatises on husbandry, accountancy, and the law, some of the manuscripts contain material that indicates that the compiler was looking beyond his obvious professional horizons. Bodleian Library manuscripts Douce 137 and 132 once formed a single compilation of six "booklets," the first five of which were first put together early in the second half of the 13th century.[37] The first three booklets contain formularies, a treatise on accountancy, and the treatise on the laws of England commonly called "Glanville." Some of the items in the formularies, such as the copy of an agreement concerning the gild merchant at Reading and a copy of a perambulation of Berkshire, indicate that the compilation was assembled by a Berkshire lawyer some time in the 1260s. The fourth and fifth booklets contain the Anglo-Norman story *Horn*, Robert Grosseteste's *Le chasteau d'amour*, the *Fables* of Marie de France, and Guillaume le Clerc's *Bestiary*. The sixth booklet, containing more legal material, was added by a later owner in the 14th century. Another Bodleian Library manuscript, Selden Supra 74, contains Walter of Henley's treatise on husbandry, Walter of Bibbesworth's treatise on learning the French language, and a morally improving work, *La desputaison du cors et de l'âme*. Bound up in the same manuscript among other pieces in a contemporary cursive hand are a courtesy poem (one of the many designed to instruct "in those externals of behaviour which indicate *savoir faire*"), an encyclopaedia of miscellaneous moral and scientific lore called *L'image du monde*, and Bozon's *Proverbes de bon enseignement*. Such material was designed to improve the reader's soul, or to multiply his accomplishments and to increase his stock of useful, even cultural, information. It reflects the pragmatic taste of the middle-class reader, and his desire to rise in the world.

Other manuscripts contain this useful and improving material but without items of strictly professional interest. Two such compilations are of special importance. Bodleian Library manuscript Digby 86, once thought to have originated in a religious community, is now known to have been the private compilation of a layman.[38] British Museum manuscript Harley 2253 was probably the private compilation of a member of a bishop's household, who may or may not have been a layman.[39] Both are well written, but in idiosyncratic cursive hands that do not closely resemble those of contemporary scribes who specialized in copying books.[40] Alongside the proverbs, recipes, memoranda, and treatises on courtesy and on dreams, the two manuscripts contain *lais, fabliaux,* and romances in French and English, and between them the bulk of the lyrics in both languages surviving from the 13th century. The contents suggest that the compilers were collecting for literate recreation, and that some pragmatic readers were becoming increasingly more cultivated.

Most of these manuscripts were written in the cursive script that had been developed in the course of preparing and drafting documents, and that came to be used in books in the second half of the 13th century.[41] Some of these manuscripts at least were probably written by the compilers themselves (who were, after all, professional scribes in one sense of the term). They used in their books the handwriting that they were accustomed to use for business purposes.* But the script was also used by scribes who specialized in writing books; and during the 14th and 15th centuries, both in England and in France, the scribes developed more dignified varieties of cursive script, some of which attained such excellence of calligraphy that they could be used in the finest books. By 1400, the cursive script was used extensively in nearly all kinds of books and documents.

The advantages of these developments for the pragmatic reader are obvious. Instead of having to master the difficult alphabets of the several varieties of the text hand, he could read a book in the alphabet with which he had become familiar in the course of reading and drafting documents. Because the cursive script could be written more quickly, it could be used by professional scribes as a cheap book hand, which (as we shall see) ultimately affected the price of books.[42] Furthermore, manuscripts containing vernacular works of general interest are comparatively free from the drastic abbreviations that occur from the beginning of the 13th century onward in specialist Latin works. The implication of these developments in the palaeography of books is that there was a steadily growing class of "general" readers.

During the course of the 14th century the rising demand for books quickly assumed commercial importance, and it was met by the growth of a more organized book trade. The best evidence is to be found in the development of the trade in London. This evidence is less ambiguous than that available in Oxford or Paris, where the book trade existed primarily to cater for the needs of the academic communities. In London in the 13th century the various craftsmen seem to have worked independently, because instances of the separate crafts of parchminer (parchment maker), scrivener, illuminator, and bookbinder are to be found in the

---

* For an example of a monk who did this, John Clive of Worcester, see M. B. PARKES, *English Cursive Book Hands 1250–1500* (Oxford 1969), pl. 23.

City records. These craftsmen were not peripatetic; they occupied important sites from which they carried out their trades. Soon, however, some, while still working as independent craftsmen, assumed financial responsibility for co-ordinating the different stages of production and for accepting commissions from patrons for completed books. These men came to be known as "stationers." The first recorded instance of a stationer in London occurs in 1311, and by the end of the 14th century the term "was not infrequently used of members of the book trade."[43] With the increasing pressure of work, a distinction gradually arose between the scribes who drafted legal documents and those who copied books. Eventually in 1373 the Writers of Court Hand, or Scriveners, broke away from the others and formed their own gild with its own ordinances. In 1403 the Writers of Text-Letter formed another gild with the Limners (illuminators) and others in the City concerned with the production of books, and from this time onward commercial book production in London was regulated by the wardens of this gild, who had power to enforce their ordinances in the sheriffs' courts.[44]

Increasing demand, better-organized production, cheaper handwriting, and the introduction of paper led in the long run to cheaper books. At the end of the 14th century, inventories of books owned by Richard II[45] and his uncle Thomas, Duke of Gloucester,[46] show that their libraries contained not only expensive Bibles and works of devotion, but also volumes of romance valued at between 6d and a couple of shillings each. The stocks of two grocers who became bankrupt in the 1390s contained four books of romance valued at a total of 11s 4d, two books in English valued at 8d, a calendar worth 8d, and a primer worth 16d.[47] These amounts suggest some cheap form of production. But if one had the time to spare, the cheapest way to acquire a book was to copy it for oneself. The most striking example of this is probably the Glasgow University Library's Hunterian manuscript U.I.I, a copy of *The Canterbury Tales* written in 1476 by Thomas Spirleng, the 16-year-old son of a prominent burgess of Norwich. Books were always a luxury in the Middle Ages, but the production of cheaper books meant that they could become a luxury for poorer people.

The 14th and 15th centuries also witnessed an expansion of literacy among the population. This is reflected in the increasing use of the English language coupled with an increase in the number of surviving vernacular manuscripts. Prior to 1300 the language of the literate laity was French, but during the course of the 14th century French ceased to be the principal vernacular in England and became a more educated accomplishment.[48] At the beginning of the century the author of *Arthour and Merlin* expresses the desirability of telling his story in English:

> Freynsche vse þis gentilman
> Ac euerich Inglische Inglische can.
> Mani noble ich haue yseiȝe
> Þat no Freynsche couþe seye.[49]

> (This gentleman uses French, but every Englishman knows English.
> I have seen many nobles who did not know how to speak French.)

In 1327 Andrew Horn, the Chamberlain of the City of London, expounded the City's new charter in English instead of French at a mass meeting at the Guildhall.[50] The earliest petition in English is dated 1344.[51] About 1350 *William of Palerne* was translated at the request of Humphrey de Bohun, Earl of Hereford:

> He let make þis mater in þis maner speche
> For hem þat knowe no Frensche, ne neuer vnderston.[52]

> (He caused this material to be fashioned in this form of speech for those
> who know no French, and never understand it.)

John of Trevisa (*fl. c.* 1370–1400) remarks that after the Black Death children were no longer taught to construe their Latin in French, but in English. In 1362 parliament conceded that henceforth pleadings in the King's courts should be made in English instead of *"la lange Franceois, q'est trop desconu en le dit Roialme."*[53] The earliest surviving deed in English is dated 1376,[54] and the earliest surviving will is that of Robert Corn, dated 1387.[55] The earliest surviving letters in English may be assigned to 1392–3, and letters in English become common in the 15th century.[56] By the end of the 14th century the term "unlettered" could well indicate ignorance of French as well as of Latin. The increase in the use of English suggests that literacy was becoming more widespread among the population and was no longer confined to the top.

The steady increase in literacy brought with it a steady increase in the number of people who wanted to read for recreation and profit. As a result, in the 14th and 15th centuries there was an increasing number of translations from French and Latin into English, as well as new works composed in English. The majority of these translations not only reflect the pragmatic taste of the middle-class reader that we have already noticed in the early compilations but indicate that this growing class was extending its interests and becoming more cultivated. The texts may be placed in two categories: those for edification and profit, and those for edification and delight. In the first category are the numerous "guides to godliness" intended to educate a varied public, both religious and lay, in conscientious belief and to foster the development of the devout life.* Also in this category are the courtesy poems such as *How the Goodwife Taught her Daughter* and *What the Wise Man Taught his Son*; the encyclopaedias, such as Trevisa's translation (in 1398) of Bartholomæus Anglicus's *De proprietatibus rerum*, and *The Booke of Quinte Essence*; the medical treatises and recipes; and the treatises on hunting. For edification and delight the reader turned to romances, "biographies," and saints' lives. The scribes and readers seem to have made very little distinction between the different kinds of narrative.[57] The copy of *Sir Isumbras* in Gonville and Caius College (Cambridge) manuscript 175 has the heading *Hic incipit de milite Ysumbras*, and the colophon *Explicit sanctus ysumbras*. In the 15th century, translations were made of the *Legenda aurea*, the standard collection of saints' lives; and new versions and collections of such lives were made by John Lydgate, Osbern Bokenham, and John Capgrave. All these narratives catered for a widespread interest in the lives of persons famous for their virtues or notorious for their vices, and were morally improving with their insistence on order, peace, sobriety and loyalty, as well as devotion.

Despite the increase in the use of English, French survived until well into the 15th century as the language of the royal court, which enjoyed a more international culture than the rest of the country. For some years after the Battle of Poitiers in 1356, the court of Edward III comprised not only the king of England and his entourage but also King John of France and many French nobles who were awaiting the payment of their ransoms. French was the common language, and a continental writer such as the chronicler Jean Froissart sought his literary fortune for a time in the English court. The international character of Edward's court led naturally, in the time of Richard II, to the adoption of what Gervase Mathew has called the "international court culture."[58] Originating in the court of King Robert at Naples in the first half of the 14th century, it spread rapidly through the courts of Europe. It was characterized by new aesthetic standards in most aspects of courtly life and culture, and in particular it brought with it a fashion for good literature, which now had to conform to international standards. The authors were mainly laymen: Boccaccio in Naples; Deschamps, Oto de Granson, and Christine de Pisan in France; and Chaucer and Gower in England. At Richard II's court, poetry was written in both French and English. Sir John Montacute composed French *balades* and *rondeaux*, which were accepted in the circle

* *The Pricke of Conscience*, a northern poem, survives in well over 100 copies.

of Christine de Pisan (who herself visited the court of Henry IV). Gower wrote the *Cinkante balades "por desporter vo noble court roial*," and—in more serious vein—the *Mirour de l'omme*. Sir John Clanvowe and Chaucer wrote mainly in English (if Chaucer wrote any French verse it has not survived), although at first much under the influence of the French court poets. But, like the bourgeoisie, the court was extending its interests. In the first half of the 15th century Humphrey, Duke of Gloucester, turned to Italy for his books, and his collection contains numerous classical Latin authors, and Latin translations from the Greek.

Thus by 1400 the principal difference between the court and the increasing bourgeoisie was one of taste, not of literacy. But there was one feature of the new culture that the two had in common: the cultivated reader's love of books. Kings and nobles collected fine libraries. Charles V of France acquired a magnificent collection of more than 900 books,[59] many of which later found their way into the collection of the English regent in France, John, Duke of Bedford. The nobles followed the king's example. The most spectacular collection was that of Jean, Duc de Berri. The epitome of conspicuous expenditure (a quality much prized in the new culture), he demonstrated an exquisite taste for artistically adorned manuscripts. The dukes of Burgundy possessed a fine library, and Jean of Angoulême collected over 150 books that, as his annotations show, he read assiduously.[60] In England, Edward III spent the enormous sum of £66 13*s* 4*d* on a book of romances that he kept in his own bedchamber (which suggests that he read it as well).[61] Richard II kept a collection of books in his private closet, and some idea of the scale of the collection can be gleaned from the fact that 19 volumes were rebound between 1386 and 1388.[62] Henry IV added to his favourite palace at Eltham a study in which to keep his books.[63] Henry V possessed books, and Thomas Hoccleve and Lydgate found it appropriate to dedicate and present works to him.[64] The most assiduous English collector was Humphrey, Duke of Gloucester. His letters are full of requests for copies of various works, and his collection, estimated at some 500 volumes,[65] was the most important in England at that time. Although he had a predilection for medicine and astrology, his tastes in literature were also instrumental in arousing interest in classical studies.[66] His successor in this field, John Tiptoft, Earl of Worcester, collected many books that show his strong humanist leanings.

In collecting books, the gentry and the bourgeoisie followed the example of the magnates, but obviously on a much more modest scale. In his will dated 1458, Sir Thomas Chaworth of Wiverton (Nottinghamshire) left five English books and one in Latin, besides service books.[67] Two further books that belonged to him have survived, although they are not recorded in his will.[68] Arthur Ormesby, gentleman, of North Ormesby (Lincolnshire) left six books in his will dated 1467–8.[69] In 1489 Edmund Rede, gentleman, of Oxfordshire left, besides service books, 14 books *"cum omnibus libris meis de lege Anglie."*[70] Citizens and merchants of London also owned books. In 1349 Robert Felstead, vintner, left a psalter written in English and Latin.[71] In 1420 John Brinchley, tailor, left two copies of Boethius (one in English, one in Latin) and a copy of *The Canterbury Tales*.[72] In 1435 William Holgrave, citizen of London, is mentioned in a will as owning a book of Chaucer.[73] William (Pelka?), citizen of London, owned what is now the British Museum's Additional Manuscript 17376, which is a copy of the Midland Prose Psalter and Shoreham's poems.[74] The Trinity College (Cambridge) manuscript R.3.21, a collection of devotional pieces and miscellaneous poems, belonged to Roger Thorney, a mercer of London, and a copy of Chaucer's works that belonged to him is now in St John's College, Oxford.[75] In 1460 John Burton, mercer, bequeathed a copy of the *Legenda aurea* to his daughter, a nun.[76]

For some of those who could not afford books in the ordinary way, or who did not have the leisure to copy them for themselves, there were compilations of religious works made at the request of pious folk "for a comyn profitte." Several of these Common Profit manuscripts[77] survive, most of them connected with the London area. They contain instructions to the holder that

> whenne he occupieth it not, leeve he it for a time to sum oþer personne, [so that the book may be passed] from personne to personne, man or woman, as longe as þe book enduriþ.

From a study of wills, Miss Deanesly has argued[78] that the population of England in the late 14th and 15th centuries was comparatively bookless. This argument cannot be accepted without some reservations. First, it implies that the books possessed by a testator would have been recorded as separate items in a will, but this need not have been so. Petrarch is known to have possessed some 300 books, but only one of them is recorded in his will.[79] A less dramatic example nearer home is that of Sir Thomas Chaworth, mentioned above. Second, a single "book" could contain many works between two covers. As we have already seen, the majority of manuscripts of middle-class interest are in fact compilations for the whole family: "libraries," as it were, of texts for edification and profit, or edification and delight. A typical compilation is Cambridge University Library's manuscript Ff. 2. 38. Written on paper in the mid-

15th century, its contents include: a verse paraphrase of the seven penitential psalms, the *Ave*, and the Commandments; the works of mercy, the five wits, the seven deadly sins, and the seven contrary virtues, all summarized in verse; the articles of faith, and the seven sacraments according to St Edmund, in prose; three saints' lives; other moral and devout pieces; *How the Good Man Taught His Son*; *How a Merchaunde Dyd Hys Wyfe Betray*; *A Gode Mater of the Marchaund and Hys Sone*; and 10 romances—*The Erle of Toulous, Sir Eglamour, Sir Tryamore, Octavian, Sir Bevis of Hampton, The Seven Sages, Guy of Warwick, La Bone Florence of Rome, Robert of Sicily*, and *Sir Degaré*. Thus between two covers we find a range of reading-matter to satisfy most of the practical and intellectual requirements of a 15th-century middle-class family.

Some of the manuscript compilations were assembled by individuals over a number of years, and represent the personal tastes and interests of the compiler. The British Museum's manuscript Egerton 1995 was compiled by a London citizen.[80] It contains a romance for entertainment, a courtesy poem, treatises on how to maintain one's health, memoranda on the properties of a gentleman and the qualities of a good greyhound, historical records, topographical material, and a chronicle by William Gregory, a London skinner. The Brome manuscript, another Common Place book (as these compilations are often called), includes a play.[81] Some of the compilers brought to the texts that they collected for re-creation the same tendency to excerpt, adapt, and enlarge the material as is found in the texts that they compiled for reference purposes in the course of their professional activities. One such compiler was a man called Rate, who wrote the Bodleian Library's manuscript Ashmole 61. The manuscript is a holster book* containing a collection of moral and didactic pieces, courtesy poems, and romances, selected and edited by Rate for family reading.[82] Collation of the texts in this manuscript with other copies indicates that Rate (in the words of one editor) was "an idiosyncratic scribe freely adapting a sound copy."[83] Cambridge University Library's manuscript Ff. 1. 6, the so-called "Findern Anthology,"[84] is a collection of poems mainly about love. It was formed by collecting "booklets," or quires already written, and the blank leaves were used, perhaps by the family, to inscribe additional pieces and memoranda. The

---

* Holster books are so called because of their long and narrow shape, the sheets being folded along the length (agenda format). Such a format would be particularly appropriate for recording accounts, and some examples of such account books survive from the late 15th century. On holster books, see G. S. IVY, "The Bibliography of the Manuscript Book," in F. WORMALD and C. E. WRIGHT, *The English Library before 1700* (London 1958); also the review by R. W. HUNT in *Archives* IV (London 1959), p. 49.

poems include an excerpt from Chaucer's *Legend of Good Women,* and excerpts from Gower's *Confessio amantis* on the Lover's wakefulness and on dreams, as well as several of the tales.

Other compilations represent the response of the bookseller to a popular demand for such anthologies. The earliest of these compilations is the Auchinleck manuscript, which was produced in a commercial scriptorium in the 1330s.[85] The similarity between the contents of the British Museum's manuscript Lansdowne 285 (the *Grete Boke* of Sir John Paston) and the New York Pierpont Morgan Library's manuscript 775 suggests that both compilations derive ultimately from the same bookseller's anthology.[86] Perhaps the most interesting example of such commercial enterprise is to be found in the activity of John Shirley, who operated from premises in St Bartholomew's Close in London.[87] Seven of his manuscripts survive, and contain pieces mainly by Chaucer and Lydgate with prologues and ascriptions by Shirley. He seems to have run something in the nature of a circulating library, because the manuscripts contain exhortations that they be returned to him.[88] The booksellers, too, were inclined to adapt their texts, particularly the anonymous ones, and introduced ingredients that would boost sales.[89]

Finally, in addition to the private and booksellers' compilations, works such as the *Confessio amantis* and *The Canterbury Tales* represent the authors' own efforts to provide a ready-made compilation. The contemporary popularity of these works must have depended at least as much upon their compendious nature—"Somwhat of lust, somwhat of lore," in Gower's words—as upon their literary merit.

Unlike the more learned Latin and French works, very few of these middle-class compilations in English found their way into monastic libraries. The majority of them passed from generation to generation and were read not only in the 15th century, but—as numerous signatures and scribbles show—during the 16th and early 17th centuries as well. In the late 17th century, when both the language and the handwriting were no longer familiar, some of them passed into the hands of antiquaries who ensured their survival.

How sophisticated was this middle-class literacy? Some impression can be gained from the style of the private letters that survive from the 15th century. Professor Davis[90] draws attention to the conscious elements of style that derive from the dictaminists, and emphasizes "grammatical forms . . . [that] are not colloquial in origin but developed in written use." The most interesting from our point of view are the parallels he draws between the phraseology and rhythms found in the Paston letters and passages from works by Chaucer, Lydgate, and Malory. John Paston uses a "flourish of superlatives" to praise a knight: a customary feature perhaps, but one that was exploited and heightened by Malory.[91] Some of the most striking parallels are of course proverbial, and therefore available to both author and letter-writer from a common stock, but the coincidence is often remarkable. About 1465 Agnes Paston wrote: "This worlde is but a thoroughfare and ful of woo. . . ." The sentiment is commonplace enough, but in one of his poems[92] Lydgate attributes it to Chaucer, and the phrase occurs in "The Knight's Tale."[93] The development in family letters of conscious *written* usage with sub-conscious literary echoes, as opposed to spoken usage, indicates a sophisticated rather than a rudimentary form of literacy.

Increasing literary awareness is also apparent in other ways. In the first half of the 15th century, wealthy citizens of London commissioned John Lydgate to produce fashionable occasional pieces. He wrote the *Lyf of Saint George* for the walls of the hall of the Armourers' Company, and perhaps his *Mesure is Tresour* for the vestibule. He wrote *The Mumming of David* for the Goldsmiths at Candlemas, and *The Mumming of Jupiter's Messenger* for the Mercers at Twelfth Night. He translated the *Bycorne and Chychevache* for a "worthy citesyn of London," and composed a poem celebrating the City's reception for Henry VI on his return from his coronation in Paris.[94]

In the 15th century there is an increasing tendency to use prose instead of verse for literature of the more pragmatic kind. With this development comes an awareness of the possibilities of verse to embellish an idea, an awareness of the "poetic."[95] Among Lydgate's minor poems are a few that by reason of their content might be called practical.[96] Yet most of them are written in rhyme royal, not couplets, and there is a conscious elegance of diction. In the Paston letters, Dame Elizabeth Brews shows a consciousness of rhyme when she quotes a proverb: "It is but a sympill ok that [is] cut down at the firste stroke."[97]

The first assessment of the extent of literacy among the population of England occurs in a statement made by Sir Thomas More in 1533. He observed that

> people farre more than fowre partes of all the whole divided into tenne coulde never reade englische yet. . .[98]

implying that by this time more than half of the total population could read English. The extent of literacy among the laity in the Middle Ages must always be a matter for debate, but in my opinion the tendency has been to underestimate it. The general pattern of the evidence indicates that from the 13th century onward increasing reliance and importance was placed upon the written word. This was accompanied by the growth of the reading habit, checked only by the high price of a book or by the necessity to write it for oneself. The growth of the reading habit gave rise to an increasing literary awareness. By the end of the 14th century the minstrel seems to have become less a transmitter of texts and more a professional musician.[99] Some of the formulas of oral delivery persisted in later mediaeval texts,* partly because old stylistic habits die hard, and partly because they would be appropriate to the situation of reading aloud,[100] especially to the whole family. The survival of these formulas, however, has helped to obscure the extent of the literate audience for such texts. The fact that a text has been preserved on the written page at all indicates that it has been transmitted by the pen of a literate person— not always by a professional scribe or a man of letters but often by one who falls more into the category of a general reader. Whatever date one wishes to assign to the emergence of the general reader, the process began in the 13th century, when the pragmatic reader began to look beyond his immediate professional horizons.

* For example, the opening formula of the type "Lystenyth all and ye shall her . . .". See c. BROWN and R. H. ROBBINS, *Index of Middle English Verse* (New York 1943), 1090–1119, 1876–1910.

References

1. Provisions for education, and the evidence that these provide for the extent of literacy in the Middle Ages, are outside the scope of this chapter. I am grateful to Mr J. A. Burrow, Professor N. Davis, Professor R. J. Dean, Dr A. I. Doyle, Dr P. O. E. Gradon, and Mr A. J. Piper for suggestions and corrections. I am solely responsible for the views expressed.
2. H. PIRENNE, "De l'état de l'instruction des laïques à l'époque mérovingienne," *Revue Bénédictine* XLVI (Maredsous 1934), p. 165.
3. M. L. W. LAISTNER, *Thought and Letters in Western Europe, A.D. 500–900* (London 1957), p. 309.
4. K. SISAM, *Studies in the History of Old English Literature* (Oxford 1953), p. 161.
5. J. W. THOMPSON, *The Literacy of the Laity in the Middle Ages* (New York 1965), pp. 141–2; cf. H. GRUNDMANN, "Literatus-illiteratus," *Archiv für Kulturgeschichte* XL (Marburg 1958), p. 10.
6. E. AUERBACH, *Literary Language and its Public in Late Latin Antiquity and in the Middle Ages*, trans. by R. Manheim (London 1965), pp. 169 ff.

7. M. D. LEGGE, *Anglo-Norman Literature and its Background* (Oxford 1963), p. 5.

8. W. STUBBS, "Learning and Literature at the Court of Henry II," *Lectures on the Study of Medieval and Modern History* (Oxford 1887), pp. 132–78; R. W. SOUTHERN, *Medieval Humanism* (Oxford 1970), pp. 158–80.

9. LEGGE, *op. cit., passim.*

10. *ibid.*, p. 28.

11. *ibid.*, pp. 22, 37.

12. H. L. D. WARD and J. A. HERBERT, *Catalogue of Romances in the Department of Manuscripts in the British Museum* (London 1883–1910), Vol. I, p. 731.

13. R. VAUGHAN, *Matthew Paris* (Cambridge 1958), pp. 170, 181.

14. LEGGE, *op. cit.*, pp. 139 ff.

15. M. BLAESS, "L'Abbaye de Bordesley et les livres de Guy de Beauchamp," *Romania* LXXVIII (Paris 1957), pp. 511–8.

16. LEGGE, *op. cit.*, p. 28.

17. See M. DEANESLY, *The Lollard Bible* (Cambridge 1920), pp. 21–2.

18. Quoted in AUERBACH, *op. cit.*, p. 291.

19. *Roman de Rou*, ed. by A. J. Holden, Société des Anciens Textes Français (Paris 1970), Vol. I, Pt 3, lines 164–5.

20. H. JENKINSON, "A Moneylender's Bonds of the Twelfth Century," *Essays in History Presented to R. L. Poole* (Oxford 1921), pp. 190, 206.

21. E. B. FRYDE, "The Deposits of Hugh Despenser the Younger with Italian Bankers," *Economic History Review*, 2nd series, III (Utrecht 1951), p. 344.

22. *The Stonor Letters and Papers, 1290–1483*, ed. by C. L. Kingsford, Camden Society, n.s. XXIX–XXX (London 1919), Nos. 39, 95, 234, 235, and 317.

23. E. RICKERT, "Extracts from a Fourteenth Century Account Book," *Modern Philology* XXIV (Chicago 1926), pp. 111, 249.

24. For a general account, see M. M. POSTAN, "Private and Financial Instruments in Medieval England," *Vierteljahrschrift für Sozial- und Wirtschaftgeschicht* XXIII (Stuttgart 1930), p. 29.

25. N. DENHOLM-YOUNG, *Seignorial Administration in England* (Oxford 1937). In this account I am indebted to my colleague Dr E. Stone for guidance and many references.

26. R. A. L. SMITH, "The Financial System of Rochester Cathedral Priory," *Collected Papers* (Cambridge 1947), pp. 48 ff.

27. DENHOLM-YOUNG, *op. cit.*, p. 121. See also Reference 36 below.

28. *Master Walter Map's Book De nugis curialium (Courtier's Trifles)*, trans. by F. TUPPER and M. B. OGLE (London 1924), p. 8.

29. W. S. HOLDSWORTH, *History of English Law* (London 1923), Vol. II, p. 313.

30. F. POLLOCK and F. W. MAITLAND, *History of English Law* (Cambridge 1895), Vol. I, p. 184.

31. *ibid.*, I, p. 195.

32. HOLDSWORTH, *op. cit.*, II, p. 315.

33. *ibid.*, II, p. 485.

34. *ibid.*, II, p. 525.

35. F. W. MAITLAND and W. P. BAILDON, *The Court Baron*, Selden Society IV (London 1891), pp. 13–4

36. D. OSCHINSKY, "Medieval Treatises on Estate Management," *Economic History Review*, 2nd series, VIII (Utrecht 1955–6), p. 308; see also her edition of *Walter of Henley and other Treatises on Estate Management and Accounting* (Oxford 1971), and the review of this edition by P. D. A. HARVEY in *Agricultural History Review* XX (London 1972), pp. 170–82

37. The compilation was first noticed by M. K. POPE, *The Romance of Horn*, Anglo-Norman Text Society IX (Oxford 1955), but the compilation has recently been analysed in more detail in P. R. ROBINSON, *Some Aspects of the Transmission of English Verse Texts in Late Mediaeval Manuscripts* (unpublished B. Litt. thesis in the University of Oxford), pp. 29 ff. and 205–15. On the circulation of texts in "booklets" and their compilation into larger manuscripts, see Miss Robinson's contribution in the forthcoming *Codicologica*, ed. by A. Gruijs (The Hague), Vol. II.

38. On manuscript Digby 86, see B. D. H. MILLER, *Annuale Medievale* II (Pittsburgh 1961).

39. N. R. KER, *Facsimile of British Museum MS. Harley 2253*, Early English Text Society, o.s. 255 (London 1964), Introduction.

40. On the hand of manuscript Harley 2253, see KER, *op. cit.*, also M. B. PARKES, *English Cursive Book Hands, 1250–1500* (Oxford 1969), pl. 1 (ii).

41. On the development and use of the cursive script, see PARKES, *op. cit.*

42. H. E. BELL, "The Price of Books in Medieval England," *The Library*, 4th series, XVII (London 1936–7), p. 331; also PARKES, *op. cit.*, p. xvi.

43. G. POLLARD, "The Company of Stationers before 1557," *The Library*, 4th series, XVIII (London 1937), p. 3.

44. *ibid.*, p. 9.

45. E. RICKERT, "King Richard II's Books," *The Library*, 4th series, XIII (London 1933), p. 144.

46. Printed in *Transactions of the Royal Society of Literature*, 2nd series, IX (London 1870), p. 180.

47. S. L. THRUPP, *The Merchant Class of Medieval London* (Ann Arbor 1948), p. 162.

48. See H. SUGGETT, "The Use of French in the Later Middle Ages," *Essays in Medieval History*, ed. by R. W. Southern (London 1968), p. 213.

49. *Arthour and Merlin*, ed. by E. Kölbing (Leipzig 1890), lines 23–6.

50. G. WILLIAMS, *Medieval London* (London 1963), p. 289.

51. R. W. CHAMBERS and M. DAUNT, *A Book of London English* (Oxford 1931), p. 272.

52. W. W. SKEAT, *William of Palerne*, Early English Text Society, e.s. 1 (London 1867), line 5532.
53. *Rotuli parliamentorum* (Rolls of Parliament) II, p. 273.
54. J. E. WELLS, *Manual of Writings in Middle English* (New Haven 1916 ff.), p. 442.
55. F. J. FURNIVALL, *Fifty Earliest English Wills*, Early English Text Society, o.s. 78 (London 1882.)
56. C. L. KINGSFORD, *Prejudice and Promise in Fifteenth Century England* (Oxford 1925), pp. 22–3.
57. See H. DELEHAYE, *Les légendes hagiographiques*, Subsidia Hagiographica 18 (Brussels 1927), especially p. 103.
58. G. MATHEW, *The Court of Richard II* (London 1968).
59. L. V. DELISLE, *Recherches sur la librairie de Charles V* (Paris 1907); also the catalogue of the exhibition held in the Bibliothèque Nationale, Paris, *La librairie de Charles V* (Paris 1968).
60. L. V. DELISLE, *Le Cabinet des Manuscrits de la Bibliothèque Impériale* (Paris 1868–81), Vol. I, p. 148.
61. F. DEVON, *Issues of the Exchequer* (London 1837), p. 144.
62. MATHEW, *op. cit.*, p. 23.
63. *ibid.*, p. 33.
64. K. VICKERS, *Humphrey Duke of Gloucester* (London 1907), p. 426.
65. *ibid.*
66. R. WEISS, *Humanism in England* (Oxford 1967), pp. 66–71.
67. *Testamenta eboracensia*, Surtees Society II (London 1835), pp. 220–9.
68. British Museum Cotton manuscript Augustus A iv, and Columbia University Library (New York) Plimpton manuscript 263, contain his arms. (Information kindly provided by A. I. Doyle.)
69. *Transactions of the Bibliographical Society* VII (London 1902–4), p. 116.
70. *ibid.*, pp. 107–8.
71. M. DEANESLY, "Vernacular Books in England in the Fourteenth and Fifteenth Centuries," *Modern Language Review* XV (Cambridge 1920), p. 351.
72. FURNIVALL, *op. cit.*, p. 136.
73. *Registrum Henrici Chichele* II, 528.
74. Information kindly provided by A. I. Doyle.
75. G. BONE, "Extant Manuscripts Printed from by Wynkyn de Worde," *The Library*, 4th series, XII (London 1932), p. 284.
76. Bodleian Library (Oxford) manuscript Douce 372.
77. E.g. British Museum manuscripts Harley 993, 2336, 6579; Bodleian Library manuscript Douce 25; Cambridge University Library manuscript Ff. 6. 31; Lambeth Palace Library (London) manuscript 472.
78. DEANESLY, "Vernacular Books. . .".
79. C. F. BÜHLER, *The Fifteenth Century Book* (Philadelphia 1960), p. 100, footnote 33; p. 106, footnote 77.
80. J. GAIRDNER, *Collections of a Citizen of London*, Camden Society, n.s. XVII (London 1876).

81. L. TOULMIN SMITH, *A Common Place Book of the Fifteenth Century* (London 1886).
82. For Rate as editor, see R. K. GINN, *A Critical Edition of the Two Texts of "Sir Cleges"* (unpublished M. A. thesis in the Faculty of Arts, Queen's University, Belfast).
83. A. J. BLISS, *Sir Orfeo* (Oxford 1954), p. xvii.
84. R. H. ROBBINS, "The Findern Anthology," *Publications of the Modern Language Association of America* LXIX (New York 1954), p. 610.
85. L. H. LOOMIS, "The Auchinleck Manuscript and a possible London Bookshop of 1330–40," *Publications of the Modern Language Association of America* LVII (New York 1941), p. 595.
86. C. F. BÜHLER, "Sir John Paston's *Grete Boke*, a Fifteenth Century Best-seller," *Modern Language Review* LVI (Cambridge 1941), p. 345.
87. For bibliography on Shirley, see E. P. HAMMOND, *English Verse, Chaucer to Surrey* (Durham, N. C. 1927), pp. 191–7; see also A. I. DOYLE, "More Light on John Shirley," *Medium Ævum* XXX (Oxford 1961), p. 93.
88. For example:

> Yee that desyre in herte and have plesaunce
> Olde stories in bokis for to rede,
> Gode matiers putt hem in remembraunce,
> And of the other take yee none hede;
> Byseching yowe of your godely hede,
> Whane yee this boke have over-redde and seyne,
> To Iohan Shirley restore yee it ageine.

89. See LOOMIS, *op. cit.*
90. N. DAVIS, "Style and Stereotype in Early English Letters," *Leeds Studies in English*, n.s. I (Leeds 1967), p. 7.
91. *ibid.*, pp. 14–5.
92. H. N. MACCRACKEN, *The Minor Poems of John Lydgate*, Vol. II, Early English Text Society, o. s. 192 (London 1934), No. 72, "A Thoroughfare of Woe," lines 184–91.
93. "The Knight's Tale," lines 2847–8; cf. DAVIS, *op. cit.*, p. 11.
94. K. J. HOLZKNECHT, *Literary Patronage in the Middle Ages* (New York 1923), p. 102.
95. For this observation I am indebted to Mrs Rachel Hands, who is preparing an article on the subject.
96. MACCRACKEN, *op. cit.*, Nos. 47–55.
97. N. DAVIS, *The Paston Letters* (Oxford 1958), No. 78; cf. DAVIS, *op. cit.*, p. 12.
98. *The Workes of Sir Thomas More* (London 1557), p. 850.
99. This is suggested by the evidence cited in J. J. JUSSERAND, *English Wayfaring Life in the Middle Ages* (London 1889), pp. 195–213.
100. H. J. CHAYTOR, *From Script to Print* (Cambridge 1945), pp. 5–21.

Bibliography

There is no satisfactory general treatment of the subject. The following are useful on particular aspects.

J. W. ADAMSON, "The Extent of Literacy in England in the Fifteenth and Sixteenth Centuries," *The Library*, 4th series, X (London 1929–30), p. 163.

E. AUERBACH, *Literary Language and its Public in Late Latin Antiquity and in the Middle Ages*, trans. by R. Manheim (London 1965), Ch. 4.

H. S. BENNETT, "Caxton and His Public," *Review of English Studies* XIX (London 1943); "The Production and Dissemination of Vernacular Manuscripts in the Fifteenth Century," *The Library*, 5th series, I (London 1946-7), p. 167.

H. J. CHAYTOR, *From Script to Print* (Cambridge 1945).

M. DEANESLY, 'Vernacular Books in England in the Fourteenth and Fifteenth Centuries," *Modern Language Review* XV (Cambridge 1920), p. 349.

L. V. DELISLE, *Le Cabinet des Manuscrits de la Bibliothèque Impériale* (Paris 1868–81).

V. H. GALBRAITH, "The Literacy of the Earliest English Kings," *Proceedings of the British Academy* XXI (London 1936).

R. IRWIN, *The Heritage of the English Library* (London 1964), Ch. XI.

C. L. KINGSFORD, *Prejudice and Promise in Fifteenth Century England* (Oxford 1925).

M. L. W. LAISTNER, *Thought and Letters in Western Europe, A.D. 500–900* (London 1957).

M. D. LEGGE, *Anglo-Norman Literature and its Background* (Oxford 1963).

G. MATHEW, *The Court of Richard II* (London 1968).

D. OSCHINSKY, *Walter of Henley and other Treatises on Estate Management and Accounting* (Oxford 1971).

H. G. RICHARDSON and G. O. SAYLES, *The Governance of Medieval England* (Edinburgh 1963), Ch. XV.

A. SAPORI, *Studi di storia economica medievale* (Florence 1946), "La cultura del mercante medievale italiano."

E. A. SAVAGE, *Old English Libraries* (London 1911).

J. W. THOMPSON, *The Literacy of the Laity in the Middle Ages* (New York repr. 1965). This book deals only with the ability to read Latin, and only up to 1300.

S. THRUPP, *The Merchant Class of Medieval London* (Ann Arbor 1948), Ch. V.

CHAPTER 17

Boccaccio, Chaucer, and the Mercantile Ethic

Aldo D. Scaglione[*]

The culture of the Greeks and Romans had grown on the rich soil of a basically agricultural society hingeing on towns that were highly developed politically but dominated by the landed gentry. The early Middle Ages saw the gradual articulation of a class of landowner-warriors flanked by the proliferating power of the clergy, which was the formidable social contribution of Christianity, the new spiritual factor in the midst of demographic and administrative upheavals. The peculiar novelty of the later mediaeval centuries, roughly after the onset of our millennium, was the virtually unprecedented emergence of a "third estate"; this middle class, committed to daring, highly diversified manufacturing and commercial enterprise, appeared strong enough to challenge the powers that were. The timid ancestors of such a new breed of men, the ancient "knights" or *equites*, seem to have produced little more than a rudimentary form of mercantile activity by comparison, even though they could, occasionally and quite individually, attain to impressive heights of wealth and influence, as in the person of the Roman triumvir Crassus (*c.* 115–53 B.C.).

The 14th century marked the culmination and crisis of the process we are envisaging. On the broad European scene, the Church being generally weakened, the three great powers of the century were the kings, the nobles, and the merchants. The former two were constitutionally at odds in the struggle that gradually led to the affirmation of centralized national administrations, while the merchants were organized on both regional and supranational bases, as in the typical—though in its way unique—

[*] W. R. Kenan Professor of Romance Languages and Comparative Literature, University of North Carolina.

Hanseatic League around the Baltic and the eastern shores of the North Sea.

More often than not, the merchant was capitalist-investor-employer-manager in one, powerful thanks to his abilities and, above all, to his organization, the gild, which the communes recognized as an official institution of economic, social, and political power as well.

The life of towns and cities rested largely in the hands of the middle class, whose relationship to the other social strata varied greatly with time and place. Let us refer to such distant and differing lands as England and Italy: it is there that we shall choose our chief literary examples. In the House of Commons one could see knights of the shire and townsmen working together—a typical English accomplishment that contrasted with the segregation of classes prevailing in the parliamentary institutions of other lands throughout mediaeval Europe. Indeed, a turning-point in English history came precisely when the knights of the shire, forsaking the social ties that naturally drew them toward an alliance with the barons, finally sat together with the burgesses as "the Commons" in the first parliament of Edward III. On the other hand, in Italy—a land of weak parliamentary traditions after the early stages of the communes—the association of urban classes could be seen at work more methodically, perhaps, than anywhere else, through the tight organisms of the "corporations," or *arti*, within which the capitalistic and managerial groups coerced, assimilated, and ultimately dominated the other elements at both ends of the social spectrum, namely the nobles and labour. Radically, yet typically, Giano della Bella's "Ordinances of Justice" of 1293 had sealed the triumph in Florence of the big burghers or *popolo grasso*, self-appointed protectors of artisans and proletarians (*popolo minuto*), by excluding the nobles (*magnati* or *grandi*) from public offices unless they individually joined the burghers' own trade gilds.

From an intellectual vantage point, appreciation of material goods was looked upon without much positive favour in the Middle Ages, but it would be a mistake to link this attitude strictly with Christian asceticism. It had been part of classical culture, considering the chiefly "rural" (that is, agricultural) basis of ancient civilization, even in its urban developments. As an eloquent testimony of the deep-seatedness of this distrust we may single out, among so many, Petronius's celebrated passage on the Civil War.[1] The fated predicament of the Roman state at the beginning of the great crisis that put an end to the republic is earnestly focussed by the poet on the stern judgment of a whole people having fallen victim to material greed, an unquenchable thirst for possession and luxury, with consequent all-engulfing corruption in public offices, debauchery in private mores, and usury in financial practices.

This indictment was written around the middle of the first century A.D. Dante, as the highest poetic "voice of ten silent centuries," repeats such charges by applying them again to his own time, under the telling symbol of "avarice." Yet the new economic orientation toward mercantilism, which started in the 11th and 12th centuries, eventually began to find its voice in literature even while the Franciscan movement restated with powerful originality the ancient ascetic ideals in moral and religious terms. Nevertheless, despite this gradually growing awareness of a new reality, the full emancipation of the "economic" point of view did not come until the ripening of humanism in the early 15th century.[2]

Economic realities sometimes emerge into the light of literature in the most unexpected manners and places. Even in such a lofty and rarefied climate as that of the Tristan legend we find such details as the following:

> [Tristan] fitted out a great ship and loaded it with corn and wine . . . , he manned it with . . . a hundred young knights of high birth . . . , and he clothed them in coats of home-spun and in hair cloth so that they seemed merchants only: but under the deck he hid rich cloth of gold and scarlet as for a great king's messengers.[3]

And later on:

> . . . but as these strange merchants passed the day in the useless games of draughts and chess, and seemed to know dice better than the bargain-price of corn, Tristan feared discovery and knew not how to pursue his quest.[4]

These exquisite brush-strokes depict a reality that the poet sees through his experience of a world in which bourgeois and mercantile consciousness is ever present, side by side with the ways of aristocracy.

Dante, "the wise poete of Florence,"[5] was notoriously unwilling and unable to espouse the mercantile core of the civilization that bore him. His declared animosity toward the *gente nova e i subiti guadagni* (the greedy lot recently come into town and quickly turned wealthy) blinded him to the economics of his time and to the relevance of those *nouveaux riches* for the prosperity of Florence and of Italy. He thus refused to acknowledge the vitality of the burghers' class as anything more than one sign of the obsessive care for material possessions and enjoyment—an aspect of avarice, the she-wolf snapping at the heels of modern Christendom. Profoundly convinced of the decadence affecting his time, he looked down upon it from the height of his aristocratic and theologically oriented idealism. Yet Dante does represent, in his own way, that very same culture of the free communes whose bourgeois spirit and inner strength he refused to recognize. Even his notion of the national vernacular bore the unmistakable imprint of the burgher's exclusivism directed against the countryside. The intrinsic quality of the *volgare illustre, cardinale, aulico e curiale,* to wit, the vernacular, enlightened and enlightening, pivotal for the life of the nation, and court-oriented (more precisely, shaped by and after the taste of the intellectuals and especially the poets who graced the noble courts with their inspiring presence), is for him *urbanitas,* the urbane virtue of courteous and refined patterns that go with living in the best city circles. The vocabulary of children, women, and peasants is excluded, and the remaining choice is clear.[6]

The same century that saw Dante rise to the heights of transcendental vision produced in Giovanni Boccaccio (1313–75) and Geoffrey Chaucer (*c.* 1340–1400) not only two of the greatest story-tellers of all time, but also two of the most delightfully "bourgeois" souls ever to leave records in literature. Indeed their masterworks, regardless of all formal aspects, happen to have one striking feature in common: both clearly and eloquently show that their respective authors grew up within the milieu of the contemporary mercantile groups.[7] Their celebrated realism owes much to this, although it encompasses literary and spiritual factors that transcend the dimensions of practical experience. To begin with, Dante himself must be held responsible for some aspects of this realism. More generally, Boccaccio must have learnt from the *Divina commedia* (?1306–21) the techniques of composition by sustained cogency of subject arrangements and by psychological playing on methodic variation through dialectical contrasts, which afford psychological relief and dramatic appeal to the reader. That he applied these criteria far less austerely and systematically is due to the difference in personalities and in the nature of the work. Rather than through the intermediary of the *Decameron* (*c.* 1352), it is in all likelihood directly from the *Commedia* that Chaucer assimilated the same procedures for his *Canterbury Tales* (*c.* 1389). Of course, the direct personal experience of the life of business and businessmen was, for both our authors, at least as relevant as any manner of literary "imitation." Boccaccio, the son of an agent of the Bardi bank (one of the financial titans of the age until its failure in 1340), grew up within Florentine business circles even while being educated at the Neapolitan court, which was practically a fief of another Florentine financial colossus, Niccolò Acciaiuoli; and Chaucer, the son of a prosperous London wine merchant, also had a successful career as businessman and government official. But it is not with biographical details that we are concerned here, except as implicit background. What matters most is the quality of the works, their inner springs and motivations.

The matter of historico-literary categories also need not detain us beyond a rather general remark. If we define humanism *stricto sensu,* Chaucer appears virtually untouched by it, whereas Boccaccio remains, a full generation earlier, a recognized master of it. Yet Boccaccio's *Decameron,* in particular, remains as much outside the progress of humanistic forms and ideals as any of his works could ever be. The distinction implied here is the one that was defined in its broadest terms by M. W. Croll while dealing with the struggle between humanism and mediaevalism, even as late as the 16th century, within the process of emancipation of the European vernaculars from the hegemony of Latin.[8] In a bold generalization Croll did not hesitate to assert that "there is little distortion in the statement that in 1550 all serious, modern thought was expressed in Latin; all that was traditional, or merely popular, in its character tended to find its way into vernacular prose."[9] If this approach is taken with a grain of salt, it will be found that the normal trend it suggests also existed, *mutatis mutandis,* as early as the mid-14th century, at least in Italy. By and large, the mediaeval element prevails in the vernacular works of Boccaccio, whereas the humanistic element permeates his Latin works.

The particular aspect that interests us is one that penetrates Boccaccio's situations in depth. Somewhat paradoxically, this relevance of the "sociological" element is strengthened, not weakened, by Boccaccio's relative neglect of "character" and individual psychology (Chaucer's strong point, conversely) in favour of the general human traits he sets in motion within his situation comedy. This is so much so that the social dimension, when it reaches its most mature stages, sometimes ceases to be an extrinsic question of auxiliary value for the fuller understanding of the context and becomes part of the intrinsic meaning of the story, an essential element of its very structure.

Consider the first story of the first day. The knave Ser Ciappelletto has been hired by a Florentine merchant for the difficult task of collecting from his debtors in the hostile milieu of "those riotous Burgundians." Upon conclusion of his mission he falls seriously ill, and his imminent death threatens to spoil his work, because it will probably expose his business associates to the embarrassing revelation of his past life, a web of unspeakable misdeeds. Ciappelletto averts this danger by making a false confession, after which he becomes widely honoured among the

583

local people as a miracle-working saint. Critics have long been concerned with the religious implications of this story, and with the question of whether the author, here as elsewhere, intended to satirize popular superstition on the subject of cult and sacrament; but the story is more subtle and complex than that. If we read it in a different key we discover that its centre may well be elsewhere, as Branca has convincingly shown in a shrewd interpretation of this "epic of the Florentine merchant," this "*chanson de geste* dei paladini di mercatura."[10] We must look beyond the splendid farce of the false confession with its preposterous outcome, to the circumstances of Ciappelletto's behaviour. Thoroughly wicked as his moral character may be, he is one of those "artists of life" whom the Renaissance will later make its heroes. Morally unscrupulous he always is, but his pride lies in a job well done. Difficulty and improbability are an irresistible challenge to him. Knowing him exactly for what he is, Musciatto Franzesi hires him in full confidence that he is the right person for that unusually difficult job. He turns out to be right, because Ciappelletto will not let him down even in the hour of direst need. His confession is the crowning achievement of a life of forgery and cheating, and—as he puts it—it does not matter much if, in the eyes of God, he will have added one more sin to so many others.[11]

Seen from the point of view of the characters involved, the employer, the employee, and the Florentine usurers who offer their hospitality to Ciappclletto "for the love of Musciatto," everything fits in terms of economic patterns of behaviour and business ethics. The hero is ready to commit his last sin at the point of death because he owes it to Musciatto and his hosts as part of his pledge to do the job for which he is paid. The confession, even artistically, becomes a means rather than an end within the tale. The story must be read against the historical background of the vicious assaults on the "Lombard dogs," which reached the violent proportions of true pogroms at least five times in France between 1277 and 1329, and became even more threatening in the two decades preceding the Black Death of 1348. The earnest consideration of questions of moral conscience adds the powerful chiaroscuro to this hilarious and yet sinister tale.

Boccaccio reacts at the same time as he discovers. His personal attitude toward the mercantile ethic is basically negative, reflecting the quasi-aristocratic orientation of his upbringing; yet he sharply feels its presence so as to represent it as a new reality. He reveals its nature by "representing" it objectively as one who has grown in its midst from his very birth. Ciappelletto violates all human and divine laws and yet remains a humorous object of amused observation. The damnation of his soul is his private tragedy: it is part of the rules of the game, a price to pay for a wanted achievement. The equanimity of the reader is neither challenged nor endangered. The story of Lisabetta (IV, v), however, is a different case. For we must note that, although Boccaccio's discovery of the mercantile ethic leads him to draw an impartial picture of it in its eventual conflicts with legal, social, and "human" morality, he does take a stand at the precise point where that conflict passes beyond legal and social criteria into a transgression against nature.

Three brothers of a family from San Gimignano attend to their firm in Messina. When they discover that their sister Lisabetta is carrying on an affair with a young shop manager—a subordinate with whom, presumably, they cannot conceive of an honourable family alliance through marriage—they quickly decide to murder him as the best and only solution. The plan backfires when Lisabetta, inconsolable over the loss, dies of heartbreak, but not before she has unearthed the body and placed the head of her beloved in a pot of basil. It is this discovery of their murderous plot and the resulting danger of their action becoming public knowledge that, together with Lisabetta's death, marks the social catastrophe, a defeat for the brothers' plan, and the end of the business enterprise they had set out to protect from what was, in their minds, Lisabetta's original blunder. From what appears to be the author's point of view, this outcome is due to the violation of no other laws but those of nature. Neither moralist nor theologian, Boccaccio reveals the "naturalist" drift in his sense of values.

The reader must note the quiet, discreet, matter-of-fact manners of the three brothers. The one who discovers the secret rendezvous of Lisabetta and Lorenzo makes no scandal, like the "wise young man" that he is, but *mosso da più onesto consiglio* (prompted by his better judgment) awaits the morning to consult with the other brothers.[12] The decision is arrived at quickly but with due circumspection, and they patiently wait for the right opportunity to carry it out. The murder is likewise committed with determined, business-like efficiency, and the narrator interjects no judgment, not a single word or twist in the representation that might arouse explicit moral participation on the part of the reader. Again, on discovering the contents of the pot of basil, the brothers quickly dispose of it, burying the head of the dead man, and get out of town "cautiously and without any more words,"[13] after giving the proper instructions to fold up their business there. Now, as before, there is not a word of consideration for poor Lisabetta. Their only concern is their business, and anything that might interfere with this exclusive goal of their lives is to be removed as an intolerable obstacle. Boccaccio does not have to express judgments to uphold his awareness of human values. He seems to be familiar with this breed of men by personal experience, and he "understands" their motives. But although he can understand them, he does not accept them. The heroine of the story is Lisabetta, and her human tragedy upholds the rights of love, the supreme value that economic forces (and their occasional ally, social prejudice, especially because we are in Sicily) have unsuccessfully attempted to crush. The social tragedy (the damage to the brothers' firm) seals the fundamental truth of Boccaccio's *Weltanschauung*: love and nature must not be—indeed, cannot be—thwarted by social institutions or economic considerations.[14] It is interesting to observe that Boccaccio's reticence here shows, for once, that he could understand such strong practical, economic considerations as those of his merchant friends perhaps more easily than mere social prejudice, which often provokes his explicit intervention.

The Mediterranean and European geography of Tuscan commerce is splendidly mirrored in many stories of the *Decameron*: of Alatiel, the Lamberti (in England), Tedaldo and Torello (in the Orient), Landolfo Rufolo, Martuccio, and so on through a large portion of the masterwork. Other relevant stories, however, draw upon experiences that are in no way limited to the sphere of commerce: for example, the baker Cisti (VI, ii) acts through his artisan's pride. The growing self-awareness of the popular classes shown in this story contains at once a mediaeval element and a Renaissance one. It reflects the "democratic" side of mediaeval society, in which every category of productive citizens could, through association into gilds, feel the full dignity of its contribution to the community and individual contentment with its lot as a stable one, as important as any other because equally necessary. At the same time, envy of others was excluded by the virtual impossibility of crossing the barriers between the orders. But Cisti's pride transcends that mediaeval fact and announces the Renaissance by virtue of its heightened individualism and "artistic" sense of value.

Cisti is discreetly but firmly proud of the superior wine he serves. He is the aristocrat of bakers, or, to be more accurate, he plies his trade with natural elegance that is the trademark of expert and conscious workmanship. Note the delightful show he puts on to impress his distinguished customers, standing on the pavement in front of his shop, and looking "like a miller" in his snow-white vest and apron fresh from the laundry. He has a newly tinned bucket of fresh water brought out to him to rinse the clear glasses "that look like silver"; then he sits down, pours some of his white wine out of a small earthen jar, and drinks it with visible relish in view of Messer Geri and his prominent guests, who are passing by. His advertising techniques are, indeed, those of a refined artist. When Geri sends to him for some of that wine, he refuses to fill the order because the large size of the container ill-advisedly produced by the servant is an insult to the quality of the wine. When Geri sees the container, he understands and in good grace accepts Cisti's refusal. The merchant-statesman and the shopkeeper are bound by the tie of sympathetic appreciation for each other's dignity. This democracy in action is reminiscent of the Venetian envoy's famous remarks on the Florentine merchant-princes not being ashamed of direct personal contacts with labour and merchandise as contrasted with the separateness of Venetian aristocratic ship-owners, the ruling class, from the toiling common people.

Human relationships are sometimes placed in social settings that are enlivened by the concreteness of technical descriptions. This is particularly interesting when we are exposed to vivid details of business mentality and practices. Take the story of "The Lover's Gift Regained" (VIII, i): this holds a double interest for us because it is one of those that reappear in Chaucer, and the comparison is instructive.

For once, Boccaccio is more circumstantial than his English counterpart in exploiting professional techniques. The tale is popular enough,[15] and smacks of the French verse tales known as *fabliaux*.[16] It is, once again, about a merchant, and is shot through with the unscrupulous spirit of calculation for gain, all other human consideration being relegated to a background role of decorative irrelevance. The cynicism of the action is clear in both authors, as is the condemnation of the woman whose covetousness is said to have been justly castigated by her lover.[17] Although the details vary, the two versions are identical in the essential plot. A merchant's wife offers herself for money to her husband's friend. The latter borrows the sum from the husband and, after the fact, tells him that he has returned the loaned sum through his wife.

Chaucer stresses the circumstances of the unsavoury covenant and simplifies the denouement through a simple declaration from borrower to creditor in the wife's absence. Boccaccio stresses the procedural details of the "repayment of the loan." The lover hands over the money to the woman in the presence of a friend of his (the woman counting the coins with business-like care), and then informs the husband of his repayment in the presence of both the wife and his own witness-friend. The language is precise in its use of business terms: *utile* (interest), *fornir la bisogna* (close

587

the deal), *dannerai la mia ragione* (close or cancel my account).[18] The explicit understanding between the narrator and his audience is that the woman got what she asked for—to wit, straight business, and at her expense and loss as deserved punishment for mixing pleasure with business, "human" with material values, ethics with economics.[19]

Boccaccio's many-shaded attitude toward the *ragion di mercatura* is conditioned both by his personal experiences and by the shattering crisis into which Italian business circles had fallen after the creatively heroic phase of the preceding generation. In the *Canterbury Tales*, on the other hand, we find the world of merchants to be a robustly, healthily advancing one, whereas the higher classes are bent on a decline, because they tend to express themselves more through the decorative and elegant than through the essential and substantial: their style is the *gothique flamboyant* of the waning Middle Ages.

The Prologue to the *Canterbury Tales* has long impressed the analyst as an almost complete survey of social types—a *comédie humaine in nuce*.[20] The first character to be portrayed is the Knight, and this charming personage well deserves a close look. As witnessed by Crécy, Aljubarrota, and later Agincourt, the knighted orders throughout Europe were becoming increasingly divorced from the realities of battlefield ethics and tactics in the course of the century, even while they withdrew more and more into the ceremonious glory of jousts and courtly rituals. The squires of France and England showed that they sensed the quixotic shallowness of the costly honour of knighthood when they started to shirk it because of its onerous public obligations. Indeed Chaucer's portrait of the Knight and his small company of Squire and Yeoman *and servantz namo* suggests, not without a brush-stroke of subtle, perhaps even melancholy, humour, that appearing in public is a costly affair for a knight, even on a holy pilgrimage. Consequently, his "array" is dignified, as is required, but it is not impressive:

> His hors were goode, but he was nat gay.

The description is not romantic but realistic in a rather bourgeois key. He still wears his campaign accoutrements, because he proceeded without delay from his latest military journey to the pilgrimage without changing his travel-stained clothing:

> Of fustian he wered a gypon
> Al bismotered with his habergeon.[21]

We are reminded of Boccaccio, who, although more disposed to invest the dream-like world of chivalry with a literary and romantic aura, cannot refrain from interjecting here and there a token of his bourgeois common sense. Think of the shattering though good-humoured effect of his intervention when he ironically encases the haunting pathos of Federigo's tale (V, ix) in the conclusive remark that, once he had reached, somewhat paradoxically, his longed-for goal of obtaining Monna Giovanna's hand, he showed himself *miglior massaio fatto* (a better manager of his affairs). At long last he gave up the magnificent liberality that had once ruined him even while it proved him a worthy knight, and developed a welcome bourgeois discretion for the management of the newly acquired household. We almost hear the narrator exclaim, with Leon Battista Alberti: *Questa santa masserizia!* (Oh, the holy art of wisely managing a patrimony!) [22] A discreet, almost casual stroke of this sort is perhaps more revealing than many a direct statement, because it works in depth and betrays something of the author's inner nature.

The world of the religious orders plays a major role in both works, and along somewhat similar lines. Chaucer's Daun Piers thinks little of St Augustine's monastic rules:

> Lat Austyn have his swynk to hym reserved.

He dislikes fasting, and enjoys good cheer and expensive clothing. Perhaps more seriously, he is a frequent *outridere*: that is, he wanders away from his cloister into the world, where, Chaucer warns us, a monk is like a fish out of water. There he takes advantage of his fast hounds and numerous horses, for he is fond of *venerie*. Equally scornful of St Francis's intent are the modern Grey or Mendicant Friars of the Franciscan Order: of the collections to which begging rights entitle him in his assigned territory (the rights of *lymytour*), Chaucer's Friar keeps more for himself as illegitimate personal *purchas* than he hands over to the Order (*rente*). Such details reveal in the author an observant and experienced man of business.* Now, among the men of the cloth there is one character who deserves our special attention. A reader of both story-tellers is immediately reminded of Fra Cipolla (*Dec.* VI, x) when reading of Chaucer's Pardoner—but with a difference. They are both, in their own way, profitably eloquent (at least at the expense of the rustic audiences they cleverly spellbind and cynically

---

* When Eustache Deschamps, in a ballad sent to Chaucer in 1386, praised the English poet by comparing him to Socrates, Seneca, Aulus Gellius, and Ovid, he was pointing out by the particular reference to Gellius the double activity of Chaucer as man of letters and man of law. See T. ATKINSON JENKINS, "Deschamps' Ballade to Chaucer," *Modern Language Notes* XXXIII (Baltimore 1918), pp. 266–78; and J. M. MANLY (ed.), *The Canterbury Tales* (New York 1928), pp. 22 ff.

589

exploit), and both operate by offering false and absurd relics for sale to the gullible. The Pardoner carries a wallet

> bretful of pardoun, commen from Rome al hoot,

including a pillowcase he palms off as Our Lady's Veil and a rag he offers as part of the sail from St Peter's boat. Fra Cipolla bears a feather from the Archangel Gabriel's wings, or, rather—as he nimbly corrects himself—coals from St Lawrence's martyrdom. He belongs to the Friars of St Anthony, long discredited for their unscrupulous practices in collecting alms and often censured as impostors, as in 1240 by Pope Gregory IX.[23] The Pardoner, in turn, is from "Rouncivale"—perhaps the famous convent of St Mary Roncevall near Charing Cross, which was involved in two scandals concerning the sale of indulgences in 1379 and 1387 while Chaucer was in London. The difference in these characterizations lies in the fact that Boccaccio shows none of the moral concern that informs Chaucer's brand of realism. For Boccaccio, the wicked ways of the swindler in religious cloth are chiefly a spectacle to be enjoyed for its artfulness. Chaucer's Pardoner, in his marvellously obsessive story against the Capital Sins, builds up the *leit-motiv* of avarice as the fountainhead of all evils. He cynically exploits all the rhetorical apparatus to bring his naive audience round to his own end—to collect alms by indirectness: Give up your greedy attachment to your money and hand it over to me. Hence the Pardoner becomes the symbolic capitalist of religion. He uses it without any scruples for the sole practical aim of personal gain.

The enjoyment of wealth takes a charming twist in the worldly side of the Prioress, who not only shows a keen decorative sense of material refinements (note her golden brooch, the pleated head-dress, even the spoiled dogs), but lets this exquisite if somewhat ambiguous worldliness pervade even her spiritual attitudes and emerge through the imagery of her language: she refers to the little martyr of her tale as

> This gemme of chastite, this emeraude,
> And eek of martirdom the ruby bright.[24]

As with Boccaccio, so with Chaucer we find technical details introduced within the characterization of men of business and in the settings appropriate to their activities. We find it first of all in the portrait of the Merchant. Just as the Major Arts of Lana, Calimala, and Cambio dominated commerce in Florence, so two companies of Merchants enjoyed the lion's share in Chaucer's London: the Merchant Adventurers (agents living on the Continent to oversee the distribution of English cloth in the local markets), and the Staplers (or Merchants of the Staple: exporters of wool, felts, and hides). Less conservative—and frequently riotous in Chaucer's day—were the lower corporations, the gilds of special retailers and craftsmen (brewers, tanners, mercers, fishmongers, blacksmiths, and the like). Different from the main craft gilds were the parish gilds, organized by territory of residence rather than by trade. Chaucer's five gildsmen (General Prologue, lines 361–2) belong to one of these latter *fraternitees*:*

> An Haberdasshere and a Carpenter,
> A Webbe, a Dyere, and a Tapycer.

The portrait of Chaucer's Merchant (lines 270–84) gives away some of his secrets. Besides concentrating his attention on *th'encrees of his wynnyng* and *bargaynes*, which is more or less normal, and of course lending at interest, which was common practice though accompanied by some pangs of conscience, he also conceals with great care the fact that he is in debt:

> Ther wiste no wight that he was in dette[25]

—an interesting revelation if we accept Miss Rickert's suggestion[26] that our character is to be identified with the enormously wealthy Merchant Adventurer Gilbert Maghfeld, who died in bankruptcy. Furthermore, he breaks the law by dealing in foreign exchange: *in eschaunge scheeldes selle* (*scheeldes*, shields; Fr. *escuz*, meaning gold coins). He is also greatly concerned that the freedom of the sea between the Dutch port of Middleburgh (the chartered base of both Staplers and Adventurers) and the English one of Orwell be kept open to traffic "at all cost":

> He wolde the see were kept for any thyng
> Bitwixe Middleburgh and Orewelle.

It has been suggested that Chaucer's declaration that the Merchant's name is unknown to him may be a shrewd hint at the anonymity a merchant in debt would try to preserve for prudence, in case he had to leave town suddenly to escape his creditors, should some alarming event be

---

* We should remember that Chaucer's London, a large busy town for its day, was less than half as large as and far less busy than the Florence of Boccaccio's youth (perhaps 40,000 people as against probably 100,000). Florence had grown from 30,000 to 90,000 during the 13th century.

temporarily feared, such as a delay in his ships' arrivals. A pilgrimage could offer as good an excuse as any for such dodging of impending danger. As to money-lending practices, one remembers that in "The Shipman's Tale" the monk and the merchant discuss *chevyssaunce* with apparent uneasiness.[27] *Chevyssaunce* was the current English term for usury, as frequently condemned as it was widely and regularly practised.

One aspect of Chaucer's realism is the pluralistic assimilation of his characters' varying ethics and points of view.[28] Similarly, his realistic method is typified by a strong interrelationship between teller and tale. Thus, using a tale to develop the character of the teller, Chaucer seems to give us in the tale of January and May a demonstration of something that stands very close to the Merchant's heart: the general unfitness of women to have the *gouvernaunce* of the household, which is the Merchant's answer to the Wife of Bath's triumphant and defiant posing as champion of feminine prerogatives. May, who might well be intended as a symbolic portrait of the Merchant's own wife, is thus, *mutatis mutandis*, a supporting role to the Clerk's Griselda, the other reply to the Wife of Bath's case.[29] What impresses us most directly is that such concern for the establishment of the rightful roles in the administration of family affairs should be expressed by the Merchant, upholder *par excellence* of the economic view of the family as the natural social "business," as it so conspicuously was in the Middle Ages. The temptation to think once again of Alberti's *Trattato della famiglia* (*c.* 1432–41) is too strong to be resisted, because the great humanist, member and illustrator of one of the prominent merchant families of Florence, introduces what, in its context, seems to be such a typically Renaissance perspective into the notion of the family as the individual's first and supreme social allegiance, to be run efficiently and pragmatically (even, in a sense, "unsentimentally") as a business firm, of which the *paterfamilias* is, of course, head, president, and manager.

We are thus confronted with the two opposite theses: that of the man as master of the family, and that of the woman as its mistress. The former appears set within the vantage point of the city merchant class, the latter within the lower class (Alisoun, the Wife of Bath, is a proud weaver, an artisan from the country). The additional supporting story of Griselda is the Clerk's discreet, implicit response to Alisoun's stand, of which he disapproves. But the Clerk is a moralist intellectual, and as such outside Alisoun's matter-of-fact world. Rather, he reflects the age-long misogyny of the intellectual, which found its adherents among mediaeval ascetics and many Renaissance humanists as well. We sense, therefore, a sort of hesitation and uneasiness on his part: he tries to limit the possibly shocking literal impact of his story, and—hiding behind the authority of his source, the "worthy clerk" called "Fraunceis Petrak, the lauriat poete"—calls attention to the story's symbolic and paradigmatic value ("be constant in adversitee"), rather than putting forward a practical standard of conduct.[30]

E. T. Donaldson has suggested that "if there is anyone [in "The Merchant's Tale"] who enjoys the Merchant's approval it is Justinus, whose hard-headed and cheaply cynical counsel makes the good mercantile point that a man ought to examine goods very carefully before he buys them. Still, his conclusion seems to be the same as the Merchant's: the goods, if a woman, will cheat you anyhow."[31] Yet Chaucer displays here more brilliantly than anywhere else his talent for "making a poem assume a meaning unknown to the fictional narrator"[32] (even while it does fit with his character). The Merchant shows through his story the tragic flaws in his own philosophy of life; people, and especially women, are not and cannot be treated like commercial goods and pieces of property, or as playthings to satisfy man's lust. Because this seems to be the only relationship he can understand, he fails, and the ignominious behaviour of May is as much the consequence of January's stupidity and "mercantilism" as of her own character.

Indeed Chaucer is a master of indirectness; he suggests more than he states. Yet Donaldson's analysis, though interesting and perhaps typical of the mercantile interpretation of this episode, appears somewhat exaggerated and not quite acceptable in all its literalness. For Justinus does not suggest that wives should be examined like goods, but rather that a future husband should

> right wel avyse
> To whom he yeveth his lond or his catel.
> And syn I oghte avyse me right wel
> To whom I yeve my good awey fro me,
> Wel muchel moore I oghte avysed be
> To whom I yeve my body for alwey.[33]

On the other hand, though not so crude and cynical as Donaldson makes it appear, Justinus's counsel does move within the same sphere of mercantile mentality as that in which both the Merchant and January move. They speak conspicuously of property, and are saddened at seeing their bargains come out short.

We turn, instead, to the surroundings of the aristocratic world when the compromise thesis is advanced in the chivalric climate of "The

Franklin's Tale." Here partnership, reciprocity, and mutual devotion in marriage are submitted as the happy mean, the perfect *gentilesse*. But again, Arveragus and Dorigen move in the remote courtly milieu that can only abstractly and ideally (shall we say literarily?) convince a woman of Alisoun's stamp. Yet note how *trouthe*—the virtue of moral integrity or honour that is the centre of the tale—is defined as a "thing," a legal contract such as might result from a commercial transaction. The bourgeois spirit, which to this extent pervades even the aristocratic climate of this "Breton lay," demands that a legal contract be kept at all costs, and in this it temporarily coincides, or can be made to coincide, with the sense of chivalric honour. Incidentally, although Aurelius matches Arveragus's magnanimity with his own sacrifice, he bemoans his indebtedness to the magician, to whom he must in faith pay "of pured gold a thousand pound of wighte" and so ruin himself. Still, pay he must and pay he will—by instalments, "yeer by yeer." He can thus keep his word as a true knight thanks to the time-honoured mercantile device of credit payment.[34]

What can one say of the economic involvement of such delightful characters as the Reeve, the Manciple, the Franklin? With curious and expert care, Chaucer underlines their professional operations. Social consciousness is likewise pervasive in the dramatic interchanges between the pilgrims. The Reeve feels insulted by the Miller's tale of a carpenter, because he has been a carpenter himself; so he tells about a miller, to repay his offender in kind: "Thus have I quyt the Millere in my tale."[35] The miller of "The Reeve's Tale" is socially conscious to an aggressive degree: he takes special delight in cheating two clerks to show that

> Yet kan a millere make a clerkes berd
> For al his art.[36]

Then, when the clerks ask him for lodging, he makes fun of them, daring them to make room where there is none by using their style of speech, of which they are such masters:

> Myn hous is streit, but ye han lerned art:
> Ye konne by argumentes make a place
> A myle brood of twenty foot of space:
> Lat se now if this place may suffise,
> Or make it rowm with speche, as is youre gise.[37]

Such a keen observer of the concrete side of life will not entirely depart from such attitudes even in less realistic works than the *Tales*. The contrasts between the different groups of birds in *The Parliament of Fowls*

594

(*c.* 1385), for example, must be appreciated first of all for their artistic and literary value: the courtly language of noble birds such as the hawks is set against the materialistic common sense of the water fowl and domestic fowl in a way that reveals Chaucer's keen instinct for comedy. Yet we cannot and must not forget that underlying all this is a clear implication of social satire on the basis of rank and status. Just as the birds of prey inexorably stand for the aristocracy, so the water fowl represent the magnates of commerce, while the worm fowl recall the qualities of the lower middle class, and the seed fowl the peasant estate. The possible derivation of this classificatory approach from Aristotle through the 13th-century scholar Vincent of Beauvais merely confirms the more-than-literary, if not directly extra-literary, overtones of the text.

So far, this discussion has stressed an aspect of their work in which Boccaccio and Chaucer find common ground. For the sake of true historical understanding, however, one must be fully aware of the contrasts as well as the parallels. Boccaccio's "objective" presentation of patterns of behaviour based on professional and business ethics foreshadows one of the most peculiar developments of the Italian Renaissance, namely the gradual and painful discarding of mediaeval absolutism toward a relativistic realization of the "autonomy" of every sphere of human activity. Even though man is always whole in his experience and action, the standards by which we understand and judge any given act of decision must be based on the particular sphere to which it more properly belongs. Thus art will no longer need defending from the charge of philosophical untruthfulness, because it belongs to the aesthetic not the logical realm; political action (witness Machiavelli) has its own "reason of state" independently of—and even contrasting with—morality and religion; and the *homo oeconomicus* virtually comes into his own, at least *in nuce*, without the feeling, which so many last wills of mediaeval businessmen clearly showed, that hard-won gain is by definition a moral sin before God. Chaucer, on the other hand, still moves within the northern concern for the harmonious unity of judgment: his representation, sympathetic and realistic though it may be, always converges toward the final goal of satisfying a firm moral need.

References

1. *Satyricon*, 119–24. This 295-line epic has been controversially regarded as an indirect critique of Lucan's style and an exposition of Petronius's own views on literature, particularly the epic.
2. Cf. HANS BARON "Franciscan Poverty and Civic Wealth as Factors in the Rise of Humanistic Thought," *Speculum* XIII (Cambridge, Mass. 1938); see also Baron's *The Crisis of the Early Italian Renaissance*, 2nd edn (Princeton 1966).
3. JOSEPH BÉDIER, *The Romance of Tristan and Yseult* (New York 1955), p. 34. The passage is from the chapter "The Quest of the Lady with the Hair of Gold," which draws upon the text of Eilhart von Oberg's *Tristrant* (see F. Lichtenstein's edition of Eilhart [Strasbourg 1877], pp. 85 ff., lines 1465 ff.).
4. BÉDIER, *op. cit.*, p. 35
5. "The Wife of Bath's Tale," III [D], 1125. All passages from the *Canterbury Tales* are quoted from *The Works of Geoffrey Chaucer*, ed. by F. N. Robinson, 2nd edn (London 1957).
6. Cf. IGNAZIO BALDELLI, "Sulla teoria linguistica di Dante," *Cultura e Scuola* 13–4 (Rome 1965), pp. 705–13.
7. Vittore Branca's studies of the textual tradition have shown how the manuscripts of the *Decameron* circulated mainly among the mercantile groups during the 15th century.
8. See *Style, Rhetoric, and Rhythm: Essays by Morris W. Croll*, ed. by J. Max Patrick and Robert O. Evans (Princeton 1966), pp. 181–7.
9. *ibid.*, p. 182.
10. VITTORE BRANCA, *Boccaccio medievale* (Florence 1956), Ch. III, "L'epopea mercantile," pp. 71–99.
11. I, i, 28 (pp. 53–4). The page numbers, here and subsequently, refer to *Decameron*, ed. by Vittore Branca, 2nd edn (Florence 1965).
12. IV, v, 6 (p. 514).
13. *ibid.*, 22 (p. 518).
14. BRANCA, *op. cit.*, pp. 85–6; see also ALDO D. SCAGLIONE, *Nature and Love in the Late Middle Ages* (Berkeley 1963), especially p. 71.
15. Cf. STITH THOMPSON, *Motif-Index of Folk-Literature* (Bloomington, Ind. 1955), K 1581.3.
16. Cf. the *fabliau, Du bouchier d'Abevile*, in ANATOLE DE MONTAIGLON and GASTON RAYNAUD (ed.) *Recueil général et complet des fabliaux des XIIIᵉ et XIVᵉ siècles imprimés ou inédits, publiés d'après les manuscrits* (New York 1963), Vol. III, pp. 227–46.
17. VIII, i, 18 (p. 880): . . . *e così il sagace amante senza costo godé della sua avara donna* (and thus the cunning lover enjoyed his greedy woman at no cost).
18. For further examples of technical jargon from commerce, see BRANCA, *op. cit.*, pp. 97–8, footnote 21.
19. VIII, i, 3–4 (pp. 876–7).

20. In his famous *Preface* to a volume of translations from Homer, Ovid, Boccaccio, and Chaucer, John Dryden, "the father of English criticism," was perhaps the first to praise *The Canterbury Tales* for the way they realistically and imaginatively mirror the English society of their day: "I see ... all the pilgrims ..., their humours, their features, and their very dress as distinctly as if I had supped with them at the *Tabard* in Southwark." See the text in W. P. KER (ed.), *Dryden: Preface to the Fables* (Oxford 1928), p. 14. For a general evaluation of the *Preface*, see J. W. H. ATKINS, *English Literary Criticism: 17th and 18th Centuries* (London 1951), especially pp. 134–8. Dryden goes on to stress the comprehensiveness of these characters, which embrace the manners and peculiarities of the whole nation as Chaucer saw it: "not one has escaped him." More specifically, each character stood out in his or her individuality, and yet qualities were invariably attributed to them that appeared becoming to their respective callings and social conditions. Indeed, this manner of social background so methodically invests the characters that it extends to the very tales they tell—a measure of artistic excellence that does not escape Dryden's sensitivity.

Of course, this very same awareness of artistic quality does not allow Dryden to stop at the realization of the social dimension. He is quick to point out that Chaucer's portraits go clearly beyond that: they are graced with a blending of the particular with the universal that makes them meaningful to Dryden's own English contemporaries and to all mankind. Furthermore, Dryden's enthusiastic response to Chaucer's poetic gifts prompted him to rank the mediaeval English poet on a par with such other classic story-tellers as Ovid and Boccaccio. Today's critic, who has come to realize how clearly and fully Boccaccio belonged to his mediaeval contemporary society, would have no hesitation in underwriting such a *rapprochement*. But to Dryden's contemporaries it must have come as a surprise, for they were accustomed to overlook the question of chronology and historical circumstances for the benefit of the Italian narrator: Boccaccio, like his contemporary Petrarch, had become identified with the "modern" tastes and criteria established by humanism and the Renaissance, of which the two Tuscans had been, in their own different ways, fathers and "princes."

21. I [A], 75–6.
22. Cf. *Della famiglia* III, p. 165, line 32, in LEON BATTISTA ALBERTI, *Opere volgari*, ed. by C. Grayson, Vol. I (Bari 1960). This is a sort of *leitmotiv* in the work; cf. *Santa cosa la masserizia ... !* (A holy thing good husbandry is!), *ibid.*, p. 163, line 26.
23. Cf. Dante's *Di questo ingrassa il porco Sant'Antonio* . . . (On this St Anthony's pigs get fattened), *Paradiso* XXIX, line 124 ff.
24. VII [B²], 1799–1800, 609–10.
25. But see OSCAR E. JOHNSON, "Was Chaucer's Merchant in Debt? A Study in Chaucerian Syntax and Rhetoric," *Journal of English and*

Germanic Philology LII (Urbana, Ill. 1953), pp. 50–7; and JOHN K. CRANE, "An Honest Debtor? A Note on Chaucer's Merchant, Line A 276," *English Language Notes* IV (Boulder, Colo. 1966), pp. 81–5.

26. EDITH RICKERT, "Extracts from a Fourteenth-Century Account Book," *Modern Philology* XXIV (Chicago 1926), pp. 111–9 and 249–56.

27. VII [B²], 1519 ff., 329 ff.

28. Cf. PAULL F. BAUM, *Chaucer: A Critical Appreciation* (Durham, N. C. 1958), pp. 108–9: "Realism is of two kinds. One is that which is confected for the common reader, who has no imagination and little memory, who asks no more than that what he is given should resemble what he knows . . . . It is preoccupied with the phenomenal world. . . . Chaucer sometimes achieves the higher realism, beyond the empirical, and along with it comes that detachment and amoral attitude which refuses to be embroiled with moral judgments, which makes his weak characters pardonable and his villains companionable."

29. Without going into the merits of Kittredge's "marriage group" theory, I find it fair to extract from this sequence of the tales the elements that respond to a contrapuntal commentary on woman's social function, whether or not they represent a systematic whole or even something central to the individual tales. Cf. G. L. KITTREDGE, *Chaucer and His Poetry* (Cambridge, Mass. 1915).

30. Cf. IV [E], 1142–8.

31. E. T. DONALDSON (ed.), *Chaucer's Poetry* (New York 1958), p. 921.

32. *ibid.*, p. 923. Donaldson's interpretation would be further undermined if we accepted Bronson's hypothesis that the connection of "The Merchant's Prologue" with "The Merchant's Tale" is only accidental, and an afterthought on the part of the author. One might insist, however, that even an afterthought must result from a way of reading—or re-reading—as Harrington has suggested. See BRONSON and HARRINGTON in Bibliography, below.

33. IV [E], 1524–9.

34. On the harmonization of ethics, courtly love, and the conjugal fulfilment in perfect equality according to Chrétien de Troyes (*fl. c.* 1165–85), see MOSHÉ LAZAR, *Amour courtois et "fin'amors" dans la littérature du XII* siècle (Paris 1964), especially pp. 241–52.

35. I [A], 4324.

36. *ibid.*, 4096–7.

37. *ibid.*, 4122–6.

Bibliography

Social and Economic Background

G. G. COULTON, *Chaucer and His England* (London and New York 1963); *Life in the Middle Ages*, 4 vols. (Cambridge 1928); *Mediaeval Panorama* (Cambridge 1939).

JOHAN HUIZINGA, *The Waning of the Middle Ages*, trans. by F. Hopman (London 1924).

J. J. JUSSERAND, *English Wayfaring Life in the Middle Ages*, trans. by L. T. Smith (London 1890).

YVES RENOUARD, *Les hommes d'affaires italiens du moyen âge* (Paris 1949).

L. R. SALZMAN, *English Trade in the Middle Ages* (Oxford 1931).

ARMANDO SAPORI, *La crisi delle compagnie mercantili dei Bardi e dei Peruzzi* (Florence 1926); *Una compagnia di Calimala ai primi del trecento* (Florence 1932); *Mercatores* (Milan 1941); *Le marchand italien au moyen âge* (Paris 1952); *Studi di storia economica medievale*, 3 vols, 3rd edn (Florence 1956).

ARMANDO SAPORI (ed.), *I libri di commercio dei Peruzzi* (Milan 1934); *I libri della ragione bancaria dei Gianfigliazzi* (Milan 1946).

HENRY OSBORN TAYLOR, *The Medieval Mind* (London 1930).

G. M. TREVELYAN, *England in the Age of Wycliffe* (London 1925).

FREDERICK TUPPER, *Types of Society in Medieval Literature* (New York 1926).

GEORGE UNWIN, *The Gilds and Companies of London* (London 1938).

RENÉ WELLEK and AUSTIN WARREN, *Theory of Literature*, 2nd edn (New York 1956), "Literature and Society," pp. 82–98.

H. F. WESTLAKE, *The Parish Gilds of Medieval England* (London 1919).

Also recommended are the more general studies of mediaeval economic history by, for instance, A. Doren, R. S. Lopez, G. Luzzatto, C. E. Perrin, A. Segre, C. Verlinden, and M. Weber.

Chaucer

MURIEL BOWDEN, *A Commentary on the General Prologue to the Canterbury Tales* (New York 1957); *A Reader's Guide to Geoffrey Chaucer* (New York 1964).

D. S. BREWER, "Class Distinction in Chaucer," *Speculum* XLIII (Cambridge, Mass. 1968), pp. 290–305.

BERTRAND H. BRONSON, "Afterthoughts on 'The Merchant's Tale'," *Studies in Philology* LVIII (Chapel Hill, N. C. 1961), pp. 583–96.

E. T. DONALDSON, *Speaking of Chaucer* (New York 1970).

THOMAS J. GARBÁTY, "Chaucer's Guildsmen and their Fraternity," *Journal of English and Germanic Philology* (Urbana, Ill. 1960), pp. 691–709.

ROBERT S. HALLER, "The Wife of Bath and the Three Estates," *Annuale Mediaevale* VI (Pittsburgh 1965), pp. 47–64.

NORMAN T. HARRINGTON, "Chaucer's 'Merchant's Tale': Another Swing of the Pendulum," *Publications of the Modern Language Association of America* 86 (New York 1971), pp. 25–31.

ALBERT E. HARTUNG, "The Non-Comic 'Merchant's Tale,' Maximianus, and the Sources," *Mediaeval Studies* 29 (Toronto 1967), pp. 1–25.

TOSHINORI HIRA, "Chaucer's Gentry in the Historical Background," *Essays in English and American Literature*, In Commemoration of Professor Takejiro Nakayama's Sixty-First Birthday (Tokyo 1961), pp. 325–44.

JOE HORRELL, "Chaucer's Symbolic Plowman," *Speculum* XIV (Cambridge, Mass. 1939), pp. 89–92.

RONALD R. HOWARD, "The Conclusion of the Marriage Group: Chaucer and the Human Condition," *Modern Philology* LVII (Chicago 1960), pp. 223–32.

MAURICE HUSSEY, A. C. SPEARING, and JAMES WINNY, *An Introduction to Chaucer* (Cambridge 1965).

G. L. KITTREDGE, *Chaucer and his Poetry* (Cambridge, Mass. 1915).

THOMAS A. KNOTT, "Chaucer's Anonymous Merchant," *Philological Quarterly* I (Iowa City 1922), pp. 1–16.

ERNEST P. KUHL, "Chaucer's Burgesses," *Transactions of the Wisconsin Academy of Sciences, Arts, and Letters* XVIII (Madison 1916), pp. 652–75.

ROGER SHERMAN LOOMIS, *A Mirror of Chaucer's World* (Princeton 1965).

JOHN M. MANLY, *Some New Light on Chaucer* (New York 1926).

CLAIR C. OLSON and MARTIN M. CROW (ed.), *Chaucer's World*, compiled by Edith Rickert (New York and London 1962); *Chaucer's Life Records* (Oxford 1966).

RICHARD J. SCHOECK and JEROME TAYLOR (ed.), *Chaucer Criticism*, 2 vols. (Notre Dame, Ind. 1960).

GARDINER STILLWELL, "Chaucer's Plowman and the Contemporary English Peasant," *English Literary History* VI (Baltimore 1939), pp. 285–90.

SYLVIA L. THRUPP, *The Merchant Class of Medieval London* (Chicago 1948).

KARL P. WENTERSDORF, "Theme and Structure in 'The Merchant's Tale': the Function of the Pluto Episode," *Publications of the Modern Language Association of America* 80 (New York 1965), pp. 522–7.

ARNOLD WILLIAMS, "The 'Limitour' of Chaucer's Time and His 'Limitacioun'," *Studies in Philology* LVII (Chapel Hill, N. C. 1960), pp. 463–78.

CHAPTER 18

The Individual in the Mediaeval World: Dante's "Divina commedia"

Anthony Thorlby[*]

> Pensa che questo dì mai non raggiorna![1]
>
> (Think: this day will never dawn again!)

No work of literature sums up the culture of mediaeval Europe more completely than Dante's *Divina commedia* (*c.* 1306–21). In so doing, however, it does not simply remain confined within the limited spheres of knowledge and understanding that it is tempting to regard, in retrospect, as "typically mediaeval." The order of those spheres, which is at the same time tidy and confused, as simple and massive in its construction as a cathedral and no less crammed with ornament and detail, is still closely observed by Dante, down to the last detail of Ptolemaic astronomy and the still active debate on the hierarchy of the heavenly hosts. But his genius is such that he can, precisely, *observe* it. In a very important sense Dante stands already outside that order. This does not mean that he is able to see anything but an entirely mediaeval picture of the world. *What* he sees is a scene that belongs altogether to the past; indeed, it illustrates very well what was regarded in Dante's day as the past, as history, as well as what counted as knowledge generally in a universe where the natural and the supernatural were so apparently contiguous in experience that it was hardly conceivable they should not be continuous in "science."[†] But the manner in which Dante presents his vision of this world is altogether distinctive. He has added the perspective of personal experience; he is present as a man in the cosmos of mediaeval realities; and although these may long since have become literally

---

[*] Professor of Comparative Literature, University of Sussex.
[†] See Ch. 7, "Christian Thought," and Ch. 8, "Mediaeval Ideas of History."

incredible, Dante's voice and mind are as real to us now as those of any character in literature.

That Dante was aware he was exploring a new dimension of experience is apparent from the number of times he calls the reader's attention to the fact that he is a real man in a realm of spirits. (This realm preserves its interest for us, despite its mediaeval costume, partly because, by comparison with Dante's role in it as a living man, it is a prototype of what we should nowadays call the "world of the imagination," and reveals a great deal about how the imagination works, as we shall see later.) This fundamental contrast between the still-mortal existence of Dante the protagonist and the immortal condition of every other person and thing he encounters is most obvious perhaps in the *Purgatorio*, where time and again Dante remarks on the fact that he casts a shadow, whereas no-one else does. Out of this simple idea Dante develops each time a different variation, which sometimes hints at a quite subtle thought and is not simply dramatic décor. For instance, when Dante meets his friend Casella, who is said to have set to music some of Dante's poems, he tries to embrace him—in vain, for Casella is an empty shade (*ombre vane*).[2] This mistaken gesture of affection is repeated on one other occasion, when Statius realizes who Virgil is, and here Statius makes a revealing comment on his mistake:

> . . . "Or puoi la quantitate
> comprender dell'amor ch'a te mi scalda
> quand'io dismento nostra vanitate
> trattando l'ombre come cosa salda."[3]

> ("Now thou canst comprehend the measure of the love that burns me for thee, when I forget our emptiness and treat shades as something solid.")

In each case two artists are involved, and the implication is that artists are particularly liable to make this mistake of "treating shades as something solid": as it were, to try to embrace figments of the imagination as real. Admittedly, it is a sign of love, as Statius says; and love is deeply associated for Dante with the prime inspiration of art, as is clear from the opening pages of the *Vita nuova* (*c.* 1292) to the summit of the *Paradiso*. But it is possible for this love to lead a man astray, so that he tries to embrace what is not real (another instance of this misuse of imaginative passion will be discussed later in connection with the Siren).

This point may be emphasized by a glance at two other passages where Virgil reproves Dante for becoming too obsessed by seeing his own shadow but no-one else's. On the first occasion, Dante's trust that he is being safely guided by Virgil is suddenly shaken and he is afraid:

> Io mi volsi da lato con paura
>   d'essere abbandonato, quand'io vidi
>   solo dinanzi a me la terra oscura;
> e 'l mio conforto "Perchè pur diffidi?"
>   a dir mi cominciò tutto rivolto:
>   "non credi tu me teco e ch'io ti guidi?"[4]

(I turned aside with fear that I was abandoned when I saw the ground darkened only in front of myself; and my comfort began to say to me, turning quite round: "Why art thou again distrustful? Dost thou not believe that I am with thee and guide thee?")

The second occasion gives rise to a still more explicit reproach from Virgil; here we see that Dante is evidently not just to be pitied for the frightening situation he finds himself in but is actually guilty of something. The incident begins because one of the spirits in Purgatory, noticing that Dante casts a shadow, cries out that here is one who "seems to bear himself like one alive."[5] Dante is brought to a near standstill by being reminded again of the difference between his mortal state and the condition of eternity (the world experienced by his imagination); and instead of committing the first error—of being carried away by love to overlook the difference—he commits the reverse one of doubt and disbelief, which sap the will with fruitless thought. Virgil protests:

> "Perchè l'animo tuo tanto s'impiglia"
>   disse 'l maestro, "che l'andare allenti?
>   che ti fa ciò che quivi si pispiglia?...
> chè sempre l'uomo in cui pensier rampolla
>   sovra pensier, da sè dilunga il segno
>   perchè la foga l'un dell'altro insolla."[6]

("Why is thy mind so entangled," said the Master, "that thou slackenest thy pace? What is it to thee what they whisper here?... for always the man in whom thought rises up upon thought, sets his mark further back, because the one thought saps the force of the other.")

In order to understand what Dante's paralysing thoughts may have been, several other details should be mentioned. One of the most obvious is the way the spirits repeatedly notice his shadow, a realistic detail that emphasizes his own sense of solitary self-hood:

> ... e vidile guardar per meraviglia
>   pur me, pur me, e 'l lume ch'era rotto.[7]

(and I saw that they looked in amazement at me, at me alone, and at the light that was broken.)

The spirit's astonishment focusses attention—Dante's attention especially, and that of the reader—momentarily on the wrong thing; or, to be more precise, it *fixes* attention on the person of the poet bringing him to a standstill and threatens to interrupt the progress of the poem. The problem posed by Dante's inspiration as a poet, which is to reconcile his spiritual gift of imagination with the fact of his being an erring man, physically alive in the world of the spirit, cannot be solved by standing still and thinking about himself and the puzzle of his situation. The *Commedia* becomes the "answer" to this problem and it is a poem about movement, a pilgrimage to the source of the light, which, by his individual presence, he "breaks." As Dante moves from the imaginative Hell of the *Inferno* to the imaginative Heaven of the *Paradiso*, the reason and purpose of his spiritually puzzling place in the world are made clearer to him. "Amazement" (*maraviglia*), along with many more painful and violent reactions, greets his appearance in Hell, most memorably perhaps in the exclamation of Brunetto Latini on seeing Dante there in the flesh: "*Qual maraviglia!*" he exclaims, and goes on to ask:

> "Qual fortuna o destino
> anzi l'ultimo dì qua giù ti mena. . .?"[8]
>
> (What chance or destiny brings thee down here before thy last day. . .?)

Brunetto asks his question in quite pagan terms (just as Dante will answer him simply that Virgil, his pagan master, has brought him here). The contrast is striking with the amazement of the souls in Purgatory, and above all those in Paradise, who increasingly comprehend, and comment on, Dante's coming to the spiritual world as a sign of grace. His privileged position is still stressed as unique, but the terms of reference for Dante's understanding of it are steadily enlarged. Thus he is asked who he is, on the second terrace of Purgatory, but at the same time told the answer as to why his presence is such a *maraviglia*:

> "O anima che fitta
> nel corpo ancora inver lo ciel ten vai,
> per carità ne consola e ne ditta
> onde vieni e chi se'; chè tu ne fai
> tanto maravigliar della tua grazia
> quanto vuol cosa che non fu più mai."[9]
>
> ("O soul who art going towards heaven while still enclosed in thy body, of thy charity give us satisfaction and tell us whence thou comest and who thou art; for thou dost make us marvel as greatly at thy grace as much as a thing must that never was before.")

Many other examples could be cited of how Dante dwells on the distinctive status he enjoys in the spiritual world of the *Commedia*. Whether it is through the way his foot kicks a stone in Hell, or the way gravity is reversed in Paradise, he never allows his readers to forget that he is there as a real man; and not just as any man, but as himself, the writer, the scholar, the intellectual whose deepest and ultimate desire is for knowledge. As a result he establishes a new sense of perspective between the mind that knows and the world it sees, a perspective that enables him to adumbrate with extraordinary intuition the whole structure of literary consciousness, and in particular the character of imaginative language, as these were to develop in the centuries to come. Not least among his psychological discoveries was the passion precisely for uniqueness itself, the desire for that distinction that comes from having seen and said something new. Again and again Dante reveals his curiosity for, and delight in, novelty: he anticipates here a major shift in the premises of art from the excellence of the work to the originality of the artist. Yet he rarely calls attention to his own personality without good reason. One further look at the use Dante makes of his "shadow," which he alone has, will illustrate the profundity of his imagination and sense of words. For it is more than mere coincidence, or lack of other choice, that has inspired Dante to make such play upon the word "shadow" (*ombra*). It describes not only the phenomenon that makes his living presence so noticeable in Purgatory, but also what the souls themselves in Purgatory actually are—shades (in English; *ombre* in Italian). The double significance of the word can scarcely be overlooked in a stanza such as the following:

> e io facea con l'ombra più rovente
> parer la fiamma; e pur a tanto indizio
> vidi molt'ombre, andando, poner mente.[10]

> (and I made with my shadow the flame appear more glowing; and even at that small sign I saw many of the shades, as they went, give heed.)

Seen in the wider context of the poem as a whole, Dante's shadow acquires a symbolic significance: it signifies his new-found ability to make the light of the spirit seem to shine more brightly by causing it to cast *his* shadow. That shadow symbolizes a degree of realism that was new to the mediaeval imagination, a realism based on self-awareness. By placing his own shadow among the shadows of the spirit world, Dante discovered an artistic dimension through which a more personal experience both of the self and of the world could be represented in literature. It may be only a "small sign," as Dante calls it, but it was enough, he felt sure, to have impressed the greatest poets of his day—the men who "give heed" in this passage

> Questa fu la cagion che diede inizio
>   loro a parlar di me; e cominciarsi
>   a dir: "Colui non par corpo fittizio."[11]
>
> (It was this that first gave occasion for them to speak of me, and they began to say to one another: "This man does not seem a fictitious body.")

There are many indications that the discovery of this perspective was the main quest of Dante's intellectual life. His two most substantial works prior to the *Commedia*—namely, the *Vita nuova* and the *Convivio* (*c.* 1304–7)—offer various points of comparison with it (most obviously the figure of Beatrice in the first, and the mass of theoretical learning in the second), and particularly interesting in the present context is their literary form. The core of each book consists of lyrical poems, which are surrounded by discursive prose that places them in a setting either of biographical narrative or of interpretative scholarship and argument. One of Dante's objects is to define a dimension of "deeper" meaning not only in these poems but in all serious literature; and in the *Convivio* he sets out a scheme of four different senses in which a book should be read: the literal, the allegorical, the moral, and the anagogical or mystical. In the latest letter by Dante to be preserved, the famous Epistle XIII to Can Grande, Lord of Verona and Dante's best-known patron in exile, this scheme is explained again, with the same example taken from Scripture (the exodus of the Israelites from Egypt) to show how a literal, historical record also signifies, respectively, man's redemption by Christ; the conversion of the soul from sin; and the resurrection from bondage to this world. Dante then goes on to apply this scheme to "the sublime canticle" of his own *Commedia*, which is to say the *Paradiso* that he now dedicates to Can Grande out of gratitude.

The result of this essay in textual analysis by the poet himself is most disappointing, to say the least. Placed beside Dante's observations and examples (from a wide range of other poets) on the use of the vernacular for lyrical poetry, in *De vulgari eloquentia* (*c.* 1304–7), his approach to his own greatest poem seems narrowly pedantic and insensitive. Is the epistle authentic, in fact? On this question scholarly opinion has been often divided; fortunately the answer is relatively unimportant. For whether Dante discovered a new dimension of imaginative experience in his *Commedia* does not depend on whether he was capable of formulating, or even of realizing, in some other conceptual or theoretical terms, what

606

such a discovery would "mean." It is almost inevitable that any theoretical pronouncement by Dante on this or any other subject will be expressed in quite conventional terms. And for almost a thousand years the mediaeval convention had been that: "Theoretical science is divided into two parts—the historical and the spiritual meaning; and the latter into three. . . ."[12] Grammar, as taught in the schools of the Middle Ages, meant the art of expressing a thing with two meanings. Dante's critical comment, if it is his, has the banality of a well-worn cliché.

To be sure, the concept of allegory may have acquired a more profound and less schematic meaning for Dante than this epistle implies. In the *Convivio* he likens allegorical meaning to "form" in the Thomist and Aristotelian sense, i.e. to the principle that makes things what they are when they pass from potentiality into actuality. Dante the writer and poet is clearly fascinated by the moment when the potentialities of impassioned thought are turned into the actualities of words, when phantasy becomes poetry. Time and again in the *Commedia* he dwells on the difficulties, the perils, and the final impossibility of this moment, warning those who expect some conventional outcome to turn back and not to try to follow him:

> L'acqua ch' io prendo già mai non si corse; . . . [13]
>
> (The water which I take was never sailed before.)

Only those, and they are evidently few, who want to do more than follow his "singing keel," who want for themselves "the bread of angels," does Dante encourage to set forth on this dangerous voyage, *per l'alto sale* (across the deep sea). In a somewhat loose sense, of course, this imagery of boats and bread might be considered to be a kind of allegory. But allegory, it should be remembered, describes properly the use of a concrete image to express an abstract, intellectual conception. What Dante is talking about does not belong at this end of the intellectual scale, but lies much nearer to what nowadays would be called existential experience: experience, that is, where the mind is not ensconced in the safety of a clear idea for which it merely lacks some graspable sign, but is sailing out into an unknown sea, the "ocean of being" (*lo gran mar dell'essere*) beyond human grasp. There the literal meanings of words fail, as Dante admits:

> Transumanar significar *per verba*
>   non si porìa; però l'essemplo basti
>   a cui esperïenza grazia serba.[14]
>
> (To pass beyond the human cannot be told in words; let the example suffice, therefore, for him to whom the experience is vouchsafed by grace.)

On the one hand, then, Dante necessarily makes great use of "examples" in his poem, which teems with schematic references and barely outlined figures whose significance is, loosely speaking, allegorical and very similar in function to that of the exempla that occur so frequently in mediaeval writing.[15] On the other hand, it would be wrong to conclude that the more profound meaning of the *Commedia*, the meaning that has given it its place for ever among the literary masterpieces of Western civilization, is due to a threefold layer of allegorical sense beneath the mere literal surface of the poem—even if that is where Dante in theory thought the importance of his poem lay. Dante has in fact found a solution in the *Commedia* to the problem of how to knit together literary utterance and spiritual significance that is the reverse of allegory as ordinarily understood. Quite plainly, the world Dante portrays in his poem is *already* the world of the spirit; here the anagogical, or mystical, significance of life on earth is visualized, touched, felt, and heard with the plainness of immediate experience; there is simply no room for allegorical teaching about what is "really" meant, and no need for it either. The whole movement of Dante's mind goes in the opposite direction, toward making the familiar details of nature (and the sometimes less familiar, but no less realistic, details of history) stand forward in vivid artistic relief—not recede into obscure depths of learned reference. Dante has discovered an artistic standpoint from which he can refer much more effectively to the facts and phenomena of this world than would have been possible by referring away from it.

The dimension in which Dante had learnt to exercise his imagination is an aesthetic one. It is the counterpart in literature to the first glimpse of a new realism that Dante could have seen in the painting of his most gifted contemporary, Giotto (*c.* 1276–1337). When Dante dwells at length on the realism of the pictures wrought in "the very marble" of the first terrace of Purgatory, he may well have been thinking of his friend's work, especially as Giotto's fame is mentioned explicitly in the following canto (XI). Admittedly Dante also says quite explicitly that this degree of "speaking likeness" (or, to be more accurate, "visible speaking"—*visibile parlar*) is new to Virgil and himself; these works of art have been made by God and are "not to be found on earth." What is nevertheless true of this long passage of appreciation by Dante of God's skill in the plastic arts is this: first, Dante *does* appreciate the artistry quite as much as the allegorical message of the pictures. Second, he appreciates them because they achieve a realism that deceives the senses: "one would have sworn," he says, that these graven figures were speaking and that one could smell the incense at their ceremonies. Third, his imagination responds so intensely to the realism of this new medium that finally one of the scenes does come to life in his mind and he hears a dramatic dialogue between Trajan and the poor widow. Dante begins by writing that she "seemed to say"; he uses the infinitive once more ("And he to answer her"); then he breaks the link with "seemed" and writes what could be a short stage script: "She: . . . He: . . . She: . . . He: . . ." The contrast is striking with the manner in which Dante introduces the words that "one would have sworn" one was hearing on looking at the first picture (of the Annunciation). There the words that spring to mind are written in Latin—which often happens when Dante wants to remind us that he is quoting from Scripture or the liturgy—so that the angel merely "says" *Ave* and Mary "answers" *Ecce ancilla Dei* (Behold the handmaid of the Lord).[16]

This remarkable sequence in Canto X of the *Purgatorio* that begins with works of art set in the context of the second use of allegory (that is, moral instruction) and ends with a dramatic dialogue as realistically "staged" as any scene in the *Commedia*, with Roman cavalry behind and their golden eagle standards moving (rather oddly!) in the wind, anticipates in miniature the future development of the artistic imagination in Europe. And, needless to say, it is a development in which Dante himself has already taken one first, decisive, and enormous stride, of which the *Commedia* as a whole is the speaking image. This does not mean that the poem is an allegory of the creative imagination, for this phrase would suggest that the thing depicted and the thing meant are separate and dual; whereas they become one in the highest kind of art that Dante can envisage. He may modestly declare that only God could accomplish such art as this, indistinguishable from reality, but we know that the dramatic dialogue must, like the other thoughts and sensations awakened in Dante, be taking place in his *own* imagination. He also indicates graphically in this same scene two other elements that were to be of crucial importance for the development of art. The first of these elements is pointed to in Virgil's brief phrase:

"Non tener pur ad un loco la mente."[17]

("Do not keep thy mind [fixed] only on one place.")

And the text goes on to insist, as the *Commedia* does so often, that Dante then moved, "crossing over" Virgil to get another of the marble pictures properly into focus. These repeated, very exact descriptions of where

Dante is standing and which way and how he moves are not just pedantic padding, but more like stage directions—or evocations of an action as solid as a play upon a stage:

> per ch' io varcai Virgilio, e fe'mi presso,
> acciò che fosse alli occhi miei disposta.[18]
>
> (therefore I crossed over past Virgil, and drew close to [the picture],
> so that it might be set before my eyes.)

The lines immediately preceding these make equally clear where Virgil is standing in relation to Dante, and where the second picture (of David dancing before the sacred ark) is situated in relation to the first. By taking this amount of care to present the complete scene in all its concreteness, Dante makes his reader aware of a second element in his art: not only that he can and must move about if he is to get close to and really see these important scenes, but also that the scenes themselves are located in different places. That Dante should go "past" Virgil in turning from an event that took place after Virgil's death (the Annunciation) to look at an event from before his birth (David dancing) has, of course, a simple historical appropriateness. When we find him devoting another whole line—

> I' mossi i piè del loco dov' io stava[19]
>
> (I moved my feet from the place where I was standing)

—to reach the "place" where the story of Trajan is enacted, the weight that now attaches to this point seems to be appropriate to something more than history in the sense of chronology. This something is history understood as cultural tradition, and Dante is aware of three distinct cultures, each of which demands a separate act of imaginative attention: the culture of the Old Testament, the culture of the New Testament, extending forward into his own time (though this has so fallen away from Christian ideals as to constitute in effect yet another "culture"), and finally the culture of pagan civilization and learning.

These cultures, then, are *seen* to be distinct in time and place, but no theoretical conflict is insisted on between them; nor does one replace another in the *Commedia* (as many mediaeval minds supposed). Each is given its due by Dante as he moves freely among them—or perhaps we should rather say that he gives them *his* due of creative insight as he "moves his feet" to the place where they are and sets each squarely "before his eyes"—so that Virgil is as real to him (and to the reader) as Beatrice, and Ulysses as the apostles James or Peter. These cultures complement one another in the poem as a whole, and each acquires its newly lifelike realism from the intensity with which Dante experiences them; and conversely, the new quality of individual experience—indeed the very poetic identity of Dante, the protagonist of the poem—is the product of this manifold cultural consciousness. In the *Commedia* we see much more than the mediaeval cosmos only; we see the birth of a modern imagination from out of its midst. Thus, Dante achieves an ultimate unity in the *Commedia* by virtue less of a coherent philosophy than of his personal artistic vision.[20] He has subjected people and ideas to the scrutiny of his own imagination, and it is there, rather than in any allegorical scheme, that their common point of reference lies. Like a man looking about him in a landscape through which he is journeying, the centre of perspective is always in himself.

The emergence of Dante as a self-conscious individual, temporarily lost, cut off from and outside the conventional scheme of things, is clearly visible from the earliest stanzas of the *Commedia*—from the celebrated *mi ritrovai* (I found, came to, myself again) of line 2, in fact, the force of which is strengthened by its position between the two-sided image of the journey and the way. Dante is right in the middle of one, at the same time as he has lost the right direction of the other (the words for "journey" and "way," *cammino* and *via*, conveniently overlap in meaning to produce a composite impression of paradox). Dante "finds himself again" (a phrase with slight overtones of "anew") in the equally celebrated "dark wood," which, coming at the beginning of a mediaeval poem, has caused much speculation as to what such an apparently allegorical image "really" refers to. What infidelity to his lady, his muse, his Church, had Dante been guilty of? It is hard to know anything more about the "facts" than what can be inferred from Dante's allusions to his perdition and salvation elsewhere in the *Commedia* and in the *Vita nuova*. It is not even clear what kind of facts we should be looking for, because the whole question of whether this is allegory in a simple biographical sense is begged. To search in this direction for an interpretation of the real Dante is to find nothing; worse, it is to turn one's back on the rich, informative details of Dante's emergent state of mind from which the whole of his new creative venture is to spring.

Dante immediately goes on to announce and stress several features of the creative state and newfound personality that will make his poetic journey possible, and these depend on no allegorical key for their comprehension. The first thing he tells us is how difficult it is to express what the dark wood was like. This might be read allegorically, of course, to mean that he is deeply ashamed of something he would rather not (but could) reveal; the disadvantage of assuming this is again obvious, in that we do not, in this sense, find out anything. We are facing the wrong way, and overlooking the fact that Dante does not here talk about shame and guilt, but (thrice) about fear and an experience that is almost like death. He also establishes, in passing, a sense of distance from this reawakening in the wood, an experience that comes back to him in thought, though just where and how it first came about is lost in a realm deeper than sleep. (This may be realistic—and surprisingly modern—psychology; but it would be bad, because impenetrable, allegory.) Two more things are certain: one, that Dante had to lose the "true path" in order to see what he has since seen; and the other, that despite the fearfulness of being in the dark wood and so near death, he will speak of these experiences "in order to treat of the good that I there found" (*ma per trattar del ben ch'io vi trovai*). The suggestion that there is a necessary psychological connection between finding himself in such a terrible predicament and expressing this "good" is reinforced by the close echo of the two relevant phrases in Italian: *mi ritrovai* and *io vi trovai*.[21] The use of repetition, echo, and rhyme in the *Commedia* is rarely without some purpose.

Finally, in this context we read that it is morning and that the fear is beginning to pass as Dante starts to struggle away from the dark wood. The last shades of some supposed allegorical content likewise fade still further as we suspect that Dante may have been talking about an actual sleep and dreams that have been as deep as death. He states that the fear has lain in the "lake of my heart all through the night," and this makes it still easier to understand the dark wood (where he spent that night) as an inner condition rather than any outward event; the psychological imagery continues in keeping with this in the following tercets:

> E come quei, che con lena affanata
>   uscito fuor del pelago alla riva
>   si volge all'acqua perigliosa e guata:
> così l'animo mio, ch'ancor fuggiva,
>   si volse a retro a rimirar lo passo,
>   che non lasciò già mai persona viva.[22]

(And like a man who with panting breath has escaped from the deep sea to the shore, turns to the dangerous water, and gazes; so my mind, which was still fleeing, turned back to see the pass that no-one ever left alive.)

Then, however, Dante encounters the three mysterious animals who bar his way. These are undeniably allegorical, and seem to challenge the interpretation we have been following so far. They can be, and of course have been, interpreted (as worldly pleasure, ambition, and avarice; or again, as Florence, France, and the Papacy), just as the greyhound to whom Virgil will shortly refer has been interpreted, although the actual creature does not appear. But the most obvious point to observe about these allegorical beasts is that they do, literally, prevent Dante from getting any further. They even make him turn back from his hard poetic enterprise so recently begun, until Virgil appears before him: a *man*, not living perhaps but recognizable and real and located in time and place. To Dante's cry for help in escaping from the beasts he replies pointedly: "For *thee* 'tis meet to take another road" (*A te convien tenere altro viaggio*). To follow the path of allegorical confrontation leads nowhere; such statements of the problem can be solved only by extending the allegory—and Virgil obligingly makes up one that can never have had, or ever will have, one clear and necessary meaning, as Boccaccio already realized, although he was barely more than a generation younger than Dante in an age that was still accustomed to allegory.* The solution to Dante's desire to give expression to the fearful world of vision he has "found himself" in (and through) lies in a quite different direction. Virgil concludes his insoluble allegorical invention by saying:

> "Ond'io per lo tuo me' penso e discerno
>   che tu mi segui, e io sarò tua guida."[23]

> ("And from this I think and do discern that for thy best good thou followest me, and I will be thy guide.")

That Dante is saved at a critical moment in his spiritual career by Virgil is the simple, basic idea—and possibly also the actual biographical fact—on which the first part of the "plot" of the *Commedia* turns. The second part is based on the saving role and the heavenly revelations of Beatrice, whose place in Dante's personal life remains rather more problematic. The connection between the two parts is consistently worked

---

* The attempt to interpret the allegorical beasts can, of course, be pursued through the later references in the *Commedia* to this opening scene. Thus, for instance, in *Inferno* XVI, 106, Dante refers to a cord he had around his waist with which he had "thought to catch the leopard with the painted skin." One 19th-century commentator (Buti) concluded that Dante must have been a Franciscan. Other commentators (e. g. Nardi) pointed out that the cord is used in the story to capture Geryon, a creature of Hell, and must therefore have a different, or at least a double, significance. The puzzle then doubles itself, because the word "capture" (*prender*) would mean something different in each case. In what sense does the Franciscan rule enable one to "capture" pleasure? What is clear, however, is that Dante in the poem uses the cord in a very realistic way; a quite detailed description is given of how he hands it over to Virgil, and how the latter throws it. He does this *instead* of employing the cord for the obscure allegorical purpose he originally had in mind.

out: Virgil comes to Dante because Beatrice asks him to, and she in her turn has been alerted to Dante's danger by Santa Lucia, who was herself commanded in the first instance by the Virgin Mary. It is into the presence of the Queen of Heaven that Dante is finally led, and through gazing upon her face, the last and closest semblance to God in human shape before Christ, that he achieves the beatific vision toward which he had struggled blindly and without yet knowing it when he fled from the fear of the dark wood.

Now, it is true that the roles of Virgil and Beatrice are so schematically prescribed on the stage of Dante's mediaeval cosmos that a reader schooled in allegorical interpretation will readily see them as personifications of Reason and Faith. It is also true that references to Dante's wanderings from the true path and need of grace and guidance to be saved suggest a moral reading: a lesson in the right and wrong use of the gift of life and the things of nature. And at a still deeper level there are many passages of mystical "science" in which Dante receives enlightenment concerning the crucial points of intersection between the natural and the supernatural realms: the chief of these is the one that (to a mediaeval mind) was visible in the stars and the celestial influence they exercise on human beings. Much stress is laid on the exact position of the heavenly bodies throughout the *Commedia,* and the doctrinal discussions can all be related to the central mystery of how God's omnipotence operatcs; whether the angels are identical with the spheres they inhabit (which would make spiritual power indistinguishable from material force); what things depend on man's free will and what on divine grace; the nature of the *prima materia* in relation God's informing light; and so on.

If these abstract considerations constituted the essential substance of Dante's poem, however, many modern readers might conclude that the *Commedia* must become duller the better they understood it. While not denying Dante's obvious and inevitable use of this mediaeval setting, we should look again to see the extent to which the poem's enduring strength springs from the informing presence in "this" world not so much of God's power (in some supposed allegory) but rather of the poet's own personality—in an altogether realistic form. The world that Dante is exploring is his own, and its reality is that of his own imaginative experience. This poem is as much about the writing of this poem as, let us say, Proust's lifelong novel is about the writing of that novel. Dante too has written about how the creative intelligence works, how memory and passion play their part in the quest for the sort of "knowledge" that only the literary imagination gives, and of its power to transform all things to its use. And what he shows us is that this knowledge is a kind of more intense seeing of what we already knew, and a transformation of the whole universe of things from the simplest glimpse of nature to the most recondite reference of "science" by the light of that more intense insight—a transformation of them into simile, metaphor, and symbol; into the stuff, that is, of poetry. When, therefore, Dante reaches the highest goal of his spiritual pilgrimage, what he sees is not God and the heavenly hosts, but a book. Speaking of this most intense moment of illumination, he says:

> Nel suo profondo vidi che s'interna,
>   legato con amore in un volume,
>   ciò che per l'universo si squaderna;
> sustanze e accidenti e lor costume,
>   quasi conflati insieme, per tal modo
>   che ciò ch' i'dico è un semplice lume.[24]

(In its depth I saw that it contained, bound by love in one volume, that which is scattered in separate leaves throughout the universe; substances and accidents and their relations [were] as if fused together in such a way that what I am saying [in words] is one simple light.)

To place so much weight on Dante's choice of this image to communicate a type of experience that he has repeatedly said is ineffable and irrecoverable may seem to stretch the argument too far. But several things may be said to support it. Dante makes no grammatical link—no "such as," no "like," not even a metaphorical extension of the meaning of any particular word—between the book and what actually was there "in the depth" of his vision. Dante writes down this image, as if it were as plainly descriptive of what he saw as the descriptions he has given of other parts of Heaven and Hell. Moreover, he is always extremely precise in his handling of comparisons, analogies, examples, and the like, so that the exact degree of "likeness" between expression and reality shall be perceived by the reader. Here, for instance, he concludes this picture of what he saw when he raised his eyes to the "light supreme" by contrasting the brightness of a single light or flame with such mere words as "substances" and "accidents," i.e. the jargon of philosophy. This has the effect, however, of making the image of the much-loved book seem yet more securely descriptive, as though it were something in its own right, far above the inadequacies of Dante's mere spoken word. A similar imaginative device is employed a little later, in the lines in which Dante compares his state of mind to that of Neptune when he saw the first man-made ship above him on the surface of the sea:

> Un punto solo m'è maggior letargo
>   che venticinque secoli alla 'mpresa,
>   che fè Nettuno ammirar l'ombra d'Argo.
> Così la mente mia, tutta sospesa,
>   mirava fissa, immobile e attenta,
>   e sempre di mirar faciesi accesa.[25]

> (A single moment makes for me a deeper oblivion than 25 centuries
> upon the enterprise that made Neptune wonder at the shadow of the
> Argo. Thus my mind, all suspended and fixed, immobile and intent,
> gazed and ever made itself enkindled with gazing.)

Here an obvious connection is established between Neptune and Dante,
who seems to be looking up for a moment in wonder, as if at his own
ship—a word that Dante has already used several times to describe the
literary "enterprise" of the *Commedia* itself. The Italian verbs at once
draw attention to this connection, and also to a difference: Neptune
wonders *at* (*ammirar*) the shadow of the Argo, whereas Dante—fixed,
immobile, intent, suspended (and long since instructed not to pay attention to the shadow but to get on with the journey)—simply gazes
passionately (*mirava ... e ... di mirar faciesi accesa*). Which is to say, there
is only an implied comparison between the objects of their wondering
gaze. This must needs be so if, as the ship-image implies, Dante is gazing
at himself, or at least at his own work; he can therefore say of his mind
both that it was "suspended" (which Neptune was not, though the Argo
was) and that it was fixed, intent, immobile (which Neptune was, but
the Argo was not). The most paradoxical aspect of this comparison,
however, lies in the contrast of time. The single instant is more over-
powering in Dante's case than 2500 years have been in Neptune's. Yet
that is not the end of the matter, because the effect of the single instant
on Dante is being compared with the effect *on the Argo* (or on the famous
enterprise of Jason's Argonauts) of the 2500 years since it sailed. The
effect is described as *letargo*—a mixture of forgetfulness and immobility.
But the Argo has *not* been forgotten: Homer speaks of it as an exploit
so famous that it is known to all men, and anyway Dante himself refers
to it here as a most striking human enterprise in order to cap it with his
own. The implication therefore is that his own poetic enterprise will be
even less likely to be forgotten, because of the superior quality of its
inner or psychological experience, than the daring nautical adventure
recorded by Homer and Pindar.

An element of paradox, ambiguity, and just plain inadequacy in the
language of the final canto of a spiritual journey into the presence of
God appears to be so inevitable and appropriate, that a reader is likely

to pay too little attention to it. He accepts too readily that human words cannot communicate the divine, and that this negative message will be all that Dante can hope to deliver. To read Canto XXXIII in this fashion, however, is once again to be facing mentally in the wrong direction, thinking of Dante's language as still essentially allegorical, as an arbitrary invention that stands for something else; and because the "something else" is now by definition beyond all human conception, it follows that whatever images Dante invents cannot have much interest. But if, as is being suggested here, the focus of Dante's attention is on his own imaginative experience, his images—and indeed, every other kind of expression he uses—are interesting in a new way: not as speculative fictions about an unknowable reality outside himself, but as much more precise psychological observations, well founded on ground that Dante had experienced directly and profoundly. This is the desire for knowledge—knowledge of that distinctive kind that art achieves, that involves the person completely, his passion and will and memory as well as his intelligence, and is quite unlike mere information. Dante may well have had some inkling of the problems that would be raised by the possibility and pursuit of knowledge that did not so unite the mind and heart of man, and in this respect the religious orthodoxy of his conception of the truth doubtless coincided happily with his artist's understanding of it.

The case of Ulysses should be cited here to illustrate a search for knowledge that did go morally astray. Ulysses appears in person in the *Inferno* (although he apparently suffers there primarily for instigating the ambush with the wooden horse), and is referred to again in both the *Purgatorio* and the *Paradiso*. Many details suggest a comparison between Dante's situation and that of Ulysses. There is the common image of the journey by ship, dangerous in both cases; but Ulysses was set on a "mad" course (*varco folla*), whereas Dante is aided by Apollo and the Muses as his song sails forth (*cantando varca*).[26] Ulysses incites his men to seek with him sensuous experience of an inhuman world behind the sun:

> "O frati," dissi, "che per cento milia
>   perigli siete giunti all' occidente,
>   a questa tanto picciola vigilia
> de' nostri sensi ch'è del rimanente,
>   non vogliate negar l'esperïenza,
>   di retro al sol, del mondo senza gente. . . ."[27]

("Oh brothers," I said, "who through a hundred thousand dangers have reached the west, do not deny to this brief vigil of your senses that remains, experience of the world without people beyond the sun. . . .")

Dante, as we have seen, urges men not to follow him unless they genuinely desire the bread of heaven for themselves, in which case they should sail in their *own* boat evidently, and not be surprised to see Dante in the end do something as different from mere sailing as ploughing land is from briefly cutting a furrow through water that "falls back again." The contrast speaks for itself, and ends with a reference to Jason that prompts the reader to think back to the 8th circle of Hell (where both Jason and Ulysses are, though in separate compartments, because they practised different degrees of deception) and also prepares for the final image of Jason's boat and Dante's greater experience:

> Voi altri pochi che drizzaste il collo
>   per tempo al pan delli angeli, del quale
>   vivesi qui ma non sen vien satollo,
> metter potete ben per l'alto sale
>   vostro navigio,   servando mio solco
>   dinanzi all'acqua che ritorna equale.
> Que' glorïosi che passaro al Colco
>   non s'ammiraron come voi farete,
>   quando Iason vider fatto bifolco.[28]

(You other few, who reached out in time for the bread of angels by which men live here but never come away sated with it, you may indeed put out your ship upon the deep, using my furrow before the water falls back level again. Those glorious ones who crossed the sea to Colchis were not so amazed, as you shall be, when they saw Jason turned ploughman.)

The other point of comparison between Dante and Ulysses lies in their both having confronted the "sweet Siren who leads sailors astray in mid-sea, so pleasurable is it to hear me."[29] Dante (whose knowledge of Homer was second-hand) thought Ulysses had succumbed, and allows his Siren to boast that "he who lives with me rarely goes away, so wholly do I satisfy him." The contrast with the peculiar property of heavenly satisfaction—which never satiates—should be noted. Dante stresses this difference: in the *Purgatorio*, for instance, he repeats that the food of Heaven, "satisfying in itself, arouses thirst for itself,"[30] because on it rests the burden of his moral psychology and his frequent distinctions between the relative value of physical and spiritual things. In this scene we may suppose that Dante too would have succumbed to the Siren, to judge from the energetic measures needed to tear him away from what, in his case, turns out to be a dream.

Again, the dream of the Siren is less interesting for its obvious moral content than for the light it sheds on the workings of the imagination.

She first appears to Dante as a "woman stammering, cross-eyed, and crooked on her feet."[31] What transforms her, so that she becomes so beguilingly beautiful in feature and voice? Dante states quite plainly that it was *lo sguardo mio* (my look). Moreover, two similes reinforce this apparently harmless-looking word for what is evidently a very remarkable power: it operates "like the sun" and "like love." They are similes that point to the basic dimensions of Dante's world, the light that governs his cosmos, and the love that governs his psyche. In other words, his inner eye finds itself here in uncontrolled possession of the keys to all existence, which it can transform at will. Because Dante's will is still very far from perfect, he not surprisingly falls into temptation, until Virgil brings him back to his senses. Or rather, Dante himself first *dreams* of a second lady "holy and alert" who doubtless represents to him what Virgil stands for at some symbolic level of his mind (in dreams, figures do become charged with that arbitrary significance from which allegories are made). We do not have to decide whether she, or he, "is" Reason, however, in order to understand that the dreamt interplay between Virgil, the lady, and the Siren is part of the process of waking up. At the same time as it has been going on, Virgil has been calling to Dante, and this dream-scene is the version that Dante "sees" of the actual words that Virgil had used. The poem does not say what these were, but the transformation of sounds —in this case one presumes they were words—into a dramatic and symbolic little scene is most realistically rendered. The power of inward seeing alone, when it is unchecked by rational understanding and deaf to language, shows what imagination is capable of in itself; it transforms ugliness into beauty as if by magic, is irresistibly seductive, and morally deluded. This gift of sight, which for Dante the poet (allegedly with weak eyesight) operates as vividly when we are dreaming as when we are awake, and is activated as much by memory, intelligence, and desire as by objects, must be recalled to the reality that is—so long as we are alive and awake—necessarily "fixed in the body" of concepts and words. Here again we perceive the underlying interest of Dante's visit to the realm of the spirit, or imagination, while he is still a living man. His story of the salvation of the soul is intimately connected with the mystery of how the infinite capacity of consciousness—which Dante equates largely with seeing, but to a lesser extent with hearing, as one might expect with an artist working with words—relates to what *can* be grasped by a finite mind and *can* be expressed in the finite medium of an actual language.

Dante's final insight into this mystery, in Canto XXXIII of the *Paradiso*, leads him to say that very little can be grasped and very little expressed of the infinite awareness of consciousness:

> Oh quanto è corto il dire e come fioco
>   al mio concetto! e questo, a quel ch' i' vidi,
>   è tanto, che non basta a dicer "poco."[32]

(O how scant is speech and how feeble to my conception! And this, to what I saw, is such that it is not enough to call it "little.")

Here are the three constituent parts of Dante's psychology—sight, concept, and word—arranged in descending order of effectiveness, each a pale shadow of the one above. Yet we have already seen how important the shadow is in throwing into relief the greater reality of what casts it. And within the characteristically tripartite structure of Dante's conceptions, each part in effect complements the other; Heaven would lose its distinctive meaning were it not *toto caelo* different from Purgatory and the natural paradise of Eden, and the possibility of moral regeneration would have no force without the recognition of how horrible unregenerate wickedness must be. Thus, the repeated protestations of verbal and conceptual failure at the summit of Paradise have the effect of inducing in the reader a contrasting sense of what inconceivable, incommunicable seeing must be like. The stanza just quoted, in which the three parts of the mind seem to fall apart revealing the gaps between them, is followed by one in which all the spiritual faculties are conjoined:

> O luce etterna che sola in te sidi,
>   sola t'intendi, e da te intelletta
>   e intendente te ami e arridi![33]

(O Light Eternal, that alone abidest in Thyself, alone knowest Thyself, and, known to Thyself and knowing, lovest and smilest on Thyself!)

Similarly, and even more explicitly, Dante tells us that he is sure he saw the whole universe gathered together in a single Book precisely because what he can actually say in words (and in the actual book he is writing) is quite inadequate to express what he saw; and he *can* state very vividly and exactly what this inadequacy is like. The relevant line here has already been quoted: the imagined "conflation" of accidents and substances is such that "what I am saying [in words] is one simple flame" (*che ciò ch' i' dico è un semplice lume*). Dante then goes on:

> La forma universal di questo nodo
>   credo ch' i' vidi, perchè più di largo,
>   dicendo questo, mi sento ch' i' godo.[34]

(I think I saw the universal form of this complex, because, in saying this, I feel that I have joy in it more greatly.)

It is important to be clear what it is that Dante is saying in the phrase "saying this" (*dicendo questo*). He is *not* putting into words "the universal form of this complex," which may be understood as the divine idea of all things, or the "unity of creation in the Creator," as one commentator puts it.[35] A wealth of supporting images in this canto—of melting snow, of dreams, of babbling babies—makes it abundantly evident that Dante cannot really state what he saw. The canto is certainly very much about the experience of seeing; in tercet after tercet Dante introduces some form of the word for sight (*vista, veder, viso,* and so on) or some reference to the eyes and to light. But at the same time he stresses that seeing is a simple, single, self-sufficient and self-illuminating thing in itself, like a light or flame, and that words and all that words refer to are not like this.

Dante uses words that describe thinking and any abstract operation of the mind fairly frequently in *contrast* to the immediate experience of vision. A very striking case occurs in the *Inferno*, where, to explain how he did not know what to make of what Virgil was showing him, he writes

> Cred' ïo ch'ei credette ch' io credesse . . .[36]
>
> (I think he thought that I was thinking . . .).

Dante's uncertainty here is cleared up by Virgil's making him see for himself, and then remarking that Dante might have believed what he had already seen once before—but "only" in Virgil's poetry, and that was apparently not enough:

> "S'elli avessi potuto creder prima . . .
>   ciò c' ha veduto pur con la mia rima . . ."[37]
>
> ("If he could have believed before what he has seen only in my verse . . .").

Looked at in the light of a passage such as this, even the phrase "I believe I saw" (*credo ch' i' vidi*) seems to contain a shade of doubt. It is in fact by recognizing the difference between the complex words he has to use about accidents and substances (*ciò ch' i' dico*) and the simple light of vision, that Dante's certainty grows. His poetry proceeds dialectically, by perceiving its own limitations; it is *this* that he is saying (*dicendo questo*) and this that is the source of his creative enjoyment.

We have already seen the same imaginative principle at work in the passage we discussed about the shadow, which made the light seem more bright, and attracted the attention of the poets in Purgatory—writers who had never seen any such thing before, and who did not "have" any shadow at their disposal, i.e. any of the realistic effects of light and shade such as Dante represents. In another sense, of course, they and their work might be said to "be" pure shadow: that is, they dwelt altogether in a world of the spirit that would be flatly fictitious without the presence of Dante, whose arrival adds a new dimension of realism to it. To the enlightened spirits themselves thought is evidently visible, but the fact that for Dante thought and vision do not coincide gives rise to the basic movement and rhythm of the poem, as the act of poetic expression strives to mediate between them. Right at the beginning of the *Commedia* Dante lays out in three lines the principal parts of his poetic psychology that will sustain the development of the whole work:

> Ah quanto a dir qual era è cosa dura
> esta selva selvaggia e aspra e forte
> che nel pensier rinova la paura![38]

> (Ah! How hard a thing it is to tell what a wild, and rough, and
> resistant wood this was which in my thought renews my fear!)

First Dante utters a cry—is it of wonder? is it of pain?—about the hard thing, which is the act of saying; and what is all poetry but an elaboration of that "Ah!"? Then he gives an image of what at that moment he sees, and does not understand, though he can particularize vividly enough its secondary qualities, its rough, resistant, savage feel. And finally he describes the state of mind that the first two factors produce in him: he is afraid. Or, psychologically speaking, does the fear in the mind come first, then the image of it, and finally the urge to express it? It is tempting to equate these three elements of the creative process with the three concepts that Dante himself employs to explain the sequence of his spiritual salvation: grace, knowledge, and love. Dante is particularly concerned to state in which order they stand, grace being the necessary precondition of all, and knowledge being the condition "upon which love follows."[39] From this it could appear either that knowledge is "higher" in importance than love, or the other way about: namely, that love is the ultimate goal. Whatever the answer to this question may be in philosophical-theological terms—and it was a live issue in Dante's day, having been debated by Aquinas and reflected in the different aspirations of the two great monastic orders represented in the poem, the Dominicans and the Franciscans—Dante has undoubtedly identified the fundamentals of the literary imagination and perhaps of the creative intelligence altogether. Whether he has named them "correctly," or set them in a theoretical framework that is still acceptable, is less important than the fact that he has perceived, and rendered visibly and vividly comprehensible, the psychological dimensions within which the world was to make imaginative and spiritual sense to the Western mind for centuries to come.

Thus, if we turn from the first to the last tercets of the *Commedia* we find the same three components of the mind interacting on one another to produce the final movement of creative experience. Only the sequence is different—which suggests that the order does not matter very much—beginning this time with what Dante has seen and ending with a final crisis in his ability to express it. He has gazed at last on the "Eternal Light" (a tercet already quoted) and has seen clearly enough its secondary qualities, especially those of colour, and he tells us how these colours appear to him and what they seem to depict. But his state of mind, which he describes next, is nevertheless one of bafflement:

> Qual è 'l geomètra che tutto s'affige
>   per misurar lo cerchio, e non ritrova,
>   pensando, quel principio ond'elli indige,
> tal era io a quella vista nuova.[40]

(Like the geometer who fixes all his mind on the squaring of the circle and with all his thinking does not discover the principle he needs, such was I at that strange sight.)

The reason for Dante's bafflement is explicitly stated: he wanted "to *see* how the image [depicted with a special colour of its own] fits the circle and how it has its place there":

> veder volea come si convenne
> l'imago al cerchio e come vi s'indova.[41]

Now, this image that will not fit the circle is an effigy of man (*nostra effige*), and the circle, which in the simile baffles the geometer because he cannot measure an exactly equivalent area in the form of a square, is raised from its status as a mere comparison or example to become descriptive of the shape of heaven that Dante has already seen as "circular" (*giri, circulazion*). This kind of shift, or deepening, of the degree of reality appertaining to Dante's imagery occurs repeatedly in the *Commedia*; it is part of the technique by which he establishes his new sense of perspective, in fact. And the result of presenting experience in the greater fullness of this realistic dimension is precisely that the human image does not conveniently fit the neatly circular schemes of mediaeval "science." The logic of the simile that Dante uses is that it is not just the radiant circles but man himself who is the incalculable mystery—*this* man being presumably Christ. Dante can evidently "see" both an ideal image of circles and an image of man; what he cannot see is how they fit together. It is the theme of the entire poem: theologically speaking, it is the mystery of how God's nature is conjoined with man's, and more broadly, how man's body is joined with his soul. What interests us here is how Dante represents this mystery psychologically, as an interaction of three functions of the mind: imagination, understanding, and expression. He comes once again to the point where he recognizes that he cannot "see" what he wants to see; but his own intellectual powers (or "wings"—*proprie penne*) are too weak. But the very act of recognizing failure brings about the experience he desires. Dante emphasizes this point in the two final tercets of the *Paradiso*, which each have the same structure: expression fails, the mind is transformed, and what is seen and what is desired, the heart and the universe, are at one:

> ma non eran da ciò le proprie penne:
>   se non che la mia mente fu percossa
>   da un fulgore in che sua voglia venne.
> All'alta fantasia qui mancò possa
>   ma già volgeva il mio disio e' l velle,
>   sì come rota ch'igualmente è mossa,
> l'amor che move il sole e l'altre stelle.

(But my own wings were not sufficient for that, had not my mind been smitten by a flash wherein came its wish. Here power failed the high imagining; but now my desire and will, like a wheel that spins with an even motion, were revolved by the Love that moves the sun and the other stars.)

It is in so many ways a fitting conclusion: religiously, because the pilgrim's heart is united with the love of the Creator; cosmologically, because Dante now moves with the stars that have hitherto wheeled about him; verbally, because each canticle ends with the same word. And at the level of our present inquiry into the literary psychology of the poem, and the basic dimensions of Dante's imaginative world, we may note that the perspective created by Dante's sense of separateness is likewise at an end. For he has been, until this very last moment, as much an outsider in Heaven as he was in Hell, or, in a different way again, in Purgatory. The same kind of significance may be attached to Dante's use of the word *nostra* to describe the human face he sees at the heart of the cosmic mystery as can be read into the opening lines of the *Commedia*, where, as Leo Spitzer pointed out, there is a noticeable change of pronoun between "the journey of our life" and the verb "I found myself again."* Of course, there are plenty of occasions when "we" and "our" are used in the poem, but they are realistic and specific occasions when what is meant is, for example, "Virgil and me," or "we in this sphere."[43] On such occasions as these, Dante is clearly moving in a reality of distinct individuals, so that his return at the end to a recognition of the common human "effigy" is appropriate to show that he is relinquishing his sense of separate identity. He does, admittedly, draw back even from this last of his visions, to reflect upon what it means and upon his state of mind (it is "like that of a geometer," and so on). This intellectual movement from thing seen to thing thought is entirely typical, as we have shown, and the reader does not have much confidence in Dante's declaration that his sight is "totally" absorbed this time by what he sees:

> per che 'l mio viso in lei tutto era messo[44]
> (wherefore my sight was totally given to it).

In fact, the pronouns here have something of the same effect that Spitzer detected in lines 1–2 of the *Commedia*; the *mio* at once establishes a sense of difference from *nostra effigie*, and the *lei* places "it" at an even more marked distance from Dante. Nevertheless, it is still remarkable that it should be this communal effigy that Dante chooses as the last on which his imagination sets eyes.

It would, of course, be absurd to imply that Dante is confusing the beatific vision with a vision of man. He is far too orthodox and mediaeval in his outlook to indulge in such gross thoughts (thoughts that were, however, to be discovered 500 years later in the irrationalistic metaphysics of the 19th century), and far too precise in his references to the form in which God did appear as man in Christ, to conclude with so unsubtle an equation, even if he does add that he cannot see how the two halves fit. We should look most carefully at those circles again to see just what Dante may have meant by them. There is a sense in which they are circles not so much of the Trinity as of his own mind. They are certainly to be distinguished from the Eternal Light in itself, for Dante says: *Quella circulazion . . . pareva in te come lume riflesso* (That circling appeared in Thee—Eternal Light—as reflected light).[45] And he subtly distinguishes between the unchanging character of "the living light," which has only

---

* Spitzer[42] is chiefly concerned to show that writing in the first person has no *biographical* significance in mediaeval literature. The present analysis of Dante's more modern understanding of how the creative imagination functions does not claim that it illustrates his biography, in the normal sense of his life story. It is possible that the experience of exile contributed to his gaining of that sense of perspective upon which the enduring life of his poem depends.

one "single aspect" (*semplice sembiante*—like the single flame already mentioned), and the development of this oneness into a manifold vision of three things *as he gazes at it*. Two tercets are here contrasted with one another, as their semantic structure shows: one begins *Non perchè* . . . (i.e. not that there is any change or plurality here), and the next begins *ma per la vista* . . . (i.e. for human sight, however, there is).[46] Dante does equate the developing vision of something that conventionally is quite outside and above the human mind with a development taking place within himself:

> . . . una sola parvenza
> mutandom' io, a me si travagliava.[47]
>
> (. . . one sole appearance, as I myself was changing, was transformed for me.)

Moreover, the first half of this tercet so places the expression for "within myself" that a nice ambiguity is achieved as regards which verb it is to be taken in conjunction with: as he gazes in himself Dante's sight (vision) grows stronger:

> ma per la vista che s'avvalorava
> in me guardando. . . .

When he tells us therefore how this "circling" is conceived, the ambiguity persists as to whether the conception is his or God's. We cannot know how God arrived at the conception of the Trinity, and as a question of abstract theology no modern reader is likely to be very interested. But Dante still holds our interest by showing us how he arrived at this conception. The circling that encompasses the human likeness is born of a contrast between man's disparate and inadequate powers (seeing, thinking, saying) and the undifferentiated oneness of being, knowledge, and love in the Eternal Light. This is the contrast that we have already looked at as typical of Dante's poetic technique,[48] and it is in *this* way that the "trinity" is conceived and still makes sense. The recognition of how consciousness divides up the totality of existence into things it can imagine, and conceptualize, and communicate—a process that breaks oneness down into ever smaller and weaker bits—evokes a glimpse of how consciousness itself is a reflected light when conceived as part of the whole. Dante can for a while run his eyes around it (*dalli occhi miei alquanto circunspetta*), and having done this the effigy of man's common humanity appears to him. The effigy is not named as Christ's, and this allows the problem it poses (of how the image fits the circle, and how the circle can be equated with a square) to symbolize more than the theological problem of Christ's place as a man in the Trinity. It can also symbolize the problem of an individual consciousness trying to grasp its place in the universe. Dante barely hints that he succeeds, but the hint is there in the final lines, where he uses the same word to describe his state as he used above to describe the "trinity" of circles. The word is *igualmente*[49] and it suggests a manner of being (for the word is an adverb) in which all aspects and movements of existence have been equalized. It recalls the state to which the water returns after Dante's "singing keel" has passed by: *equale.*[50]

The concluding sequence of tercets, with their alternation of personal confession and suprapersonal vision that both are approaching the realm of the unsayable, signals the end of the dimension in which the poetry of the *Commedia* has made its way through a great new world of literary experience. The dimension that has made human affairs, whether of public history or inward reflection, stand out with extraordinary vividness finally collapses on itself, as it were, and the orderly unity of God's "uni-verse" is no longer disturbed by Dante's "lost" individuality from which the poem began. Repeatedly in the *Paradiso* Dante approaches this condition of oneness, which will absorb his self-hood into the greater whole, but each time until the last he draws back to reflect, or ask questions, or submit to instruction and examination from the saved to prepare him for the end. For it will mean the end of his poetic vision, as he well knows: in Canto **XXXIII** he repeats the thought that after this he will never again be able to *look at* anything else:

> Io credo, per l'acume ch' io soffersi
>   del vivo raggio, ch' i' sarei smarrito,
>   se li occhi miei da lui fossero aversi.[51]

(I think, from the keeness I endured from the living ray, that I should have been dazzled if my eyes had been turned from it.)

And again:

> A quella luce cotal si diventa,
>   che volgersi da lei per altro aspetto
>   è impossibil che mai si consenta;
> però che 'l ben, ch'è del volere obietto,
>   tutto s'accoglie in lei, e fuor di quella
>   è defettivo ciò ch'è lì perfetto.[52]

(At that light one becomes such that it is impossible for him ever to consent that he should turn from it to another sight; for the good which is the object of the will is all gathered in it, and apart from it that is defective which there is perfect.)

From our preceding discussion the principal parts of Dante's spiritual psychology should catch our attention at once: we note the interplay of sight and thought, but we see also that the familiar third component, the concern with poetic expression, is absent. There is neither explicit declaration of how difficult or inadequate words are, nor (in this context) one of those marvellous great similes by which Dante so often transcends the difficulty that he says defeats him. Instead, in these tercets the emphasis falls on the moral will: true perfection consists in the good that is sought by the heart and the will—*il mio disio e 'l velle*, as Dante says in the end—and the shift of emphasis implies that this is not the same thing as the "good" pursued by poetry and imagination. For Dante, poetry "leads" somewhere; and if, having reached his goal, he were to turn aside from the "living ray," to see perhaps how the world looks by its light, he would be lost: *smarrito*. It is the word he first used to describe the reason for his poetic venture: "that the straight way was lost" (*chè la diritta via era smarrita*). That reason no longer exists, or perhaps he has learnt to turn his back on it; imagination made it seem that it was the "way" that was lost, projecting onto the circumstances of the world an error that really lay within himself.*

Posterity has tended to prefer the imaginative projection to the approach to perfection, and the *Inferno* has enjoyed the reputation of being poetically superior to the *Paradiso*. Taste in poetry (particularly such modern and Romantic taste) reveals more about the taster than about the poem, and it is equally arguable that the *Inferno* is superficial in its dreadful details by comparison with the subtle psychology of the second and third canticles. If the stage and its actors become less lurid, there can be no doubt that Dante's own development and the poetry

---

* There was error enough too in the ways of the world, of course, as Dante is reminded by St Peter's tirade against the Papacy in *Paradiso* XXVII. St Peter stresses, however, what Dante's task as a writer must be on returning to earth: he must speak out against corruption in the Church, in other words use his gifts of vision and expression to a moral end. That is the only reason for his having been given this privileged, "superhuman" view of earth. The point is emphasized when Dante turns back to Beatrice and the goal of his spiritual pilgrimage. Art, by comparison, is nothing:

> e se natura o arte fè pasture
>   da pigliare occhi, per aver la mente,
>   in carne umana o nelle sue pitture,
> tutte adunate, parrebber nïente
>   ver lo piacer divin che mi rifulse
>   quando mi volsi al suo viso ridente.[53]

(And if nature or art ever made food to catch the eyes, in order to catch the mind, either in human flesh or in pictures, [this] all united would seem nothing approaching the divine delight that glowed upon me when I turned myself to her smiling face).

of his spiritual growth become much more interesting. And there is certainly no decline in the quality or the frequency of his feats of imaginative expression. To suppose otherwise is to overlook the basic distinctions that we have been insisting on here between vision, reflection, and expression. Certainly Dante "sees" a more colourful landscape in Hell, and this if anything lessens the need for subtle simile; there are, in fact, fewer similes, metaphors, and other poetic figures of speech in Hell than in Purgatory and Heaven, and those that there are illustrate physical sensations in a generally bestial way: wounded bulls, flea-ridden dogs, and hunted boars are the kinds of comparison that are most appropriate there.[54] The distinctive strength of the *Inferno* consists in the contrasts that Dante creates between the (as yet) disparate and discordant constituents of his mind. Above all there is the long and deepening shadow of unnaturalness that falls across the whole canticle as regards its "literal" aspect. It might scarcely seem necessary to point this out, but for the tendency of modern readers to take this very partial poetry of gruesome sights for the whole, or at least the best part, of Dante's genius; even readers who protest against the mediaeval cruelty of Dante's imagination fail to see the larger context in which it is working. The opening of Canto II may conveniently be quoted to remind ourselves of Dante's feeling of being cut off and outside the natural order as he embarks on this unheard-of imaginative journey:

> Lo giorno se n'andava, e l'aere bruno
> togliea li animai che sono in terra
> dalle fatiche loro; e io sol uno
> m'apparecchiava a sostener la guerra
> sì del cammino e sì della pietate
> che ritrarrà la mente che non erra.[55]

(The daylight was going and the dark air was taking the animals that are on earth from their toils; and I, one alone, was preparing to bear the war both of the journey and of the pity which the mind shall recall that does not err.)

Here is Dante setting out alone (because his companion, Virgil, is only a "shade") at the moment when evening brings rest, and sleep promises reconciliation with the world, to all other creatures, animals and men. And he draws attention at once to *three* aspects of the ordeal that lies before him: the journey itself (*il cammino*), the pity aroused in him by the sufferings he is to recall (*la pietate*), and the work of the mind—or "memory," as *la mente* is usually understood here, rather too narrowly— which has to sustain the "war" (*la guerra*) between what Dante sees and what he feels. The metaphor could hardly be more explicit, and should dispel suspicions that Dante perversely took pleasure in imagining his enemies being tortured in Hell. Such suspicion anyway accords badly with the fact that friends, or figures whom Dante evidently admired, also appear in Hell, and it distracts attention again from the repeated utterances of pity, pain, and simple fright that provide the essential polarity, the perspective of truly human interest, for the *Inferno*.

A yet more vivid comparison follows, which serves to explore the significance of this new perspective that takes Dante as if in reality into the underworld. The comparison is voiced by Dante the personage in the poem—who does not, until the very end, coincide with Dante the author of the poem (else the effect of realism would be wanting); he points out the difference between his own position and that of Aeneas and St Paul, who likewise visited regions beyond the grave while still alive, Aeneas infernal ones, and St Paul heavenly ones.[56] "But who am I that I should go," he asks Virgil, "and who permits it?" (*Ma io perchè venirvi? o chi 'l concede?*)[57] Now, it has to be remembered that for Dante the visit of these two men, famous as founders of the Roman Empire and the Christian Church, were "facts" of equal reality and reliability one with the other and thus conceivably with his own. In which case, what great enterprise does he expect to follow from his own visit to the underworld, which he knows to be an inner or imaginative one? Dante (the personage) takes the question literally and is afraid; Dante the author realizes that "he" is making a mistake and that the realism of his journey is of a literary and psychological kind. A literal equation of inner vision and historical reality is no longer the way forward for him. Such a "new thought" will bring him to a standstill almost before he has even started:

> E qual è quei che disvuol ciò che volle
> e per novi pensier cangia proposta,
> sì che dal cominciar tutto si tolle,
> tal mi fec'io in quella oscura costa,
> perchè, pensando, consumai la 'mpresa
> che fu nel cominciar cotanto tosta.[58]

(And as a man who unwills what he willed, and with new thoughts changes his purpose, so that he wholly leaves the thing commenced, such I made myself on that dim coast; for with thinking I wasted the enterprise, that had been so quick in its commencement.)

This simile evokes the danger that Dante's inspired readiness to look upon the things of the imagination as though they were real, and as though he were really witnessing them in person, might paralyse him with perplexing thoughts. (The metaphysical thoughts that were to

630

grow from the new kind of artistic self-consciousness that Dante was initiating could indeed be dangerous and perplexing.*)

Virgil rebukes Dante for "shameful cowardice" and puts forward a simile of his own—that of an animal scared by something it has seen but not recognized for what it is. It is a nice simile because it contains a play on the word *ombra*, which has just been used to describe himself (*del magnanimo quell'ombra*) and also describes the beast that "takes fright" (*ombra*, i.e. *si adombra*), as a result of "seeing falsely" (*falso veder*). It further serves to make Dante trust what he does see—namely, Virgil's shadow—which he now discovers has been sent to him by Beatrice. In other words, Dante is encouraged to go on with his journey into the underworld of the imagination, for which the "real" equivalents will be found in the great vistas of references to this world—its history, its institutions, its geography, its natural phenomena, and above all its men and women—that form one of the most memorable aspects of the *Commedia*. A passage such as the one just quoted, however, should remind us that Dante's poem has more than one "aspect"; that there is both a literal surface (which is, as it were, flat) and also a dimension of realistic depth, which is certainly not produced by an allegory lying directly underneath the text, but by Dante's self-conscious reflections on where he stands and what he is doing. The "depth" of the *Commedia* does not lie in the receding and abstract meanings of mediaeval thought, but stands out towards us still in the shape of a recognizable person's experience. To begin with, Dante represents himself as utterly perplexed by his own position, and calls on Virgil to help him again here, as he had helped him to give up the fruitless struggle with the allegorical beasts in Canto I:

> "se' savio; intendi me' ch'i'non ragiono."[59]
>
> ("thou art wise; thou understandest better than I can argue.")

There are, of course, innumerable gradations of aspect or surface in the poem, and it is often difficult to say whether an image lies more nearly in the flat plane of "literal" vision or in the poetic dimension of imaginative expression in depth. But to speak of two distinguishable planes in the composition of Dante's poetic realism is as necessary for an appreciation of its artistic character as such terms are in considering realistic painting. Moreover these two planes make possible some quite precise psychological observations concerning the "angle" between them, what might be called an angle of comprehension. To comprehend the

---

* See Volume V, "Irrationalism."

relationship between the two dimensions, which taken apart or separately would represent flat literal surface and abstract signification in "depth"—that is the secret wherein Virgil is "wise" and can correct Dante's first misapprehension. As the poem continues, Dante's comprehension struggles to bring his visionary surface into harmonious alignment with his imaginative expression, and this turns out, as we have seen, to produce the same kind of difficulty: if a point of complete *rapprochement* is approached, the sense of personal difference, the distinction of individual experience, must finally disappear. By contrast, many scenes in the *Inferno* achieve an effect of great imaginative vividness where the angle of comprehension is painfully sharp. Here the mediaevally hellish tortures Dante sees are quite out of alignment with the imaginative dialogue that ensues, while the "rational" explanations offered by Virgil on the one hand, and the painful feelings aroused in Dante on the other, are stretched to the limit in an effort to comprehend the scene. One example must suffice to illustrate how the *Commedia* spans the enormities of Hell.

In Canto XXXIII of the *Inferno* Dante presents Count Ugolino to us as a traitor of the second degree, than which there are only two degrees worse in all Hell. Because the subdivisions of this lowest ring are designed to show that to betray one's relatives, one's country, one's friends and guests, and one's lord and benefactor is in each case a distinct and more serious crime, Ugolino is placed here specifically because he "betrayed" some of the castles belonging to Pisa into the hands of Florence and Lucca. Historians may produce other grounds on which he might have been accused—with regard to his grandson Nino, for instance—but these are not relevant to Dante's scheme. The act of treachery itself is barely mentioned in the poem, however, and although it is possible that Dante knew more about this incident than he tells, and counted on his audience likewise needing no further persuasion regarding Ugolino's wickedness—ancient history by more than a quarter of a century at the time he was writing—it is still remarkable that he does no more than refer obliquely to Ugolino's blame. Indeed, he plays it down, not even stating what it is before allowing Ugolino to tell his own story. Dante even encourages him to argue that the world may have misjudged the affair,[60] and afterwards concludes that even if "he had the fame" (*aveva voce*—a phrase what has since acquired overtones of mere opinion) "of having betrayed Pisa's castles," what Ugolino had to suffer through his children's suffering was unwarranted.[61] Was there already doubt on the subject in Dante's day? And would not public memory of Ugolino's story recall that he was just as much a victim of treachery as guilty of it—an impression confirmed by the gruesome punishment of his gnawing the body of his political rival and betrayer? This detail in particular highlights the problem exhibited by the passage as a whole, a problem that in no way signifies failure on Dante's part, but rather adds to the complexity and interest of the scene.

The punishment meted out to the traitors here has a simple twofold character: it is in the first place "physical," even though the shades in Hell are as insubstantial as those elsewhere in the *Commedia*, and the reader is by this time becoming grateful that Dante does not expatiate on the frightful details of their suffering as fully as he might. This is the flat, mediaeval picture that first greets his eyes. Dante often asks flatly realistic questions about the physical workings of what he sees, and he is answered by being *shown* some more of Hell's landscape. In this canto, for example, he asks Virgil how there can be a wind down here, where all heat is extinguished. To which Virgil replies;

> ". . . di ciò ti farà l'occhio la risposta
> veggendo la cagion che 'l fiato piove."[62]

> (". . . of that thine eye shall give thee answer seeing the cause why the wind blasts.")

Dante does "see" the explanation for this infernal wind in the next canto: it is caused by the grotesque wings of Satan, who flaps them where he lies jammed into the ice at the bottom of Hell.[63] These details are far from meaningless: the "fact" that there is no heat, light, or movement in Hell is perfectly explicable in terms of Dante's mediaeval cosmos, in which light and movement originate in God, are dispensed by the various orders of angels, and are variously reflected by the whole scale of created things on earth. Such are the explanations of mediaeval science, which displays the literary characteristic of being plainly symbolical; that is to say, the explanation can be seen—the physical phenomenon and its significance are made to coincide. Similarly, with the physical punishment imposed on Ugolino, as on the rest of the damned, there is a reason why it is as it is: it fits the crime. A modern reader may be no more convinced that Dante's morality does actually fit than he is that Dante's science does actually explain anything, but there can be little doubt that Dante assumed that his readers would recognize the truth and justice of the sufferings endured in both Hell and Purgatory. He was simply elaborating on a well-established theological tradition for which there was ample biblical precedent.[64] This, then, is the second characteristic of Dante's system of punishments, its purely rational component; taken together, they would constitute little more than a lengthy allegory, and in no wise justify the high esteem in which the *Commedia* is held. This stems, as we have argued, from the presence of a third factor that quite transforms and redeems the other two.

The third factor is, to repeat, the new dimension of imaginative expression that Dante opens up by his living presence in the poem. One sentence of Canto XXXIII sums up the effect of his presence. In answer to a cry for help from one of the damned frozen up in ice, Dante (the personage) says:

> "Se vuo' ch'i'ti sovvegna,
> dimmi chi se', e s'io non ti disbrigo,
> al fondo della ghiaccia ir mi convegna."[65]

> ("If thou wouldst have me aid thee, tell me who thou art, and if I do not extricate thee may I go to the bottom of the ice.")

Dante "liberates" his mediaeval characters from their condition within the fixed laws of contemporary understanding and belief, which would represent them allegorically at best, and he does so by talking to them and getting them to tell him who they are. In dialogue with himself, the poet standing apart, they become individuals in their own right—albeit for only a few moments, but they are moments that have their own kind of literary "eternity" and one that has to be snatched away from the eternal course of things, as several of these characters make clear to Dante. Now, in the case of Ugolino, the individual who emerges through his spoken discourse is a very different person from the traitor formally condemned. As he tells his story, the agony of a despairing father and the pathos of his loving children, naively and horrifyingly ready to sacrifice themselves to his hunger, reveals an utterly contrasting aspect of his "case." Even the crude picture of the punishment that ostensibly he *inflicts* on Archbishop Ruggieri, the man responsible for betraying Ugolino and starving him to death, is transformed by the end into a symbol of painful rage and desperation instead of remaining merely an allegory of fit—but surely bestial?—retribution.

Dante carries this technique forward into the *Purgatorio* and *Paradiso*, where we have already had occasion to mention examples of it in a different context. Indeed, the changed visual and spiritual context of the later canticles makes it natural that the contrast between the individual and his environment should appear less and less striking. This does not mean, however, that Dante makes less effective use of his new perspective the higher he mounts towards Heaven. In Purgatory, certainly, some individuals have as vivid a personality as any of those in Hell, even if their story is less lurid. And Dante has other ways of exploiting his imaginative position that yield a richer poetic canvas than the sensational scenes in Hell. For instance, a very large number of images are concerned with the theme of orientation. Even the importance attaching to Dante's shadow, which we discussed at the outset, involves the question of where Dante is standing in relation to the sun, and the theme of orientation itself is basic to both the landscape and the doctrine of Purgatory. Which way to go, what is on the left and the right, who goes first, how high the pilgrims have ascended: these are the visual equivalents of the doctrinal task of the *Purgatorio*, which is to teach the true adjustment of man's energy and appetite to the will of God—his libido, as we might now say, to the "Love that moves the sun and the other stars." Simply to have made the description of climbing a mountain stand for stages in a psychological development, however, would have produced no more than a straightforward allegory. If we ask what else Dante's poetry achieves (besides further dramatic encounters of a type generally familiar to us from the *Inferno*), we shall discover a wealth of beautifully observed pictures of how men and animals move, whose expressiveness depends not at all upon how well they communicate an idea, but rather the other way round: how well an idea has enabled Dante to recall scenes from actual life, which he depicts for their own sake. Lack of space confines us to one example, but the following may serve to illustrate Dante's superlative gift not so much for making up the contours of another world but rather for seizing the reality of this one:

> Quando si parte il gioco della zara
>   colui che perde si riman dolente,
>   repetendo le volte, e tristo impara:
> con l'altro se ne va tutta la gente;
>   qual va dinanzi, e qual di dietro il prende,
>   e qual da lato li si reca a mente:
> el non s'arresta, e questo e quello intende;
>   a cui porge la man, più non fa pressa;
>   e così dalla calca si difende.
> Tal era io in quella turba spessa. . . .[66]

(When the game of hazard breaks up the loser is left disconsolate, going over his throws again, and sadly learns his lesson; with the other all the people go off; one goes in front, one seizes him from behind, another at his side recalls himself to his memory; he does not stop but listens to this one and that one; each to whom he reaches his hand presses on him no longer, and so he saves himself from the throng. Such was I in that dense crowd. . . .)

Here is Dante separating himself once again from the crowd, richly conscious of his gifts and the "wealth" he can bestow upon other men. As regards the story, this scene illustrates Dante in the pilgrim's position among souls unknown to him in Purgatory, who are anxious that he shall make their fate known among the living. And Dante the poet has done so, of course, in the very act of reporting their request. But the poetically crowning achievement of his interview with them (in Canto V) occurs in the passage above, with which Canto VI opens. Dante's imagination passes beyond their individual stories, and beyond their value as a moral object-lesson about late repentance, to find this image of his own more general relationship to the world. And how brilliantly he expresses his mood in the likeness of a lucky gambler, knowing also the disconsolate wisdom of the sad loser, and the readiness of most men to take whatever they can get. But Dante escapes alone to seek the highest prize.

Dante reaches the summit of perfection as regards his natural powers, his genius, at the top of Mount Purgatory, where Virgil bids him farewell with his famous words:

> "Non aspettar mio dir più nè mio cenno:
> libero, dritto e sano è tuo arbitrio,
> e fallo fora non fare a suo senno:
> per ch'io te sovra te corono e mitrio."[67]

> ("No longer expect word or sign from me. Free, upright, and whole is thy will, and it were a fault not to act on its bidding; therefore over thyself I crown and mitre thee.")

Virgil has brought him to this point by means of his creative understanding and art (*con ingegno e con arte*), and beyond this he can see no further; here imagination alone, and self-insight, reach their limit. This passage may be read in conjunction with two others, in order to plot the course of Dante's development to this moment and then beyond it. The first is Dante's last experience in Hell, where he sees Satan himself. Satan's three heads and two wings (which send forth three winds) have given rise to much allegorical speculation, thereby diverting attention from Dante's more interesting and clearer description of his own psychological state:

> Io non mori', e non rimasi vivo:
> pensa oggimai per te, s'hai fior d'ingegno,
> qual io divenni, d'uno e d'altro privo.[68]

> (I did not die and did not remain alive; now think for thyself, if thou hast any grain of ingenuity, what I became, deprived of both death and life.)

Dante's state here could almost be compared with the one he will experience at the height of Paradise, where he will find that expression fails him just as it does here:

> Com' io divenni allor gelato e fioco,
>   nol dimandar, lettor, ch'i'non lo scrivo,
>   però ch'ogni parlar sarebbe poco.[69]
>
> (How icy and chill and hoarse I then became, ask not O reader! for I
> write it not, because all speech would fail to tell.)

The vital difference between these two extreme moments is that in Heaven Dante will feel himself taken up into, and made one with, the source of all life, which is infinitely greater than himself and above all outside himself. In Hell, Dante is driven back to an innermost point of consciousness inside himself that leaves him uncertain whether he is living or dead—he cannot say positively that he is either, only that he is neither. And to express this utter inwardness in himself, he cannot communicate even with his reader, but has to ask him to evoke an idea of this state likewise "for himself" and in himself. Satan, of course, symbolizes a spirit next to God who rebelled, wanting to possess his given spiritual power in his own right; hence the very thing that once was so beautiful and good becomes the epitome and source of ugliness and evil.[70]

Through this experience, too, Dante must pass, and in doing so he anticipates the desperate self-awareness of being nothing, neither dead nor alive, and utterly isolated from all living beings, that was to be a permanent, not a passing, discovery of many a poet of more modern times totally committed to art.* Without insisting on a new allegorical reading of Satan's three heads, the obvious remark may be made that they correspond in the manner of a travesty to the Trinity in Heaven; and they therefore also reflect, without specifically standing for, the tripartite structure of Dante's psychology. On Satan, they are unnaturally joined; they emit a vile mixture of tears and blood; the wings beneath them flap but do not fly; and their staple diet, which they have ever in their mouths, are traitors and rebels. Many social and political comments have been made in connection with this passage, and with the one above where Virgil "crowns and mitres" Dante sovereign lord over himself. It is doubtful, however, whether the *Commedia* as a whole allows us to arrive at a programmatic statement of what Dante's political views were (the *De monarchia, c.* 1312, and the *Epistolae* present his views much more explicitly). The crucial fact about the *Commedia* is that it is a poem,

* See Volume V, "The Cult of Art."

somewhat resembling an epic and in some respects a play, and that it *moves*. Its perspective changes with the changing state of mind and situation of its chief protagonist, Dante. He descends through all the depths of human perversity that imagination can plumb; and what more reprehensible act, in the face of all the wickedness that men are capable of, than to rebel and kill the emperor? But then Dante purges his imagination of all sinful imaginings and can conceive again of human innocence; what need has he then of emperor or priest—is he not perfect lord over himself, and in himself most "free, upright, and whole"? Yet this is not the end, as Dante is quickly to be reminded. His inward will may be restored, but there remains the inexplicable desire that draws the mind beyond itself; Dante will feel again the "ancient flame"[71]—a phrase deliberately taken from the *Aeneid* because, as he says, he wants to tell Virgil what it is he feels, that is, to refer the experience back to the kind of love-story told in literature (where individual passion must remain subject, tragically or peacefully, to the laws of social and historical necessity).* But Virgil has gone, and Dante must follow his love into another realm of knowledge where an unearthly Beatrice will be his guide. The ascent through which she will lead him will take him as far beyond his naturally perfected self as the descent into inner isolation had taken him in the other direction. The words with which she announces herself are as striking as those with which Virgil had left:

> "Guardaci ben! Ben son, ben son Beatrice."[72]

The line demands above all that Dante look there, outside himself, at her, at her who truly is Beatrice.

An avalanche of disputation threatens to descend at the mere mention of the role that Beatrice plays, bearing with it the weight of other evidence provided by the *Vita nuova* and the *Convivio*. It may be avoided by observing simply that, whatever she may signify, what she *does* is to carry Dante far above the earth to a vantage-point from which he can see all physical and spiritual aspects of the universe as a whole. Wholeness is the dominant figure of Dante's poetry in the *Paradiso* as orientation was in the *Purgatorio*. The reader is reminded again and again of this perspective by metaphors, similes, and plain statements of unity; and just before Beatrice ushers Dante into the starry Heaven, she makes him look back through all the circles of Heaven to show him just where he stands:

---

* See Vol. I, "Virgil's *Aeneid*," p. 323.

> e però, prima che tu più t'inlei,
>   rimira in giù, e vedi quanto mondo
>   sotto li piedi già esser ti fei.[73]

(And therefore, before thou goest further into [Heaven], look down and see how much of the universe I have already put beneath thy feet.)

And five cantos later, she tells him again to look down on the earth, which is very precisely located, before opening his eyes to the mystery of the Empyrean itself, which "has no other *where* than the divine mind" (*non ha altro dove che la mente divina*).[74] It is in this context that Dante's "political" view must be judged, for it reflects his creative experience as a poet. It is not a programme or a solution, least of all a taking of one side against another, no matter what Dante the man may have done during his active political life—a period that was past by the time he came to write the *Commedia*. What Dante moves towards through the poem is a gradual resolution of opposites, in which love and law, the individual and history, the Church and the Empire, are imagined ideally as one. His political vision, in the great poem of the *Commedia*, is no longer that of a Ghibelline or Guelf; it is the vision of a poet, of the uniquely gifted man who *sees*. Verbs of seeing and of movement dominate the vocabulary of the poem. They tell us how Dante's imagination has been moved to see the mediaeval universe as a whole, as no other man had ever seen it: from the outside.

References

1. *Purgatorio* XII, 84. The text quoted throughout is that of the Società Dantesca Italiana, ed. by G. Vandelli (Milan 1965). The translations are adapted from several English versions to suit the needs of my argument.
2. *ibid.*, II, 79.
3. *ibid.*, XXI, 133–6.
4. *ibid.*, III, 19–24.
5. *ibid.*, V, 6.
6. *ibid.*, 10–2, 16–8.
7. *ibid.*, 8–9.
8. *Inferno* XV, 46–7.
9. *Purg.* XIV, 10–5.
10. *ibid.*, XXVI, 7–9.
11. *ibid.*, 10–2.
12. CASSIANUS, *De spirit. scient.* VIII; quoted in *The Banquet*, trans. by K. Hillard (London 1889).

13. *Paradiso* II, 7.
14. *ibid.*, I, 113 and 70–3. The italics are mine.
15. See the discussion of this question in E. AUERBACH, "Figura," in *Scenes from the Drama of European Literature: Six Essays* (New York 1959).
16. *Purg.* X, 28 ff.
17. *ibid.*, 46.
18. *ibid.*, 53–4.
19. *ibid.*, 70.
20. See the discussion of this question in E. GILSON, *Dante and Philosophy*, trans. by D. Moore (London 1948).
21. *Inf.* I, 2 and 8.
22. *ibid.*, 22–7.
23. *ibid.*, 112–3.
24. *Par.* XXXIII, 85–90.
25. *ibid.*, 94–9.
26. Cf. *Par.* XXVII, 82, and II, 3. Ulysses himself uses the word *folle* (mad) in *Inf.* XXVI, 125.
27. *Inf.* XXVI, 112–7.
28. *Par.* II, 10–8.
29. *Purg.* XIX, 19 f.
30. *ibid.*, XXXI, 129.
31. *ibid.*, XIX, 7 f.
32. *Par.* XXXIII, 121–3.
33. *ibid.*, 124–6.
34. *ibid.*, 91–3.
35. See the notes in J. D. Sinclair's translation (London 1948).
36. *Inf.* XIII, 25.
37. *ibid.*, 46 and 48.
38. *ibid.*, I, 4–6.
39. *Par.* XXVIII, 111.
40. *ibid.*, XXXIII, 133–6.
41. *ibid.*, 137–8.
42. See LEO SPITZER, "Note on the Poetic and the Empirical 'I' in Medieval Authors," *Romanische Literaturstudien 1936–1956* (Tübingen 1959).
43. See, for instance, *Inf.* VII, 39, or *Par.* III, 111
44. *Par.* XXXIII, 132.
45. *ibid.*, 127–8.
46. *ibid.*, 109 and 112.
47. *ibid.*, 113.
48. See references 31 and 32 above.
49. *Par.* XXXIII, 120 and 145.
50. *ibid.*, II, 15.
51. *ibid.*, XXXIII, 76–8.
52. *ibid.*, 100–5.
53. *ibid.*, XXVII, 91–6.
54. *Inf.* XII, 22 f.; XVII, 49; XIII, 112.

640

55. *Inf.* II, 1–6. Thomas Mann used these lines as a frontispiece for his novel *Doktor Faustus* (1947), his own journey through all the perversities of the modern mind, especially those relating (like Dante's) to art and society.
56. See VIRGIL, *Aeneid* VI, and Corinthians II: xii.
57. *Inf.* II, 31.
58. *ibid.*, 37–42.
59. *ibid.*, 36.
60. *ibid.*, XXXII, 133 f.
61. *ibid.*, XXXIII, 85 f.
62. *ibid.*, 107–8.
63. *ibid.*, XXXIV, 46 f.
64. See Exodus XXI: 24; Leviticus XXIV: 20; Deuteronomy XIX: 21; Matthew VII: 2.
65. *Inf.* XXXIII, 115–7.
66. *Purg.* VI, 1–10.
67. *ibid.*, XXVII, 139–42.
68. *Inf.* XXXIV, 25–7.
69. *ibid.*, 22–4.
70. *ibid.*, 34 f.
71. *Purg.* XXX, 37 f.; cf. *Aeneid* IV, 23.
72. *ibid.*, 73.
73. *Par.* XXII, 127–9.
74. *ibid.*, XXVII, 109 f.

CHAPTER 19

"Piers Plowman" and the Ricardian Age in Literature

Stephen Medcalf*

I

"We need a new thing," wrote G. K. Chesterton, "which may be called psychological history. I mean the consideration of what things meant in the mind of a man, especially an ordinary man. . . . I have already touched on it in such a case as the totem. . . . It is not enough to be told that a tom-cat was called a totem; especially when it was not called a totem. We want to know what it felt like. Was it like Whittington's cat or like a witch's cat? Was its real name Pasht or Puss-in-boots? . . . What did vassals feel about those other totems, the lions or the leopards upon the shield of their lord? So long as we neglect this subjective side of history, which may more simply be called the inside of history, there will always be a certain limitation on that science which can be better transcended by art."[1]

There cannot be many poems as well suited for this kind of understanding as William Langland's *Piers Plowman*. For perhaps no other book is so individually marked, so concerned to be a public communication, didactic and outward, while being also so inward and so personal. Langland opens his poem (at least in the first version, the A-text, *c.* 1370, and in the second, the B-text, *c.* 1377-9[2]) with a scene at once magical and exactly located in time and place. The first ten lines are about a shepherd's or hermit's clothes—May morning—the Malvern Hills—faery—weariness—a stream under a broad bank—water moving and laughing; the language is conversational, off-hand, but compelling, partly because of the sliding effect of alliteration. This extraordinary combination of roughness and a delicate magic ("I shope me in shroudes · as I a shepe

* Lecturer in English, University of Sussex.

643

were . . . I slombred in a slepyng · it sweyued so merye"[3]) gives already the peculiar effect, at once surprising and insistent, that one is entering the mind of the man who wrote it—the effect of what J. A. Burrow has called the "drastic simile," as when Haukyn must either avenge himself openly

> . . . other frete my-selue
> Wyth-inne, as a shepster shere . . .

(like "the grating and wearing of shear-blades on their inside surface"[4]). Not only Langland but also Chaucer and the author of *Sir Gawain and the Green Knight* (*c.* 1380) are fond of this kind of simile; and C. S. Lewis noted in Dante's similes

> the suggestion of a curious intensity of sensibility in directions where modern sensibility is, I believe, much weaker: the intensity which compares the gratification of curiosity to an infant sucking at the breast, which can feel *fasciato*, muffled or wrapped up, in joy, or in light, which feels love pulling with ropes or biting with teeth, which can see spiritual or even local transitions as knots tied or untied.[5]

What one is getting from Langland is "inscape," but without effort, without the sense of intense momentariness and strain that it has in Gerard Manley Hopkins; likewise Hopkins' effect of a peculiarly individual encounter with the "thisness" of objects, but in a completely public language. There is nothing exquisite or searched-out in Langland's style, which is perhaps why Helen Gardner would deny him the "auditory imagination" of Chaucer or T. S. Eliot.[6]

None of these effects is peculiar to Langland among the poets of his time. One finds the same kind of attack, at once idiosyncratic and public, in *Pearl* (*c.* 1380), though there the language *is* exquisite and overlaid with images of colours and flowers alien to the *grisaille* world of Langland. These effects arise partly from a deliberately personal reshaping of genre. Langland comes before us offering a story of faery, something like the rich and marvellous *Sir Orfeo* of the generation before his: a man enchanted into sleep on a May morning in the countryside—one of the traditional beginnings for a Celtic fairy-tale. But thereafter the story slides into a quite different genre, that of the dream that shows us truth. Perhaps he is deliberately manipulating his readers into accepting a kind of story that they might otherwise be reluctant to pursue: but the pressure of Langland's own spiritual concerns is so great that the magical dream and the vision are grafted together into a new genre.

Similarly, at the opening of *Pearl*, we are offered a garden full of *luf-daungere*,[7] of the power of frustrated love, a garden like that of the *Roman de la rose* (1225–37 and *c.* 1275), with spices, clove-gilly flowers, and ginger growing in it. A pearl has been lost, and we begin to expect a love-allegory. But other echoes inhabit the garden: we hear that

> . . . vch gresse mot grow of grayneʒ dede,
> No whete were elleʒ to woneʒ wonne;[8]
>
> (. . . each stalk must grow from dead grains,
> No wheat would otherwise be brought home;)

in reminiscence of Christ's saying (John XII:24): "Except a corn of wheat fall into the ground and die, it abideth alone: but if it die, it bringeth forth much fruit." And when presently we are given a vision of Paradise, we know that the garden is perhaps also Eden or Solomon's garden in the Song of Songs, in which spices also grew. Or it may, indeed, be a graveyard.[9]

In both *Pearl* and *Piers Plowman* we are given something like an hallucination that ripens into a vision. In *The Parliament of Fowls* (*c.* 1376) Chaucer, with his unvaryingly self-conscious art, deliberately points out the workings of this land of dream even while he constructs it. Dreams, he says, go by habit and wish-fulfilment:

> The wery huntere, slepynge in his bed,
> To wode ayeyn his mynde goth anon. . . .
> The syke met he drynketh of the tonne;
> The lovere met he hath his lady wonne.[10]

Yet, when once he sees Nature sitting in judgment at the parliament of the birds, the poem seems to have turned from phantasy to vision: although it is again characteristic of Chaucer that we cannot so easily make the distinction here as in *Piers Plowman* or *Pearl*.

But in all three poems the sense of being shown the truth when one was composing oneself to enjoy illusion is strong. The feeling is rather like that in Frederick Rolfe's novel *Hadrian the Seventh* (1904), and especially in Peter Luke's dramatization of it: the paranoid hero, dreaming that he had been accepted into the Roman Catholic priesthood, finds himself in the confessional answering "No!" to the question "Do you love your neighbour?"[11]

Gower exploits the confessional within a vision in somewhat the same way in the *Confessio amantis* (1390), although here we have journeyed through eight books before the lover, who has been hunted through all the possible psychological reasons for his ill-success in love, is finally brought to the simple (or not so simple) realization that he is too old. Some things, particularly for those who easily defend themselves in phantasy, can be faced or understood only in a dream, a ritual situation, a work of art, or all three.

The suggestion of beginning in phantasy or faery is much stronger in the *Piers Plowman* A- and B-texts than it is in the poem that may have inspired Langland (and is certainly *Piers'* closest analogue): *Winner and Waster* (1352):

> Als I went in the weste, · wandrynge myn one,
> Bi a bonke of a bourne, · bryghte was the sone. . . .[12]

Here the noise of the stream, together with the chattering of birds, listed at length, delays the dreamer from falling asleep. But when he does so, he is immediately in a symbolic dream. The natural detail, of colours and birdsong, is much more abundant but much less forceful than in Langland's spare description; and there is no sense of enchantment at all. *Winner and Waster*, in fact, reads more like a didactic poem or debate dressed up in pleasing circumstance, and one sees by contrast how carefully Langland has created a poem that echoes in the mind, suggesting much more than the didactic.

But it was a form that, having created, he abandoned. After 1390 he made his final revision, the C-text. In this, he pared away both the suggestion of faery and the bemusing brook, and adopted the form of *Winner and Waster*. This is characteristic of a general trend in the C-text: ambiguities, tensions, and as much as possible of what might impede the significance and didactic intent of the poem were cut away. It is as if Langland, having completed his search in the course of composing the B-text, felt that nothing—no elusiveness, doubt, or overtone—should obscure the view of the world he had gained.

After the opening 10 lines of the Prologue we move into the first dream. But oddly enough, although the dreamer (like the author of *Winner and Waster*) tells us that he "wist never where" he was, we do not seem quite to have left the waking landscape behind. We are still on a hill and below a hill as before: above us to the east

> . . . an hiegh to the sonne,
> I seigh [saw] a toure on a toft · trielich [excellently] ymaked;
> A depe dale binethe · a dongeon there-inne,

With depe dyches and derke · and dredful of sight.
A faire felde ful of folke · fonde I there bytwene,
Of alle maner of men · the mene and the riche,
Worchyng and wandryng · as the worlde asketh.[13]

The visionary landscape is very like the actual. They are made more like by Langland in naming the first, actual landscape. It is that of the Malvern Hills, which are even better described in the dream—the second landscape—than in the first. R. W. Chambers, writing to Allan Bright about Bright's identification of the spot where Langland places his dream, describes the first and second together:

> As you shewed it to me, it seemed certain. There was the Primeswell, and certainly it "sweyved so merye," as it is the nature of a brook to do. If you look up to the right hand, the east "an hiegh to the sonne," you see the Herefordshire Beacon towering above you, with its mighty entrenchments. It must have been even more of a "tower on a toft" in the fourteenth century, with its Norman work standing out much more boldly than, after so many centuries of denudation, it does now. There is the vale beneath; the "dungeon"—the Old Castle—has disappeared, but its "deep ditches and dark" remain. Between, is the fair field.[14]

One need not make so precise an identification (although this one is fairly convincing) to recognize that significance is being seen in, with, and under the physical landscape. Landscape and meaning are being fused together in a way that has been experienced at various levels by other visionaries. George Fox, for instance, says, "When first I set my horse's feet atop of Scottish ground, I felt the seed of God to sparkle about me like innumerable sparks of fire. Not but that there is abundance of thick cloddy earth of hypocrisy and falseness that is atop, and a briery, brambly nature, which is to be burnt up with God's Word, and ploughed up with His spiritual plough, before God's Seed brings forth heavenly and spiritual fruit. . . ."[15] The actual Scottish heath becomes partly a metaphor, partly a prophecy about the spiritual condition of Scotland. At a deeper level Isaiah, standing in the Temple at Jerusalem, saw it become the vehicle of divine glory: "In the year that King Uzziah died I saw also the Lord sitting upon a throne, high and lifted up, and his train filled the temple."[16] Langland's Prologue describes something between the two, not unlike Fox's, but with a greater supersession of the physical by vision. Elsewhere he describes visions that are closer, variously, to Fox's— as in the ploughing of Piers' field[17]—or to Isaiah's—as when, during the mass at the offertory, Piers Plowman, "painted al blody"

647

> . . . come in with a crosse · bifor the commune peple
> And riȝte lyke in alle lymes · to oure Lorde Iesu.[18]

Although visionaries have talked in such ways in all ages, it seems easier for them to do so in some periods than in others. T. S. Eliot has more work to do in our own time in describing visionary landscapes than Langland had in his. The landscapes of mediaeval literature are landscapes of meaning, brimming with significance. They relate at once to human meanings and purposes; and they lend themselves naturally to the mystic's vision. They can also easily be abolished altogether in favour of significance. Once again, in the C-text, Langland destroyed as much topographical detail as he could—the "toft" on which the tower stood, the "dongeon" that stood in the dale beneath, and the "depe dyches and derke" that surrounded it. Instead he makes at once explicit what in the B-text must await an interpreter—that Truth was in the tower, and Death and wicked spirits in the dale.[19] We have something that, if it is physical at all, is more akin to the arranged scenery of a morality play or of the Cornish mysteries,[20] with God, the World, and Hell sitting above or beside the main action, than to the visionary landscape under the Malvern Hills. The impression is no longer of an actual thing seen symbolically, *sub specie essentiae*, but of a thought that, as in some of the "drastic similes" mentioned before, easily embodies itself concretely: mediaeval allegory works equally happily in both directions.

Between the tower and the dale, Langland sets the world, filled with people "worchyng and wandryng, as the worlde asketh." From the beginning, ploughmen come first among crafts to his mind, and those in this field who

> . . . wonnen that wastours · with glotonye destruyeth[21]

evoke *Winner and Waster*, with the difference that the earlier poem allows more argument to the consumers, whereas Langland never gives an inch, here or elsewhere, in demanding that every man work

> Or in dykynge or in deluynge · or trauaillynge in preyeres.[22]

So he contrasts the ploughmen with the vain, who dress according to their vanity, and then—as if to make sure that he does not seem to confine working to the lay, active life—contrasts these in turn with those who

> In prayers and in penance · putten hem manye.[23]

This phrase *putten hem* (apply themselves)—to the plough, to pride, or to prayer—is used only with the first three classes: the workers, the rich and ostentatious, and the religious, who account for the majority of mankind. Langland turns to classes who might perhaps be difficult to identify with any of the three. The contemplatives of prayer and penance he has just mentioned seem to bring to his mind Christ's phrase to Martha—in mediaeval thought, the type of the active life—about her sister Mary, the contemplative: "Mary has chosen the best part"[24]; for Langland's next lines make an ironic contrast:

> And somme chosen chaffare · they cheuen the bettere,
> As it semeth to owre sy3t · that suche men thryueth;
> And somme murthes to make · as mynstralles conneth.[25]

In the A- and B-texts Langland thinks minstrels are guiltless, in contrast to "iapers" and "iangelers"; in the C-text he decides more austerely that minstrels are as guilty and idle as the rest.

Thus far Langland's association of ideas has proceeded by a tangling with ethics: now the dream moves more swiftly into a chaos, still without colours but with unending, meaningless motion, like the lives of Dante's futile people at the gates of Hell, who have chosen neither good nor evil. The resemblance is a matter of values common to the two poets, for there is no evidence that Langland, or anyone else in England, knew anything of Dante before Chaucer's mission to Italy in 1372–3:

> Bidders and beggeres · fast aboute 3ede. . . .
> Slepe and sori sleuthe · seweth hem eure.
> Pilgrymes and palmers · pli3ted hem togidere
> To seke seynt Iames · and seyntes in rome.
> Thei went forth in here wey · with many wise tales,
> And hadden leue to lye · al here lyf after. . . .
> Heremites on an heep · with hoked staues,
> Wenten to Walsyngham · and here wenches after.[26]

> (Beggars and mendicants rushed about quickly. . . . Sleep and sorry sloth always pursue them. Pilgrims and palmers banded together to go after St James and saints at Rome. They went out on their way with many clever stories, and had leave to lie all their lives after. Hermits in a mob with hooked staves went to Walsingham, and their girl-friends followed them.)

The minstrels perhaps suggested to Langland this glimpse of the wayfaring life of the Middle Ages,* and we are now well into one of the crowd scenes that, as Burrow has pointed out, are characteristic of the

* Other chapters have noted it as typical of the period; see, for instance, Ch. 12, "Courts and Courtly Love."

writing of Langland's contemporaries—Gower's *Confessio, Sir Gawain and the Green Knight*, and especially Chaucer's work, culminating in the extended crowd scene that is the background of *The Canterbury Tales* (*c.* 1387 ff.).[27] The crowd scene suited the way writers of the time portrayed the world—at once realistic and a way of summing up or caricaturing all humanity in bulk: a kind of natural allegory, because each man necessarily tends to become Everyman in a crowd—he can be either confounded with or set off by his companions. Eliot has done the same thing for our time in *The Waste Land* (1922); significantly, he borrows one of Dante's lines about the futile to make the crowd's meaning apparent:

> A crowd flowed over London Bridge, so many,
> I had not thought death had undone so many.[28]

Langland's pilgrims and hermits once more suggest a moral theme in their misuse of religion, and we pass—through friars, pardoners, clergy who desert their parishes for better money in London, and bishops who turn civil servants—to another use of allegory altogether, which adumbrates one of the great issues of Christian civilization. In a passage added in the B-text for its topicality (but retained in the C-text), Langland points out, with something more than a pun, that Christ left the power of Peter's keys to love and the cardinal virtues, and not to the cardinals who have just (September 1378) presumed to elect an anti-pope in Peter's succession. He does not quite impugn them: at some level of his mind, he seems to be aware of what C. S. Lewis has pointed out: that it is in the nature of Catholicism to be allegorical, to embody penitence in penance, man's peregrine status in pilgrimages, and grace in sacraments.[29] Langland was a sacramentalist and by no means anti-Catholic; moreover, in his poem he is searching into "that region of the mind where the bifurcation"[29] between spiritual and material, and hence between the Protestant and Catholic emphases of Christendom, had not yet occurred. In the institutional world of churches and sects it had not occurred at this time either: it was in fact at just this time (the years 1378 and 1379) that Wyclif began to clarify his position about the bifurcation by attacking the doctrine of transubstantiation. One cannot really talk of Catholics and Protestants until decisive positions had been taken up in those matters. So Langland (neither Catholic nor Protestant but simply a mediaeval Christian) makes jokes against bad cardinals but is not sure whether to deny their right to their title, nor the right of the pope to hold the gates of Heaven so long as he acts in obedience to love, the real vicar of Christ

("Countrepleide it no3t," Langland adds in the C-text, "for holy churches sake"[30]).

This historical world, in which allegory was not simply a literary device but the key to real, worldly meaning, authority, and power, gave Langland a much wider range of acceptable significance than was available to Eliot. When Eliot offers some kind of light and order to set against the dim crowds of London the effect is local and inaccessible:

> . . . where the walls
> Of Magnus Martyr hold
> Inexplicable splendour of Ionian white and gold.[31]

Langland, living in an age of acted symbolism—that is, ritual—has available an image in which the whole people takes part and which almost sacramentally describes their whole political life. His equivalent to Eliot's image of a peaceful backwater of London is a formal picture of an ideal state (secular power balancing the power of the pope), bound together by a social covenant in the symbolism of a coronation (the king's bond in such a state was expressed in his coronation oath: to render justice in compassion and in truth, as is evident both in the care taken in framing Richard II's oath in 1379 and in the proceedings for his deposition 20 years later):[32]

> Thanne come there a kyng · kny3thod hym ladde,
> Mi3t of the comunes · made hym to regne,
> And thanne cam kynde wytte · and clerkes he made,
> For to conseille the kyng · and the comune saue.[33]

The four estates—king, knighthood, clergy, and commons—arrange the state among them: ploughmen (again their craft is given dominance) are ordained to "trauaile as trewe lyf asketh." Four variants on the demand for justice between the people and their king are then cried out. A lean lunatic (the leanness suggests Langland himself, for it is a feature he stresses in himself elsewhere) prays:

> Crist kepe the, sire kyng · and thi kyngriche,
> And leue the lede thi londe · so leute the louye,
> And for thi ri3tful rewlyng · be rewarded in heuene.[34]

> (Christ keep you, Lord King, and your kingdom, and let you rule your country so that loyal folk may love you and that you for your right ruling may be rewarded in heaven.)

The notion of reward in Heaven suggests the counterbalancing thought that an angel in the air on high stoops out of Heaven to utter: a king, too, is subject to fortune, may be deposed, and will die. (He speaks in Latin, for this is business in which unlearned men cannot join—whether for good or ill, Langland does not say.) Because it is the law of the archetype of kingship, Christ, that the king administers, justice demands in its nakedness that he clothe it with mercy (*pietas*). The law of measure for measure applies to him too: naked justice for naked justice, mercy for mercy.

Next, a satiric jester, a glutton for words, plays with the word *rex*, answering the angel in apparent offence: since *rex* is a word from *regere*, a king has the word without the thing unless he studies to maintain the laws.[35] This is ambiguous; does he mean that a king who falls below justice is no king and deserves to be deposed, or that a king should maintain an iron rule without mercy if he is to be a real king? What is clear is that the jester is introducing a discord into the balanced picture of the good king. The discord is resolved by the fourth voice, that of the commons, who cry out: "The king's words are the bonds of law to us."[36] But this, too, is ambiguous, and this time Langland means it to be: "construe ho-so wolde," he comments.[37] Is it good or bad that the king's commands should constitute absolute law? And do the commons wish to be chained by them, or not?

So far we have a picture rather like an illumination to the text of a coronation ritual: king, lean lunatic, angel on high, satiric jester, and commons, with the king's council of bishops and knights attending.[38] But Langland wants to allow—just as he allows with the passage from faery dream to vision—a hint of quite a different picture to shadow the scene. And immediately, in the fable of belling the cat, we have it. Crazily, grotesquely, the rats and mice run on, and a rat demands that someone should bell a cat of the court that

> . . . pleyde with hem perilouslych · and possed hem aboute.[39]

In April 1376, a year before Richard II's coronation, Thomas Brunton, bishop of Rochester, had used this fable in a courageous sermon demanding action against the corruption of the government under John of Gaunt; and Langland may have taken the story from this occasion.[40] But if so, his application is very different; for the rat is answered by a mouse that it is better to let the cat be, for after all

> There the catte is a kitoun · the courte is ful elyng [miserable][41]

—that is, where a boy is king, government will suffer; which seems to be a clear reference to the youth of Richard II, who was 11 years old when he ascended the throne. Where there is no cat to keep control, argues the mouse, there is intolerable anarchy; the mice and rats destroy everything. Here is a reductionist theory of politics, a belief in the necessity of absolute control, in keeping with the shift in allegory from high to low, from ritual to caricature. But after all it, too, is ambiguous; for the mouse may, as in the original fable, be speaking out of mere cowardice —no one is brave enough to bell the cat. And Langland leaves it so, saying

> What this meteles [dream] bemeneth ·3e men that be merye,
> Deuine 3e, for I ne dar · bi dere god in heuene![42]

This allegory of the rulers of Church and state was no doubt occasioned by the election of the anti-pope and the accession of Richard II, for Langland added it all in the B-text. In 1390 he excised from the C-text everything between the jester's speech and the end of the fable of belling the cat—the whole of the passage shadowed by caricature—whether as part of his removal of all ambiguities, or because after the Peasants' Revolt the implied criticisms were abhorrent to him or, during Richard II's personal rule, inappropriate.[43]

At any rate we revert to the straightforward crowd scene of the A-text, now more definitely a London street, to lawyers who will give no opinion except for money (appropriately, because in the B-text the obscurity of the laws has been discussed), and to all the trades; and the Prologue ends in the clamour of idlers singing, of cooks crying hot food and taverners their wine.

The dream has been offered to the reader so convincingly that the whole scene, alien as it is in time and dress, seems familiar even today. There are difficulties in it, but even these work by nettling the reader into attempting their solution; and apart from any political reasons Langland may have had for covering his meaning, it is possible that Blake's opinion is true of him:

> The wisest of the ancients considered what is not too explicit the
> fittest for instruction, because it rouses the faculties to act.[44]

On the other hand it is likely that Langland could see no solution to his basic problems, and used the concrete and active form of allegory to tease out his latent meanings. This is almost certainly true of later passages in the poem.

The technique of the Prologue thus conspires to involve the reader in two enduring problems—first, the way in which men live carelessly while eternity (the choice of tower and dungeon) surrounds them; and second, the difficulty of making a satisfactory society out of a crowd—the dialectic of whose investigation will keep him searching throughout the poem.

II

Langland's capacity for drawing the reader in, together with his peculiar way of perceiving phenomena as significant, are very striking. He was obviously aware, at some level of his mind, of both these aspects of his work, as his use of shifting genre and allegory of several kinds shows. Both elements pervade what Burrow has called Ricardian literature,[45] that marvellous body of literature that sprang up soon after English replaced French as the chief language of educated people, which happened relatively suddenly in the period immediately following the Black Death. It was produced almost entirely, though not exclusively, during the reign of Richard II (1377–99). It includes the books of Langland, Chaucer, Gower, and the author of *Sir Gawain and the Green Knight* and *Pearl* among major poets; the prose writings of the three great English mystics, Walter Hilton, Julian of Norwich, and the author of *The Cloud of Unknowing* (*c.* 1370); the sermons and other writings of John Wyclif; the works of such writers as Thomas Usk, John Lydgate, the translator of Sir John Mandeville's *Travels*, Margery Kempe, Thomas Chestre, John of Trevisa, Thomas Hoccleve, Sir John Clanvowe, Nicholas Hereford, and John Purvey; and anonymous works among mediaeval lyrics, miracle plays, and romances, some of which (especially the lyrics) bear comparison with the greatest works of the period.[46] Before we discuss the way in which Langland explores the mystery presented to us in his Prologue, it will be worth while to consider the characteristics of some of this contemporary literature, together with the society that produced it, with particular regard to the two characteristics of Langland's art just mentioned.

III

Owen Barfield has noted that many of the words that came over from France with the Normans "seem to have a distinctive character of their own, and even now . . . they will sometimes stand out from the printed page with particular appeal. Perhaps this is especially true of the military vocabulary. That sharp little brightness, as of a window-pane flashing just after sunset, which belongs to the ancient, technical language of heraldry, such as *argent, azure, gules* . . . somehow seems to have spread to more common Norman words—*banner, hauberk, lance, pennon,* . . . and—in the right mood—we can even catch a gleam of it in everyday terms like *arms, assault, battle, fortress, harness, siege, standard, tower,* and *war*."[47]

In its first two lines, *Sir Gawain and the Green Knight* enters the world that spoke this language, and sets it alongside another:

> Siþen þe sege and þe assaut · watz sesed at Troye,
> þe borȝ brittened and brent · to brondez and askez. . . .[48]

> (After the siege and the assault had ceased at Troy, the city wrecked and burnt to charcoal and ashes . . . .)

In the first line the stressed words *sege, assaut,* and *sesed* are Norman French; in the second line, every word is Old English, with some overlay of Norse in the grammar and pronunciation. Compared with the technical and chivalric atmosphere of the first line, the second is domestic and everyday: none of its words is exclusive to the vocabulary of war. This effect may well have been one that the poet was conscious of: the evidence of first-known use is consistent with all the French words having entered English within the century before he wrote, so that they would have retained a very obviously contrasted feeling.

Throughout the poem the sense of a union between two worlds continues: on the one hand the world of French speaking, of courts, of courtly love and manners, of studying heraldry and books of romance, with an aesthetic taste for the sharp and bright, as when Gawain sees a castle clustered with so many pinnacles among the battlements

> þat pared out of papure · purely hit semed . . .[49]

and on the other hand the world of a countryman from the borders of Staffordshire and Cheshire, speaking a rough dialect and accustomed to listening to heroic stories in alliterative verse, dominated by strong physical sensations, by warmth and cold, the vigour of the hunt, the weather, the turn of the seasons, and the habits of animals. And, as in the repetition of sense in the first pair of lines, each world gives the other an added dimension of significance, concreteness, and acute self-consciousness.

The self-consciousness is probably not something the poet expected his readers or listeners to share at this stage of the poem, or they might be too discomforted by the mention of treachery in the next two lines—

> þe tulk [man] þat þe trammes [tricks] · of tresoun þer wroȝt
> Watz tried for his tricherie · þe trewest on erthe[50]

—and by the ambiguity, perhaps intentional, of *trewest* (most utterly treacherous? or, despite his treachery, most upright?); for although the poet is capable of slovenliness, he is also capable of subtle effects, and in this case the ambiguity of truth is to become the dominant theme of the poem.

The poem hurries on from Troy into an opening full of purposive movement, as Aeneas and his followers radiate out from Troy to found the kingdoms of the west, until Brutus founds Britain, and we abandon movement through space for movement through time—to the reign of Arthur, where we move down from our high position above history into involvement with the New Year feast of the court at Camelot.[51] But even now we are reminded that this was long ago:

> For al watz þis fayre folk · in her first age,
> On sille [in the hall],
> þe hapnest [luckiest] vnder heuen,
> Kyng hyȝest mon of wylle.[52]

It is not improbable that, like Langland, the *Gawain*-poet took his departure from *Winner and Waster:* his two opening verses are simply an expansion of the first four lines of that poem:

> Sythen that Bretayne was biggede, · and Bruyttus it aughte [possessed],
> Thurgh the takynge of Troye · with tresone with-inn,
> There hathe selcouthes [marvels] bene sene · in seere [various]kynges tymes
> Bot neuer so many as nowe, · by the nyn[d]e dele [ninth part].[53]

This may have come from a common stock of motifs: another alliterative poem of the Ricardian age, the northern English *Morte Arthure*, ends by tracing Arthur's line to Brutus and Troy.[54] But there is more striking common detail in *Winner and Waster:* treason, for instance, and the many wonders that have befallen Britain since, under different kings.

But in *Winner and Waster* this is a mere opening flourish, whereas the *Gawain*-poet uses it to convey a sense of time contained in time, and of an age before the last age: of histories and peoples perishing and surviving. It is a sense that Professor Tolkien has noted as native to fairy-tale— "distance and a great abyss of time"[55]—and to *Beowulf*—"already the long ago had a special poetical attraction [and] its maker expended his art in making keen that touch upon the heart which sorrows have that are both poignant and remote."[56] It is in fact something native to the alliterative tradition, not only in *Beowulf* but in *The Wanderer* and *The Ruin*, and in the early-13th-century *Brut* of Laȝamon.[57]

There seems also present in this opening something that the author might have found associated with the fall of Troy in the *Aeneid*, and that Chaucer conveys in *Troilus and Criseyde* (*c.* 1380)—a sense of the pressure of war and of the precariousness of peaceful habits. All these nuances are appropriate to the story he has to tell. For into the joyful noise of Arthur's hall comes the Green Knight, at once gay and ominous, to challenge

> þe reuel and þe renoun · of þe Rounde Table[58]

with a wager. Any knight may strike him now with his great axe if he will swear to suffer a return blow in a year's time. Arthur moves to accept the wager, but Gawain claims the right, because the game is too *nys* (silly) for a king. When the Green Knight's head falls and the red blood gleams on his green body, the knight picks it up, and his severed head charges Gawain to stand the return blow next New Year's morning at the Green Chapel.

The manners of Arthur's court are sufficient to sustain this violent outrage—Arthur gently tells Guinevere that it is only a Christmas game— but the year until Gawain must be tested passes in deliberately pointed suspense: a year in which natural phenomena are treated, like the Malvern Hills in *Piers Plowman*, as symbolic. The Christian year of Christmas, Lent, and Michaelmas is mixed with the changing of the seasons; and, underlying the seasons, are combat, happiness, the alternation of life and death, with a slight playing on the colour green: for in the spring

> Boþe groundez and þe greues · grene ar her wedez

and in autumn

> Wroþe [angry] wynde of þe welkyn [heaven] · wrastelez with þe sunne,
> þe leuez lancen [fall] fro þe lynde [linden trees] · and lyȝten on þe grounde,
> And al grayes þe gres · þat grene watz ere;
> Al rypez and rotez · þat ros vpon fyrst,
> And þus ȝirnez [passes] þe ȝere · in ȝisterdayez mony,
> And wynter wyndez aȝayn, · as þe worlde askez.[59]

Langland employs the oral tag *as þe worlde askez* with a stress on *worlde*— the world over against eternity—whereas the *Gawain*-poet perhaps stresses *askez*, emphasizing the tension; but both poets use it with a sense of distraction from some *kairos*, some critical time of judgment, and both give it, by its place in the syntax of their sentences, a conscious weight such as an everyday oral poet might not aspire to.

Gawain arms himself for the journey: his arming demonstrates both the ideal balanced perfection of mediaeval chivalry and his own claim to be the perfect knight. His device is the pentangle: his five faultless senses and five fingers, his trust in the five wounds of Christ and in the five joys of Mary, and the five qualities of his character—all five fives balanced, interlocking, and supporting. The five qualities of character are the most important because they are unfolded in it:

> . . . fraunchyse and fela3schyp · forbe al þyng,
> His clannes and his cortaysye · croked were neuer,
> And pité, þat passez alle poyntez. . . .[60]

Fraunchyse (magnanimity, the quality of a hero) balances with *fela3schyp* (good companionship)—the two qualities that show that Gawain, like the Black Prince, knows the "doctrine of largesse,"[61] and also the two qualities that Shakespeare presented later in Henry V as essential to an ideal leader; the qualities, moreover, that have led Gawain to accept the dangerous game of the Beheading. *Clannes* (chastity) and *cortaysye* were almost opposed in the system of courtly love, but, as the story is to show us, they are never *croked* in Gawain. The single and unpaired *pité* may (like the *pietas* of Langland's king) mean mercy, but in terms of the story is more likely to be piety—the devotion to Christ and the Virgin Mary that Gawain displays in bearing Mary's image on his shield, and that is to help him at two crucial points in his adventures.

So the knight sets forth, and thus far, apart from the vigour of the telling, we may seem to have a courtly romance that conforms to what Erich Auerbach and D. W. Robertson have variously said of the type. "In charmingly graceful, delicately pointed, and crystalline verses, knightly society offers its own presentment," celebrating its values, "refinement of the laws of combat, courteous social intercourse, service of women . . . all directed toward a personal and absolute ideal—absolute both in reference to ideal realization and in reference to the absence of any earthly and practical purpose."[62] In so doing it celebrates no more than its own existence, the existence of a class that no longer has any real social or economic function: its stories are about the only two themes worthy of a knight—"feats of arms, and love"—adventures that happen for no other end than to prove the knight in a land without "geographical relation to the known world and in a time which apart from them passes 'without leaving a trace'."[63] In such stories, aristocratic society uses to

celebrate its own qualities the general characteristics of mediaeval literature singled out by Robertson: in that literature, he claims, a man's
"feelings are not specifically displayed before us; instead his condition
is described with reference to an objective scheme of moral values. . . .
Mediaeval characters are frequently exemplary—either of wise or of
unwise action—but mediaeval authors do not usually invite us to share
their experiences."[64]

In so far as this is a true description of mediaeval romance, it begins
to seem as if the *Gawain*-poet is doing something novel with his genre (as
Langland does with the faery dream) in the verses immediately following
the arming. Gawain, with "no gome [man] but God·bi gate [road]
wyth to" talk, rides into an exactly located country, over the Dee at a
ford called "The Holy Head"—probably the holy well where (one of
the author's minute effects) St Winifred, like the Green Knight, had her
severed head restored to her shoulders[65]—and onward into the Wirral,
some 30 miles from the area where the poem, as its dialect shows, was
written or conceived. He fights with wild beasts and wild men:

> And etaynez, þat hym anelede · of þe heȝe felle;
> Nade he ben duȝty and dryȝe, · and Dryȝtyn had serued,
> Douteles he hade ben ded · and dreped ful ofte.
> For werre wrathed hym not so much · þat wynter nas wors,
> When þe colde cler water · fro þe cloudez schadde
> And fres er hit falle myȝt · to þe fale erþe;
> Ner slayn wyth þe slete · he sleped in his yrnes
> Mo nyȝtes þen innoghe · in naked rokkez,
> Þer as claterande fro þe creste · þe colde borne rennez,
> And henged heȝe ouer his hede · in hard iisse-ikkles.[66]

(And ogres, that came breathing down after him from the high fell;
had he not been brave and enduring, and a servant of the Lord,
without doubt he would have been dead, and killed many times. For
war troubled him not so much but that winter was worse, when the
cold clear water was shed from the clouds, and froze before it could fall
to the pale brown earth. Nearly slain by the sleet, he slept in his
armour, more nights than enough in bare rocks, where clattering
from the crest the cold stream ran and hung high over his head in
hard icicles.)

Like the landscape at the beginning of *Piers Plowman*, this one is exactly
portrayed and recognizable (it is most probably the writer's locality,
the Peak District)[67]; at the same time it is a *significant* landscape, brimming
with response (even if hostile response) to human meanings and purposes.
"Nature," wrote C. S. Lewis, "has that in her which compels us to invent

giants: and only giants will do. Notice that Gawain was in the northwest corner of England when 'etins aneleden him,' giants came *blowing* after him on the high fells. Can it be an accident that Wordsworth was in the same places when he heard 'low breathings coming after him'?"[68] One is tempted to think that the landscape is a "romantic" one, responding to the hero's, or the poet's, feelings. It is, in a way: but it is also more than that. The giants are physically real: Gawain has no inward guilt, as Wordsworth had, that might co-operate with nature in evoking them from the landscape.

Against this very mediaeval landscape Gawain moves, more timelessly, like the Old English *Wanderer*, and also like Kierkegaard's Abraham or the Old Testament's: alone with God. And what is most striking is that his winter sufferings are so described as to persuade us into empathy. The author, consciously or unconsciously, does invite us to share Gawain's plight. This empathy is continued, and even extended to the world about us: the author is surpassed only by Keats in his gift for transferring us under other skins, as of the

> . . . mony bryddez [birds] vnblyþe · vpon bare twyges,
> Þat pitosly þer piped · for pyne of þe colde.[69]

On Christmas Eve Gawain prays to Christ and Mary to hear Mass of

> . . . þat syre, · þat on þat self nyȝt
> Of a burde [girl] watz borne · oure baret [troubles] to quelle.[70]

Almost at once, he comes upon a pinnacled castle, where he is invited to spend the week until New Year (his host tells him the Green Chapel is nearby). He may rest in the castle, although his host will go hunting: and the host proposes that they exchange whatever they gain during the day. And now both our admiration for Gawain as pattern, and our empathy with him, are exercised in a most singular way: for on three successive days his host's wife attempts to seduce him, and each day we feel like cheering him as, in the intricate and delicately recounted conversations, he maintains both his *cortaysye* and his *clannes*, each day receiving one or more kisses, which he duly gives his host. Each day his host hunts and kills a beast: and on the last day in particular the poet seems to use empathy with the animal world to enforce empathy with Gawain, when the fox (like Gawain, with death before his eyes) thinks he has eluded the hounds: for a moment we see through his eyes as the hounds come on him again:

> He blenched [swerved] aȝayn bilyue [quickly]
> And stifly [undaunted] start on-stray [out of his way],
> With alle þe wo on lyue
> To þe wod he went away.[71]

On this last day, indeed, the lady presses Gawain so hard that if it were not for the Virgin Mary's care for him, his *cortaysye* would have overcome his duty to his host. But the lady sadly admits defeat, and offers him an enchanted green silk girdle, which has the power to protect its wearer against violent death. Gawain (with an eye to his ordeal in the Green Chapel) accepts the girdle, goes to confession, and is shriven as "clene as domezday schulde · haf ben diȝt on þe morn."[72] On New Year's Day he rides out through the snow to the Green Chapel. The Green Knight makes two feints at him, at each of which he flinches, then at the third blow wounds him slightly in the neck. Gawain leaps back, seizes his weapons, and challenges the knight to fight. But the reader is disconcerted by a curious shift in the narrative: for the first time we look through the Green Knight's eyes, as he sees Gawain,

> How þat doȝty, dredles, · deruely þer stondez
> Armed, ful aȝlez: · in hert hit hym lykez.[73]

Then he shouts cheerfully that not only is the wager fulfilled but he himself is the host of the castle and had set his wife to tempt Gawain. Each feint with the axe has paid for a kiss, and the cut is Gawain's punishment for accepting the magic girdle. He was caught, like the fox, when he least expected it.

At this humiliating revelation Gawain breaks down in violent self-accusation for his cowardice, covetousness, treachery, and *untrawthe*. The Green Knight laughs and tells him that his sins are known, that he has done penance, and is *clene* (which perhaps refers to Gawain's extra fault in making a false confession, clearly concealing his intention to break his agreement by not yielding up the girdle). But Gawain's idea of himself is too deeply shaken: he even departs from knightly habit so far, while asking to be recommended to that *cortays* (the knight's wife), as to compare his treatment by her with that which women gave to Adam, Solomon, Samson, and David.[74]

When the knight allows him to keep the girdle, Gawain says he will wear it in penance and, after one final trivializing touch—the Green Knight explains that the whole affair was a trick of Gawain's aunt, the witch Morgan la Faye, to frighten Guinevere (which, we recall, Arthur's courtesy in consoling his wife had forestalled)—he rides back to Camelot, again confesses to cowardice, covetousness, and *untrawthe*, and insists that he will wear the girdle as a token of treachery that cannot be undone. Arthur comforts him, and the members of the Round Table all agree to wear a green girdle for Gawain's sake. The story is set back once more in its frame of adventures that have happened—

> Syþen Brutus, þe bolde burne · boȝed hider fyrst,
> After þe segge and þe asaut · watz sesed at Troyeȝ[75]

(once again, the lines divide into Old English and Norman French)—and the poem ends with a prayer:

> Now þat bere þe croun of þorne,
> He bryng vus to his blysse.[76]

It is probably no more than a coincidence, but *Abraham and Isaac* (a play preserved in a Common Place book from Brome Manor in Suffolk), also about the testing of truth, ends with almost the same couplet: the *Gawain*-poet may have known it.[77]

Consciously or unconsciously, then, the poet has offered his audience what seems to be a straightforward romance; has with great skill persuaded us to applaud Gawain's dishonest attempt to conceal the girdle and to ignore his false confession; and has then torn the foundation from under our feet by showing all this as it looked through the Green Knight's eyes, and shifting the whole poem for a moment into a comic key. All this, indeed, we might have predicted, for at the very start the poet warned us that truth in man cannot be trusted: Troy fell so.

Perhaps, then, it was the poet's deliberate intention to shock us into sharing not only Gawain's adventure but also his moment of self-recognition and his penitence. (The defeat of our expectations about a hero with whom we tend to identify is the same device that William Golding used in *Pincher Martin* [1956].) We are to realize that the most formidable temptation always comes when we are not looking for it, and that we ourselves are not secure. The only final wisdom is in confession and penitence. Yet we are not even left there: we are reminded that repentance itself can be excessive and that the values of Arthur's court are good values, in so far as they centre on *felaȝschyp* and recognition of our shared fortune. But we cannot expect to live up to them. And finally we are persuaded to see the whole adventure in a historical pattern, perhaps from a little outside time. Our pride is attacked on all sides.

662

This interpretation of *Sir Gawain and the Green Knight*, and in particular the point about the reader's identification with Gawain, may seem a little far-fetched. Yet the notions of a phantasy that becomes truth and of a dream that shows us a mirror of ourselves were familiar enough in Richard II's time, as we have already seen. And self-consciousness mediated through the confessional was a natural theme for literature, especially religious literature, after 1215, when the fourth Lateran council enjoined yearly confession and communion.[78]

The same point might be illustrated from Gower's *Confessio amantis*, but we may appeal to the other poems that are almost certainly the work of the *Gawain*-poet. In *Patience* and in *Clannesse* (Purity) he attempts straightforward sermons, with illustrative *exempla*, in alliterative metre: and in *Patience* we find his characteristic devices to make us participate—as when Jonah enters the whale's belly. It is at least possible that he then took the steps outlined by Gabriel Josipovici in relation to Chaucer:

> At the heart of St Augustine's theology lies the distinction between *amor sui* and *amor dei*. All evil springs from a wrong choice of the will, from putting oneself instead of God at the centre of the universe. Pride is the basic sin. . . . Clearly this presents a problem for the preacher; it is not enough to tell a man that he is proud, since all too often his pride consists in the belief that only he of all men is humble. To exhort the proud man by moral example is not enough, since what is required is a redirection of the will, not the performance of good works. The only way is to take men off their guard, to bring them to recognize of their own accord that they too are fallible, and that they had been keeping this from themselves.[79]

Sir Gawain and the Green Knight offers this recognition, perhaps especially to knights, through the kind of story that that class liked (whether or not because, as Auerbach implies, such stories enabled the knight to hide from himself the growing uselessness of his class), precisely at the period of the Indian summer of chivalry, when it was concerned to assert its way of life "with such worldly pomp, as ear hath not heard neither hath it entered into the heart of man," as Adam of Usk says of the meeting of parliament in 1398.[80] And again we must remember that Gawain is not condemned as either a knight or a man: he remains as much a pattern, if not as Chaucer's "verray parfit gentil knight," at least as his "curteis . . . lowely and servysable"[81] son the Squire, one of whose heroes is indeed "Gawayn, with his olde curteisye." (The opening of this story somewhat suggests that of *Sir Gawain and the Green Knight*.)[82] The lesson is not condemnation but the insistence that *all* Christian virtues must be founded on penitence.

The fourth poem in this group, *Pearl*, begins by shifting the genre from love-allegory to vision. But it does more: as in *Gawain* (and in *Patience*), the poem employs the device of the framing line at beginning and end. The first line—

> Perle plesaunte to Prynces paye [pleasure]

—is taken up into the love-allegory: the pain, the jealousy, and the frustration. When it appears that what the narrator is lamenting is a girl who died at less than two years of age, the love longing is only slightly shifted, and the sense of doubt and jealousy relates itself to her absence in Heaven: perhaps, indeed, to the doubt whether she can be in Heaven at all, because she is too young to have done anything to deserve it. This is not stated, but it may underlie the question actually posed: how it is that—although she has done nothing to deserve it—she is a queen in Heaven. She explains patiently and beautifully the nature of God's grace, changing as she does so the meaning of the poet's beloved word *cortaysye:* in heaven it does not suggest hierarchy, but the paradox of equal supremacy. The underlying notion of the absoluteness of God's grace in choosing and bringing mankind to Heaven had become the centre of Christian thought since 1344, when Thomas Bradwardine finished his book on God's power, *De causa Dei*, and it pervades Chaucer and Langland as much as *Pearl*. Pearl herself brings the narrator to rejoice in this, until he is able to see the City of God, Jerusalem, and the Lamb. In longing for Jerusalem he tries to cross the river that lies between him and it. As he fails, he awakens, with his head on his Pearl's grave. But the love that he is now most conscious of is not his for the Pearl, but God's for him: thus the poem ends with the prayer (more integrated with the story than the prayer for the same ends at the close of *Gawain*, more integrated as the device of the framing line is):

> He gef vus to be his homly hyne [household servants],
> Ande precious perle3 unto his pay.[83]

Christ's symbol of the pearl of great price, for which one would give up everything else, has shifted in meaning from the lost daughter, through the kingdom of Heaven, to the narrator's own self. The poem becomes partly a means of realizing the intensity of God's love for us, like the love of a frustrated court-lover; the ends and the means are not unlike those that we have suggested in *Gawain*.

The transition from jealousy to charity has been similarly made in Grahame Greene's *The End of the Affair* (1951) and—as in the former analogy between *Gawain* and *Pincher Martin*—the reason for this is clear. In all four works there is an attempt to bring self-realization to a society that lives by one set of values while half-recognizing another, by juxta-posing the knightly code, or human love, or possessive individualism, with the ethic that derives from the love of God for man.

IV

The *Gawain*-poet judges the worlds he depicts and their values, but he by no means rejects them. The acute criticism that springs from deeply held and delighted love informs his description of the life of courtesy of the 14th century. He displays both the capacity for drawing the reader in and the way of perceiving phenomena as significant that we found in Langland. He shares, moreover, another quality with Langland: a high degree of consciousness of the self. It is symbolized in the way in which Gawain and the narrator of *Pearl* stand out against the significant land-scapes around them.

Both the world that the *Gawain*-poet assumes and loves, and the degree of his detachment from it, become apparent when one turns to Thomas Usk's *Testament of Love*.[84] Usk had been clerk to John of Northampton (mayor of London, 1381–3, and a protégé of John of Gaunt) and had dabbled in politics, "helping to certain conjuracions and other grete maters of ruling of citizens," first because he thought it "bothe profit were to me and to my frendes," and second because common profit in a community cannot exist unless "pees and tranquilite, with just govern-aunce proceden from thilke profit." Subsequently he decided that North-ampton's schemes were only "of tyrannye purposed," and, being obliged to give evidence under oath, was the means of his employer's imprisonment, for the sake of peace and the City of London ("and more kyndely love have I to that place than to any other in erthe. . .").[85] His evidence, which survives in the Public Record Office, of various conspiracies to power held in a tavern at Bow, sounds circumstantial enough, and he refused to withdraw it even when, on 4 March 1388, he was sentenced to a peculiarly brutal judicial murder by Bolingbroke (Gaunt's son) and the other Lords Appellant. He made a devout end, reciting psalms and the prayers for the dying.[86]

But clearly he felt a need to justify himself, both for his turncoat behaviour toward Northampton and for the way he had earlier assisted him; and in particular (perhaps because this assistance had involved a

665

certain parade of moral reform) for some involvement in Lollardry and Wyclifism. Hence, perhaps during his last imprisonment, he wrote his *Testament*, an allegory of how love explained to him the conditions of his service to a certain Margaret. The book is a charming one, although it has arid passages, partly because Usk seems to have been a deep and earnest but careless thinker, and partly because the surviving text is exceedingly corrupt.

Usk, like most mediaeval writers, was a great adapter and copier, and the book seems to have connections with most of the literature of his time. Chaucer he heartily admires, making Love call him "the noble philosophical poete"[87] and praise his treatment of free will and predestination in *Troilus and Criseyde*. The whole *Testament* is an emulation of Chaucer's translation of Boethius' *De consolatione philosophiae*, and he also paraphrases Chaucer's defence of women against the fickleness of men from the story of Dido and Aeneas in *The House of Fame* (*c.* 1379). *Piers Plowman* may be echoed in various statements about the state of society and about the nature of love, and it is even possible that he alludes to *The Cloud of Unknowing* when he apologizes for being clothed "in the cloudy cloude of unconninge."[88] He seems indeed to be consciously part of the movement to "shewe our fantasyes" not in French or Latin but "in suche wordes as we lerneden of our dames tonge."[89]

But notably, for our purposes, it looks as if there is some connection (probably as a result of imitation on Usk's part) between Usk's Margarite-perle, as he calls her ("Margaret" means "pearl") and the Pearl of the *Gawain*-poet. When at the end of his book he makes a classic exposition of figural allegory, Usk's interpretation fits both Pearls:

> How was it, that sightful manna in deserte to children of Israel was spirituel mete? Bodily also it was, for mennes bodies it norisshed; and yet, never-the-later, Crist it signifyed. Right so a jewel betokeneth a gemme, and that is a stoon vertuous or els a perle. Margarite, a woman, betokeneth grace, lerning, or wisdom of god, or els holy church. If breed, thorow vertue, is mad holy flesshe, what is that our god sayth? It is the spirit that geveth lyf; the flesh, of nothing it profiteth. Flesshe is flesshly understandinge; flessh without grace and love naught is worth. "The letter sleeth; the spirit geveth lyfelich understanding." Charité is love; and love is charité.[90]

When he says of pearls, then, that they are engendered by heavenly dew in mussels on the coast of Britain and show the nature of their making by their colour, he means real pearls: but he also means what the word also means: Margaret and her fineness of virtue. Further, he says:

> Made not mekenesse so lowe the hye heven, to enclose and cacche
> out thereof so noble a dewe, that after congelement, a Margaryte,
> with endelesse virtue and everlasting joy, was with ful vessel of
> grace geven to every creature, that goodly wolde it receyve?[91]

Here he recognizes that the mussel and the pearl, the very things themselves, stand for the Virgin and for Christ. For all nature is one work of
God:

> Kyndely heven, whan mery weder is alofte, apereth in mannes eye
> of coloure in blewe, stedfastnesse in pees betokening within and
> without.[92]

Again, when he speaks of Margaret he means a woman (else there would
be no sense in his saying that idiots "wene, forsothe, that suche accord
may not be, but the rose of maydenhede be plucked. Do way, do way;
they knowe nothing of this. For consent of two hertes alone maketh the
fastening of the knotte").[93] "Margaret" means also the Church from
which he fears he is alienated, and perhaps means also his good name;
but it always means the jewel that "[al other left] men sholde bye, if
they shulde therfore selle al her substaunce," which applies at all levels.
"Wherto shulde I seche further?"[94]

Above all, when he speaks of love, Usk also means grace: and here his
thought is wise and beautiful. Grace, like love, comes from no desert in
the lover, and it may be unwelcome. "Certes, it was harde grace; it hath
nyghe me astrangled," he says; and Love replies:

> ... thou that were naked of love, and of thyselfe none have mightest,
> it is not to putte to thine owne persone, sithen thy love came thorow
> thy Margaryte-perle. . . . Al the thoughtes, besy doinges, and
> plesaunce in thy might and in thy wordes that thou canst
> devyse, ben but right litel in quytinge of thy dette . . . . And kepe wel
> that love, I thee rede, that of her thou hast borowed, and use it in
> her service thy dette to quyte; and than thou art able right sone to
> have grace; wherfore after mede in none halve mayst thou loke.
> Thus thy ginning and ending is but grace aloon. . . .[95]

There is no valuable reward for grace or love: they are value itself.
When love has explained this, "with that, this lady al at ones sterte into
my herte: 'her wol I onbyde,' quod she, 'for ever . . .'"[96] and needs to say
no more, for she has possessed his will:

> This may never out of my mynde, how I may not my love kepe,
> but thorow willinge in herte; wilne to love may I not, but I lovinge
> have. Love have I non, but thorow grace of this Margarite-perle.
> It is no maner doute, that wil wol not love but for it is lovinge, as
> wil wol not rightfully but for it is rightful itselve. Also wil is not
> lovinge for he wol love; but he wol love for he is lovinge. . . .[97]

Usk's universe, like that of Boethius, of Bradwardine, and of the author of *Pearl*, is altogether filled by grace and (Love says) all good. When Usk objects, "often han shrewes me assailed, and mokel badnesse therin have I founden; and so me semeth bad to be somewhat in kynde," Love replies that, apart from "suche maner badnesse whiche is used to purifye wrong-doers," and is therefore good, and apart from the less fair things that, like "blacke and other derke colours commenden the golden and the asured paynture," evil is either ill will, guilt, or non-being. Good is a participation in God: "Every creature cryeth, God us made," and "Our noble God, in gliterande wyse, by armony this world ordeyned."[98]

More positively than Langland, Usk makes it clear, in the ending paragraph quoted earlier, that this view of the world centres on the sacraments. God's grace was apparent in manna; and manna was real in itself, but was also a prophecy of Christ in the Eucharist; as the author of *Pearl* also says in the ending words of his poem, Christ

> . . . in þe forme of bred and wyn,
> Þe preste vus scheweȝ vch a daye.[99]

Real bread becomes Christ's real flesh: and Christ's flesh profits only through the spirit. The world is grounded in spirit and meaning: the meaning of the world is love, and the meaning of earthly love is heavenly love.[100]

If, then, his book is a "testament of love," it is so called, he says, because of love for Margaret, because of love for natural creation, and because of love for God. For this, men study natural science (Bradwardine's *De causa Dei*, with its insistence on the all-pervasiveness of God's grace, was dedicated to his friends at Merton College, Oxford, and was written at the centre of the liveliest scientific thinking of the Middle Ages in that college, including the advances in physics on which Galileo was to build): "by thilke thinges that ben mad understanding here to our wittes, are the unsene privitees of God made to us sightful and knowing," says Usk. "Considred, forsoth, the formes of kyndly thinges and the shap, a greet kindely love me shulde have to the werkman that hem made."[101]

But everything, in fact, is "understanding here to our wittes," and man is at home in creation:

> Is nat every thing, a this halfe God, mad buxom to mannes contemplation, understandinge in heven and in erthe and in helle? Hath not man beinge with stones, soule of wexing with trees and herbes? Hath he nat soule of felinge, with beestes, fisshes and foules? And

> he hath soule of reson and understanding with aungels; so that in
> him is knit al maner of lyvinges by a resonable proporcioun. Also
> man is mad of al the foure elements. Al universitee is rekened in him
> alone; he hath, under God, principalité above al thinges. Now is
> his soule here, now a thousand myle hence; now fer, now nygh; now
> hye, now lowe; as fer in a moment as in mountenaunce of ten winter;
> and al this is in mannes governaunce and disposicion. Than shewith it
> that men ben licke unto goddes, and children of moost heyght.[102]

Man, then, is the microcosm, centre, and lord of the world: he unites in himself the irrational creatures below him with whom he shares being, vegetative growth, and sentience, and the incorporeal creatures above with whom he shares reason. His understanding of the whole world likewise unites delight in physical form with spiritual and moral contemplation. So Usk, in an allegorical description of how he first found the pearl, says that once

> in tyme whan Octobre his leve ginneth take and Novembre sheweth
> him to sight . . . gan I take in herte of luste to travayle and see the
> wynding of the erthe in that tyme of winter. By woodes that large
> stretes wern in, by smale pathes that swyn and hogges hadden
> made as lanes with lades [byways] their maste to seche, I walked
> thinkinge a wonder greet whyle. . . .[103]

Contemplating him on his winter walk, one is very much tempted to jump the difficulties presented by arguing from aesthetic convention to form of consciousness, and exclaim with Owen Barfield:

> In his relation to his evironment, the man of the Middle Ages was
> rather less like an island, rather more like an embryo, than we
> are. . . . If [he] could be suddenly transported into the skin of a man
> of the twentieth century, seeing through our eyes and with our "figur-
> ation" the objects we see. . . , "Oh," he would say, "look how they
> *stand out!*". . . In such a world the convention of perspective was
> unnecessary. To such a world other conventions of visual repro-
> duction, such as the nimbus and the halo, were as appropriate as to
> ours they are not. It was as if the observers were themselves *in* the
> picture. Compared with us, they felt themselves and the objects
> around them and the words that expressed those objects, immersed
> together in something like a clear lake of—what shall we say?—of
> "meaning" if you choose. It seems the most adequate word.[104]

This is not so unlike the way in which mediaeval philosophers talked. They had, for example, no word exactly equivalent to our "objective," with its connotation of trying to perceive objects as they would be if we were not conscious of them. For them, what one sees is not an interpretation of an object but the very object itself present to the mind (however mediated by the senses) under the mode of intelligible or sensible species.[105]

The difference from ourselves need not be more than a difference of emphasis. Usk, for example, assumes that knowledge of God is knowledge, whereas it can be only opinion "if the sonne be so mokel as men wenen, or els if it be more than the erthe" (which applies not only to the kind of scientific and theological knowledge we actually have, but also to the degree of certainty that knowledge in either field can even theoretically confer). But the difference has far-ranging effects on what one is prepared to believe or imagine: for example, it underlies that easy commerce between Heaven and Earth, which goes so far that Mandeville can say that of the Earthly Paradise "ne can I speak properly. For I was not there. It is far beyond. And that forthinketh me. And also I was not worthy,"[106] naturally combining physical and ethical reasons. It is a passage that probably lay at the back of the *Pearl*-poet's mind when he described his dreamer standing outside Paradise. One might compare this with the Franciscan John Marignolli, who in about 1349 had journeyed to Ceylon, of which he says:

> from Seyllan to Paradise, according to what the natives say after the tradition of their fathers, is a distance of forty Italian miles; so that, 'tis said, the sound of the waters falling from the fountain of Paradise is heard there.[107]

Altogether, *The Testament of Love* gives perhaps the fullest picture, along with the wall-paintings of about 1330 at Longthorpe Tower[108] (near Peterborough), of the habitual thought of a 14th-century mind: a little static, but complex, meaningful, and beautiful.*

<h2 style="text-align:center">V</h2>

Langland, the *Gawain*-poet, and Chaucer shared Usk's world. But against that world they stand out strongly, in three ways: as artists, in the detachment from their works that comes out in their easy exploitation of genre (especially their shifting of it); as men, in the self-consciousness that makes their chief characters isolated as well as inquiring; as thinkers, in the sense that all three seem to have the conviction that writing about religion or humanity ought to be not only descriptive (moving within an objective scheme) but also existential (having its meaning less in what it says than in what it does to the reader).

* See also Ch. 15, "Mediaeval Religious Drama." The Wakefield Master plays in this field the role of detached, ironic creator that the greater Ricardians play elsewhere.

For this last conviction they had a model in Boethius, who—when he has expounded objectively the essence of the world, and brought the reader to grant that he will understand the world better and be more free the nearer he approaches to "thilke devyne thought that is yset and put in the tour . . . of the simplicite of God,"[109] because there in eternity all time is the present—suddenly at the end turns the idea of God's vision of the world quite around upon the reader:

> Withstond thanne and eschue thou vices; worschipe and love thou
> vertues; areise thi corage to ryghtful hopes; yilde thou humble
> preieres an heygh . . . syn that ye worken and don . . . byforn the
> eyen of the juge that seeth and demeth alle thinges.[110]

Chaucer in his translation renders this sudden end with a demand accurately, although his English is looser and less urgent than Boethius's Latin. Usk does not imitate it.

An even more likely model lay in the parables of the Bible, especially in the parable—a *locus classicus* that Usk mentions, though not to make this point—in which Nathan persuades David to take sides in his story, and then, when David has condemned the principal character, says simply: "Thou art the man."[111] This is something more than the ordinary application of an anecdote in a sermon, and more like the procedure of involvement that we have suggested in *Sir Gawain and the Green Knight*.

For the aesthetic and human detachment, and the underlying self-consciousness, there can be no doubt that some impulse came from Dante. It is Dante who first surveyed the mediaeval universe from outside, and with it his own poem,* and who established that distinction between the all-knowing poet and his persona in the story, the pilgrim, that we also find in *Pearl* and in *The Canterbury Tales*. It is in the *Divina commedia* (*c.* 1306–21) that we find most poignantly the little grey trivial figure on the outside of the universe, going his way drawn by the terrific love, by the interest of infinity in the finite, until finally he apprehends the world's inwardness. It is Dante who attempted the task of purifying the vernacular so as to provide metaphors that could describe the hidden things of God and the world in which they are expressed, as he was led to see the earth again in God's sight,

> Cleansed of its stiff and stubborn man-locked set.[112]

This of course is not a complete explanation. Langland, on the one hand, can scarcely have known Dante's work; but then it is precisely Langland

---

* See Ch. 18, "The Individual in the Mediaeval World: Dante's *Divina commedia*."

who does *not* distinguish between poet and pilgrim, but makes his own questions and the pilgrim's, his own life and his persona's, keep pace in his own poignant way. Chaucer, on the other hand, had made this distinction in *The Book of the Duchess* before he journeyed to Genoa and Florence in 1372–3 and discovered Petrarch, Boccaccio, and Dante. But the distinction in that early book, though important, exists primarily to play the author off against the knight whom he meets (probably John of Gaunt, for whom he wrote the poem). It does not yet have the almost confessional overtones of man's incapacity in face of the universe that appear (though in a wholly comic mode) in Chaucer's first Dantean work, *The House of Fame*.

The most striking example of Dante's impact is in *Pearl*: it seems likely, from the similarity of theme (the man, lost by losing his beloved, having both his passion and his man-locked view of the world transformed by his vision of her in Heaven) and picture (Pearl, like Matilda in the *Purgatorio*, seen beyond the stream in the wood and field of Eden), that the *Pearl*-poet knew the *Commedia*. Both the glory and the homely exactness of his diction and vision are like Dante's, though in a tighter, smaller mode.[113]

It is, however, of great interest that he should have known Dante's work. Before the 19th century the only English poets who show familiarity with Dante are those, such as Chaucer and Milton, who had sojourned in Italy. Other poets merely mention him (Gower in the Ricardian period, for instance, though Gower's knowledge was fairly certainly derived from Chaucer). We are left with three possibilities: that at that time there existed a translation from Dante, since lost (Lydgate ascribes a "Daunt in English" to Chaucer, who is the only likely translator; but there is no other trace of it, and he may mean *The House of Fame*[114]); that the *Pearl*-poet had been to Italy (which might explain the similarity of *Pearl* and Boccaccio's *Olimpia* [*c.* 1358], although common sources in Dante and the Bible could suffice); or that he knew Chaucer well enough to have had a detailed account of Dante from him. The last might be the case even if the first or second were established: Chaucer's hypothetical translation cannot have been widely diffused, and even a journey to Italy would tend to suggest a common circle for the two poets.

Personal friendship of the *Pearl*-poet with Chaucer is an exciting possibility. One might associate *The Book of the Duchess* with *Pearl*, for elegy in the form of a dream is not a common genre; and the slight likeness between *Gawain* (because the *Pearl*-poet and the *Gawain*-poet were probably the same person) and "The Squire's Tale" might be due to more than a coincidence based on the taste of squires.[115]

Moreover, one might after all identify the *Pearl*-poet with the friend to whom, along with Gower, Chaucer dedicated *Troilus and Criseyde*—a lawyer and writer on logic and theology called Ralph Strode.* Strode was a man with some of the interests, it seems, and with the subtlety of mind required for the turns and twists that we have looked at in *Gawain* and *Pearl*. Something very like a Ricardian literary movement would then emerge, centred on Chaucer, Strode, and Gower, and with Usk and others as followers, devoted to making English rival Latin and French, and inspired by Dante.

VI

In Chaucer again we find the paradox of a complete acceptance of the mediaeval world—Usk's world—combined with detachment from it. The result is a perennially disturbing irony. It is at its height in the language of *The Canterbury Tales*. In this poem Chaucer seemingly can produce any effect he wants. He can pass from unaffected sublimity,

> O martir, sowded to virginitee[123]

to a brutal physicality,

> My throte is kut unto my nekke boon[124]

within 60 lines of "The Prioress's Tale." This, however, almost any Ricardian poet can do: such comprehensiveness is a quality of the language and perhaps of the life of the time. Chaucer does more: he can, and

---

* This is an old identification of Sir Israel Gollancz's. Briefly, Strode was a Fellow of Merton College (Bradwardine's college) in 1359–60, and a note in the 15th-century catalogue of Fellows tells us *nobilis poeta fuit et versificavit librum elegiacum vocatum Fantasma Radulphi* (he was a noble poet and composed an elegiac book called *Ralph's Dream*).[116] Among surviving poems, this could scarcely be anything but *Pearl*, although *elegiacum* is ambiguous—it might mean a Latin poem in the elegiac metre—and *fantasma* might mean, besides "dream," simply "ghost" or the "phantasy" that the *Pearl* begins as, rather than "vision." Strode was a notable logician and corresponded with Wyclif: what can be gathered from Wyclif's answers (for Strode's letters have not survived) suggests that he was a critical but conservative man theologically and socially, tolerant, a believer that tares should not be rooted up till the harvest, a lover of the rites and ceremonies of the Church, and concerned with the question of grace and works, notably in the case of children who die newly baptised.[117] He also probably had a daughter called Margery— that is, "pearl"—though she did not die young. He was a man of some versatility, for from 1373 he was Common Serjeant to the City of London until he resigned on the re-election of John of Northampton in 1382; during this period he knew and lived near Chaucer. He died in 1387.[118] *Pearl*, if it comes after Mandeville's *Travels* and before the *Testament of Love*, would be dated *c.* 1370–85. Objection has been raised to Gollancz's identification, partly because of doubts as to the identity of Chaucer's neighbour with the Mertonian, partly because Merton was primarily a college of southerners, whereas the author of *Pearl* was certainly a northerner. However, the London Strode twice stood surety for Merton and its Fellows,[119] and a count of Fellows of Merton of Edward III's reign whose origins are identifiable shows 14 from the north

deliberately does, produce opposite effects with the same line. Arcite, at the end of "The Knight's Tale," cries out as he dies:

> What is this world? what asketh men to have?
> Now with his love, now in his colde grave
> Allone, withouten any compaignye.[125]

This—simple, sensuous, and passionate as it is—is infinitely more moving than Dryden's heightened version:

> Vain men! how vanishing a bliss we crave,
> Now warm in love, now withering in the grave,
> Never, O never more to see the sun!
> Still dark, in a damp vault, and still alone.[126]

It has, rather, the accent of Shakespeare's Juliet:

> Or, if you do not, make the bridal bed
> In that dim monument where Tybalt lies.[127]

Yet Chaucer chooses to parody it at the very beginning of the next tale, when the Miller says of Nicholas the Oxford clerk:

> A chambre hadde he in that hostelrye
> Allone, withouten any compaignye . . .[128]

and in this different context the line works just as well; with the same skill as P. G. Wodehouse uses when he brings a cliche just enough to life to kill it: "I inspected my imagination. He was right. It boggled."[129]

Of course, the difference tells us something about the Knight's gentility and the Miller's coarseness. But the combination tells a great deal about Chaucer's human and inhuman detachment, and his breathtaking sense of humour. It is breathtaking because he makes both the passion of Arcite and the Miller's flatness ring true.

---

as well as 48 from the south.[120] Another argument arises if not only *Clannesse, Patience, Gawain,* and *Pearl* are by one author but also the poem *St Erkenwald*—as two of its recent translators agree.[121] Although in the dialect of *Pearl*, it is a London poem based on a London legend, probably written in 1386, when St Erkenwald's feasts were made major festivals in London. In other words, it would bring the *Pearl*-poet, like Strode, to London in 1386. This poem also deals with the power of God's grace, this time in relation to the salvation of the good pagan who lived before Christ, a judge of New Troy (London) miraculously preserved in suspended life, to be baptised by Erkenwald's tears. This is reminiscent of Dante's Trojan Ripheus, the good pagan in heaven. Finally, John Gardner has pointed out some resemblances between *Gawain* and *Troilus*, although they do not prove any direct connection.[122] No more can be said than that the identification of Strode with the *Pearl*-poet is attractive and consistent with the evidence, but still only a speculation.

Chaucer can translate Dante's sublime passages so as to transfer nearly all the effect into English:

> Thow Mayde and Mooder, doghter of thy Sone . . .
> Thow humble, and heigh over every creature,
> Thow nobledest so ferforth oure nature,
> That no desdeyn the Makere hadde of kynde
> His Sone in blood and flessh to clothe and wynde.
> Withinne the cloistre blisful of thy sydis
> Took mannes shap the eterneel love and pees. . . .[130]

Yet when he first copies Dante, in *The House of Fame*, he parodies him. An eagle whose feathers are like gold, whose flight is like lightning, and whose voice reminds him of his wife, only more kindly, carries Chaucer up to Heaven, and lectures him at some length on the propagation of sound; and as Chaucer, quaking with fear in his claws, answers the question whether he has understood with a monosyllabic "Yis," it begins to dawn on the reader that the satire has fastened itself accurately on the weakest point in the *Commedia*—the way in which Beatrice lectures Dante.[131]

But "satire" is the wrong word; the right one is "humour." Chaucer is less concerned to mock Dante than to give his own version in the comic mode of the penitential theme of his own littleness and the noble theme of the ascent to see what God has created—the God who also created him:

> "O God," quod y, "that made Adam,
> Moche ys thy myght and thy noblesse!"[132]

He also means to work out some paradox at his own expense as a writer, and also at the expense of what one might suppose was the general mediaeval tendency to write about the universe from books and not from observation: "For though thou have hem ofte on honde," says the eagle of the stars, "Yet nostow not wher that they stonde."

> "No fors," quod y, "hyt is no nede.
> I leve as wel, so God me spede,
> Hem that write of this matere,
> As though I knew her places here;
> And eke they shynen here so bryghte,
> Hyt shulde shenden [destroy] al my syghte,
> To loke on hem."[133]

It would surely be too much to suppose that here Chaucer has in mind Dante's comparison of the world in God to a book bound up by love, although he probably does have in mind the dazzling that Dante experiences in Paradise before his human sight is made heavenly. But one can point out that Dante thinks that when the sight is purged, the world will be like "a book written by the finger of God,"[134] perhaps with the implication that it confirms what authority, centring on the Book (the Bible), tells us: Chaucer, however, sure though he is that books are "of remembrance the key," is at pains to contrast their authority with experience. Even more than Dante, he sees the mediaeval world from outside.[135]*

This poem, however, he abandoned. Even in the comic mode, he cannot vie with others who have ascended to see earth from Heaven—Boethius, Dante, or the Scipio of Cicero's *Somnium Scipionis*. But he was to return to the theme: it is Scipio himself who leads him to the garden of *The Parliament of Fowls*, over whose gate is written a parody of the inscription at the gate of Hell where Dante began his pilgrimage; and Chaucer suggests that indeed the dream may be no more than the effect of reading the *Somnium Scipionis* before going to sleep.[136] The vision again seems to be an attempt to see nature whole. But Chaucer tries a new device for this, which was to be fruitful: each of the birds, echoing one of the orders of society, gives his own view about love. However, Nature, sitting as judge, says that all this is only an *entremes*—an intermediate course—and defers sentence.[137] It is as if only at a point of convergence of all the opinions, outside this world, could truth be found.

Thereafter Chaucer turned to translating Boethius's *De consolatione philosophiae*, the profoundest treatment of the theme of the approach to truth by ascent from the world to God; and this work influenced *Troilus and Criseyde*. Here he takes a fairly thin and worldly love-story of Boccaccio's, *Il filostrato* (*c.* 1335), tilts at authority again by never mentioning Boccaccio, while continually complaining that he cannot tell the story in any other way because he must follow "myn auctour Lollius" (whom he certainly never read, because Lollius exists only as a misreading of a line by Horace).[138] He follows Boccaccio fairly closely, but profoundly meditates his story through his own categories of courtly love and the conflict of free will and fate—whence, perhaps, the reason for his dedicating *Troilus* to "moral Gower" for the treatment of love and "philosophical Strode"[139] for the treatment of fate. Gradually he works through the character of Troilus to present him in both categories, and in both as passive: the servant of his lady, who would better have been mastered; and the believer in Fate without free will—or could Fate have been

* See Ch. 18, "The Individual in the Mediaeval World: Dante's *Divina commedia*."

mastered? But he gives him one of the finest stories of happiness in our literature, succeeded by the greatest story of misery. When he has brought him through this single turn of Fortune's wheel, he takes Troilus to look down on "this wrecched world" from "the pleyn felicite" of Heaven,[140] and he concludes the whole poem with a translation of the hymn of which Dante says that its melody is a just reward for all merit and an answer to our lament that to live there we must die here:

> Thow oon, and two, and thre, eterne on lyve,
> That regnest ay in thre, and two, and oon,
> Uncircumscript, and al maist circumscrive . . . .[141]

Chaucer carefully distances the story (even commenting, as mediaeval writers rarely do, at the beginning of Book II that the language and customs so long ago must have been very different, although love must have been much the same*) and places it in its time—the time of the war of Troy (in a stronger but similar way to the framing of *Sir Gawain and the Green Knight* in the same war). He exploits, through our knowledge of the inevitability of the story, a sense of fate, of surveying the whole story from above, that makes the Boethian conclusion of seeing the world from Heaven also seem inevitable.

And yet in another way this conclusion seems not inevitable, but a violent turning against the current of the story. For Chaucer involves us so closely with the secular world and its issues (although I think he creates less empathy with Troilus, of the kind we have with Gawain, than a heart-breaking sympathy) that their rejection in favour of Heaven can seem unsatisfying. Furthermore, the break is too absolute: there is no sense in which what happens to Troilus in this world is figurally consummated by what happens to him in Heaven, as there is—at least in theory—in Dante. Chaucer begins Book II with an adaptation of the opening lines of the *Purgatorio*:

> Owt of thise blake wawes for to saylle,
> O wynd, o wynd, the weder gynneth clere.[142]

He may have thought of Troilus's sufferings as a purgatory, but this remains true in a purely secular and allegorical sense: the sufferings prepare him for Criseyde but not for Heaven. Chaucer approaches what Auerbach calls "creatural" style, the style that has lost eternity.[143]

In a way, Chaucer recognizes the tension between his earth and his

---

* Cf. Ch. 8, "Mediaeval Ideas of History."

Heaven by the beauty of the image he gives to the transience of this world when at the conclusion he bids

> O yonge, fresshe folkes, he or she,
> In which that love up groweth with youre age . . .
> . . . thynketh al nys but a faire
> This world, that passeth soone as floures faire[144]

("upgroweth" in the second line has prepared us for the flowers). One might quote George Herbert:

> Say that fairly I refuse
> For my answer is a rose.[145]

But the dichotomy remains. At the beginning and end of Book III, the book in which the heaven of Criseyde and Troilus is described, Chaucer tells us, following Boethius, that love, the love of Troilus and Criseyde, is the same by which

> God loveth, and to love wol nought werne.[146]

But at the conclusion he opposes them, telling the young, fresh lovers

> Repeyreth hom fro worldly vanyte,
> And of youre herte up casteth the visage
> To thilke God that after his ymage
> Yow made. . . .[147]

He does not resolve the contradiction, although when he brings in God's creation, and therefore love, of man, and continues it in the next verse by an appeal to consider the passion of Christ, one can feel him labouring with the paradoxes of the doctrine of creation: that the world is separated from God, but loved by him.

In the *ballade* "Truth," which he wrote about this time, he takes the path of rejection: to those who trust Truth, he says,

> Her is non hoom, her nis but wildernesse:
> Forth, pilgrim, forth! Forth, beste, out of thy stal!
> Know thy contree, look up, thank God of al.[148]

The chronology would be consistent with supposing that he has in mind here the intention of embodying this pilgrimage in *The Canterbury Tales*. Yet it is not immediately apparent in the *Tales* that the pilgrimage is a linear one to a heavenly goal. As in *The Parliament of Fowls*, he sets off person against person, view against view. *Troilus and Criseyde* is the one poem in which he made a linear progress to a goal; but compare his treatment of love and fate in this poem with that in "The Knight's Tale," where these themes are accommodated and their conclusions made relative, as being the sort of thing a knight might say. Moreover, Chaucer changes direction: Arcite's soul, like Troilus's, goes somewhere; but this time Chaucer refuses to say where.[149] Palamon who, in his service of Emelye, more resembles Troilus, learns to accept this world. Theseus tells him to "maken vertu of necessitee"[150]: and *vertu* in this context is akin to the *vertu* of the Prologue, of which "engendred is the flour."[151] The phrase, as Theseus's speech expounds, means "to create sap, life," from knowing how the "faire cheyn of love" binds the world. This is an opposite moral to that at the end of *Troilus*. But in any case we immediately pass on to "The Miller's Tale," beginning the series of views about love and marriage.

It might very well be argued that this series in fact converges on what must have been the centre of mediaeval English thought on sexuality, the promises of the marriage-rite: "to have and to holde fro this day forwarde, for better, for wors, for richer, for poorer, in sykenesse and in hele, to be bonere and buxum [cheerful and responsive] in bedde and at the borde tyll dethe us departhe . . ." and "With this rynge I the wed, and this gold and silver I the geve, and with my body I the worshipe, and with all my worldely cathel [property] I the endowe."[152] But Chaucer does not say so, although the ideal of "The Franklin's Tale" is not unlike this balanced statement.

In one way the structure of the *Tales* is like that of the *Confessio amantis*, a build-up of stories to a particular point: but equally strong is the impression of a huge extension of the crowd-picture in which each portrayal serves to give richness to every other. The linking passage between "The Squire's Tale" and "The Franklin's Tale," for example, is certainly a study in character. The Franklin compliments the Squire, and wishes that his son had equal *gentillesse*, in a way that, as Chesterton says, is "as quiet and as real as Jane Austen."[153] But it also serves a purpose in relation to the build-up of opinions, although this purpose too is an ambiguous one: it underlines the way in which "The Franklin's Tale" is both an exemplary story in its own right about the true nature of *gentillesse*, and a manifestation of the Franklin's slightly uneasy place in society between the (both socially and ethically) *gentil* Knight and the rest:

"Straw for youre gentillesse!" quod oure Hoost.[154]

679

Comparable dualities occur in "The Pardoner's Tale." At the beginning we seem about to enter a figural or allegorical landscape as the young men swear

> Deeth shal be deed, if that they may him hente!
> Whan they han goon nat fully half a mile,
> Right as they wolde han troden over a stile,
> An oold man and a povre with hem mette. [155]

—at first sight a terrifyingly symbolic figure, Death himself, or the old man of sin, or the Wandering Jew.[156] Yet Chaucer has been careful to make all the remarks that give these impressions susceptible of a natural explanation. Because the appearance of symbolism comes first, and the realization of this possibility of naturalism second, it does not read like a figural vision. The old man's quality of suggestion rather than symbol and the deliberate uncertainty about him surprisingly resemble the death figures of Thomas Mann's *Death in Venice* (1911); for Chaucer, like Mann, preserves an ironic detachment from any set symbolism. The old man is Chaucer's own addition to the tale, and by his sinister quality helps to shift the moral from "Greed is the root of evils" to "the wages of sin is death." The young men are caught by their own attempt to kill death, to break out of nature, as well as by their greed.

But these are only the beginning of the ironies that surround this tale. The Pardoner, who believes that he can exploit for his own profit the superstitions that he has seen through, does not perceive that the tale reflects directly on himself. And when at the end he seems to try to practise on his audience the tricks of eloquence he has exposed, and the Host responds with bitter insult (the Knight having to remind them both to "laughe and pleye"[157]), we no longer know who is taking whom seriously. Chaucer seems determined to make us realize how uncertain interpretation is, and how much we are prey to self-deception.

That at some point the treatment is meant to go further and to jolt us into self-awareness—as Josipovici has suggested in the passage quoted earlier in application to *Gawain*[158]—is indicated by the treatment Chaucer accords to himself. Of his tale, "Sir Thopas," the Host says rightly,

> **Thy** drasty rymyng is nat worth a toord![159]

Yet it parodies not only bad ballads but, as Burrow has pointed out,[160] also those features that Chaucer uses in straightforward narrative, although no doubt often with irony or a Wodehousean joy in cliché. In fact we have in the comic mode the picture of one's own inadequacy that Dante, Langland, and the *Pearl*-poet give in other modes.

But the matter is more complex even than this. After all, Chaucer created all the *other* stories. He "is mocking not merely bad poets but good poets; the best poet he knows; 'the best in this kind are but shadows,'" says Chesterton, who is perhaps not going too far when he adds: "It has in it all the mystery of the relation of the maker with things made. There falls on it from afar even some dark ray of the irony of God, who was mocked when He entered His own world, and killed when He came among His creatures."[161]

In this way, the *Tales* does what Auden suggested all good books do when he said that one should ask, "Have you been read by any good books lately?" It builds up for the reader the sense of confessional search; and ends very naturally in the Parson's sermon on penitence. In this way the book does have a direction, and the pilgrimage is properly consummated in the Parson's promise

> To shewe yow the wey, in this viage,
> Of thilke parfit glorious pilgrymage
> That highte Jerusalem celestial. . . .[162]

> Manye been the weyes espirituels that leden folk to oure Lord Jhesu Crist, and to the regne of glorie. Of whiche weyes, ther is a ful noble wey and a ful covenable, which may nat fayle to man ne to womman that thurgh synne hath mysgoon fro the righte wey of Jerusalem celestial; and this wey is cleped Penitence. . . .[163]

This end is utterly outside the book, which even here does not claim to go beyond setting the reader on the right way. So far as the book itself is concerned, and perhaps so far as Chaucer's opinions of what one can achieve in this world go, we are left with his haunting statement (written about 1396, characteristically at the beginning of a not very serious poem on the Wife of Bath, as a warning against marriage) of the relativity of Truth:

> My maister Bukton, whan of Crist our kyng
> Was axed what is trouthe or sothfastnesse,
> He nat a word answerde to that axing,
> As who saith, "No man is al trewe," I gesse.[164]

Not even Christ? With all his Boethian emphasis on the grace, power, and omniscience of God, Chaucer makes no steady connection between God and the world of which he is foundation and creator. This is perhaps natural for a man who (certainly) had read Bradwardine and may have read William of Ockham.*

VII

Walter Hilton, in *The Ladder of Perfection* (*c.* 1390), develops the allegory of the pilgrimage, of the traveller telling himself "Thu wuldes be at Jerusalem."[165] He likewise gives a rationale of the relation between the phantasy by which we defend ourselves in everyday life and the reality that faces us in other modes of consciousness, quoting the Song of Songs:

> I sleep and my heart waketh. . . . The more I sleep from outward things, the more wakeful I am in knowing of Jesu and of inward things. I may not wake to Jesu, but if I sleep to the world.[166]

Another of the mystics, Julian of Norwich, in the vision ("shewing") she had on 8 May 1373—a fortnight before Chaucer returned to London from his diplomatic business in Italy—resolved the paradoxes of creation that perplex the end of *Troilus and Criseyde*:

> I saw that he is . . . all thing that is good, as to mine understanding. Also in this he shewed me a little thing, the quantity of an hazel-nut, in the palm of my hand; and it was as round as a ball. I looked thereupon with eye of my understanding, and thought "What may this be?" And it was answered generally thus "It is all that is made." I marvelled how it might last; for methought it might suddenly have fallen to naught for littlenes. And I was answered in my understanding "It lasteth and ever shall: for that God loveth it. And so All thing hath the Being by the love of God."[167]

The most striking thing about Ricardian society, as mirrored in its literature, is its wholeness, the continuity of theme that exists (as in *The Testament of Love*) between politics or sexuality and mysticism. It appears, from the *Book of Margery Kempe* (1432–6) and from the mystical tracts, that one of the functions of anchorites was to give ordinary people advice. They had a peculiar position in society, at once its centre (even its aim) while yet standing outside it. The mystical writers have a similar position in the world of thought.

The author of *The Cloud of Unknowing* in particular overgoes even Chaucer in using the structures of his age while finding them something from which he is completely free. All means to God are only means, he says (and that may include the whole Catholic system of devotion, which straddles allegory and the literal), advising us to be careful of following any means "in an ape manner."[168] Both he and Walter Hilton are

* See Ch. 7, "Christian Thought."

particularly concerned to modify the influence of Rolle, a hermit who died in 1349 (the year of the onset of the Black Death), to whose writings indeed they owe the possibility of writing of mystical experience in vivid metaphorical English prose, but who never quite makes clear the distinction between inner and outer. Rolle laid much stress on experiences of warmth, sweetness, and the song of angels.[169] The *Cloud* does not quite condemn these things but says they should be held suspect. And then, commenting on the word *up*, it says of some visionaries:

> For ʒif it so be þat þei ouþer rede, or here redde or spoken hou þat men schuld lift up here hertes unto God, as fast þei stare in þe sterres as þei wolde be aboven þe mone, and herkyn when þei schul here any aungelles synge oute of heven. þees men willen sumtyme wiþ þe coriouste of here ymaginacion peerce þe planetes, and make an hole in þe firmament to loke in þerate. . . .[170] Heven goostly is as neigh doun as up, and up as doun, bihinde as before, before as behynde, one syde as oþer, in so moche þat whoso had a trewe desir for to be at hevyn, þen þat same tyme he were in heven goostly. . . .[171] For þof al þat a þing be never so goostly in itself, neverþeles ʒit ʒif it schal be spoken of, siþen it so is þat speche is a bodely werk wrouʒt wiþ þe tonge, þe whiche is an instrument of þe body, it behoveþ alweis be spoken in bodely wordes.[172]

On the other hand, we are not to despise physical expressions or revelations in bodily likeness "as þees heretikes done, þe whiche ben wel licned to wode [mad] men havyng þis custume, þat ever whan þei have dronken of a faire cup, kast it to þe wall and breke it. . . . For men wil kysse þe cuppe, for wine is þerin."[173] The *Cloud*'s author is perhaps the century's greatest master of metaphor. Usk's thoughts of the gratuitousness of the gift of love, and of its absoluteness, and Chaucer's of the relativity of truth in this world are taken up by him into the tradition of negative mysticism; and the meditation that he enjoins, with a cloud of forgetting between himself and earth and a cloud of unknowing between himself and God, is expressed in a purged language of economical and powerful metaphor, when he says:

> What weri wrechid herte and sleping in sleuþe is þat, þe which is not waknid wiþ þe drawʒt of þis love and þe voise of þis clepyng [calling]?[174] . . . But now þou askest me and seiest: "How schal I þink on himself, and what is hee?" and to þis I cannot answere þee bot þus: "I wote never." For þou hast brouʒt me wiþ þi question into þat same derknes, and into þat same cloude of unknowyng þat I wolde þou were in þiself. . . .[175] Fonde [Try] for to peerse þat derknes aboven þee, and smyte apon þat þicke cloude of unknowyng wiþ a scharp darte of longing love, and go not þens for þing þat befalleþ.[176]

Underlying his purged diction and the pressure of his style is the prayer with which he begins his book, which expresses accurately the piercing self-awareness of Ricardian literature: characteristically of that literature's balance of individual and society, it is a translation from the liturgy:

> **God,** unto whom alle hertes ben open and unto whom alle wille spekiþ, and unto whom no prive þing is hid, I beseche þee so for to clense þe entent of myn hert wiþ þe unspekable gift of þi grace, þat I may parfiteliche love þee and worþilich preise þee. Amen.[177]

VIII

Langland puzzles his way in *Piers Plowman* through most of what the other literature of his age contains, never as free of his time as is Chaucer or the author of the *Cloud*, but the more poignant for that. After the Prologue, a lady comes down from the castle and explains his vision to him. And when he asks her "How I may save my soul?"[178] she answers him that God is love, and explains (in another metaphor for Julian's theme of the love of God for creation) that

> . . . heuene myȝte nouȝte holden it · it was so heuy of hym-self
> Tyl it hadde of the erthe · yeten [eaten] his fylle.
> And whan it haued of this folde [earth] · flesshe & blode taken,
> Was neuere leef vpon lynde · liȝter ther-after,
> And portatyf [mobile] and persant · as the poynt of a nedle
> That myȝte non armure it lette [prevent] · ne none heiȝ walles.[179]

In a sense this contains all he ever learns: but it does not yet touch Langland. Instead, the field of folk merges through several visions into a dream in which the Seven Deadly Sins—realized with a vigour of motion and line that is not quite Chaucer's concretion of accumulated detail, and more than a little like Blake—confess themselves before Reason. They wish to go on pilgrimage to find Truth, but do not know the way. This is the occasion for the appearance of Piers the ploughman,[180] the ordinary good man who, as earlier passages of the poem have suggested, is the foundation of a good society. For he knows the way to Truth and will show it to them if they will first help him plough his field. Thus he organizes a society ideal for this earth. It would seem that this is all we need, and indeed Truth sends a pardon to enable us not to go on pilgrimage. Only, when the pardon is open, it is

> . . . do wel, and haue wel · and god shal haue þi sowle,
> And do yuel, and haue yuel . . .
> Þe deuel shal haue þi sowle.[181]

Perhaps this was inexplicable even to Langland. In the A- and B-texts it is succeeded by a scene in which Piers in anguish tears the pardon in two, and declares that he will cease to labour but pray and do penance instead. The C-text cancels this passage, probably because it prefers to take Piers throughout as a model and guide without ambiguities.[182] In the A- and B-texts he is at this stage a more ordinary character who can be prone to doubt. It is possible that at the back of Langland's mind was the image of Moses breaking the tables of the law.[183] He does not say so, and yet the scene is so puzzling that we may well suppose things were happening in it, pressures from some hidden part of his mind, that he did not fully understand. The scene does bring to an end, as it were, his Old Testament. The ideal society has been founded, and found wanting: because, apparently, it can give no answer to guilt, and no meaning to mercy, other than justice. Soon after this, the crux of the poem, the original poem (the A-text) ends.

The later poems then describe a long puzzling over the riddle offered, which becomes the only means to understanding. Thought suggests that Langland may look not only for Dowell, but for Dobetter and Dobest. He does, and gets a great many answers as to what they may be—some foolish, some wiser. But the basic interpretation that he gradually riddles out is that Dowell is what he knows already—that is, doing one's duty. Dobetter is to go beyond that, and Dobest is to enable other people to do well and do better.

It is oddly empirical, but it works. In the end it leads him to see Piers again and to see through Piers many meanings, as Usk does through Margaret. But just as one could say of Margaret that she was always the thing for which one would give everything else, so of Piers one can say that he seems always to be the capacity for Christ in every man.[184] At some stage in the poem, we realize that he was that from the beginning, even when he was an ordinary ploughman. Chaucer tried to create a character of this kind in the Prologue, and failed dismally:

> A trewe swynkere and a good was he
> Lyvynge in pees and parfit charitee[185]

and so forth. His method of concretion does not lend itself to creating ideal figures. Langland does not create an ideal figure: he presents in rough caricature a figure you can identify:

> "I have no peny," quod peres · "poletes forto bigge,
> Ne neyther gees ne grys · but two grene cheses."[186]

685

The contrast is the same as that we remarked on with the Deadly Sins: but there one could say only that Langland had a superiority in vigour, but Chaucer in everything else—individuality, colour, depth of implication, even humour. In the case of Piers, Langland's obsession comes into play: and Langland's obsession is Christ. All through the poem the pressure of Christ is felt, embodying God's grace in everyday life:

> For oure ioys and owre hele · Iesu Cryst of heuene,
> In a pore mannes apparaille · pursueth vs euere.[187]

From the beginning this means that all men are brothers in society: "'They are my blody bretheren' quod pieres · 'for god bouȝte vs alle.'"[188] But under the pressure of Christ and the discovery of Christ in every man, the poem circles round and round the picture of everyday life with which it began, going always inward, until we see the true meaning of the conflict of Truth and Falsehood, as Christ before the gates of Hell makes Piers' original statement, in the form:

> And to be merciable to man · thanne my kynde it asketh. . .
> For blode may suffre blode · bothe hungry and akale,
> Ac blode may nouȝt se blode · blede, but hym rewe . . .
> Ac my riȝtwisnesse and riȝt · shal reulen al helle,
> And mercy al mankynde · bifor me in heuene.[189]

This is nothing less than universal salvation, the final inevitable triumph of God's grace and love. It is also the triumph of Dobest, solving the riddle of Dowell, so that Truth, who must always demand Justice, can dance with Mercy. For Christ in Piers' armour, in humanity, has jousted for and won man's soul:

> And al that man hath mysdo · I, man, wyl amende. . . .
> For I, that am lorde of lyf, · loue is my drynke,
> And for that drynke to-day · I deyde vpon erthe.
> I fauȝte so, me threstes [thirst] ȝet · for mannes soule sake. . . .[190]

In such passages, the language becomes transparent to the meaning. The alliteration seems to touch those deep levels of the mind where sound echoes sense: sometimes simply by linking words as if to suggest that they have a necessary affinity (Lorde . . . lyf . . . love . . .); sometimes by exploiting identifiable sound associations—

> And portatyf and persant · as the poynt of a nedle. . .[191]

—and sometimes quite inexplicably.

686

Piers Plowman is a very great poem: but it is only a poem, or at best a vision, and Langland was unusually aware of that. It embodies a vision one can appropriate: at Mass, when Christ enters as conqueror, but bloody in Piers' coat of armour; in the Church, which Piers as Peter the Apostle founded; in the Church's year at Palm Sunday, when Christ rides in to joust—

> Olde Iuwes of Ierusalem · for Ioy thei songen[192]

—and at Easter, when Mercy and Truth, Justice and Peace dance together for ever—

> Tyl the daye dawed · this damaiseles daunced,
> That men rongen · to the resurexioun . . .[193]

—the high point of the liturgical year, the ringing of bells at the Easter Mass: all at once a personal and a liturgical expression of man in society, the society of the Church.

But the poem does not end there. It ends in Langland's own time with the Church failing, because friars are dispensing cheap grace, and with Conscience crying out for the real grace:

> ". . . sende me happe and hele · til I haue Piers the Plowman!"
> And sitthe he gradde after grace · til I gan a-wake.[194]

This is Langland's version of the existential turn, the transcendence of the aesthetic in the ethical, the demand for action. And this is what Langland expects of his readers.

One result seems to have been that the poem was used as a watchword in the Peasants' Revolt. John Ball's letter to the peasants speaks of letting Piers Ploughman go to work, and tells them to Dowell and Dobetter and to flee sin.[195] The use of these phrases is enigmatic, and it is not possible to know exactly what part Langland's poem played, or what approval he could have given the revolt. Gower and Chaucer feared it as an example of horror and chaos:

> Myn is the strangling and hangyng by the throte,
> The murmure and the cherles rebellyng . . .[196]

says Saturn in "The Knight's Tale." It might be argued—from the fact that, after the revolt had used it, Langland did not suppress his poem but issued another recension—that he did not wholly disapprove. On the other hand, he seems to have tried to modify the poem's revolutionary tendency; for instance, in the C-text he adds a piece of advice from Piers to his son:

> Consaile nat the comune · the kyng to displese
> Ne hem that han lawes to loke [watch over], · laike [play with] hem
> nat, ich hote
> Let God worthe with al, · as holy writ techeth.[197]

Perhaps a mixed attitude is the most likely. In any case, although all three versions demand a change in society, Langland's intention in the B- and C-texts at least could not be confined to that: both society and the individual stand, under judgment and in need of grace, before God.

IX

So far as I understand Erich Auerbach's categories, the literature of the Ricardian age would seem to fall between his figural and his creatural categories: that is, it has begun to lose the vision of time being consummated in eternity and to be obsessed only with time. Auerbach seems to allude to *Piers Plowman* when he says "[Men] are equal before death, before creatural decay, before God. . . . We find individual instances (in England especially of a very forceful kind) where politico-economic conclusions are drawn from this doctrine of equality."[198] He seems to mean such lines as

> For in charnel atte chirche · cherles ben yuel to knowe,
> Or a kniȝte fram a knaue there · knowe this in thin herte.[199]

But his remarks, true so far as they go, hardly seem adequate to explain the force of Ricardian literature. For Auerbach, Christian art breaks itself with Dante:

> The image of man eclipses the image of God. Dante's work made man's Christian-figural being a reality; and destroyed it in the very process of realising it. The tremendous pattern was broken by the overwhelming power of the images it had to contain.[200]

That is, Christianity created the concept of the importance of the individual, because every individual is important to eternity: but individuality is too strong for eternity. The literature of the Ricardian age in England suggests, however, a very different conclusion. It is true that it does not lay down paths, or, for the most part, give a vision of Heaven and Hell. It is the product of a failing society. For all that, it is radically

Christian: its pressure is that of the demand for judgment, repentance, and grace. So far from Christianity paling before secular society, one would apply to Langland and to the bulk of the greater Ricardian writers the words of Lord Salisbury:

> He quoted Professor Clifford's accusation against that religion that it had destroyed two civilizations and had only just failed in destroying a third—and he quoted it with agreement. . . . We had been warned that Christianity could know no neutrality and history had verified the warning. It was incapable of co-existing permanently with a civilization which it did not inspire and any such as came into contact with it withered. How much more must this be so with one that had been formed under its auspices and had subsequently rejected it. Such a society must inevitably perish.[201]

References

NOTE: All citations of passages from Chaucer are followed by page numbers in parentheses; these refer to *The Works of Geoffrey Chaucer*, ed. by F. N. Robinson, 2nd edn (London 1957).

1. G. K. CHESTERTON, *The Everlasting Man* (London 1925), pp. 156–7.
2. WILLIAM LANGLAND, *The Vision of William Concerning Piers the Plowman, in Three Parallel Texts, &c*, ed. by W. W. Skeat (Oxford 1886), reprinted in 2 vols. (Oxford 1954) with bibliographical note by J. A. W. Bennett; the line references below are to this edition. See also *Piers Plowman: the "A" Version*, ed. by G. Kane (London 1960), and selections from the C-text in *Piers Plowman*, ed. by E. Salter and D. Pearsall (London 1967). For chronology, see J. A. W. BENNETT, "The date of the A-Text, &c," *Publications of the Modern Language Association of America* LVIII (New York 1943), and "The Date of the B-text, &c," *Medium Ævum* XII (Oxford 1943).
3. B-text, Prologue 2 and 10.
4. J. A. BURROW, *Ricardian Poetry* (London 1971), p. 136; B-Text, Passus XIII, 330–1.
5. C. S. LEWIS, *Studies in Medieval and Renaissance Literature*, ed. by W. Hooper (Cambridge 1966), p. 92.
6. H. GARDNER, *The Art of T. S. Eliot* (London 1949), pp. 4–5.
7. *Pearl*, ed. by E. V. Gordon (Oxford 1953).
8. *ibid.*, 31–2. See W. R. J. BARRON, "Luf-daungere," in *Medieval Miscellany Presented to Eugène Vinaver*, ed. by F. Whitehead *et al.* (Manchester/New York 1965), pp. 1–18.
9. Cf. P. M. KEAN, *The Pearl: an Interpretation* (London 1967), pp. 31–52.

10. *The Parliament of Fowls* 99–100 and 104–5 (p. 311).
11. P. LUKE, *Hadrian the Seventh: a Play* (London 1968), p. 17.
12. *Winner and Waster* 32–3, ed. by Sir I. Gollancz, 2nd edn revised by M. Day (Oxford 1930); see also *The Age of Chaucer*, ed. by B. Ford (London 1954), pp. 315–33.
13. B-text, Prologue 13–9.
14. A. H. BRIGHT, *New Light on "Piers Plowman"* (Oxford 1928), pp. 11–2.
15. G. FOX, *The Journal*, ed. by N. Penney (London 1924), p. 163.
16. Isaiah VI:1.
17. B-text, Passus VI, 107 ff.
18. *ibid.*, Passus XIX, 6–8.
19. C-text, Passus I, 13–8.
20. Cf. F. E. HALLIDAY, *The Legend of the Rood* (London 1955), pp. 18–43.
21. B-text, Prologue 22.
22. *ibid.*, Passus VI, 250.
23. *ibid.*, Prologue 25.
24. Luke X: 42 (Vulgate).
25. B-text, Prologue 31–3.
26. *ibid.*, 40, 45–9, and 53–4; cf. DANTE, *Inferno* III, 22–69.
27. BURROW, *op. cit.*, pp. 122–5.
28. T. S. ELIOT, *The Waste Land* (London 1922), 62–3; cf. DANTE, *op. cit.*, 55–7.
29. C. S. LEWIS, *The Allegory of Love* (Oxford 1936), pp. 322–3.
30. C-text, Passus I, 138.
31. ELIOT, *op. cit.*, 263–5.
32. Cf. A. STEEL, *Richard II* (Cambridge 1962), p. 283; M. MCKISACK, *The Fourteenth Century* (Oxford 1959), pp. 399 and 497; B. WILKINSON, *Constitutional History of Medieval England*, Vol. II (London/New York/ Toronto 1952), *passim*.
33. B-text, Prologue 112–5.
34. *ibid.*, 125–7.
35. *ibid.*, 141–2.
36. *ibid.*, 145.
37. *ibid.*, 144.
38. See, for instance, the miniature from a *Coronation Order* (early 14th century) in Corpus Christi College (Cambridge) MS 20, folio 68r, reproduced in J. EVANS (ed.), *The Flowering of the Middle Ages* (London 1966), p. 13.
39. B-text, Prologue 151.
40. G. R. OWST, *Literature and Pulpit in Medieval England*, 2nd edn (Oxford 1961), pp. 582–4.
41. B-text, Prologue 190.
42. *ibid.*, 208–9.
43. Cf. E. T. DONALDSON, *Piers Plowman, the C-text and its Poet* (Yale 1949), pp. 111–20.
44. WILLIAM BLAKE, letter to Dr Trusler, 23 August 1799, in *The Letters of William Blake*, ed. by G. Keynes, 2nd edn (London 1968), p. 29.

45. BURROW, *op. cit.*
46. The fullest account of these writers is in B. COTTLE, *The Triumph of English, 1350–1400* (London 1969).
47. O. BARFIELD, *History in English Words*, new edn (London 1954), p. 51.
48. *Sir Gawain and the Green Knight* 1–2, ed. by J. R. R. Tolkien and E. V. Gordon, 2nd edn revised by N. Davis (Oxford 1968). Editions available for the modern reader include that in *The Age of Chaucer*, ed. by B. Ford (London 1954).
49. *Gawain* 802.
50. *ibid.*, 3–4.
51. *ibid.*, 37 ff.
52. *ibid.*, 54–7.
53. *Winner and Waster* 1–4.
54. *Morte Arthure*, ed. by J. Finlayson (London 1967), 4342–6.
55. *Essays Presented to Charles Williams*, ed. by C. S. Lewis (Oxford 1947), p. 57.
56. J. R. R. TOLKIEN, "Beowulf: the Monsters and the Critics," *Proceedings of the British Academy* XXII (London 1936), pp. 245–97; this essay has also been published separately (London 1936).
57. *The Wanderer* and *The Ruin* are included in *A Choice of Anglo-Saxon Verse*, selected and trans. by R. Hamer (London 1970), and *Brut* in *Selections from Laʒamon's Brut*, ed. by G. L. Brook, with Preface by C. S. Lewis (Oxford 1963).
58. *Gawain* 313
59. *ibid.*, 508 and 525–30.
60. *ibid.*, 652–4. I owe the main points in the next paragraph to Miss M. E. Griffiths.
61. *Life of the Black Prince by the Herald of Sir John Chandos*, 74–9, cited in J. A. BURROW, *A Reading of Sir Gawain and the Green Knight* (London 1965), p. 6.
62. E. AUERBACH, *Mimesis*, trans. by W. Trask (paperback: Princeton 1968), pp. 132 and 134.
63. *ibid.*, pp. 140 and 130.
64. D. W. ROBERTSON, JR, *A Preface to Chaucer* (Princeton 1962), pp. 36–7.
65. Cf. BURROW, *A Reading . . .* , pp. 190–4.
66. *Gawain* 723–32.
67. Cf. R. W. V. ELLIOTT, "Sir Gawain in Staffordshire," *The Times* (London), 21 May 1958, p. 12; reprinted in *Twentieth Century Interpretations of Sir Gawain and the Green Knight*, ed. by D. Fox (Englewood Cliffs, N.J. 1968), pp. 106–9—the same country, rather gratifyingly, as that in A. GARNER, *The Weirdstone of Brisingamen* (London 1960). Cf. also BURROW, *A Reading . . .*, pp. 176 ff.
68. *Essays Presented to Charles Williams*, p. 95.
69. *Gawain* 746–7.
70. *ibid.*, 751–2.
71. *ibid.*, 1715–8.
72. *ibid.*, 1883–4.

73. *Gawain* 2334–5; cf. A. C. SPEARING, *The Gawain-Poet: a Critical Study* (Cambridge 1970), pp. 231–5.
74. *Gawain* 2411–28.
75. *ibid.*, 2524–5.
76. *ibid.*, 2529–30.
77. *Abraham and Isaac* 464–5, in *Non-Cycle Plays and Fragments*, ed. by N. Davis (Oxford 1970), p. 57. The Brome play was probably known in Chester, since it bears some relation (probably antecedent) to the Chester *Abraham and Isaac*: see *Non-Cycle Plays . . .*, p. lxiv.
78. W. A. PANTIN, *The English Church in the Fourteenth Century* (paperback: Notre Dame, Ind. 1962), pp. 191 ff.; cf. BURROW, *A Reading . . .*, pp. 107 ff. and 127 ff.
79. G. D. JOSIPOVICI, "Fiction and Game in *The Canterbury Tales*," *The Critical Quarterly* VII (London 1965), p. 196.
80. ADAM OF USK, *Chronicon*, ed. by E. M. Thompson, 2nd edn (London 1904), pp. 18 and 163, cited in H. F. HUTCHISON, *The Hollow Crown* (London 1961), p. 188; cf. A. B. FERGUSON, *The Indian Summer of English Chivalry* (Durham, N. C. 1960).
81. *The Canterbury Tales*, General Prologue 72 and 99 (p. 18)..
82. *ibid.*, "The Squire's Tale" 95 and 58–109 (pp. 128–9); cf. J. GARDNER, *The Complete Works of the Gawain-Poet* (Chicago 1965), pp. 8–9, and C. O. CHAPMAN, "Chaucer and the *Gawain*-Poet: a Conjecture," *Modern Language Notes* LXVIII (Baltimore 1953), pp. 521–4.
83. *Pearl* 1211–2.
84. THOMAS USK, *The Testament of Love*, included in *Chaucerian and Other Pieces*, ed. by W. W. Skeat (Oxford 1897); page numbers included with references to the *Testament* below refer to Skeat's edition. It should be noted that no treatment of the *Testament* has yet done it justice, perhaps because no one who has written on it has read it as Usk clearly asks, as a figural allegory relating sexual love and grace.
85. *Testament* I, vi (pp. 26–8).
86. The Appeal of Thomas Usk in *A Book of London English 1384–1425*, ed. by R. W. Chambers and M. Daunt (Oxford 1931), pp. 18–31 and 238–43.
87. *Testament* III, iv (p. 123).
88. *ibid.*, I, Prologue (pp. 3–4; cf. pp. xxv–xxviii and 452).
89. *ibid.* (p. 2).
90. *ibid.*, III, ix (p. 145).
91. *ibid.*, II, xii (p. 93).
92. *ibid.* (p. 92).
93. *ibid.*, I, ix (pp. 40–1).
94. *ibid.*, I, iii (pp. 17 and 16).
95. *ibid.*, III, vii (p. 136).
96. *ibid.* (p. 137).
97. *ibid.*, III, viii (pp. 137–8).
98. *ibid.*, II, xiii (pp. 95–7).

99. *Pearl* 1209–10.
100. *Testament* III, ix (p. 145).
101. *ibid.*, I, Prologue (pp. 2–3).
102. *ibid.*, I, ix (p. 39).
103. *ibid.*, I, iii (p. 15).
104. O. BARFIELD, *Saving the Appearances* (London 1957), pp. 78 and 94–5.
105. Cf. E. GILSON, *The Christian Philosophy of St Thomas Aquinas*, trans. by L. K. Shook (London 1957), p. 227. This paragraph is based on my remarks in *The Vanity of Dogmatizing: the Three "Versions" by Joseph Glanvil*, ed. by. S. Medcalf (Hove 1970), pp. xxxviii-xli.
106. *The Travels of Sir John Mandeville*, ed. by A. W. Pollard (London 1900 and 1964), Ch. XXXIII, p. 200.
107. *Recollections* of Marignolli, in *Cathay and the Way Thither*, new edn by H. Yule and H. Cordier, Vol. III (London 1914), p. 220.
108. See E. C. ROUSE, *Longthorpe Tower* (London 1964).
109. BOETHIUS, *De consolatione philosophiae* IV, vi, ed. by H. F. Stewart and E. K. Rand (London/New York 1918). Chaucer's translation of this passage is in Robinson's edition of the *Works*, page 368.
110. BOETHIUS, *op. cit.*, V, vi (p. 384).
111. II Samuel XII: 7 (Authorized Version).
112. WALLACE STEVENS, "Angel Surrounded by Paysans," *Selected Poems* (London 1965), pp. 141–2; cf. G. JOSIPOVICI, *The World and the Book* (London 1971), p. 39.
113. Cf. KEAN, *op. cit.*, pp. 208 ff.
114. Cf. J. A. W. BENNETT, *Chaucer's Book of Fame* (Oxford 1968), p. 51.
115. Cf. J. GARDNER, *op. cit.*
116. *Merton Muniments*, ed. by P. S. Allen and H. W. Garrod (Oxford 1928), pl. XVII and p. 37. Cf. SIR I. GOLLANCZ, *Pearl* (London 1921), pp. xlvi-xlix; also Gollancz's article on Strode in the *Dictionary of National Biography*, Vol. XIX (London 1898–9), pp. 57–9, and A. B. EMDEN, *A Biographical Register of the University of Oxford to A.D. 1500*, Vol. III (Oxford 1959), pp. 1807–8, and the article cited therein.
117. *Johannis Wyclif opera minora*, ed. by J. Loserth (London 1913), pp. 175–200.
118. *D.N.B.*, *ed. cit.*, article on Strode; EMDEN, *op. cit.*
119. EMDEN, *op. cit.*
120. G. C. BRODRICK, *Memorials of Merton College* (Oxford 1885), pp. 200–18, and EMDEN, *op. cit.*, *passim*, collated.
121. J. GARDNER, *op. cit.*, p. 342 and *passim*, and B. STONE (ed. and trans.), *The Owl and the Nightingale—Cleanness—St Erkenwald* (London 1971), pp. 247–8.
122. J. GARDNER, *op. cit.*, p. 11.
123. "The Prioress's Tale" 579 (p. 62).
124. *ibid.*, 649 (p. 163).
125. "The Knight's Tale" 2777–80 (p. 44).
126. JOHN DRYDEN, *Palamon and Arcite* III, 794–7: in *The Poems of John Dryden*, ed. by J. Kinsley (Oxford 1958), Vol. IV, p. 1520.

127. *Romeo and Juliet* III, v, 201–2.

128. "The Miller's Tale" 3203–4 (p. 48).

129. P. G. WODEHOUSE, *Right Ho, Jeeves* (London 1934), p. 207; cf. P. TOYNBEE in *The Observer* (London), 29 October 1972.

130. Prologue to "The Second Nun's Tale" 36 and 39–44 (p. 207); cf. DANTE, *Paradiso* XXXIII, 1–9.

131. *The House of Fame* II, 529–864 (pp. 287–90); cf. DANTE, *Paradiso* (especially Canto II), and BENNETT, *Chaucer's Book of Fame, passim.*

132. *The House of Fame* II, 970–1 (p. 291).

133. *ibid.*, 1011–7 (p. 291).

134. HUGH OF ST VICTOR, *Eruditionis didascalicae libri septem*, VII, iv, in *Patrologia latina*, ed. by J. P. Migne (Paris 1844–64), CLXXVI, col. 814; cf. DANTE, *Paradiso* XXXIII, 86, and JOSIPOVICI, *The World and the Book*, p. 29.

135. See Ch. 18, "The Individual in the Mediaeval World: Dante's *Divina commedia*"; also JOSIPOVICI, *The World and the Book*, pp. 54 ff., R. O. PAYNE, *The Key of Remembrance* (Yale 1963), *passim*, and GEOFFREY CHAUCER, *The Legend of Good Women* 26 (p. 483).

136. *The Parliament of Fowls* 29–170 (pp. 311–2).

137. *ibid.*, 665 ff. (p. 318).

138. *Troilus and Criseyde* I, 394, and V, 1653 (pp. 393 and 477): see the edition by R. K. Root (Princeton 1926), pp. xxxvi–xl; also Chaucer's references to "myn auctour" or "the storie" cited by Root, p. xxxvii.

139. *ibid.*, V, 1855–6 (p. 479).

140. *ibid.*, 1817–8 (p. 479).

141. *ibid.*, 1863–5 (p. 479); cf. DANTE, *Paradiso* XIV, 25–30.

142. *Troilus* II, 1–2 (p. 401); cf. DANTE, *Purgatorio* I, 1–3. I owe this point to Mrs Dorothy Bednarowska.

143. AUERBACH, *op. cit.*, pp. 246 ff.

144. *Troilus* V, 1835–6 and 1840–1 (p. 479).

145. GEORGE HERBERT, "The Rose" 31–2: in *The English Works of George Herbert*, ed. by F. E. Hutchinson (London 1941), p. 178.

146. *Troilus* III, 12 (p. 421).

147. *ibid.*, V, 1837–40 (p. 479).

148. "Truth" 17–9 (p. 536).

149. "The Knight's Tale" 2809–15 (p. 44).

150. *ibid.*, 3042 (p. 46).

151. General Prologue 4 (p. 17).

152. Sarum marriage-rite: see *The Annotated Book of Common Prayer*, ed. by J. H. Blunt, 7th edn (London 1876), pp. 267–9; and F. PROCTER and W. H. FRERE, *A New History of the Book of Common Prayer*, 3rd imp. (London 1905), pp. 614 ff.

153. G. K. CHESTERTON, *Chaucer*, 2nd edn (London 1948), p. 175.

154. "The Squire's Tale" 695 (p. 135).

155. "The Pardoner's Tale" 710–3 (p. 152).

156. See *The Works of Geoffrey Chaucer*, p. 731; cf. R. P. Miller in R. SCHOECK and J. TAYLOR, *Chaucer Criticism: The Canterbury Tales* (Notre Dame, Ind. 1960), pp. 221–44.

157. "The Pardoner's Tale" 967 (p. 155).

158. JOSIPOVICI, "Fiction and Game. . .," p. 196.

159. "Sir Thopas" 930 (p. 167).

160. BURROW, *Ricardian Poetry*, pp. 12–23.

161. CHESTERTON, *Chaucer*, pp. 21–2.

162. Prologue to "The Parson's Tale" 49–51 (p. 228).

163. "The Parson's Tale" 75 ff. (p. 229).

164. "Envoy to Bukton" 1–4 (p. 539).

165. WALTER HILTON, *The Ladder of Perfection* II, Ch. 22; see the translation by L. Sherley-Price (London 1957), p. 160.

166. *ibid.*, II, 40 (p. 228 of trans. cited above).

167. See *Revelations of Divine Love Recorded by Julian*, ed. by G. Warrack (London 1901), Ch. V, p. 10.

168. *Epistle of Discretion of Stirrings*, in *Middle English Religious Prose*, ed. by N. F. Blake (London 1972), p. 124.

169. See P. HODGSON, *Three 14th Century English Mystics* (London 1967). For examples of Rolle's work, see *English Writings of Richard Rolle*, ed. by H. E. Allen, rev. edn (Oxford 1963), and *The Fire of Love*, trans. by C. Wolters (London 1972).

170. *The Cloud of Unknowing, &c*, ed. by P. Hodgson (London 1944), Ch. 57, p. 105. The page numbers given below refer to this edition.

171. *ibid.*, Ch. 60 (p. 112).

172. *ibid.*, Ch. 61 (p. 114).

173. *ibid.*, Ch. 58 (pp. 107–8).

174. *ibid.*, Ch. 2 (p. 14).

175. *ibid.*, Ch. 6 (p. 25).

176. *ibid.* (p. 26).

177. *ibid.*, *ad. init.* (p. 1).

178. B-text, Passus I, 84.

179. *ibid.*, 151–6.

180. *ibid.*, 544.

181. *ibid.*, Passus VII, 113–5.

182. C-text, Passus X, 284 ff.

183. Exodus XXXII: 19.

184. Cf. A. M. HADFIELD, *An Introduction to Charles Williams* (London 1959), p. 144.

185. General Prologue 531–2 (p. 22).

186. B-text, Passus VI, 282–3.

187. *ibid.*, Passus XI, 179–80.

188. *ibid.*, Passus VI, 210.

189. *ibid.*, Passus XVIII, 373 and 392–5.

190. *ibid.*, 339 and 363–5.

191. *ibid.*, Passus I, 155.

192. *ibid.*, Passus XVIII, 17.

193. *ibid.*, 424–5.
194. B-text, XX, 383–4.
195. See R. B. DOBSON, *The Peasants' Revolt of 1381* (London 1970), pp. 379–83.
196. "The Knight's Tale" 2458–9 (p. 41).
197. C-text, Passus IX, 84–6.
198. AUERBACH, *op. cit.*, p. 250.
199. B-text, Passus VI, 50–1.
200. AUERBACH, *op. cit.*, p. 202.
201. LADY G. CECIL, *Life of Robert, Marquis of Salisbury* (London 1921), Vol. I, p. 108. I owe this quotation to Professor Martin Wight.

Index

Page numbers in *italics* refer to footnotes. The letters þ (thorn) and ð (eth) are indexed as *th*; the letter ȝ (yogh) is indexed between letters *g* and *h*.